The Psychology of Reading

The Psychology of Reading

INSUP TAYLOR

Division of Life Sciences
Scarborough College
University of Toronto
West Hill, Ontario, Canada

M. MARTIN TAYLOR

Defense and Civil Institute of Environmental Medicine
Downsview, Ontario, Canada

ACADEMIC PRESS 1983

A subsidiary of Harcourt Brace Jovanovich, Publishers

New York London
Paris San Diego San Francisco São Paulo Sydney Tokyo Toronto

ACADEMIC PRESS, INC.
111 Fifth Avenue, New York, New York 10003

United Kingdom Edition published by
ACADEMIC PRESS, INC. (LONDON) LTD.
24/28 Oval Road, London NW1 7DX

Library of Congress Cataloging in Publication Data

Taylor, Insup.
Psychology of reading.

Bibliography:p.
Includes index.
1. Reading, Psychology of. I. Taylor, Maurice M.
II. Title.
BF456.R2T37 1983 153.6 83-11855
ISBN 0-12-684080-6

PRINTED IN THE UNITED STATES OF AMERICA

83 84 85 86 9 8 7 6 5 4 3 2 1

To Wendell R. Garner and G. Ernest MacKinnon
for their faith and encouragement

Contents

III

Learning to Read

Preface

Everybody in an industrialized country should be able to read. How does a child learn to read, and why do some children never learn? How does a skilled reader recognize letters and words, and understand sentences and passages? How do the striking differences among writing systems of the world affect reading processes? The psychology of reading attempts to find answers to such questions.

We hope to achieve three main objectives in this book:

- To relate reading to writing systems—We investigate a variety of writing systems, emphasizing the English system but examining also a few that are very different.
- To analyze the process of reading from several viewpoints using research from diverse disciplines—We emphasize the latest research but do not neglect the small body of classic work.
- To develop a model of reading—With a single model we try to explain reading processes all the way from letter recognition to reading whole texts.

Reading instruction is one of the main tasks of early schooling, and so the theory and practice of reading were for a long time the province of educators. Recently, however, reading research has been attracting psychologists, linguists, computer scientists, and neuroscientists. Research activities from such diverse disciplines are bound to produce complex results. Sometimes experimental results seem to conflict; where possible, we try to resolve the differences. Other times several experiments point to the same conclusion, thus strengthening our confidence that we understand what is happening. Using both kinds of result we strive toward a fair and coherent overall picture of how reading is done and how it is best taught.

Research in reading has not been confined to languages which, like English, use the Roman alphabet; research using other writing systems often sheds new light on results from English. As the noted linguist Whorf (1941) pointed out, an exotic language is a mirror held up to our own. This text breaks new ground in its coverage of three quite different Oriental systems: Chinese that uses a pure logography; Japanese that uses many logographs and two syllabaries; and Korean that uses an alphabetic syllabary and some logographs. But the bulk of the text is on English reading, as practiced and studied in the United States.

We describe how children learn to read in different scripts, by different methods, and at different ages. We discuss different components of reading—

eye movements, letter and word recognition, sentence and prose reading, and so on, in beginning readers, in skilled or unskilled readers, as well as dyslexic readers. Brain-damaged patients with selective impairment of different components provide us with a "natural laboratory" where we can compare reading processes within one script as well as across different scripts. The more types of readers, scripts, and components we examine, the better picture of reading processes we can draw.

This book is a text for college students as well as a reference book for professionals in psychology, education, linguistics, and other related fields. With students in mind, we try to make the text readable; with professionals in mind, we try to be comprehensive in our coverage of writing systems and reading research; with sexists in mind, we try to use *he* and *she* interchangeably.

Now, it is our pleasant duty to thank many friends and colleagues, in Canada and elsewhere, who helped us in making this book.

Dr. G. Ernest MacKinnon of the University of Waterloo is responsible for the conception of the book: he asked Insup Taylor to write a chapter ("Writing Systems and Reading") for *Reading Research: Advances in Theory and Practice* (2), which he and T.G. Waller were editing. His enthusiasm for that chapter inspired Insup Taylor to begin this book.

Dr. Edmund B. Coleman at the University of Texas originally intended to be one of the authors of this book but had to withdraw from authorship because of other commitments. His contribution can still be found, especially in the two chapters on learning to read.

Dr. In-mao Liu in Taiwan, and Dr. Jae-ho Cha in South Korea, helped with Chinese and Korean respectively, and Drs. Giyoo Hatano, Shozo Muraishi, and Danny D. Steinberg in Japan kept us supplied with up-to-date Japanese studies on reading.

Several colleagues commented on various chapter drafts (in alphabetical order): Jim Baek, Herman Bouma, Brian Butler, Anthony Cheung, Annabel Cohen, Zhang Jian, Yukiko Kimura, Marcel Kinsbourne, Paul Kolers, Betty-Ann Levy, Colin MacLeod, Sharon McFadden, Lochlan Magee, Morris Moscovitch, David Murray, Karalyn Patterson, and Mary Rees-Nishio, among many others.

At Scarborough College, Dr. Joan Foley, the principal, and Dr. John M. Kennedy, the associate chairman of Life Sciences, gave their support and assistance to the project. At home, our children, Mia and Ian, had to put up with author-parents for two (or, was it three?) years.

So, thank you all, for your support, and just as important, for your cogent criticisms.

Some years ago, MacKinnon, Coleman and the two authors first met as graduate students in the Psychology Department of the Johns Hopkins University under the inspiring Chairmanship of Dr. Wendell R. Garner (now at

Yale University). Dr. Garner admitted both authors to the Department under unorthodox (and quite different) circumstances; we owe our careers as psychologists to him. In 1983, the Johns Hopkins Psychology Department will celebrate the centenary of its founding by G. Stanley Hall as the first psychological laboratory in North America. In honour of the Centennial, and for their faith in us, we dedicate this book to Wendell Garner and Ernest MacKinnon.

(I.T. held Grant A6400 from the Natural Sciences and Engineering Council, Canada, while writing this book.)

1

Introduction

Through reading we journey to times long ago and places far away.

—Insup Taylor

The cultures of the world have developed a multitude of writing systems, but they must all resolve the same questions: How can ideas be set down on paper, stone, or clay? How do readers pick those ideas up again? How do people learn to read? This book is in three parts, one for each of these three questions. Here we introduce some concepts and terms needed for the book. We also describe briefly the organization of the three parts into their 16 chapters.

Written and Spoken Language

It has been said that writing is a way of representing speech visibly. The eighteenth-century French philosopher Voltaire observed: "L'écriture est la peinture de la voix; plus elle est ressemblante, meilleur elle est." ('Writing is the painting of voice; the better the likeness, the better it is.') According to the noted American linguist Bloomfield (1933), "Writing is not language, but merely is a way of recording language by means of visible marks [p. 21]." Writing is not merely visible speech; it is more than visible speech in some ways, and less in others. As Weber (1977), a researcher in reading, observed: "When language is fixed in writing it takes on a separate identity, serving different functions and following different principles of organization from its spoken counterparts [p. 7]."

Differences Between Speech and Writing

Speech is processed while it is spoken. Once spoken, speech is gone, leaving no physical trace. Writing was invented partly to overcome this evanescent quality of speech. Written language can be read slowly or quickly, now or later, and here or somewhere else.

For spoken language, speech sounds and auditory processing are important; for written language, the shapes of letters and words and visual processing matter. Differences between the two types of language do not end at this initial input stage.

Oral speech has intonation patterns that impart linguistic as well as emotional signals. Punctuation marks in written language are only pale imitations of intonations. A speaker in a conversation receives instant feedback from the listening partner. A writer who communicates to an absent audience has no such luxury—if there is any feedback at all, it usually happens sometime later. The speaker and listener share an immediate situational context, but the writer and the reader do not.

Because of these differences between speech and writing, a transcript of a casual conversation may be hard to understand. The transcripts of ex-president Richard Nixon's infamous tapes had to be heard, not just read, in order for the meanings of words to be understood at all, as the House Judiciary Committee learned. Moreover, the committee required information on the situational context of the conversation (Hirsch, 1977).

To compensate for the absence of interpersonal contact and situational context, writing tends to be expressed more fully and formally than is speech. The writer has time to read what he has written many times over and to revise it to make it ever more effective. William James, renowned both as a psychologist and as a writer, remarked that once he had his composition in a crude shape, he could "torture and poke and scrape and pat it until it offends me no more." A product of such intense and long mental work ought to surpass speech in elegance, organization, and other qualities. On the other hand, it may lose spontaneity and simplicity. A reader, in turn, can read and reread a piece of writing, underlining important points and savoring beautiful expressions.

Writing is more stable than speech and is less vulnerable to changes in pronunciation across space and time. Literate Chinese in different parts of China can understand the same written text, even though the text may be read aloud in many mutually unintelligible dialects. Chinese text written in antiquity can be read today without much difficulty, even though the sounds of the language may have changed somewhat. The same may be said for English, whose various dialects are spoken in many parts of the world. If English spelling were to be simplified to fit the pronunciation of some one dialect, written English might become unintelligible to speakers of other dialects. The move in China toward Romanized spelling could have similar effects.

Speech is acquired, but reading and writing are learned. Children "pick up" their native tongue in the streets and at home without formal instruction, but they are usually instructed in the art of reading and writing by professional teachers. No "normal" children fail to learn to speak, but some fail to learn to read and write. Millions of people in the world have never had even the opportunity to learn to read and write.

Written language is peculiarly suited for studying science, law, and other cultural achievements, as D. R. Olson (1977) observed. In the study by L. Walker (1977), mature readers scored higher than did listeners on precision of comprehension, whether reading at their normal rate or in a controlled time (to match the time required for listening). This was so even though the test material consisted of transcriptions of speeches. In a study by Hildyard and Olson (1978), for Grades 4 and 6 children, reading tended to bias comprehension toward verbatim information explicit in the text, and listening, toward the gist of the story.

On the other hand, listening ability predicts reading comprehension, once decoding skills develop. The correlation between listening and reading ability increased from Grades 1 to 4 and remained stable thereafter at around .60 (Sticht, Beck, Hauke, Kleiman, & James, 1974). The correlation between listening and reading comprehension was as high as .80 for college students (Palmer, MacLeod, Hunt, & Davidson, 1980). Carver (1977–1978) goes so far as to propose a theory that reading comprehension be considered part of a more general language comprehension called rauding (reading + auding).

Throughout this book, we shall see that experimental manipulations sometimes affect listening and reading differently, and sometimes similarly.

Reading Popularity

The importance of oral speech can be taken for granted. Is written language also important, in this age of electronic communication? Is reading still the main means of acquiring communal knowledge? In the United States, Robinson (1980) answers no, and reports a decline in reading time from 50 min per day in 1954 to 30 min in 1975–1976. Bormuth (1978), on the other hand, gives a resounding yes. In items checked out of libraries, newspaper material purchased per household, number of pieces of mail per person, number of days spent in a school year, number of people in white-collar jobs, and so on, the level of reading activity has increased in the past 25 years or so. For example, in 1972 the exchange of information through print consumed about 29% of the average worker's time on the job and 17% of his waking hours.

The advance of technology and the increased complexity of social organization make the communication of information more crucial than ever. Bormuth (1978) concludes: "Although we have developed many other media for communicating some of this information, the written word has borne and continues to bear a large fraction of the load [p. 157]."

Similar increases in reading may be found in other developed and developing countries. In Denmark, a survey by the National Institute of Social Research found a steady increase in the number of books borrowed from libraries between 1959 and 1977. The rate of increase was higher for children than for adults. For example, in 1960 a child borrowed an average of 20 books a year; today, the average has risen to 100 books per year (M. Jensen, 1979).

Japan, which boasts the world's highest literacy rate, could easily surpass the United States in reading. Taiwan and Korea, where illiteracy is almost eradicated, are not far behind Japan. Mainland China seems to have drastically reduced illiteracy from 80% before the revolution to about 20% around 1980. The sight of ordinary people reading wall posters in the streets of Chinese cities has become familiar to Westerners.

Communication of information is not the only purpose of reading and writing. What about the communication of nobler sentiments? George Bernard Shaw retorted to those who complained that his 25-year romance with Ellen Terry existed "only on paper": "Let them...remember that only on paper has humanity yet achieved glory, beauty, truth, knowledge, virtue and abiding love."

Linguistics in a Great Hurry

This section gives a quick and superficial look at some of the linguistic terms and concepts we use throughout the book. Linguists for a long time considered the sentence to be the highest and biggest grammatical unit of language. (Recently, text or dialogue has been awarded this status.) Sentences are composed of phrases and clauses, which are made of words. Words have subunits, of which some are syllables, morphemes, phonemes, and speech sounds (phonetic elements). All of these are units of language.

Phoneme

Following the linguistic convention, 'p' as a letter is written as 'p'; as a phoneme, /p/; as a speech sound, [p] or [p^h]. (The superscript [h] after a stop consonant indicates aspiration.) Table 1-1 lists the conventional symbols for some common sounds used in various languages.

A phoneme, an English speaker may think, is the sound of a letter. This thinking can be only partially correct, for English uses about 44 phonemes, but its alphabet has only 26 letters.

A **phoneme** is a label given to a class of speech sounds regarded as being the same by speakers of a given language.[1] Listening carefully, you can hear the slightly different speech sounds of the phoneme /p/ in *pat* (a puff of breath after it) and *spat* (no puff). This phonetic difference is not phonemic in English, and English speakers hear both [p] and [p^h] as one phoneme /p/. In

[1]We use boldface to make new terms stand out at the place where we first define them.

Table 1-1 *Some International Phonetic Symbols*

Symbol	Key word	Symbol	Key word
æ	fat	k	kin
e	date	l	let
a	car	m	me
ɛ	ten	n	no
i	meet	p	pin
I	is	r	raw
o	go	s	sit
ɔ	hall	t	ten
u	tool	v	veal
U	took	w	wet
ʌ	up	y	yes
ə	ago	z	zip
		tʃ	cheek
b	bee	ŋ	sing
d	done	ʃ	ship
f	fit	θ	think
g	game	ð	this
h	hen	ʒ	azure
d	jump		

other languages, two such sounds may be used as two different phonemes, enabling speakers of these languages to hear the difference better than can English speakers.

In ascertaining whether two sounds belong to the same phoneme in a given language, the crucial criterion is not whether they sound different but whether one sound can substitute for the other without changing the meaning of a word. A phoneme change is the smallest sound change that can convert one word into another. A change between /k/ and /p/ in *kin* and *pin* causes a change in meaning, whereas a change between [p] and [pʰ] in *pin* does not. As is well known, /r/ and /l/ are not distinguished in Japanese, so *maru* and *malu* do not differ in meaning. In English, of course, *red* and *led* do differ in meaning, so that /r/ and /l/ are different phonemes in English.

All languages have two main classes of phonemes: consonants and vowels. To produce a variety of **vowels** such as /a, e, i, o, u/, speakers leave the vocal tract unobstructed but mold the cavities of the mouth and throat into different shapes and sizes by movements of the tongue and the lips. A **diphthong** is a smooth sequence of two vowels, such as in the words *oil* and *day*.

To produce a **consonant,** speakers obstruct the air flow through the oral cavity in a particular way. By closing the vocal tract completely, building up air pressure behind the closure, and then abruptly releasing the air, speakers produce stop consonants. Depending on whether speakers use the lips or front or back of the tongue to block the air flow, they produce /p/, /t/, or /k/. When speakers produce siblants such as /s, z/, the passage in the mouth through which the air must pass is narrow, causing turbulence, hissing noise.

Speakers produce voiced consonants /b, d, v/ by vibrating the vocal folds and voiceless consonants /p, t, f/ by not vibrating the folds. If speakers close the oral cavity and let the air flow out through the nasal cavity, they produce nasal consonants such as /m, n/. If they do not completely block the vocal tract, they produce semivowels such as /l/.

Syllable, Morpheme, Word, and Grapheme

A **syllable** may loosely be defined as a unit whose sound contains one and only one vowel or diphthong. Often it contains one or more consonants (C) before or after a vowel (V)—/ki/, /et/, /bot/ (CV, VC, CVC).

The **morpheme,** the smallest meaningful unit of a language, is a word stem or an affix. In the word *un-friend-ly,* the prefix *un-* and the suffix *-ly* are called **bound morphemes,** and *friend* is called **free morpheme.** Free morphemes can stand by themselves, whereas bound morphemes are found only in connection with free morphemes. A morpheme contains at least one syllable, but one syllable, such as /ka/, is not necessarily a morpheme.

In English, a word can consist of from one (*man*) to about five (*un-gentle-man-li-ness*) or even more morphemes and syllables. Since the concept of a word as a unit is familiar to most readers, we will not dwell on its precise definition, which can be surprisingly complicated and elusive (e.g., Lyons, 1968). Chapters 8 and 9 discuss how these linguistic units are used in reading.

A **grapheme** is a unit of writing: In an alphabet it can be a letter or letter cluster ('sh') that represents a single phoneme; in a syllabary, a grapheme represents a syllable, and in a logography, it represents a morpheme or word. In this book, we often use the terms "letter," "sign," "symbol," or "character," for the minimum unit of writing in a particular script.

Syntax

In this book, by **syntax** we mean nothing more abstract and deep than various devices by means of which linguistic items are connected and built into larger units. It is syntax that differentiates *A man bites the dog* from *The dog bites a man* and either from *Is the dog biting a man?*

Common syntactic devices available in English include:

- Using **function words** to indicate how the **content words** (noun, verb, adjective, adverb) that carry the meaning are related in a sentence. In the earlier examples, *bite, man,* and *dog* are content words, and the rest (*a, the,* and *is*) are function words.
- Using word order such as noun–verb–noun to indicate that the first noun is the subject and actor, the second the object and the acted-upon, with the verb relating the two.
- Using order inversion and/or special morphemes to indicate questions, negations, passives, and so on: *Why isn't the dog bitten by a man?*
- Inflecting words to indicate number and tense, as in *Men were biting dogs.*

More about English syntax is covered in Chapter 12, and a little about English morphology and phonology, in Chapters 6, 10, and 14. Other languages have other kinds of syntactic devices at their disposal. For example, Latin relies heavily on inflection and only slightly on word order; the opposite is true for Chinese. Korean and Japanese use postpositions instead of prepositions to indicate relations among words. Their basic word order is subject–object–verb rather than the English subject–verb–object. These three Oriental languages use question morphemes rather than word-order inversion for interrogative sentences. By whatever devices, all languages ensure that messages get across, usually unambiguously.

Memory and Reading

Memory underlies all our behavior. In reading, it is involved from the simple and mundane act of recognizing the letter 'B' to comprehending a sentence and a passage. If a writer's purpose is achieved, a reader will retain a portion of what is read and comprehended. One conventional, though by no means undisputed, way of discussing memory is to divide it into three separate but continuous and interrelated stages or stores: sensory registers, short-term memory, and long-term memory (e.g., Atkinson & Shiffrin, 1971).

Sensory Registers and Icon

A sensory register holds a stimulus in a raw, unanalyzed state for a fleeting fraction of a second, and it does so regardless of whether a person is paying attention to it. Separate registers may exist for separate senses. A visual image that persists briefly after a stimulus is gone is called **icon.** An icon decays rapidly, within 1 sec, but for the short time it lasts, it is graphic—it holds all that is seen. Some of its information may be ignored in the subsequent stages of analysis (Sperling, 1960).

Short-Term or Working Memory (STM)

Short-term memory receives information from sensory registers and holds it briefly. It can hold a limited number (about seven) unrelated items, such as words and digits (Ebbinghaus, 1885; G. A. Miller, 1956). It can hold more items when they form chunks, meaningful units people impose on the incoming material. Simon (1974), using himself as subject, measured the amount of verbal material he could immediately recall without error. Glanzer and Razel (1974) studied college students' immediate verbatim recall of proverbs and unfamiliar sentences. Here are the results from the two studies:

7 one-syllable words
7 two-syllable words
6 three-syllable words

4 two-word phrases (e.g., *Milky way, differential calculus*)
3 longer phrases (*forescore and seven years ago; all's fair in love and war*)
2 proverbs (*Beggars can't be choosers; Honesty is the best policy*)
1.4 sentences (*Men can't be mothers; Love is the most beautiful accident*)

In one study, a long-distance runner could train himself to hold at least 79 digits in short-term memory, but only by chunking items into groups and these groups into supergroups. Yet, his mnemonic or rehearsal group still contained 4 digits, e.g., *3492*, "3 min and 49.2 sec, near world-record time for running a mile" (Ericsson, Chase, & Faloon, 1980).

Verbatim recall of items does not feature prominently in reading or speaking. Murdock (1972), among others, points out: "[Multiple store] models posit perfect memory for a very small number of items, while the redundancy of language demands a short-term memory system capable of holding imperfectly a large number of items [pp. 91–92]."

Another term for short-term memory is "primary memory." As James (1890) described: "It [an object of primary memory] never was lost; its date was never cut off in consciousness from that of immediately present moment [p. 647]." Contemporary psychologists have resurrected the term to refer to a memory process rather than a store, especially an attending process. For example, Craik and Levy (1975) observe: "The information is in PM [primary memory] only by virtue of the continued allocation of attention . . . and forgetting from PM reflects the diversion of attention to other events [p. 166]." Neisser (1967) describes primary memory or "active verbal memory" as part of the speech comprehension process.

Short-term memory can also be considered as a flexible "workspace," whose limited capacity can be allocated to either storage or processing. To emphasize this aspect of short-term memory, some psychologists use the label **working memory** (Baddeley & Hitch, 1974). The material may remain in memory just so long as it is being worked on. Working memory is heavily involved in reading: Verbal items are integrated and comprehended while being held in this memory (see Chapters 10–13 and 16 for more on working memory).

Long-Term Memory (LTM)

Long-term memory is the repository of more permanent knowledge and skills. As Plato observed, all knowledge is but remembrance. Stored in your long-term memory are knowledge of the alphabet, thousands of words, linguistic rules, your own phone number, and so on. Memory for such items, independent of the particular occasions in which they are acquired, is semantic memory; the memory for how, when, where, and so on, the items were acquired is then episodic memory (Tulving, 1972).

The storage capacity of LTM is effectively unlimited: One learns one's native language storing 50,000 words in LTM and then learns a second language storing an additional 50,000 words, and so on. Information in long-term memory has to be well organized for efficient retrieval; information that is hard to retrieve is more likely to have been mislaid than lost, for it may often be retrieved with an appropriate cue.

Long-term memory serves as a data base into which information is inserted through STM, and from which information is retrieved to be used in STM.

Cortical Function and Reading

Two Hemispheres of the Cortex

The human cerebral cortex is divided into a **left hemisphere** and a **right hemisphere** that have different but complementary functions. In almost all right-handed people, as well as in most left-handed people, verbal material is processed by the left hemisphere (LH), and nonverbal, visual–auditory material, by the right hemisphere (RH) (e.g., Kimura, 1961; Levy & Trevarthen, 1976; Milner, 1975; Moscovitch, 1979; Sperry, Gazzaniga, & Bogen, 1969). It may be more appropriate to distinguish the two hemispheres by modes of processing than by types of material processed. LH function has analytic and sequential capabilities, whereas RH function is imagic and wholistic.[2] As language requires sequential and analytic processing, it is usually processed by the LH. But language processing by the LH may be helped by the wholistic and imagic processing of the RH.

The following areas of the brain, especially in the LH, are heavily involved with speech and reading (see Figure 1-1):

- Angular gyrus: integrates visual and phonetic information
- Broca's area: produces speech
- Wernicke's area: comprehends verbal material
- Motor area: executes motor activities
- Supplementary motor area: plans motor activities, including speech
- Auditory area or temporal lobe: processes auditory information
- Visual area or occipital lobe: processes visual information
- Corpus callosum: a thick bundle of nerve fibers that connects the two hemispheres (not shown in Figure 1-1)

Damage in any of these cortical areas can lead to speech and/or reading impairment. Hemispheric differences in processing appear often in this book, in particular, in Chapters 3, 4, 10, 11, and 16.

[2] *Wholistic* or *holistic*? Following Henderson's (1980) argument, we opt for the former: *wholistic* relates to its parent *whole,* and also serves to differentiate it from the philosophical concept of *holism.*

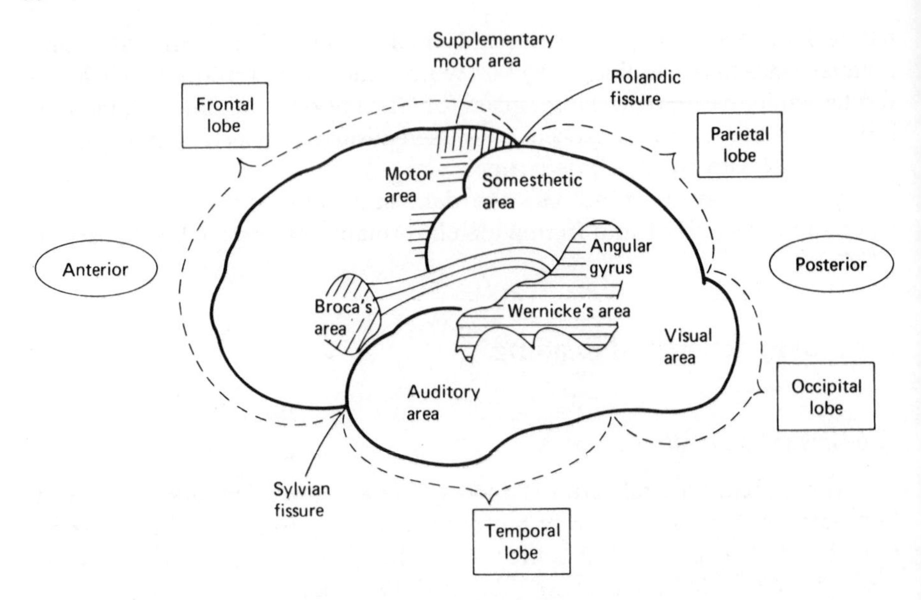

Figure 1-1. *Speech areas (shaded) in the left hemisphere of the human brain (side view). The figure also shows sensory and motor areas, four lobes, and two fissures (from I. Taylor, 1976, p. 361, reprinted by permission of Holt, Rinehart and Winston.)*

Visual Representation in the Cortex

The visual image of the world is focused on the eye's retina, a complex network of neural receptors. The retina is connected by way of several intermediate stages to the visual area at the back of the cortex.

Researchers have several methods for studying which hemisphere processes what kind of information in what way. In one method, they ensure that initial processing is done in the left or right hemisphere by presenting the material to the right or left half of the visual field. Things seen in the left half of the visual field (LVF) of either eye are represented in the RH; things seen in the right half of the visual field (RVF), in the LH. A strip about 1 or 2 degrees down the middle of each eye is represented in both hemispheres, so that things seen centrally are simultaneously available to both hemispheres (Cowey, 1979).

English words are typically recognized faster and more accurately when presented in the RVF (**right visual-field advantage**), implying initial LH processing, whereas faces, pictures, and single Chinese characters are processed faster and better when presented in the LVF, implying initial RH processing.

T-scope (Tachistoscope)

Visual stimuli may be presented for a controlled duration and following a controlled sequence in a simple instrument called a **T-scope.** Experimenters can vary the number and kind of stimuli. For each stimulus, they can manipulate brightness and the sequence of exposure durations. Sometimes they mask a stimulus with an immediately following pattern. One T-scope exposure is usually too short to allow the subject to change the point at which he is looking (the fixation point).

T-scopes have been used in studying recognition of letters and words since the turn of the century. They or their modern equivalents—computer displays—have been used in many of the experiments described in this book.

Why Three Parts and Sixteen Chapters?

Under such a title as *Psychology of Reading*, one could write about a practically limitless range of topics. However, our knowledge, time, and interest are limited; so are our readers' time and tolerance. Thus, we limit our coverage to reading of text (not of maps, blueprints, musical scores, floor plans, graphic signs, circuit diagrams, palms, tea leaves, minds, etc.). On text reading, we have chosen the topics described in the following subsections.

Part I: Writing Systems

This introductory Chapter 1 is followed by Part I, which consists of five short chapters about the writing systems of the world.

Chapter 2 reviews the 5000-year history of writing, which developed through a variety of stages. How writing systems developed not only is interesting in its own right but also provides a perspective on the writing systems discussed in the following chapters.

The next few chapters deal with specific writing systems and the languages that use them. The chosen ones meet one or more of the following criteria: The language is reasonably important; the writing system is a good representative of its type; it has some interesting features; and it has generated research into reading processes.

Chapter 3 discusses the Chinese system, the best existing example of a logography, in which each character represents a morpheme. In this respect, the Chinese systsem contrast sharply to the two kinds of phonetic writing systems, syllabaries and alphabets.

Chapter 4 describes the Japanese system, which uses two kinds of syllabary, along with many Chinese characters. It provides a fertile ground for comparing the processing of the two writing systems.

Chapter 5 describes the Korean system, a unique alphabetic syllabary, in which a small set of symbols for phonemes can be built into a few thousand syllable-blocks. Koreans also use Chinese characters.

Chapter 6 describes English, which is the most important international language and is used either as the first or as a second language by more than half of the world population. Furthermore, English uses an alphabet—specifically the Roman alphabet—that today is the most widely used writing system in the world.

A brief "Interlude" after Part I summarizes differences among 10 writing systems and discusses what these differences imply for reading processes. It sets the stage for Parts II and III.

Part II: Reading Processes

Part II is the heart of this book, in both its content and its location. It is the largest of the three parts and contains seven chapters, each discussing a major issue in reading. It deals mostly with reading research in English, which is prodigious in extent. (Is it the complexity of the orthography or the availability of large research funds that inspires these research activities?)

Chapter 7 describes the activities of the eyes during reading. Recently, computer technology has enabled researchers to make significant advances in the study of eye movements. What cognitive processes do eye movements reveal?

Chapter 8 discusses reading units, sequential constraint, and context. All linguistic units can be used as reading units under different conditions. Sequentially constrained letters and words can be read in large units, especially by skilled readers.

Chapter 9 considers letter and word recognition. The shapes of letters may be analyzed into configurational features such as "outer diagonal parts" or "parallel verticals." The shapes of words can be analyzed into outer contour, length, interior features, and so on. People can use word shape and letter features to recognize familiar words, or they can figure out unfamiliar words from their letters.

Chapter 10 describes phonetic and visual coding. Familiar words are recognized by a fast visual route; unfamiliar words, by a slow phonetic analysis. More importantly, phonetic recoding is used as a means to hold words in short-term memory during text comprehension. Some people subvocalize while they read "silently." Why?

Chapter 11 develops a model of reading processes, after considering many pieces of evidence, both from normal readers and brain-damaged readers of different scripts. Reading involves two cooperating series of processes: One track does fast pattern matching to recognize familiar words and to discover the meanings of text; the other track does slow, but accurate, phonetic analysis to recognize unfamiliar words, and does syntactic analysis of sentences.

Chapters 12 considers how people write, read, understand, and remember sentences. How do syntactic structure, case roles of words, semantic content, and general knowledge interact in sentence processing? It also contains ten suggestions for writing effective sentences.

Chapter 13 discusses narrative and expository prose. It explores concepts such as story grammar and schema in narrative prose and paragraph and text structure in expository prose. It also explores ways to measure a reader's comprehension and retention of text and ways to increase learning from text.

Part III: Learning to Read

Part III has three chapters on how children learn to read.

Chapter 14 describes young children who have learned to read before entering school. It also examines the concept of "reading readiness": What perceptual, cognitive, and linguistic capacities must children possess to begin reading?

Chapter 15 compares several different teaching methods and materials used for school instruction, mostly in the United States but some in other parts of the world. It also traces the development of several reading skills throughout primary and high schools.

Chapter 16 describes symptoms and causes of developmental dyslexia, a difficulty experienced by intellectually normal children in learning to read. Why is dyslexia more prevalent in some countries than in others? How does it compare with acquired dyslexia in adults?

Finally, in an Epilogue, we dare to summarize reading processes in a single page!

I

Writing Systems

2

Development of Writing Systems

The palest ink is better than the best memory.

—Chinese proverb

We start this chapter with a quick look at some precursors of writing—pictures, identification marks, and clay tokens. We then have a leisurely look at writing systems proper.

Precursors of Writing

Long before there was written language, people used markings or objects to keep records of events, identify owners, or invoke magic.

Pictures

Humans carved or painted animals and other objects on rocks as early as the Stone Age (20,000–10,000 B.C.) (H. Jensen, 1970). The animals drawn on the walls of dark caves may have been meant for magic: Perhaps hunters believed that those paintings would bring good hunting. Drawings of slightly more elaborate hunting scenes found in more accessible places could have been records of hunting: How many and what animals were killed, and in what manner.

When people wish to describe an object to somebody who is not there, the natural thing is to draw it. They do not have to learn much in order to draw and decipher a few simple common objects. However, as they try to express more abstract and complex ideas, picture drawing becomes increasingly inadequate. Not only are many events and concepts unpicturable, but also drawing requires some artistic skill and time. Try to draw a picture of soul or democracy.

Pictures of even concrete objects may be misinterpreted. First, a viewer must identify a picture as depicting certain animals. Then, he must ask: Is a drawing meant for decoration? For magic? As a record? As a message? Even when it is understood to be a message, the content may be ambiguous, as the following anecdote shows. When the Persian general Darius invaded the land of the Scythians in 512 B.C., a herald came to him with a message from the enemy. The message contained a picture of a mouse, a frog, a bird, and three arrows. Darius interpreted the message to read:

> O Persians, we surrender our land and our water [the mouse and the frog]. We fly [the bird] from the might of your legions. We are ready to turn over to you all of our arms [the arrows].

That night the Scythians attacked the Persian camp—to the great consternation of the Persian invaders.

After the battle, Darius discovered from a Scythian commander that the message had really meant:

> O Persians, unless you can turn yourselves into birds and fly through the air, or become as field mice and burrow under the ground, or be as frogs and take refuge in the swamps, you shall never escape to return to your native land but will die by our arrows.

Identification Marks

From the Stone Ages down to modern times, simple geometric designs have been put on objects of daily use, such as pots and weapons. Potters' marks are found on pottery of ancient Egypt, and masons' marks have been seen on ancient buildings in Anatolia, Turkey. Some marks are triangles, arrows, diamonds, and vertical or horizontal lines.

Other marks, such as those shown in Figure 2-1, uncannily resemble the letters of the Roman alphabet. Nevertheless, scholars consider these ancient letter-like marks to be no more than offshoots of an art striving toward stylization (H. Jensen, 1970), or "the result of a schematic development from real pictures [Gelb, 1963, p. 27]." Marks found on pots used in China 6000–7000 years ago are also geometric shapes, but a few are indistinguishable from characters used today (see Chapter 3).

Figure 2-1. *Identification marks on flints from Azilian Paleolithic period (12,000–8000 B.C.) (found by E. Piette, 1896).*

Clay Tokens

There is material evidence in the form of **clay tokens** for a record-keeping system indigenous to western Asia from early Neolithic times onward—some 11,000 years ago (Schmandt-Besserat, 1978, 1981). Clay tokens from Susa, a city site in Iran, were small, 1–2 cm in diameter, and varied in color and shape. Some bore simple markings. They were used for many centuries as invoices, to keep track of trade.

An impressed tablet was a sort of written document dating from about 3150 to 2900 B.C. About 200 have been found in Iran, Iraq, and Syria. Their signs have been decoded to be units of grain metrology, land measure, animal enumeration, and other economic units. The signs seem to be pictures of the older clay tokens, which had been in use with little change for several thousand years. The substitution of two-dimensional portrayals (pictures) of the tokens for the tokens themselves could have been the crucial link between the archaic recording system and Sumerian cuneiform writing.

The Variety of Writing Systems

The development of full writing systems was a relatively recent event in human history: It happened no earlier than some 5000 years ago. Note that we are now considering not just a collection of objects or symbols but a writing system that can represent a spoken language in its entirety. At different times, in different places, humans have developed a variety of writing systems, most of them influenced by earlier systems. Languages and their scripts have intimate relations: A certain kind of script is more suitable for one language than for another. Sometimes a script is loaned from one language to another, in part or whole. Sometimes a language adopts two or more scripts and uses them in a mixture. Sometimes the implements used for writing control the form of a script.

Some writing systems have a vertical arrangement of graphemes, others a left-to-right or right-to-left horizontal arrangement, or left-to-right and right-to-left on alternate lines (a style known as boustrophedon). Figure 2-2 shows specimens of several different writing systems. In some writing systems, graphemes look compact and complex, whereas in others they appear simple and spread out.

Writing systems differ in less obvious, more technical and fundamental ways, which have important effects on the way the writing is used. The systems differ in the basic linguistic unit they adopt for their scripts: Some take a phoneme, some a syllable, some a morpheme, and some a word. The first two are sound-based units, and the last two are meaning-based units. Humans become aware of individual meanings more easily than they do of individual sounds. After all, conveying meaning is the primary use of speech and writing;

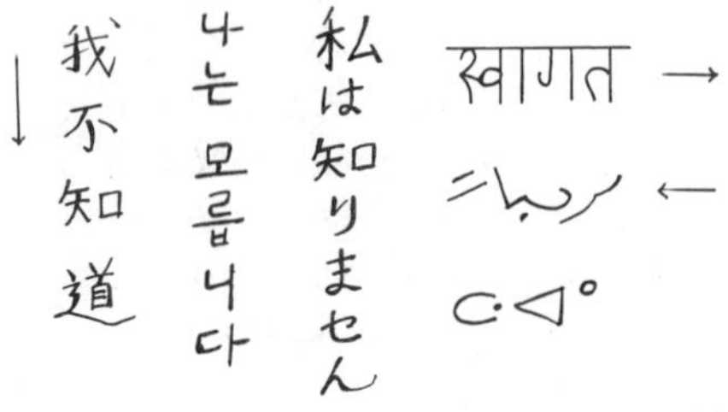

Figure 2-2. *A few different writing systems. From left to right: Chinese, Korean, and Japanese I do not know written vertically. From top to bottom: Devanagari, Arabic, and Cree Welcome written horizontally (from I. Taylor, 1981, p. 2, reprinted by permission of Academic Press.)*

speech sounds and syntax are merely vehicles by which meanings are conveyed. Historically, the units adopted for the earliest scripts were based on meaning. Soon enough, people became aware of speech sounds as units, starting with the more accessible syllables and eventually discovering phonemes.

Let us see what roles linguistic units have played in the development of writing systems. We base our developmental history on Gelb (1963), Diringer (1968), and H. Jensen (1970), who do not always agree, as may be expected in discussions of ancient and mostly extinct writing systems. Our discussion progresses from larger, meaning-based units to smaller, sound-based units. Table 2-1 gives a few examples of each writing system to be discussed. At the same time, it summarizes a 5000-year history of the development of writing systems.

Logography: Word or Morpheme Unit

A writing system in which one grapheme represents primarily the meaning (and sometimes secondarily the sound) of one word or morpheme may be

Table 2-1. *Development of Writing Systems*

Type	Unit	System	Sign	Direction	Number	Time
Logography	word (syllable)	Sumerian cuneiform	sun [glyphs]		600 (150)	3100 B.C. – A.D. 75
		Egyptian hieroglyphic	sun ⊙, man [glyph]	← ↓	700? (100)	3000 B.C. – A.D. 400
		demotic	[glyph]			
	morpheme	Chinese	sun ⊙ ⊖ 日	↖ ↓	45,000?	well developed by 1400 B.C. – present
Syllabary	syllable	Semitic		←		
		Proto-Sinaitic	[glyphs]		31?	1600 B.C.
		Byblos linear	daleth ⊿		22	1000 B.C.
		Phoenician	daleth ⊿, [glyph]		22	
		Japanese	da ダ, だ	→ ↓	71	A.D. 900 – present
Alphabet	phoneme	Greek	d Δ	⇄ →	23?	900 B.C.
		Arabic	ti ط	←	28	A.D. 500
		Latin	D	→	23	700 B.C.
		English	d, D	→	26	A.D. 700
		Cyrillic	d Д	→	43	A.D. 900
	phoneme/ syllable	Korean	d, a 다	→ ↓	24	A.D. 1500

Source: I. Taylor, 1981, p. 3, reproduced by permission of Academic Press.

called a **logography.** Originally, a picture might have been drawn to represent a concrete object. Later, the same picture could represent a less concrete word with a meaning related to the original concrete object. Eventually, the picture itself, gradually simplified and stylized over time, might have lost any resemblance to the original object. For example, both ancient Chinese and ancient Egyptians drew a picture—a small circle with a dot inside—to represent the sun. Later, the same picture represented the concept "day" as well. Subsequently, in Chinese, the picture itself became stylized as a square with a horizontal bar inside.

Early on, a limited degree of phonetization (phonetic transfer or rebus writing) arose from the need to express words and sounds that could not be adequately depicted by pictures. As an example from English, to express *I saw,* a picture of an eye and a saw might be drawn. In Chinese, the character representing 'wheat' is used for the less easily depictable 'come' because the two words used to share the same sound /lai/. (Now, 'wheat' is /mai/.)

Sumerian, Egyptian, and Chinese are historically the three most important logographies, according to Gelb.

SUMERIAN

The Sumerian system was used in Mesopotamia (modern Iraq) between 3100 B.C. and A.D. 75. As it was the first true writing system to emerge, it is instructive to trace its development.

Writing implements and material influenced the type of symbols adopted by most early writing systems. The Sumerians at first used a stylus to draw pictures but later made wedge-shaped marks called **cuneiforms** on wet clay tablets. They developed writing mainly to keep records of commercial transactions and tax collections, baking hard the most important documents for preservation. The story up to this point may be linked to the clay tokens discussed earlier.

Here is the story of how the Near Eastern scribes refined their scripts over a period of 2400 years. Figure 2-3 shows the scripts in four stages of development:

1. To show that the tax was in the form of an ox, a scribe drew a picture of an ox (first drawing). At first, clay tablets were small enough to be fitted into the palm of the hand.

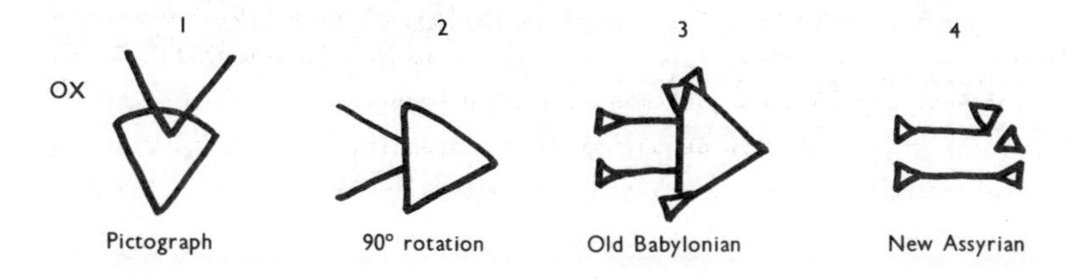

Figure 2-3. *The ancient symbol for ox used in the Near East. It underwent four stages of development.*

2. Around 2800 B.C., as the tablets became larger in order to record more information, the scribe found writing easier if the tablets—and the symbols—were turned sideways (second drawing). At the new angle, writing that had formerly run in vertical columns now ran horizontally from left to right. Many signs lose resemblance to objects after they are turned 90 degrees and after curves (which are difficult to draw on clay tablets) are eliminated.
3. Because a pointed reed raised ridges and bumps in the clay as it was drawn across the soft surface, the scribe began to use a blunter instrument that could simply be pressed on the tablet. The resulting wedge-shaped impressions or cuneiforms (third drawing) kept some remote resemblance to the original pictographs.
4. But by 1500 B.C., any lingering attempts to maintain realism had yielded to abstract symbols (fourth drawing) (Claiborne, 1974).

Any respectable writing system must, sooner or later, solve the problem of how to express abstract and complex concepts. The Sumerians from the beginning had some non-pictorial, linear symbols for concepts such as "to protect" (a squat or flattened 'X'). For some concepts that are complex or hard to picture, compound signs were possible: "to eat" = 'bread + mouth.'

Words have sounds as well as meanings. A sign for a word such as 'fish' could be used for another word 'may' that does not stand for an object but has the same sound as 'fish', namely, /ha/. This phonetic loan is a secondary version of rebus writing, substituting the sign for 'fish' instead of the picture of a fish.

The Sumerian city-state Uruk had between 1500 and 2000 word signs, according to Claiborne (1974) and Schmandt-Besserat (1978), or only about 600 logographs, according to Gelb (1963) and Trager (1974). Whichever number the system had, it must have represented only some key words, not the entire vocabulary. In the Sumerian language, many words were only one syllable long, and signs were invented for these words first. Then, to make words that were two-syllables long, two one-syllable signs were put together. There were 100–150 syllabic signs. The syllabic system did not distinguish between voiced, voiceless, and emphatic consonants and indicated vowels inadequately, so that there might have been confusion among similarly coded syllables.

In time, as speakers of other languages adopted the Sumerian signs to the sounds of their own tongues, the signs began to change. And as people made wider and wider use of phonetics, they began to introduce their own syllabic signs to take the place of word signs. As that happened, the number of signs diminished from thousands to hundreds, because the same syllable sign could now stand for parts of many words (Claiborne, 1974).

EGYPTIAN

Around 3000 B.C., Egyptian writing either developed from the Sumerian system (Gelb, 1963) or arose independently (H. Jensen, 1970). Most likely, the

Egyptians got the notion of writing from the Sumerians, for there is evidence of contact between the two peoples. On the other hand, the Egyptians did not borrow the writing system from the Sumerians, for the symbols of the two systems differ. For example, the picture of "mouth" is an oval shape in the Egyptian system, but it is a whiskered face in the Sumerian system.

By around 500 B.C., there were three related forms in the Egyptian system: **hieroglyphic** (sacred inscription on stone) for public display, and two cursive systems, hieratic and demotic, for everyday practical purposes. Throughout its history, between 3000 B.C. and A.D. 400, the Egyptian system was a word-syllabic writing.

In its developed form, the Egyptian system had about 700 signs for words and 100 signs for syllables. It consisted of three types of signs:

- Ideograms are pictures of objects, symbols of abstract ideas, and compound pictures:

  𓇯 'sky, heaven'

  𓇼 'star'

  𓇰 'sky + star = night'

  Some abstract concepts could still be expressed with pictures of objects: "to rule" with a scepter and "to lead" with a staff of office.
- Phonograms indicate one to three consonant sounds of a word. They are used on the rebus principle. "Basket" 𓎟 codes /nb/, pronounced as /neb/. It can be used to write other unpicturable words with the sound of /nb/, such as /nib/ or /nob/.
- Determinatives emerged when the combination of word signs with phonograms created a wealth of words with the same consonantal frame. Each determinative indicates or delimits the conceptual sphere to which a word belongs. For example, the determinative for "seated goddess" added to the phonogram for /st/ indicates a goddess's name.

According to Meltzer (1980), a written word can be characterized as an incomplete phonetic representation that is supplemented by, and even subordinated to, visual and mnemonic priorities. The standard orthography ensured that a given word was written in a consistent and recognized way in order to minimize confusions among similar sounding or meaning words.

The reading direction was flexible: One read from the direction toward which the hieroglyphs faced. Thus, if the signs faced to the right, the text was read right to left (the most common direction), and vice versa. With all these varied means available to represent a single word, a word to our eyes appears quite unwieldy and complex. Nevertheless, it was an effective writing system that lasted longer than almost any other so far in the history of writing.

In the first century A.D., the Coptic script, which was largely based on the Greek alphabet, gained ground in Egypt, and after the seventh century, the Coptic script itself gave way to Arabic.

CHINESE

Independently of the Near Eastern development of writing systems, China developed its own unique logographic system. Its origin is shrouded in mystery, but material evidence suggests that it was in a fairly developed stage by 1400 B.C. By this stage, the system contained at least 4000 characters, whose pictorial origins were clearly recognizable. Over centuries of continued use, the number of characters kept increasing, up to 50,000 (some say 80,000), and the pictorial origins of many became blurred.

Complex as it is, a logography still survives in China because it is singularly suited to represent the Chinese language. Chapter 3 is devoted to the Chinese system. A large number of Chinese characters were borrowed by Vietnam (until 1910), Japan (see Chapter 4), and Korea (see Chapter 5).

LOGOGRAPHIES: EVALUATION

Because a logograph represents a word's meaning primarily and its sound secondarily, or not at all, a logography is easy to devise, learn, and use, as long as there are only a handful of words to be coded. The set of 130 colored plastic shapes the chimpanzee Sarah used to "read and write" represents the simplest kind of logography (Premack, 1971). Each colored shape as a whole visual pattern is directly associated with its meaning, which is usually concrete ("apple, give"). The sound of a word is completely bypassed, and the shape need not be analyzed in any way.

A proper logography that represents an entire spoken language has to be exceedingly complex. It requires a large and unspecified number of signs, for there have to be as many signs as there are morphemes or words. Witness the varied estimates of the number of Chinese characters—from 50,000 to 80,000. One can always invent a sign for a new morpheme or for a slight variant of an old morpheme. Typewriters, typesetting, and electronic communication are cumbersome for a proper logography. Writing is a burden for the users of such logographs as Chinese characters: They must remember an arbitrary configuration of strokes for each of several thousand logographs, even if they confine themselves only to common ones.

Further, in a full logography most of the signs have to be complex to ensure that they can be discriminated from one another. Some signs have an internal structure analyzable into two or more components; some signs act as determinatives for other signs; some picture signs come to represent sounds. All these trends are discernible in the Sumerian, the Egyptian, and the Chinese logographies. For these reasons, writing systems invented in modern times have rarely been logographies. An exception is the set of **Blissymbols,** which was originally invented as a universal written language but is now used mainly by children with cerebral palsy who cannot speak (Bliss, 1965; Kates, MacNaughton, & Silverman, 1978). Some Blissymbols are simple line drawings of objects; some are abstract and arbitrary symbols; and some are compounds of several symbols. And, the system is far from representing a complete language.

A logography is manageable, even effective, when a limited portion of it is used along with a phonetic script, as was done in the archaic Egyptian system, and as is done in the modern Japanese and Korean systems. Even a full logography by itself can obviously be effective. In China the written language's independence from actual sounds has permitted speakers of diverse dialects to be held together for thousands of years.

Syllabary: Syllable Unit

Words have sounds as well as meanings. At some point in the history of writing, people realized that an entire writing system could be devised to represent sounds directly and meanings secondarily by way of the sounds. If a spoken word has to be analyzed phonetically, the first natural step is to divide it into its constituent syllables, as in *to-ma-to.* An English speaker, if asked to sound out the word, is likely to break it up in this way. Each of the three syllables is easy to pronounce and can be used in other words, as 'to-' is used in *toboggan.* Thus, the first phonetic writing system to be developed was a **syllabary** in which each sign represents a syllable.

A language usually has far fewer different syllables, as few as 100, than it has morphemes. Thus, a syllabary can manage with far fewer signs than can a logography. In fact, the number of different signs is often a clue to the type of an extinct writing system awaiting decipherment: If it has fewer than 100 different signs and more than 20–30, it is likely to be a syllabary. Michael Ventris in the 1950s used this clue in determining the ancient Greek Minoan script called Linear B to be a syllabary. It had 88 characters.

Some notable syllabaries are the ancient Semitic, the two contemporary Japanese systems, and various syllabaries invented in modern times for some African and Amerindian languages.

SEMITIC SYLLABARIES

In the last 2 millenia before Christ, syllabaries were used in the northwest Semitic countries, stretching from Sinai to Syria. They consisted of a limited number of signs (22–30), of which 24 were identical to 24 of the 100 syllabic signs of the Egyptian system. Out of the complicated Egyptian system, the Semites evolved a simple system of their own by discarding all word signs and phonetic signs with two or more consonants but retaining those with one consonant. Their syllable signs were restricted to a small number of open syllables, that is, vowel or consonant–vowel (V or CV).

As in the Egyptian system, each of the 22–30 signs in the Semitic system expressed the exact consonant but not the vowel. Non-expression of vowels did not pose a serious problem in the Semitic and Hamitic (Egyptian) writings because Semitic and Hamitic languages use consonants for the roots of words and vowels for grammatical variations of these words. By analogy, consider the English *sing-sang-sung* or *live* (adjective) and *live* (verb).

The Proto-Sinaic syllabary (1600–1500 B.C.) of about 30 signs was definitely pictorial. Other syllabaries used nonpictorial signs: Ugaritic cuneiform (fourteenth century B.C.) with 30–32 signs and the Byblos syllabary with 22 linear, geometric signs (1000 B.C.). When a syllabary has such a limited number of signs, it cannot have a sign for every syllable of a language.

At this point, a syllabary is hard to distinguish from an incomplete alphabet. In fact, we will take up the Ugaritic system again in "Alphabet: Phonemic Unit."

AMERINDIAN SYLLABARIES

A number of writing systems invented in modern times for Amerindian and African languages are syllabaries, with good reason. Word-based picture signs may be easy to invent, but they are cumbersome to use. On the other hand, the abstraction of phonemes, which is a prerequisite to devising an alphabet, is relatively difficult, as is discussed later in this chapter.

The most important and oldest American Indian writing is the Cherokee script, invented by Sequoyah in North Carolina around 1820. At first, he experimented with a system of pictographic signs, each of which stood for a word of his tongue. Realizing the difficulty of using the system, he gave it up in favor of a syllabary. The signs were no longer pictures. Some were invented, and others were borrowed from English, such as 'H' and 'h', which represented /mi/ and /ni/, respectively. Sequoyah eventually settled on 85 signs. His system is the writing in which books and newspapers of the Cherokee nations were published. Apparently, the Cherokee were 90% literate in the 1830s using the Sequoyah syllabary (W. Walker, 1969).

The Cree system is also a syllabary, invented by the Reverend J. Evans in the 1840s for the use of the Cree Indians and other neighboring tribes of the Algonquins in Canada. The syllabary has 44 basic signs for 44 open syllables (V or CV) in simple, familiar geometric forms. The Cree language contains some closed syllables (CVC), for which small markers have to be attached to the basic signs. About 1885, the Reverend Peck modified the system (48 symbols) for the Eskimos of the eastern Arctic.

The Cree syllabary entails some analysis of each syllable into its initial consonant, medial vowel, and final consonant. However, the medial vowels

Table 2-2. *A Part of the Cree Syllabary*

Consonant \ Vowel	a	e	i	o
p	< (pa)	V (pe)	Λ (pi)	> (po)
k	P	q	P	d
n	ᓇ	ᓀ	ᓂ	ᓄ

do not have their own independent signs; instead, they are indicated by varying the orientation of the consonant signs, as illustrated in Table 2-2. Given the syllables of the first row, you are invited to deduce the syllables of the second and the third row.

On the surface, the Cree–Eskimo system appears extremely simple. Yet, simple shapes distinguished only by left–right and up–down orientation are highly confusable, as is seen in the difficulty of English-speaking children in distinguishing 'b/d' and 'p/q' (see Chapter 16). The Canadian government is replacing the syllabary with the Roman alphabet.

TWO JAPANESE SYLLABARIES

Between the eighth and fourteenth centuries A.D., Japan developed two types of syllabary based on Chinese characters. The Japanese syllabaries do not entail analysis of syllables into initial consonants and medial vowels. The two syllabaries are used to supplement Chinese characters (see Chapter 4).

SYLLABARIES: EVALUATION

Languages differ enormously in the number and variety of syllables they use. English and Korean use several thousand syllables, whereas Chinese uses about 400 and Japanese only 100. Obviously, a syllabary is suitable for Japanese but not for English or Korean.

When it can be adopted, a syllabary has many good features. Because a syllabary is a phonetic system, a word can be sounded out instantly and accurately even if it is unfamiliar or nonsense. Since a syllabary needs only a limited number of signs, the signs need not be complex. In these features, a syllabary has advantages over a logography. It also has some advantages over another phonetic system, an alphabet. The unit of a syllabary, the syllable, is phonetically larger and stabler than is the phoneme. Thus, historically syllabaries were developed before alphabets, and for children, a syllabary is easier to learn than is an alphabet (see Chapters 4, 14, and 16.)

Alphabet: Phoneme Unit

In an **alphabet,** each sign or letter represents a phoneme. An alphabet has been invented only once in the world; all other alphabets (except possibly the Korean) derive from this single original invention. Today alphabets are the most popular scripts.

ABSTRACTING PHONEMES

When words are phonetically decomposed into syllables, the first step toward a sound-based writing system has been taken. To go the next step to an alphabet requires the analysis of a syllable into its phonemes. Such analysis is relatively difficult, both in historic cultures and for modern children. In Japan, even adults have difficulty isolating the phonemes of their syllables. To illustrate the problem, the phoneme /p/ has to be mentally isolated or abstracted from the many syllables in which it occurs in different guises. The phoneme /p/ by itself cannot be pronounced, and a vowel has to be attached to it to form a pronounceable syllable such as /pi/. Furthermore, /p/ by itself has no meaning, although it has the potential of differentiating the meanings of such "minimal pairs" (a pair of words differing only in one phoneme) as *pin* versus *tin* or *pin* versus *pit*.

Historically, abstraction of consonants seems to have preceded that of vowels, perhaps because consonants are more stable and prominent than are vowels. In most languages, consonants tend to be articulated more precisely and consistently than are vowels. An English vowel sign is associated with a far more varied range of pronunciations than is an English consonant (see Chapter 6). Not surprisingly, sound changes occurring across dialects and over time often involve vowel rather than consonant variations. Furthermore, consonants tend to be more numerous and important in many languages, especially in the Semitic and Hamitic languages, which played such vital roles in the development of alphabetic writing systems.

SEMITIC SYLLABARY–ALPHABET

According to Diringer (1968), the North Semitic system of the second millennium B.C. is the first writing that is an alphabet rather than a syllabary, as it abstracted and represented individual consonants adequately. Its 27 signs were pictorial, bearing some resemblance to Egyptian hieroglyphs, but the names and order of the symbols were unmistakably related to the Phoenician syllabary–alphabet. Geographically, the Sinai Peninsula lay between Egypt and the Phoenician ports.

Most of the tablets found in Ugarit, the ancient port of Syria, date to 1400–1500 B.C. Among the many religious texts, some bore striking similarities to the stories of the Old Testament. The Ugarit script (*Ras Shamra* alphabet), consisting of 30–32 cuneiform characters, is the oldest known list of signs written in a standard order. The script disappeared with the city soon after 1200 B.C. H. Jensen (1970) describes it as "a true alphabetical script, though one that represents consonants only [p. 118]."

The **Phoenician syllabary–alphabet** had come to full flower by 1000 B.C. It had 22 consonant signs but no vowels. The names of the first four letters were *aleph, beth, gimel,* and *daleth,* which were the Semitic names of the common objects ox, house, camel, and door, respectively.

GREEK ALPHABET

The **Greek alphabet** is considered to be the first genuine alphabet in that it had symbols for both Cs and Vs. Around the ninth century B.C., the Greeks streamlined the cumbersome representation of the Semitic system, and converted into vowels a number of Semitic signs for "weak consonants" that did not occur in Greek. Thus, Semitic *he* became Greek 'e' or *epsilon*; Semitic *yodh* became Greek 'i' or *iota,* and so on. In this way, consonants were truly isolated, and vowels were differentiated and represented separately.

Of a number of possible Semitic systems, the Phoenician syllabary–alphabet seems to have been the source of the Greek alphabet. Greek *alpha, beta* (from which the term *alphabet* came), *gamma, delta,* and so on, correspond to Phoenician *aleph, beth, gimel,* and *daleth.* The alphabet was created by taking the initial sound from each of these common words.

OTHER ALPHABETS

Since its initiation by the Greeks (according to Gelb), or by the Semites (according to Diringer), the idea of an alphabet has spread all over the world. Gelb (1963) attaches great importance to the representation of vowels, distinguishing three types of alphabets based on this feature. In type one, which includes Greek, Latin, Runic, and Slavic, vowels have their own signs on an equal footing with consonants. In type two, which includes the Semitic writing of Palestinian Hebrew and Arabic, the vowels are indicated by small strokes, dots, or circles, placed either above or below the consonant signs. These diacritic marks are written separately in Hebrew and Arabic, but in the third type, represented by Indic and Ethiopic alphabets, they are attached to consonants.

The **Latin alphabet** deserves a special mention. It once served as an almost international script throughout the Roman Empire, which covered much of Europe and northern Africa. It descends from the Greek alphabet via the Etruscan alphabet, taking 21 of the 26 Etruscan letters with their Etruscan names. The oldest Latin inscription found dates back to the seventh century B.C. The letters 'Y' and 'Z' were added around the first century B.C., and 'J', 'U', and 'W' in the Middle Ages. The Latin alphabet had only capital letters and did not leave spaces between words. The Latin alphabet is also the ancestor of the **Roman alphabet,** the most common alphabet in the world today. The Roman alphabet is the script for such diverse languages as English and Spanish (Indo-European language family), Finnish (Finno-Ugric), Turkish (Altaic), and Vietnamese (Sino-Austric). The Roman alphabet is used to transcribe Chinese, Japanese, and Korean.

The first Cyrillic alphabet was developed by the Greek missionary Saint Cyril around the ninth century A.D. Of its 43 letters, 24 are the Greek letters of the ninth and tenth centuries. Cyrillic alphabets are used by speakers of such Slavic languages as Russian and Bulgarian. Other Slavic languages such as Polish use a Roman alphabet. Serbo-Croatian uses either, depending on whether the writer is Serbian or Croatian.

The **Devanagari alphabet** used in India has 49 letters, which are more complex than those of the Roman alphabet, and which may change shape when combined into CV groups. The Tamil script used in southern India has 12 vowels and 18 consonants which combine and transform into over 200 composites that resemble their parent letters but are not simple combinations.

The blended forms create a set of characters that code the first halves of syllables, the CV component.

The Korean script is an alphabet because its 24 symbols represent all the phonemes of the language; at the same time, it is a syllabary because 2–4 of these symbols are packaged in a block to represent a syllable, which is the unit of reading. Unlike the CV component of the two East Indian scripts, a Korean syllable-block codes a full syllable, including CVCC, and preserves the shape of its constituent symbols.

ALPHABETS: EVALUATION

An alphabet is the latest invention in the history of writing systems and hence should be the best. Is it? The answer is yes and no. The number of phonemes in any language is small, usually around 30. And hence, any language can have a full alphabet that requires a small number of letters. A set of about 30 signs can afford to be simply shaped without limiting visual discriminability. The phoneme, being a small unit, has great combinatorial possibility and flexibility. In short, with only a handful of simple signs, any sound or word of any language can be represented fully. F. Smith (1978) thinks that the alphabet system is a help more to the writer than to the reader. Certainly, writing with an alphabet, even with a complex orthography such as English, is faster than writing with a logography. Typewriters, typesetting, and electronic communication are easier to make and use with a small set of symbols than they are with a large set.

The difficulty of abstracting and using phonemes is not the only undesirable feature of an alphabet. In some alphabets, such as Hebrew and Arabic, tiny dots are "tucked under" consonant letters to indicate vowel sounds. They can cause difficulty for beginning readers (see Chapter 15).

A single word in an alphabet tends to require a long array of letters, longer than a word in a syllabary. For example, *alphabet* requires eight letters in English but three syllable-blocks in the Korean script. A long array not only presents more material to be processed visually but also poses a problem in sequencing and grouping letters and sounds for word identification. People often have trouble seeing and remembering the orders of things in lists.

For an alphabet to be a useful representation of speech, its letters have to code their sounds consistently and accurately. In some alphabets, notably English and French, the letter–sound correspondence is irregular and complex, thus causing trouble for beginning readers, if not for mature readers. On the other hand, by maintaining a close letter–sound correspondence, a script may preclude the possibility of keeping a link between letter patterns and meaning when sounds of words change. The ideal is to have perfect letter–sound correspondence in a language whose sounds do not change unless meaning also changes.

We shall take up a specific writing system in each of the next four chapters and see how it is designed, learned, and used by readers and writers.

Summary and Conclusions

The first writing systems to emerge in different parts of the ancient world were logographies, such as Sumerian cuneiform, Egyptian hieroglyphs, and Chinese characters. Each logograph represented the meaning of a word or morpheme. At the beginning, each sign was a picture of an object, but later it became a stylized design. Some signs came to represent the sounds of words.

The next systems to emerge were syllabaries, in which each sign represents the sound of a syllable. The ancient Semitic syllabaries used cuneiforms, pictures, and linear signs. They represented only consonants. Contemporary syllabaries represent full syllables, including the vowels. Each Japanese sign represents a full syllable, but its shape cannot be analyzed into V and C parts. Each Cree–Eskimo sign likewise represents a full syllable, but it can be analyzed into C (the sign's shape) and V (the sign's orientation).

The most recent type of system to develop was an alphabet, in which each sign approximately codes a phoneme. The Greek system is considered to be the first true alphabet in that it had signs for both Cs and Vs. It is the ancestor of the Roman, Cyrillic, Devanagari, and other alphabets.

Each writing system has desirable and undesirable features. In a logography, the association between a sign and its meaning is direct, but there must be a large number of signs, and so some of them have to be visually complex.

In a syllabary, a small number of signs can represent all the words of a language, but a syllabary is practical only for a language with a small number of different syllables. Syllable signs can be visually less complex than logographs.

In an alphabet, an even smaller set of simple signs can represent the entire language, but the association between a sign and its meaning is still more remote than in a syllabary. Because its sound unit is unstable, letter–sound correspondence can become poor, and because the sound unit is small, a word may require a long array of letters. Nevertheless, alphabets have conquered the world of writing.

3

Logography: Chinese Characters

Thus, the sign for woman next to that for a child means "love" or "good."... Such a language is already half way to poetry.

—E. Glahn (1973, p. 16)

The Chinese writing system is important and interesting for a number of reasons. It appears to be the only full and pure logography used in the modern world. It is used by a huge number of people: One billion Chinese speakers, who form one-quarter of the world population. Chinese characters are used also in Japan and Korea along with native phonetic scripts. The Chinese system is the medium through which a unique, ancient, and influential culture has flourished. It intrigues psychologists, educators, linguists, and computer scientists in the West because in appearance and use it contrasts sharply to Roman alphabets.

Characteristics of Chinese Characters

Origin of Chinese Characters

The origin of Chinese characters is shrouded in mystery, but it may be linked to symbols used in farming communities during Neolithic times 6000–7000 years ago. The number of characters devised up to that time was small, perhaps fewer than 400, which seem to have been mostly numerals and clan names put on pottery and spades (shoulder blades of oxen). Most of them were simple geometric shapes, such as ×,–, +, I, but a few of them are indistinguishable from the modern characters.

Characters had reached a fairly advanced stage of development by around 1400 B.C. About 100 years ago, a large number of oracle bones inscribed with characters were found in An-yang, the last capital of the Shang dynasty (*ca.* 1400–1100 B.C.). The characters were written on the shoulder blade of an ox or the shell of a turtle. When the bones were heated, irregular cracks radiated from the characters, and fortunes were divined from the way the cracks formed. Though there have been some stylistic changes, about half of the original 4000 Shang characters still can be read today (Chou, 1979; Ohara, 1980; W. Wang, 1973). The Chinese system is the only writing system in the world today that has been continuously used since its invention in antiquity.

One Character—One Morpheme—One Syllable

One **Chinese character** represents one morpheme, which is always one spoken syllable—one character, one morpheme, one syllable. (English *potato* is one morpheme, but it consists of three meaningless syllables and is written in six alphabetic letters.) The majority of Chinese morphemes are "free," that is, each can be used by itself as a word. Only a handful of Chinese morphemes are "bound" morphemes such as suffixes and particles, which also are written as single characters.

Chinese morphemes do not inflect but remain invariant. Thus, one character may serve as 'I, me' and 'my', and another as 'go, goes, went, gone', and 'going', occasionally aided by bound morphemes. Neither is it always obvious whether a particular character represents a noun, adjective, verb, or other part of speech. The character for the adjective 'large' might be used as 'largeness', 'largely', or 'enlarge'. However, in some other kinds of word, meanings may determine word classes. For example, the character for 'book' can be only a noun. In general, the way characters are used in a sentence defines their grammatical classes and functions.

One character is always one morpheme. But a Chinese word is not always only one character: It may consist of from one to as many as eight morpheme-characters. The character for 'fire' /huo/ is a one-morpheme word; so is the character for 'vehicle' /che/. When these two morphemes are combined, a new word 'train' /huo-che/ is created.

Logographs that represent monosyllabic and noninflecting morphemes are well suited for the Chinese language. They are also invaluable to Chinese speakers in two ways. First, since the Chinese language uses only 400 different syllables, it has many homophones. But each of the numerous homophones pronounced /fu/ would have its own unique character. Secondly, characters enable speakers of different dialects to communicate, because the meanings of characters remain more or less the same while their pronunciations may vary across the dialects. Even speakers of different languages, such as Japanese, Korean, and Chinese, can communicate to some extent through writing in Chinese characters.

Number of Characters

When each character represents a morpheme, there must be as many characters as there are morphemes in a language. The authoritative *K'ang-hsi Dictionary* of the early eighteenth century lists between 40,000 and 48,000 characters, depending on the edition. However, most of these characters, over 34,000, are archaic, or "monstrosities of no practical use [Wieger, 1965, p. 7]." Only several thousand characters are in active use in mainland China. For example, the *New Chinese Dictionary* published in 1971 contains 8500 characters. The four volumes of *Selected Works of Mao Tsetung* contains 3000 character types, or different characters, of which about 750 account for 95% of all the character tokens occurring in the four volumes (660,000) (Seybolt & Chiang, 1978–1979). (**Types** count different words or characters; **tokens** count all words or characters, whether new or repeated. *Row, row, row your boat* has 5 tokens but three types.) The typical typesetting tray of a printing press contains 2500–3500 different characters. Chinese can manage with a relatively small number of character types because of great freedom in combining them into words. By contrast, in English about 2000 word types account for 95% of word tokens in adult writing (Horn, 1954). This book contains about 8000 word types, of which 2600 account for 90% of words.

Remember that the use of 3000 or so characters does not mean that there are only 3000 words: Characters combine to form multi-character words, such as /huo-che/ ('fire + vehicle = train') given earlier. According to the count made in Taiwan, the number of characters in daily use is 4532, but the number of words is 40,032 (Liu, Chuang, & Wang, 1975). Some Western scholars are not aware of this important fact, as can be seen in the following statement of Rozin and Gleitman (1977): "An Australian second grader [who encounters 2747 different words in his reading series] is reasonably expected to recognize nearly as many words as a Chinese scholar acquires in a life time [pp. 67–68]."

Complexity of Characters

If several thousand characters are to be visually discriminable, many of them must be complex. To print alphabetic letters as configurations of dots on a display screen, a 7 x 11 dot matrix is often used, but to print Chinese characters, a 50 x 40 dot matrix is common.

The complexity of a character can be measured as the number of strokes. A **stroke** is a dot, an L-shape, or a line—horizontal, vertical, or diagonal—that is written in one brush stroke. There is no circle or circular stroke, although a diagonal stroke can be slightly curved. A stroke is strictly a building block of a character's shape, with no phonetic or semantic function whatever. There are about 20 stroke types, according to W. Wang (1973), or 17, according to Wieger (1965).

In machine recognition, characters are often analyzed into their strokes. In one scheme, strokes are extracted and classified for their type, size, and position (W. Stallings, 1976). Dictionaries are arranged according to the radicals in the characters, and under each radical according to the number of strokes (see "Phonetic and Radical," below).

The character with the smallest number of strokes is one horizontal bar (which appropriately represents 'one'); a complex character can have over 30 strokes. Exceedingly complex characters may have been invented for esoteric meanings, which are used rarely. Table 3-1 gives a few examples of characters with increasingly complex and esoteric meanings, and possibly with uncommon uses. For example, the simple character for the common word 'insect' has 6 strokes; the complex character for the uncommon word 'short-legged spider' has 27 strokes.

The average number of strokes is 16 for a few thousand common characters in the original form, but only 10.3 for the 2238 "simplified" characters (C.-C. Cheng, 1977; see Table 3-2 below). These numbers are derived by averaging over types, not allowing for the varying frequencies with which characters are used. Cheng also points out that characters having fewer than 11 strokes comprise 56.6% of the 2500 most common characters.

Intuitively one would think that complex characters are harder to process than simpler ones. Yeh and Liu (1972) in Taiwan did find an adverse effect of complexity on recognition: Recognition threshold was longer for complex characters (15 or more strokes) than for simple ones (10 or fewer strokes). Each of the test words consisted of two characters, both were either complex or

Table 3-1. *Progressively More Complex Characters with Increasingly More Specific and Infrequent Meanings*

Character	*Meanings*	*Character*	*Meanings*
虫	insects	言	words; to speak
虱	louse	訃	to announce death
螢	a glow worm	誓	to swear
[illegible]	a big caterpillar	讛	to speak in one's sleep
蠾	a short-legged spider	讞	to decide on judicial cases

Source: I. Taylor, 1976, p. 159, reproduced with permission of Holt, Rinehart and Winston.

simple. Research in Japan, however, shows that complexity scarcely affects learning and using characters (see Chapter 4). The complexity of character (within limits) should not adversely affect its recognition, for a character is not processed stroke by stroke, on the one hand, and a complex pattern often contains more cues for discrimination, on the other.

Reforming the Writing System

For the all-powerful Chinese Character Reform Committee of the People's Republic of China, the overriding concern is a spread of the National (standard) Language and literacy throughout the vast territory of China. The most authoritative exposition of the whole reform program was presented by the late Premier Chou Enlai in a speech delivered in 1958: "The immediate tasks in writing reform are simplifying the Chinese characters, spreading the use of the standard vernacular, and determining and spreading the use of phonetic spelling of Chinese." This statement is included in the documents on language reform edited by Seybolt and Chiang (1978–1979, p. 1). In that volume, there is a heated debate among politicians and scholars on language reform but little evidence of research.

The problem of representing characters phonetically has concerned Chinese as well as Western scholars for the past 2 decades. Since January 1, 1979, the Chinese government has been pushing the use of the national Romanized language of China, called **pinyin** ('spell sound'), which uses all the letters of the Roman alphabet. To give a few examples of the well known names in the pinyin (and also in the older Wade–Giles system), Deng Xiaoping (Teng Hsiap'ing), Mao Zedong (Mao Tsetung), and Beijing (Peking). The pinyin is used for various purposes in China: to teach sounds of characters to children, to arrange words in dictionaries or books in libraries, for telegraph, Braille, computers, and so on. The pinyin brings an overall uniformity of spelling in anticipation of the final move to do away with characters altogether, if it ever occurs.

As part of writing reform, many frequently used characters have been simplified, by abolishing hundreds of variants (characters with the same sound and meaning but different forms), and by reducing the number of strokes in complex characters. Simplifying common characters may be desirable so long as the meaning-conveying radicals and sound-cuing phonetics are retained, esthetic quality and visual discriminability are not sacrificed, and similarity to the original forms are discernible. Attention has been paid to these points in some cases but not in others, as can be seen in Table 3-2. Simplification is judicious in the first example, but injudicious in the remaining five examples, which retain only the hollow shells and are hard to distinguish from one another.

The rules of calligraphy say that a well-shaped character should fit and fill one of the four basic forms: triangle, circle, rectangle, diamond. Some simplified characters shown in Table 3-2 are top-heavy and unbalanced—

Table 3-2. *Simplification of Characters*

燈	15	灯	6
廣	14	广	3
產	11	产	6
廠	14	厂	2
嚴	21	严	8
病	10	疒	5
Mean Stroke	14		5

Source: I. Taylor, 1981, p. 11, reproduced with permission of Academic Press.

surely a blow to the ancient and venerated art of calligraphy. Drastic simplification of many characters—from an average of 14 to 5 strokes in Table 3-2—is achieved at the expense of discriminability. An individual character, which has to be discriminated from several thousand other characters, may require more than 4–5 strokes. Sadly, some of the characters so drastically simplified are no longer recognizable to overseas Chinese, Japanese, and Koreans. On simplification, the Chinese psychologist Ai (1950) observes:

> It is my finding as well as that of Professor Chai Loh-Sen, in different laboratories at different times, that when the characters are produced for recognition, it does not matter whether they are simple or complex in form, or whether they contain too many strokes or only a few, because the subjects perceive them as a whole [p. 212].

China's illiteracy rate in the prerevolution days was reported to be 80%, but now this figure has been reduced dramatically. The mammoth 1982 census shows that there are 1,031,882,511 Chinese including the population in Taiwan, and there are 235 million in China over 12 years of age who cannot read or can read only a few characters. The revolution in the political–social–economic structure could be more responsible for this felicitous event than the reforms in the writing system. Taiwan, without drastic simplification, has also reduced its illiteracy rate from 20% in 1950 to 0.43% today (Ministry of Education, 1978; cited in Liu, 1979).

Six Categories of Characters

Characters appear hopelessly complex, numerous, and arbitrary to those who do not use them. The American linguist Halle (1969) observed: "Since

Table 3-3. *Six Categories of Characters*

Category	Example
Pictograph	⊙ 日 sun
	☽ 月 moon
Simple Ideograph	丄 上 above
	丅 下 below
Compound Ideograph	日, 月 → 明 bright (sun, moon)
	女, 子 → 好 good (woman, child)
Analogous or Derived	网 fish net; extended to any network, cobweb
Phonetic loan	來 來 /lai/ wheat ↓ come
Semantic – phonetic compound	女, 馬 → 媽 (woman) /nu/+ (horse) /ma/ = (nurse) /ma/

Source: I. Taylor, 1981, p. 12, reproduced with permission of Academic Press.

strokes are arbitrary symbols the writer's task is equivalent to that of a person trying to remember telephone numbers [p. 18]." Not exactly. The characters are conventionally grouped into six categories based on their origins, which in turn provide some information on their sounds and meanings. Most of the 4000 characters used in the ancient Shang dynasty were invented according to five of the six principles (Chou, 1979). Table 3-3 lists the six categories or principles.

1. Pictographs, the oldest category, are iconic representations of concrete objects such as sun and moon. In some characters, the iconic origins are still discernible, in others, less so, and in a great many others, not at all. Fewer than 3% of all characters are pictographs (Tsien, 1962).
2. Simple ideographs express relational or abstract concepts that cannot be easily depicted by pictures.
3. Compound ideographs contain two to four ideographs or pictographs. The two pictographs, one for 'sun' and one for 'moon', join in the character for 'bright'. Occasionally, a compound ideograph is made up with one character repeated twice or thrice. Thus, the character for 'tree' repeated twice is 'forest' and thrice is 'dense forest'.
4. Analogous and derived characters can be ignored, as this category is not clearly defined, and applies to only a minute number of characters.
5. Phonetic loans are seen in the characters for 'wheat' and for 'to come', which were homophones in Archaic Chinese, both being pronounced

as /lai/. Because an iconic representation is far easier for 'wheat' than for 'to come', the character for the former was loaned for the latter.

6. Semantic and phonetic compounds form by far the most numerous and important category. About 80–90% of the characters are estimated to fall into this category. By compounding sound-cuing phonetics and meaning-conveying radicals, many new characters have been created since antiquity. The same component can be used either as a radical or a phonetic in different characters.

Phonetic and Radical

There are about 800 **phonetics**, which cue the sounds of characters. In the beginning, the pronunciation of a phonetic and the character containing it might have been identical for some dialect or other. But differences developed over time, so that a phonetic allows experienced character users to guess, but not to ascertain, the sound of a character. Also, tones may not correspond in morphemes that otherwise sound alike. For example, the phonetic /kung/ may be pronounced as /kung, kang, hung, kiang, chiang/, and so on, in different characters. In a monosyllabic language such as Chinese, a slight change involving a single sound or tone can destroy phonemic likeness between characters. The success rate of using a phonetic to predict a character's sound is estimated to be 0.39 (Zhou, 1978).

There are 214 **radicals,** which cue meanings of characters. (In mainland China, the number has been reduced to 189.) The radicals serve as important classifiers of characters: In dictionaries characters are arranged according to their radicals, and then within each radical, according to the number of strokes. In Table 3-1, the radicals 'insect' and 'word' appear on the left or at the bottom in a number of characters that have related meanings. (A radical can occur on the right or at the top of a character as well.)

Radicals are not always accurate clues to meaning. For example, the radical 'insect' appears in each of the two characters that together make up the word for 'bat', a mammal. It also appears in the characters for 'snake' and 'crab', perhaps because these creatures crawl like worms. The radical 'wood' appears in the character for 'cup', which is seldom made of wood in modern times. Considering that the system of radicals has existed for 2000 years, these slight anomalies and anachronisms may be excused.

The radicals can be grouped into four major semantic categories (T'sou, 1981): nature (earth, wind, etc.), flora (grain, rice, etc.), fauna (horse, pig, etc.), and man (man, woman, etc.), reflecting the way Chinese dissect the world events. Similarly, compound ideographs and semantic–phonetic compounds provide an intriguing glimpse into the ways Chinese view the world. For them, a woman joined with a child symbolizes 'good', and a woman under a roof symbolizes 'peace'. But a compound character made of 'woman' repeated twice means 'quarrel' (two women cannot be on good terms), and repeated thrice means 'intrigues among and with women.' As Glahn (1973) observes, "Such a language is already half way to poetry [p. 16]." And to psychology.

Learning Characters

Chinese Children Learn Characters

Over a period of 5 or 6 years in primary school, 2500–3000 characters are taught, 700 of them in Grade 1; over the next 5 years in middle school, an additional 2000 characters are taught. About 30% of the time at school is devoted to mastering characters, according to the director of the Language Research Institute (cited in Ohara, 1980).

Characters are numerous and must be learned batch by batch, starting with "easy" ones and progressing to more "difficult" ones. The easy characters have the following characteristics (partly based on Ai, 1950): They contain fewer than 10 strokes; they have "balanced" forms—when a complex character contains two subparts, each subpart should contain a similar number of strokes (compare the first example of complex characters with its simplified version in Table 3-2); they are easy to discriminate from other characters containing the same subpart; they contain vertical and horizontal strokes rather than diagonal ones. In addition to these visual factors, they should be common and with few homophones.

Ai (1950) reports that the use of the six categories (see Table 3-3) facilitated children's learning of characters: The children scored three times higher when the six categories were explained than when they were ignored. This was so whether the children were tested immediately or 3 months after learning. Liu (1978) in Taiwan also observed a dramatic increase in acquisition of vocabulary by Grade 4 children when the principles were taught to them.

Characters are learned by the **look–say** or **whole-word method**: A character as a whole visual pattern is associated with its sound (syllable) and meaning (morpheme). Van and Zian (1962) studied first graders learning characters in Shanghai primary school. In the first stage, the children related previously learned sound–meaning associations with only the global shape of written characters. In the second stage, they associated sound–meaning with subparts of characters and often wrongly substituted subparts from similarly shaped characters; they confused characters sharing a subpart. In the third and final stage, they were able to make the correct associations between sound–meaning and the assemblage of strokes. Character learning throughout the three stages was dominated by the visual aspects of the characters.

This kind of **three-phased learning** often occurs for complex materials such as characters and alphabetic words. At first, a handful of items are learned by their global form; next, the items are analyzed into parts; and finally, the parts come together again in wholistic perception, based on securer knowledge of the parts (see Chapter 15).

The child must learn the sounds of characters, usually in the pronunciation of the standard language. Sound learning is done with the aid of the pinyin: New characters are annotated with the pinyin written small above characters arranged horizontally. The pinyin itself is learned quickly within a few weeks at school: In less than 3 months, beginning Chinese readers (aged

7), even those toward the bottom of the class, are on the verge of achieving literacy in the pinyin. The pinyin itself apparently is forgotten quickly upon leaving school (DeFrancis, 1977; Ohara, 1980; Unger, 1977).

The pinyin is not used in Taiwan; instead, a set of 37 indigenous pronunciation signs called "The National Phonetic Symbols" is used. The system is based on the traditional Chinese phonology, which divides a syllable into three parts: initial (C or semi V), final (medial V and final C), and tone. Thus, /ian/ is expressed in two phonetic signs as /i-an/ plus its tone. The phonetic signs appear on the right side of characters written vertically. Liu and Chen (1980) in Taiwan studied the effect on reading of annotating characters with the phonetic signs, using college students as subjects. When the overall degrees of comprehension were about equal, characters alone or characters annotated with the phonetic signs were easier to read than phonetic signs alone. Having the phonetic signs on the right side of characters was more effective than having them on the left side. For long-term retention, simultaneous acquisition of the meaning and pronunciation of new words is the best strategy. The meanings of individual characters, like those of English words, are learned more securely in the context of sentences than they are by themselves.

In a large-scale cross-cultural study, Stevenson and his team found that the reading achievements of elementary schoolchildren are comparable in Taiwan, Japan, and the United States (Stevenson, Stigler, Lucker, Lee, Hsu, & Kitamara, 1982). Taiwanese children are disciplined in the classroom, despite their class size that is twice as large as that in the United States (average in Taiwan is 47 pupils versus 21 in the United States).

Unger (1977), a British educator, visited primary schools in mainland China and reports that a vast quantity of rote learning remains a part of the primary school syllabus. This emphasis on memorization continues, despite Mao Zedong's opposition to "stuffing students with memorized passages like Peking ducks." A fair portion of each reading session is occupied by the children's recitations, chanted boistrously in unison. The contents of the primers are heavy with moral and political lessons. For example, during the cultural revolution, one Grade 1 basal reader seen by Unger started with *Long live Chairman Mao!* in Lesson 1 and *Study well, progress daily* in Lesson 2.

Non-Chinese (and Apes) Learn Logographs

In one foreign resident's words, "most foreign kids took happily to characters. The younger the children, the more enjoyable it was for them to learn to write characters." A moderately intelligent European adult has to spend a good 2 years of full-time study to learn enough of the language and characters to read the *People's Daily* with modest fluency (compared with 1 year for Russian) (Bonavia, 1977).

Turning to research in the United States, American children with reading problems could learn to read a handful of words represented in Chinese characters (Rozin, Poritsky, & Sotsky, 1971). Subjects were disabled readers from Grade 2, selected because of their inability to read a series of six simple CVC trigrams, such as PIP and LAG, and after being given the pronunciation for AT, a set of rhyming words (CAT, FAT, MAT, and SAT).[1] The children learned 30 Chinese characters in six stages. In final tests, they had to arrange the individually mounted characters to form orally presented sentences such as 'A good brother does not give a man a red car.' After an average of 4 hours of individual tutoring in the characters, they were able to negotiate the final sentence and one story with few errors and some comprehension.

Why did the American children succeed in learning characters after having failed to learn to read English syllables? Rozin *et al.* attribute this success partly to the novelty of characters and partly to an intrinsic property of characters, namely, "the complete absence of sound mapping in Chinese [p. 1267]." The researchers used the English syllables and the Chinese characters in unnatural ways: They ignored the meanings of the English syllables and words on the one hand, and the sounds of the characters, on the other. Their endeavor amounts to a demonstration that meanings of soundless words are easier to learn than are the sounds of meaningless syllables. Nevertheless, the research demonstrates how easy it is for children to learn a handful of logographs by the whole-word method, especially if the sounds are bypassed.

Chimpanzees can learn to "read and write" by exactly the same method. Premack's (1971) chimapanzee, Sarah, learned in 2 years over 130 plastic symbols that varied in color, shape, and size. Each stood for a word. She could string several of these symbols together to construct sentences, such as 'Mary no give chocolate Sarah,' which is not unlike the Chinese sentence learned by the American children with reading problems. In her mastery of syntax, Sarah went even further than these children: She could read such conditional relations as 'Sarah take apple if-then Mary no give chocolate Sarah.'

Again by the same method, 10 mentally retarded adults (mean IQ 37) could learn 16 logographs (simple line drawings) (House, Hanley, & Migid, 1980); some low-IQ cerebral palsied children learned a handful of logographic Blissymbols (Vanderheiden & Harris-Vanderheiden, 1976); and some Japanese language-disabled preschoolers (e.g., congenitally deaf, autistic) learned a few hundred words, mostly in Chinese characters (see Chapter 4). In some of these cases, the manipulation of visual symbols is the main means of communication.

Chinese System versus Other Logographs

Chimpanzees and speech- or reading-disabled children have learned a severely limited number of Chinese characters or other logographs, of necessity bypassing sounds completely. Moreover, the logographs represent mostly concrete and simple objects and events. Notwithstanding Sarah the chimp,

[1]We write stimuli in capitals, if they were in capitals during the experiment.

syntax tends to be rudimentary. The kind of communication possible with these types of logographs is limited. For example, Sarah uses her reading and writing to manipulate her immediate environment; she does not appear to use reading to learn about events in distant places and times (as far as we know, she was not given an opportunity to use reading in this way.) Obviously, learning some logographs in this manner is remarkably easy.

Even though Chinese children also learn logographs, and learn them by the whole-word method like the chimpanzees and speech- or reading-disabled children, the two types of learners differ in fundamental ways. The Chinese system is closely tied to oral speech, and Chinese children must learn to associate a shape to its sound (syllable and tone) as well as to its meaning. In order to represent the Chinese language adequately, the Chinese system requires several thousand characters, some of them representing abstract and complex concepts. For such a large number of logographs to be discriminable from one another, some of the characters must be complex. On the other hand, characters are not totally arbitrary: A radical and a phonetic give a clue to a character's meaning and sound, respectively, and some characters are related by a shared phonetic, radical, or both.

The chimp (and the speech or reading disabled) might "write" by arranging her plastic shapes (or characters), and the cerebral palsied, by pointing to the required Blissymbols in the correct sequence. But Chinese children must be able to write each character, stroke by stroke, in the prescribed order. That is, they analyze a character into an ordered set of strokes when they write (but not necessarily when they read). Character writing is regularly assigned as homework. Syntax becomes somewhat more complex as the ideas to be expressed get complex.

For all these reasons, learning the Chinese writing system takes some time, and it progresses differently from learning by the chimpanzee and by the speech or reading disabled. Recall that 10 years of schooling are needed to learn it.

Processing Characters

Chinese characters and alphabetic letters differ in the ways they look, code sounds, and map meanings. How do such differences affect the ways in which characters and alphabetic letters are processed—perceived, remembered, read, and so on?

Wholistic Recognition of Characters

Since one character by itself represents one intact morpheme, its perception should be wholistic. The Chinese word for 'mountain', 山 /shan/, is one morpheme, one syllable, and one character, that defies decomposition into subunits. A reader either identifies it as a whole or fails to identify it. One character may consist of several strokes (three in /shan/), but the strokes do not have individual semantic and phonetic functions, as do English letters or letter groups. A stroke is merely a building block for the shape of a Chinese character.

By contrast, an English word consists of a number of subunits, each of which has a semantic and/or phonetic function. Consider *mountains.* It is decomposable into two morphemes plus *ain,* 2 syllables, 7 phonemes, 7 spelling units, and 9 letters, in the following way:

[(m.ou.n.t) ai.n (s)] /maun-tənz/.

Various kinds of suffixes, infixes, and prefixes can be attached to a word. Reading is sometimes taught by such subunits, from small to large units—that is, from letters to words. In short, English words are potentially decomposable into a few levels of subunits; whether they are actually so decomposed in processing depends on the reader's skill with the given material (see Chapters 8 through 11).

Once again, each character is processed not stroke by stroke but as a whole visual pattern. At most, some characters may be decomposed into a radical and a phonetic. As Wieger (1965) points out:

> The analysis must end when it has separated and isolated these formal elements [radical and phonetic]. To go further, to decompose into strokes, would add nothing to knowledge... Just as... an iron ingot can be smashed with a hammer, and yet this is not a decomposition, but a breaking up [pp.13–14].

Hemispheric Processing of Characters

Letters and words of a phonetic script, be it an alphabet or a syllabary, are processed faster and better when presented in the right than in the left visual field of each eye (implying left hemisphere processing; see Chapter 1). Which hemisphere processes Chinese characters? To answer the question, numerous experiments have been carried out, mostly in the United States, employing Chinese–English bilinguals (referred to as Chinese speakers in the following discussion).

In one experiment, Chinese speakers verbally identified single characters shown in a T-scope (Tzeng, Hung, Cotton, & Wang, 1979). A strong left visual-field advantage (RH processing) was obtained, regardless of whether the characters contained a phonetic clue. When stimuli were multi-character words (such as 'train = fire-vehicle'), the opposite result—namely, evidence of LH processing—was obtained. In another experiment, Chinese speakers decided: "Do characters form a meaningful word?" by pressing a key to indicate yes or no. In this task that did not involve verbal identification, evidence of LH processing was again obtained.

Tzeng *et al.* attribute the results to wholistic recognition of single characters by the right hemisphere and sequential–analytical processing of character strings by the left hemisphere. Contrary findings—LH processing of single characters—have also been reported (Nguy, Allard, & Bryden, 1980). On balance, however, the evidence for RH processing of single characters is stronger than the contrary evidence, if we consider also several Japanese studies involving a large number and variety of characters, subjects, and tasks (see Chapter 4).

Stroop tests can be used to reveal differences between Chinese speakers processing characters and English speakers processing alphabetic letters. The **Stroop** effect occurs because people cannot help but perceive the meaning of the word, say, *green,* when they have to name only the ink color (red) in which the word is written (Stroop, 1935). When Chinese subjects tried to name the ink color of characters that represented conflicting color words, they showed more interference than did English-speaking subjects doing the same task with English words (Biederman & Tsao, 1979).

Single characters tend to be processed by the RH, which is involved also for processing color. Thus, reading Chinese characters and using color information may be competing for the same perceptual capacities, whereas reading English letters—a mainly LH activity—and color naming are executed by different mechanisms. Tsao and Wu (1981) confirmed that Chinese speakers experienced more Stroop interference when color words were presented to the right hemisphere, whereas English speakers showed more Stroop interference when color words were presented to the left hemisphere.

Typically, interlanguage color naming produces less Stroop effect than does intralanguage color naming (Dyer, 1971; Preston & Lambert, 1969). Chinese–English bilinguals showed greater reduction of the effect than did Spanish–English bilinguals (Tzeng & Hung, 1980). Switching from one language to another very different language enabled the Chinese–English bilinguals to be released from the Stroop interference.

The easiest way for a Westerner to understand how a Chinese character is processed is to think of how an Arabic numeral is processed: The symbol *4,* as one whole visual pattern, is associated with the concept 'four' in whatever language it is used. Its sound, however, changes from language to language: It is *quatre* in French, *vier* in German, *shi* or *yotsu* in Japanese, *net* or *sa* in Korean, and *si* in Mandarin Chinese. Similarly, the character for 'man' can be read either as *nin* or *hito* in Japanese, *ren* in Mandarin Chinese, and *in* in Korean. The similarity between Chinese characters and numerals does not end here. Single characters are preferentially processed by the right hemisphere; so are single numerals (Teng & Sperry, 1973). Some Japanese brain-damaged patients who have trouble reading phonetic scripts may retain the ability to process characters (see Chapter 4); likewise, some English- or French-speaking patients who have lost the ability to read may still be able to recognize numerals (Geschwind, 1965; Hécaen & Kremin, 1976).

Sensitivity to Radicals and Phonetics

Characters sharing either a radical or a phonetic will appear similar. This visual clue is useful in learning and processing characters. It can also be a source of errors: Characters sharing the same component may be confused (Van & Zian, 1962; see also Chapter 4).

In a pioneering experiment, Hull (1920) asked American college students to learn nonsense names of characters containing radicals. He gave the same name to all the characters containing the same radical and then divided the characters randomly into six packs, each containing 12 characters. In the first pack, Hull said the name of each character, which the student then repeated. Thereafter, the students had to guess the names of the characters in each of the five other packs. Students' correct guesses of the names of the characters increased from pack to pack, indicating that they were using radicals as clues.

In Kuo's (1923) experiment, American college students learned the English meanings of several characters containing the same radical. Each student was then questioned to ascertain whether he had noticed the radical and divined its meaning from the meanings of the characters in which it was a part. For example, a radical meaning 'mouth' was present in characters meaning 'bite, kiss, whistle, cry, sing, bark', and so on. Though instructions made no reference to radicals, the majority of the students spontaneously discovered the meaning of 'mouth' and of other radicals. However, as Woodworth (1938) points out, fully as interesting was the failure of the minority to reach any generalization. The common element of form or meaning is not necessarily obvious from a collection of specimens, when their attention is directed to the individual specimens. Matsuda and Roffins (1977) used terminology that is more in keeping with that of contemporary cognitive psychology: a prototype for a radical and examplars for characters that contain it. However, the point they make is the same as those made in the other studies: A prototype is abstracted and used as a cue for recognizing old and new exemplars.

In I. Taylor's (1980) experiment, when possibilities for pairing by meaning or by sound were available, two characters sharing a radical tended to be grouped as being similar in meaning, whereas two characters sharing a phonetic tended to be grouped as being similar in sound, more than did pairs of characters with similar meaning or pronunciation without sharing any component. In Tzeng and Hung's (1980) experiment, Chinese subjects read a passage, circling all characters containing certain grapheme components. The subjects detected more characters in which the designated grapheme component was a phonetic than characters in which it was not a phonetic.

Considering all the useful information radicals and phonetics provide, it is not surprising that they are regularly used as teaching aids wherever characters are taught (Ai, 1950; Leong, 1973; Liu, 1978; see also Chapter 4). And, one laments the disappearance of some of them in the simplification of characters in mainland China.

Phonetic Recoding of Characters

Tzeng and Hung's (1980) experiment, just described, serves also as evidence of phonetic recoding of visually presented characters. In English, visually presented letters and words seem to be phonetically represented in short-term memory so that similar sounding, rather than similar looking, letters are confused. For example, 'B' rather than 'X' is a more likely memory error when 'V' is visually presented (R. Conrad, 1964). Chu-Chang and Loritz (1977) demonstrated that written Chinese characters, too, are represented phonetically in short-term memory. They showed, very briefly, 15 isolated characters to Chinese high school students. The characters then had to be recognized among 90 response characters, 15 of which were homonyms (homophones? phonetic distractors), 15 synonyms (semantic distractors), 15 shape mates (visual distractors), and 45 correct items. The largest number of errors in recognition was phonetic, next was visual, and then semantic.

Phonemic similarity of of visually presented characters adversely affects short-term retention (Tzeng, Hung, & Wang, 1977). Recall was worst for those characters that shared an initial consonant as well as the following vowel and about the same for those that shared either only an initial consonant or only a final vowel. Furthermore, the more phonetically similar an interference list was to a target list, the worse the recall of the target list. (An interference list is learned between the presentation and the recall of a target list.) In judging whether a sentence was grammatical or not, reaction times depended on the degree of phonemic similarity among characters constituting the sentence: They were faster for phonemically variegated sentences, especially for ungrammatical ones, than for phonemically uniform ones.

Between Chinese reading and English reading, which shows more phonetic coding? American and Chinese subjects silently read two types of sentence, in their own language, and judged their truth or falsity (Treiman, Baron, & Luk, 1981):

1. *A pair is a fruit.* (homophone sentence)
2. *A pier is a fruit.* (control sentence).

Both groups of subjects took longer to respond to the homophone sentences than to the control sentences. But English speakers made more errors, whereas Chinese speakers made fewer errors, on the homophone than on the control sentences. Chinese speakers used phonetic recoding, but to a lesser extent than did English speakers.

Yik (1978) manipulated some single character pairs in acoustic similarity, others in visual similarity. In addition to a strong acoustic similarity effect, he obtained a strong visual similarity effect on memory. The visual effect was particularly pronounced in the absence of acoustic similarity between the characters. In other words, if characters sounded similar, visual dissimilarity had less effect.

In sum, Chinese characters, once their sounds are learned, are phonetically recoded in short-term memory, just as are alphabetic letters and words. Chapter 10 discusses phonetic recoding in English, the language in which a large number of experiments on this topic have been carried out. In that chapter we will discuss phonetic recoding as a means to access words' meanings and/or to hold already processed words in short-term memory as part of the business of comprehending sentences.

How Many Characters in a Chinese Word?

Examine the Chinese sentence in Figure 3-1.

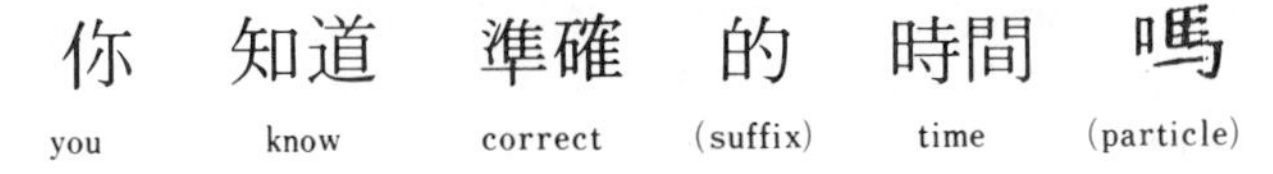

Figure 3-1. *Chinese sentence 'Do you have the time?'*

The sentence literally says, 'Do you know the correct time?' Each of the two words 'know' and 'time' require two characters; 'correct' has either two or three characters, depending on whether the suffix (which turns the noun into an adjective) is included in the count. The last character is a particle that transforms a declarative sentence into an interrogative one. The sentence contains six words in English and 7 character–morphemes in Chinese. If 7 Chinese characters are needed for 6 English words, roughly 1.2 characters must be counted per English word. Gray (1956), in his comparison of English and Chinese reading processes, used equivalent passages in the two languages. The English passage contained 146 words, and the Chinese one, 233 "words." Gray's Chinese "words" were probably "characters." If so, roughly 1.6 characters might be counted per English word.

The number of multi-character words has increased, partly due to an increase of technical terms in modern times, and partly due to an increase of homophones around 500 A.D. when syllable structures became simpler with dropping of consonant clusters and final consonants (Karlgren, 1962). Over 80 different morphemes, including 'husband, rich, wife, putrid' share the same monosyllable /fu/, and 188 morphemes share the syllable /yi/. Even with several levels of tone variation, homophones are hard to distinguish. Combining two or more morphemes to form a multi-character word is one way to minimize ambiguity. Some multi-character words merely repeat a synonymous morpheme, or even the same morpheme, as in 'road-route' for 'street', 'house-building' for 'house', and 'sister-sister' for 'younger sister' (or 'older sister', depending on the character used.) Such practice has crept into Chinese pidgin English, in words such as 'look-see'.

Two-character (two-morpheme) words seem preponderant in a certain type of language. In Kratochvil's (1968) casual counts of 1000 words each of three different types of speech, the number of two-morpheme words was six times greater than that of one-morpheme words in political speech, but in a casual dialogue between two speakers, it was somewhat smaller than the number of one-morpheme words. Huang and Liu (1978) in Taiwan estimate that two-character words in all types of speech comprise 65.15%. Some words contain three or four characters, and a few rare words have as many as eight. Such long words are almost phrases, like the four-character "word," 'no voice, no echo'.

In Chinese writing, characters are uniformly arranged with a space after each character but no extra space after a word. One wonders whether an extra space after each word, as in Figure 3-1, might facilitate word recognition. Liu's team investigated this question and found, unexpectedly, that it made the sentence hard to read (Liu, Yeh, Wang, & Chang, 1974). Reading habits may partly explain the result: Chinese readers are not accustomed to reading with space between words.

To interpret further this unexpected result, perhaps we need to look closely into multi-character words, in which each of the constituent characters contributes to the overall meaning of the word:

sky + screen = tent
mind + logic + study = psychology
dry + cup = bottoms up, cheers
sister + sister = younger sister (repetition)
right + exact = correct (synonym compound)

To process a Chinese word character by character is to process it morpheme by morpheme. This mode of processing is not comparable with letter-by-letter processing of an English word, in which each letter has no meaning. The Chinese way is comparable to processing such words as *blackboard* as *black + board,* but only few English words are formed in this way, and the semantic composition of some of them (*brachycephalic = brachy + cephal + ic*) is obvious only to scholars. A more comparable object is a telephone number such as *555–1212,* in which each digit needs attention.

There are some multi-character words whose constituent characters do not contribute to a word's meaning or, worse, produce a misleading meaning (an analogous example in English is *cocktail*): 'east + west = the thing'. We have not come across a survey of such illogical words; nor have we come across a study on how hard it is to learn them. We note only that this particular Chinese word has been adopted neither by Koreans nor by Japanese, who have adopted all the logical words (except 'sister + sister'), listed earlier.

Writing and Printing Characters

Most people who can read can write, and vice versa. Different processes are involved in the two skills, however: In reading, a person recognizes letters, whereas in writing, she recalls them. Recall is more difficult than recognition, because recall includes a search as well as recognition (Anderson & Bower, 1972). Recall is difficult also because it needs complete information about an object, whereas recognition needs only sufficient information to distinguish an object from others. When a writing system contains many complex characters, writing is adversely affected far more than is reading. But remember, each character represents a morpheme, which in English may require as few as one or as many as nine or more letters (*a character*).

One way to measure the relative complexity of characters and English words is to compare the time required to write "equivalent" content in English and Chinese. I. Taylor (1981) reported that it took three times longer to write a Chinese page than its English equivalent. On that bilingual text, 1.6 characters were counted per English word. According to a survey cited in C.-C. Cheng (1977), it takes one-third less time to copy a text of 500 characters in simplified than in original form. It makes sense that, in Taiwan, people simplify characters when they write but normally do not use simplified characters in printing (Liu, 1979). But then, what one writes, someone else may have to read.

Learning to write characters takes time and patience because of their variety and complexity. The strokes of each character must be written in an authorized, fixed order. However, the order of writing strokes, once learned for a handful of characters, can be applied to writing any new character. Basically, write a character from top to bottom, and from left to right. Finish one subpart, be it a radical or a phonetic, before tackling another. For example, to write the character for 'bright' (see Table 3-3), write the part for 'sun' first, and then that for 'moon'. This kind of writing order may promote the unit property of a subpart. If a writer follows the rules, the finished product has a better chance of being a well-balanced character than if he does not.

For typing and typesetting, characters are cumbersome mainly because of their great variety. As of today, there is no character typewriter for home use. A Chinese "typewriter" found in business offices is actually a sort of a printer's typesetting machine, having a few thousand common characters plus a reserve of a few more thousand uncommon ones. A typist must first search for a required character and then punch it. The search among so many choices can seldom be automatic, especially when characters cannot be arranged in a perfectly systematic manner. In Taiwan, C.-M. Cheng (1978; 1982) is experimenting on a typewriter with the 37 signs of the National Phonetic Symbols. The abundance of homophones ought to present a formidable obstacle for readers when the Chinese language is represented purely phonetically. If one considers only common characters and takes into account tone variations as well, the number of homophones is drastically reduced, but there are still 30 homophones of /yi/ instead of 188.

Vertical and Horizontal Eye Movements

Chinese characters are suitable to both horizontal and vertical directions of reading, because a one- or two-character word is well within a horizontal as well as a vertical perceptual span (see Chapter 7). Chinese is traditionally written vertically: Characters are arranged in a column, every column starting from the top of a page. Columns are arranged from right to left so that a page of a book is turned from left to right (the opposite of the Western manner). In Taiwan, the vertical direction is used for ordinary writings, but the horizontal direction is used for technical writings in order to accommodate Arabic numerals and Roman letters. In mainland China, the horizontal direction is now used in most writings—textbooks, magazines, and newspapers, including the official *People's Daily.* People read faster in the direction to which they are accustomed (see Chapter 4).

The eyes of a reader do not glide along the lines of print but instead perform a series of jumps called **saccades** with **fixation pauses** between them. Only during the fixation pause does visual perception of print take place. Each fixation lasts on average a quarter of a second, and fixations account for 90% of reading time. In mature reading, fixations move forward more or less rhythmically, but occasional **regressions** occur for retakes of missed material.

Do eye movements differ in reading Chinese and English? In a modern study carried out in the United States, Chinese readers averaged 10 saccades (frequent fixations) per line, compared with American readers, who averaged 4 per line (Stern, 1978). Fixation durations did not distinguish the two groups. The Chinese text used in the experiment was written horizontally, in the same width as the English text. The Chinese readers, if they came from Taiwan, were less accustomed to reading Chinese horizontally than they were vertically. In reading English, Chinese students in the United States (with 7–14 years of English) made 10 saccades per line of print, with many regressions. They were reading English the way they read Chinese. Many regressions indicate that the Chinese readers found English reading difficult.

F.-C. Wang (1935) suggests why eye movements tend to be more smooth, but frequent, in reading Chinese than in reading English. Each character is of a similar size and occupies the same amount of space regardless of the number of strokes. This uniformity of characters causes other striking differences in the spatial distributions of fixations along a line: The square shape of the characters and their compact arrangement in a line demand smaller and more frequent eye movements than is required in the reading of English.

We suggest other reasons for frequent fixations in Chinese reading: In Chinese, almost every character is meaningful and important and hence needs processing. *Know person not say, say person not know.* Compare this sparse and lean sentence (written by Laotzu in the classical style) to its English equivalent, 'He who understands does not talk, and he who talks does not understand.' The English sentence contains more items, but some of them are function words with little meaning, such as *does, who, and,* and the suffix *-s* that the eyes tend to skip during reading (see Chapters 7, 11, and 12).

Another reason for frequent fixations has to do with the non-use of **peripheral vision.** In reading English text, a reader, while fixating on one word, can note in her peripheral vision gross features of next word and blank space, which may guide her eye movements. On the other hand, she wastes, though not entirely, the vertical span of three lines. The Chinese-character reader may do the opposite: He wastes horizontal peripheral vision but makes full use of his vertical visual span. As characters are by and large uniform in gross appearance, there are few prominent features to be noted in peripheral vision. The visual density of a character might be noted, but its usefulness in perceiving characters is limited.

Summary and Conclusions

Chinese characters are suited for representing the Chinese language, whose morphemes are monosyllabic and noninflecting. Since characters represent meanings primarily and sounds secondarily, they permit communication among Chinese speakers of mutually unintelligible dialects.

A character as a whole visual pattern represents a meaning and a syllable. Hence there is little problem in learning and using a ***limited*** number of them. Even severely speech- or reading-disabled children can learn a handful of Chinese characters by look-say, bypassing their sounds.

Chinese characters have unfavorable features: To represent the Chinese language in its entirety there must be a large number of characters, as many as there are morphemes in the language. To ensure discriminability, some characters have to be complex, posing problems for learners and users, especially for writers. Typewriters and typesetting are cumbersome. As a ***system,*** Chinese is not so easy to learn and use. For all these reasons, the government in mainland China is deeply involved in reforming the writing system. All the same, it is possible for a society to attain near 100% literacy in Chinese, as is seen in Taiwan.

To be literate, Chinese children learn about 3000 common characters. They learn characters' sounds using phonetic symbols and learn to write each character according to rules for sequencing strokes. They learn to read characters in three phases: first, as global visual patterns; next, analyzed into subparts; and third, again as whole patterns, now made from familiar subparts.

Research into processing of characters is gaining momentum in the North America, Taiwan, and Japan, though not in China itself. To cite only a few recent research findings, single characters tend to be processed as whole visual patterns by the RH, whereas multi-character words are processed as a sequential linguistic materials by the LH. In short-term memory, Chinese characters are coded phonetically, just as are phonetic letters. People, whether they read Chinese or not, show sensitivity to meaning-cuing radicals and sound-cuing phonetics.

What future do Chinese characters have? Half-hearted attempts at discarding the logographic system in favor of an alphabet have not made much headway. A writing system that represents several thousand years of high culture, and that is used by over 1 billion people, cannot easily be changed, much less discarded. Among the writing systems that exist in the world today, the Chinese is undoubtedly the most unique and picturesque, if not the most practical, system. It is safe to assume that Chinese characters—streamlined and digitized for electronic communications—will be with us for a long time, to be cherished by those who use them.

4

Logography and Syllabary: Japanese

i ro ha ni ho he to chi ri nu ru [w]o
wa ka yo ta re so tu ne na ra mu
u [w]i no o ku ya ma ke fu ko e te
a sa ki yu me mi si [w]e hi mo se su

'Its colours dazzle, even as it lies there fallen.
Of our generation, who can be for ever?
Today I will cross the far hills of creation,
Waking from the shallow dream—and sober too!'

Writing System: Kanji and Kana

The poem at the head of this chapter uses all 47 letters of the old Japanese syllabary, each letter only once, thus providing Japanese speakers with an excellent mnemonic for learning the syllabary. It is said to have been written by a Buddhist priest in the tenth century and has been translated into English specially for this book by William Skillend of London University.[1]

Japan is a chain of small, mountainous islands forming an arc in the Pacific Ocean. Densely packed in this chain of islands are 117 million people speaking a single language, Japanese (not counting a small group of aborigines

[1]Two other translations, the first one by Chamberlain (1905), and the second by Kinda (1978), follow:

'Though gay in hue, flowers flutter down, alas!/ Who then, in this world of ours, may last forever?/ Crossing today the uttermost limits of phenomenal existence,/ I shall see no more fleeting dreams,/ Neither be any longer intoxicated.'

'Though flowers bloom, they soon fall,/ to everyone this world is transient./ Crossing the mountains of life's vicissitudes today,/ we shall not have light dreams or be intoxicated again.'

who speak Ainu, a language unrelated to Japanese). On its west, Japan faces the giant land mass of China, to whom it owes its writing system, thousands of words, Buddhism, and many other elements of its culture. Japanese reading is interesting for two reasons: Japan enjoys one of the highest literacy rates in the world, and it uses a mixture of various writing systems, the two important ones being Chinese characters and a syllabary. Japanese writing has been described by Chamberlain (1905) as "a backbone of Chinese characters with Kana [syllabary] ligaments [p. 5]."

Kanji (Chinese Character or Characters)

Chinese characters used in Japan are called **Kanji** ('letters of the Kan dynasty'). Japan borrowed characters from China at several times between the fifth and fourteenth centuries A.D. Of special importance was the year A.D. 404, when two Korean scholars became tutors to the Japanese heir to the throne. From then on, Chinese was studied zealously in Japan.

Chinese and Japanese are totally unrelated languages, just as unrelated as are English and Japanese. The two differ in sound system, vocabulary, and syntax. Chinese is monosyllabic, whereas Japanese is polysyllabic; Chinese is tonal, whereas Japanese is not; Chinese has about 400 syllable types, whereas Japanese has about 100; Chinese has phonemes that are not found in Japanese.

Because of the differences in the sound systems among Chinese, Korean, and Japanese, the borrowed characters retain by and large their original meanings, but their pronunciations are modified to suit the sound system of each language. To illustrate this point, the Kanji for *bamboo* is pronounced as:

/chu/ in Mandarin Chinese,
/chuk/ in Korean, and
/chiku/ in Japanese.

Only the Chinese pronunciation requires tone variations. (The Korean pronunciation may be the way this character was pronounced in certain old Chinese dialects, which once permitted /k/ as a final consonant.) Both Chinese and Japanese sound systems require that a word end in a vowel or /n/ (or /r/ in Chinese).

The majority (about two-thirds) of the Kanji used in Japan have at least one Chinese-derived and one Japanese-native pronunciation (henceforth, simply "Chinese pronunciation" and "Japanese pronunciation"). Take *bamboo* again: In addition to its Chinese pronunciation of /chiku/, it also has a Japanese pronunciation /take/, or its variant /dake/, which is a native Japanese word for *bamboo.* To get the flavor of this practice, imagine English speakers adopting this character and pronouncing it /chu/ and also /bæmbu/. In earlier times, when the Japanese wrote a Kanji, they would sometimes juxtapose a Japanese word to explain its meaning. The Kanji for 'correct', has no fewer than 14 Japanese readings (*akira, kami, masashi, sada,* etc.) and 2 Chinese ones (*sho* and *sei*) (Takebe, 1979, p. 53).

To complicate the picture further, one is not always sure when a Kanji is to be read in a Chinese or a Japanese way, or in which Chinese and Japanese way. Muraishi and Amano (1972) studied 5-year-old preschoolers who could read a limited number of Kanji. Some single Kanji, such as for numerals ('one, five'), were read by all children in the Chinese way, others ('rain, summer') in the Japanese way. Some other Kanji ('old, fire') were read in either of the two ways equally often. Chinese pronunciations of some Kanji vary, depending on where in China these Kanji came from and when. A word may be made up of more than one Kanji, and it is not uncommon for each of the Kanji to be pronounced by a different method. We point out this somewhat chaotic state of Japanese pronunciation of Kanji to show that to read Japanese like a highly educated person is not as easy as one might imagine from the simplicity of its syllabaries.

Perhaps not all is chaos. According to Nomura's (1978) study on adult readers, Kanji with Japanese pronunciation were read faster than were Kanji with Chinese sounds. Recall was also better for the Japanese-sound than for the Chinese-sound Kanji. Japanese people tend to attach a meaning to a single Kanji through its Japanese pronunciation. If the Chinese reading is specifically required, they appear to translate the Japanese reading to the Chinese one, perhaps because it is the Japanese pronunciation that gives the character's meaning. Multi-Kanji words tend to be read in the Chinese way, because they are often loan words from Chinese or words created according to the pattern of Chinese words.

In the 1950s, 1850 Kanji were designated in Japan as "official." Recently, several more have been added. As everybody is aware, linguistic matters are notoriously untamable by official decree. Most educated Japanese find the official list insufficient and learn at least 1000 additional Kanji. According to a large-scale survey carried out in 1976, 1000 Kanji account for 91.3% of all Kanji used in Japan; 2000 Kanji, for 98.8%; and 3000 Kanji, for 99.8% (reported in Watanabe, 1976).

As long as the Japanese continue to use a substantial number of Kanji, they face the same problems in typesetting and electronic communications as do the Chinese. Thanks to Kanji, ordinary Japanese are denied the convenience and pleasure of writing on a typewriter, although business offices may be equipped with a cumbersome Kanji–Kana typewriter. Like a Chinese typewriter, a Japanese typewriter has 2000 common characters plus a reserve of a few thousand more uncommon ones. For the latter, a typist gets a type slug from a bin, puts it on the machine, types, takes it off, and puts it back in the bin. An average Japanese typist can type only 20–30 words per minute, compared with an English-speaking typist, who can type 50–60 words.

Problems with computer terminals are only slightly less daunting than those with typewriters. After a 3-year development program, IBM's Canadian research laboratory is exporting to Japan a terminal with 254 keys and 12 shift keys that give access to 2500 common characters including both Hiragana and Kanji. A further 9000 characters are available with an alternate numeric call-up system. Even with a keyboard that looks as if it were designed by a crazed crossword puzzle fanatic, the designers have not scratched the surface of the complexity of Japanese writing (the *Globe and Mail*, Toronto, January 16, 1981).

But the advantages of Kanji for reading outweigh these disadvantages in writing and printing, as we shall see.

Two Kana (Syllabaries)

The first writing of Japanese was done by scholars who used Kanji exclusively. For a few hundred years this system continued, although it was awkward. For one thing, Japanese syntax requires grammatical morphemes that inflect, but Chinese characters are totally unsuitable for representing such morphemes. All but a handful of Chinese characters are for writing content morphemes (see Chapter 3). For this and other reasons, the Japanese developed two kinds of syllabaries over a long period, starting in the eighth century and culminating in the twelfth to fourteenth centuries A.D. The two syllabaries were modernized and standardized in 1946.

The Japanese syllabary is called **Kana** ('false name'), and the two types of syllabaries are called **Katakana** ('fragment, side Kana') and **Hiragana** ('cursive, smooth Kana'): Each Katakana sign is a fragment or side of a Chinese character, and its Hiragana version is a cursive and greatly simplified form of the same character, as shown in Table 4-1. These particular characters served as models for the Kana signs because they have sounds like those of the required Japanese syllables, and at the same time are simply shaped. In fact, Kana are fragments of Chinese characters used only for their sounds, disregarding their meanings and tones. Thus, Kana is variously translated as 'false name,' 'expedient name,' or 'borrowed name,' Kanji being the 'true name.' Hiragana duplicates Katakana exactly in the number and phonetic values of the letters, just as capital letters duplicate the small letters of the English alphabet.

The shapes of the Kana signs give no indication of their sounds. For example, the five syllables /ka, ki, kú, ke, ko/ share the same initial consonant, but their Kana signs have nothing in common. Nor do the signs for /hi, mi, ki/, which share the same vowel. Unlike the Cree syllabary (see Table 2-2) or the Korean alphabetic syllabary (Chapter 5), the Japanese syllabaries do not permit any analysis of a syllable into its initial consonant and following vowel and hence can be considered a "true" syllabary.

A syllabary is well suited for the Japanese sound system, which has a small number of syllables and no consonant clusters. Every syllable ends in a vowel, the only exception being /n/ as a final consonant. The number of phonemes is small—five "canonical" vowels (/a, e, i, o, u/) and about a dozen simple consonants (see Table 4-2 for eight of them.)

Not only the Japanese syllables but also the Japanese syllabaries that represent them are simple. First of all, each letter represents the same syllable

Table 4-1. *Katakana and Hiragana*

Sound	Katakana	Kanji	Hiragana	Add (゛)	Sound: voiced	Add (゜)	Semi voiced	
ha	ハ	八波	は	ば	ba	ぱ	pa	
hi	ヒ	比	ひ	び	bi	ぴ	pi	
f, hu	フ	不	ふ	ぶ	bu	ぷ	pu	take both (゛) & (゜)
he	ヘ	阝部	へ	べ	be	ぺ	pe	
ho	ホ	保	ほ	ぼ	bo	ぽ	po	
ka	カ	加	か	が	ga			
ki	キ	幾	き	ぎ	gi			
ku	ク	久	く	ぐ	gu			take only (゛)
ke	ケ	介計	け	げ	ge			
ko	コ	己	こ	ご	go			
na	ナ	奈	な					
ni	ニ	仁	に					
nu	ヌ	奴	ぬ					take neither (゛) nor (゜)
ne	ネ	祢	ね					
no	ノ	乃	の					

Source: I. Taylor, 1981, p. 21, reproduced with permission of Academic Press.

consistently. Second, the sound of a syllable sign serves also as the name of the sign ("ka" for /ka/ to compare with English "aitch" for /h/). Third, each letter is simple in shape, containing no more than six strokes, with three being the most common. The shape of letters is reasonably distinct between the two types of syllabary: Katakana is squarish containing many straight lines, whereas Hiragana is cursive, containing many curved lines and is suited for rapid handwriting. Letters are distinct also within each syllabary. For example, there may be similar letters but no exact mirror-image letters, such as the notorious 'b/d' or 'p/q'.

Fourth, the number of letters in each syllabary is small: Each has 46 basic letters representing 46 syllables. Originally, there were 50 letters, but 5 redundant ones have become obsolete, and 1 ('n') has been added. Two kinds of diacritic marks can be attached to the 25 basic letters to create secondary letters (see Table 4-1). Counting both the basic and the secondary letters, 71 short syllables can be represented by 71 letters of either Katakana or Hiragana. In addition, there are 35 modified signs, which are the basic symbols written small to represent "assimilated" (doubled consonants) and contracted sounds as in *ge.k.ki.yu* ゲッキュ (Kana for the first 'k' is 'tsu' written small).

Table 4-2 *Arrangement of 46 Basic Kana*

a	*ka*	*sa*	*ta*	*na*	*ha*	*ma*	*ya*	*ra*	*wa*	
i	*ki*	*si*	*chi*	*ni*	*hi*	*mi*	—	*ri*	—	
u	*ku*	*su*	*tsu*	*nu*	*hu,fu*	*mu*	*yu*	*ru*	—	
e	*ke*	*se*	*te*	*ne*	*he*	*me*	—	*re*	—	
o	*ko*	*so*	*to*	*no*	*ho*	*mo*	*yo*	*ro*	*wo*	*n*

As far as the basic and the secondary syllables and their symbols are concerned, the principle of "one symbol for one syllable" holds. However, a few of the syllables present problems: /n/ as a final consonant, assimilated consonants, and lengthened vowels. To deal with them, a Kana is said to represent not a syllable but a **mora,** which is a short sound uttered in the same length of time as an ordinary short syllable. Thus, /hon/, 'book', though it contains one syllable, is written in two Kana (*ho.n*), and *gakkō*, 'school', a two-syllable word with an assimilated C and a long V, in four Kana (*ga.k.ko.o*).

The basic Kana signs are often arranged in 10 columns, the 5 vowels by 9 consonants, as in Table 4-2. The arrangement is said to be based on the Devanagari alphabet (R. A. Miller, 1967).

Learning to Read in Japanese

A mixture of writing systems borrowed and developed from various sources in bits and pieces over centuries might be expected to play havoc with reading. In his book on the Japanese language, R. A. Miller (1967) even goes so far as to describe this mixture of scripts as "fatal intermingling." Contrary to his view, the mixture, so awkward for typing, turns out to be a blessing for reading.

High Literacy and Mixed Scripts

Makita (1968) reports that the literacy rate in Japan is 99%, with illiteracy confined largely to the mentally retarded. Based on teachers' responses (covering over 9000 children) to his questionnaires, Makita also reports an extremely low rate (0.98%) of reading disabled children. According to Duke (1977) and Sakamoto and Makita (1973), there are no remedial reading classes or teachers in Japan.

Makita attributes the high literacy rate to:

1. The Japanese people's respect for education
2. Compulsory education from Grades 1 to 9, with 99.9% enrollment
3. Ready availability of good but inexpensive reading material
4. Movements to stimulate reading, such as National Reading Week
5. Initiation into reading with Kana

The first reason has little to do with writing systems. One can only speculate that the Japanese respect for education, coupled with their disciplined classroom behavior, may largely explain their extremely low rate of illiteracy. Taiwan, which uses Chinese characters exclusively, and South Korea, which uses its own phonetic script along with some Kanji, also have low illiteracy rates, perhaps for the same reason.

As for the second reason, free and compulsory education is available in most advanced countries. What distinguishes education in Japan from that of North America is the low dropout rate in Japan, where 98% of children go on to complete 3 noncompulsory years of senior high school, perhaps in part because they ***can*** read.

For the third reason, the availability of reading material, one may argue that much good and cheap reading material is published in Japan because there is a great demand for it. At any rate, many advanced countries do even better than Japan, in that they have neighborhood libraries available to all citizens free of charge. The U.S. equivalent to the fourth reason is "Right to Read," which has become a national goal since the 1970s.[2]

The fifth reason, namely, the use of Kana, is unique to Japanese. Kana codes a syllable, a simply structured one at that. A syllable is intrinsically easier to isolate and use than a phoneme. By age 4, some Japanese children, regardless of their knowledge of letters, can segment words into syllable–moras (Muraishi & Amano, 1972). Even for English-speaking children, the ability to segment words into syllables develops much faster than their phoneme segmenting ability (see Chapter 14, "Linguistic Awareness").

In addition to Makita's (1968) five reasons, we suggest that reading is made easy by the mixed use of logographic Kanji and phonetic Kana for different purposes. This factor will be discussed later. All in all, Makita's five reasons for the high literacy rate might equally well be caused by the ease of reading in Japanese.

Learning Kana

Considering the simplicity of the Japanese syllables and the two syllabaries that represent them, it is not surprising that almost all Japanese children learn some Hiragana even before they enter school at age 6. They learn Hiragana letters at home and kindergarten, often without any formal instruction but with some help from their families and teachers. They absorb Hiragana simply by being exposed to printed materials such as comics, story books, letter blocks, labels on objects, TV, and so on.

Between 1967 and 1970 the Japanese National Language Research Institute conducted a nationwide survey of reading abilities of preschoolers,

[2]The "Right to Read" office was set up in the spring of 1970. Its objective was to ensure that by 1980, 90% of those over age 16 would possess and use literacy skills.

covering over 2000 4- and 5-year-olds. The results of the survey are published in a book (National Language Institute, 1973) and also in a short report (Muraishi & Amano, 1972). By the age of 4, one-third of the preschoolers could read at least 60 Hiragana letters, and only 9.3% were unable to read any letters. (A decade previously, these levels of ability had been reached only by Grade 1 children at age 6.) By 5, two-thirds of the children could read 60 or more letters, and only 1.1% could read no letters. The majority of the 5-year-olds could also write 21 or more letters. A month before entering school, the percentage of 5-year-olds who could read 60–71 Hiragana jumped to 88%. (Note that this survey was conducted more than a decade ago; 5-year-olds' reading performances when they enter school might be even more impressive if tested today because of the trend to improved test and IQ results in Japan.)

Besides age, preschoolers' reading achievements were influenced by their sex, the number of years in kindergarten, and the levels of their fathers' education. Girls read more than boys, time in kindergarten helped, and children with better educated fathers read more, as shown in Figure 4-1. In kindergarten, reading is not formally taught, but writing is used to identify owners of objects, to give brief instructions to children, and so on. Also children's questions about letters are answered. If writing is used in this way to convey vitally important information to children, it is not surprising that the children want to read.

Learning to read Hiragana is completed quickly once the child starts to learn. To give two typical cases: In 1 month after learning their first letters, Child A learned 8 letters and Child B 10 letters; in the next 5 months, Child A learned 65 letters, and Child B learned all 71 letters (Ishikawa, 1970; Murata, 1974). In other words, once a child grasps the idea of Kana, she quickly learns all the letters.

Recall that Kana consists of 46 basic and 25 secondary letters. With knowledge of 60–71 Hiragana letters, preschoolers can negotiate simple stories written in Hiragana only. Actually, some 5-year-olds know Katakana, a limited number of Kanji, the Arabic numerals 0–9, and even some letters of the

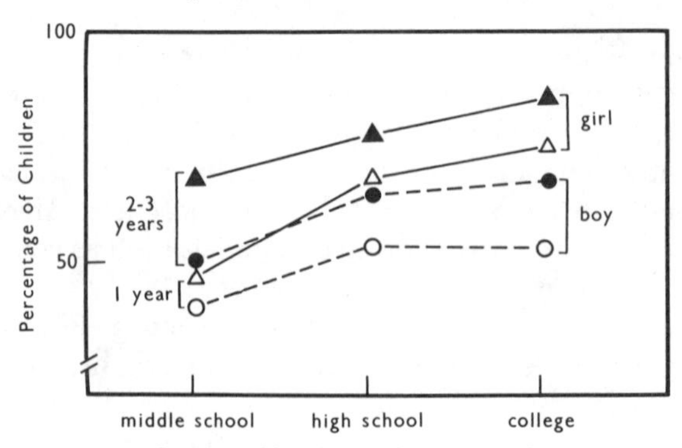

Figure 4-1. *Percentage of 5-year-olds who read over 60 Hiragana, as a function of sex, years in kindergarten, and fathers' education (from Muraishi & Amano, 1972, p. 21, reproduced with the authors' permission).*

English alphabet. In one test, 5-year-olds could read 50% of the sentences found in Part 1 of a Grade 1 primer (Muraishi & Amano, 1972). Contrast learning Japanese Kana to learning English orthography: Knowledge of the English alphabet by itself does not guarantee story reading, even word reading, because English-speaking children have to grapple with complex and irregular sound–letter relations as soon as they start reading. See how the sound of 'o' changes and 'b' becomes silent in *come, rob, comb,* and *bomb.*

Those Japanese children who have not mastered Hiragana before they start schooling do so in a short time at school. Each Kana letter is associated with its own unique sound, a syllable, which need not be analyzed into phonemes. There is no need for phonic blending, either, since each Kana codes a stable syllable, which can be combined with other syllables with no change in its sound value. The syllables /sa/ and /ra/ do not change, whether they occur in /sa.ra/ 'dish', /sa.ku.ra/ 'cherry blossom', /sa.yo.na.ra/ 'good-bye', or in any other word. One Grade 1 basal reader examined by one of us starts with two simple phrases in the first lesson and progresses to two simple sentences in the second lesson.

There is an order in learning Kana: Usually Hiragana are learned before Katakana, simply because the former are far more useful and hence are taught earlier. The basic Kana can be learned in the order shown in Table 4-2, column by column starting from the vowel column. The order of Kana is worth remembering because it is the order in which words are listed in dictionaries. In the Grade 1 basal reader just mentioned, the basic Hiragana table is made into a song and put somewhere in the middle of the reader. Japanese college students show evidence of having internalized the order of the syllables (Itsukushima, 1981), as English readers do the ABCs.

In a large-scale cross-language study comparing reading achievements of children in three countries, Grade 1 children in Japan scored higher in sentence comprehension and oral reading of text than did Grade 1 children in Taiwan and the United States (Stevenson *et al.* 1982). This finding is not surprising, considering that many Japanese children already read most Hiragana even before they start Grade 1. In vocabulary and letter tests, however, the Japanese children scored no higher than did the children in Taiwan and the United States, perhaps because the test materials were more difficult.[3]

To conclude, initiation into literacy is painless in Japan because of the simplicity of its Hiragana. Almost all preschoolers "pick up" some Hiragana before entering school at age 6.

Learning Kanji

A Japanese cannot be considered literate without knowing many Kanji, since daily newspapers, popular magazines, and street signs use them. As in

[3]In the test lists, the Hiragana letters were crowded, whereas the English letters, in boldface, were spaced. We thank Stevenson and his team for letting Insup Taylor examine their test materials and the Grades 1 and 2 basal readers used in Japan and Taiwan.

China, Kanji are taught batch by batch: 76 in Grade 1; 145 more in Grade 2; 194 more in Grade 3, and so on, until about 1000 Kanji have been mastered by the end of 6 years of primary school. By the time children finish the compulsory 9-year education, they have mastered most of the official 2000 Kanji. Many people learn an additional 1000 or so "unofficial" Kanji.

The Kanji for early grades were selected with the following four criteria in mind, according to a 1958 report of the Ministry of Education:

1. Common occurrence in printed materials
2. Relevant to children's life
3. Basic characters (containing few subparts?)
4. Easy to remember (based on empirical findings?)

Initially, single-Kanji words are favored over multi-Kanji words.

The complexity of Kanji seems not to have been an explicit criterion. Nevertheless, according to our own calculation, Kanji for Grade 1 are far simpler than those for Grades 2 and 3, as shown in Table 4-3.
In general usage, frequently occurring Kanji tend to be simpler than infrequently occurring ones, according to the 1950 survey by a leading Japanese paper *Asahi* (Ono, 1967).

The sounds of Kanji are annotated with Kana to aid initial learning. The pictorial origin of some Kanji and meaning-bearing radicals are also useful aids to teaching Kanji. Kanji are taught by the whole-word method, as in China: Each Kanji as a visual whole is associated with its meaning and sound.

For the past 20 years, the Japanese educator Ishii (1967) has been championing the massive teaching of Kanji, as many as 1000, even to preschoolers as young as 3 years of age. His method is to teach Kanji systematically, making full use of semantic and phonetic relations among Kanji. Most Kanji are composed of phonetics and radicals. Thus, by learning one basic Kanji, many other Kanji sharing either a radical or a phonetic, or both, can be easily learned. Ishii also teaches multi-Kanji words in groups that share the same Kanji and have related meanings. According to Sakamoto (1975), Ishii's method has been accepted by more than 200 kindergartens since 1968. Even without much instruction, a month before entering school 5-year-olds who could read most Hiragana could also read on average 53 (range 8–168) Grade 1 and some Grade 2 Kanji (Muraishi & Amano, 1972).

Kanji can be successfully taught to language-disabled (e.g., deaf, autistic, delayed speech) preschoolers as young as 1 year and 5 months old. The child associates the whole visual pattern, be it a single- or multi-Kanji word, with an object, picture, or an event, bypassing sounds. In fact, a language-disabled

Table 4-3 *Kanji for Three Early Grades*

Grade	*Number of Kanji*	*Average strokes*	*Range of strokes*
1	76	4.9	1–12
2	145	8.4	2–17
3	194	9.2	2–18

child should be highly motivated to learn to read, since reading is her main means of communication. Rees-Nishio (1979, 1981) taught seven language-disabled preschoolers to read over 200 Kanji and Kanji–Kana words. Difficulty in learning a Kanji word appeared to depend on its conceptual difficulty rather than on its visual complexity. Thus, Kanji for 'apple' was easier than Kanji for 'bookstore', which in turn was easier than the category word 'clothing'. In 20 months, Steinberg's team taught one profoundly deaf toddler, aged 1 year and 5 months, to recognize about 200 words, as well as 100 phrases and short sentences, mostly in Kanaji but some in Kana (Steinberg, Harada, Tashiro, & Yamada, 1982). These researchers' method is similar to the one used to teach reading to nonhuman primates (Premack, 1971) and to reading-disabled American children (Rozin *et al.*, 1971), as described in Chapter 3.

Learning Kanji versus Kana

Which are easier to learn, Kana or Kanji? In the article entitled "Learning to Read Kanji is Easier than Learning Individual Kana," Steinberg and Oka (1978) showed that preschoolers aged 3 and 4 learned Kanji faster than they did Kana. Each child learned four items—1 Kanji noun, 1 Kanji adjective or verb, 1 Hiragana, and 1 Katakana—in 10 trials of paired-associate learning. The test materials included 84 Kanji (taken from Grades 1–4 Kanji), 42 basic Hiragana, and 42 basic Katakana (4 Kana letters that look similar in the two syllabaries were not used). Differences between the two types of Kana, as well as between Kanji verb/adjective and Kanji nouns, were negligible. Furthermore, the complexity and length of material made no difference. But whether the item was Kanji or Kana made a difference, in favor of Kanji. Kanji of all kinds were learned twice as fast and correctly as either kind of Kana. Over one-third of the Kanji words were learned within three trials. Some Kanji, even complex ones with 16 strokes, were learned on the first trial. In another study, the Kanji words were also retained better than the Hiragana letters when tested 1 week later (Oka, Mori, & Kakigi, 1979).

Do these results tell us that Kanji are easier to learn than Kana, or that meaningful words are easier to learn than meaningless syllables? The Kanji stimuli were all meaningful words, whereas the Kana stimuli were all meaningless syllables. As Steinberg (1977) points out, "If we have learned anything in 100 years of psychological experimentation, it is that meaning is a very important variable in verbal learning." In fact, differences in learning scores between Kanji and Hiragana disappeared when Hiragana letters were learned as part of familiar meaningful words ('sa' in *sakura*, 'cherry blossom') (Oka *et al.*, 1979). The differences disappeared also when each of five monosyllabic words (*me, ha, to, ki, su*) ('eye, teeth, door, tree, nest') was taught either as a single Kanji or Katakana (Imai, 1979). Furthermore, the 42 Kana used by Steinberg and Oka (1978) represent almost all the basic Kana letters to be learned, but 84 Kanji represent a tiny portion of the 2000–3000 Kanji that must be learned eventually.

What these studies do show is not that the Kanji system is easier to learn than the Kana system, but that even preschoolers can learn a ***limited*** number of judiciously selected Kanji. The best teaching method should use the customary script, be it Kanji, Hiragana, or Katakana. But the age-old tradition persists: Kanji are treated as complex and difficult material to be introduced to young children gingerly.

Learning a large number of Kanji is difficult, as many Japanese educators attest. Makita (1968) found that in each of the first four grades, reading disabled children had more trouble with Kanji than with either kind of Kana. Kanji are difficult to master because of their quantity and complexity (visually, phonologically, and semantically). Accordingly, both in primary and middle schools, considerable time and money are expanded on teaching Kanji, but without satisfactory results (Yoshida, Matsuda, & Shimura, 1975). Stevenson *et al.*, 1982) found that whereas Japanese children outperformed Taiwanese and American children in Grade 1, the children from the three countries performed similarly by Grade 5. Beyond Grade 1, learning to read in Japan is concerned with learning more Kanji and more complex uses of Kanji.

Sasanuma (1975) observes: "Even a highly educated person sometimes finds himself unable to recall some low-frequency Kanji words, and represents them in Kana instead. The converse situation never happens [p. 370]." We ourselves observe some highly educated Japanese who do not know unusual pronunciations of some Kanji.

Reading in Japanese

Complex versus Simple Kanji

In Japanese text, Kanji are more important than are Kana. Accordingly, the Japanese direct considerable research into learning and processing Kanji. Kanji are simplified in Japan, but not so extensively and drastically as in mainland China. According to Takebe (1979), 90% of the official Kanji have between 6 and 14 strokes, and the mode (the most common number) is 10.

It is true that Kanji for Grade 1 are far simpler (average 4.9 strokes) than those for Grade 2 (8.3), as shown in Table 4-3. But there is no evidence that complex Kanji are harder to learn than are simpler ones. In the studies described earlier, the complexity of Kanji did not influence preschoolers' ability to learn a small number of them.

Kawai (1966) tested Japanese adults reading 160 "less complex" and 160 "more complex" single Kanji, which were taken from 3328 Kanji used in Japan. Adult subjects had to give two pronunciations, one Japanese and the other Chinese, as well as the meaning, of each Kanji. The errors were fewer for more complex than for less complex Kanji, with frequency of use controlled. Frequency had its own effect: The higher the frequency of usage, the more easily and correctly they were read. Kawai found similar results with figure–word paired associates: The more complex nonsense figures were learned faster than were less complex ones. With children, Fukuzawa (1968) found that familiarity but not complexity of stimuli had an effect on learning.

To investigate errors in Kanji use, Yoshida *et al.* (1975) asked a large number of middle school children to fill blanks in phrases with Kanji. The complexity of Kanji was a weak predictor of form-based errors, which were caused not so much by dropping or adding a stroke or a dot, but more by confusing an entire component, such as a radical or a phonetic. Here are two frequently confused Kanji, 鋼 and 鑛, sharing the radical 'gold' and the sound /kō/ (by chance, not because of a shared phonetic). Both Kanji mean 'hard metal' and can be used in a similar context. Yoshida *et al.* found some errors to be sound based: The subjects filled in a semantically wrong Kanji with the same sound as the correct one. Contextual difficulty of meaning, as determined by independent judges' ratings, was a good predictor of sound-based errors. Furthermore, the kinds of error changed according to the contexts.

All the studies cited so far show convincingly that visual complexity per se is not the cause of difficulty in learning and using Kanji. On the contrary, it may even aid learning, because a complex pattern—be it Kanji or a nonsense figure—contains more cues for discrimination than does a simple pattern.

Complexity may help in recognizing or reading Kanji, but not necessarily in recalling and writing them. Writing involves not only recalling but also motor execution of strokes. It takes longer to write a complex Kanji with many strokes than it takes to write a simple one with fewer strokes. The best compromise is to have the characters complex enough to ensure easy discriminability, but not so complex as to slow writing. This solution may entail using up to 15 strokes and arranging them in maximally varied configurations to produce about 3000 efficient Kanji.

Different Uses of Five Scripts

In Grade 1, children learn Arabic numerals along with the two Kana and some Kanji. Later, at about Grade 4, they learn Roman letters or the English alphabet. Actually, even preschoolers pick up some English letters and the Arabic numerals (Muraishi & Amano, 1972). Text written in a judicious mixture of the five different writing systems becomes easy to read, because the type of writing by itself tells the reader something about the meanings of words. Figure 4-2 shows a Japanese sentence in mixed scripts.

鶏肉とベーコンは1.5cmの角に切る。

chicken BACON cube cut

Figure 4-2. *A Japanese sentence in mixed scripts of Kanji, Hiragana, Katakana, Arabic numerals, and Roman letters.*

Words written in Kanji (e.g., *chicken*) tend to be roots of nouns, verbs, adjectives, and adverbs. Most, but by no means all, are of Chinese origin. Names of persons and places are usually in Kanji. Insup Taylor counted 285 Kanji, or 57%, in a 500-grapheme newspaper article (the first part of the political news in *Asahi Shinbun*, October 11, 1981). Hiragana is the most important script in Japan, next to, or along with, Kanji. In the preceding count, Hiragana accounted for 42% of the graphemes. Words of Japanese origin tend to be written in Hiragana, although suitable Kanji for them may be attempted. But the most important use of Hiragana is in expressing all kinds of syntactic morphemes.

In Japanese, there are two basic kinds of syntactic morphemes: postpositions (postpositional particles) and endings of verbs and adjectives. The postpositions come after nouns to indicate their grammatical functions in sentences. For example, nouns functioning as subjects of sentences take the postpositions *-wa* or *-ga*; as direct objects, *-o*; and as indirect objects, *-ni*. Thus, *Peter-**wa** book-**o** Mary-**ni** give.* The basic word order is subject–object–verb, in contrast to the English order of subject–verb–object. In Japanese sentences, verbs and adjectives (when used in predicates) come at the ends of sentences or clauses, and their endings vary enormously with tense, level of politeness, degree of formality, type of sentence (e.g., interrogative or declarative), and connection to the next clause. These grammatical items are indispensable and occur frequently in any text.

Words written in Katakana are European loan words and onomatopoeic words. The proportion of words in Katakana fluctuates greatly from one type of text to another. For example, it is relatively large in a cookbook of Western dishes, which require words such as *butter* constantly, and small in a cookbook of Japanese dishes. In the above count of 500 graphemes there was only one Katakana word, which had 5 letters.

The Roman alphabet is used only for personal names and technical terms of European origin such as *Taylor* and *cm* (centimeter). Arabic numerals are used in arithmetic calculations and technical writings; a Kanji set of numerals are used for other purposes.

Horizontal versus Vertical Reading

Japanese writing uses both the traditional vertical and the modern horizontal directions, making it an ideal system for comparing the relative advantages of the two directions, with reading habits reasonably controlled. In one study on discriminability of single graphemes, a horizontal arrangement yielded a higher score than did a vertical one for all three scripts: Kanji, Katakana, and Hiragana (Tanaka, Iwasaki, & Miki, 1974).

Ultimately, one must compare the two directions of writing in real text. In Sakamoto's study, for meaningless patterns, eye movements were smoother for horizontal than for vertical arrangements, but for real text, they were smoother for vertical than for horizontal directions (cited in Sakamoto & Makita, 1973). Shen (1927) also found that Chinese readers read comparable passages faster vertically than they did horizontally. In Japan, the vertical seems still to be the prevalent direction, and reading habits influence the relative ease of horizontal or vertical reading. Gray (1956) compared readers of 14 writing systems, written in various directions, and found that the directions did not greatly affect reading. One reads best in one's accustomed direction, be it vertical or horizontal, left to right or right to left.

Different Processing of Kanji and Kana

In Nomura's (1981) study on pronunciation, latency was shorter for Kana than for Kanji words, and it was faster for Kanji annotated with Kana than for Kanji alone. The stimuli were familiar one- or two-Kanji (two- or four-syllable Kana) words. Increased number of syllables had a greater effect on Kana than on Kanji pronunciation. Nomura concludes that Kanji pronunciation is generated on the basis of meaning; Kana's pronunciation too is generated on the basis of meaning but in addition is directly constructed from the data—the sound of each syllable-sign. He describes Kana pronunciation as data-driven, in contrast to conceptually-driven Kanji pronunciation.

In Stroop tests, color words written in single Kanji ('green') interfered with naming the ink color (red) more than did the same words written in two or three Kana signs, even though the Kana words were pronounced faster than the same words in Kanji (Morikawa, 1981; Shimamura & Hunt, 1978). The results may have four explanations: (*a*) Color words are cutomarily written in Kanji; (*b*) A color word has one Kanji but two to four Kana; (*c*) Meaning is extracted faster from Kanji than Kana words; and (*d*) Both color and single Kanji tend to be processed by the RH, thus competing for the same resources.

Kana can represent the entire Japanese language adequately. Moreover, they are extremely easy to learn. Why then do Japanese keep Kanji? There are several reasons, which are cultural, visual, and semantic.

Kanji can help a Japanese reader to retrieve the meaning of an unfamiliar word. Confronted with a word such as *dolichocephalic,* an ordinary English speaker has no way of guessing its meaning. In Japanese, it is written in two familiar Kanji, 'long' and 'head'. Any Japanese who knows these two Kanji can figure out that it means 'long-headed' (Suzuki, 1975).[4] Sometimes the meanings of learned words become transparent when the correct constituent Kanji are found. The Japanese word for 'limnology' is *koshōgaku.* When Japanese college students retrieved the correct Kanji for the term, it was correctly identified as 'lake-pond study'; when they retrieved Kanji that had the same

[4]An English speaker familiar with the Classical roots of words might also be able to use the same technique, since the word derives directly from the Greek for "long-head." But few English readers today are Classics scholars.

sound but different meanings, the term was incorrectly identified as 'old-evidence study' or 'old-name study' (Hatano, Kuhara, & Akiyama, 1981).

Kanji differentiate homophones. In general, each Kanji is associated with only one morpheme, whereas one syllable may stand for several different morphemes because of the small number of syllable types available in Japanese. For example, the syllable /kō/, with a lengthened vowel, stands for over 60 different morphemes ('go, high, mouth, think', etc.) each of which has its own Kanji. Suzuki (1977) suggests that a Japanese speaker and a listener can differentiate ambiguous homophones by recoding them into Kanji—by "writing Kanji in the air." The celebrated example *shikaishikaishikai* is hard to understand when spoken but easy to understand when written, for each of the syllables has its unique Kanji with its unique meaning. The phrase seems to have at least two translations: 'dentists' teachers' conference' and 'chairmanship of the dentists' conference'.

To represent one morpheme, one can use either one Kanji or a few Hiragana letters. For example, *I* requires one Kanji but three or four Hiragana letters *wa.ta.shi* or *wa.ta.ku.shi*. Physically, each Hiragana letter occupies roughly the same amount of space as each Kanji. Thus, a mixed script tends to be somewhat shorter than the same text written only in Hiragana. Furthermore, a single Kanji can be processed wholistically but a string of two or more Kana might be processed letter by letter.

Kanji are easy to discriminate not only from Kana but also from other Kanji. Tanaka required school children to cancel one or two target Kanji or Kana among distractors of their own kinds (Kanji distractors for a Kanji target). Recognition and discrimination scores were higher for Kanji than for either Hiragana or Katakana, but only for older children (Tanaka, 1977; Tanaka *et al.*, 1974). The older the children, the more experienced they are with the use of many Kanji.

A mixture of Kanji and Hiragana performs the function of visually separating words, since no extra space is made between words. (Extra space, along with either a comma or a period, is left between clauses and sentences.)

Last and most important, key words are quicker and easier to identify in mixed than in all-Hiragana text, because most Kanji in which key words are written are complex and dark, standing out from the background of simpler Hiragana. Sakamoto photographed the eye movements of college students reading short sentences of identical meaning but written in Hiragana only or Hiragana mixed with Kanji. The all-Hiragana text required twice as much time and showed a shorter perceptual span, more frequent fixations, longer fixation pauses, and more regressions (cited in Sakamoto & Makita, 1973). In short, all-Hiragana text is much harder to read than is text that uses both Hiragana and Kanji. These results are not surprising. Texts intended for mature readers are written seldom only in Hiragana but almost always in a mixture of Kanji and Hiragana, and possibly some Katakana. Japanese readers are far more experienced in reading a mixed script than a Hiragana-only text. Mixed text should definitely be easier to read than all-Kana text, most likely even when reading habits were controlled.

Hemispheric Processing of Kanji and Kana

The Japanese writing system is ideal for comparing hemispheric processing of a logography to that of a phonetic script. Researchers present stimuli in a T-scope either to the right or left visual field of each eye. Visual stimuli seen in the right visual-field (RVF) project to the left hemisphere (LH), and vice versa (see Chapters 1, 3, and 11). Subjects are usually right-handed adult Japanese speakers of both sexes.

Kanji showed a LVF advantage, implying RH procesing, in the following conditions:

- When two single Kanji were matched physically (Hatta, 1981a); or when two to five individual Kanji were judged same or different (Nishikawa & Niina, 1981; see also Chapter 11).
- When single Kanji were verbally identified (Hatta, 1977a, 1977b, 1978). Concrete Kanji were more correctly identified than abstract Kanji, but both were processed faster by the RH in Hatta's studies. By contrast, only concrete nouns, but not abstract ones, were processed by the RH in the study done in the United States with Japanese-English bilinguals (Elman, Takahashi, & Tohsaku, 1981).

The opposite results were obtained—Kanji seemed to be processed by the LH—in the following conditions:

- When Kanji–Kana words or multi-Kanji words were recognized (Hatta, 1978).
- When single Kanji were processed phonologically (Are two single Kanji the same in sound?) (Sasanuma, Itoh, Kobayashi, & Mori, 1980).
- When a single Kanji had to be given "deep" semantic processing—deciding whether the single Kanji with the meaning of 'left' or 'right' was displayed in the correct position with respect to a bar (Hatta, 1979).
- When single Kanji had to be judged to belong to one of the three semantic categories—animal, plant, body—for Kanji with concrete meanings, and—numeral, emotion, warmth—for Kanji with abstract meanings (Hayashi & Hatta, 1982). Concreteness and abstractness did not make any difference.

No RH–LH differences were found with Kanji stimuli in the following conditions:

- When two or more Kanji forming a nonsense word had to be recognized (Sasanuma, Itoh, Mori, & Kobayashi, 1977).
- When a task involved memory, and single Kanji ranked high in concreteness: Subjects had to move the right or the left index finger leftward for

two of four Kanji, and rightward for the other two (Endo, Shimizu, & Nakamura, 1981a).

- In a task where subjects had to categorize each Kanji as either bona fide or counterfeit (containing an inappropriate subpart). Reaction times were faster for the bona fide, but no RH–LH differences were found (Hatta, 1981b).

Kana are processed by the LH under the following conditions:

- When two- or three-letter Hiragana words (transliterations of single Kanji) were verbally identified (Hatta, 1977b). (In the same study, single Kanji tended to be processed by the RH).
- When two-Kana nonsense words were recognized (Endo *et al.*,1981a). (In the same study, no RH–LH difference was found for the Kanji stimuli.)
- In visual matching of single Hiragana (Which of three alternatives is the same as the standard?) (Hatta, 1976).
- When two to five Kana were judged same or different (In the same study, Kanji showed RH processing) (Nishikawa & Niina, 1981).
- In records of evoked potentials from the scalps of normal people, reading of Hiragana words activated the angular gyrus in the LH, whereas reading of two-Kanji words did not. These results were most clear when both scripts were presented together (Hink, Kaga, & Suzuki, 1980).

At least for simple recognition, single Kanji are processed preferentially by the RH and multi-Kanji words by the LH. Why? Hatta (1978) hypothesized that for a single Kanji with multiple readings, visual rather than phonetic processing is advantageous. When more than two Kanji join to form a word, usually one particular reading becomes clearer, and hence phonetic processing dominates visual processing. Hatta's explanation is not convincing. First, Chinese speakers (who have one reading for each character) also tend to process single Kanji by the RH (Tzeng *et al.*, 1979). Second, Japanese adults tend to read single Kanji in a Japanese way at first glance (Nomura, 1978; Hatta, 1981c).

Processing differences between single Kanji (by the RH) and multi-Kanji words (by the LH) also have been explained as follows: A single Kanji tends to be recognized as a wholistic visual pattern by the RH; two or more Kanji forming a word tend to be recognized as sequential linguistic material by the LH (Hatta, 1978; Sasanuma *et al.*, 1977; Tzeng *et al.*, 1979). Hiragana, which code sounds, are processed by LH whether used singly or with other Kana or Kanji.

Hatta (1978) observed: "Japanese people need the integrated action of both hemisphere processing systems in reading their text; to a far greater extent than would the Westerner reading his language [pp. 58–59]." At the moment there is no evidence for or against Hatta's observation, but there is an increasing amount of evidence implicating RH involvement in reading by Westerners (see Chapter 11).

Selective Impairment of Kanji and Kana

When Japanese speakers suffer brain damage, are they selectively impaired in either logographs (Kanji) or syllabaries (Kana)? Sasanuma and Fujimura (1971) studied two types of aphasics with right-sided paralysis and two types of nonaphasics with either right- or left-sided paralysis. **Aphasics** have speech impairment caused by damage in the speech areas of the LH. In visual recognition tasks, the patients matched written words shown on a T-scope to line drawings of the objects that the words represented. There were three sets of words:

1. 10 multi-Kanji words ('child, radish', etc.)
2. 10 European loan words in Katakana ('bus, necktie', etc.)
3. Hiragana versions of the Kanji words ('child, radish', etc.)

The nonaphasic groups made practically no errors on any of the three types of test words. Between the two aphasic groups, the simple aphasics made some errors, and to similar degrees, on all three types of words. But the aphasics with apraxia of speech (articulatory difficulties) made far more errors on the two kinds of Kana, especially on Hiragana, than on Kanji (on which the two groups of aphasics were similar). Their high error rate on Kana relative to Kanji was even more pronounced in writing tests.

According to the researchers, Kanji can be directly identified with a word, bypassing its sounds, whereas Kana must be phonologically processed before the word is identified. Thus, an impaired phonetic ability would affect Kana processing more than it does Kanji processing. Between two kinds of Kana, there was a tendency for all groups of patients to make more errors on Hiragana than on Katakana in visual recognition tasks, perhaps because the Hiragana words were transcriptions of words ordinarily written in Kanji, whereas the Katakana words, being European loan words, were in their customary script.

In writing tests, aphasics' Kanji errors tended to be graphic confusions, whereas their Kana errors tended to be phonetic confusions (Sasanuma & Fujimura, 1972). There was no correlation between the respective levels of performance in the Kanji and the Kana tasks, suggesting that the processing of two scripts can be impaired independently of each other in different patients. In reading, regardless of the degree and type of reading impairment, semantic errors tended to be produced with Kanji words, and phonological errors with Kana words. Visual errors occurred in both Kanji and Kana words.

Sasanuma (1974) made an in-depth study of one LH-damaged adult who showed serious impairment in reading but only minor impairment in other speech functions and writing. With Kanji, the patient showed normal, instantaneous comprehension of many words with two or more Kanji. With Kana, he had difficulty in decoding a word of more than two Kana signs as an integrated visual pattern. He made a detour: He first sounded out individual Kana signs (signing in the air, if necessary), then combined these sounds to form an integrated pattern of the word, and finally arrived at the meaning. In another study, after section of the splenium of the corpus callosum, impaired reading (oral and silent) of isolated words was restricted to the RH, and was more pronounced and persistent for Hiragana than for Kanji (Sugishita, Iwata, Toyokura, Yoshioka, & Yamada, 1978).

There is a small group of patients who can read Kana better than Kanji, comprehending poorly what they read. Aphasics with Kana trouble have lesions in the two speech areas in the LH (Broca's and Wernicke's), whereas aphasics with Kanji trouble have diffuse lesions in the areas that surround the two speech areas (Sasanuma, 1974; see Figure 1-1 for the speech areas). Hagiwara's (1983) review of the literature covering between 1901 and 1980 suggests that there may be as many cases of selective impairment of Kana as of Kanji.

Summary and Conclusions

Japan is a nation of readers. Five different scripts are used in Japan. They are, in order of importance, Kanji, Hiragana, Katakana, Arabic numerals, and Roman letters.

About 3000 Kanji are used in Japan, and about 2000 of them are "official." A limited number of judiciously selected Kanji can easily be learned even by preschoolers and language-disabled children. In primary school, Kanji are introduced, batch by batch, starting from Grade 1. In middle and high schools, Kanji learning consumes much of students' time and effort, because Kanji are numerous and are used in a far more complicated way than in either China or Korea. Each Kanji usually is pronounced in two or more ways.

On the other hand, the two Japanese syllabaries—Hiragana and Katakana—are exceedingly simple in form and sound. Each has 46 basic, 25 secondary, and 35 modified Kana signs.

The reading unit is the syllable, and syllable-to-Kana correspondence is highly regular. A syllable is stable and does not change its sound value when it combines with other syllables. For all these reasons, Kana are learned—rather, "picked up"—rapidly and effortlessly even by preschoolers. It is the simplicity of the Japanese sound system that makes the simple syllabaries possible. The sound system uses only a small number of phonemes to make its 100 or so V and CV syllables.

Single Kanji tend to be recognized as whole visual patterns by the right hemisphere, but multi-Kanji words tend to be recognized as sequential linguistic materials by the left hemisphere. Kana, being phonetic signs, are better processed by the LH, whether they are presented singly or along with other Kana. Brain damage can impair Kanji and Kana processing selectively: Damage in the speech areas of the LH leads to impairment of Kana processing, whereas diffuse damage outside them leads to impairment of Kanji processing.

The use of logographic Kanji for roots of key words, and phonetic Hiragana for grammatical items, is the most prominent feature of the Japanese writing system. This feature is a bane to typing, for it calls for a large number of keys and shifts, but it is a boon to reading, for it helps readers to pick out and attend to key items in text.

5

Alphabetic Syllabary: Korean Hangul

The bright can learn the [Korean] system in a single morning, and even the not so bright can do so within ten days.

—a Hangul scholar (1446)

Hangul Alphabetic Syllabary

Hangul—the 'Great Letters' of Korea—is a writing system that can be considered as an alphabet, a syllabary, or even a logography.[1]

HISTORY OF HANGUL

Hangul was invented in the middle of the fifteenth century A.D. by King Sejong, with the assistance of a royal commission. Until then, the only writing available to Koreans was the Chinese system, which was extremely ill-suited to represent the Korean language. (Korean is polysyllabic and inflecting; Chinese is monosyllabic and noninflecting.) The Chinese system was also too difficult for ordinary people to learn. The king's noble sentiment was to invent a script that could be learned easily by ordinary people. The original name for Hangul, *Hunmin-jongum,* bespeaks the king's intention: It translates to 'Correct pronunciation of letters for teaching ordinary people.' For the purpose of

[1]The second vowel in "Hangul" is 'ŭ', which is a high central vowel with lips spread; it sounds like a vowel between /i/ and /u/. For convenience of typing, we use 'u' for it. Romanization of Hangul is basically, but not entirely, according to the McCune–Reischauer system. International phonetic symbols (see Table 1-1) are used when they closely code required Korean sounds.

creating a new script he founded The Hall of the Learned Assembly and gathered together eight scholars to assist him. The scholars, under the king's supervision, made a careful study of other writing systems, traveled to other countries to consult experts in various systems, and after several years of deliberation came up with an alphabet of their own. Their end-product amply justifies their effort and time.

When Hangul was first introduced to the public, the privileged class, deeply entrenched as they were in the Chinese culture, mounted stiff resistance to its use. For many years Hangul was mainly used by the less privileged and by women. During the Japanese occupation of Korea in the first half of the twentieth century, Hangul and the Korean language were not allowed in schools. Today, in North Korea it is the sole scripts, and in South Korea it is the main script. The day Hangul was proclaimed by King Sejong, October 9, is now celebrated as Hangul Day.

Hangul is appreciated among Western scholars too. In his two-volume book *Alphabet,* Diringer (1968) describes Hangul as the most perfect phonetic system that has been called on to stand the tests of time and actual use. H. Jensen (1970) states: "I would fully and wholly endorse the praise which H. F. J. Junker bestows on the Korean script: 'One cannot describe the script-system... as other than brilliant, so deliberately does it fit the language like a glove [p. 215].'" Martin (1972) comments on its construction: "The Korean script is remarkable for its internal structure and for its graphic origin [p. 82]." The American linguist Bolinger (1968) praises its "sheer creativeness."

Hangul Alphabet

The principle of an alphabet is that one symbol codes one phoneme, and this principle is almost realized in Hangul. Three unique and rational features of Hangul as an alphabet are:

1. The shapes of simple symbols suggest the manner in which the symbols' sounds are produced by the articulatory organs.
2. Simple C and V symbols are used as bases for increasingly complex symbols that code Cs and Vs having added articulatory features.
3. The few phoneme-symbols are used as elements in building a few thousand syllable-blocks.

CONSONANT SYMBOLS

To represent 14 single and 5 doubled consonants, Hangul starts with five basic consonant symbols, which are shaped to suggest the articulators pronouncing them. For example, a small square depicts a closed mouth pronouncing /m/. Figure 5-1 shows the other four basic consonant symbols and their articulation.

ㄱ /g/ : the root of the tongue as it closes the throat passage and touches the soft palate

ㄴ /n/ : the shape of the point of the tongue as it touches the ridge behind the teeth

ㅅ /s/ : upper (/) and lower (\ ) tooth get together

ㅎ /h/ : unobstructed throat passage in producing /o/ is joined by two strokes

ㅁ /m/: the shape of the closed mouth

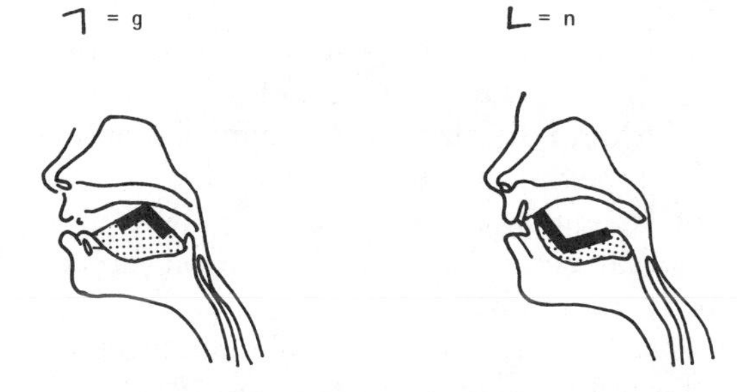

Figure 5-1. *The shapes of five Hangul symbols depict the manner by which the symbols' sounds are produced (from I. Taylor, 1981, p. 29, reproduced by permission of Academic Press.)*

Based on the five basic symbols, several related consonant symbols are created:

- /d/ is articulated in the same place as /n/; its symbol is created by adding a stroke to the n-symbol.
- /b/ is articulated in the same place as /m/; its symbol is created by adding two small strokes to the m-symbol.

For the articulatory feature of aspiration, a stroke is added:

- inside the g-symbol to create the k-symbol;
- over the d-symbol to create the t-symbol;
- under the b-symbol to create the p-symbol.

For the articulatory feature of tenseness, each of the g-, d-, b-, s-, and ch-symbols is doubled to make symbols for sounds that do not exist in English. (The Korean sounds of 'gg' and 'dd' are close to French "qu" and 't', respectively.) Table 5-1 is a complete list of Hangul consonants.

The linguist W. Wang (1981) points out that, of all current writing systems, the Korean script comes closest to a feature representation of speech, a remarkable achievement in 1443. Deese (1981) suggests that Hangul might be called an alphabetic-feature syllabary.

The names of consonant symbols are useful: Each name contains the

Table 5-1. *Hangul Consonant Symbols*

Velar			ㄱ	¯	ㅋ		ㄲ
Lingual	ㄴ	¯	ㄷ	¯	ㅌ	ㄹ	ㄸ
Bilabial	ㅁ	ʼʼ	ㅂ	ʼʼ	ㅂ̄ → ㅍ		ㅃ
Sibilant	ㅅ	¯	ㅈ	ˋ	ㅊ		ㅉ, ㅆ
Glottal	ㅇ			⁼	ㅎ		

Source: I. Taylor, 1980, p. 69, reproduced by permission of Plenum.

symbol's sound at both initial and final positions, flanking the same two basic Vs, as in "giug, biub, mium . . ." for the symbols 'g, b, m . . .' The symbol for 'l' is appropriately named "riul," reflecting that the symbol is pronounced as /r/ at the initial and as /l/ at the final positions of a word.

The creation of Hangul was steeped in Oriental philosophy. That the same initial consonant can be used again as the final one in such CVC as /gag/ is supposed to embody "return to the sources," one of the principles of the *Book of Changes* (one of Five Confucian Classics): "As all things have sprung from the earth, so must they return to the earth (see Lee, 1972)."

VOWEL SYMBOLS

The three basic vowels represent the three elementary beings or the trinity of Oriental philosophy, namely, the heaven, earth, and man, represented by a dot (now, a short bar), a long horizontal bar, and a long vertical bar, respectively. The vowel symbols are remarkable not so much for their esoteric philosophical origin as for their simplicity and versatility. Increasingly complex vowel symbols can be created by attaching the short bar, the marker, to the two basic ones. To create a symbol for /o/, attach the marker above the horizontal bar ㅗ ; to create a symbol for the related /yo/ (as in *yonder*), attach an additional marker ㅛ . To create a symbol for /a/, attach the marker to the right of a vertical bar ㅏ ; to create a symbol for the related /ya/, attach an additional marker ㅑ . If the symbols for /o/ and /a/ are combined, we have the compound symbol for /oa/ ㅘ .

Altogether, 21 vowel symbols (10 simple and 11 compound) are created in this manner. (Table 5-3 lists 16 of the 21 vowel symbols.) Note that the consonant and the vowel symbols are differently shaped: The consonants are geometric forms, whereas the vowel symbols are bars.

Hangul Syllable-Blocks

RULES FOR FORMING SYLLABLE-BLOCKS

In Hangul, a consonant symbol is always used in combination with a vowel, as a CV. When a vowel is required by itself, an empty circle takes the place of a consonant symbol, thus ensuring that a V syllable-block is constructed by the same rule as a CV block. A Hangul block then represents a syllable, which may be V, VC, CV, CVC, or CVCC. For this reason, Hangul should be called an **alphabetic syllabary**; that is, the unit coded in Hangul is a syllable, which is represented by a block built by combining two to four alphabet symbols.

There are rules for packaging alphabetic symbols into syllable-blocks. The syllable containing Vs /o, yo, u,/ etc. require the horizontal-bar V symbol, which is placed under a C symbol. The syllables containing Vs /a, ya, i, e/ etc. require the vertical-bar V symbols, which are placed to the right-hand side of a C symbols (see Table 5-2, and also Table 5-3 later). To form CVC or CVCC, the initial CV part goes over the final C or CC symbol.

Syllable-blocks, like Chinese characters, have more-or-less the same overall size despite varied internal structures that can be analyzed into top, bottom, left, and right components. Unlike a Chinese character, however, a Hangul block contains alphabetic symbols, and these symbols are arranged in a fixed pattern. Although a huge number of syllable-blocks are possible, only about 2000 occur in practice (Hahn, 1981). The beauty of Hangul is that although an experienced reader can process a syllable-block as a single unit, a beginner does not have to memorize a few thousand blocks by rote; he merely learns a handful of alphabet symbols and the simple rules for packaging them.

The Hangul syllabary can be further illuminated by comparing it with the two Japanese Kana. In the Hangul blocks for the syllables 'ga, gi, go', it is possible to identify the same consonant symbol, and in the blocks for the syllables 'ga, ma, da', the same vowel symbol. By contrast, a Japanese Kana (see Figure 4-1) cannot be analyzed into its constituent consonant and vowel. Japanese can afford to have a true syllabary because it uses only about 100 syllable types. For Korean with its rich variety of syllables, an alphabetic syllabary is the only system which allows the good features of a syllabary without having the problems of memorizing thousands of individual shapes.

HANGUL TYPEWRITER

The different levels of complexity are a boon for reading but a bane for developing typewriters. Still, home use of a typewriter is far more feasible in

Table 5-2. *Hangul Syllable-Blocks in Three Complexity Levels*[a]

I		ㅏ		아	V/a/	suffix;ah
I	ㄷ	ㅏ		다	CV/da/	all
II		ㅏㄹ		말	VC/al/	egg
II	ㄷ	ㅏㄹ		달	CVC/dal/	moon
III	ㄷ	ㅏㄹ	ㄱ	닭	CVCC/dalg/	hen

Source: I. Taylor, 1980, p. 70, reproduced by permission of Plenum.

[a]All the syllable-blocks in this table, except the level 3 block, could represent both native morphemes and Chinese loan morphemes; only the native ones are given here.

[b]"Complexity" is based on visual complexity, which is partly confounded with syllabic complexity.

[c]In V and VC blocks, the empty circle is required to show that a vowel is alone in a syllable. The circle depicts the shape of the throat in vowel production— it is empty and wide open.

Korea than in either China or Japan. To limit the number of keys, a Hangul typewriter might contain only the 24 alphabetic symbols and produce words in linear arrangements in the same way the Roman alphabet does. This arrangement would lose one of the more useful features of Hangul for reading, namely, syllable-blocks. It would also produce a visually unfamiliar text.

Modern typewriters have keys for all vowel and consonant symbols used at the initial, top positions of syllable-blocks. Keys for consonant symbols used at the final, bottom positions are on a separate, bottom row of keys. This type of machine will produce Hangul syllable-blocks in familiar forms, although a final C or CC might be slightly misplaced under an initial CV.

These placement problems with mechanical typewriters are easily solved with electronic typewriters. Word processing on a computer is as easy with Hangul as with English alphabet. A writer simply types in Korean words symbol by an alphabetic symbol, and a computer automatically packages the symbols into syllable-blocks. Automatic packaging is possible because Hangul has only three possible syllable structures (CV, CVC, and CVCC), within which the alphabetic symbols are placed systematically. Because the computer also adjusts the position and size of the symbols within a syllable-block, Hangul text on a display screen or printout can be of high quality. An advanced word processer, called the Hangul Processor III, is ready for marketing (Chong, Han, & Kang, 1983).

SEQUENCING SYLLABLE-BLOCKS

In alphabetic writing, a word contains several letters arranged in a line, and their order can sometimes be confused. This problem is alleviated in Hangul: Each Hangul block represents a syllable, which codes in one complex symbol a group of sounds that might take three to six English letters arranged in a row. An example is /dalg/, which requires four linearly arranged letters in English but one complex block in Korean (see 'hen' in Table 5-2). The Korean way of arranging blocks is particularly advantageous for long words with CVC or CVCC syllables: *ungentlemanliness* has 17 letters in English but transcribes into 7 syllable-blocks in Hangul. The longer a sequence, the more likely it is to cause sequencing errors, especially in the middle. In English, transposition errors involving letters in medial positions, such as '-er-' and '-re-' in *there* and *three,* are most intractable among Grade 2 poor readers (Park, 1978–1979). Each of these 5-letter English words is reduced to a 2-syllable word in Hangul.

In a syllabary like Hangul, the syllable breaks within a word are always apparent, as opposed to linear alphabetic writing, in which even experts may disagree as to where the syllable breaks may occur. In Hangul text, extra spaces are provided between words. No syllable-block has more than four symbols, and most words have no more than four blocks (six blocks with attached postpositions). All in all, readers of Hangul should not have many problems related to sequencing and grouping sounds, letters, and words.

HANGUL AS A LOGOGRAPHY

In a logography one character represents one meaningful unit such as a morpheme or a word. Though Hangul is a phonetic script, some single Hangul syllable-blocks represent morphemes as well, as do the English syllables *up, see, hat,* and so on.

Spelling has been standardized to preserve the logographic property of Hangul. For example, the Korean words for 'mouth' and 'leaf' sound the same when spoken alone, but are nevertheless distinguished in spelling: *ib* and *ip,* respectively. The phonetic difference between the two words becomes apparent when a V postposition is attached to them: *ib.i* /ibi/ and *ip.i* /ipi/. (A dot indicates the separation of syllable-blocks in spelling.) (In English, *but* and *butt* are distinguished in spelling, but they never differ in sounds.) As a second example, /l/ in *dalg* ('hen') becomes silent when the word combines with a postposition starting with C, /dagdo/, but is fully pronounced with a V postposition, /dalgi/. In either case, 'l' is kept in spelling so as to maintain the visual form of the block. This spelling practice is analogous to English *hymn-hymnal,* where 'n' is pronounced when possible but is ordinarily silent.

Beginning readers of Hangul tend to spell words as they sound but learn easily the standardized spelling, because spelling is nonarbitrary as well as being useful. They merely have to test the sounds of words with a V and a C postposition.

The likelihood of a syllable-block being a morpheme increases with its complexity: Level 3 blocks (four phonemes) are always morphemes; level 2 blocks (three phonemes) are often morphemes; and level 1 blocks (one or two phonemes) are occasionally and ambiguously morphemes, mostly as postpositions or sounds of Chinese characters.

This writing arrangement shares the benefit of Chinese characters in that a skilled reader can associate one unique shape with its morpheme. Hangul logographs do not contain semantic components comparable with radicals in Chinese characters. At the same time, Hangul is better than, or at least different from, the Chinese system in that it spells out the constituent phonemes of each syllable-block fully, clearly, and consistently. Because of this phonetic property, single Hangul blocks tend to be processed by the left hemisphere, whereas single Kanji tend to be processed by the right hemisphere of the brain (see "Hemispheric Processing").

Processing Syllable-Blocks

There have been only a few experiments that explicitly study Hangul as a writing system, and even these few have mostly been done in North America and Japan. In South Korea itself, researchers investigate such practical problems as improving reading speed and teaching methods.

THREE LEVELS OF COMPLEXITY

Hangul is unique among phonetic scripts in having letters in three levels of structural complexity. In perceiving shapes, the distinctiveness of shapes matters, and complex shapes have better chance to be distinct than do simple ones. One Japanese study shows that Kanji are more discriminable than are Kana (Tanaka *et al.*, 1974; see Chapter 4). Hangul syllable-blocks are intermediate between Kanji and Kana in complexity; would their discriminability be also intermediate? Would complex and simple syllable-blocks differ in discriminability? While these questions await answers, I. Taylor (1980) tackled still another question: Are three levels of complexity better than only one level for discriminating and recognizing blocks? A target Hangul block was indeed better recognized and discriminated against the background of other blocks when the background includes all three complexity levels rather than only the complexity of the target.

BLOCK VERSUS LINEAR ARRANGEMENT OF SYMBOLS

Brooks (1977) compared a word written in sequentially arranged, discrete letters with the same word written in a "glyph," in which the same discrete letters are packaged into one integrated form, as in: SEAT = IUV∞ which is written in a glyph . English-speaking subjects identified words in their glyph form better than they did the same words in discrete letters.

Each of Brooks's glyphs appears similar to a Hangul syllable-block in that it packages four alphabetic symbols into a single form. Examined closely, glyphs and Hangul syllable-blocks differ: (*a*) One glyph maps one or two syllables, whereas each Hangul block maps one syllable; (*b*) alphabetic symbols are arranged in a glyph following no particular rule, whereas they are arranged in Hangul according to a rule; and (*c*) glyphs do not vary systematically in their complexity, whereas Hangul letters do—in three levels.

To compare linear arrangement with packaged form of Hangul, I. Taylor (1980) taught four CVCV and four CVCCVC Hangul words to English-speaking subjects, who learned to read them fluently in 5 min. The subjects initially read the Hangul words faster in a linear than in a packaged arrangement. But over 18 trials, which gave them about 80 min experience, the differences between the two arrangements gradually narrowed and then almost disappeared. The data, though inconclusive, suggested that a study involving longer words and Korean subjects, run over many more trials, might show the packaged arrangement to be superior.

HEMISPHERIC PROCESSING

Which hemisphere of the brain is better at processing Hangul? In Japan, Korean–Japanese bilinguals showed a right visual-field advantage (LH processing) in recognizing single Hangul syllable-blocks, which were CVC nouns (Endo *et al.*, 1981a). The finding shows that single Hangul blocks, even when they represent morphemes, tend not to be processed by the RH, as single

Chinese characters tend to be (see Chapters 3 and 4). Because each of its constituent symbols codes a phoneme, a Hangul block is processed by the LH, like any phonetic sign. Japanese speakers unfamiliar with Hangul showed a left visual-field advantage (RH processing), presumably because they processed Hangul stimuli purely as shapes.

In another study, when some of the Japanese subjects learned the sounds and the meanings of the Hangul stimuli, they showed no RH–LH differences. Their performance was between that of Koreans with good knowledge of Hangul and that of Japanese with no knowledge of it (Endo, Shimizu, & Nakamura, 1981b). Both the Japanese and the Korean–Japanese bilingual subjects showed a right-field advantage (LH processing) for two-Kana nonsense words.

Reading in Hangul and Kanji

Learning to Read in Hangul

EASE OF LEARNING

Because of the simplicity and rationality of its design, Hangul can be learned painlessly and rapidly. According to one of the scholars on the committee for the invention of Hangul, "the bright can learn the system in a single morning, and even the not so bright can do so within ten days." In his book *A Guide to Korean Characters,* Grant (1979) spends a mere half page on Hangul, claiming: "The Korean alphabet is so simple that its sixteen totally distinct letters can be learned in ***minutes*** with the aid of the hangul-in-a-hurry charts [p. 12, emphasis added]." Grant's consonant chart is similar to Table 5-1, except that it gives an English sound for each Hangul symbol. His second chart shows some syllable-blocks. He devotes the rest of his book to explaining the Chinese characters used in South Korea. Learning the Hangul alphabet and some syllable-blocks may require a little more time than a single morning or minutes, but not much more.

Illiteracy is negligible, being confined to the mentally retarded and to the very old, who have not benefited from modern compulsory education. As in Japanese and Chinese, there is no label for developmental dyslexia in Korean, and there are no remedial teachers. At the end of Grade 1, in private schools all children in a class of 60 read well, whereas in public schools 2 or 3 out of 60 have slight difficulty only with complex syllable-blocks. Note the large size of a classroom: It is twice or thrice as large as that in North America. Yet children in a classroom are disciplined. No first grader can be described as a nonreader, in the sense of lacking a grasp of how letters code sounds (see Chapter 16). The absence of nonreaders was confirmed in tests given to Korean first graders who have just arrived in Toronto, Canada.[2]

READING INSTRUCTION AT SCHOOL

In South Korea, children enter school at age 6, almost all of them already reading some words in simple syllable-blocks. Primary education is compulsory, and practically all eligible children enter primary school. Most of the children who finish 6 years of primary school go on to 3-year middle school. The government plans to introduce 9-year compulsory education by 1983.

Up-to-date teaching in Korea includes meaning-centered teaching but concentrates on sound decoding. Noh (1975) compared the two methods of teaching Hangul: One group of kindergartners was taught by the meaning-centered method, and the other group by sound decoding, by the same teacher for 2 months. In pronouncing test words, substitution errors made by the sound group were predominantly sound-based; that is, they were nonsense syllables that shared the initial and/or final sounds with the correct words. By contrast, substitution errors made by the word group tended to be meaning based; they were meaningful words taught in the class. These results are comparable with those obtained in some American studies (e.g., Barr, 1975; see Chapter 15). All in all, the sound group performed better than the word group in the pronunciation tests. However, even the word group showed some awareness of the letter–sound relations.

In South Korea, there is one standard series of basal readers for primary school. The basal reader of each grade consists of two parts, each to be used for a half year. The first part of the Grade 1 reader starts with pictures, words, and then quickly progresses to phrases, short sentences, and stories (Aesop's fables). It has provisions for drill in word recognition and letter writing. About 400 words, all in Hangul, are introduced in this first half of Grade 1. (In the United States, at the end of Grade 1, children have learned about 500 words; see Chapter 15.) Part 2 contains more new words, longer stories, and comprehension-recall questions. The contents of basal readers tend to be moralistic, as the title of the 1982 readers, *Correct Living,* suggests.

LEARN HANGUL AS AN ALPHABET OR A SYLLABARY?

Hangul, being an alphabetic syllabary, can be taught as an alphabet or as a syllabary. In earlier times Hangul was taught more as an alphabet than as a syllabary. That is, children learned individual alphabet symbols and their phonemes, plus the rules for packaging them into syllable-blocks. In modern days, syllable-blocks, the actual reading units, tend to be used as teaching units (based on Noh, 1975). The syllable being a larger and more stable phonetic unit than is the phoneme, learning to read is a lot easier with a syllabary than with an alphabet.

[2]We thank Jae-Ho Cha in Seoul for conducting this informal survey on our behalf, and also for sending us a copy of the Grade 1 (part 1) reader. We also thank Yong-Hi Yoon for information on Korean immigrants in Toronto.

In the first 2–3 months in Grade 1, children learn familiar words in simple sentences. Once they become interested in reading, the sounds that make up words (syllables) are taught. This way, from the very beginning, children learn to read for meaning, as well as how to decode words.

In teaching Hangul, whether as an alphabet or as a syllabary, a teacher can use the **syllable matrix,** which lists all the vowels across each row and all the consonants down each column. Table 5-3 lists part of the syllable matrix, with 16 of the 21 Vs and 9 of the 19 Cs.
Knowing these vowels and consonants, any child can deduce the sound of any V or CV syllable within the matrix. (V syllables are constructed in the same way as CVs.) For example, he can combine the first consonant /g/ with each of the 16 vowels to produce /ga, gya, gɔ, gyɔ.../, and can repeat the same process with the second consonant /n/ to produce /na, nya, nɔ, nyɔ.../. In this way, he learns through deduction, instruction, and practice all 399 V or CV syllables. The more complex syllable types that contain final consonants can be easily derived from the matrix, by placing a final C or CC at the bottom of any V or CV. (Not all the possible complex blocks occur in the language.) At the same time, individual V or C symbols can be analyzed out of the syllables in the matrix.

The CV Syllable Matrix is possible because of the near perfect grapheme–phoneme correspondence and because of the systematic placement of phoneme-symbols in building syllable-blocks. Once these 399 systematically constructed syllables are learned, a child has no trouble pronouncing any syllable string, whether familiar, unfamiliar, or nonsense. There is no need to consult a dictionary for pronunciation and spelling.

In reading text, however, Koreans face the same problems that readers of any writing system do. That is, they must learn to read rapidly and flexibly with good comprehension and retention. To become a good reader, one must read a lot.

Table 5-3. *Part of Hangul* CV *Syllable Matrix*
(with 9 of the 19 Cs and 16 of the 21 Vs)

	a	ya	ɔ	yɔ	o	yo	u	yu	ŭ	i	æ	e	oa	œ	ui	ŭi
C \ V	ㅏ	ㅑ	ㅓ	ㅕ	ㅗ	ㅛ	ㅜ	ㅠ	ㅡ	ㅣ	ㅐ	ㅔ	ㅘ	ㅚ	ㅟ	ㅢ
g ㄱ	가	갸	거	겨	고	교	구	규	그	기	개	게	과	괴	귀	긔
n ㄴ	나	냐	너	녀	노	뇨	누	뉴	느	니	내	네	놔	뇌	뉘	늬
d ㄷ	다	댜	더	뎌	도	됴	두	듀	드	디	대	데	돠	되	뒤	듸
r ㄹ	라	랴	러	려	로	료	루	류	르	리	래	레	롸	뢰	뤼	릐
m ㅁ	마	먀	머	며	모	묘	무	뮤	므	미	매	메	뫄	뫼	뭐	믜
b ㅂ	바	뱌	버	벼	보	뵤	부	뷰	브	비	배	베	봐	뵈	뷔	븨
s ㅅ	사	샤	서	셔	소	쇼	수	슈	스	시	새	세	솨	쇠	쉬	싀
vowel ㅇ	아	야	어	여	오	요	우	유	으	이	애	에	와	외	위	의
dz ㅈ	자	쟈	저	져	조	죠	주	쥬	즈	지	재	제	좌	죄	쥐	즤

Chinese Characters (Kanji)

Chinese characters were adopted by Koreans early in their writing history, perhaps in the first century A.D., and then were introduced by Koreans to Japan a few centuries later. Chinese characters were the only writing system available to Koreans until Hangul was invented in the fifteenth century. Today, even though Chinese characters are abolished in North Korea, and are relegated to a supplemental role in South Korea, they cannot be ignored.

KANJI IN SOUTH KOREA

The Korean pronunciation of the Japanese term "Kanji" is Hanja. Both terms translate into 'letters of Kan/Han [Dynasty]' or 'Chinese characters'. Since "Kanji" is by now familiar to our readers, we will use this term. In Korea, knowledge of Kanji is useful but not vital. North Korea stopped using Kanji after World War II, and South Korea designated 1800 of them as "official." The complexity of official Kanji ranges from 1 to 26 strokes, 11 strokes being most common. Almost all of the Korean official Kanji are the same as the Japanese official Kanji.

In South Korea, Kanji definitely are supplemental to Hangul: They do not appear in government papers or textbooks for primary schools, but start to appear in textbooks for middle schools and high schools. In daily newspapers, Kanji tend to be used in text on weighty topics (i.e., politics and economics), and fewer Kanji, sometimes none, are used in text on light topics.

Each Kanji usually has only one reading in Korean, in contrast to its multiple readings in Japanese and its dialect variations in Chinese. Korean readings of Kanji are similar to Chinese (classic Mandarin) reading in being monosyllabic and in containing similar sounds; they are dissimilar to Chinese readings in having closed syllables (CVCs), and being atonal (e.g., Korean /chuk/, Chinese /chu/ with a tone, and Japanese /chiku/ for *"bamboo."*)

To compare the use of Kanji in Korea and Japan, Korean has numerous native content words for which there are no Kanji equivalents and hence must be written in Hangul, whereas Japanese try to find and fit Kanji to most native content words. Thus, the sentence *I don't know* in Figure 2-2 contains two Kanji in Japanese but none in Korean. In Insup Taylor's count of a 500-grapheme passage, Kanji constituted 11% in Korean and 57% in Japanese. The passage was the first part of the political news in the *Korea Times* (October 21, 1981) and in *Asahi Shinbun*, a leading Japanese paper (October 11, 1981). South Koreans need not learn 1000 Kanji in addition to the official 1800, as Japanese must (Chapter 4). All in all, Kanji are used far less in South Korea than in Japan.

Methods of teaching Chinese characters are the same wherever characters are taught (see Chapters 3 and 4). In a nutshell, Kanji are taught batch by batch, starting with simple yet visually distinct ones representing familiar morphemes. Meaning-cuing radicals, sound-cuing phonetics, and pictographic origins are useful teaching aids for some Kanji. Note that each Kanji must be learned for its shape, meaning, and sound, all at once. In China and Japan, Kanji are taught from Grade 1; in South Korea, they are taught in middle and high schools, 900 at each stage.

KANJI VERSUS HANGUL

The Korean and Japanese systems provide effective means for comparing logographs with phonetic signs. Park and Arbuckle (1977) compared Kanji and Hangul using Korean–English bilinguals in Canada. Korean words presented in two Kanji were remembered better than were the same words presented in two Hangul syllable-blocks on recognition and free recall tests but not on paired-associate recall or serial anticipation. Note that the Hangul stimuli were not native words but were transliterations of Kanji words, and hence were not in their customary script.

Our research team has compared Kanji and Hangul reading using a natural text (Kang, Chong, & Taylor, in preparation). Korean adult subjects read either a Kanji–Hangul (53%–47%) mixed text or an all-Hangul text. The text was displayed on a computer screen one word at a time as the subject pressed a key. Subjects' silent reading time was recorded, and their comprehension (gist extraction) was tested.

In the mixed text, Kanji words were read slower than Hangul words. In Korean, Kanji words are always content words, whereas Hangul words are sometimes content words and sometimes function words. When reading time was recalculated without the Hangul function words, the difference in reading time between Kanji and Hangul was reduced, but Kanji time was still longer. Readers may process Kanji words longer than Hangul words because they are aware that Kanji words are always content words and hence are important.

After the reading experiment, the subjects were asked to recognize whether printed test words had been read on the computer. The test words were presented among an equal number of foils selected from a different section of the same article. The Kanji words were recognized better, with higher hit rates and lower false alarm rates, than were the Hangul words. Better recognition of Kanji cannot be due to the fact that they were read longer than were the Hangul words, for the same result obtained even when both types of stimuli were presented at a constant rate (Park & Arbuckle, 1977).

According to Park and Arbuckle, pictures are richer in information content and hence are more memorable than are verbal labels, and Kanji occupy a position between pictures and labels in information content and memorability. Pictures provide ambiguous messages (Chapter 2), and Chinese characters can no longer be equated to pictures (Chapter 3). More likely, Kanji words are recognized well because they are easy to discriminate from other Kanji. The large range in stroke number and the variety of possible patterns makes each Kanji visually distinctive, discriminable, and recognizable. On average, a Hangul block has only half as many strokes as a Kanji. Hangul blocks have a lesser range of complexity, and hence discriminability, than do Kanji.

KANJI–HANGUL MIXED TEXT

In text, Kanji are used in the same manner in Korean and Japanese, which have similar syntax, requiring similar kinds of grammatical items—postpositions after nouns and a rich variety of endings for verbs and adjectives. Kanji are used for stems of key words, with native phonetic signs added for grammatical endings.

The mixed use of two types of script should make reading easy. Because semantically important words are in Kanji, which are visually distinct and prominent (dark and complex objects), readers may develop a strategy whereby they attend mainly to Kanji. Kanji are figures against the background of phonetic signs. Japanese and Korean readers accustomed to mixed texts find pure phonetic text hard to read. Gray's (1956) Korean subjects read all-Hangul text with more fixations and a slower rate than Hangul–Kanji mixed text, to which they were accustomed. By contrast, a research team in South Korea found that their college student subjects read a mixed text more slowly than they did an all-Hangul text (Noh, Hwang, Park, & Kim, 1977). This result perhaps arises from the late introduction of Kanji in schools (middle and high schools) and the limited use of Kanji in general publications in Korea now, as opposed to 26 years ago.

Korean text, whether mixed or all-Hangul, can be written either vertically or horizontally. In one Korean study, eight college seniors initially read faster vertically than horizontally. Their reading speed in both directions improved dramatically after an intensive speed reading training, but the final speed was greater in the horizontal than vertical direction (Noh *et al.*, 1977). A horizontal span is intrinsically longer than a vertical one (Salapatek, 1968; see Chapter 7). Also, horizontal writing is becoming popular in South Korea to the extent that it is adopted in most school textbooks.

Since Koreans have an excellent phonetic script like Hangul, why should they keep using Kanji? Because of the useful function Kanji play in Korean text, because of the existence of many Chinese loan words, and because of the links they provide to Chinese and Japanese writings, learning a limited number of judiciously chosen official Kanji is well worth a Korean reader's time and effort. On the other hand, since North Korea seems to manage well with Hangul only, Kanji are not indispensable to Koreans.

Summary and Conclusions

Hangul was invented in the fifteenth century by King Sejong for his less privileged subjects. Hangul is unique in that it is at once an alphabet, a syllabary, and perhaps a logography. As an alphabet, in Hangul a small set of symbols codes phonemes unambiguously, and at the same time, the symbols reflect the articulation of their phonemes. The names of the symbols teach their sounds. Complex consonant symbols are created by starting with five basic symbols and adding extra strokes for additional articulatory features. Compound vowel symbols are created by varying the combination of two basic symbols and a marker. As a result, related sounds have related symbols.

As a syllabary, in Hangul from two to four of these alphabet symbols are packaged—again, according to a set of rules—into a two-dimensional block that represents a syllable. The complexity of syllable-blocks varies in three levels, aiding discrimination. Home typewriters and electronic communication are possible with Hangul.

As a logography, in Hangul a single syllable-block, especially a complex one, represents a morpheme. Spelling has been standardized to preserve the logographic property of Hangul: A set of morphemes, even though they sound the same in certain phonetic context, may be distinguished in spelling.

The rich sound system of the Korean language requires a few thousand different syllable-blocks. Yet, these blocks can be learned efficiently: Their sounds can be deduced by a simple algorithm or, better, by noting the pattern formed when they are arranged in a syllable matrix that reveals their highly regular interrelations. Thanks to all these rational features, word decoding is painlessly learned in Hangul, usually within a few months. Illiteracy is negligible, and remedial teachers are unnecessary.

South Korea uses 1800 Kanji, each of which has only one reading, always a monosyllable. In text, Hangul may be supplemented by Kanji: Hangul letters express grammatical items as well as some content words of native origin, whereas Kanji are used to write Chinese loan words. The admixture of Kanji assists rapid reading by visually breaking the texture of the printed page in a syntactically useful way.

6

English Alphabet and Orthography

How on earth do you spell pearl—and don't ask me to look it up in the dictionary because I've already looked under "pir," "pur," and "per" without finding it.

—a child[1]

English Alphabet and Spelling

English Alphabet

The Anglo-Saxon alphabet was adapted from Roman letters in the seventh century by Christian missionaries from Ireland. Originally, there were two extra letters to represent the two sounds of 'th' in *this* and *think.* The English alphabet now has 26 uppercase and lowercase letters and can be written in print or cursive forms. In whatever case or form they are written, letters of the alphabet are simple compared with logographs like Chinese characters. Unfortunately, 'p/q' and 'b/d' are mirror images of each other, causing confusion errors for beginning or disabled readers. Most letters have names that contain the letters' sounds: Thus, "bee" for 'b' and "ou" for 'o'. A few names, however, have no relation to their letters' sounds: "aitch," "wye," and "doubleyou" for 'h', 'y', and 'w'.

The most serious defect of the English alphabet is that only 23 letters are available to represent about 44 phonemes. (Of the 26 letters, 'c, q, x' are superfluous.) This gross mismatch between the letters and phonemes plays

[1]Quoted in Rosewell and Natchez (1971, p. 103).

havoc with English **orthography,** the rules or conventions for using letters to spell words. One letter can represent a variety of sounds, and one sound can be represented by several different letters or letter groups. On the other hand, the simplicity of the alphabet, without the variety of diacritic marks of French or Arabic, makes typewriters easy to design and use.

History of English Orthography

As the English alphabet is imperfect, so is English orthography. How did the present complicated orthography all begin? Old English (A.D. 700–1100) was roughly phonetic in its spelling, but early Middle English in the fourteenth century had already lost some of its phonetic character, perhaps in response to the wide regional variations in English pronunciations. Geoffrey Chaucer lamented in *Troilus and Criseyde*:

And for ther is so grete dyversite
In English, and in writyng of our tonge,
So preye I God, that non myswrite the,
Ne the mysmetere for defaut of tonge.

At the beginning of English writing, having no standard spelling conventions, scribes sometimes spelled words according to their own individual whims. For example, French scribes improvised 'gh' for the then English guttural 'h' in words such as *right* (Old English *riht* and modern Scots *richt*). These 'gh' sounds became silent in most English dialects in the late fifteenth century.

When printing came to England around the middle of the fifteenth century, pioneer printers such as William Caxton, who worked many years on the Continent, would spell words in Continental ways when in doubt. The 'gh' in *ghost* is perhaps inherited from Flemish. Printers also frequently justified lines (straightening the right hand margin) by adding extra letters rather than spaces. This practice persisted until well into the sixteenth century. Spelling could be changed for financial gain as well: Lawyers' clerks lengthened spellings, because they were paid by the inch for their writing.

Poets and scholars played their parts in perpetuating nonphonetic spelling. When poems were written to be read, some poets used so-called visual rhymes, such as John Milton's *foul–soul.* Edmund Spencer's rhymes include *quight* (*quite*) to rhyme with *fight,* and *arre* (*are*) with *farre* (*far*). As well, there have always been pedantic scholars who delight in tracing words to their "original, classical" spellings. Thanks to their zeal, English has been left with such irregularly spelled words as *comptroller, debt, island, sovereign.* The Renaissance was the heyday of such etymologizing in English orthography. Samuel Johnson's prestigious 1775 dictionary standardized or made official many illogical spellings of his day. In Dewey's words, "rigor mortis" had set in in English orthography (based on Dewey, 1971; Downing & Leong, 1982; Scragg, 1974; Wrenn, 1949).

English has been blessed, or should we say, cursed, with a profuse infusion of loan words. Sometimes original foreign spellings are retained, sometimes not. In particular, the influence of French orthography, itself burdened with irregularities, has been disastrous. Scragg (1974) estimates that about 40% of the words in a dictionary count of present-day vocabulary would show French derivation. Lawrence of Arabia, when asked by his perplexed publisher to spell his foreign words and names more uniformly, is said to have answered: "I spell my names anyhow, to show what rot the systems are." Who can blame him?

Representing speech in a phonetic, as opposed to logographic, writing system presents one fundamental problem: How should changing speech be represented? Speech sounds, in particular long vowels, are unstable and tend to change across regions, over time, and in word derivation. The **Great Vowel Shift** that occurred several centuries ago changed the English vowels gradually but comprehensively, affecting many vowels in relation to one another. The Great Vowel Shift continued even after spelling stabilized substantially, thus rendering vowel spelling non-phonetic. Table 6-1 shows some typical vowels affected by this shift.

Finally, slight differences exist between British and American spellings: Americans tend to use simpler spellings, thanks to the lexicographer–educator Noah Webster's efforts in the years around 1800. *Colour, judgement, programme,* and *levelled* in Britain became *color, judgment, program,* and *leveled* in the United States. Canada is, as usual, between Britain and United States, spelling some words in the British way and others in the American way, and some in both ways.

Complex Spelling Rules

Having several letters for one sound makes correct spelling difficult, and having several sounds for one letter makes oral reading difficult. In Dewey's (1971) count based on 100,000 running words, English orthography has 219 spellings for 24 consonants (9.1 spellings per consonant), and 342 spellings for 17 vowels (10.7 spellings per vowel).

Table 6-1 *The Great Vowel Shift*

Middle English		Modern English	
spell	say	spell	say
bite	/bi:tə/	—	[bait]
bete	/be:tə/	beet	[bi:t]
bete	/bɛ:tə/	beat	[bi:t]
abate	/aba:tə/	—	[əbeit]
foul	/fu:l/	foul	[faul]
fol	/fo:l/	fool	[fu:l]
fole	/fɔ:lə/	foal	[foul]

Source: Jespersen (1933, p. 232).
Middle English = 1150-1500; Modern English = since 1500.

Following spelling patterns found in real words, *supper, sour,* and *suffer* could each be spelled *psougholo*:

ps:	s, as in	psychology
ough:	up, as in	hiccough
	ow, as in	bough
	uf, as in	enough
olo:	er, as in	colonel

A real word of the same kind is *gaol* /dʒeil/. The town in which Dylan Thomas's *Under Milk Wood* is set has a name that is simple in sound but complex in spelling: /la:n/ = *Laugharne.* As Pitman and St. John (1969) observed: "They [some English printed words] represent sounds which we would be horrified to utter [p. 40]."

Are there spelling rules to guide us? Consider the simple matter of whether to double the consonants in an English word. This matter can seldom be inferred from the sound of the word and becomes one of the frequent causes of misspellings. The only helpful rule deals with just one point: the doubling or not of the final consonants of a word to which a suffix has been added. The rules, as given by Dickinson (1976?) are:

> When a suffix commencing with a vowel is added to a word ending in a single consonant, the final consonant is doubled—
>
> (a) If the word is a monosyllable; *swimming, running.*
>
> (b) If the last syllable of the word is accented; *forgetting, beginning.*
>
> But final 'l' is doubled in any case except before a suffix beginning with 'i' (unless it is *-ing*): *travelled, marvellous,* but *devilish, liberalism, naturalist,* but again, *modelling.* Words ending in 'll', as *befall, enthrall, install, recall,* and those which sometimes end in 'l' and sometimes 'll', as *appal(l), distil(l), enrol(l),* double the 'l' before a suffix beginning with a vowel. Derivatives of the word *parallel* do not double the final 'l', due to the preceding 'll' in the same syllable; *unparalleled, paralleling* [p. 19].

In the initial position of a word, no English consonants double, but vowels do in these five words: *aardvark, eel, eerie, oodles,* and *ooze.* In other positions, only 15 letters can double; those that do not are 'a, i, j, k, q, u, v, w, x, y' (*yakking* and *revving* are exceptions).

In another spelling lesson by Dickinson, some nouns ending in 'o' form their plurals by adding *-s*; others, without any apparent reason, add *-es*: thus, *altos* and *dynamos* but *cargoes* and *echoes.* One might as well resort to a mnemonic: *potatoes* and *tomatoes* have *toes.* As for Latin plurals, they can be formed in either a Latin or an English way: *formula, formulae, formulas* and *fungus, fungi, funguses.*

Spelling rules are numerous, and most are complex. What is worse, they account for only some words. In computer simulation, the use of over 200 phonemic rules led to about 50% correct spelling in the 17,000 words examined (Hanna, Hanna, Hodges, & Rudorf, 1966). The rule table for a given phoneme lists a number of different spellings for one phoneme, and states conditions (position, stress, surrounding phonemes, etc.) under which each is used. Most misspellings could be accounted for when morphological and etymological factors were considered. Hanna *et al.* chose to conclude that English orthography, far from being capricious, is substantially more systematic than is commonly regarded. But is 50% correct spelling of a small vocabulary with 200 rules a good performance?

Development of Spelling Strategies

The variety of words calls for a variety of spelling strategies. A strategy based on letter names is used by preschoolers as well as first graders. Such spelling errors as "DA" (*day*) and "TIGR" (*tiger*) reflect the names of the vowel letters (Beers & Henderson, 1977; Read, 1971; Zutell, 1981). The letter-name strategy seems to have been used also by some older dyslexic children, who spelled *road* as "rode" (Thomson, 1981).

Here is a well-known nursery rhyme, as written by a 5½-year-old:[2]

liti miss miofit
sat on a tof fit
eding crand was
alag cam a spidr
and sat don be
sidr and scod
miss mafit a
way

—Sara Butler

Spelling based on vowel name can be seen in "cam," "spidr," and "be sidr," but other manners of spelling are also evident. "Liti" uses the common sounds of its letters, but "eding" uses the name-sound of 'e' and the conventional pattern of *-ing*. Has *-ing* already been learned as a unit? Some words, such as *miss* and *way* suggest that whole-word patterns have also been learned, but the main pattern is phonetic in one way or another.

Bryant and Bradley (1980) tested the reading and spelling ability of normal and backward readers with a reading age of around 7½ years. Occasionally, a child could spell a word he could not read, or vice versa. Most of the words that could be read but not spelled were phonetically irregular, whereas the ones that could be spelled but not read were phonetically regular (e.g., *bad, fit*) and could be spelled letter by letter. From this and other evidence, Bryant and Bradley argued that children learn to read visually and to spell phonetically, and only as they mature do they apply both strategies to the two tasks.

To name a few of the strategies used by older spellers, sequential sound–letter decoding is sufficient for spelling CVC words such as *mat* and *cut*; "hierarchical decoding" (a later item influences the sounds of earlier items) is

[2]We thank Brian Butler for this example.

necessary for CVCe words such as *mate* and *cute.* A special rule such as the 'c' rule must be learned for spelling /k/ as 'c' before 'a, o, u' (*cat, cot, cut*); analogies are useful for irregularly spelled words (the familiar word *nation* leads to the unfamiliar *spallation*) and also for derived words (*critical—criticize* to *metrical—metricize*) (Marsh, Friedman, Welch, & Desberg, 1980). Marsh, *et al.* assessed the use of these strategies by children from Grades 2 and 5, and also by college students. The subjects spelled **pseudowords,** which, though not real words, are pronounceable (*jat, jate, jation, cazical, cazicize*) to dictation.

Fig. 6-1 shows that certain strategies are acquired much earlier than others. Compare the three top curves to the bottom two: The top three are based on phonemic coding rules for regular words while the bottom two are based on analogies for irregularly spelled words. Unfamiliarity does not explain entirely why analogies develop later, because a Grade 2 vocabulary contains irregularly spelled words. The figure also shows a clear developmental trend: The use of each of these strategies increases with age, especially between Grades 2 and 5. One exception to the trend is a slight decrease between Grade 5 and college on the 'c'-rule. Marsh *et al.* attribute it to college students' knowledge of rare exceptions to the 'c' rule (*kayak, kudos*).

Because of complex orthography, spelling errors are unavoidable, even among skilled readers. H. D. Brown (1970) showed that even college students do not seem to have a powerful set of phoneme–grapheme rules that might help them to spell such unfamiliar but regular words as *bucolic, calumny, churlish,* and *feldspar.* In 5000 college English compositions, Alper (1942) found over 1000 different words misspelled, usually in one particular "hard spot" in a word (e.g., "nickle" for *nickel*). The majority of errors made sense phonetically.

Simon and Simon (1973) suggest a "generate-and-test" process: Generate a few spellings by phonemic rules and then test by visual recognition, which has been acquired as a by-product of reading. Recognition requires only sufficient information, whereas recall requires complete information. Skilled spellers rely on visual or rote memory in spelling irregular words (e.g., Barron, 1980; Sloboda, 1980). Even beginning readers, at least more successful spell-

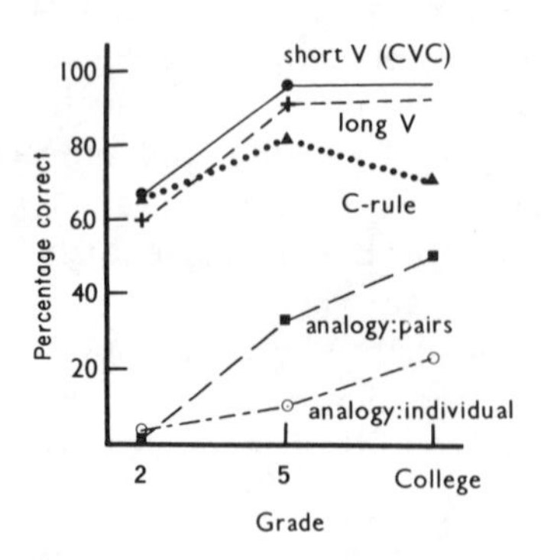

Figure 6-1. *Development of spelling strategies (based on Marsh, Friedman, Welch, & Desberg, 1980).*

ers, learn to store printed words as orthographic images, visual forms of words that include both silent as well as pronounced letters (Ehri, 1980). In Tenney's (1980) experiment, in deciding which of two alternatives "look right," subjects found it less helpful to imagine the alternatives than actually to see them. According to Hodges (1981), spelling-bee contestants, aged 10–14, use semantic, syntactic, morphological, and phonological information in their spelling, relying on phoneme–grapheme strategies only when no other clues elicit from memory the particular word in question.

Learning to spell and pronounce many common English words is not unlike learning the so-called arbitrary Chinese characters. In both systems, memory for visual shape plays a large role.

Recovering Sounds from Orthography

Brush up Your English[3]

I take it you already know
Of tough and bough and cough and dough.
Others may stumble but not you,
On hiccough, thorough, lough and through.
Well done! And now you wish, perhaps,
To learn of less familiar traps.

Beware of heard, a dreadful word
That looks like beard and sounds like bird,
And dead—it's said like bed, not bead.
For goodness' sake, don't call it deed!
Watch out for meat and great and threat:
They rhyme with suite and straight and debt.

A moth is not a moth in mother,
Nor both in bother, broth in brother,
And here is not a match for there,
Nor dear and fear for bear and pear,
And then there's dose and rose and lose—
Just look them up—and goose and choose,
And cork and work and card and ward,
And font and front and word and sword,
And do and go and thwart and cart.
Come, come, I've hardly made a start.

A dreadful language? Man alive,
I'd mastered it when I was five!

—T. S. Watt (1954)

[3]Reproduced with permission of *The Guardian*.

How do you pronounce words such as *phlought*, *victuals*, and *Pontefract*? In each case, you would try to use an analogy. People sound out almost all English words by analogy, according to some psychologists (see Chapter 10). An analogy with *phase* and *brought* would lead you to pronounce *phlought* as /flɔ:t/. (But then you might just as easily say /flufd/ in analogy with *through* and *laughed.*) For *victuals,* you may use analogies with *victim* and *actual,* when it is pronounced like neither of them: It is /vitəls/. As for *Pontefract,* you are unlikely to have guessed that it can be pronounced as /pʌmfri/.

Many Sounds from One Letter

In English orthography, several sounds can be represented by one letter. Dewey (1971) counts 2.4 sounds on average per consonant letter, and 8.2 per vowel letter. See how 'c' is pronounced in *city, car, social, indict, cello, eczema,* and *discern,* or how 'a' is pronounced either alone or in a digraph in *about, farm, fat, fall, face, fare, hurrah, feat, instead, boat, oar, aisle,* and *learn.* A letter by itself cannot be a reliable clue to its sound. Being aware of a few patterns, such as that the consonants 'j, k, m, n, q, v, z' have one consistent sound and 'c, g, s, t' have several different sounds (as well as no sound), may be of some help. As for the vowel letters, every one has more than one sound.

Because recovery of sounds from written words is not straightforward, dictionaries such as *An English Pronouncing Dictionary* (D. Jones, 1917) and books such as *Rules for Pronouncing for the English Language* (Wijk, 1966) exist. Even ordinary dictionaries give sounds, spellings, and syllable breaks for all the words they list. In his book on English pronunciation, Wijk assures the reader that 90–95% of the total vocabulary does in fact follow regular spelling and pronunciation patterns. And yet, on the matter of whether to pronounce the five simple vowels short or long, he devotes 26 pages to rules, examples, and exceptions to the rules. He admits that the exceptions to the rules are numerous, especially among the commonest words. Here is the first of eight categories describing when simple vowels ('a, e, i, o, u') are pronounced short:

> Usually in monosyllable words ending in one or more consonants and in such disyllabic or polysyllabic words as are stressed on the last syllable and end in one or more consonants. [For example, see (a) below.] Further in words which end in two consonants plus silent 'e' the preceding vowel most often has its short pronunciation [see (b)]. The long pronunciation occurs, however, in such words as [see (c)]. There are also various other groups of words which form exceptions to the above rules [see (d)]. A detailed account will be given in Section B, p. 28 etc. below under each individual vowel [pp. 17–18].

Have you grasped the rules well enough to give examples of these rules and exceptions to the rules? Here are some: (a) *glad, distinct*; (b) *pulse, involve*; (c) *change, taste*; and (d) *craft, chance.*

Rules not only are hard to grasp but also presuppose the reader's knowledge of vowel–consonant distinction, syllabification, stress, etymology,

Table 6-2 *Factors that Determine Sounds of Letters*

Factor	Letter	Sound	Example	Contrast
POSITION				
initial	s-	/s/	*say*	*sure*
medial	-s-	/s/, /z/	*basal, bosom*	*tension*
LOAN WORD				
Italian	c	/tʃ/	*cello, vivace*	*cell*
French	ch-	/ʃ/	*chic*	*chin*
SILENT E				
vowel	a	/ei/	*mate*	*mat*
consonant	g	/dʒ/	*rage*	*rag*
STRESS				
before	x	/ks/	*appróximate*	
after	x	/gz/	*exámple*	
WORD CLASS				
noun	a	/e/	*dúplicate*	
verb		/ei/	*duplicáte*	
function word	th-	/ð/	*the, though*	
content word		/θ/	*thin*	*through*
CONTEXT				
before a,o,u	c	/k/	*cat, scold, cut*	*facade*
before e,i,y		/ʃ/, /s/	*ocean, city, cycle*	
MORPHEME				
within	-th-	/ð/	*father*	
between		/t-h/	*fathead*	
WORD DERIVATION				
stem	ea	/i:/	*heal*	
derived		/e/	*health*	
SYLLABLE				
one	i	/i/	*live*	
two		/ai/	*alive*	*living*
PRONOUNCING EASE				
	n	(silent)	*hymn*	
		/n/	*hymnal*	

morphology, phonology, and so on.[4] Table 6-2 lists several factors that, singly or in relation with others, determine the sound of a letter or a letter cluster.

The Kurzweil reading machine developed for the blind is a miniature computer: The machine scans a printed page, reading out words. Stored in it are rules for figuring out how English words are pronounced. What interests us about this machine is the enormous number of rules that must be stored—1000 rules, plus 1500 exceptions to the rules!

In developing the MIT speech synthesis system known as MITALK, Allen and his coworkers developed over 800 orthographic rules for English (Allen, Carlson, Granstrom, Hunnicutt, Klatt, & Pisoni, 1979). Even so, to make the speech sound reasonable, the most common 2000 words were treated as

[4]Even knowledge of the distinction between vowels and consonants cannot be taken for granted. When Insup Taylor asked "mature students" in a continuing-eduction class about it, the answer was, "one is short and the other is long."

exceptions, and the computer was programmed precisely how to pronounce them. The rules were then adequate to deal with 98% of the less common words. The remaining 2% were pronounced by using letter-to-sound rules.

Pronunciation Skill

Considering that 'c' is pronounced in so many ways and conditioned by so many factors, it is not surprising that English speakers, even in college, have not completely mastered its varied sounds. In one study, 561 children (from Grades 2, 4, and 6) and college students pronounced, one at a time, English words or pseudowords (Venezky, Chapman, & Calfee, 1972). The words contained the letter 'c' at initial, medial, or final positions, as in *cade, cyfe; mecal, hacen; dac, zyc.* The most difficult was 'c' before 'i, e, y' (pronounced as /s/); it was correctly pronounced by only 22.4% (initial) and 39.3% (medial) of Grade 2 children, and 69.8% (initial) and 73.8% (medial) of college students. On the other hand, 'c' before 'a, o, u' (/k/) was easier and was pronounced correctly 82.4% of the time by Grade 2 children, and 88.1% by college students.

The sounds of 'g' (*get, gem*) are even more difficult than those of 'c'. Although readers acquire the 'c' pattern usually by the end of elementary school, 'g' is treated as having the single, invariant sound of *get* even by college students (Venezky, 1976). Poor readers of Grades 7 and 9 have not fully mastered variant predictable and unpredictable vowels and vowel clusters (Ryder & Graves, 1980).

In English, one can distinguish between **regular words** (spelling gives clues to standard pronunciation) and **irregular words** (spelling misleads to wrong pronunciation, including stress). Schoolchildren in England, aged 9–12, made 10 times more errors in reading irregular words (e.g., *attorney*) than in reading equally infrequent but regular words (*certificate*) (Gasper & Brown, 1973). Even college students in the United States took longer to pronounce irregular but short words than to pronounce regular words of similar length

Table 6-3 *Pronunciation of Regular and Irregular Words*

Regular	Irregular	Pseudoword
glue	*vise*	*laf*
loan	*beige*	*caik*
chant	*epoch*	*skail*
fresh	*should*	*secks*
.	.	.
.	.	.
.	.	.
	TIME (msec)	
428	594	778
	ERROR RATE (percentage)	
0.5	4.5	5.6

Source: Based on Baron & Strawson, 1976.

and frequency (Baron & Strawson, 1976). On the irregular words, the subjects made many errors, almost as many as on pseudowords. Table 6-3 shows some of the test words, along with pronunciation time and error rates.

Functional Spelling Unit

Since the grapheme–phoneme correspondence is so irregular in English, some linguists look for other ways to predict sounds from spellings. Venezky (1967, 1970) derived 65 spelling-to-sound correspondences, or functional spelling units, for the 20,000 most common English words. A functional unit is a string of one or more letters that acts as a unit in predicting a sound. It does not transcend morpheme boundaries. For example, the sound of 'ph' in *sapphire* and *shepherd* differs: In the former, it occurs within one morpheme and is pronounced as /f/, and in the latter, at a morpheme boundary and is pronounced as /p/.

Functional units are divided into markers and relational units. A marker does not have its own sound value but indicates the pronunciation of a preceding grapheme. When a silent 'e' follows a single consonant after a single vowel, it usually makes the vowel sound long, as in *mate* and *hide* compared with *mat* and *hid.* When silent 'e' follows the consonants 'c', 'g', 'th', it again determines their sound values: Compare *farce, rage,* and *breathe,* with *arc, rag,* and *breath.* The 'i' in *city* can also be thought of as a marker since it marks the sound value of 'c' as /s/.

A relational unit is a string of one or more letters that is pronounced as a unit. Examples may be single letters such as 't, k', or letter clusters such as 'ch, gh, sh, th, tch, oi'. But the concept of relational unit becomes complex when the same cluster 'gn' is counted as one or two units depending on its use: It is one unit in *cognac* and *poignant* but two units in *signal* and *malignant.*

Venezky's morpho-phonemic "solution" for regular prediction of sounds from spellings is interesting but turns out to be complex: His book contains over 70 pages of rules, and inevitably, many exceptions to the rules. A morpheme boundary may not always be a reliable clue to the sound of a two-morpheme word. For example, in pronouncing *shepherd,* which consists of *sheep* and *herd,* /h/ in *-herd* is dropped, whereas in *goatherd,* which consists of *goat* and *herd,* /h/ in *-herd* is retained.

Phonological Rules and Orthography

Underlying Phonological Representation

Chomsky and Halle (1968) contend: "The fundamental principle of orthography is that phonetic variation is not indicated where it is predictable by a general rule. Thus, stress placement and regular vowel or consonant alternations are generally not reflected [p. 49]." In their theory, every word has its underlying and surface phonetic representation and a set of phonological rules that derive surface from underlying representation. Even a word as simple as *spa* is supposed to have been derived from its underlying representation through no fewer than five phonological rules.

In an orthography that is based on an underlying representation, correspondence between semantic units and orthographic representations is maintained when sounds change in word derivation. That is, when a sound changes from one word to its derived word, the sound's spelling does not change, as in *anxious–anxiety.* Underlying representations are also fairly resistant to historical and regional sound changes. For all these reasons, Chomsky and Halle made the celebrated claim that English orthography is a "near optimal" system for the lexical representation of the English language.

Vowel-Shift Rule

Among all the phonological rules, Chomsky and Halle (1968) place great importance on the vowel-shift rule, which they describe as "without doubt the pivotal process of Modern English phonology." The **vowel-shift rule** changes a vowel under specified conditions, that is, when the vowel is both tense and stressed. Take *linear*:

1. Underlying vowel /li:n/
2. Apply diphthongization rule to produce [lain]
3. Apply vowel-shift rule and laxing rule to produce *linear* [liniə]

Here are a few more examples of front vowel shift from [+tense] to [–tense]:

derive–derivative; divine–divinity
profane–profanity; grateful–gratitude
obscene–obscenity; receive–receptive

For back vowels, the way the "rule of unrounding" applies to *profound–profundity* is as follows, in Chomsky's (1970) own words:

> In the word *profundity* the underlying /ū/ [as in *shoe*] becomes nontense [u] by a rule that applies in a syllable followed by an unstressed nonfinal syllable; it then lowers to [o] and unrounds to [ʌ] just as the /ū/ of profound, after diphongizing to /ūw/, lowers and unround to [a]. . . Rules of tensing, lowering, raising, rounding, unrounding, and others interweave to determine complex relations between the abstract underlying forms and the phonetic output [p. 9].

As Moskowitz (1973) points out, those word pairs that show alternating vowels constitute a small percentage of the total vocabulary. These words are also among the most literary and abstract types and occur rarely in speech. In 6385 words in the basic spelling list used in Australia, only 168 pairs showed alternating vowels (Yule, 1978).

In children's speech, 1000 common words account for 96% of their verbal production (Rinsland, 1945). Of these, we found only 12 words that preserve vowel spelling while sounds change (e.g., *hear–heard, lose–lost, dinner–diner, live–life, bite–bit, suppose–supposition, line–linear,* etc.) Against this meager crop of words that preserve spellings, several from the 200 most common words change pronunciation ***and*** spelling: *get–got, know–knew, come–came, see–saw, take–took, find–found.* Much the same pattern holds also for the next most frequently used 800 words. So, when English words change pronunciation, they often change their spelling as well.

Moskowitz (1973) points out a few more complicating factors. Some semantically related word pairs do not show the vowel shift, as in *valid–validity.* On the other hand, in some word pairs with a vowel shift, the semantic relations are not always clear: *rape–rapture.* (The semantic relation is there, but distant. *Rapture* comes from the same root as *raptor,* a bird that, like a falcon, captures its prey. In *rapture,* one is captured by one's emotion, in *rape,* by another person.) Some word pairs that are related neither semantically nor historically also follow the same phonological pattern: *comply–complicity.*

Enough about suffixes; what about prefixes? Prefixes do not normally seem to "trigger" vowel shifts, as in *decent–indecent.* But sometimes they do, as in *famous–infamous* and *face–preface.*

English seems prone to sound changes: A slight variation in word form, such as adding a suffix, causes shifts in vowels, consonants, and stress. Let us look at word derivation in German, a sister language of English. No sound change is involved in the following word pairs: *äusserst–Äusserste(s),* 'extreme–extremity'; *göttlich–Göttlichkeit,* 'divine–divinity'.

It might be instructive to ponder how the other phonetic writing systems considered in this book solve the problem of sound changes. The Japanese and Korean systems solve it by usually representing sounds as they sound. In these two languages, there tends to be little sound change within the roots of words across different dialects and in word derivation. Even if there were, the roots of words are frequently written in Kanji, which are impervious to minor sound changes. Adding a suffix seldom triggers sound changes in these languages.

Vowel-Shift Rule and Readers

According to Moskowitz (1973), although children have implicit knowledge of the vowel shift, the knowledge develops gradually, through learning to spell. Her subjects had to say *sepity* to the experimenter's *sipy.* All 7-year-old and some 9–12-year-old children tolerated any kind of vowel alternation, whereas other children aged between 9 and 12 tolerated only the major alternation pattern of English.

Steinberg (1973) did not find evidence that adults know the vowel shift rule. Subjects selected one of two suffixes, attached it to a given base, and then pronounced the derived form. The suffixes were arranged so that either selection should have triggered vowel shifting, as hypothesized by Chomsky and Halle (1968). For example, *A trout is a fish* [after two more sentences]. *It swam in a true* _____ *fashion.* Subjects had to repeat the final sentence, filling the blank with *trout* plus either *-cal* or *-ify.* No subject said [tr∧tikəl], as in *pronunciation*; all subjects said [traʷtikəl].

Crowder (1982) claims to have obtained high rates of vowel shifting using Steinberg's design with such modifications as testing nonsense words instead of real words. MacKay's (1978) adult subjects took longer, with more errors, to produce *decision* from *decide* (which involves a vowel shift) than to produce *conclusion* from *conclude* (no vowel shift).

Consonant and Stress Shift

Here are examples of consonant and stress shifts, which appear to be triggered by addition of a syllable in word derivation: *anxious–anxiety,* [ks–gz]; *expedite–expeditious,* [t–ʃ]; *prodigal–prodigeous,* [g–dʒ]; and *critical–criticize,* [k–s]. Note, however, in *governer–gubernical,* both vowel and consonant change in spelling.

One important aspect of English pronunciation is stress, even though it is not expressed in orthography. As shown in Table 6-2, stress can determine the sound values of some letters. Stress, in turn, is determined by sound values of letters and by such other factors as syllables.

- Vowel quality. In two-syllable words, a tense (long) final vowel attracts stress: *témpest* versus *domáin.*
- Number of consonants. Two-syllable words ending in two consonants have stress on the second syllable: *édit* versus *eléct.*
- Affix. A prefix such as *com-* is a signal to move stress to the second syllable: *cáncel* versus *compél.*
- Silent 'e'. Final silent 'e' attracts stress on the preceding vowel in 3-syllable words: *dámask* versus *arabésque.*
- Noun versus verb. Stress on the second syllable on verbs derived from nouns: *súrvey* (noun) versus *survéy* (verb). The same rule applies to *désert* (noun; arid land) and *desért* (verb; leave the army illegally), even though the verb is not derived from the noun.

Smith and Baker (1976) tested adults and Groat (1979) tested 7-year-old children for their abilities to use these factors. All factors had large effects on the assignment of primary stress in the word. Similar results were obtained for the adults and the children, except on the silent 'e', to which the adults were far more sensitive than were the children. There was no strong evidence in either study for the underlying phonology suggested by Chomsky and Halle (1968).

Trammell (1978) tested how adults assign primary and secondary stress in unfamiliar words such as *elenctic,* on which subjects tended to agree, and *agee,* on which they tended to disagree (even two large dictionaries disagree). Overall he found a high degree of consistency in stress assignment but no significant differences in pronouncing words of different origin—Latin, Greek, and Germanic. The number of different sounds produced per test word ranged from 1 to 10, with the average for all 30 words being 5.

We conclude, along with Trammell (1978), that although "the orthography may be 'near optimal' for a formal system of rules, the speaker–reader's internalized rules are not nearly so well defined or consistently applied as those of SPE [Chomsky and Halle's book] [p. 93]."

Some Advantages of Nonphonetic Spelling

Preserving the same spelling for a word and its derivation (*sane–sanity*) may be helpful for indicating semantic relations between the two, as discussed earlier. But these are learned words that occur infrequently. Readers are more likely to encounter inflected words than derived words. The sounds of suffixes for past tense and plural number change, depending on the final sounds of words to which the suffixes attach, but their spellings (*-ed, -s*) remain unchanged:

picked / -t/	*cats* / -s/
housed / -d/	*dogs* / -z/
trotted / -id/	*buses* / -iz/

The invariant spellings for these suffixes aid readers in using them as perceptual units (see Chapter 8).

English is spoken in widely separated parts of the world, in a vast range of dialects, some mutually unintelligible. English sounds, especially vowels, change also in dialects (British *train* /trein/ versus Australian /train/). No orthography could do justice to all of them. By not catering to capricious sound variation, English orthography serves well a wide range of people who use different sound patterns, just as the consistent logography does in China.

Conversely, different spellings of the same sound differentiate semantically unrelated words with the same sounds, namely, homophones: *right, rite, write,* and *wright,* as in this limerick:[5]

A right-handed fellow named Wright
In writing "write" always wrote "rite"
Where he meant to write right.
If he'd written "write" right,
Wright would not have wrought rot writing "rite."

This ability of spelling to differentiate homophones provides the same advantage as having a unique Chinese character for each of the numerous homophones in Chinese and Japanese morphemes.

Lest we get too smug, Dewey (1971) points out that against a few hundred homophones distinguished by different spellings, there are many thousands that are not, and there is no demand to create distinctions for them. Think of the many different meanings of the word *bay*: a color, a tree, a part of a

[5]Quoted in *The Complete Limerick Book,* compiled by L. Reed (1925). Reprinted with permission of Hutchinson of London.

building, a body of water, a prolonged (dog's) bark. *The American College Dictionary* lists 76 meanings for *take,* 83 for *round,* 93 for *turn,* and 104 for *run.* According to Fries (1963), for the 500 most used words of English, the *Oxford Dictionary* records 14,070 separate and different meanings, an average of 28 for each word. There are also words that are spelled the same, but differ in sounds as well as meanings: *shed a tear/tear a coat; blowing wind/wind a clock.*

A handful of content words and function words, when they sound the same, can be differentiated by their spellings: The content words are three-letters long because of a doubled consonant or vowel, or of a silent 'e', whereas the function words have two letters: *be–bee; by–bye; in–inn; or–ore; so–sow*; and *to–two* (Albrow, 1972). Shortness of function words is a useful feature in guiding eye movements in text reading (see Chapter 7).

Some short, frequent, and irregularly spelled words (*the, of, by, come, laugh*) are learned, recognized, and memorized (for spelling) as whole patterns. For these words at least, whether each constituent letter regularly codes its own sound becomes unimportant.

Reforming English Orthography

Considering the complexities and difficulties of English orthography, it is not surprising that there have been numerous attempts to standardize or reform it, starting perhaps as early as the twelfth century and still continuing. Such influential people as George Bernard Shaw, Isaac and James Pitman, and Andrew Carnegie lent their names and fortunes to the cause of reforming spelling. Vachek (1973) distinguishes two strands of reform, both of which can be traced to the sixteenth century. One strand attempts to reform the alphabet itself to make it more phonetic, whereas the other attempts to regularize spelling while keeping the alphabet as it is. The following history is based partly on Vachek.

Augmented and Modified Alphabet

In the sixteenth century, John Hart proposed modifying the alphabet by adding several letters and changing some existing ones. In the 1960s, Sir James Pitman suggested a similar modification, which has come to be known as the **initial teaching alphabet (i.t.a.).** The i.t.a. contains 44 graphemes, 24 of which are identical to those in the traditional alphabet (eliminating 'q, x') and 20 of which are new graphemes. Some of the new ones are ligatured (connected by a loop to each other). It has no uppercase letters, and sentences begin with larger versions of the lowercase letters. The sounds are based on a "standard" dialect. See whether you can decipher the following i.t.a. words: *enuf, woz, laf, sed, hav, dog, cat, hot.*

The principle of i.t.a. is to have one grapheme for one phoneme, but without drastically changing the traditional grapheme shapes. Several of its letters are awkward for handwriting and deviate too much from the existing letters. Downing (1967) recommends modifications, such as using 'sh' for i.t.a. ʃh. We find another shortcoming: Not only are the two mirror-image letters 'b/d' left unmodified, but also two additional confusable letters 'z/ʒ' (*zebra/daisy*) are created.

The i.t.a. is not meant to replace or reform traditional orthography but is meant for mediating a child's introduction to traditional orthography. It has proven useful as a transitional alphabet, according to some educators (e.g., Downing, 1967; Gasper & Brown, 1973), but not according to others (e.g., Chall, 1967; Gillooly, 1973; Thackray, 1971) (see Chapter 15).

Unlike i.t.a., Shaw's 40-letter phonetic alphabet bears no resemblance to the traditional alphabet. English readers must learn the new script as they would, say, shorthand, which it resembles, before they can read Shaw's (1962) *Androcles and the Lion* written in the new script. To psychologists, Shaw's alphabet is as inefficient as a script can be, because it is replete with left–right and up–down mirror-image letters for pairs of similar sounds: C : Ↄ for /l : r/; ⟋:⟍ for /m : n/; V : Λ for /U : u/. See Chapter 16 for how mirror-image letters give trouble to some reading-disabled readers. The script has never caught the public's fancy.

Regularized or Simplified Spelling

Some reformers want to keep the alphabet but simplify or regularize spelling. Toward the end of the sixteenth century, the real driving force for standardizing English orthography came from the writings of schoolmasters and printers. In the twentieth century, there have been several reform attempts, two of which are described here.

Zachrisson (1931) surveyed the reforms proposed over the preceding 4 centuries and then presented his own proposal, which he called *Anglic*. The chance of a spelling reform proposal being accepted will increase if the appearance of the texts written in the new spelling does not deviate too much from what it was under the old spelling rules. Thus, he kept the old spelling for some common function words (e.g., *as, be, by, do, I, she, the*). He thus could claim that the texts in *Anglic* preserve between 60–70% of words essentially unchanged.

The Simplified Spelling Society was founded in the United States in 1906 and in Britain in 1908. It has secured the sympathies and cooperation of many distinguished linguists such as Henry Sweet and Walter Ripman and the financier Andrew Carnegie. It boasts the patronage of His Royal Highness Duke of Edinburgh (or Edinboro). The simplified spelling proposal keeps the well-established English digraphs and adds to them several new ones ('dh' for *this*; 'ae' for *make*): *whot kan be mor familyar dhan dhe form ov wurdz dhat we hav seen and riten mor tiemz dhan we kan posibly estimaet?* Wijk (1959) too uses 'dh' in *udher* and *faadher* but not in *the* and other common function words, which he spells traditionally.

Neither Zachrisson nor the Simplified Spelling Society pays due regard to the morphemic relations in noun and verb endings. For example, a plural ending is spelled phonetically as either *-z* (*wurdz, tiemz*) or *-s* (*shoks, kats*). Wijk respects morphemic unity in noun and verb endings but disregards the unity in past tense endings, which he spells phonetically *-t, -d, -ed*, as the case may be. This practice blurs the visual image of the morphological structure, thus depriving the written language of the possibility to perform one of its essential functions, namely, "to speak quickly and distinctly to the eyes," to borrow Vachek's (1973) phrase.

To conclude, every proposal for a wholesale reform has become no more than one chapter in a long but vain effort at spelling reform. On the other hand, in the eighteenth and nineteenth centuries, Noah Webster succeeded in having his spelling reform adopted in the United States perhaps because his proposal was modest yet sensible.

Summary and Conclusions

Some problems of English orthography can be traced to the fact that it does not adhere consistently to the basic principle of an alphabet—namely, one letter for one phoneme. The alphabet has 26 letters (3 of which are superfluous) to represent 44 phonemes of the language. One letter represents several sounds, and one sound is represented by several letters, in a complex and irregular manner.

Historical accidents seem to be responsible for much of the irregularity and complexity of English orthography. The Great Vowel Shift in the Middle Ages changed many vowels, thus rendering vowel spelling nonphonetic. Since the English sound system is prone to changes over time, regions, and word derivation, it is difficult to adopt a regular and uniform orthography to cover all English speech for any length of time.

English words can be divided into regular words (spelling gives clues to standard pronunciation: *dog, Don*) and irregular words (spelling misleads to wrong pronunciation: *come, comb*). Understandably, irregular words are harder than regular words both to spell and to pronounce. The less common sounds of certain letters ('c, g') are not fully mastered even at a college level. For spelling, a phonetic strategy is adequate for regular words, but a visual strategy and analogies must be learned for irregular words.

Because of its complexity, English orthography is difficult to learn, and it produces some reading casualties, as documented in Chapter 16. In J. Feldman's (1978) words, "In a vast conspiracy, history has mined the child's road to literacy with hundreds of exceptions and minor rules [p. 57]." Even as mature reader–writers, English speakers have to consult dictionaries for the pronunciation and spelling of uncommon or irregular words. English orthography represents the English language in many levels: at the phonemic level (*dot, lot*); at the morphophonemic level (*sapphire* versus *shepherd*); at the morphemic level (*dogs, cats, heal–health*); at the logographic level (*sight* versus *site*; *to* versus *two*). By not faithfully coding sounds, spelling sometimes indicates semantic relatedness (*heal–health*) or unrelatedness (*way–weigh*) between words. But these advantages are outweighed by the disadvantages.

However erratic it may be, English orthography is the key to the vast treasures of printed material accumulated over many centuries, in many regions of the world. Obviously, English orthography is not something to be tinkered with, but neither is it something to be exalted; it is simply something to live with or suffer through.

Interlude: Writing Systems and Reading Processes

Writing Systems Compared

The five chapters of Part I have introduced several writing systems. On the surface, it may seem that such varied writing systems must be read differently, but we believe these differences come down to a question of balance among a small set of fundamentally similar processes. The balance, however, has a bearing on the relative ease of learning to read in the various writing systems.

Visual Elements

All writing is visual. In text printed in any script certain visual patterns occur repeatedly. In English, there are 52 uppercase and lowercase letters, plus 10 numerals and several punctuation marks. In all, an English reader has to be able to recognize about 80 different patterns. Of course, each of these 80 patterns comes in an amazing variety of physical shapes.

In Japanese, many more different fundamental visual patterns must be recognized: the Arabic numerals, the Chinese characters, and the two sets of Kana. A literate Japanese must recognize upward of 200 basic visual forms for Kana alone. This number seems too large for immediate visual recognition, and we should perhaps look for an even lower level of visual analysis.

There are thousands of different Chinese characters, but they are all composed of about a dozen basic strokes that occur in overlapped combinations. The elements recognized in Chinese are probably frequent patterns of strokes rather than the individual strokes themselves. The characters are many, and the strokes are too few, to be the fundamental visual elements in reading Chinese.

Sound Coding

All writing systems code for the sounds of their languages, in one way or another. Japanese Kana code sounds directly and reliably, syllable by syllable. The Korean Hangul codes sounds in three levels: The shape of its symbol codes an articulatory feature; its symbol codes a phoneme; and its symbol block, a syllable.

Chinese characters code for sound in two ways: indirectly, by knowledge of the meaning of the character, and directly but unreliably, through the phonetic of the character. Not all characters have phonetics, and among those that do, the 800 or so different phonetics give clues rather than unique codes for the sounds. Chinese characters code syllables just as precisely as do Japanese Kana or Korean Hangul, but there are thousands of characters to code only about 400 different syllables. The characters are said to code meaning primarily and sound secondarily.

The sound-coding capabilities of alphabetic writing systems are varied. Some orthographies, such as Finnish and Serbo-Croation, code phonemes regularly. Others, such as English and French, code them irregularly so that in about half of the words the letters give only clues to the sounds of the words. English orthography codes letters visually but is closer to phonetic coding of syllables or morphemes than of phonemes.

Meaning Units

English writing uses spaces and punctuation marks to set off words but not morphemes. Chinese writing visually separates morphemes but not words. Japanese writing provides some visual breaks between the Kanji content morphemes and the Kana function morphemes. All-Kana text does not code directly for meaning, as it does not visually separate morphemes or words. Korean Hangul syllable-blocks, especially CVC and CVCC, tend to code morphemes. In addition, words are set off by extra space.

Units Coded in Ten Scripts

The following table shows some of the elements coded in 10 different orthographies mentioned in Part I.

In the bottom row of the table "Function/content" indicates whether there is a visually marked distinction between function and content words or morphemes. In the languages that use Kanji for most content words, the native

Units Coded in Ten Scripts[a]

Unit	Logographies		Syllabaries				Alphabets			
	Chinese	Egptian hieroglyphics	Japanese Hiragana or Katakana	Japanese orthography including Kanji	Korean Hangul	Korean Hangul plus Kanji	Devanagari (Hindi)	English	German	Serbo-Croatian
Phoneme	0	+	0	0	++	+	+	+	++	++
Syllable	++	+	++	++	++	++	0	0	0	0
Morpheme		++	0	+	+	+	0	+	+	0
Word	0	+	0	+	++	++	++	++	++	++
Meaning	+	+	0	+	0	+	0	0	0	0
Function/content	0	0	0	+	0	+	0	0	Nouns	0

[a]++ = strongly coded; + = weakly coded; 0 = not coded.

phonetic script often indicates a function word or morpheme. These are mixed texts of Kanji and Kana in Japan and of Kanji and Hangul in South Korea. Among the alphabetic scripts, German denotes nouns by a capital letter. This useful feature might beneficially be copied by other alphabetic scripts.

The row marked "Meaning" asks, Can a reader find a clue to the meaning of a new symbol? In Chinese characters the radical gives a semantic clue, and hence Chinese and the mixed scripts of Japan and Korea are weakly coded for meaning. In Egyptian hieroglyphics the determinatives give semantic clues. Meaning is not directly coded in alphabetic writing, but "morpheme" is weakly marked in English and German, as some familiar bound morphemes (*-ing, un-*) can be extracted from a word by using their spelling patterns.

The table makes the point that there is a great variety in what different writing systems code visually, phonetically, and semantically.

Implications for Reading Processes

All reading processes must start with visual feature extraction of some kind. Most likely, this process is identical to the visual feature extraction a human uses for perception in general. No matter how many signs a reader has to distinguish—80 in English text or a few thousands in Chinese text—he starts with extracting 10–20 features, such as "diagonal outer parts," "parallel verticals," and so on. At the next level, these features are combined to form some kind of entity, be it a radical, a letter, a pictograph, or a syllable sign. Outside shapes are more important than are inner details, as a human tends to perceive an object outside-in.

Are words perceived as a whole or through analysis into individual letters? Viewed from the perspective of many writing systems, the question seems ill-conceived. A more appropriate question is, When are writing units perceived as a whole, and when are they analyzed into subelements to be organized by rules? In an alphabetic script, if a reader is looking for misprints, she may analyze words into their letters, but in reading for meaning, perhaps not. Chinese characters are normally perceived wholistically. But some of them are analyzed at least into a radical and a phonetic during learning. Errors often involve confusions between characters that share these subparts. Characters need not be analyzed into individual strokes in reading, but they need to be so analyzed in writing. The features of Japanese Kana, like those of English letters, are indivisible attributes of the whole symbol. Hence, Japanese syllables are perceived wholistically, but morphemes or words must be created by extracting an appropriate cluster from a sequence of Kana—this process is analytic.

In a text, a reader in any script has the same goal: to comprehend its content and retain its gist. To do so, he organizes incoming material into larger units, distinguishes important from unimportant units, draws inferences, and much more.

Reading Processes and Learning to Read

Reading is really a miracle: Your eyes pick up groups of words in split-second time and your mind keeps these words in delicate balance until it gets around to a point where they make sense.

—Flesch (1949, p. 182)

In the next seven chapters we elaborate on this single sentence. We shall examine various kinds of visual, linguistic, cognitive, and neural processing during reading. We describe reading processes in mature readers and trace the development of children in becoming mature readers. Our discussion is based heavily on experiments, because reading processes are surprisingly hard to observe directly or by introspection. Most of these experiments are on English reading, for two reasons: First, more work has been done on reading in English than in any other language; second, we covered in Part I much of the research on several other writing systems. However, where possible we will mention other systems, in the belief that comparison is a valuable route to insight.

The first chapter of Part II looks at the initial stage of reading, eye movements, which tell us how readers deploy their visual and cognitive resources over a text. The second chapter considers how readers of varying skills use different levels of reading unit and context.

The next three chapters consider how readers recognize letters and words and how they code words into phonetic and visual representations. The middle chapter introduces the Bilateral Cooperative model of reading, in which the LEFT and the RIGHT tracks perform different but complementary processes. The last two chapters of Part II consider how people read and write sentences, paragraphs, stories, technical papers, and textbooks.

The three chapters of Part III discuss how children learn to perform the miraculous task of reading, and how some children have great difficulty learning to read at all. Learning to read is easy or difficult, depending on which unit a script codes, how regularly it does its coding, and how reading is taught.

II

Reading Processes

7

Eye Movements in Reading

The gaze of man is free to move around
From place to place where'ere the eye does will.
It flicks about to give the mind its fill
and make the image whole within the head.
—John W. Senders

Types of Eye Movement

Recording Eye Movements

You read, not by sweeping your eyes along a line of print, but by moving your viewpoint in a series of little jumps called saccades. Emile Javal (1906), a French oculist, made this important and surprising discovery simply by watching a school child who was reading. You can easily see the effect—just watch a reader's eyes.

At the turn of the century, the psychologist Dodge invented a photographic technique for recording eye movements (Dodge & Cline, 1901). In its modern version, a harmless beam of infrared light is directed into the reader's eye, and the reflection of this light from the cornea is recorded on a photographic film. The film may be a moving picture that also records the scene, so that the direction of looking can be monitored frame by frame. Most modern techniques use corneal reflection in one form or another, often using several

[1]Quoted in Monty and Senders (1976, p. viii); reprinted with the author's permission.

beams of light reflected from different parts of the eye for added precision. These methods usually require either that the subject wear a specialized helmet or that the head be fixed in place on a chin rest. In either case, the measurement could interfere with normal eye-movement patterns.

Another technique uses recordings from electrodes placed above, below, and at the sides of the eye. These electrodes record a change of voltage as the eye moves from side to side and up and down. This method does not determine precisely where the eye is pointed; rather, it measures eye position in its orbit. It is little affected by the reader's head movements, and hence does not require any cumbersome apparatus that might obscure part of the visual field.

In modern research using either method, a computer can provide continuous on-line recording of eye movements, enabling researchers to score and identify locations and durations of fixations accurately and easily. With a computer, a text display can be modified as a function of where the reader is looking. Doing so has yielded valuable data on the functions of eye movements.

Fixations

In order to see, a reader focuses the image of an object upon the **retina,** a screen of photosensitive neural receptors at the back of the eyeball. The retina as a whole covers a visual angle of 240 degrees (Llewellyn-Thomas, 1968). Acuity is sharpest in the center of the visual field, the **fovea,** where the receptors are densely packed. The fovea is a tiny area, subtending an angle of only about 1–2 degrees; the region just outside it, subtending about 10 degrees, is the **parafovea**; the rest is the periphery. Actually, parafovea and periphery blend smoothly into each other, with no clear distinction between the two. The farther away from the fovea, the less densely packed are the receptors and the less clear is vision.

As one reads, a target word is brought into the fovea by a saccadic jump. The eyes then fixate on the word for about a quarter of a second, during which time the image of the object is more or less stationary upon the retina. It is mainly during the fixation that a reader acquires information on the fixated word. At the end of the fixation, the eye saccades to the next target word. On the average, 90% of reading time is spent in fixations. Although the eyes generally move forward in the left-to-right direction (in English), they occasionally jump back, or regress, to fixate on words insufficiently perceived earlier.

The best fixation point from which to perceive a whole word should be near its center, and this is where a fixation tends to occur (Dunn-Rankin, 1978; Erdmann & Dodge, 1898; Rayner, 1979a). If the eye first fixates near the middle of a long word (9–14 letters), the fixation is long and is followed by a saccade to the next word; if the eye first fixates near one end of a word, it shortens the fixation and then makes another fixation near the other end of the word (O'Regan, 1981).

Certain kinds of reading, such as proofreading or copy typing, require frequent fixations and regressions. Reading aloud requires longer and more frequent fixations than does silent reading (Wanat, 1976). The more difficult the reading matter, the more fixations there are and the longer each fixation is (Tinker, 1958). The number and duration of fixations, both forward and regressive, increase dramatically for sections of a long passage that are specifically assigned for learning (Rothkopf & Billington, 1979). All in all, the easier the text and task, the fewer and shorter are the fixations, and the longer are the saccadic jumps.

Eye movements may be intrinsically inefficient: People seem to read faster, without impairing comprehension, when eye movements are bypassed. In the technique called **rapid serial visual presentation** (RSVP), words of a sentence are presented in rapid sequence one at a time at the point of fixation (Forster, 1970). The words are presented two to three times faster than the speed at which people normally read (6 words per sec). Subjects could read and recall individual sentences better when presented at a rate as high as 12 words a second than when they read the text at the same speed off a normal display (Potter, Kroll, & Harris, 1980). "The active eye movement patterns of a skilled reader are not necessarily the optimal way to sample information from text [Juola, Ward, & McNamara, 1982; p. 226]." Nevertheless, when confronted with words on a page, the reader has little choice but to move the eyes; moving the book would be much more cumbersome.

Saccades

Saccadic jumps carry the eye from one fixation to another. They start quickly and stop quickly: The long return movement to the beginning of the next line takes about 40 msec, and the movement between fixations within a line about 30 msec. The eye moves ballistically to its target position so that once a saccade is initiated, its speed and goal cannot be altered. Visual sensitivity is reduced during the saccade, and the blur due to eye motion does not affect the perception of the world. Saccades may serve to "reset" the visual system's analysis processes.

When a saccade is initiated, the eye is being sent to a specific location in the text. Landing at the wrong position can trigger corrective eye movements. Such corrective eye movements were observed when a text on a computer screen was shifted two letter positions to the right during certain saccades (McConkie, 1978). A corrective regression was more likely after a left shift than after no shift or a right shift (O'Regan, 1981). The subjects did not notice that the text had been shifted in either study.

The mean length of a saccade is about eight character spaces in reading ordinary text (Rayner & McConkie, 1976). The length of a saccade is influenced by the length of the word immediately to the right of the fixated word: If the word is longer, the eye tends to jump further than if it is shorter (O'Regan, 1979).

McConkie and Rayner (1976) looked for a relation between the length of a saccade and the duration of the fixation that follows or precedes it. Finding no relation, they concluded not only that saccades and fixations represent independent aspects of eye-movement control but also that successive fixations and saccades are controlled by some momentary state that does not endure beyond the time of one fixation.

Eye–Voice Span

In reading aloud, when the voice is speaking one word, the eyes are fixating a later word. The distance between the fixation point and the speaking point, called the **eye–voice span** (EVS), can be measured in letter spaces, words, or time. Quantz (1897) pioneered an elegantly simple technique of measuring EVS: He suddenly covered the page that a reader was reading aloud and asked the reader to continue to say the words for as long as possible. A variation on the technique is a "light-out"—the reading light is suddenly turned off.

Eye–voice span, like eye movements, concerns visual processing of text and often is studied together with eye movements. The patterns of EVS and eye movements match: Where linguistic patterns are predictable, EVS is long, and fixations and regressions are few and brief. Buswell (1920) obtained simultaneous records of eye movements by photography and of the voice by a dictaphone, and synchronized the two records. EVS goes down almost to zero when the eyes encounter an unfamiliar or ambiguous word and continue to fixate it until the meaning is discovered or resolved. Where the material reads along smoothly, the span lengthens to as many as eight words. EVS varies also according to reading purposes: It is shorter in reading for details and longer in reading for general ideas (Levin & Cohn, 1968).

Like eye movements, EVS varies according to the skill and age of readers. For example, at Grade 2, EVS was 11.0 letter spaces for good readers and 5.4 for poor readers; by Grade 12 it was 15.9 and 12.4, respectively (Buswell, 1920). For reading aloud with good intonation and comprehension, long spans are essential.

Wanat and Levin (1968) examined subjects' EVS in reading passive sentences:

1. *The ball was hit by the bat.* (instrument included)
2. *The ball was hit by the park.* (instrument deleted)

When the light was turned off immediately prior to the critical phrase (*by the bat/park*), the mean EVS was 5.8 letters for sentence 1, compared with 5.2 letters for 2. The deleted instrument in 2 caused a regressive fixation in Wanat's

(1976) eye-movement study on the same passive sentences (see "Regressions on Unclear or Important Information"). There is a possible scoring artifact: Suppose that the last word was not seen in either case but that the subject guessed the more predictable *bat*. If sentence 1 had been presented, this guess would have been scored as one extra word on the EVS, but not if 2 had been presented.

Unlike eye movements, EVS is partly a measure of information being held in the reader's short-term memory at the light-out instant (Mackworth, cited in Wanat, 1976; Resnick, 1970). Wildman and Kling (1978–1979) also consider EVS to be a memory report rather than a perceptual one: Failure to report words beyond phrase or clause boundaries may reflect simply a loss of unintegrated information, if integration occurs at these boundaries. Whether EVS reflects a memorial or perceptual process, it makes an excellent tool for demonstrating that mature readers read not word by word but phrase by phrase or clause by clause. We present more EVS studies in the next chapter, which discusses reading units and sequential constraints.

Integrating Information Between Parafovea and Fovea

Perceptual Span and Parafoveal Vision

The parafovea is the region just outside the fovea. Though it has less sharp vision than does the fovea, it plays a vital role in visual perception. In visual search and picture perception, information obtained in parafoveal vision is critical in determining the locations of following fixations (Gould, 1967). How is parafoveal vision used in reading?

By **windowing** text, Ikeda and Saida (1978) manipulated the number of characters (horizontally printed Kanji and Kana) visible to their Japanese readers. They found a critical visual-field size: Increasing the size of a window through which the text could be seen resulted in faster reading rate, but only up to a certain critical window size. The value of the critical size varied among subjects, ranging from 10 to 17 characters, but even in a large visual field, it was always much larger than the mean size of saccades, which was 2–5 characters. Fixations were long with a small field and shortened as the field was enlarged, until the field was widened beyond the critical field size. Apparently, subjects were getting some information from words on which they would not fixate until two or more saccades later.

For Dutch text, the critical window size has a value of 25–31 character positions, or 12–15 positions to the right and left of the fixation point, equaling 4–5 degrees of visual angle (Buurman, Roersema, & Gerrissen, 1981). Vertically, the window covers three lines. The researchers tried to simulate normal reading conditions by having their subjects read typescript passages. Still, the

Dutch value is close to the English value (21–31 positions) obtained by McConkie and Rayner (1975), who used computer characters and restricted their subjects' head movements. Like Japanese readers, Dutch and English readers seem to be getting information from material they will not fixate until later.

Perceptual span is not symmetrical about the fixation point: In Hebrew reading (right-to-left), the span is asymmetric to the left; in English reading, it is asymmetric to the right (Pollatsek, Bolozky, Well, & Rayner, 1981).

Information from the Parafovea

To study what information is picked up in the parafovea and how it is used, researchers manipulate text displayed on a computer while subjects read (McConkie & Zola, 1979; Rayner & McConkie, 1976; Rayner, 1979b). The experiments work as follows. When the computer judges the subject's eye to be in a saccade, it removes a word in parafoveal vision and replaces it with another word. The subject is not aware of the display change. The subject's task is, in effect, to name the new word by continuing to read. Is the fixation following a display change longer than one following no change? Yes, it is, demonstrating that information picked up in the parafovea influences the forthcoming fixation. Disruption in fixation depends on several factors, such as the distance of the display change from the fixated point, and the similarity between the word originally seen and the word seen after the change.

Information picked up in the parafovea is about gross visual features, such as length and shape of a word and blank spaces between words. Information on word length is picked up farthest into the periphery, at least 13 or 14 character positions from the fixation point. This information is used primarily for eye guidance: The eye is more likely to fixate on longer than on shorter words. The shapes of words and letters are picked up at a shorter range, 10–12 character positions to the right of the fixation point. Changes in word shape affect fixation durations, and changes in word length affect saccadic length. In addition to these gross features, some letters—the first one or two and the last—are identified in the parafovea.

Information is integrated between parafovea and fovea: Gross physical information picked up in the parafovea is used in acquiring detailed information in the next fixation. Eye movement per se is not important for integration. The effect occurs even when saccades are simulated by sequentially moving words to the fixation point. Nor is there evidence that information integration is based on a common visual pattern: If a word appeared as "cHeSt" before the saccade and as "ChEsT" after the saccade, the visual shape is "drastically" changed between what is picked up in the parafovea and at the fovea. And yet, integration occurs.

But is the shape so "drastically" changed in case-alternating words? Word length, the most important information about word shape, is still the same.

Also some uppercase and lowercase counterparts share features—round as in C–c, O–o, U–u, S–s, or angular as in—X–x, V–v, K–k, Z–z. Furthermore, people can use a whole-word, quasi-visual route based on abstract letter information to recognize a mixed-case word (see Chapter 9). Since the subjects were reading a text, they were able to anticipate the kind of word (not necessarily the exact word) coming up even in the alternating-case condition. In short, case alternation may not constitute a drastic change, except to the outer contour of a word.

The parafovea covers at least one line above and one below the line of print being read so that information on the unattended lines may be partially processed. When subjects were required to read a passage that contained irrelevant words between text lines, their answers to the questions following each passage were influenced by the "unattended" material, though they could not recall its specific words (Willows & MacKinnon, 1973). In reading a newspaper, Martin Taylor made an amusing mislocation of a word from one line to the preceding line. The original text (about Hitler's supposed diaries) read:

> A personal secretary has
> maintained since his suicide in
> a Berlin bunker that he never
> made notes by hand.

The misreading moved "that" to precede "since," thus assuring the reader that after Hitler killed himself he ceased making handwritten notes. Most of us have probably had the experience of noticing a misprint, without at first being able to find what word was misprinted. On searching, the misprint turns out to be on a different line from where we are reading. There seems to be no research on how material on following lines is processed to aid in reading those lines when the time comes.

Braille for the blind is read by touch. By varying the number and configuration of six raised dots in each cell, Braille can express 63 symbols (26 capitals, 26 small letters, 1 space, and 10 other symbols, including punctuation marks). In the primary grades, Braille readers and sighted readers read at about the same speed, but in the upper grades Braille readers lag far behind the sighted. Even skilled Braille readers can read only 100 words per min (WPM), compared with the sighted readers' 300 WPM (Aschcroft, 1967; Hampshire, 1981). In the lower grades, both the blind and the sighted read words letter by letter without using the parafovea; in the upper grades, only the sighted can read words wholistically and use the parafovea.

Word Identification

During one fixation lasting a quarter of a second, the number of words identified is on average 1.2, according to Just and Carpenter (1980), and 1.12, according to Hogaboam and McConkie (1981). Words seem to be identified only as far as 4–6 character positions to the right of the fixation point. That is, readers can interpret words that begin 1–6 letter positions to the right of fixation (Rayner, 1975). At this time, of course, they are fixating a previous word. According to Hogaboam and McConkie, with normal print size, the fixated letter plus 2–5 additional letters will fall on the fovea. Therefore, it is not only the word fixated that is identified; often, the word to the right of the fixated word lies partially, and sometimes wholly, on the fovea itself, thus permitting identification.

A word is identified easily if what was previously seen in the parafovea is similar to what is now fixated. In Rayner's (1979b) study, *palace* was named faster if a visually similar word (*police*) or nonword (*pcluce*) was previously seen in the parafovea; it was named slower if a dissimilar shape was previously seen (*qcluce, pflyce*). Interestingly, there was no great difference between nonword distractors such as *pcluce* and real words such as *police.* Detailed information apparently is not picked up in the parafovea, at least from words to the right of fixation. As further support of this conclusion, the word *table* seen in the parafovea did not facilitate naming it's semantic associate *chair.*

By contrast to the above finding, a word such as TREE or HAND, presented in the periphery, biased interpretation of ambiguous word PALM presented on the fovea, even though neither of the biasing words could be reported (Bradshaw, 1974). As another counterexample, remember that when "ChEsT" was changed to "cHeSt," the change did not affect fixation patterns. The jury is still out on what information is used from words seen in the parafovea.

Individual Differences in Eye Movements

Individuals differ in eye-movement patterns, depending on their ages and skills but not on their visual acuities.

By School Grade

Several decades ago, Buswell (1922) studied the eye-movement patterns of readers from different school grades, ranging from Grade 1 to college. As is seen in Figure 7-1, the number and duration of fixations and regressions steadily decline from Grade 1 to college. The steepest decline occurs between Grades 1 and 2, and only a gentle decline occurs after Grade 5, at which time eye-movement patterns seem to have all but stabilized. According to Ballentine's (1951) reexamination of his own and Buswell's data, eye movements continue to develop as late as Grade 10.

In a modern study, Fisher and Lefton (1976) found a developmental trend in letter recognition: The recognition speed became progressively faster from Grade 2 to adult. The difference in speed between the age groups was greater

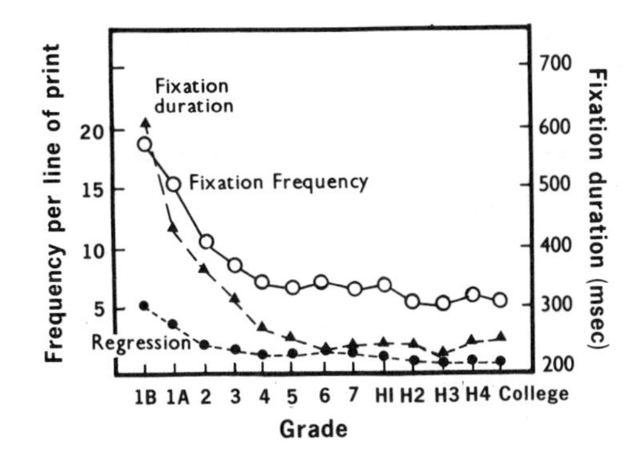

Figure 7-1. *Eye movements become efficient at higher school grades (based on Buswell, 1922).*

when the letters were presented parafoveally than when they were presented foveally. When spaces between words were filled with 'X's and &'s, thus eliminating one of the most effective peripheral cues, oral reading of Grade 2 children was affected only slightly, whereas that of Grade 5 children was affected greatly (Fisher & Montanary, 1977; Hochberg, 1970).

Eye movements differ qualitatively between prereaders and readers. Nodine and Simmons (1974) compared the eye movements of kindergartners and Grade 3 children while they were matching letter-like symbols (something that looked like 'C' or 'G'). The prereaders required twice as many fixations and cross-comparisons per pair as did the readers. The readers fixated proportionately more on features that specifically differentiate the two symbols, such as a tiny crossbar that was present in the 'G'-like symbol but absent in the 'C'-like symbol. According to the researchers, the older, reading child calls upon memory for identifying and matching symbols, whereas the younger, prereading child relies on a purely perceptual strategy. Alternately, readers can use analysis to differentiate the symbols, whereas prereaders concentrate on their global similarity.

An older, skilled reader makes longer saccades (or fewer fixations), fewer regressions, shorter fixations, and better use of the parafovea than does a younger, unskilled reader. For these and other reasons, reading speed increases from an average 80 WPM in Grade 1 to 300 WPM and up in college students.

Skilled Adult Readers

Even skilled readers from the same grade level differ in eye-movement patterns. For example, 10 college students—skilled readers with good comprehension—differed considerably. Their fixation duration ranged from 190–255 msec; saccade length, 6.7–9.5 character spaces; regression, 1–20% of total fixations; and reading rate, 230–382 WPM. Saccade length and fixation were highly correlated across readers: The faster readers had shorter fixation durations and longer saccades (Rayner, 1978).

Fast (451–855 WPM) and slow (200–300 WPM) college readers differed in their ability to pick up information from each fixation (Jackson & McClelland, 1975). The percentage of letters, words, and indeed, whole sentences correctly reported from a single fixation increased dramatically with increasing normal reading speed. The fast readers seemed to be able to encode more of the contents of each fixation. The two groups did not differ in identifying letters farther into the periphery, or in their susceptibility to interference from neighboring letters.

Skilled readers use a flexible strategy to suit their reading goals. I. Anderson (1937) studied the eye movements of 50 good college readers (highest decile on a reading test) and 50 poor readers (lowest quartile) reading under three different instructions. Under "gist instruction" (read to get only the general idea of the content), good readers read faster, with fewer regressions and shorter fixations, than they did for neutral instruction. Poor readers responded in the opposite way!

Poor or Dyslexic Readers

In many studies, poor readers show shorter saccades, longer fixations, and more regressions than do good readers. In Mackworth's (1977) study on oral reading, poor readers from Grades 2, 4, and 6 made four times as many fixations as did good readers, and their average fixation time was twice as long as that of good readers. Fixation times correlated highly with the time taken to select a missing word among six alternative possibilities for completing a sentence.

Let us consider dyslexic readers, people with severe and specific reading difficulties. In some studies, dyslexic children and adults did not show a consistent left-to-right scanning pattern or showed a reverse scanning pattern, and they made many short pauses (Lesevre, 1968; Pirozzolo & Rayner, 1979; Zangwill & Blakemore, 1972). Vellutino's team, on the other hand, found the left-to-right scanning of dyslexic children to be no different from that of normal readers. Both groups made more omission errors at the right end of words, compared with normal readers of Hebrew, who made more errors at the left end of words (Vellutino, Pruzek, Steger, & Meshoulam, 1973).

Pirozzolo (1979) distinguishes two subtypes of dyslexia: "auditory–linguistic" and "visual–spatial." The first group does not show abnormal eye movements in reading easy text, whereas the second group shows atypical patterns, with many instances of faulty, right-to-left scanning and return sweep inaccuracies.

A poor eye-movement pattern is considered to be a symptom rather than a cause of dyslexia (Rayner, 1978; Tinker, 1958). Thus, training a poor reader to move the eyes more efficiently does not improve reading efficiency, according to Tinker's review of the literature. More likely, poor eye movement may be a symptom in some cases and a cause in others. Some individual dyslexics have abnormal eye movements and experience difficulty in reading because of them; other dyslexics have normal eye movements, yet experience difficulty in reading; and still others have abnormal eye movements because of their reading difficulty (see Chapter 16).

Speed Readers and Skimmers

A **speed reader** can read over 1000 WPM, supposedly with good comprehension. President John F. Kennedy was reputed to have read detective novels at 18,000 WPM, or about one page per sec. Adequate comprehension tests are rarely given to such readers, and reading materials are easy. Carver (1971) points out that common sense and guessing are all that is needed in order to do respectably on typical true–false comprehension tests given after speed-reading courses.

The speed readers studied by Llewellyn-Thomas (1962) and McLaughlin (1969) differed from non-speed readers in frequency and distribution, but not in duration, of fixation. One speed reader typically read a page of 260 words in 14 fixations (21 words per fixation), distributed in a rough zigzag down the page. Other speed readers moved their eyes down the middle of the left-hand page and up the middle of the right-hand page, skipping a number of lines per saccade. S. E. Taylor (1962) observed little evidence of a vertical line of progression among graduates of a speed-reading course. Furthermore, those who showed the greatest tendency to move down the center of the page had the poorest scores on a true–false test. He concluded that eye-movement patterns of speed readers closely resemble those of non-speed readers skimming text. Possibly, however, the graduates of the course had not learned true speed reading.

Masson's (1982) skimmers found it difficult perceptually to select important information, because there are few physical cues for such information in a narrative passage. The skimmers seemed adventitiously to sample parts of a story and read those sampled parts in a manner similar to the normal reading process. They verified faster and recalled gist information better than they did details. Some skimmers slow down for difficult material, but others do not, and the two groups differ in other ways as well (Eisenberg & Becker, 1982; see Chapter 11).

In our own introspection on skimming, we seem to abort the effort to comprehend any sampled part as soon as we deem it to be unimportant. We also find many visual cues for skimming, at least in expository text: Topics are likely to be introduced at the beginning and conclusions at the end of a paragraph or a passage; figures, tables, and pictures stand out; important terms may be in boldface or italics, whereas incidental items, including references, are enclosed in parentheses. Some of the most prominent and useful cues are headings.

In one study, trained speed readers fixated content words quite regularly, in contrast to untrained readers skimming text at the same high speed.

Skimmers fixated as many words as did the speed readers, but the fixated words were less regularly distributed (Just, Carpenter, & Woolley, 1982). Normal readers, when forced to read fast in RSVP, report content words better than they do function words (Forster & Ryder, 1971; Potter *et al.*, 1980). And they process the semantic content better than the syntactic structure of a sentence (French, 1981).

According to our Bilateral Cooperative model of reading, speed readers should be able to understand gists of sentences by sampling the critical content words without using much syntax. Syntactic operations are analytic and slow compared with the construction of meaning from content words. As the content words become abstract or ambiguous, or as syntax becomes important to disambiguate meanings, so speed reading should be more difficult (see Chapters 11 and 12).

Linguistic Factors Influence Eye Movements

Fixations on Long and/or Informative Items

A reader's fixation patterns vary greatly over a text, depending on the physical and linguistic characteristics of the words. The longer a word, the more likely it is to be fixated, and the longer is the fixation. For example, the probabilities of fixating 2-, 6-, and 10-letter words were .201, .724, and .922, respectively (Rayner & McConkie, 1976). These probabilities are close to what would be expected if the eyes were targeted randomly, but the following pieces of evidence suggests that the targets are by no means randomly selected.

Function words and content words differ in their influences over saccades. O'Regan (1979) found that the eye tends to make longer jumps when approaching *the* than when approaching less frequent three-letter verbs (*ate, ran, met*). The closer the eye is to the word *the* on the prior fixation, the higher is the probability that it will be skipped. He calls this phenomenon, appropriately, "the-skipping" effect. On less frequent three-letter function words (*had, was, are*), the length of the saccadic jump is intermediate between the saccade for *the* and for a three-letter verb. Such short function words may well be identified and processed during the prior fixation.

Even content words are differentially fixated depending on how predictable they are in a passage. Ehrlich and Rayner (1981) found that the same target word (e.g., *shark*) was less likely to be fixated when it was in a highly constrained position (predictable from context) than when it was in a poorly constrained position. When they were fixated, the predictable target words were fixated for shorter durations than were unpredictable ones. Jacobson and Dodwell (1979) found a greater tendency to regressive saccades with low-redundancy, poorly constrained material.

In a study by Shebilske and Reid (1979), sentences that directly form "macro-propositions" (gists of passages) were read faster and with fewer fixations than were sentences that had to be integrated with others to construct a macro-proposition. When the same sentences were read out of context, the reading rates did not differ between the two types.

Eye movements are affected by whether information is old (already mentioned) or new. In the following sentence, [ ] marks old information, and ( ), new: *(There once was a man) [who] (loved money very much.) [He loved money] (so much) (that) [he] (would not spend a penny) (if) [he] (could help) [it].* Scinto's (1978) five college student subjects read a fable that starts with this sentence. (They read unmarked text.) The fixations of all five subjects were shorter on old than on new information. The results held when length was controlled.

Shebilske and Fisher (1981) asked two adult subjects to read twice a long excerpt from a Grade 10 biology text. In the first reading, the subjects modulated their reading rate according to the familiarity of information, spending more time on new than on familiar information. In the second reading, they modulated the rate according to the importance level of idea units (roughly, clauses), reading important units more slowly than unimportant ones. They made longer fixations and more regressions on important idea units than on unimportant ones in both readings.

The importance or unimportance of a unit is perceived in relation to the theme of a passage; hence, it should be reduced or eliminated when the unit is read out of context of the passage. In a later study, six college students read 9 important units and 9 matched unimportant units, one at a time, along with 42 filler units. The reading rates for the two types of units no longer differed, confirming the hypothesis that the perceived importance of units influences reading rate (Shebilske & Fisher, 1982). According to the researchers, variations in eye-movement patterns are sometimes determined by the text and at other times by the subjects' views of what information is important. Good readers are better at adopting such flexible strategies than are poor readers.

Semantic contents, predictability, and importance of words and clauses, over and above their physical lengths, seem to affect eye movements.

The Rocky Road from Eye Fixations to Comprehension

Just and Carpenter (1980) developed a model of text comprehension based solely on readers' eye-movement patterns. In doing so, they made two assumptions: A word is a unit of processing, and processing occurs immediately and completely at the time the word is encountered. They computed "gaze" durations, which are summed durations of consecutive fixations on the same word by an individual subject. The gaze duration is assumed to reflect processing time.

Gaze durations were long on long words, infrequent words, novel words, and words with "important" case roles, such as Agent and Instrument. Gaze durations were long also at certain locations—the beginning of a line, the last word in a sentence, and the last word in a paragraph. The last word is presumably where a sentence or a paragraph is wrapped-up and integrated. Within a paragraph, gaze durations were longer on thematically important definition clauses than on unimportant detail clauses. In another study, Just *et al.* (1982) required subjects to press a button to see the next word of a passage on a display. The pattern of times spent on the various types of words was similar to the pattern of gaze durations obtained in text reading, even though the absolute times were about twice as long.

Just and Carpenter (1980) assigned gaze durations only to words that receive direct fixations. Hogaboam and McConkie (1981) point out that not all content words are fixated and not all function words are skipped. In their own data, about 25% of content words and 70% of function words were skipped. If so, it is unlikely that only the fixated word is processed; rather, the skipped word is also likely to be processed, on the preceding fixation. More than one word may be processed during a fixation. They conclude that eye movement records do not directly provide a measure of processing time. (Hence, the title of their critique "The rocky road. . . ," which we borrowed for the heading of this section.)

Ehrlich and Rayner (1983) question Just and Carpenter's assumption that a word is processed completely at the time it is encountered. When pronouns such as *she* and *he* are encountered, all that can be retrieved from a mental lexicon or dictionary are their number and gender. To complete the processing of a pronoun, a reader must find its referent, a word matching the pronoun in number and gender (e.g., *the girl* for *she*) in other (sometimes distant) part of the text. Ehrlich and Rayner found evidence that this complex integrating process is completed during a later fixation.

Just and Carpenter's (1980) variables (physical and functional characteristics of words and clauses) influence processing time, but perhaps only to some extent. On the one hand, their data do not completely match the data obtained from studies using other techniques (see Chapters 12 and 13), and on the other, their variables are not the only ones that influence processing time, as can be seen from the pattern of regressions, which they ignored in their model.

Regressions on Unclear or Important Information

Ambiguous, unexpected, complex, or important information, be it semantic or syntactic, can cause regressions. Read the following passage constructed by Buswell (1920):

> The boys' arrows were nearly gone so they sat down on the grass and stopped hunting. Over at the edge of the woods they saw Henry making a bow to a little girl who was coming down the road. She had tears in her dress and also tears in her eyes. She gave Henry a note which he brought over to the group of young hunters. Read to the boys it caused great excitement. After a minute but rapid

> examination of their weapons, they ran down the valley. Does were standing at the edge of the lake making an excellent target [p. 87].

Did you trip over some words? The eye–voice span (EVS) measures the number of words read aloud after the light is turned off or the text is removed. Buswell's subjects with a large EVS had less difficulty in reading the words of the preceding passage than did his subjects with a small EVS. The latter made frequent regressive eye movements and often assigned the wrong pronunciation to the words with two sounds because they were not looking far enough ahead to grasp the meaning of these words in context before it was time to say them.

In a more recent study, reading times were shorter for sentence 1 than for 2, which is syntactically ambiguous (Frazier & Rayner, 1982) (the ambiguous region is in bold italics; the disambiguating region covers two words after it):

1. *Since Jay always jogs* **a mile and a half** *this seems like a short distance to him.*
2. *Since Jay always jogs* **a mile and a half** *seems like a very short distance to him.*

Readers fixated long on the disambiguating regions, and made a regression to the ambiguous region or to the beginning of sentence 2.

The following passive sentences, which you have seen before, appear identical on the surface but differ in the underlying semantic relations, especially in the final phrase:

1. *The ball was hit by the bat* (instrument included)
2. *The ball was hit by the park* (instrument deleted; locative)

In Wanat's (1976) study, the readers spent more time on regressive fixations and made more regressions in sentence 2 than in 1. Remember, the readers also had a shorter EVS on 2 than on 1 (see "Eye–Voice Span"). Furthermore, many regressions occurred after the final adverbial phrase, and these regressions were directed back toward the area of the sentence where the phrase occurred. It is as though the structure of the sentence led the readers to search for an instrument of action, and when they realized that the phrase was a locative rather than an instrument phrase, they reread it. Generally, the subjects read more smoothly in active than in passive sentences, with fewer and briefer forward fixations and less regressions.

Holmes and O'Regan (1981) found an effect of syntactic structure on regression using French sentences with relative clauses. More regressions were made for the object-relative sentence 1 than for the subject-relative sentence 2:

1. *L'auteur que l'editeur connait a rencontré mon ami.* ('The author whom the editor knows has met my friend.')
2. *L'auteur qui connait l'editeur a rencontré mon ami.* ('The author who knows the editor has met my friend.')

Other linguistic variables that can cause regressions are a lack of clarifying punctuation (Bayle, 1942), and importance of words and idea units in a passage (Shebilske & Fisher, 1981, 1982; Mandel, 1979). Besides linguistic factors, overshooting or undershooting a target seems to cause regression. The saccadic system undershoots the beginning of the line and then makes a regression to bring the eyes back to the intended location. This kind of regression occurs not only for texts but also for alphanumeric displays (Shebilske & Fisher, 1982).

Fixations both before and after a regressive movement are shorter than are other fixations (Stern, 1978). Readers must abort information extraction in the fixation preceding a regression because they realize that it is not making sense and they must regress. They must know exactly where the required information is displayed, for they make single regressive movements. They must also have a good idea about what it is they are looking for, accounting for the shortness of the regressive fixation.

Models of Eye Movement

Eye movements are sensitive to the information content of a text: The eyes fixate on informative words and parts and make regressive fixations when words and parts are ambiguous, important, complex, or not as predicted. The relative importance of a word must be predicted mostly before the reader's eye arrives at it. "Prediction-before-fixation" is necessary because the reader moves the eyes rapidly; it is possible because the reader uses syntactic and semantic context to predict what is coming, and because the readers use their peripheral vision efficiently. Decision-at-fixation also occurs, as is seen in forward and regressive fixation patterns.

What controls the reader's decision as to when and where to move the eye? Two contrasting models for eye-movement control are the "global control model" and the "current fixation model" (Rayner & Pollatsek, 1981). According to the global model, the reader selects a rate for moving through the text based on her skill and perceived difficulty of the text. The variations of fixation duration and saccade length randomly fluctuate around this preset rate. According to the "current fixation model," the decision of how long the eye is to remain at a fixation and where to move the eye next are completely controlled by information extracted from the text processed on the current fixation.

Using a computer-driven display, the text can be obscured just as each saccade occurs and then restored after a short delay. Rayner and Pollatsek found that the length of the fixation increased by roughly the duration of the masking period. This finding is taken as evidence that some control of when to move the eye occurs during the same fixation. When the experimenters made the text illegible outside a window of a certain size around the fixation point, the length of the window affected the length of the next saccade instead of the fixation duration: The wider the window, the longer the saccade. If the window size was randomly varied from one fixation to the next, both the size of the current window and the one that had been available on the previous fixation affected the length of the saccade.

Based on these results, Rayner and Pollatsek (1981) support a mixed control model, in which the decisions of when to move the eye and where to move it next are controlled partly by information extracted during the current fixation and partly by information extracted previously and held in memory buffers. The buffer contains traces of information from previous fixations not yet fully processed. Although the durations of successive fixations are unrelated, the duration of each fixation depends on information gained on previous fixations.

Writing Direction and Eye Movements

One striking difference among the writing systems of the world is writing direction, which can be left to right, right to left, or top to bottom. Writing direction should influence eye movements, with the most obvious influence being the direction in which the eyes move. Let us first compare vertical with horizontal writing.

The visual field is wider horizontally than vertically. According to Salapatek (1968), the visual scanning of the newborn is more widely dispersed in the horizontal than in the vertical dimension of the field, regardless of what kind of figure is viewed. The infant makes more and larger horizontal than vertical shifts in gaze. In an early study using single English letters, the extent of fairly clear vision was smaller in the vertical direction—half or two-thirds of the horizontal extent—but was still large enough to include at least two lines of print above and below the line on which the eyes were fixated (Ruediger, cited in Woodworth, 1938). In this experiment, the exposed field was empty except for the fixation point and a single letter. With other letters in the field, lateral masking will occur, reducing the size of the effective visual field (see Chapter 9). A modern Dutch study found the vertical span to be three printed lines (Buurman *et al.*, 1981).

Reading habits influence eye movements. With meaningful text, Chinese, Japanese, and Korean readers accustomed more to vertical than to horizontal writing read faster in the vertical direction than in the horizontal. But when the material consists of unrelated letters or figures, they read better in the horizontal direction than in the vertical (see Chapters 3, 4, and 5).

Horizontal writing can run either left to right, as in English, or right-to-left, as in Hebrew. When subjects read Hebrew, the perceptual span is asymmetric to the left, and when they read English, it is asymmetric to the right (Pollatsek *et al.*, 1981). Hebrew readers' right–left scanning is not as strong as English readers' left–right scanning, perhaps partly because Hebrew readers at school must read left–right materials such as Arabic numerals and English books (Nachshon, Shefler, & Samocha, 1977; Orbach, 1967). Gray (1956) compared reading skills in 14 different writing systems, concluding that reading direction, if it is the habitual one, does not appreciably affect reading efficiency.

Eye Movement in Other Scripts and Languages

Chinese readers make frequent fixations (F.-C. Wang, 1935; see Chapter 3). In a modern study done in the United States, Chinese readers averaged 10 saccades per line, compared with English readers, who averaged 4 saccades per line (Stern, 1978). Fixation durations did not distinguish the two groups. Because less useful information can be obtained about a Chinese character than about an English word from a given distance in the periphery, more frequent fixations are required so that most characters can be seen foveally and identified. Moreover, in Chinese text, almost every character is a content morpheme and is important.

For guiding the eye in reading, the ideal text may be mixed scripts in which informative words are in a visually prominent script whereas less informative words are in a less prominent script. Precisely this kind of mixed script is used in Japan and Korea: Visually complex Kanji are used for key words, and simple phonetic signs are used for grammatical endings.

Orthographic conventions may influence content–function word processing. Frequent French function words such as *la* and *de* are very short. When they merge with content words, as in *d'accord, l'eau, t'aime,* function words are less easy to pick up in the parafovea, and content words become obscured. On the other hand, in German text, nouns are visually prominent because they have capitalized initial letters. In all these European languages, a possible way to enhance the distinction between function and content words is to capitalize the initial letters of all content words, as is sometimes done in headings of articles.

What about reading in a foreign language? Foreign languages that are not fully mastered require close examination. Futch (1935) studied Latin reading by English-speaking Latin students. There were more regressions in reading Latin, but the fixation durations were similar for the two languages. In Stern's (1978) study, Chinese students in the United States (with 7–14 years of English) made 10 saccades per line of English print, with many regressions, showing that they found English reading difficult. Skilled Japanese readers (professors and graduate students) have large saccades in reading their own native text but small saccades (i.e., many fixations) in reading even easy English text (Bebko, Saida, & Ikeda, 1978). These are the same kinds of differences as are found between good and poor English readers.

As a reader of several writing systems (with varying fluency), written horizontally or vertically, Insup Taylor may be allowed to introspect a little. I may make some, but not large, mental adjustments in switching from one script to another, suggesting that my reading is governed more by higher-order cognitive skills than by the strikingly dissimilar visual patterns. In texts written in any system except Chinese, I can use the strategy of fixating on informative words and parts.

Summary and Conclusions

The study of eye movements flourished in the early twentieth century but was almost forgotten for some decades, along with reading research in general. Recently it has been resurrected by contemporary psychologists armed with computers.

During reading, a target word is brought to the fovea by a saccade; the eyes then fixate on the word for a quarter of a second to identify it. About 90% of reading time is spent in fixations, including some regressions to an earlier misperceived word.

A reader can pick up in the parafovea information on length and shape of a word, spaces between words, and the first and last letters of a word. When the word is fixated, he can devote attention to the rest of the word, sometimes identifying more than one word.

Chinese reading contrasts sharply with English reading: In Chinese, information content is dense, and the use of peripheral vision is limited. Accordingly, fixations are more frequent in Chinese than in English reading. Fixation durations do not distinguish reading in the two scripts.

The eyes take in printed material by alternately jumping and fixating, and reconnoitering ahead. How the eyes do their job is determined to a large extent by how the reader digests what her eyes take in. This is why, when the reader's mind wanders off, she does not grasp the word even though her eyes are dutifully "reading." This is also why complexity and importance of words and clauses, on the one hand, and the skill and task of a reader, on the other, influence eye movements. The better the reader and the easier the text and task, the fewer and shorter are fixations (both forward and regressive), and the larger is eye–voice span. In reading a foreign language, a skilled reader mimics the eye movements of an unskilled reader of the native language.

At one time eye movements were thought to be autonomous: The eyes moved to their own rhythm, influenced neither by variations in text nor by the reader's comprehension processes. That view of eye movements seems to have been superseded by the view that eye movements are under on-line, moment-to-moment cognitive control. Fixations tend to occur on informative words and clauses, and on the last words of sentences or paragraphs; regressions tend to occur on ambiguous or unexpected words.

Eye movements may not be required for comprehension, as shown by RSVP studies. When they do occur in normal reading, they reveal how the interpretation of the printed material progresses during reading. But what they reveal must be corroborated by other techniques before being fully accepted.

8

Reading Unit, Constraint, and Context

We read by phrases, words, or letters as we may serve our purpose best.

—E. B. Huey (1908)

Units of Reading

WHAT IS A READING UNIT?

A reader's task is to understand what the writer is trying to say. But on the page there are letters, lots of them. To get from the letters to the whole text, the reader chunks them together into larger units. Smaller chunks are easier to make than are bigger ones, but having made them, the reader still has a great many chunks to deal with. So chunks are themselves chunked. Different readers may have varying skills in using ever larger chunks, but they all use this multilevel construction of reading units. As Huey (1908) observed, ease and power of reading come through increasing ability to read in large units.

A **reading unit** has one or more of the following properties: It may be physically separable from others of its kind; it may have a sound; it may have a name; it may have a meaning. It may be something that can be counted, deleted, added, and moved around as a piece. It may be learned, recalled, and forgotten as a piece. It may be something that is taken in at one glance, or whose correct sound or meaning may emerge when processed as a whole. A reading unit might be a letter, a letter cluster, a syllable, a morpheme, a word, a phrase, a clause, idea unit, a sentence, a paragraph, a story, an article, or a book. This chapter deals with smaller units, up to phrases, leaving the others to the later chapters.

Small Meaningless Units

Letters, letter clusters, and syllables are usually meaningless in themselves. Such units have to be dealt with on their own terms and in the end must be put together into a larger unit that may have some meaning.

LETTER

The letter is the smallest unit of an alphabet and is familiar to everyone who can read. Learning to read often begins with reciting the alphabet. Yet, letter-by-letter processing is the least efficient way of reading. It may be used by some beginning or poor readers. One class of brain-damaged patients can read only letter by letter, taking several seconds to read a single word (Patterson & Kay, 1982).

Readers differ in their abilities to identify letters. Fast-reading college readers are quicker than slower readers in judging whether two letters have the same or different names (Jackson & McClelland, 1979). This fast access to letter codes allows fast readers to capture more information from each fixation than do slow readers. In a study of children (Grades 2 and 6) and adults, older and better readers were faster than younger and poorer readers in naming individual letters and words, despite the normal use of larger units by the better readers (Biemiller, 1977–1978).

Skilled readers may revert to letter-by-letter processing when presented with strings of unconnected letters or long unfamiliar words. When you confront a string such as 'TXN', you have no choice but to read it letter by letter. People use such strings of random letters and digits for telephone numbers, postal codes, car licenses, and so on. Acronyms for some organizations, complex chemical names, and common phrases often are strings of unconnected letters—FBI, RCMP, DNA, LSD, TNT, RSVP.

Reading theorists are divided about the role of letters in word recognition: Some claim that word recognition does not require letter identification, whereas others claim that it does. This dispute is the subject of Chapter 9, where we show that individual letters are not normally identified in recognizing words but that letters sometimes help word recognition.

LETTER CLUSTER

A **letter cluster** that has an invariant pronunciation might be a useful reading unit. The letter cluster 'sh' is usually pronounced the same way, as one phoneme, wherever it appears within a morpheme (*ship, push, bushel*). Gibson and Levin (1975) point out that '-ati-' is a frequent trigram but is not a unit for reading, because it is pronounced differently depending on context (*relation* versus *relative*). The reason may instead be that '-ati-' is usually split across two syllables.

Santa and Santa (1977) asked subjects to judge whether a probe (which was a word fragment) was contained within a word. For a yes judgment, the fragment was in the word; for a no judgment, it was not. A probe could be a single letter such as 'L', a two-letter cluster such as 'BL' or 'LA', a three-letter cluster 'LAS' or a whole word BLAST. Stimulus examples might be:

BLAST : BL (yes)

BLAST : BC (no)

Initial consonant clusters were processed as quickly as single letters and slightly faster than whole words. In Santa's (1976–1977) study, Grade 5 children and adults used the initial clusters as perceptual units, but Grade 2 poor readers relied on single letters as units. The final consonant cluster was found to be a weak unit for all ages.

To ensure that a consonant cluster, and not the initial position, speeds perception of 'BL-', Santa and Santa (1979) tested words having two unrelated letters rather than a cluster at the initial position. The initial consonant cluster 'BL-' in BLAST produced a faster response than the unrelated initial 'PA-' in PAINT. Furthermore, the medial vowel cluster '-AI-' in PAINT produced a faster response than did the medial '-LA-' in BLAST. In short, when the probe corresponded to an obvious cluster, reaction time was shorter than when it crossed a cluster border.

Jorm (1977), on the other hand, found no evidence that letter clusters act as units: Words and pseudowords with and without common letter clusters had the same latencies and errors of pronunciation. Perhaps his 8-year-old subjects were too young to use letters clusters as units, being only slightly older than Santa's Grade 2 children who had not yet learned to use clusters.

According to Marcel (1980b; see Chapter 10), letter clusters are analyzed from left to right in reading, with larger clusters superseding smaller ones. In a reasonable context, clusters that frequently appear in real words will be analyzed quickly.

SYLLABLE

A syllable is a good candidate to be a reading unit: People can easily pronounce an isolated syllable such as /da/ or /di/. A whole syllable, but not a part syllable, may be omitted or added in speech and reading. Young children may omit an unstressed syllable in their speech: *giraffe* → /raf/, *elephant* → /efənt/. Some disabled readers by habit omit or insert a syllable (Cotterell, 1972). Some Russian preschoolers can segment phrases into syll-ables before they can segment them into words (Karpova, 1977). The syllable is the unit of writing in a syllabary, such as the Japanese Kana, and syllables represent morphemes in the language and writing of China.

In word recognition, splitting a word into syllable units permits subjects to overcome the effect of time separation between presentation of parts of the word, whereas splitting into similar sized non-syllable clusters does not (Mewhort & Beal, 1977; see Chapter 9). Long words like the German *Aufmerk-samkeitsschwankung* appear fearsome, until they are divided into syllables. A series of familiar syllables, whether it forms a real word or not, is particularly easy to read. Zeitler (1900) found that from a 10 msec presentation his German subjects could report: 4–7 letters of consonant strings, *vcpfnglw;* 5–8 letters if vowels were interpersed, *vicopefunigalow;* and 6–10 letters of a meaningless string of familiar syllables, *losverkungweit.*

In an early study, Wilkins (cited in Woodworth, 1938) typed some familiar names in two lines, interchanging the final syllables of the words, and exposed them to her subjects briefly, for 50–100 msec:

WOODSON
WILROW

The words were misread, as you can guess, as "Woodrow Wilson," who was at that time President of the United States. Familiar syllables instantly suggest a word or phrase. In this case the extreme familiarity of the phrase or name itself must have exerted a powerful influence on the subjects' reading.

Jorm (1977) found children's pronunciation latencies to be shorter for pseudowords consisting of familiar syllables than for those consisting of unfamiliar ones, although pronunciation errors did not differ between the two types of pseudowords. For words, and especially for pseudowords, pronunciation latencies were longer for two-syllable strings than for one-syllable strings of the same length. Remember that Jorm found familiarity of letter clusters to have no effect either on latency or errors in the pronunciation of words or pseudowords. His results point to syllables rather than common letter clusters as units, at least for young children.

In English, German, French, and other languages that use a Roman alphabet, writers must be aware of rules for syllabification in order to break a word correctly at syllable boundaries when it crosses the end of a line. However, the rules in English are so complex that no completely satisfactory scheme for computer hyphenation has yet been produced. Nevertheless, most of us could divide words into syllables satisfactory to ourselves most of the time.

Small Meaningful Units

MORPHEME

A morpheme is the smallest meaningful unit; it may consist of a few alphabetic letters or one Chinese character. The following studies show that both stems (free morphemes) and affixes (bound morphemes) are recognized as units.

Murrell and Morton (1974) trained subjects with particular words (e.g., READ) and then required them to detect the same word, one with the same stem morpheme (READER), or one with as much visual similarity but semantically unrelated (READY). Training on READ facilitated recognition of

READER, but not of READY. This kind of training did not work with the bound morphemes (-ER).

The word *rejuvenate* consists of *re-* and *-juvenate,* meaning "again make young." The word *repertoire* cannot be analyzed into a prefix and a stem in the same manner. Taft and Forster's (1975) subjects took longer to classify strings like *-juvenate* as nonwords than they did strings like *-pertoire,* even though both types of strings are nonwords. When an inappropriate prefix was added (*dejuvenate, depertoire*), they still took longer to classify the strings that had real stems. The subjects' task was **lexical decision,** to decide whether or not a letter string is a word. The less wordlike is a string, the quicker it is classified as a nonword.

Bound morphemes are perceived as units under some conditions. How a final letter string *-ing* or *-ed* is processed depends on whether it is part of a one-morpheme word (*spring, speed*) or an inflectional ending of a two-morpheme word (*spying, spied*). In a **letter-cancellation task,** in which subjects must cancel all occurrences of a designated letter, 'i's and 'e's are more likely to be left uncancelled in inflectional endings than in one-morpheme words. Non-cancellation implies that these frequent inflectional endings are scantily processed, perhaps because they are unimportant or unstressed, or more likely because *-ed* and *-ing* are processed as a unit rather than as '-e-d' or '-i-n-g' (Drewnowski & Healy, 1980; Smith & Sterling, 1982).

Gibson and Guinet (1971) prepared three kinds of words: real words, pronounceable pseudowords, and unpronounceable nonwords (*put* → *tup, ptu*).[1] A verb ending (*-s, -ed, -ing*) could be added to any of the strings. The errors made in recognizing a letter string in a T-scope show that the endings serve as units. First, when the strings were real words or pseudowords, errors in the endings were often substitutions of other endings. Second, there were far fewer errors in the verb endings than in the final letters of equal-length strings without suffixes. Third, the number of errors in the endings did not depend on the length of the ending (*-ing* produced the same number of errors as did *-s*). When the strings were real words, the root morpheme seemed to dominate the ending, but when they were pseudowords, the ending served more strongly as a perceptual unit. When the stems were unpronounceable, the endings were not perceived as endings.

In speech, people sometimes produce errors called **slips of the tongue.** In one type of error, a bound morpheme is shifted one or more words (Garrett, 1976):

1. *They get weirder every day* → "They get weird everier day"
2. *He goes back to* → "He go backs to"

[1]The astute reader may notice that *tup* is actually a real English word. It has eight distinct meanings in the *Oxford English Dictionary*, four as a noun, and four as a verb. Two of the other pseudowords used, *nair* and *trast*, also appear in the OED, albeit marked as rare or obsolete. Nevertheless, for a subject, these letter strings will be pseudowords if she does not know them as real words. The question is how an experimenter can be sure that she does not know them.

In lexical decision, prefixed words (*absent*) took longer to be recognized than similar looking single-morpheme words (*abbey*), when subjects were responding to predominantly prefixed words but not when responding to mostly single-morpheme words (Rubin, Becker, & Freeman, 1979). Words are not automatically decomposed into their morphemic constituents prior to recognition.

Whether a suffix or prefix is responded to as a unit may depend partly on how clear-cut and familiar it is. The suffix *-ing* is extremely familiar; it was the most frequent syllable in 5000 common words examined by Sakiey (1979). The prefix *un-* can be joined with a wide variety of stems, carrying the same meaning "not," whereas *ab-* has a limited occurrence. Among 28 prefixes taught in Grades 2–6 primary readers, *un-* is one of the most frequently taught; *ab-* is not even included (Stotsky, 1981). *Un-* is much less common than *-ing*: In this chapter's 10,000 words, there are over 300 *-ing* endings but only 40 *un-* prefixes. (In this whole book, there are even more *-ed* endings than *-ing*. But this is fairly technical writing.)

In current printing practice, hyphens tend not to be used, even though they might facilitate word recognition by separating prefixes from stems. For example, *multisyllable* or *subthreshold* appears as a long, unfamiliar word, until it is segmented into *multi-syllable* or *sub-threshold.* When a word is long, readers tend to parse it into affix + stem (Smith & Sterling, 1982). In this book we have retained a hyphen in several long and infrequent words such as *multi-character* and *pseudo-homophone.*

WORD

A word is a familiar and meaningful reading unit. Words in print are separated by a space in modern alphabetic writings, but not necessarily in syllabic or logographic writings. Since words, along with letters, have a chapter by themselves (Chapter 9), in this chapter we merely provide a few pieces of evidence that a word is used as a unit.

In a classic experiment, Cattell (1886) found that readers could identify in a 10-msec T-scope exposure the following items: (*a*) 3–4 unconnected letters; (*b*) 2 unconnected short words (about 8 letters); and (*c*) 4 connected short words (12 letters). Zeitler's (1900) German subjects read that 25-letter word *Aufmerksamkeitsschwankung* after a 10-msec exposure. When asked to read other strings of consonants or familiar syllables in 10 msec, they could manage only between 4 and 10 letters. Presumably, subjects process letters forming a word as one familiar unit, whereas they process unrelated letters individually. Alternately, they might guess and remember better letters that form a word than those that do not.

Another line of evidence that a word is a unit comes from its resistance to fragmentation and segmentation. Try to solve the following anagrams (make a real word different from the initial letter arrangement): *sauce; bleat.* Now try these: *sucae; belta.* You see how much harder it is to break up the two words in the first pattern to solve anagrams than it is to solve them from the same letters in random arrangements (Beilin & Horn, 1962; Ekstrand & Dominowski, 1965).

A familiar word has a better chance to be perceived as a unit than does an unfamiliar word. In a letter-cancellation task, Healy's (1976) subjects missed the letter more often in frequent nouns than in infrequent ones. The two types of nouns were equated in length and in the location of the target 't' (e.g., *plant* versus *yacht*).

The ability to use a word rather than its letters as a unit increases with age and reading skill. Hoffmann (1927), using a T-scope, measured the increase in perceptual span for unconnected consonants, nonsense syllables, unfamiliar words, and familiar words. His subjects were children selected from eight different Grades, from 1 to 8, divided into good readers (best 25% of the classes) and poor readers (worst 25%).
In Figure 8-1, the span increases with advancing grade; it does so most dramatically with words, especially with familiar words, and barely with nonsense syllables and consonant strings. For good readers, the gain is from 5 to 20 letters in words, and for the poor readers, from 3 to 12 letters. In both cases, the rise is most rapid from Grades 1 to 3. Learning to read is, partly, learning to group material in larger and more meaningful units.

In one study, subjects from Grades 2, 4, 6, and college judged whether single words belonged to animal or non-animal categories (Samuels, LaBerge, & Bremer, 1978). Words varied in length from three to six letters (e.g., *hog, pony, whale, cattle*). The younger the subjects, the more slowly they judged the words. Further, the young children's reaction times increased as the word length increased. But college students' reaction times were more or less the same for different word lengths, suggesting that they processed a six-letter word as a whole.

PHRASE

A few words may combine to form a syntactic and semantic unit called a **phrase.** On the Moabite Stone (Semitic script) dating from 850 B.C., scholars can detect the first punctuation marks, which were vertical lines separating phrases. The sentence *With a big bang/ the universe/ was born* consists of one adverbial phrase, one noun phrase, and one verb phrase, in that order. Syntactically, a phrase is a coherent unit: Words within a phrase are closely

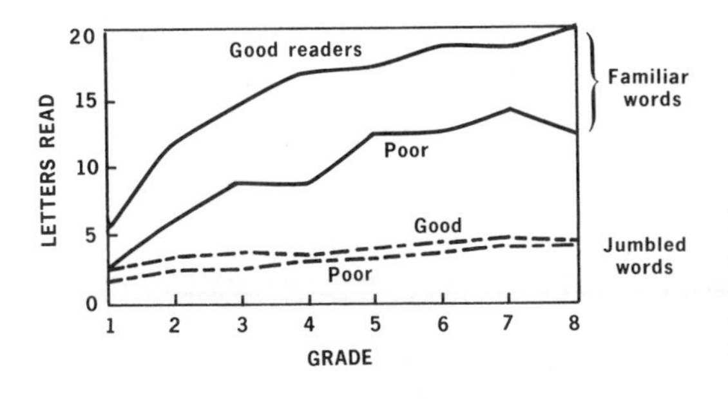

Figure 8-1. *Increase in number of letters perceived in a T-scope as a function of school grades and reading skill (based on Hoffmann, 1927, and Woodworth, 1938).*

related to one another in their proper order, and when rearranged sound strange and ungrammatical—*with a big bang* cannot become *a with bang big.* On the other hand, the phrases in this sentence can be rearranged into the prosaic but perfectly grammatical *The universe was born with a big bang,* or the stilted but still grammatical *The universe with a big bang was born.*

A phrase makes an excellent processing unit. Older studies, with good reason, refer to the phrase as a "thought unit." A few short words are within the perceptual and short-term memory span. The sound and meaning of a word is often clarified within a phrase. Schlesinger (1968) studied subjects reading Hebrew passages. The eye–voice span (EVS) tended to coincide with phrase boundaries, and when errors were made, they tended to take the form of completed phrase units. Levin and Turner (1968) found the same tendency in English reading. Further, fast readers were more likely to show EVS ending at phrase boundaries than were slower readers. Not only did subjects tend to read up to phrase boundaries, but they also changed the words in a phrase in such a way as to make a phrase boundary. That is, if the final phrase was *next to the house,* the subjects might have read *next door.* The ability to read in phrases kept improving with advancing grades until Grade 4, at which time it seemed to have stabilized. Resnick (1970), on the other hand, found that though Grades 3 and 5 children had this ability, it was greater in college students.

The type of phrase has an influence on EVS. Rode (1974–1975) studied EVS in children from Grades 3, 4 and 5 reading second-grade readers. Each age group's EVS terminated at the end of three-word and two-word verb phrases more frequently than at noun phrases of the same lengths. In each case, the verb phrase followed the noun phrase, completing a clause, as in *The man/wants to go,// but...*

During oral reading, people tend to pause at syntactic breaks such as phrase and clause (Goldman-Eisler, 1972). Reading purpose influences where readers pause: Aaronson and Scarborough's (1976) subjects read, at their own pace, a sentence displayed on a computer scope one word at a time. The subjects who had to recall the sentence (rather than take a comprehension test) read with short pauses within phrases and longer pauses at phrase boundaries. Word length influences the size of optimal segmentation. Pynte and Noizet (1980) presented on a video screen French sentences segmented at various levels. For sentences with short words, the fastest reading times were obtained with segmentation by noun phrase and verb phrase; for sentences with long words, optimal presentation was almost word for word.

Finally, reading skill influences the size of reading unit: Grade 5 good readers organized incoming words in phrase units, whereas poor readers tended to read word by word (Steiner, Weiner, & Cromer, 1971). In New Zealand, the best Grade 3 readers (top one-quarter) read, on the average, 7 words between pauses and 4.7 words per stress, compared with 1.3 words between pauses and 1.1 words per stress for the poorest readers (Clay & Imlach, 1971). In college, slower readers required more time to organize words into phrase units than did fast readers (Aaronson & Scarborough, 1977).

These experiments, using different techniques, all show that readers organize incoming material in phrases. If so, organizing the layout of the text by phrases should make reading faster. Frase and Schwartz (1979) segmented complex technical sentences into phrases and clauses and arranged them with indentation, as follows:

The cable may be
air-core or
waterproof design;
however, in the case of
buried air-core PIC cables,
the double-sheath types are recommended.

Adults read the arrangement-by-phrases much faster than they read the regular text.

Processing by phrase means that individual words within a phrase are accumulated with varying degrees of partial processing until the entire unit is completed. The meaning of the phrase is obtained as one unit and then is integrated with the meaning of the other phrases in a sentence. This method of processing is efficient because the meaning and the sound of an individual word is sometimes ambiguous until other words provide a context. Organizing by phrase may also facilitate retrieval: When one salient word of a phrase is retrieved, the rest of the words in the phrase quickly join it (Wilkes & Kennedy, 1969).

The same mode of processing occurs in dealing with larger units, such as clauses, sentences, and paragraphs. The smaller units are understood as far as possible, disambiguated using following units, and accumulated to form larger units. We describe syntax and then discuss sentence processing in Chapter 12; we describe text structure and then discuss text processing in Chapter 13.

Sequential Constraint

Predictable patterns emerge when objects are arranged according to rules, and any rules imply constraints. We now discuss a particular kind of constraint, **sequential constraint,** the pattern that emerges because linguistic items are arranged in ways that reflect, to varying degrees, their sequences in normal texts. In learning a language, one not only learns linguistic items and rules but also gains implicit knowledge about how frequently certain items occur, and in what sequence they tend to follow one another.

Constraint Between Words

ORDERS OF APPROXIMATION

People implicitly know the **transitional probabilities** among words, the probabilities that particular words will follow any given sequence of words. Given the word *goes,* people know that *down, up,* or some other location word

Table 8-1 *Orders of Approximation to English (Words)*

Approximation	Example
Zero order	combat callous irritability migrates depraved temporal prolix alas pillory nautical...
First order	day to is for they have proposed I the it materials of are its go...
Third order	family was large dark animal came roaring down the middle of my friends love books passionately every kiss is fine...
Fifth order	house to ask for is to earn our living by working towards a goal for his team in old New York was a wonderful place wasn't it even pleasant to talk about and laugh hard when he tells lies he should not tell me the reason why you are is evident...
Seventh order	then go ahead and do it if possible while I make an appointment I want to skip very much around the tree and back home again to eat dinner after the movie early so that we could get lunch because we liked her method for sewing blouses and skirts is...

Source: Based on Miller & Selfridge, 1950.

follows it with high probability, and given *goes down, there* has a higher probability than does *roses* or *electromagnetism.* In order to study people's sensitivity to sequential constraints, psychologists prepare strings of words or letters of different **orders of approximation.** To get a **zero-order** approximation, pick words randomly from a dictionary; for first order, pick words at random, but from text, thus ensuring that probabilities of chosen words are proportional to their frequencies in text; for **fifth order,** give four sequentially constrained words to a person who then adds a fifth one. The point of what looks like an idle exercise is to calibrate precisely the degree of sequential constraint and then relate it to processing difficulty. See Table 8-1 for some examples.

As the order of approximation becomes higher, the word string becomes more sequentially constrained. In a way, it becomes textlike, although even with very high order of approximation the content of the string rambles like a dream without a theme, as does the fifth- or seventh-order approximation in Table 8-1. Such a string is not necessarily grammatical. Over and above the transitional probabilities between words, syntax and theme impose a structure.

ORDERS OF APPROXIMATION AND PROCESSING

People can read, write, transmit telegraph, and so on, more quickly and accurately for higher- than for lower-order approximation. Sumby and Pollack (1954) instructed subjects to copy written material with the fewest possible glances. A glance was necessary for every 3 words of zero-order approximation, but only one for every 10 words in ordinary prose. Morton's (1964) adult subjects read higher orders of approximation (up to the eighth) faster than they did lower orders. Fast readers, who use contextual cues effectively, increased their speed up to the sixth order, and slower readers, up to the fifth order. Eye–voice span increased up to the eighth order, especially for the fast readers. Vanacek (1972) confirmed that it is the contextual constraints that reduced the number of fixations; word frequency had an effect only when the words were very rare, probably in zero order.

In Coleman's (1963) study, the mean number of words correctly recalled continued to increase up to the ninth order, the highest order studied. He also scored recall of words according to different sizes of sequences of correct words—correct single words, two-word sequences, and so on, up to correct 17-word sequences. The advantage for the higher order approximations became greater as recall was scored in longer sequences. At higher-order approximations, sequential constraints package words into familiar phrases and clauses.

Klein and Klein's (1973) subjects had an unusual but interesting task. They had to draw slashes at each word boundary without leaving any letter dangling, in letter sequences such as: *towindadjustedear.* This string of letters is a part of a passage that contained up to 250 words, printed without spaces between words. The correctness of boundary marking depended on the approximation to English: The first order yielded the lowest score, and a prose passage, the highest, pointing out the importance of high-level constraints in recognition of low-level units.

In sum, the more constrained a sequence of words, the more speedily and accurately it can be processed. Sequentially constrained items tend to form familiar units of various sizes. Fast readers take better advantage of constraints than do slow readers.

Constraint Between Letters

"**Information** is something we get when some person or machine tells us something we didn't know before [Garner, 1962, p. 2]." In English text, after 'q', 'u' certainly follows; in that case, the appearance of 'u' conveys no information; it is completely predictable; it is 100% **redundant.** According to Garner, redundancy for printed English is about 50%: Given the optimal length of letter sequence (12–16 letters), the next letter is only half as uncertain, or informative, as it would be without the context.

WITHIN-WORD CONSTRAINT AND PROCESSING

Within-word constraint is largely phonetic: Consonant and vowel letters tend to alternate for ease of pronunciation. In English some clusters of three consonants are allowed, as in 'str-' and '-nds'. The word *constraint* itself has a four-consonant cluster. In some languages such as Japanese, no consonant cluster is allowed anywhere in a word, and in some other languages such as Korean and Finnish, a few types of consonant clusters are allowed but only in the final position of a syllable.

Three further sources of within-word constraint are: (*a*) the tendency of some letters to occur more frequently than others; (*b*) the tendency of particular letters to follow others; and (*c*) the tendency of letters to occur in characteristic positions in words. For example, 'e' is by far the most frequent letter, and 'x' the least. After 'q', 'u' will almost certainly occur, but after 'a', any of 26 letters can occur. In one count, the letter 'r' was more or less uniformly distributed over all positions of a sample of 20,000 five-letter words, whereas 'h' had an uneven distribution, being found in the second position (as in 'sh-') 608 times and in the third position only 55 times (Mayzner & Tresselt, 1958). In the draft of this book 'h' does indeed appear strongly in the second position among words of all lengths. The effect probably comes from frequent words such as *the* and 'wh-' words *when, which, where.*

People use within-word constraint not only to read but also to solve anagrams or crossword puzzles, break codes, win Scrabble games, and so on. In recognizing words, knowledge of letter distribution may be useful in the early stages if sufficient letter-feature information has been perceived to specify the letter, but the letter's serial position is unresolved (Katz, 1977). Skilled readers of Grade 6 use this kind of positional information on letters, but poor readers do not (M. Mason, 1975).

Table 8-2 lists eight-letter sequences in four orders of approximation to English. In zero-order approximation, there is virtually no constraint between letters. The higher the order of approximation of a letter sequence, the more pronounceable it becomes, and hence the more word-like it is, though it may still be meaningless. These meaningless but pronounceable letter sequences are pseudowords, much favored in psychologists' experiments.

Miller *et al.* presented such eight-letter sequences to subjects in a random order using a T-scope. The subjects wrote the letters they saw, in the correct order, in the eight blanks on the answer sheet. The higher the order of approximation, the higher the percentage of letters correctly placed. However, in lower orders, letters correctly perceived and wrongly placed would have been counted as errors; in higher orders, position errors would often be correctable and would not have been recorded. Perceptual errors of position frequently occur in this kind of task (see Chapter 9).

With Japanese letters, the eye–voice span increased from zero order (2.8 Hiragana) to third order (3.7), and to text (7.6). Oral reading errors decreased from zero order to text (Ohnishi, 1962).

Hershensen (1969) found that accuracy in reporting perceived English letters decreased linearly from letter position one to seven. This decrease was

Table 8-2: *Orders of Approximation to English (Letters)*

Approximation	Example
Zero order	YRULPZOC
First order	STANUGOP
Second order	WALLYLOF
Fourth order	RICANING

Source: Based on Miller, Bruner, & Postman, 1954.

slight for English words but steep for zero order. Training reduced the effect of approximation sharply, suggesting that order of approximation did not affect iconic storage but did affect subsequent cognitive processing.

Sequential constraint between letters helps also a letter search task. Krueger's (1970) subjects searched more rapidly for a target letter through real words and pseudowords with a high order of approximation than through scrambled letter strings. Subjects exploit sequential letter dependencies to search faster, indicating that they are not restricting their attention to the letter shape being sought.

NOT LETTER BY LETTER

Is the use of sequential redundancy based solely on the transitional probability between letters? Mewhort (1966) answers no. He used fourth-order and zero-order sequences with different amounts of space between letters. With normal spacing, he obtained the increase in recognition expected with higher order. When the spacing between letters was widened, recognition of the fourth order was impaired, whereas recognition of the zero order was not. The widened spacing disrupted the subjects' ability to use the redundancy in the higher order sequences, suggesting that larger structural segments were perceived as visual units when spacing allowed perception of letter context. Similar effects occurred in learning to read text with inverted letters (Kolers, Palef, & Stelmach, 1980): The benefit of higher order of approximation was obtained only with closely spaced letters (see Chapter 9). Mewhort (1974) obtained similar results by manipulating time intervals between letters: Increasing the interletter interval from 0 to 50 msec did not change recognition of first-order strings, but it impaired recognition of fourth-order strings.

So, in discussing sequential constraint, we come around again to the idea of a processing unit. Groups of letters in a highly constrained sequence tend to be processed as units if they are normally spaced and presented simultaneously.

CHILDREN'S SENSITIVITY TO LETTER SEQUENCE

The ability to take advantage of redundant letter sequences, or orthographic structure, improves with age and with reading and/or spelling skill. The studies described in this section trace the development of this ability, using similar materials but dissimilar tasks.

Lott and Smith (1970) studied children's ability to recognize a letter in isolation and in three-letter words. Although there were improvements from Grades 1 to 4 in the ability to use orthographic structure, Grade 1 children were still able to recognize a letter more easily in a word than in isolation. In another procedure, children from Grades 1, 2, and 3 selected from a set of three letter-strings the one that was most similar to a real word. The stimuli were eight-letter sequences of zero-, second-, and fourth-order approximation to English. Sensitivity to orthographic structure was acquired rapidly during the second half of Grade 1, and continued to progress slowly during Grades 2 and 3 (Niles & Taylor, 1978).

A slightly more difficult task involved seven-letter pseudowords, either first-order or fourth-order approximation to English. Children were asked to fill in one missing letter in the words, taking as long as they wished. Grade 1 children showed no difference in correctness of guessing across the two orders of approximation; Grade 3 children showed a great increase in accuracy for the fourth as compared for the first order; and Grade 5 children performed almost as well as adults (Lefton, Spragins, & Byrnes, 1973).

Sensitivity to orthographic structure develops through reading. Naturally it is lacking in prereading kindergartners. It can be found in Grade 1 children who have started reading, but only for simple and easy tasks. Children's sensitivity steadily improves with schooling, perhaps up to Grade 3 for easy tasks and up to Grade 5 for difficult ones. Apparently, it is word-recognition ability per se, rather than age, grade level, or simple exposure, that correlates highly with orthographic knowledge (Allington, 1978; Leslie & Shannon, 1981).

Words in Context

Context is such an important factor in reading that it is discussed in a few different chapters of this book: identifying a letter in isolation versus in a word (Chapter 9); recognizing a word in isolation versus among other words (Chapter 11); and understanding a sentence in isolation versus among other sentences (Chapter 12). Here, we discuss how other words in a sentence provide a context for restoring, recognizing, and reading a target word.

Target Word in Context

WORD PERCEPTION AND TYPES OF CONTEXT

Appropriate context, especially a long context, enables readers to recognize a word quickly and accurately. Conversely, incongruent context interferes with or inhibits word recognition. Tulving and Gold (1963) studied how quickly subjects recognize nouns presented in a T-scope under three conditions: no context, congruent context, and incongruent context. In both kinds of context, the preceding context varied in length: 8, 4, 2, and 1 words of a 9-word sentence. An example of the 8-word congruent context, with the ninth word as the target: *The actress received praise for being an outstanding PERFORMER.* Compared with no context, recognition was easier in the congruent context and harder in the incongruent one. The longer the context, the better the thresholds were for the congruent context, but worse for the incongruent one.

Schuberth and Eimas (1977) showed a word or a pseudoword either alone or preceded by a sentence fragment or by 4 spelled-out digits. The sentence context helped detection of the words and the pseudowords, unless the word was incongruous with the sense of the fragment, in which case it inhibited recognition. The digit context inhibited detection of both congruous and incongruous words. Context aids detection of even a pseudoword with which it has no possible semantic or syntactic relationship. There seems to be some "framing" or settling effect about a sentence context that just makes it easier to see word-like objects.

Ehrlich and Rayner (1981) studied the effect of context on reading target words, which were 5-letter common nouns (e.g., *shark*). The same target word was less likely to be fixated, or was fixated for a shorter duration, in a highly constrained than in a poorly constrained passage. A misspelling was less likely to be detected in the highly constrained passage than in the less constrained one. Contextual information allows readers to reduce their reliance on visual information.

RESTORING WORDS IN CONTEXT

You should have no trouble filling in the missing letter and the missing word in the following sentence: *Time flies l__ke an ____*. What factors can help you to fill in the missing items in this sentence? You are probably familiar with this maxim; if not, you try to think of things that can fly. As the article is *an,* the word for this thing must start with a vowel; it must also be singular; it must be a noun. With so many clues, *arrow* or *eagle* is an obvious solution. To fill in the missing letter in *l__ ke,* you consider only vowels; possible English words to fit the frame are *like, luke,* and *lake; like* comes to your mind first because it is commoner than the others, and it happens to fit the slot syntactically and semantically.

Such filling in is not an idle academic exercise: In daily speech and reading, people constantly have to fill in faintly heard or seen items, without being conscious of it. Items may be faint either because people are momentarily inattentive or because the materials come in unclear forms. Think of different individuals' handwritings: Some letters or words taken out of context, or even in context, may be illegible, but the whole text can be read accurately.

Several factors influence how well a correct word is found for a deletion. When a single word was deleted in the middle of a sentence, 11-word sentences provided a more effective context than did 6-word sentences, but 25-word sentences were no better than 11-word ones (Aborn, Rubenstein, & Sterling, 1959). Words were equally restorable when every 24th, 12th or 6th word was omitted, but not when every 3rd word was omitted. Words omitted in pairs were easy to restore but words omitted in groups of four were not (MacGinitie, 1961).

Does contextual constraint operate only within a sentence, or does it operate between sentences as well? Miller and Coleman (1967) found that readers' correct restorations of deleted words, **cloze scores**, increased fairly steadily from the first to the last word within a sentence but not beyond it. (The word *cloze* comes from *closure*.) In Kibby's (1980) cloze tests, subjects read two paragraphs whose sentences were in a regular or scrambled order, or were given in isolation. Cloze scores did not differ between the regular and the scrambled orders. The scores were lower for the isolated sentences than for the regular text, but by only 10–15%. The effect of context appeared not to extend strongly beyond a sentence boundary.

Syntactic constraint may operate only within a sentence, but semantic constraint may operate between sentences (see "Prediction and Comprehension" below). Naturally, conjunctive relations (*and, yet, so, then,* etc.) depend most on intersentence relations, and lexical items (*dog* repeated as *dog* or *animal*) least (Bridge & Winograd, 1982).

Still another question is the relative effectiveness of preceding versus subsequent context. According to Information Theory (e.g., Garner, 1962), a word should be equally predictable from either kind of context. In practice, words before the missing word are far more helpful than are words following it. More interestingly, preceding context plus a single following word makes the target word much more predictable than would be expected from independently combining the results for just the prior context with those for just the following word (Rubin, 1976). The words surrounding the target appear to work in harness, rather than providing independent information about it. This effect is conceptually similar to the "word superiority effect" (a letter is recognized better in a word than by itself) or to the "line in letter effect" (a line is better recognized in a letter than by itself; see Chapter 9). In all three effects, the existence of an appropriate context permits better detection, recognition, or prediction of an item than one might expect from the information that is apparently available.

Other factors—contextual richness, frequency of target words, and readers' grade level—were studied together in one experiment by Pearson and Studt (1975). Subjects had to fill in missing words in sentences. Suppose a target word pair was *song* (frequent) and *tune* (infrequent). Here are three kinds of context for the target word:

1. Rich context: *In music class we chose to sing a happy* _____ .
2. Moderate context: *The choir got to choose its own* _____ .
3. Poor context: *In school today we voted for our favorite* _____ .

All three factors and their interactions had effects. For example, the rich context was more effective than the moderate, which in turn was more effective than the poor context. This contextual effect was stronger for the frequent than for the infrequent word. Grade 3 children were more successful on this task than were Grade 1 children, especially with the frequent target words.

Individual Differences in Using Context

All the studies cited in the preceding section, without exception, showed that good (and/or older) readers are better than poor (and/or younger) readers in reading in large units, being sensitive to sequential constraints, and making good use of context.

INTERACTIVE–COMPENSATORY MODEL OF CONTEXT USE

According to Stanovich's (1980) "interactive–compensatory model of context use," superior reading is not associated with a greater use of the redundancy to speed word recognition; instead, it is associated with rapid context-free word recognition. Poor readers compensate for a deficit in lower-level processes, such as letter or word recognition, by relying more on higher-level processes (i.e., hypothesis testing based on contextual expectancies): "Word recognition of good readers is ***less*** reliant on conscious expectancies generated from the prior sentence context. The result is that more attentional capacity is left over for integrative comprehension processes [p. 64, emphasis added]." Stanovich discounts numerous findings on better readers' good knowledge of orthographic structure on the ground that "they all measured conscious knowledge of orthographic constraints rather than the ability to use orthographic structure to actually ***speed*** word recognition [p. 38]."

Stanovich's position is perverse, surely. Good readers are skilled both at using context and at context-free word recognition; the two skills work together, not in opposition. Attentional capacity is not apportioned between the use of context and integrative comprehension processes, as Stanovich maintains; rather, integrative comprehension processes entail the efficient use of context. Knowledge in any aspect of text (or of the world), whether conscious or implicit, leads to its use in reading. For example, in recognizing words, skilled Grade 6 readers use their knowledge of positional probabilities of letters better than do unskilled readers (M. Mason, 1975). In reporting letters of briefly exposed words, good high school readers, but not poor readers, improved their scores when orthographically regular pseudowords were substituted for unpronounceable nonwords (Frederiksen, 1981a).

MUTUALLY SUPPORTIVE MODEL OF CONTEXT USE

We now present our own explanation of the use of context by good and poor readers. For want of a better term, we shall call it "mutually supportive model of context use." To recognize a word in context, both higher-level contextual information ***and*** lower-level graphic information must be used efficiently. A good reader is good at using both types of information. It is the poor readers, not the good, who may have to divert resources or attention from one process to another. According to Singer and Crouse (1981), making letter and word decoding automatic may permit readers to devote more attention to higher-level units. In their study, nonverbal IQ, vocabulary, and decoding skills were correlated with the ability to use context, but even with these variables accounted for, context-using skills still had a positive effect on comprehension.

As compared with a poor reader, a good reader uses context efficiently in several ways:

- By narrowing down alternatives rather than by guessing one specific word to be expected
- By using both preceding and following context rather than just the preceding context
- By correcting erroneous hypotheses that do not fit the total context
- By using long- as well as short-range context
- By not using context when using it is not the best strategy

A good reader uses graphic information efficiently too. He uses it in a feedback loop with contextual information. He is good at perceiving distinctive features of letters (Nodine & Simmons, 1974), at analyzing graphemic patterns (Kolers, 1975), at making use of orthographic structure of words (e.g., Lefton, et al. 1973; Niles & Taylor 1978), and at identifying letters (Biemiller, 1977–1978; Jackson & McClelland, 1979). Here are some experimental findings supporting our position.

ORAL READING ERRORS AND SPEED

Oral reading errors reveal a host of interesting data. Fairbanks (1937) analyzed the oral reading errors of freshmen, who were divided into good and poor readers according to their silent reading performance. The poor readers made on average 5.8 errors per 100 words, the good readers, only 2.1. Substitutions were the most frequent type of error for both good and poor readers. However, 51% of the substitutions made by the poor readers seriously changed the meaning, but not one of the good readers' substitutions did. Further, the good readers corrected their errors more often than did the poor readers.

Several contemporary studies compared good and poor readers from Grades 1 through 6 for their abilities to use context. Let us first consider beginning readers. Biemiller (1970) observed three stages in the development of the use of graphic and contextual information by children who were taught by a whole-word method. (See Chapter 15 for whole-word and phonics methods.) In Stage 1, context guides the children's "wild" guesses: *John was cold, so he put on his hat* (*hat* was read as "sweater" or "glove"). In Stage 2, children prefer to make no response rather than to make wild guesses. In Stage 3, they use both graphic and contextual constraints. Cohen (1974–1975) examined oral reading errors made by Grade 1 children taught by a phonics method. The three stages observed were No response, Nonsense errors, and Word substitutions. Near the end of Grade 1, contextually acceptable substitutes were .70 for good readers, but only .19 for poor readers. Unacceptable errors were .15 for good readers and .21 for poor readers. Good and poor readers differ in the use of subsequent context. Though 90% of the reading errors of both good and poor Grade 1 readers were grammatically acceptable when taken with the preceding text, the good readers were more likely to correct errors that did not fit into the subsequent context of the sentences (Weber, 1970).

Let us now consider older schoolchildren. Christie (1981) studied miscues (oral reading errors) of good and poor readers (one grade level above and below their real grade) from Grades 2, 4, and 6. The percentage of miscues acceptable in context increased as a function of both grade level and reading ability. Self-corrections of unacceptable miscues tended to be higher for the good than for the poor readers (with the exception of Grade 6 good readers, who perhaps corrected silently). Errors of graphic similarity did not greatly distinguish the groups.

Willows and Ryan (1981) studied oral reading by intermediate graders (4–6), who were divided within each grade into skilled and unskilled readers based on the discrepancy between a score on a reading test and a score predicted by IQ. Oral reading errors were scored in terms of syntactic and/or semantic acceptability, both for total context and for preceding context only. Subjects also read text in which letters were transformed, thus preventing automatic word decoding. For this text, corrected errors and nonword substitutions were examined. On every measure scored, the skilled readers were better than were the unskilled readers. But there was no significant improvement across grades in the proportion of acceptable errors. According to the researchers, other studies failed to find differences between skilled and unskilled readers in the use of context, because they compared children at all reading levels in one grade as a group with those in another grade.

A good reader is flexible: He will rely more on graphic than on contextual information for some kinds of task and material. Juel (1980) presented Grades 2 and 3 readers with target words that varied in decodability, frequency, and number of syllables. The words were presented in isolation, poor context, and moderate context:

1. *She sees a couch.* (hard-to-decode, high-frequency word in poor context)
2. *That is a bobcat.* (easy-to-decode, low-frequency word in poor context)

Good readers were predominantly "text driven" (relied on stimuli), whereas poor readers were "concept driven" (top-down, or relied on context), and average readers fluctuated. Note that the readers' task was to pronounce the target words, which could be infrequent and hard to pronounce, on the one hand, and the preceding context available was brief and uninformative, on the other. The best strategy for minimizing errors would be to pay most attention to graphic information. A good reader, being flexible, can adopt this strategy. In these special conditions, Stanovich's (1980) hypothesis holds.

Other researchers also measured pronunciation latencies of target words but used a story as a context (Perfetti, Goldman, & Hogaboam, 1979). Subjects were Grade 5 skilled readers and less skilled readers. The less skilled readers were slower than the skilled readers in pronouncing the target words, whether the words were in isolation or in context. But both groups of readers benefited from context, pronouncing the target words faster in context than in isolation. Schwantes (1981) found similar results, using similar procedures. Furthermore, context had greater effects on the pronunciation speed of Grade 3 children than on that of Grade 6 children.

As Perfetti *et al.* (1979) point out, skilled readers are already so good at identifying words that context is of little consequence. This observation holds also for Schwantes's research: The target words were easy (*her, came, help,* etc.), and so were the three stories (Grade 2 level) that provided their context. In short, simple tasks (oral reading) and material (easy words in short sentences or easy stories) are inadequate for fully revealing the better use of context by good readers than by poor readers.

Goodman (1965) found a developmental trend in the use of context in the first three grades: In a story, Grade 1 children were able to read two-thirds of the words that they had missed on a list; Grade 2 children, three-fourths of the words; and Grade 3 children, four-fifths of the words. In testing a child's ability to use context, Goodman (e.g., 1982) advocates selecting materials that are somewhat difficult for the child.

PREDICTION AND COMPREHENSION

Let us consider tasks that are more demanding than oral reading of easy material. Cloze scores, which reflect how well a reader can restore deleted words in a passage, correlate positively with scores on tests of comprehension (e.g., Divesta, Hayward, & Orlando, 1979; Entin & Klare, 1978; Grundin, Courtney, Langer, Pehrsson, Robinson, & Sakamoto, 1978; see also Chapter 13). Guthrie (1973a) found that disabled readers were inferior to normal readers on a sentence-completion task, which involved selecting one of three alternatives provided (see Chapter 16).

Poor or disabled readers seem to be helped better by training them to read in context than by training them in rapid word decoding. In one study, poor comprehenders in Grades 4 and 5 still remained poor even after extensive training in rapid word decoding (Fleisher, Jenkins, & Pany, 1979–1980). On the other hand, training in context (so as to maintain meaning) was helpful for disabled readers (mean age 10:6) who had achieved at least Grade 2 reading level (Pflaum & Pascarella, 1980).

Mackworth (1977) asked good and poor readers from Grades 2, 4, and 6 to search for the word missing from a sentence such as *He could not carry the* _____. The sentence appeared along the bottom of a slide display. Above the sentence were two lists of three words well separated, one list consisting of nouns (e.g., *books, year, sky*), the other of verbs (*ran, threw, makes*), the missing

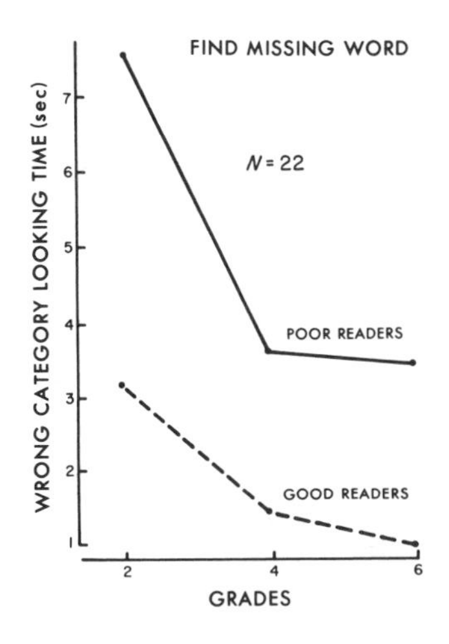

Figure 8-2. *Predicting the last word (a noun or a verb) in a sentence by poor and good readers (from Mackworth, 1977, reproduced with the author's permission).*

word being either a noun or a verb. To do this task, the children must be aware of both syntactic and semantic constraints. In eye-movement data, both the ability and age of the readers influenced the time spent looking at the wrong category: The good readers from each grade spent far less time than did the poor readers, as can be seen in Figure 8-2.

As Perfetti *et al.* (1979) point out, for processing that is more demanding than word pronunciation—such as drawing inferences quickly or encoding an entire phrase or sentence in a brief exposure—skilled readers' superior knowledge of contextual constraints may be a distinct advantage. In studies by Frederiksen (1977, 1978), skilled high school readers, more than less skilled readers, were able to take advantage of context to recognize sentences presented very briefly, at subthreshold exposure. Skilled readers benefited from sentence context even when it provided only subtle cues, regardless of whether the target word was high or low frequency. In contrast, low-skilled readers showed an ability to use context only when it was semantically constraining and the target was high in frequency.

Skilled or older readers can make use of long-range context, such as information from preceding sentence(s), paragraph(s), or a title. In predicting target words, Perfetti *et al.*'s (1979) subjects, skilled or unskilled, did equally well in highly constrained text and did equally dismally in poorly constrained text. But the skilled readers' predictions were more accurate than those of the unskilled readers in moderately constrained text such as the following:

When I got home from work, I wanted to eat a fruit. I went to the refrigerator and got a ____ (pear).

Although the unskilled readers produced 14 of the 16 different words produced by the skilled readers, their total also included 9 items that could not be classified as fruits but that fit the refrigerator constraint (e.g., *cake, pie, pizza*). They used constraints from the current sentence but not from the previous one.

Reading ability is even more strongly correlated with the use of intermediate-range, subsequent information (Divesta *et al.*, 1979). If you were to restore the words deleted in the following paragraph, how would you do it?

> I once had a _____ I suspected of being able to _____ . He was a big _____ with brown eyes with whom I lived in a New York apartment. One day I had just finished writing to a lady whome I loved and left the _____ on the table. I was called to the telephone for a few minutes. When I returned, my cat was sitting on the table examining the letter. I was certain that he had read it.

Poor readers (from middle and high schools) scored somewhat lower than good readers in restoring words deleted in the last half of a paragraph, but they scored much lower than the good readers in restoring words deleted in the first half of a paragraph. When the subjects were stratified into six levels of comprehension skill based on a standard test, there was a linear relation between the skill and the use of context: The higher the comprehension skill, the better the use of subsequent context.

Let us now consider long-range context that spans across paragraphs. In reading a story with 16 paragraphs, Grade 3 children, but not Grade 5 children, made fewer inferences when premises for an inference were located in separate paragraphs than when they occurred in the same paragraph in the story (Johnson & Smith, 1981).

Titles and headings in a passage or a book also exert long-range constraints, as does a reader's knowledge about the subject matter or about the world. The more you know about a subject, either from prior knowledge or from context, the better you can comprehend and recall a passage on it.

In sum, a good reader is more skilled than a poor reader in all aspects of reading, including the use of both graphic information and context.

Summary and Conclusions

A reading unit is what a reader processes as one piece. Small and meaningless units are letters, letter clusters, and syllables; small but meaningful units are bound and free morphemes, and words; the largest units considered in this chapter are phrases.

Which unit is used most heavily in reading? The answer depends on reading task, reading material, and readers' skill. Proofreading demands attention to letters; verbatim recall, to words; and comprehension, especially gist extraction, to clauses and larger units. The more skilled a reader, the larger are the units he can use efficiently.

The more sequentially constrained are letters and words, the larger are the units in which they are processed. The letter string *nrdki* (zero-order approximation to English) is both unpronounceable and meaningless, and must be processed letter by letter. The higher-order approximation, *kindr,* is pronounceable, though still meaningless, and is processed with an efficiency between the zero-order string and the real word *drink*. *Drink*, being short and familiar, tends to be processed as a visual whole by skilled readers. Children become increasingly sensitive to sequential constraints between letters, or orthographic structure, as they learn more words; word learning, in turn, is aided by knowledge of orthographic structure.

A large processing unit enables readers to gather a lot of contextual information at once. To be effective, context must be sufficiently long, syntactically and semantically congruent with a target, and should surround the target; it enables the readers to expect a certain type of item, and what they expect, they perceive readily, with reduced reliance on visual information. The more the readers knows about what has gone and what is to come, the more accurately and speedily they perceive what is at hand.

The efficient use of context entails the use not only of preceding but also of subsequent context, correcting errors unacceptable in this total context, making use of short- as well as long-range context, and much more. Poor readers and beginning readers may in some cases compensate for poor word recognition by excessive but inefficient use of context, but good readers use word recognition and context to aid one another. The good readers' word recognition is automatic enough to leave considerable resources available for the use of context.

To read skillfully is to read in large units, make use of context efficiently, and be sensitive to sequential constrains between letters and words.

9

Letter and Word Recognition

In the beginning was the word, the word
That from the solid bases of the light
Abstracted all the letters of the void;
And from the cloudy bases of the breath
The word flowed up, translating to the heart
First characters of birth and death.

—Dylan Thomas[1]

Two small but basic units of reading in English are letters and words. How are they recognized? If you have not thought about the question, it may seem obvious that people read by recognizing letters and forming them into words. And yet, researchers over the last century have disputed this very view of reading, claiming that skilled readers rarely pay attention to letters in words, although it is possible to do so.

In the first part of this chapter, we show that a letter is recognized by its features, under the influence of neighboring letters. In the second part, we show how a word can be recognized from its shape or from its letters.

Isolated Letters

Although letters might not be individually identified in reading text, enough information must be taken from them to permit words and meanings to be extracted from the page. People are usually able to identify individual

[1]The fourth stanza of "In the Beginning" from Dylan Thomas: *The Poems of Dylan Thomas*, copyright 1953 by Dylan Thomas. Reprinted by permission of New Directions Publishing Corporation.

letters on request (in print, if not in handwriting). There has been a great deal of experimental work on letter recognition; let us follow a few of the main themes.

Fragmental Features versus Configurational Features

A **feature** is some characteristic of an object that puts it in a class with one set of things and differentiates it from another set. For example, an object that possesses the feature "wings" might be a butterfly, an airplane, or a bird, or perhaps even an English country house, but it could not be a person, a tree, or a cloud. If it also possessed the feature of being about 20 cm long, it would not be a house, an airplane, or a butterfly. Identifying enough such features would permit an ornithologist to determine precisely what kind of a bird it might be, although no single feature would give much information.

For letters, we consider two kinds of features: A **fragmental feature** is a part of the letter, such as a "central crossbar," which is a feature shared by 'A, H, B, e' and a few other letters; a **configurational feature** depends on the relationships among the parts of a letter, such as "open on the bottom," which is shared by 'A, H, h, n' and a few other letters. People use mostly configurational rather than fragmental features to recognize letters.

INTUITIVELY DETERMINED FEATURES

The letters of the Roman alphabet have obviously different shapes, but some are more different than others. There is something in common among 'l, d, f, k, b . . . t' that is not shared by 'a, x, s, c, . . . m'. The first group is "tall" whereas the second group is "short." Among capital letters, 'E, T, L, or H' differ from 'O, C, Q, or S', and both groups from 'V' or 'W'. Disregarding ornamental flourishes such as serifs, the first group has only vertical and horizontal straight lines, the second only curves, and the third only diagonal lines. According to some accounts, these differences represent features of the letters.

Features of letters may be described, abstractly and arbitrarily, by looking at them and noticing that some features are owned by this set of letters and some are owned by that set. If enough different features are described, each letter may be uniquely identified by the set of features it owns. For example, the only letter that is short, curved, closed, and without inner parts is 'o'; the letter 'c' shares all these features except "closed." Instead of "closed," 'c' has "open right side," which it shares with 'e'. Another person looking at the letters might select a different set of features to describe them. Lists of this kind, using both fragmental and configurational features, have been produced by many authors (e.g., Gibson & Levin, 1975; Lindsay & Norman, 1972), but psychologically they all have only the validity bestowed by an insightful analyst.

In general, when the type style changes, so do the features that can be ascribed to the letters. If an 'A' is described as having a left diagonal side and a right diagonal side, a sharp angle at the top, and a central crossbar and being open at the bottom, is ᗩ an 'A' or not? Perhaps it would be possible to improve the feature list to describe several varieties of 'A', but a better course might be to do experiments to see what aspects of an 'A' give it its identity.

CUE VALUES OF FEATURES: LOWERCASE LETTERS

Various experiments have given us some information about the probability that one letter is confused with another in different typefaces. Modern statistical techniques can take these confusion matrices and generate groupings of letters that are similar to one another in different ways. By looking at these clusters, it may be possible to see what features they seem to have in common, and in what ways letters that are perceived differently really differ.

Bouma (1971) produced such clusters of similar lowercase letters and analyzed to what extent various proposed features could have accounted for the data. Assuming that the chosen features did play a part, he could determine their maximum influence on letter discriminations. For each feature, he computed a ***maximum cue value,*** which ranged from zero for a cue that could not have discriminated between two given sets of letters to unity for a cue that would have resulted in perfect discrimination. A high maximum cue value proves not that a feature is important, but that it is potentially important: People might not use it, even though in principle it could serve very well to discriminate letters. On the other hand, a low cue value proves that a feature is unimportant

Bouma's highest cue values were mostly for the tall letters:

- tall letter: 0.92 (almost perfectly discriminable from short letters)
- slender letter: 0.90
- left upper extension: 0.89
- right upper extension: 0.88

Among short letters, except for the feature "oblique outer parts," cue values were lower:

- oblique outer parts: 0.92
- shortness: 0.84
- lower gap: 0.80
- double vertical: 0.77
- left part round: 0.74
- upper dot: 0.70

Features such as "filled inside," "gap right side," or "upper gap" had appreciably lower maximum cue values. That is, people do not see them as well as they see the other features. All of the potentially important features were configurational, except for "upper dot," which distinguishes 'i' and 'j' from other letters.

CONFUSION ERRORS ARE NONSYMMETRIC

Bouma's features were based on similarity, which is normally considered to be a symmetrical measure: 'c' is as similar to 'e' as 'e' is to 'c'. If similarity were a valid measure of the confusability of two letters, then confusion errors should be equally likely to go in either direction, unless the observer had a preference for reporting one or other of the letters (a response bias). This is spectacularly not true in real letter confusion data, as Bouma was careful to note.

In one confusion matrix, 'Q' was called 'O' more often than it was given correctly, but the reverse error almost never occurred (Gilmore, Hersh, Caramazza, & Griffin, 1979). No matter what the response bias, 'Q' should still be more like itself than like another letter. In another confusion matrix 'G' was called 21 times when 'C' was presented, but the reverse error happened only once; 'G' was called for 'O' 8 times, with no reverse errors (Kinney, Marsetta, & Showman, 1966). The bias towards reporting 'G' cannot be due to the frequency with which the letters occur, since of all letters, 'O' comes fourth, 'C' twelfth, and 'G' seventeenth in frequency of occurrence (Zettersten, 1969). What then accounts for the bias to say 'G'? The distinguishing feature for 'G' is a little bar or irregularity by the gap. People often see such small irregularities instead of smooth lines if they have to look very carefully at something. Thus, a 'C' can look like a 'G', but this does not mean a 'G' will look like a 'C'. Symmetric similarity measures are obviously deficient in describing such data.

Tversky's Feature-Based Model

Tversky (1977) has presented a recognition model based not on symmetric similarity but on feature sharing and discrimination. In comparing two letters, some features are shared, some not. Four independent factors determine the probability of choosing one letter when another is presented:

- The intrinsic importance of each individual feature
- The importance of having features in common
- The importance of owning a feature not owned by the other
- The importance of not owning a feature owned by the other

Tversky's model is especially valuable, because it can account for two experimental findings: (*a*) it is more important for a letter to own a feature than to lack one, and (*b*) common features make two letters confusable more than different features make them discriminable.

CONFUSION: NUMERALS AND UPPERCASE LETTERS

Keren and Baggen (1981) tested Tversky's model against two confusion matrices. In the first, the figures to be discriminated were numerals, in the bar-segment form much favored for hand calculators and other electronic displays. They chose as (fragmental) features the seven individual segments and were able to reproduce the actual confusion matrix very closely using only 11 parameters to model the 100-element matrix, although the confusions were far from symmetric. In contrast, Luce's (1959, 1963) popular choice model, which involves symmetrical similarity and response biases, required 54 parameters to achieve almost the same degree of fit.

In their second test of Tversky's model, Keren and Baggen used the confusion data for uppercase dot-matrix letters published by Gilmore *et al.* (1979). This test is more interesting, because Keren and Baggen both derived the features and assessed their relative importance from the same data. This procedure has the benefit of being able to demonstrate objectively the relative importance of the selected features. Using a novel multidimensional scaling technique (Sattath & Tversky, 1977), they found 14 important features. In this analysis, the weight of a feature directly represents its importance in making the discrimination, so that a ratio of 10 between two weights means that the higher weight has 10 times the significance of the lower. The 14 important features and their weights were:

VERY IMPORTANT FEATURES

- Diagonal lines not framed by verticals: 2.94
- Parallel vertical lines: 2.53
- Single vertical line: 2.36
- Non-closed letters standing on a broad base: 1.75

MODERATELY IMPORTANT

- Whole figure closed: 1.36
- Circular elements: 1.34
- Horizontal symmetry: 1.21
- Open towards bottom: 1.01
- Facing to right: 0.99
- Upper part closed element: 0.80

LESS IMPORTANT

- Open angle in vertical position: 0.44
- Horizontal line in center of letter: 0.34
- Open towards top: 0.32
- Non-closed letters standing on a broad base: 0.30

Although the most important of these features is more important than the least by almost a factor of 10, even the weakest is stronger than other features that might be used to describe the letters

In both parts of Keren and Baggen's study, items with many features in common tended to be confused, regardless of the features that distinguished them. For both numbers and letters, erroneous responses tended to be due to omission of a feature rather than to the addition of a feature, whether the features were configurational or fragmental. That is, a letter or a number tends to be confused with another that has one fewer feature. For example, in bar segment form, '9' can be turned into '3' by omitting the upper left segment, or into '8' by adding the lower left; '9' is more likely to be seen as '3' than as '8'. The preference for losing features is quite general: It has been noted by Garner and Haun (1978) in letter discrimination studies, and by Healy (1981) in searching a text for misprints.

D. A. Taylor (1976) asked observers to report whether block letters were the same as or different from a probe letter. If the probe had four segments (e.g., 'E'), reaction time was longer and errors more frequent than if it had three segments (e.g., 'H'), but only for the "different" judgments. "Same" judgments were insensitive to the number of segments. In this task, as well, it was easier for a letter to lose than to gain a segment. As with the bar-segment numerals, features in common between two letters diluted the influence of features that differed. This kind of dilution effect has also been observed in perceptual studies far removed from letter recognition. It even exists in the social perception of human characteristics (Nisbett, Zukier, & Lemley, 1981). It implies that we tend to perceive what agrees with a pattern we are looking for, rather than what discriminates among patterns.

Features and Perceptual Processing

Letters and words are identified through perceptual processes that presumably were evolved before humans had to read. One should expect, therefore, that psychologically useful lists of features have something in common among themselves, despite differences in type styles. Effective features are those that can be handled easily by our perceptual processes, and these should not depend on what kinds of letters we are reading, or even whether we are reading alphabetic or logographic characters. Of course, some type styles eliminate the use of some features. One cannot, for example, use ascenders and projections below the line with CAPITAL LETTERS.

GENERALITY OF FEATURES IN LETTER PERCEPTION

There is a difference between descriptive feature lists, which anyone can make up to describe sets of letters, and recognition feature lists, which people actually use in recognizing letters. It is difficult to determine a priori what features are important in recognition, because the process is unconscious. Keren and Baggen's (1981) list of 14 important features covers an order of magnitude in weight. Other obvious features chosen from descriptive lists presumably would have even smaller weights. The exact importance of particular features probably would not be replicated with other typefaces. For example, "circular elements" had a relatively low weight for the dot-matrix uppercase letters. Such a low value might arise in part from the difficulty of simulating circular arcs in dot-matrix letters. With a more classical typeface, "circular elements" might well have a much higher weight, as they did in similarity data for Swedish lowercase letters (Kuennapas & Janson, 1969).

Despite these reservations, Keren and Baggen's strong features for dot-matrix uppercase letters have something in common with Bouma's (1971) high value cues and Kuennapas and Janson's (1969) similarity factors for lowercase letters. "Diagonals not shielded by vertical lines" (e.g., 'w, A, v, Z') are clearly important, as this feature was the strongest in both discrimination studies and was an important factor in the similarity analysis. Double vertical was also important in all three studies, but there is nothing in lowercase letters to compare with the "single vertical" feature, unless it is "tall," "slender," or "upper extension," all of which had high maximum cue values for Bouma and appeared on the similarity factor list. The generality of the feature "tallness" is attested anecdotally by the child who told his teacher: "All I see when I look at a page of print is some tall thin letters and some short fat ones. [W. Watt, 1964, p. 543]."

Similar factors seem to be important in the recognition of Kanji in Japan. Kaiho and Inukai (1982) asked 554 subjects to rate the 881 Kanji taught in primary school on ten descriptive dimensions. A factor analysis of the results gave three major dimensions:

- Symmetric characters with long or rectilinear strokes versus asymmetric characters with short and diagonal strokes.
- Open characters with few strokes versus complex, dense characters.
- Elongated versus square or round characters.

The first of these dimensions corresponds to the "outside diagonal" feature that is important for alphabetic letters, and the third to the "tall" feature. Since alphabetic letters are simpler than most Kanji there is no important alphabetic feature to correspond with the complexity (density) dimension of similarity for Kanji.

Inner parts had low weight in both Bouma's and Keren and Baggen's discrimination studies, and do not appear in Kuennapas and Janson's similarity factor list. They were less important than outer shapes in scanning a text for misprints (Healy, 1981). Even in a strictly perceptual experiment in which subjects had to discriminate differently shaped rectangles with a central horizontal or vertical bar, the central bar was far less important than the outer shape (Keuss, 1977).

Keren and Baggen (1981) observe:

> [Previously published feature lists] have used mainly what may be labelled "basic features," namely, specific line segments, and have included relatively few "global features," which refer to properties of the entire gestalt, such as openness, symmetry, etc. In contrast, the list proposed. . . is mainly composed of global features and relatively few basic features. We speculate that this feature list reflects more accurately the nature of the perceptual process where global features play the more important role [p. 243].

We need a description of the perceptual principles underlying letter recognition, rather than a catalogue of features used for each individual typeface.

LETTER RECOGNITION AS A FOCUSING PROCESS

Lupker (1979) has characterized the growth of information about a letter as a "focusing" process. The perceptual system rapidly acquires gross information about the general shape of a letter (or word, presumably), and over time refines this impression. Lupker used four two-fragment letters ('T', 'L', 'X', and 'V'), their fragments, and four pseudoletters built from pairs of the fragments. He measured the identification of the different items as a function of the time between the onset of the stimulus and that of a masking pattern. The masking pattern was designed to mask all fragment types equally, but its effects differed sharply among fragments and among characters. For all items, recognition increased rapidly with masking delay, up to a delay of about 50 msec, and then increased more slowly to at least 200 msec (the longest delay tested). Fragments were not acquired sequentially, judging from the pattern of confusion errors over time. Rather, the letters were seen as if defocused for the first few milliseconds and gradually focused over time. Lupker's "global-to-local" model may well be a reasonable first approximation to what happens in letter recognition, but it should not be treated as if real focusing were going on.

Rather than defocusing, Brady (1980) invokes a series of five visual channels that detect edges at different resolutions. The resolution of each channel varies as a function of position within the visual field, all having good resolution in the fovea, and progressively coarser resolution in more peripheral regions (Marr, 1976, 1982; Marr & Hildreth, 1980). If the model is correct, then Lupker's (1979) results might be accounted for by successive invocation of finer channels. The finer the channel, the longer it takes to gather the information it requires. Letter (and word) choices may be suggested by information from the early, coarse channels, and the choices finalized by improved information from the finer ones. In the parafovea, the resolution of the finest of the five channels is adequate only to see the overall shape of the words in the neighborhood of the next fixation, and sometimes to identify the first and last letters. Interference from their neighbors prevents the identification of internal letters of words in the parafovea.

Successive refinement of resolution by no means denies the value of a feature analysis of the letters. It simply provides a mechanism whereby one can understand the greater importance of the outsides than the insides of the letters. For example, the outside diagonals may be important because there is no external masking element to disturb early detection of the diagonality. With adequate viewing time and large enough letters, internal features can be clearly seen. These features are not usually necessary, however, because before they can be seen, the letter or word has already been identified from its grosser configurational features.

TWO PROCESSES IN LETTER RECOGNITION

An additional explanation for the focusing effect involves two cooperating processes. A quick process takes a gross view of the letter as a whole, concentrating on its outer shape and the balance of its parts. This process is essentially complete by 50 msec. The second, slower process analyzes the parts of the letter, possibly using the results of the first process as a guide. It may take as long as 200 msec. Evidence for the two processes comes from a number of studies. In D. A. Taylor's (1976) letter-matching experiment, the reaction time for a "same" judgment was fast and was independent of the number of segments in the probe letter; for "different" judgment, reaction time was longer, the more segments in the probe letter.

Jones (1982) presented letters for identification in one or the other visual half-field. He distinguished two groups of subjects, one who were better with LH processing (right visual-field presentation), the other with RH processing. The two groups showed quite different error patterns: The RH-preferred group tended to confuse letters with similar outer shapes, whereas the LH-preferred group confused letters which differed in the placement or presence of a feature. Only 4 of the 26 different two-way confusions ('M–W', 'O–Q', 'C–G', and 'F–P') were made by both groups.

Two processes also seem to be involved in perception of simple free-form shapes: A wholistic matching process is responsible for similarity judgments, whereas an analytic difference-detection process is responsible for checking identity judgments (Cunningham, Cooper, & Reaves, 1982). Subjects differed in the extent to which they used the analytic process, but not in their use of the wholistic matching process.

Throughout the next few chapters, we shall find examples of such cooperating process pairs. One is always a fast, global process preferred by the RH, the other a slower, analytic process usually performed by the LH. At higher levels of processing, the evidence for two processes is stronger and comes from more diverse sources (see Chapter 11).

Letters and Lines in Context

We have analyzed in detail the recognition of a single letter, despite our belief that a normal reader rarely performs this task consciously. We did this because the principles that apply to letters can be extended to words, at least in some degree, and because the notion of feature will turn out to be important in dealing with words. The features of the letters within a word may be crucial to recognizing the word, even though the individual letters are not fully identified. In this section, we still deal with letters, now in the company of other letters or letter-like forms. Studies on the recognition of letters among other letters show two strong but opposed effects: the word superiority effect and lateral masking.

Word Superiority Effect

The basic statement of the **word superiority effect** (WSE) is: Letters are better perceived in words than in strings of unrelated letters. For example, 'C' is more easily perceived in the context 'ACE' than in the context 'VCH'. This effect has been shown in a variety of situations in which the detection of individual letters has been made difficult by masking, by shortening the presentation time, or by blurring the print. The WSE occurs whether the letters are lowercase, uppercase, or mixed in case or type style.

The WSE has also been found when letters in words are compared with isolated letters. Reicher (1969) observed that letters may be easier to detect in words than by themselves. His results have since been replicated several times (e.g., Carr, Lehmkuhle, Kottas, Astor-Stetson, & Arnold, 1976; Johnston & McClelland, 1973). The WSE has also been found for Japanese Hiragana syllabics (Miura, 1978), demonstrating that the effect does not arise only from the words being pronounceable, as was suggested by Spoehr and Smith (1975). Hiragana syllabics are individually quite pronounceable, and so are nonsense strings made from them

The WSE has been found under tightly controlled observing conditions (Purcell, Stanovich, & Spector, 1978; Purcell & Stanovich, 1982). The observer had to determine whether a 'C' or a 'P' was presented in the context 'ACE–APE' or 'VCH–VPH', knowing exactly where the target letter would be presented, and what the two possibilities were. Important factors in determining whether the WSE occurs are the overall size of the stimulus display and the interletter spacing. Of these effects, interletter spacing is probably the more important. Whenever the letters in a string are separated by more than about one character-width or so, context effects such as the WSE are much reduced. Such a space is the distance between words in normally typed text, although in print the interword spacing may be smaller.

The WSE often disappears when the subjects know where in the letter string the alternatives will appear. It was at first expected that the WSE would vanish under these conditions because performance would improve with the nonword strings when the subject knew just where to look and what alternatives there might be. In fact, when the WSE did vanish, it was for the opposite reason: Focusing on a particular location caused performance with the word stimuli to drop to the nonword level. The observers seem to concentrate on just the position they will be required to judge, eliminating possible beneficial influences when the letter string is a word, while retaining the detrimental effects of lateral masking (Holender, 1979; Johnston, 1981; Silverman, 1976; Spector & Purcell, 1977).

WORD SUPERIORITY EFFECT WITH MUTILATED WORD SHAPES

The WSE occurs even when the letters are in a variety of type styles, mixed in case, or even in mixed Cyrillic and Roman script, though with diminished strength (Adams, 1979; Feldman & Kostic, 1981; Friedman, 1980; McClelland, 1976). That the WSE occurs at all under these conditions shows that letter identities are used in word perception; that the size of the effect is diminished shows that the visual shape of the words is also used.

Subjects sometimes cannot report which font a target letter is in, despite being sure which letter it is. In Friedman's (1980) experiment, subjects were especially asked to observe the font. On rare occasions they became quite disturbed because they knew which letter had been presented (say, a "gee") but could not tell which of two very dissimilar shapes ('G' or 'g') it had been. Despite the rarity of this problem, the fact that it could happen even occasionally is interesting. In Adams's (1979) study, which used quite bizarre letter shapes, subjects sometimes reported seeing the correct words, in normal print! At least from the subjects' point of view, the words were being perceived through the abstract representation of the letters, and not simply through the general shapes of the words. The letter shapes they perceived must have been reconstituted from a knowledge of the letters' identities, which itself might have been based in part on recognizing the words.

INDEPENDENCE OF LETTER AND WORD RECOGNITION

Johnston and McClelland (1980) predicted and found another situation in which the WSE did not occur when it might have been expected. They compared the recognition of a letter within a word with its recognition in isolation. They presented the targets in a T-scope for a brief duration, followed by presentation of a mask. The character of the mask was a strong determiner of the size of the WSE: If the mask consisted of letters or words that appeared in the place where the target had been, little or no WSE was found; if, however, the mask consisted of quasi-letters made with the scrambled parts of real letters, then a strong WSE was observed. Johnston and McClelland (1973) had previously found that failure to mask the stimulus led to equal recognition for single letters and letters in words. Introduction of a patterned mask that hardly affected perception of a letter in a word substantially reduced the detectability of single letters. Different masks seem to interfere with different stages in word recognition.

In a series of studies, Jacobson showed that the masking of words and their constituent letters could be drastically varied by changing the character of the mask (1974, 1976; Jacobson & Rhinelander, 1978). Words were poorly masked by associated words but strongly masked by homophones. Disoriented or broken letters were poorer maskers for words and for letters than were strings of complete letters. Letters, but not words, were strongly masked by strings of geometrically similar letters, whereas words were more strongly masked by randomly chosen letter strings. Most interestingly, words were poorly masked by letter strings that were anagrams of the target word. Using a different procedure, Kolers and Katzman (1966) presented the letters of a word sequentially. With rapid presentation, the words were recognized better than were their letters, but with slow presentation, the reverse was true.

These results show that there must be at least two interacting stages in word recognition: One at which letters are analyzed and another at which words are recognized. It is possible to recognize a word by way of its letters or the letters by way of the word. In normal reading, words seen during one fixation will not be masked by the words fixated at the next. Stimuli presented for a very short time are susceptible to backward masking from masks presented several tens of milliseconds later, but stimuli presented for more than 100–150 msec are not (e.g., Di Lollo, 1980). The 30-msec duration of the saccade is sufficient to protect the pattern perceived in one 200-msec fixation from being disrupted by the next. Masking studies on the WSE are important for sorting out the various processes that occur in word recognition, but they do not apply directly to effects that might occur in normal reading.

Related Context Effects

LINE-IN-LETTER EFFECT

If letters are more easily detected and identified in the context of a word than by themselves, then what about the parts of a letter? In the **line-in-letter effect,** letter fragments are more easily identified when they are part of a letter than when seen by themselves. Consider, for example, the letters 'N' and 'H', written in a simple block style, consisting of two verticals connected by a diagonal or a horizontal stroke respectively. The only difference between the 'N' and the 'H' is the location of the connecting stroke. The presence of the vertical lines should not affect a subject's ability to discriminate between the horizontal and the diagonal stroke, but it does. Under conditions where subjects could discriminate 'H' from 'N' at over 90% correct, they could barely make 60% correct in discriminating the strokes presented without the vertical lines (Schendel & Shaw, 1976).

The line-in-letter effect is itself an example of a general but sometimes elusive perceptual effect whereby a line in the context of other lines is discriminated sometimes better and sometimes worse than the same line by itself (Earhard, 1980; Earhard & Armitage, 1980; Pomerantz, Sager, & Stoever, 1977; Williams & Weisstein, 1978).

LATERAL MASKING

Lateral masking refers to diminished perception of an object when something else is nearby in the visual field. It is a fundamental property of vision, not just a property of letter recognition. Visual acuity for simple targets is reduced when other edges are nearby in the visual field. For example, Flom and Weymouth (1963) measured visual acuity using the Landolt C figure. This procedure is one of the most basic tests of visual acuity. For subjects with both good and poor eyes, acuity was drastically reduced by the presence of a black bar near, but not too near, the target. The most effective distance between the bar and the target was proportional to the acuity for the individual subject. The distance involved was similar to the distances among letters in normal text read at a normal distance.

Lateral masking is affected by the similarity between target and masking letters or forms. If the target letter has as neighbors forms with similar features, it will be masked more than if it has dissimilar neighbors. For example, White (1981) tested the ability to discriminate a circle from a square when the target was flanked by forms like an elongated 'D', made from half a square completed by a semicircle. Circles were harder to see when the round side of the

'D' faced them than when they were flanked by the straight side. For squares, the situation was reversed. Using letters, Santee and Egeth (1980) found an 'A–E' discrimination harder when the letters were surrounded by a frame of similarly sized "tic-tac-toe" marks than when surrounded by a frame of 'P' characters. Discrimination of 'B' from 'R' was worst with the surround of 'P's. Wolford and Chambers (1983) showed that lateral masking had several causes: feature interference was prominent only when the letters were close together; distribution of attention was more important for wider spacings; and perceptual grouping affected accuracy of target location at all levels.

The lateral masking effect is pronounced for letters. Under some experimental conditions, flanking the target letter by two others can reduce its correct recognition score from perfect to 40% correct. Even when letters are spaced well apart, they can interfere with one another. According to Bouma (1970), the effect can extend over as many as five to eight letter spaces. Lateral masking must be reckoned with in any account of reading that asserts the basic units of recognition to be letters (see Bouma, 1978, for a review).

Text is apparently laid out badly if the object of reading is to identify letters. Fortunately, that is not at all the object of reading; the object is to get the message in the text.

Feature Detectors

The initial processing of letters is thought to be done by a series of **feature detectors,** starting in the retina and continuing in the cortex. A feature detector is a processing unit that responds to some property of its input: If the input pattern looks like the one to which the detector is tuned, it will respond strongly; otherwise, it responds less strongly or not at all. The input pattern might be an edge, a horizontal line, or something more complex, depending on the processing stage. These feature detectors are interconnected in a fairly regular way, in a hierarchy of levels.

Feature detectors should not be confused with the features of letters, discussed earlier. It is unfortunate that the same word *features* has been applied to two related but different concepts. The letter features are properties that the letter either has or does not have, whereas the feature detectors respond in a ***graded*** way to patterns matching to a greater or lesser degree the patterns to which they are tuned. It is quite possible, and even likely, that there exist feature detectors whose patterns correspond to the important letter features, but there is no a priori reason for such a correspondance.

PANDEMONIUM

Selfridge's (1959) recognition system, "Pandemonium," is based entirely on hierarchically organized detectors called "demons." Each low-level demon looked out for some aspect of a pattern, such as a diagonal line. For example, if a letter 'X' was presented, then the low-level demons looking for left-diagonal, right-diagonal, and crossing lines would all shout, but the demons looking for vertical lines, horizontal lines or curves would be quiet. A demon at the next level looking for 'X' would shout very loudly, and the demons for 'V' and 'A' and perhaps 'W' would shout less loudly. The top-level demon would decide that 'X' had happened.

Selfridge's demons did not talk to one another, except to their superior officers, and Pandemonium was only moderately successful, at least for complex patterns. It was, however, influential and has served as the basic concept for many subsequent pattern recognition schemes. We will not attempt to cover the hundreds of simulations, theoretical analyses, and applications based on similar devices, often called "Perceptrons."

Two major concepts were missing from the original Pandemonium and early Perceptrons: lateral inhibition and feedback.

FEATURE DETECTORS, FEEDBACK, AND INHIBITION

Lateral inhibition (mutual inhibition among detectors at the same level) can be used to make the set of detectors adapt to the type of input currently being encountered, in such a way as to make the most efficient possible analysis of the data. In other words, with lateral inhibition used appropriately, the detectors are able to tune themselves to those features that most effectively describe the data (M. M. Taylor, 1973). It is not clear whether this kind of dynamic tuning happens with low-level feature detectors. It may well be that there are sets of feature detectors that have mutual inhibitory connections and sets that do not. In our Bilateral Cooperative model of reading (see Chapter 11), we propose that there are two kinds of linked process: one with inhibition and one without.

Feedback can have important effects in controlling what is detected by feature detectors. If a higher-level detector anticipates a pattern, either because of a tentative version coming from the lower levels or because of contextual expectations, it may send feedback to the lower-level detectors feeding into it, so that they would become more sensitive to their own patterns. Contextual expectation can, of course, be expressed in just the same kind of feedback from an even higher level detector. This kind of feedback would have the effect of confirming noisy or uncertain patterns, a process known as "perceptual clarification" when it occurs in humans (M. M. Taylor, 1974). It would also give rise to the some of the contextual effects discussed in the following chapters.

McClelland and Rumelhart (1981) use feedback as an important component of their model for the word superiority effect. In their model, visual feature detectors (for lines, edges, and so on) feed into letter detectors, which in turn feed into word detectors. Features inappropriate to a letter inhibit the detector for that letter: A horizontal line is incompatible with an 'I', so the horizontal line detector will inhibit the 'I' detector. Also, the different letter detectors inhibit one another: If a 'G' was detected, there could not have been an 'H' at that position. Feedback comes from higher to lower levels: If there is some evidence for 'N', then the vertical line and the diagonal line detectors will be sensitized, and the rest of the 'N' will be readily detected. The model has been simulated by computer under various assumptions about the degree of inhibition and excitation provided by the various kinds of interconnection. It gives reasonable results in explaining the WSE and some other phenomena. The model can explain the finding that the WSE occurs if the feature detectors are masked by letter fragments, but fails to occur if the letter or word detectors are masked by letters or words (Jacobson & Rhinelander, 1978; Johnston & McClelland, 1980).

What about features inconsistent with the detector? In most of McClelland and Rumelhart's simulations, inhibition was given quite a high weight. In fact, the existence of one feature incompatible with a letter was sufficient in some cases to eliminate that letter from consideration. Their inhibitory possibilities ranged from three times to about half the excitatory value, depending on whether the simulated subjects were expecting words only or were anticipating some pseudowords. Their high inhibition values have the function of letting only assuredly correct letters into their word-level detectors. These high values, however, conflict with experimental evidence we presented earlier: In human perception, incompatible features usually play a much weaker role than do compatible features (Healy, 1981; Keren & Baggen, 1981; Nisbett *et al.*, 1981).

McClelland and Rumelhart's model explains certain basic properties of word recognition and has already become popular, but it is not a fully adequate model. It does not account for left–right scanning, the effects of letter positional probability, outside-in recognition, or location uncertainty of features and letters. These aspects of word recognition are discussed later in this chapter.

To conclude, feature detectors transform the patterns of light and dark on the page into something resembling an abstract representation of letters and possibly words. Each detector responds to its own special pattern more than to others. Detectors may interact with one another through mutual inhibition and by feedback from higher levels. Feature detection is reasonably complete by 50 msec (Lupker, 1979), although word recognition may not be. Feature detection forms the first stage of letter and word recognition but is not the whole story. In the second half of this chapter, we argue that word recognition may sometimes be based directly on patterns of letter features detected by word detectors but that other ways of recognizing words may be even more important.

Contextual Effects: Interpretation

Context can either mask or enhance lines in letters or letters in words. It may seem paradoxical that stimulus patterns so nearly alike should produce such different effects, but the effects can be reconciled. First, we show that the WSE is perceptual, and does not arise from higher-level cognitive processes.

NOT "SOPHISTICATED GUESSING"

A once popular model known as "sophisticated guessing" says that the target is in some way more predictable in an appropriate context than by itself. According to this model, the observer sees the letter no better (and no worse) in context than by itself, but the context restricts the number of reasonable responses. For example, if the stimulus was 'ACE', and the observer saw 'A' 'something round' 'E', the only reasonable (word-making) responses for the "something round" would be 'C' or 'G'; without the context, however, the same partial perception of 'C' could lead to responses 'O', 'Q', or 'G'. In context, the observer might get 50% correct, as compared with 25% correct when the letter was presented by itself. For the letter-in-word effect, at least, this model appears to be untenable.

Geoffrion (1976) looked for tendencies to give word responses to nonword (three-letter) stimuli, and vice versa. If the sophisticated guessing model were correct, subjects would tend to give word responses where they were unsure of a letter, more than they would the reverse. This possibility, however, did not happen; if anything, there was a tendency away from word responses, despite the subjects showing the usual WSE.

Purcell *et al.* (1978) went to great lengths to control all kinds of uncertainty in their stimuli. In all conditions, the subjects knew they had to distinguish between, say, a 'C' and a 'P' and knew also just where the target letter would be presented. The only variation in the stimulus was that sometimes the letter was presented in the context 'A–E' and sometimes in the context 'V–H'. In both conditions the context letters had similar shapes. Despite these precautions, 'ACE' and 'APE' were more distinguishable than 'C' and 'P', and these in turn were easier than 'VCH' and 'VPH'.

Silverman (1976) required subjects to discriminate between letter strings, knowing both what and where the alternatives would be. Word strings differing by two letters were more easily discriminated than were word strings differing in only one letter. For nonword strings, on the other hand, it made no difference whether they differed in one or two letters. If letters in words were identified independently, or if nonwords were seen as simple visual patterns, there should have been no difference between words and nonwords.

When Johnston (1981) told his subjects exactly where the target letters would be, identification of letters in nonword strings improved. Identification in words declined, however, to the point that no word advantage remained. Paying particular attention to a letter position both reduces lateral masking (in the nonword strings) and eliminates the benefits of the letter being in a word. To obtain the WSE, the subject must pay attention globally to the word.

The WSE is a perceptual phenomenon, although one can imagine other, postperceptual processes that further enhance the word advantage if circumstances permit. A letter is ***perceived*** differently in a word than it is by itself.

UNCERTAINTY OF FEATURE LOCATION

The context effects have been explained by theorizing that feature detectors compete with one another, or that spatially neighboring similar features inhibit one another (Bjork & Murray, 1977; Bouma, 1970; Estes, 1975; Walley & Weiden, 1973; Wolford, 1975). The inhibition of ***spatially neighboring*** feature detectors is not the same as the mutual inhibition of detectors for different features in the ***same spatial*** location. Logically, two incompatible features cannot occupy the same place, so it makes sense for their detectors to inhibit one another. But there is no logical reason why two detectors for similar features in nearby places should inhibit one another, as these researchers suggest. Whether features do inhibit similar neighbors is a matter for subtle experimentation.

An alternative explanation hinges on **location uncertainty:** Features of objects, including letters, are not well located in their initial processing; features are coalesced at a later stage into meaningful objects and in the process may get replicated, combined, or misplaced so that they produce a result different from the way they were initially sensed (e.g., Gilmore, 1980; Mason, 1978; Treisman, 1977; Treisman & Gelade, 1980). Treisman calls the combination of features into something that was not there "illusory conjunction."

These two views, mutual inhibition and location uncertainty, may be reconcilable, as follows. Regard the feature detectors as being much like the point detectors of the retina. If two points of light are too close, they seem like one point. Similarly, if two identical features are physically too close, they can be confused. If the context requires a feature to be near a second similar feature, then the visual system cannot easily tell whether there are one or two of them, and may mislocate them if it does detect both. The feature analysis of words may result in a floating field of features, tied only loosely to their proper locations, as a field of buoys may move around even though anchored to the bottom of the sea.

Estes (1982) has examined his own and other studies that bear on feature inhibition and location uncertainty. He concludes that the similarity of neighboring letters to the target has no effect on the ability to discriminate the target from a specified nontarget letter Thus, 'DOD' is no harder to distinguish from 'DQD' than 'HOH' is from 'HQH', although both 'O' and 'Q' are detected more readily when flanked by 'D' than when flanked by 'H'. If the subject is just trying to guess which letter is present, features from the neighboring letters will bias the subject to guess that the target is a letter with those features ('DOD' will bias the subject to guess 'O' or 'Q' rather than, say, 'K', whereas 'HOH' will bias the subject against guessing either 'O' or 'Q'). It is as if a vague impression of the features of neighboring letters was added to the initial perception of a letter: If it truly had the same features, they would be perceived more quickly and surely, whereas if it did not, their absence would be detected only slowly and with less certainty. Estes did find evidence for location uncertainty of recognized letters, as well as of features, but the effect was not important to his results. Estes's work pulls together similar results obtained by other researchers, all of whom concluded that location uncertainty accounted for their results better than did mutual inhibition of neighboring features (e.g., Gilmore, 1980; M. Mason, 1978; Santee & Egeth, 1980).

Wolford and Shum (1980) looked deliberately for feature migration across symbols, using letter-like forms in which migrating features would cause a distinct pattern of errors. They found evidence both of feature location uncertainty and of location uncertainty for correctly recognized forms. Butler and Morrison (1982) concluded that errors scored as feature migration were simple errors unrelated to the neighboring characters. Their characters, however, were about twice as large as characters seen at a normal reading distance, and were separated by two whole character widths. Both the large character size and the wide intercharacter spacing would have reduced or eliminated any featural drift that might normally occur. Interletter spacing has to be normal for the WSE to occur and for words to be recognized well in actual reading (as will be discussed shortly).

Not only features but also letters can be uncertain in their perceived locations. A letter recognizer (letter-level feature detector) will gather features that might belong to its letter, provided that they are not too far away; if it claims a detection, the location of the letter itself may well not be certain. A word recognizer similarly will gather letters and features appropriate to itself and try to fit them if they are not too far away from where they belong.

According to Estes (1975), both the WSE and lateral masking might arise from the possibility that letters could be transposed in perception (e.g., "ate" for *tea*). Geoffrion (1976) showed that many errors in reporting constrained three-letter strings were in fact a result of letter transposition. These errors were more likely when two irrelevant flanking letters were added at the ends of the string. Mewhort and Campbell (1978) showed that transposition errors for letter strings were independent of the order of approximation to English, in contrast to intrusion errors, which decreased with the more wordlike higher orders of approximation. (See Table 8-2 for examples of different orders of approximation to English).

The effect of context probably has several causes, besides the uncertainty of feature location. One obvious possibility depends on the outside-in focusing discussed earlier. Letters seen in isolation differ in both their low- and high-resolution patterns. When they are seen in company of other letters, their low-resolution patterns are mixed with those of the neighboring letters and are therefore less useful for discrimination, but the high-resolution patterns remain useful. In a word context, two things happen: First the distortions of the low-resolution patterns have a familiar form, and second the word itself may be recognized from the high-resolution components. Both effects could result in a WSE. If the neighboring letters do not form a word, and if they are orthographically irregular, the low-resolution pattern of the letter may interfere with recognition, causing the lateral masking effect.

Context effects are important at higher levels of reading, where uncertainties other than spatial location must dominate, and visual resolution cannot be a factor (see Chapters 8, 11 and 12). Indeed, context effects seem to occur quite generally in perception. For example, if one takes a photograph of a scene and cuts it into smaller (but not too small) squares, objects that fall wholly within one of the small squares will be less well identified if the squares are randomly rearranged (Biederman, 1972). Effective perception demands an appropriate contextual frame. Featural location uncertainty or variable resolution may explain the WSE and lateral masking, but are too specialized to explain context effects in general perception and in reading.

WORD SUPERIORITY EFFECT AND LATERAL MASKING: SUMMARY

A letter presented by itself is perceived with some measureable speed and accuracy. Other shapes nearby make the letter more difficult to perceive, unless those other shapes are letters that combine with the target letter to form a word. The decrement in perception is called lateral masking, the improvement, word superiority effect. These effects disappear if there is extra space between letters in the words or nonwords, if the letters are too big, or if the pattern is rapidly masked by a pattern of letters or words. None of these exceptional conditions apply in normal reading, where the letters are small and close together and the time between fixations is too long for effective masking. Apparently, reading is done under conditions that maximize both the WSE and lateral masking.

Both lateral masking and the WSE can be understood in terms of location uncertainty of features and letters. If feature detectors (and letter detectors) gather their information from a fairly wide area, then two effects happen: First, the detectors do not know precisely where in the visual field the pattern that they detected occurred, and second, they find it difficult to distinguish between two or more occurrences of the feature they detect. When the stimulus pattern is a real word, the mislocation of features or letters does not matter much, because the overall pattern is one that is known to belong to that word. If it is not, then the constituent letters must be extracted from a mush of interfering features, any of which could conceivably have come from the letter being examined.

The word superiority effect may also be derived from feedback between word-level detectors and letter-level detectors and between letter- and feature-level detectors. Such feedback could serve to clarify the perception of the individual letters by fixing the location of uncertainly located features or letters. These "fixed" features might then provide less interference to neighboring features than "floating" features would do. Such a reduction in masking would occur in addition to any clarification of letters or features arising from the redundancy of letters in words.

Word Recognition

Since we have examined in detail the problems of identifying letters, let us now consider the other extreme in word identification, the shapes of words as a whole. Later we shall bring letters into words, and present an overall view of how words may be recognized.

Readers' Use of Word Shape

Word shape can be analyzed into word length, initial and final letters, internal features, and outer contour. Do people use word shape to help them recognize words? Both anecdotal evidence and experimental studies suggest that they do.

MISREADING

In normal reading, people occasionally misread words. Sometimes they realize their misreadings, and other times they do not. Next time you realize that you have misread a word, stop and analyze your misreading. How does it differ from the correct, printed word? Flesch (1949) was reading Arnold Toynbee's *Study of History* late at night after a tiring day. He was suddenly pulled up wide awake by a word that simply did not belong in Toynbee. The word was *horseradish.* "We know very little about them, but we know that they produced, in Pelagius, a heresiarch who made a stir throughout the Christian world of his day [p. 184]." Insup Taylor read *current belief* as *correct belief.* One of Sigmund Freud's patients was so anxious to have a baby that she habitually misread *stocks* as *storks.*

People also tend to read misprints as correct words. Pillsbury (1897) found that misprints were detected most often at the beginning of a word, and least often in medial positions. If the word exposed with a misprint was *foyever,* subjects might read it as *forever.* The misprint *fashxon* was seen as *fashion*, and *verbati* as *verbatim.* Sometimes the misprinted words were seen as if they had flecks of dirt or other marks on them.

In one's misreadings, unfamiliar words tend to be read as familiar words, and pseudowords as real words. Interestingly, these tendencies are among the more marked effects shown by the phonemic dyslexic patients who cannot derive sounds from the letters of words, and who may substitute erroneous words for similarly shaped words (see Chapter 11). There are also much higher level, motivational effects, as Freud's example demonstrates.

For whatever reasons words are misread, the misread words tend to preserve the initial and final letters and approximately the length of the printed words. These are precisely the elements that are visible in peripheral vision during the previous fixation and could have been processed at that time (see Chapter 7).

WORD LENGTH

Recall that Flesch misread *heresiarch* as *horseradish*, a discrepancy in length of 1 letter in 10. For long words, people can estimate length only approximately; for more common, shorter words, they tend to substitute words of the same length for those misread (*storks* for *stocks*; *correct* for *current*). In errors made in reading transformed (rotated or mirrored) text, substituted words and printed words were approximately the same length (Kolers, 1970).

How accurately do people estimate word length in experiments? For long words (more than 10 letters), Zeitler (1900) found that people added, on average, about 1 letter in a misreading. Modern studies have reached the opposite conclusion: Erroneous word responses are generally shorter than the correct word by a small amount (Bouma & van Rens, 1970; Nooteboom & Bouma, 1968). In agreement with these results, Schiepers (1976a, 1976b) found that subjects underestimated letter strings presented in a T-scope by 5% for real words and 10% for nonwords. In simply estimating the number of letters in a string, they underestimated by 15%. Saying the number of letters is not equivalent to saying a word that has the wrong number of letters, so these two kinds of study may not be directly comparable.

OUTER CONTOUR

The outer contour, or "envelope," of a word is defined by the sequence of tall letters, short letters, and letters that project below the line. It is roughly the same as a casually drawn outline of the word. For example, the outer contour for *dog* is the same as for *bay* (tall–short–projecting). To study the use of outer contour, several researchers asked children and adults to select the string most like a target nonword such as *cug* from the set *owj, jun, cqg* (Marchbanks & Levin, 1965; Rayner & Habelberg, 1975; Williams, Blumberg, & Williams, 1970). The stimuli might be 3-letter or 5-letter nonwords. If the subjects selected *owj*, they used the contour as the cue. Prereading kindergartners used outer contour as much as they used the first letter, but Grade 1 beginning readers used it much less than the first letter. With 5-letter stimuli, poor Grade 1 readers ignored contour altogether, but good Grade 1 readers used it together with the initial letter. Adults again used outer contour effectively, but less than they used the letters in the strings.

Haber and Haber (1981) report that deleted words were somewhat better restored if their contours were provided than otherwise. They point out that the syntactic and semantic constraints, along with the word contour, more often than not provide a unique choice among all possible common English words of the same contour. It would be hard to gather statistical evidence to support this assertion. In a later study, restoration of some types of function words was improved from about 50% to nearly perfect when length and contour were provided. Restoration of most other parts of speech increased by about 10% when length was provided, and another 10% when contour information was added (Haber, Haber, & Furlin, 1983). Letters really do not seem to be needed for recognition of some function words in context.

College students reading a passage of text were able to report misspellings in 81% of the cases in which outer contour was changed but in only 68% of the cases in which it was maintained (Ehrlich & Rayner, 1981). In the same study, misspellings were much more likely to be detected if they involved the initial letter of a word than if they involved a middle or ending letter. Haber and Schindler (1981) examined proof reading errors for three different classes of words in text, both when the misprint preserved the outer contour and when it did not. For long content words, it did not matter whether the misprint preserved the word contour. The probability of missing the error was about 25% in both cases. For short (three to four letters) content words and for function words, contour did matter: In both kinds of words, contour-preserving errors were missed twice as often as contour-changing errors. Misprints are missed twice as often in function words as in content words of similar length, no matter what changes in contour the misprint causes.

Contour is used, at least in reading short words. It is especially important for function words: In many cases, people identify the function word only by its outer contour, even when the readers are looking for misprints. Presumably the use of the outer contour would be even more pronounced if they were just reading for sense.

McClelland (1976) used a T-scope to present words, pseudowords, and nonwords in mIxEd CaSe or in the same case. Mixing the case reduced accuracy in reporting words and pseudowords but did not affect nonwords. Words were better than pseudowords in all conditions but were more strongly affected by case-mixing. Both the visual appearance of the words and the identities of their letters affected word recognition.

WORDS WRITTEN IN CAPITAL LETTERS HAVE NO VARIATION IN OUTER CONTOUR, EXCEPT FOR LENGTH AND POSSIBLY SOME SLOPE OR CURVATURE ASSOCIATED WITH THE FIRST OR LAST LETTER. READING CAPITAL LETTERS BECOMES QUITE TEDIOUS AFTER A WHILE, AS ANYONE KNOWS WHO HAS SPENT A FEW HOURS READING COMPUTER PRINTOUTS WRITTEN ALL IN CAPITALS. CAPITAL LETTERS DO HAVE INTERNAL FEATURES, BUT AS WE HAVE SEEN, THESE ARE HARDER TO DISCRIMINATE THAN ARE EXTERNAL FEATURES. NEVERTHELESS, THEY ARE WHAT WE HAVE TO DEAL WITH WHEN WE READ TEXT WRITTEN IN CAPITALS.

Although it is tiresome and tedious to read long passages of capitalized text, short texts in capitals can be read almost as quickly as normal text. Even material written in AlTeRnAtInG cAsE can be read almost as fast, provided the interword spacing is normal. If, however, the interword spaces are filled with nonletter signs or, worse, eliminated, then text written in CAPITALS or aLtErNaTiNg CaSe is very much harder to read than normal text with similar treatment of the spaces (Fisher, 1975). Contour apparently makes it easier to see the shapes of words in such a text, so that the words can be partially segregated before the letters are recognized. Compare for yourself:

Thisisapieceofelidedtextinnormalprint
WHICHISQUITEHARDTOREADBUTNOTASHARDASTHIS
AnDcErTaInLyEaSiErThAnThIsMeSsWhIcHiSvErYhArD.
ItmightbebetterifContentWordswereCapitalized.
bUtitismUChhaRderifthesizekeepSchaNging

The last example is from Kolers and Rudnicky (1982), who find that changes in size can also have a strong effect on readability.

INTERIOR FEATURES

Distorted text is obviously harder to read than normal text, but some distortions matter more than others. Try to read the following two garbled sentences:

1. Il ix easj tc sqct miatakes.
2. Earors mre tarler to sxe.

Most people find sentence 1 easier than 2, despite that it contains 7 errors in 21 letters, compared with only 5 errors in 20 letters for sentence 2. Each sentence maintains the outer contour (sequence of tall, short, or projecting letters). In 1, it is easy to spot mistakes, because the distorted words have the same "Bouma shape" as the originals, whereas in 2, errors are harder to see, because the letter substitutions are from a different class. Table 9-1 shows the seven groups of mutually confusable lowercase letters found by Bouma (1971).

The **Bouma shape** of a word can be defined by listing the group numbers of its letters: *at* has the shape *16* (short–filled, tall–thin), and *dog* is *527* (tall–fat, short–round, projecting). Words with the same Bouma shape (*dog, beg; met, not*) tend to be confused.

Using text distorted in different ways, Frith (1979) examined the relative importance of word shape and sound for rapid reading. The distortions and the corresponding reading speed were:

- (Fast)—Mix up the type styles of the letters but keep the same letters.
- (Fast)—Change the letters, but substitute only ones from the same confusion group
- (Slow)—Change letter clusters for ones with the same sound but different appearance.

Table 9-1 *Bouma's Seven Groups of Letters*

Short	Tall	Projecting
1. a s z x	5. d h k b	7. g j p q y
2. e o c	6. t i l f	
3. r v w		
4. n m u		

If either the letters in the word or the general shape of the word were maintained, reading speed was quite good. Identifying the words from their sounds was substantially slower than it was from their shapes. Unfortunately, Frith did not include a condition that maintained the outer contour of the words while distorting the interior shape, as in our second example sentence earlier.

Internal features of letters do play a role in recognizing a word, albeit a smaller role than outer contour. Rayner and Kaiser (1975) asked college juniors and Grade 4 children to read text that had been mutilated in various ways. When the letters had been replaced with letters that shared features and hence were visually similar, subjects took less reading time and made fewer errors than when the words had been altered by replacing letters with letters that were not so visually similar.

SHAPE, LETTERS, AND SOUND

The Stroop effect refers to the interference by a word, such as *red,* on naming the color of the ink (green) in which the word is printed, but the term has been expanded to cover other similar interferences, such as the fact that a word written inside a picture can interfere with naming the picture.

Rayner and Posnansky (1978) used the picture–word Stroop effect to study the early stages of word recognition. They masked both the word and the picture with a pattern of overlapping 'I', 'X' and 'O' characters after a brief exposure. In six experiments, they varied the visual, the phonological, and the semantic character of the "word," which was in most cases a nonword distortion of the word that would correctly label the picture. For example, if the picture showed a horse, the letter string might be *horse*, *hcnae* (keeping the shape and the initial and final letters), *hgpke* (keeping initial and final letters but not the shape), and so forth, through many variations. They also controlled the phonetic similarity between the "word" and the appropriate label, by using pseudo-homophones (*hauce*).

Rayner and Posnansky measured only the time it took to name the picture under the various conditions. The picture was named fastest if the word was the appropriate label and slowest if it was an inappropriate label. The nonword distortions of the correct label gave intermediate naming times for the picture, and different distortions had their strongest effect at different exposure durations. Comparing all their results is a complex business, but our reanalysis of their data suggests the following statements to be reasonable (we will use *horse* as an example):

- Stroop effect with incongruous label (*radio*) At an exposure time of 20 msec, the Stroop effect increased naming latency by 100 msec; the effect increased by 75 msec for each doubling of exposure time up to the longest exposure tested, 160 msec. (All exposure times are given as increments over a threshold exposure for identifying the picture, usually about 20 msec.)

- Outer contour same as correct label (*kcnas*) For short exposures, nonwords sharing the outer contour with the appropriate label gave response latencies perhaps 20-30 msec shorter than nonwords with a different outer contour. The outer shape affects word perception early if at all, and by 160 msec, its effect has vanished.
- Initial and final letters same as correct label (*hgpke*) This manipulation produced a stronger effect than outer contour, improving latency by about 50 msec for short exposures, but like outer contour, it had no effect for 160 msec exposures.
- Initial and final letters as well as shape (*hcnae*) For exposure durations less than 80 msec, this was as good as the correct label. Apparently, middle letters are not seen until 80 msec into the presentation.
- Anagram keeping initial and final letters same (*hrsoe*) If the nonword was constructed from the correct label by scrambling the middle letters, then there was an improvement over just keeping the first and last letters, but only for exposures at least 80 msec long. (No longer exposure was used in this test.) This result shows in a positive way that the middle letters really are used after 80 msec.
- Phonetic similarity (*hauce*) If phonetic similarity had any effect, it was only beginning to show up by 160 msec exposure.

Visual recognition processes can operate on outer contour in combination with outermost letters, though not very effectively on contour by itself. Wrong contours inhibit correct recognition, but correct contours are insufficient to produce it. Contour and outer letters are used early, before the inner letters can be recognized. Next, all letters are recognized, and, finally, much later, the sound of the word begins to take effect.

Information Available from Different Refinements of Shape

What aspects of word shape uniquely identify a word? This question can be answered from analyses of text and has nothing to do with how readers actually use the available information. Consider the word *dog*. It has a shape, which can be defined at various levels of precision:

- At the coarsest level, it is three letters long: *dog = the.*
- With little more refinement of description, it has a contour defined by a tall letter, a short letter, and a projecting letter: *dog = lap ≠ the.*
- Still more refinement may take into account the gross features of the letter forms, such as Bouma shape: *dog = beg ≠ lap.*
- At the most refined level of shape description, the actual letters of the word are listed: *dog ≠ beg.*

To supplement data available in the literature on word shape, we conducted some statistical analyses of the text of this book, at a particular stage in its drafting. In our analysis, we used only the words that had no capital letters

Table 9-2 *Distribution of Word Length in this Book*

Length	Number of tokens	(%)	Number of types	tokens per type
1	4440	(3.0)	1	4440
2	25,285	(17.1)	30	842
3	26,304	(17.8)	237	111
4	22,308	(15.1)	645	34.5
5	15,433	(10.4)	852	18.1
6	11,617	(7.8)	1054	11.0
7	12,620	(8.5)	1104	11.4
8	10,959	(7.4)	1106	9.9
9	7069	(4.7)	909	7.8
10	5614	(3.8)	761	7.4
>10	5722	(3.8)	1149	5.0
Totals	147,371	(100)	7848	18.8

(thus eliminating names, acronyms, and words that started sentences; we also eliminated foreign words and nonsense words). At that stage, there were about 147,000 valid word tokens, consisting of 7848 different word types. First, we analyze word length, as shown in Table 9-2.

The table shows that there are, for example, 1054 different words of 6 letters, but only one of 1 letter. Word length, by itself, is sufficient to identify only one word type, namely "a." The table further shows that there are more 3-letter tokens than tokens of any other length, and that there are more 7 or 8 letter types than longer or shorter ones. Shorter words are repeated more often than longer ones, as the column "tokens per type" shows. On average, a 3-letter word is repeated 111 times in the book, but an 8-letter word is repeated only about 10 times.

WORD LENGTH PLUS INITIAL LETTER

Dunn-Rankin (1978) asked adults to sort into groups words they thought looked most alike. The stimuli were 100 words chosen from a newspaper article. The subjects based their groupings firstly on the initial letter, then on the length, followed by particular word endings like *-ing* and *-ed*, and only lastly by internal letters. Dunn-Rankin suggested that word length plus initial letter might contain enough information to identify most words. To test this idea, he examined elementary school textbooks and found that all but about 1% of the words could be uniquely identified. Analysis of our own book has a different result, probably because of the much larger number of word types involved. Only 44 of our 7848 different words (0.6%) have a unique combination of word length and initial letter. There were only 321 different combinations, over half (182) of which contained at least 10 word types, and over 50 contained more than 50 different word types.

Word length plus initial letter is certainly not adequate to identify many words uniquely. It does, however, provide a lot of information. Even in a very poor case, it serves to reduce the number of possibilities from over 7000 to around 100. With appropriate context, a unique identification might sometimes be possible using just the initial letter and the word length.

OUTER CONTOUR AND BOUMA SHAPE

Bouma (1970) analyzed the most frequent Dutch words in terms of their outer contour. Counting the *N* most frequent words (those with frequencies greater than 1 in 10,000, 2 in 10,000, 5 in 10,000 or 1 in 1,000), approximately 30% had unique outer contours within their own frequency group. Another 25% were defined down to two or three possibilities. Our analysis of this book agrees closely with Bouma's numbers. Approximately 30% (2304 of 7848) of our words have a unique outer contour, and 20% more are defined down to two or three choices. Allowing for contextual constraint, probably a considerable proportion of the words in an actual text could be identified purely by their outer contour. In our calculations on this book, we found the probability of words having the same outer contour plus the same initial letter, following Dunn-Rankin's suggestion: 4088 of the 7848 types (52%) are uniquely determined, and another 27% are determined down to two or three choices.

What aspects of the contour provide the information? For the outer contour, the top half of the word carries much more information than does the bottom. The amount of information is measured in **bits.**[2] In our analysis of this book, letters were distributed 33% tall, 61% short, and 6% projecting. Information in the upper contour is about 0.9 bits per character (not allowing for contextual constraints), whereas in the lower contour it is only 0.33 bits. When the two are combined, the total contour information is 1.20 bits per character. According to Garner (1962), the information value of each character in words is 2.02 bits on average. Assuming that contour information, like letter information, is 50% redundant, we may guess that contour carries about 0.6 bits per character, leaving 1.4 bits to be provided by further processes of identification.

Huey (1908) pointed out that the upper half of a lowercase word is more important than the lower half. This effect is often illustrated in science books for children, where sentences may be displayed with the top or bottom half blanked out. The importance of different parts of the word varies in different scripts, and probably across languages using the same script. For example, in Hebrew letters, the lower parts are more important than are the upper

[2]A bit is a unit of information, the amount you can get from a single yes–no choice if each alternative is equally likely. For example, a coin toss can give one bit of information. With two yes—no questions, one can decide among four (2^2) choices; with three questions, among eight (2^3). Put another way, four equally likely possibilities can provide 2 bits of information, eight can provide 3 bits, and so forth. The roll of a die, with 6 possibilities, gives between 2 and 3 bits. Redundancy is the amount by which the information is reduced below what is possible from a given set of choices. If a 'q' appears in English text, it is almost certainly followed by 'u'. Almost no information is conveyed by the 'u', and the redundancy is almost 100%. Selections from the 26 letters of the alphabet could give over 4 bits of information each, but in English orthography the redundancy is enough to reduce the information by about 50%. (See also Chapter 8, "Constraints Between Letters").

(Shimron & Navon, 1980) and the left halves more than the right (Navon & Shimron, 1981), both characteristics being opposite from English.

If we refine the shape definition another stage and group those letters found especially confusable by Bouma, most words become uniquely identifiable. We know of no such counts other than our own analysis of this book. Among our 7848 word types, 6953 (88.5%) are uniquely determined by their Bouma shape, and another 10% are determined to within two or three choices. From the viewpoint of information theory, the Bouma shapes are substantially better than are the outer contours. Not considering redundancy, they carry 2.66 bits per character, compared with 1.20 bits for outer contour. Allowing for 50% redundancy, they probably carry 1.33 of the 2.02 bits available per character in words.

When we add information about the initial letter to the Bouma shapes of the words, almost all words are uniquely identifiable (94.6%). More to the point, 97.3% of the shapes correspond to a unique word, and all shapes but one determine the word down to two or three choices. If a reader can see the Bouma shape and the initial letter of a word peripherally, in principle only 1 in 40 shapes need be examined foveally to identify it exactly.

Table 9-3 shows the occupancies for different kinds of shape. For example, consider the number *452* in the second column of the line "outer contour." There are 452 different outer contours, each of which has 2 words of that contour. Put another way, there are 904 words (452 × 2), each of which has a partner with the same outer contour. Now consider the number 15 in the fourth column of the line "Bouma shapes." There are 15 Bouma shapes, each of which has 4 words of that shape. For example, the shape *5271* (from Table 9-1) has *begs, hogs, boys,* and *bogs,* and *565* has *bid, did, kid,* and *hid.* Finally, consider the last entry of the same row, the 1 in column 7: There is only 1 shape that has 7 words: *5216* (the words are *beat, heat, deaf, boat, best, host, deal*).

LATERAL MASKING AND SHAPE DISTORTION

In explaining the WSE and lateral masking, we invoked "location uncertainty," the idea that there is often uncertainty as to just where in a word a letter or letter feature may be located. Furthermore, it is difficult to see how many times a feature or letter is repeated. A word like *little* (Bouma shape *666662* in Table 9-1) has five consecutive letters from the same confusion class. To see how important this problem might be, we did a new analysis in which no letter class is allowed to occur more than twice in a row, by eliminating all occurrences after the second: *little* would now belong in the same compressed Bouma shape group (*662*) as *lie, tie, tile,* and so forth. One might expect a drastic reduction in the proportion of words with unique compressed Bouma shapes, but the reduction was actually small: from 88.5% to 87.3%. It seems that the length of sequences of similar letters is of little consequence.

Text could, in principle, be read when the letters are too small, blurred, or distant to be consistently identified correctly, provided their gross features could be seen. These are the conditions that prevail during parafoveal viewing

Table 9-3: *Occupancy Number for Different Classes of Word Shapes*

	Number of Word Types Sharing the Same Shape									
Type of shape	1	2	3	4	5	6	7	8	9	10+
Outer contour	2304	452	209	103	64	48	40	19	16	91
Outer contour plus initial letter	4088	694	248	113	55	35	21	17	11	23
Bouma shapes	6953	323	50	15	4	2	1	—	—	—
Bouma shapes plus initial letter	7431	185	14	1	—	—	—	—	—	—

of words to be foveated at the next or the second following fixation. Word recognition does not require letter identification, except, possibly, for the initial and final letters.

HANDWRITING

Handwriting could be considered as distorted print, although print is actually a way of systematizing (and speeding) writing. The overall shape of a handwritten word is usually like that of the printed word, in that the sequence of tall, short and projecting letters is preserved. Often the first letter is quite legible in isolation, but depending on the elegance of the hand, the other letters may be missed, or misshapen, or be represented only by one or two salient features. It is frequently unclear exactly where one handwritten letter ends and the next begins. Nevertheless, people can read most handwritten material.

In a T-scope experiment, handwritten words were recognized only 26% of the time, whereas printed words were recognized 41% of the time under the same conditions (Corcoran & Rouse, 1970). These results were obtained when either printed words or handwritten words were presented with none of the other kind in each block of recognition trials; when printed or handwritten words might follow one another at random, the recognition probabilities dropped drastically, to 14% and 19% for handwritten and printed words respectively. However, when words in upper and lowercase print or in two widely different types of handwriting were intermixed, there was no difference, or possibly even some improvement, over the blocked presentation. There must be at least two different strategies for word recognition, one used mainly for print, and one for handwriting.

Ford and Banks (1977) studied the reaction time for determining whether a presented word had been one of 2, 3, 4, or 5 previously given. The more words in the memory set, the longer was the reaction time, a standard result in the memory literature. If the presented word was handwritten, the reaction time was about 100 msec longer than if it was printed, regardless of how many words were in the memory set. To see whether this difference was due to extra time needed for recognizing the handwritten word, the researchers asked subjects simply to name the presented word. Again, handwritten words took about 100 msec longer than printed words.

Does practice in reading a particular handwriting help in reading that specific hand? It does to some extent, but reading one's own handwriting is not necessarily easier than reading somebody else's. Some people are good writers; their handwriting is easy for everyone to read. Others are good readers of handwriting; they can read what most people write. But how easy it is to read one's own handwriting depends on how good a writer and reader one is. Practice in reading one's own very bad handwriting may help one to become a good reader of any bad handwriting (van Jaarsveld, 1979).

In reading handwriting, one problem is not knowing where the boundaries lie between letters and between words. Van Jaarsveld (1982) has investigated the effects of irregularities in the rhythm of handwriting. Taking a naturally written letter string or word, he systematically varied the width either of a letter or of an interletter connection, and asked subjects to recognize the string or word. Variations within the letter seemed to be more disruptive than variations in the space between connected letters.

Figure 9-1 has been prepared following a suggestion by Bouma (1982). It shows that one does not need much more than shape and the initial letter to read handwriting in context.
If one looks at Figure 9-1 from a distance, it resembles normally legible (illegible) handwriting. Most people can read it after a little trying. Close up, however, the only thing that is left is one or two wiggles to represent each letter, plus the initial letter itself and projections above and below the line. Real handwriting is more legible. It contains features approximately correctly placed to represent most of the letters, so it is closer to the Bouma shape representation than to the outer contour plus initial letter shown in Figure 9-1. To recognize handwriting one needs no more than letter features in roughly the right places; presumably to recognize print requires no more precision.

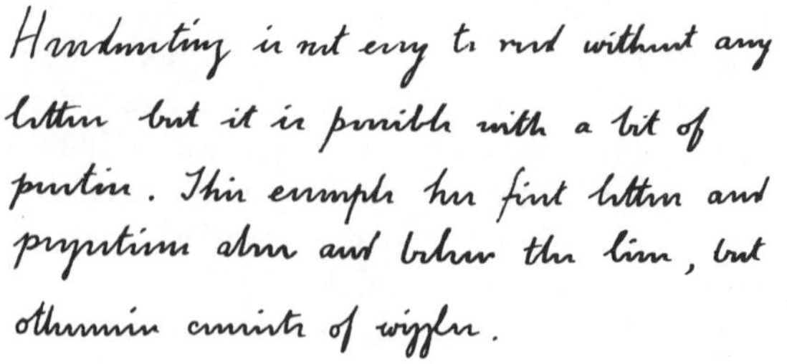

Figure 9-1. *Handwriting is not easy to read without any letters but it is possible with a bit of practice. This example has first letters and projections above and below the line, but otherwise consists of wiggles (example prepared following Bouma's suggestion).*

READING WITHOUT KNOWLEDGE OF LETTER SHAPES

People can read even when they are unable to name the letters that compose the words. Over the years, Kolers and his associates have experimented on reading transformed material, in which the letters and words are rotated, inverted, or mirror-imaged. In the experiments discussed here, the individual letters were inverted (flipped upside down but not rotated), leaving the words otherwise unchanged.

Kolers and Magee (1978) required subjects either to read several pages of inverted text or to name the scrambled and spaced-out letters of the same text. Both groups were very poor at their respective tasks initially, but both learned rapidly. After several sessions, the letter-naming group was switched to reading. There was little transfer from one task to the other, although they did learn to read a bit faster than the original reading group had done. After several more sessions, both groups were asked to name inverted letters. There was no detectable transfer from the reading task to letter naming: The reading group was as poor at naming as the naming group had been before training. As for the naming group, they had not improved since they transferred to reading. Whatever had been accomplished by training in reading, it was not familiarity with the individual letters. Relatively fluent reading requires familiarity with the shapes of words, but not with the letters in those words.

In a second study, the material was first- or fourth-order approximations to English, presented with normal letter spacing (Kolers *et al.* 1980). The more word-like fourth-order letter strings (e.g., *wallylof* or *edesener*) were learned faster than were first-order strings (e.g., *yrulpzoc* or *eapmqzcn*) and transferred better to reading. Neither type of training transferred to naming spaced-out letters. In a second experiment, training with spaced letters in a first-order or fourth-order approximation did not transfer to reading normally spaced letters, and there was no difference between the orders of approximation. (Remember, spacing the letters was enough to eliminate the word superiority effect.) In a final transfer stage, changing the typeface of inverted letters was more important than was the order of approximation in initial training.

It is possible, but unlikely, that the subjects identified the individual letters without learning to name them when they were reading the transformed text. More probably, they learned the way features group in words and the way certain patterns of features correspond to certain letter groups or words. Identifying letters in isolation is a different task from reading, but practice in seeing letters grouped the way they are in text can help reading.

Letters need not be identified for a word to be recognized, but they are useful, as we discuss in the following section.

Word Recognition from Letters

Bouwhuis has developed a theory of word recognition based on the identification of individual letters. His theory predicts well the accuracy with which each three-letter Dutch word is recognized and deserves serious consideration (Bouwhuis, 1979a; 1979b; Bouwhuis & Bouma, 1979).

POSITIONAL PROBABILITIES OF LETTERS: DUTCH

Bouwhuis's theory looks at the confusion probabilities of letters in each successive position of the word, in an appropriate visual context. Of all the letter patterns thus derived, some will represent words. For example, the word *cut* might possibly be seen with the 'c' altered to an 'e', and the 'u' to an 'a', giving *eat*, or with the changes 'c' to 'o', 'u' to 'i' and 't' to 'l', giving *oil.* There are many possible words, some of which will be generated by highly probable confusions, such as 'c' to 'e', some by improbable confusions such as *cut* to *hag.* The probabilities for the word confusions are given by the combined probabilities of the letter confusions.

Bouwhuis refined the simple model in two ways. First, he took into account the probabilities that the different letters occur in particular positions of the words. In Dutch three-letter words, over 80% of the first and last letters are consonants and over 80% of the middle letters are vowels, and the probabilities of digraphs (letter-pairs) are highly predictable from those of the individual letters. Second, he allowed for the fact that readers are not equally familiar with all three-letter words. Although Dutch has 713 three-letter word types, the average subject was familiar with only 493 of them. Hence, not all the words will be likely to occur as responses from a given subject. In English, *col* would be an unlikely response to *cut*, although the letters are readily confused and *col* is a real word (a depression in the ridge line of a mountain, possibly forming a pass). On the other hand, *out* is a very likely response, based on both confusion and familiarity. Of course, it is hard to think of a sensible textual context in which either *col* or *out* would be a likely substitute for *cut*

In the Bouwhuis model, the effects of lateral masking are taken into account by gathering confusion data in the appropriate visual context. A real three-letter word is transformed into a nonword by changing either the middle letter or the two outer letters. The changed letters are always selected from the same Bouma confusion groups as the original letters, so that the one to be tested has almost the same visual context as it does in the real word. Confusion matrices can then be generated from the results, with separate matrices for each visual environment, and used to predict letter confusions in reading the word.

Bouwhuis's model depends solely on letter recognition and does not require an independent word recognition process. There are a certain number of words in a recognition lexicon, and one will be selected by a given stimulus pattern with a probability dependent only on the probability that its particular letters will be identified from the input.

POSITIONAL PROBABILITIES OF LETTERS: ENGLISH

The probability of occurrence for a given letter changes drastically as a function of its position in the word. Tables of frequencies of letters and letter groups have been published (Massaro, G. A. Taylor, Venezky, Jastrzembski, &

Lucas, 1980; Mayzner & Tresselt, 1965; Mayzner, Tresselt, & Wolin, 1965a, 1965b, 1965c).

We have analyzed the draft of this book to look for strong or unexpected positional probabilities of individual letters. We counted the number of occurrences of each letter at each position in a word, counting either from the start or from the end of a word. Overall, of course, some letters are more common than are others. As everyone knows, 'e' is by far the most common letter. In the book draft, 'e' outnumbers the second most common letter, 't', by 95,386 to 66,164. This is not true at several positions in the word, however. The letter 'e' is only fifteenth most probable as the first letter of a word and fourth most probable in the third position from the end (beaten out by 'i, a, t').

If we consider the probability of a letter occurring in a given position only as compared with its overall probability, there are large variations across positions in words. Some of the anomalies for this book are shown in Table 9-4.

Almost three-quarters of all occurrences of the letter 'y' are the last letter of a word, and over half of all the occurrences of 'h', 'b', 'd', and 'j' are at a particular position in a word. There are many other anomalies not listed in Table 9-5, that are probably known implicitly to skilled readers, though most would be a surprise when pointed out. The rarity of 'm' and 'w' in the last position may be a surprise, since it is easy to think of words like *show*, *now*, *seem*, *him*, and so forth, but these words hardly appear in this book (*show*- occurs often, but usually with the addition of -*s* or -*ed*). A comprehensive list of positional frequencies for letters, digraphs, trigraphs and tetragraphs for words of seven or fewer letters has been published (Massaro *et al.*, 1980). In that analysis, 'w' and 'm' are indeed rare last letters, except in three- and four-letter words, in which they occur reasonably often as the last letter.

According to Bouwhuis (1979a), positional probabilities of letters in Dutch are used in assessing the familiarity of letter strings that might be

Table 9-4 *Positional Frequency Anomalies for Letters*

High Probability Positions for Letters			
Letter	Position	Probability	Comment
y	last	0.74	
h	second	0.61	*th- sh- wh-*
b	first	0.57	
d	last	0.51	*-ed*
j	fourth	0.51	??

Rare Positions for Letters

Letter	Position
b f h j k o p w	sixth and later positions
a b c i m u v w	last
c d g k m	second
j p q	last three positions
y	sixth to second from end

words, and thereby in identifying the words. For English, as well, M. Mason (1975) concludes: "The orthographic structure of strings of letters can usefully be defined in terms of the spatial frequency of individual letters within the string, ignoring the successive order of the letters [p. 164]." In other words, sequential constraints among letters matter less than do letters' positions in words, considered independently of one another. Mason showed that skilled Grade 6 readers make more use of such positional frequency distributions than do unskilled readers, both for words and for nonwords. Mason's results were confirmed in an experiment that controlled for her confounding of positional frequency with orthographic regularity (Massaro, Venezky, & Taylor, 1979).

Henderson and Chard (1980), in a lexical decision task, varied the positional frequency of single letters. In this task, the more a letter string deviates from any familiar word, the faster subjects can decide that it is not a word. Children from both Grades 2 and 4 made faster decisions on nonwords with low (*kugafp*) than with high positional frequency (*turild*). The two groups differed in one respect: Grade 4 children could reject nonwords with low positional frequency regardless of absence or presence of vowels (*sprnth; juwfac*), but Grade 2 children's rejection was faster for nonwords with vowels.

Bouwhuis (1979b) and M. Mason (1975) both found that positional frequencies of digraphs (letter pairs) gave no improvement over positional frequencies of letters in predicting how well words are recognized. Massaro *et al.* (1980), on the other hand, found that digraph frequencies gave better prediction of their results than letter frequencies, perhaps because they used longer letter strings. People may be aware of patterns of digraphs in different positions, but for three-letter words digraphs just do not matter much.

The positional probabilities could often be used by a reader to guess an imperfectly seen letter. A tall letter at the end is very likely to be a 'd', and at the beginning a 't'. Two tall letters at the beginning of a word are probably 'th-', and a word beginning 'short–fat tall–fat' probably starts 'wh-'. A projecting letter at the end of a word is most likely to be a 'y' but might well be a 'g' (in *-ing*).

WORD FREQUENCY AND FAMILIARITY

The words and nonwords used in lexical decision and word-matching experiments tend to be short, and the real words are usually of high frequency. C. P. Whaley (1978) collected lexical decision times for 100 words and 100 nonwords that were less restricted than those used by previous researchers. He calculated multiple regressions for the words and nonwords separately. For the words, by far the most powerful predictor was frequency; the next was richness of meaning (a composite factor involving the number of associates a word elicits, concreteness, imagery, and age of acquisition); and the third predictor was the number of syllables in a word. By contrast, for nonwords, and perhaps for new or unfamiliar words, the important predictor was interletter probability structure (degree to which letters in sequence follow predictable patterns).

The **familiarity** of a word is measured by the proportion of people who know it; the frequency is measured by counting the number of times a word occurs in ordinary texts. Bouwhuis (1979b) showed that familiarity was more important than frequency. He used a lexical decision experiment that included all official Dutch three-letter words. Of the 713 words, subjects on average knew only about 493. Neither response speed nor familiarity varied as a function of word frequency between over 1000 and 10 per million. Over this range of high frequency, familiarity was uniformly high, 95%. For words of a frequency less than 10 per million, familiarity averaged 60%, and responses were appreciably slower. When response times were plotted as a function of familiarity rather than of frequency, there was a smooth increase in time as familiarity decreased.

To determine the familiarity distributions of words and nonwords, Bouwhuis used the probabilities of incorrectly judging nonwords to be words, in a signal detection analysis.[3] The familiarity of a nonword, like that of a word, was taken to be the proportion of subjects who "recognized" it as a word. Regular and irregular words were narrowly distributed, but the regular nonwords were more familiar than were the irregular ones. Words had twice as wide a range of familiarities as did nonwords, and their familiarity distribution overlapped the nonword distributions at the low end.

Also in a signal detection paradigm, the confidence with which subjects of different verbal ability discriminated words from nonwords was shown to correlate well with their verbal scores on the Scholastic Aptitude Test (Zimmerman, Broder, Shaughnessy, & Underwood, 1973). As in Bouwhuis's study, the distribution of familiarity for words was twice as wide as that for nonwords. Associative strength and word frequency were the most important variables in producing "word" responses, but orthography and pronounceability also played a part.

Hayman (1983) gave subjects a lexical decision task preceded by a dummy task in which half of the words and half of the nonwords had been used. He also used a signal detection analysis and found that visual, orthographic, and semantic factors all played a part in the lexical decision. If the subjects had seen the visual shape before, they were biased toward calling it a word (faster responses and fewer errors for words, slower responses and more errors for nonwords). The same applied, but less strongly, if the letters were maintained but the typeface changed.

[3]Signal detection analysis allows for the possibility that one may be uncertain as to whether a string is a word or a nonword. It separates the response into two underlying processes: A discrimination process that determines how well words can be distinguished from nonwords, and a bias that determines how willing the subject is to say "yes" when uncertain. In the analysis, stimuli can be arranged along some continuum that defines the discrimination. Stimuli falling above some threshold receive a yes response, others receive a no. In the case of Bouwhuis's words, this continuum provided another way of defining "familiarity."

In Butler and Hains's (1979) study college students with large vocabularies were faster in word naming but were slower in lexical decision than were subjects with smaller vocabularies. Presumably, the extra words in the larger vocabularies of the good readers were all of low frequency and hence were difficult to discriminate from nonwords. The good readers' extra words may have slowed their lexical decision, as the association levels required for a yes decision to a word would necessarily be rather low. The large vocabulary subjects were also less affected by word length than were the small vocabulary subjects, suggesting that they take a more wholistic approach to word recognition.

Lexical decision differs from word recognition during normal reading in an important respect: A reader assumes that the pattern of letters on the page represents a word, and tries to determine which word it is; in lexical decision, the subject decides whether the pattern of letters is a word at all. A misspelled word is a word when one is reading, but not in a lexical decision task. We pursue this matter further in Chapter 11.

LEFT-TO-RIGHT SCANNING

Words are defined by the order of their letters. This statement seems too trivial to make, but it is worth making because it touches on an important point in word recognition. When the eye is fixated on or near a word, all its letters are available at the same time, but they are not always used simultaneously in identifying words. For English readers, there is a left-to-right scanning pattern which seems to be invoked in phonemic coding, but not in direct visual recognition of the word.

The **scan-parse** mechanism links letters from left to right, presumably developing the phonetic code as it goes along. Here is a set of experiments that demonstrate a left–right scan-parse mechanism. Mewhort, Merikle and Bryden (1969) masked the left side or the right side of first-order and fourth-order approximations to English before the other side was masked. Delaying the left-side masker enhanced the effect of approximation order for letters on the right, but the reverse did not hold. Lefton and Spragins (1974) replicated and extended this result, showing that both the speed of processing and the effect of approximation order increased with age. No matter what the age, however, the effect of approximation order was almost zero if the stimuli were masked after only 50 msec. The stimulus had to be presented for at least 100–150 msec for the higher order of approximation to be effective. Performance continued to improve up to about 200 msec.

When arbitrary visual stimuli are presented in rapid visual sequence, there is a tendency for English-speaking subjects to see them as being presented from left to right rather than the reverse. Right-to-left time differences in the presentation of two circles had to be about 10 msec longer than left-to-right time differences in order to be equally discriminable from a simultaneous presentation (Sekuler, Tynan, & Levinson, 1973). There may be a perceptual, rather than a linguistic, explanation of the scanning effect.

Using letter groups as well as letters, Mewhort and Beal (1977) showed that syllables can be important in integrating the letters of a word. They presented the potential units of the word (individual letters or letter groups) laid out either in the normal left-to-right order or reversed (by letters, ORDER might become REDRO; by groups it might become ERORD). They then showed the letters or groups sequentially either from left to right or from right to left. In this way, words could be shown in the right spatial order but the wrong temporal order, or vice versa, or with both spatial and temporal order correct or reversed. For letters, performance was poor at 125 msec spacing regardless of the spatial layout or time order, and if the time order were reversed the performance remained poor for all longer spacings. For spatially reversed letters, however, performance improved when the spacing reached 250 msec in right-to-left presentation order. With letter groups, reversing the temporal order caused difficulty no matter how the letters were grouped, but if the groups were syllables, the effect of reversing the order could almost be eliminated by lengthening the intergroup interval to 500 msec.

These results give the impression that syllables can be used as a unit in integrating the letters of a word, and that this integration can be performed in at least two different processing levels. When the syllables are presented in reverse order with sequential delays of 250 msec between them, they interfere in some way with one another. If the delay is longer, however, they can be processed into some internal (presumably phonetic) form and integrated at a higher level. Nonsyllabic groups cannot be processed individually and so cannot be prepared for this higher-level integration process. If they are to be integrated, it must be done visually. As Di Lollo (1980) has shown, all the parts of a stimulus pattern must have their onset within 100–150 msec for such visual integration to occur.

Left-to-right scanning is important only if the stimulus is displayed for some 150 msec. It is no coincidence that this time is the same as that needed for phonetic coding to begin, because the scanning pattern is part of the phonetic coding process (Rayner & Posnansky, 1978; see "Shape, Letters, and Sound" earlier in this chapter; see also Chapters 10 and 11).

OUTSIDE-IN ANALYSIS

Letters are visually perceived from the outside inward, as we discussed earlier. The same process happens for words: In addition to being scanned left to right, words are processed from the ends in toward the middle. Outside-in-analysis is a much quicker process than left-to-right scanning and may be part of the direct visual recognition of words, as well as a stage in letter recognition.

Butler (1978) asked subjects to report all the letters they saw in five- or eight-letter strings masked by blank squares after 100 msec presentation. About 50 msec into the presentation, however, one of the letters might have been abruptly changed. No subjects reported seeing the change, though occasionally both of the two letters in the altered position were reported. Subjects were more likely to see the original letter if it was near the end of the string and to see the replacement near the middle of the string. The outer positions were apparently processed earlier, within the first 50 msec, and the middle positions later.

Using the Stroop effect with T-scope exposures, Rayner and Posnansky (1978) showed that the middle letters of words were used only after about 100 msec, whereas the initial and final letters were used as early as 40 msec into the exposure. Several other studies agree in showing that the outer letters are used before the inner ones, at least in 4-letter words. Typical timing delays in these experiments have been around 50 msec, rather than the delays of 100–300 msec that affect left-to-right scanning (e.g. Bradshaw, Bradley, Gates, & Patterson, 1977; McCusker, Gough, & Bias, 1981).

Keuss (1977) reached a similar conclusion in an experiment using nonverbal material. He asked subjects to compare two simple patterns composed of a rectangle with an internal line. The outer shape was detected much faster than the orientation of the inner line and could interfere with detection of the line orientation, whereas the line did not interfere with judgment of the outer shape. He observes: "Subjects appeared to perceive outline aspects of figures, formed by size and form, wholistically. An internal characteristic, such as an interior line, was apparently processed as a separate attribute [p. 371]." Also working with nonlinguistic figures, McClelland and Miller (1979) concluded that "perceivers use processing heuristics . . . for determining the structure of the final figure, working primarily from the outside in [p. 221]."

In word recognition, as well as in general figure perception, there appear to be two processes: One works fast on the outsides and structurally important elements of a shape, including the initial (and possibly the final) letters of words; the other performs a slower analysis of the whole structure or word. If a stimulus is presented in such a way as to prevent the use of familiar shape, or if a letter string does not form a word, then only the slower analytic process is available.

Paths to Word Recognition

We have mentioned only a handful of the overwhelming number of studies on word recognition. How çan we make sense of all this confusion? We must accept that word recognition, which seems so easy when one reads, is truly complex. Any model that can be written down is probably oversimplified. All the same, we will rush in where so many before us have trod, and try to describe what we think happens during word recognition.

WHOLE-WORD PROCESSES

There are clearly two separable ways of dealing with letters and letter strings: One deals with the whole word as a familiar pattern, the other with its parts. The same word may be processed as a whole or as a series of letters, depending on how it is presented. Terry and coworkers found wholistic, parallel processing of familiar words containing from 3 to 6 letters (Terry,

1976–1977; Terry, Samuels, & LaBerge, 1976). The subjects reverted to serial letter-by-letter processing, however, when the words were presented in unfamiliar mirror-image print. Time to recognize words increased as words became longer for the transformed but not for the regular print. Even when the words in regular print were blurred, response time did not increase for longer words, suggesting that each of these words was processed as a whole.

For a short word of six or fewer letters, the whole-word process deals with the whole word equally (Schiepers, 1976b), but for a longer word it seems to take into account only the beginning of the word. This whole-word visual recognition process does not worry about the inner features of letters, or even about letter identification. Its primary data are the outer contour and the initial letter or two. It completes its work within the first 50–100 msec after a word is presented.

After the initial shape-based recognition is completed, letter identities are becoming available to the whole-word recognition system. The identities of outer letters are determined by about 50 msec, those of inner letters perhaps 30–50 msec later. The letter identities can be used to confirm the earlier word recognitions or to make a new attempt. This second, letter-based whole-word recognition is essentially complete by 150 msec (Rayner & Posnansky, 1978).

The whole-word processes, whether shape-based or letter-based, cannot work accurately for long words. But long words tend to have stereotyped endings, such as *-ing* (the most common of all syllables), *-ment*, *-ically*, *-tion*, and so forth.[4] Prefixes and suffixes, as well as stem morphemes, can be recognized as units (see Chapter 8, "Small Meaningful Units"). If the ends of long words convey much less information than the beginnings, then the visual information required to identify them does not have to be so accurate. A good visual recognition of the root morpheme at the beginning, plus enough information to select a suffix from a small set of candidates, may well be enough for word recognition.

To see whether this intuition was technically plausible, we performed additional statistics on the book draft. We computed the amount of information conveyed by the first letter, the first 2 letters, and so forth, and similarly for the last letter, the last 2 letters, and so forth. In each case, we assumed that the word length was known and computed information only for words of a given length. It turned out that letters at the ends of words are indeed less informative than those at the beginning and that this effect was stronger the longer the word was. For words of 6–10 letters, the first 3 letters conveyed as much information as the last 4; for 11–13 letter words the balance was 3 letters to 5; and for words longer than 13 letters the balance was 3 letters to 7, despite

[4]Here are a few others of the more common endings, not all of which are morphemes: *-ed* 6258, *-ing* 5398, *-es* 4723, *-er* 4592, *-al* 3082; there are 3188 *-on-*, but almost all of these (2399) come from *-tion*. Apart from *-ing*, the most common 3-letter ending is *-ers* (2257). *-ed* is more frequent than *-ing* in this book, probably because of its technical nature, which demands many past participles.

the fact that very long words often have stereotyped prefixes (*un-*, *in-*, *pre-*, etc.) as well as suffixes.

The second (letter-based) whole-word process may well work satisfactorily even for long words, even though its accuracy is reduced for their endings.

SCAN-PARSE PROCESS

The third route to word recognition begins with the same analysis of the individual letters as is used for the second whole-word process. Initial and final letters are recognized first, then the inner letters. When the letters have been recognized, they are made available not only to the whole-word recognition system, but also to a scan-parse system that takes them sequentially, left to right, for transformation into a phonetic form. This scan-parse operation has at least two stages: One in which the letters are grouped into clusters that have familiar spelling implications, such as 'th-', and a second that converts them into sound form. This process is just beginning to produce results by about 150 msec after the word has been presented. The scan-parse route based on letters supplements the two whole-word routes based on visual features and on letters.

THREE ROUTES TO WORD RECOGNITION: CONCLUSION

There are three routes to word recognition: A direct but approximate visual whole-word recognition; a whole-word recognition based on the identities of the letters in the word; and a scan-parse mechanism that works left-to-right and slowly using the letter identities to provide a phonetic transcription of the letter string, whether or not it is a word. The third process also serves to verify the faster work of the other two. The visual mechanisms are strongly influenced by context and expectation, the scan-parse mechanism less so.

In summary, the sequence of events in word recognition is as follows:

1a. The visual feature patterns excite whole-word detectors, especially those for which prior context is appropriate. The precise locations of the features are not too important, and inner features are ignored. The result of this phase is the excitation of several word recognizers as "possibles."

1b. The visual feature patterns simultaneously excite letter detectors and create many "possible" letter recognitions.

2. The excited word recognizers feed back to the letter recognizers, enhancing the consistent letters and inhibiting the inconsistent ones. At the same time, the letter recognizers are passing their information on to the whole-word recognizers, further exciting those having the recognized letters and not exciting (but not inhibiting) those missing them. At the end of this phase, if the letter string represented a familiar word, one word recognizer and its participating letter recognizers are firmly in control, having excitation values substantially higher than other possibilities.

3. As the letter recognizers clarify their detections, they pass information over to a scan-parse process (which may or may not involve a buffer to store

some of the processed and unprocessed information). This process attempts to match the letter strings, left to right, to a phonetic transcription.

4. If the whole-word process has arrived at a satisfactory result, or perhaps a small number of possibilities, it can excite the phonetic system for that word (those words). The scan-parse system then merely provides confirmation. If, on the other hand, the letter string was not a familiar word, then the scan-parse operator provides a phonetic transcription, which may be recognized (e.g., HORL = *hall* or *haul*).

5. At the end of these processes, there is a (usually) unitary representation of the word, if the letter string represented a word. This unitary representation quickly divides into phonetic and meaningful components, as well as into function and content aspects, but at that stage, we can say that the word has been "recognized."

Summary and Conclusions

Letters can be described in terms of features. We consider two kinds of features: A fragmental feature is a part of the letter, such as a central crossbar ('A, H, e', etc.); a configurational feature depends on the relationships among the parts of a letter, such as "open on the bottom" ('A, h, n', etc.). People use mostly configurational features for letter recognition.

For discrimination of lowercase letters, certain features have high cue values, whereas others have low values. The cue "tall letter" discriminates well a group of letters ('f, l, t', etc.) from short letters ('m, o, e', etc.), whereas the cue "upper gap" ('u, y') discriminates poorly the letters that have this feature from those that do not. People see "tall letters" quite well, but not "upper gap." For both uppercase and lowercase letters, one of the most important features is "diagonal lines not framed by verticals" ('w, A, v, Z'), whereas a less important one is "open on the bottom."

A letter is more easily confused with another that lacks some of its features than with one that has additional features.

Initial processing of letters is performed by feature detectors in the retina and the cortex. Each detector responds, in a graded manner, to its own stimulus feature (an edge detector to an edge.) Each can inhibit others on the same level and can be sensitized or inhibited through feedback from others in a higher level.

Letter fragments are not acquired sequentially; rather, letters are seen as if defocused for the first few milliseconds, and gradually focused over time. Thus, people normally identify a letter (or a word) from its outside features, which are seen before the internal features. The inner features may be analyzed by a process separate from the one that discovers the gross shape of the letter.

When letters are recognized among other letters, two context effects occur: word superiority effect and lateral masking. In the WSE, letters in words are more easily identified than alone, or than among unrelated letters. The letter 'C' is better recognized in 'ACE' than alone or in 'VCH'. The WSE occurs even when letters are in mixed case ('AcE'), but with a diminished force, showing that both letter identities and word shape are used in word recognition. The WSE is eliminated if there is extra space between letters in the words or nonwords, if the letters are too big, or if the pattern is rapidly masked by an unpatterned glare of light. None of these conditions apply in normal reading, which is done under conditions that maximize the WSE.

Because of lateral masking, a letter is harder to identify among other letters than alone. Flanking the target letter by two others can reduce its recognition by half. Text is apparently laid out badly if the object of reading were simply to identify letters.

Both lateral masking and the WSE can be accounted for in part by the idea that the visual system localizes letter features poorly. When letters form a word, the features are consistent with a familiar pattern and can be correctly identified with the letters to be named, but if they are not a word, then misplaced features can mask the target.

Does perception of a word build up from the perception of its letters? Or, are words perceived by their shapes, with no intervening interpretation of the letters? Both are used; sometimes one works better, sometimes the other.

Word shape can be analyzed into word length, outer contour, initial and final letters, and interior features. A misread word tends to share these properties with the correct word, although longer words and words with narrow letters tend to be underestimated in length. Common words deleted in text can be somewhat better restored if their outer contours are provided than otherwise. Outer contours are useful especially in recognizing short function words.

Based on letter confusion data, Bouma (1971) has grouped lowercase letters into seven groups: two tall, four short, and one projecting. By outer contour alone, *dog* = *beg* = *leg*. By Bouma shape, *beg* is no longer the same as *leg*, since 'b' and 'l', though both tall, belong to two different groups—one fat and the other thin. Bouma shape plus initial letter uniquely identify many words in text.

Interior features of letters do matter. When the shape of a word is maintained by replacing letters with letters that share features, they are easier to read than when the shape is not maintained. But interiors matter less than exteriors, as people tend to process letters, words, and figures from the outside in toward the middle.

What readers learn is not identification of individual letters but the way features group in words. But letters can help word recognition. Readers can make use of the probabilities with which letters occur in particular positions of words. For three-letter words, the majority of the first and last letters are consonants and the medial letters are vowels. In English, 'y' is common at the end and 'h' at the second position of a word.

When words are recognized by their letters, they are (in English) scanned left to right, by letter clusters forming "spelling groups," by syllables, and by morphemes. When they are recognized directly by shape, as is most often the case for short familiar words, there is no scanning, and the letters are not individually recognized.

There are three main paths to word recognition: (*a*) directly from visual features (word shape) to a wholistic detector; (*b*) via letter recognition to the same wholistic detector; and (*c*) via letter recognition through a scan-parse operation to a phonetic code. This last route usually serves merely to confirm a recognition made by one of the other routes, or to select among alternatives suggested by the faster routes, but for pseudowords it is the only available route. These three processes usually result in a single representation of the word, ready for use by higher level processes.

10

Phonetic and Visual Coding

We shall find this [inner speech], too, a powerful factor in welding together what is seen, and in keeping it together before the mind's eye until the full meaning dawns.
—Huey (1908, p. 116)

Inner Speech and Subvocalization

Huey's "Inner Speech"

Huey (1908), in his classic *The Psychology and Pedagogy of Reading*, devoted two chapters to "inner sppech." As the term implies, inner speech is hard to observe directly from outside, and in the late nineteenth century, experimental procedures were insufficiently developed to demonstrate its existence. We need not dismiss Huey's observations just because they were based largely on introspection. Today, many of his observations are still subject to experiment and debate, and direct introspection sometimes provides more insight into some of the issues than does indirect experimentation. Some of Huey's salient points follow.

Inner speech involves both hearing and pronouncing: "Although it [**inner speech**] is a foreshortened and incomplete speech in most of us, yet it is perfectly certain that the inner hearing or pronouncing, or both, of what is read, is a constituent part of the reading of by far the most of people [p. 117]."

Huey claims that inner speech may (*a*) support visual perception, (*b*) get words' meanings, and (*c*) hold words in short-term memory:

> (*a*) The visual range is itself enlarged and its content supported by the more stably organized inner utterance into which the visual percepts are constantly being translated. The carrying range or span of the inner speech is considerably larger than that of vision [p. 144].
>
> (*b*) And as meaning inheres in or is fused with the word's sound or utterance, so to get the meaning we naturally utter the word, incipiently for the most part, actually when the meaning is obscure [p.164].
>
> (*c*) It is of the greatest service to the reader or listener that at each moment a considerable amount of what is being read should hang suspended in the primary memory of the inner speech. It is doubtless true that without something of this there could be no comprehension of speech at all [p. 148].

On direct visual coding and visual–phonetic dual coding, he describes a mathematician friend who could read a 320-page novel in 2½ hours. Huey thought that at such a speed "The meanings suggested immediately by the visual forms suffice for all but the more important parts . . . the more important places themselves having a fleeting inner utterance to vivify their meanings [pp. 180–181]."

In the rest of this chapter we shall discuss modern experiments that test Huey's observations. However, unlike Huey and some modern researchers, we divide "inner speech" into subvocalization and phonetic recoding. We try to clarify three common confusions: (*a*) between subvocalization and phonetic coding, (*b*) between phonetic coding in word recognition and in sentence comprehension, and (*c*) between a phonetic route and a visual route to meaning. The chapter enlarges on word recognition, which is discussed in Chapter 9, and touches on sentence processing, which is described in Chapter 12.

Subvocalization

Children at first learn to read aloud and then carry over some of the speech movements into silent reading, first as audible whispering and later as inaudible lip and tongue movements. As Quantz (quoted by Huey) observed, reading without lip movement is an acquired habit, the natural thing being to use the lips. Even as adults, people tend to sound out unfamiliar or difficult words. By **subvocalization** we mean the muscle activities in the articulatory organs—the tongue, chin, lips, larynx (voice box)—that accompany silent reading.

In the literature on memory, the distinction between subvocalization and articulatory rehearsal seems to be blurred. An articulatory loop, which is considered to be one component of working memory (the other being a central executive), is "entirely synonymous with subvocalization [Baddeley, Thomson, & Buchanan, 1975, p. 587]." In contrast to Baddeley *et al.*, we distinguish subvocalization that accompanies reading from vocalized rehearsal that occurs as a part of memorizing words. Rehearsal is one means of delaying the loss of information in short-term memory and of integrating information into long-term memory. When you look up a phone number, you may say it over and over to help you remember it until you dial. Subvocalization occurs only ***while*** words are being read, but (sub)vocalized rehearsal may go on ***after*** reading has ceased.

MEASURING SUBVOCALIZATION

One can easily observe the articulatory movements of overt vocalization but not so easily those of subvocalization. Subvocalization can be picked up and amplified for better observation by a technique called electromyography. Either by inserting needle electrodes inside the muscles or by placing electrodes on the surface of the speech organs, researchers can record the tiny action potentials of the muscles, which they amplify and integrate to prepare electromyographic records (EMGs). EMGs taken during silent reading are then compared with those taken at rest, which provide a baseline for comparison. EMG amplitude increases during speech but does not vary in an obvious manner for different speech sounds. In other words, EMGs show a reader's overall degree of subvocalizing throughout a passage but do not show which sounds, or even which words, the reader is subvocalizing. McGuigan (1970) reviewed 27 studies carried out between 1900 and 1969 in Sweden, Britain, the Soviet Union, and the United States. All studies but one answer yes to the question: "Is there an increase in vocal muscle activity during a language task?"

EMGs are affected by reading conditions. Sokolov (1972) in the Soviet Union observed subjects who were translating Russian into English. The more difficult translations resulted in larger amplitude EMGs than easy translations. Instructions such as "Read it more attentively" or "Memorize it more accurately" also resulted in greater EMGs than did a first reading of the text without instructions of this kind. When rereading the native Russian passages without specific instructions, the subjects' subvocalization was very weak, and at times it disappeared altogether. Edfeldt (1960) found that EMG increased for difficult text, for blurred text, and in poor readers. As compared with native text (Danish), EMG increased also when reading intelligible foreign text (Swedish), especially if subjects were unaccustomed to reading the foreign language.

Children show more subvocalization than do adults. In McGuigan's (1967) study, three subjects—children aged 10, 11, and 11—showed substantial subvocalization when tested for the first time. Over two or three sessions, however, their subvocalization decreased rapidly. When they were retested two and three years later, their EMG amplitudes were still low and similar to those of college students who had been tested but once (McGuigan & Bailey, 1969).

REDUCING SUBVOCALIZATION BY EMG FEEDBACK

Full-fledged vocalization, even when inaudible, presumably slows reading, because articulatory movements are slower than normal visual and cognitive processing. Most people can pronounce no more than 150–200 words per minute (WPM), but they can silently read 300–800 WPM. EMG can be used along with biofeedback in reducing excessive subvocalization: Subjects receive instant feedback on their EMG level so that they can control it. In one study, a single session of feedback was sufficient to eliminate subvocalizaton altogether in students from a remedial reading class (Hardyck, Petrinovich, & Ellsworth, 1966). Following this single session, there was no evidence of subvocalization after 1 month, or even after 3 months. Similarly, Aarons (1971) reported that adults were responsive to feedback training and that the reductions in subvocalization lasted beyond the training trials.

Hardyck and Petrinovich (1970) recorded laryngeal EMG from the surface of the thyroid cartilage, chin–lip, and right forearm flexor. Their subjects were freshmen from a remedial English class. The reading materials were two essays: a brief biography of John F. Kennedy (easy), and an article on the culture of cities (difficult). There were three experimental conditions:

1. Normal condition: Subjects read the essays while all the EMG recordings went on.
2. Feedback condition: The subjects read the essays as they did in the "normal" condition, but any increase in the amplitude of laryngeal EMG over a predetermined relaxation level resulted in a 500 Hz tone. They were told to keep the tone off as much as possible.
3. Control: This condition was the same as the feedback conditon except that the tone was triggered by any increase in the amplitude of the forearm flexor over its predetermined relaxation level.

EMG activity in all three conditions was higher with the difficult text. Laryngeal and chin–lip EMGs were most responsive to difficulty level, and the arm muscle least so. When laryngeal activity was reduced by the feedback, comprehension of the difficult passage suffered. This result does not necessarily imply, however, that the laryngeal muscle activity was essential for comprehension. (Can you read while you eat?) Comprehension might have suffered simply because the subjects had to pay attention to the task of learning to eliminate laryngeal activity.

In a study by Riley and Lowe (1981), subjects who ***enhanced*** subvocalization with the aid of biofeedback read with the same level of comprehension as controls and two other experimental groups who reduced subvocalization either by biofeedback or by instruction. Incidentally, instruction alone was as effective as biofeedback in reducing subvocalization, and hence in increasing reading speed. The amount of subvocalization apparently had no effect on comprehension.

PRECURSORS OF SUBVOCALIZATION

Measurements of blood flow to the brain, using radioactive xenon, show that silent reading activates four areas in the cortex in addition to the primary visual area (which is not reached by this technique): the visual association area, the frontal eye field, the supplementary motor area, and Broca's speech center (Lassen, Ingvar, & Skinhøj, 1978; see Figure 1-1 for the areas of the cortex). Reading aloud activates two more centers: the mouth area and the auditory area. Presumably, the auditory area is activated by hearing the speech and the mouth area by producing it. Both cortical hemispheres show the same pattern of activity.

One may guess that the subjects were not actually subvocalizing; if they had been, the cortical area that controls the mouth should have shown some activity. The radioactive xenon technique may therefore detect an even more subtle residue of vocalization than does the EMG method. EMG shows actual activity in the articulatory musculature, which must be controlled by the motor area; radioactive xenon shows the related cortical activity, which may include not the actual mouth area, but only the activity of the supplementary motor area.

The measurement of blood flow may be subtle enough to distinguish levels of subvocalization: Of two studies in which the subject imagined counting from 1 to 20, one (Lassen *et al.*, 1978) found involvement of the supplementary motor area, whereas the other (Orgogozo & Larsen, 1979) did not. Perhaps, the subject in the former study was partway to subvocalizing, whereas the subject in the latter was not even close to it. Subvocalizing may possibly be eliminated in stages.

PURPOSE OF SUBVOCALIZATION

Written language represents oral speech, not vice versa. People first learn to speak and to understand speech. Only much later—after the oral speech is reasonably developed—do they learn to read. Furthermore, reading is usually taught orally. Even after they have learned to read, most people probably spend more time speaking than reading. Thus, speaking and listening to speech is far more practiced than is reading.

For these reasons, people first develop the auditory channel for analyzing speech. When people talk, they hear what they say. Even before people learn to read, they can associate movements in the mouth, the tongue and the larynx with the sounds of known words. Hence, these control movements may themselves come to be associated with the sounds as if they had been actually spoken; the control movements may serve as a surrogate for speech.

Later, when a reader comes across a difficult word, it may be easier to speak it aloud, or to subvocalize. One Japanese patient who had lost his ability to read Kana could sometimes recognize one if he traced it with his hand

(Sasanuma, 1974; see also Chapter 4). His kinaesthetic channel for writing could substitute for his failing visual analysis channel. The articulatory control patterns of speech may substitute similarly for actual speech in aiding the integration of the sounds of a difficult word. Even though a skilled reader rarely needs to sound out a word in order to get its meaning, the process may help with difficult words. People fall back on a well-practiced method in time of difficulty.

Phonetic Coding

Phonetic Coding in Word Recognition

Phonetic coding has many labels—*inner speech, speech coding, phonemic coding, phonological encoding,* and *acoustic coding,* to name only a few. These various labels sometimes may indicate subtly different forms of phonetic coding, but more often they reflect simply individual researchers' preferences. For the sake of simplicity, we will use mainly the label **phonetic recoding,** or **phonetic coding,** which means converting a printed word into a phonetic internal representation. According to phonetic recoding theorists, printed words are routinely recoded into phonetic forms (*a*) because phonetic forms are the means by which meanings can be accessed; and/or (*b*) because phonetic forms are the means by which words can be held in working memory or short-term memory.

SENSITIVITY TO PHONETIC FORM

Many experiments show clearly that readers are sensitive to the phonetic qualities of the words they read silently. The experiments are not so clear, however, on how people use these phonetic qualities. Here is a sampling from the dozens in the psychological literature.

1. A reader takes longer to recognize printed words whose sounds contain more syllables than to recognize other words of identical graphemic length but fewer syllables (Eriksen, Pollack, & Montague, 1970; Klapp, 1974; Pynte, 1978). Similarly, in recognizing words presented in a T-scope, accuracy decreases as the syllable and phoneme length increases for a given number of letters (Spoehr, 1978). In an alphabetic representation, a word of a given length probably has a more regular vowel–consonant alternation if it has more syllables. This characteristic should make it easier to recognize the words with more syllables, but the results show the opposite.

2. Readers searched through a prose passage for words spelled incorrectly. Some were misspelled in a phonetically compatible way (e.g., "hurd" for *heard*), others in an incompatible fashion (e.g., "borst" for *burst*).

The readers were more likely to detect a misspelling that was phonetically incompatible than one that was compatible (MacKay, 1968).

3. In a letter cancellation task, if the target occurs in an accented syllable, it is more likely to be detected than if it occurs in an unaccented one (Drewnowski & Healy, 1982; Hatch, Polin, & Part, 1974; P. T. Smith & Groat, 1979). Two groups of profoundly deaf, one congenitally and the other adventitiously, did not miss silent 'e's (*nin***e**) as much as did the other two groups, the hearing and the hard-of-hearing. In fact, the two profoundly deaf groups missed the silent and pronounced 'e's about equally (Chen, 1976). Locke (1978) found the same kind of difference between hearing subjects and deaf subjects, using 'c, g, h' as target letters.

4. Subjects tried to name words presented in a T-scope when the words were masked by other words presented immediately afterward. The target words were strongly masked by homophones but poorly masked by semantically related words (Jacobson, 1976; see also Chapter 9).

5. Subjects tried to recall a string of 9 digits presented sequentially on a computer display while hearing, but not attending to, spoken words. The words interfered with recall of the digit sequence, but much more strongly if they were phonetically similar to digits (*tun, gnu, tee, sore,* etc.) than if they were not (*tennis, jelly, tipple,* etc.). The words had no effect on the perception of the digits, as tested by immediate copying (Salame & Baddeley, 1982).

6. In writing, misspellings are phonetically constrained. Sears (1969) examined the spelling errors identified by the publications department of an aerospace company over a 1-year period. Of more than 100 errors, over 92% were phonetic (e.g., "murge," "priar"), proving to the author that "engineers spell acoustically." Non-engineers, some good and some poor readers and/or spellers, also misspell acoustically (e.g., Alper, 1942; Barron, 1980; Bryant & Bradley, 1980; Frith, 1979; Thomson, 1981). Similarly, in Japanese publications in the English language, one occasionally finds 'l–r' substitutions (e.g., crunk for *clunk*), reflecting Japanese speech, in which these phonemes are not distinguished.

LEXICAL DECISION VIA PHONETIC RECODING

In a lexical decision task, reaction times to nonwords increased in the following order (Rubenstein, Lewis, & Rubenstein, 1971):

1. illegal unpronounceable (crpwe)
2. illegal pronounceable (gratf)
3. legal pronounceable (strig)
4. legal homophonic (brane)

The less wordlike a nonword is, the faster subjects can decide that it is not a word. According to the researchers, a pseudoword sounding like a real word takes longer to be rejected because a search for it is carried out in a mental dictionary or lexicon, whereas no search is necessary for unpronounceable nonwords.

Rubenstein *et al.*'s study has been criticized on methodological grounds (e.g., H. H. Clark, 1973; Fleming, 1976; Meyer, Schvaneveldt, & Ruddy, 1974). Subsequent researchers have effectively countered these objections, and the basic findings have been replicated and extended in other studies (e.g., Coltheart, Davelaar, Jonasson, & Besner, 1977; Glushko, 1979; Gough & Cosky, 1977; Miller & Coleman, 1978; Patterson & Marcel, 1977; Rubenstein, Richter, & Kay, 1975).

According to Rubenstein *et al.* (1971), phonetic recoding is achieved by segmenting a word into letters and almost simultaneously converting each letter to its corresponding phoneme. Word recognition is then achieved by comparing the phonemic form of the stimulus with the representations of the words in the lexicon. However, letter-by-letter coding into sound is impossible for many English words, especially for irregularly spelled ones, which tend to be frequent; nor is this stage necessary for phonetic coding (see Chapters 6 and 9).

In a different but related theory of phonetic coding, Marcel (1980b) suggested that successively longer segments of the word are matched to patterns of letters having known sounds. If the entire string matches, then it will be a word and will be correctly pronounced, whether its spelling is regular or irregular. If the letter string is a pseudoword, the match will fail at some point and must be restarted. For example, BLATE would be matched with (BLA) or even (BLAT) but the E would not match, forcing a re-analysis as (BL)(ATE). A lexical no decision could be made very quickly by this mechanism, because it can be done as soon as the matching process fails. In actual experiments, yes decisions are usually faster than no ones.

Taft (1982) argues that what seems to be phonetic recoding really is not. Instead, letter groups (graphemes) are automatically recoded into other graphemes which sometimes have the same sound, thus making many possible spelling patterns for any given letter string. Sound patterns are constructed from all the candidates, especially if they make words. For example, the nonsense string KOALD might be transformed as follows: K → {K, C}, OA → {O, OA, O_ E}, D → {D, ED}, to make many possible spelling patterns, including KOLDE, COLD, COALD, COALED, and so forth. At least two of these patterns are real words; both happen to have same pronunciation. Through this process, pseudo-homophones generate some real words, which then have to be rejected in lexical decision. Non-homophones do not generate real words and hence can be rejected quickly.

Acronyms like RCMP (Canadian), IBM, FBI have a borderline status between being and not being words. On the one hand, they have semantic meaning, but on the other, they are not phonologically or orthographically legal words. One says "eff bee eye," not /fbi/. These "words" cannot be analyzed phonetically, and yet it takes longer to respond that they are nonwords than to respond for meaningless clusters of letters (Novik, 1974). Familiarity with the whole letter group is used, despite orthographic irregularity. Hayman (1983) suggests that any kind of familiarity, whether it be graphemic, orthographic, phonetic, or semantic, can affect lexical decision by making the "word" response more likely and quicker and the "nonword" response less likely and slower.

RECODING BEFORE OR AFTER LEXICAL ACCESS?

On intuitive grounds, some authors suggest that phonetic recoding occurs after rather than before meaning is accessed. To use the jargon of the literature, "post-lexical phonology," not "pre-lexical phonology" occurs. Each author cites a different type of word as appropriate for post-lexical phonology. Massaro (1975) points out that many words cannot be pronounced until their meaning is determined. These are words that are spelled the same but pronounced differently (e.g., *lead,* metal, versus *to lead,* to guide). Allen *et al.* (1979) ask: How are homophones out of context disambiguated if lexical access is always done via phonetic recoding? One could not distinguish *way* from *weigh* by sound. This question may be spurious: A reader may adopt one strategy for homophones and another for ordinary words. At any rate, there are only a few hundred homophones in English. Coltheart (1980b) considers exception (irregular) words such as *yacht* and ideographs like '$' to be candidates for post-lexical phonology because they cannot be pronounced by grapheme–phoneme conversion. Both Glushko (1979) and Marcel (1980b) argue that phonetic recoding is neither before nor after lexical access but is a part of it.

Let us consider experimental findings on this issue. Kleiman (1975) measured the effect of shadowing (subjects repeat each digit as they hear it) on several kinds of decision about words and sentences. Given a pair of words, subjects might decide whether they sounded alike, or were spelled alike, and so on. Given a sentence, the subjects decided whether it was semantically acceptable. Shadowing did not impair the synonym decision any more than it did the spelling decision. It did substantially impair, however, the decision on sentence acceptability. Kleiman concludes that phonetic recoding is not necessary for lexical access: It is used ***after*** lexical access, in order to facilitate temporary storage of words necessary for sentence comprehension.

Others also consider phonetic recoding to be a storage strategy for words, even for individual words, but not to be a part of lexical access (Shulman, Hornak, & Sanders 1978). In their study, phonetic similarity influenced lexical decisions only when words were to be discriminated from nonwords that followed English orthographic conventions. Such words have to be kept in short-term memory while a protracted search goes on in long-term memory. When consonant strings or random letter strings were used as nonwords, phonetic similarity effects were absent, and graphemic similarity exerted a powerful effect.

In lexical decision used by Venezky (1981), letter–sound regularity had no effect on real words, but it had an effect on pseudowords. Irregular nonwords were rejected faster than all other types of nonword. Furthermore, irregular nonwords homophonic to real words (*brij, ckuf*) failed to show a "homophone effect," that is, they were not rejected more slowly than non-homophones. Phonetic coding presumably would come after lexical decision in these cases.

In a study investigating the locus of phonetic coding, subjects repeated "blah" while making various judgments about words they were reading: Were the words homophonic to one another? Did they rhyme? Was a pseudoword homophonic to any real word? Saying "blah" slowed phonological segmentation, thus slowing detection of word rhymes, but it did not slow lexical access or the detection of either homophones or nonword rhymes; saying "blah" increased errors in judging whether the items were words (Besner, Davies, & Daniels, 1981). According to Besner *et al.*, there are at least two different phonetic codes, one corresponding to storage of phonological information, which must be used when words have to be segmented, and one for lexical access, which may be used for entire words. Lexical access is not affected by saying "blah," but the storage mechanism is.

Using both lexical decision and naming tasks, Mitterer (1982) identified two different populations of poor Grade 3 readers: One group relied heavily on phonetic coding, the other on whole-word recognition. His control group of good readers did not rely so strongly on either route. The phonetic coders coded before lexical access, the whole-word readers after lexical access if they did any phonetic coding at all. Good readers presumably have their choice of routes, and can code before or after lexical access, depending on the task demands and the letter strings being tested.

Phonological and Orthographic Factors

In a sense, all English words follow spelling rules, or are orthographically regular, and all nonwords are irregular because their letter combinations are by definition legal and illegal, respectively. Usually, a less strict definition is used for orthographic regularity. Clusters of a few (perhaps two to four) letters are examined, taking into account their position in a letter string, to see whether they occur in English words. For example, an initial 'Vl-' is illegal because no English word starts that way, not because English speakers are unable to say such words as *Vladivostok.*

In real words, orthographic irregularity tends to mean that the letters are pronounced differently from the normal expectation. For example, '-are' at the end of a word is usually pronounced to rhyme with *care,* but the word *are* rhymes instead with *car.* Let us look at some studies that examine one or another facet of orthographic regularity in the perception of words and pseudowords.

REGULAR, EXCEPTION, AND INCONSISTENT WORDS

The connection between spelling and sound seems important for reading aloud. Glushko (1979) asked subjects to pronounce as fast as possible a letter string that might be a word or a pseudoword. Words were regular (e.g., DEAN) or exception (e.g., DEAF), and the pseudowords were derived from them by changing one letter (e.g., HEAN, HEAF). The latency was longer for the exception words, and more interestingly, it was longer for pseudowords derived from exception words than for ones derived from regular words. Also, rather than following the regular pronunciation pattern, the subjects' pronunciations often rhymed with the exception words from which they were derived (e.g., HEAF was often rhymed with DEAF rather than SHEAF or LEAF).

In another experiment, Glushko used only real words but divided them into three classes:

1. Regular words words whose pronunciation agrees with almost all words of similar spelling (e.g., WADE, HAZE).
2. Exception words words whose pronunciation differs from most words of similar spelling (e.g., HAVE).
3. Inconsistent words words that follow the pronunciation rules but that have similar spellings to words of more than one kind of pronunciation (e.g., GAVE, which has partners HAVE and WAVE).

Inconsistent regular words took as long to pronounce as exception words. Only the consistent regular words were faster.

Glushko explains the effect as follows: Letter clusters in either a word or a nonword tend to evoke pronunciation patterns based on the known pronunciations of similarly spelled words. If a letter string is an irregular word, it resembles other words that have different pronunciations (e.g., HAVE looks like WAVE and SAVE). Although it will eventually activate its own pronunciation most strongly, in the process of doing so it will have activated competing pronunciations, which must be overcome before a final pronunciation can be derived. Inconsistent words also evoke competing pronunciations (e.g., GAVE evokes HAVE and SAVE) with the same result, whereas consistent words evoke the same pronunciation both from their own representation and from their similar partners. Consistent words therefore can develop a unique pronunciation faster than can either exception or inconsistent words. Orthographically irregular but unique words, such as *yacht*, should evoke no competitors and should be as fast as regular words. This prediction appears not to have been tested.

Glushko considered only words ending in -VCe, and matched them with other words of the same form. A more comprehensive theory would match HAVE not only with words like SAVE, but also with words like HIVE or HAVEN. But it would be difficult to find and evaluate all the partners and competitors for any given word. Some would be close matches, some distant; would SHAVEN be expected to have a strong influence on HAVE?

The digram 'th-' at the beginning of a word has an unusual status in English. If 'th-' begins a function word, it is voiced, as in *the*, *this*, and *those*, whereas if it begins a content word, it is unvoiced, as in *thank*, *thimble*, and *thought.* Campbell and Besner (1981) used this characteristic to show that phonetic coding can depend on syntactic context. If a nonsense word beginning with 'th-' was put into a sentence frame where it should have been a function word, the 'th-' was usually voiced, even if the sentence was itself nonsense (e.g., *Stibby blooped on thock one*), whereas if it should have been a content word, it was unvoiced (*Stibby thocked on bloop one*). Glushko's theory must be modified to permit the set of "partner" words to depend at least on the syntactic context, and possibly on semantic context as well.

PHONOLOGICAL–ORTHOGRAPHIC INTERACTION

Orthographic and phonetic representations interact in a complex way: On the one hand, visually presented material is coded into phonetic form, in at least two functional stages; on the other, auditorily presented material may be recoded into orthographic form. We consider first orthographic to phonetic coding.

Chastain (1981) asked subjects to identify the central vowel of a CVC syllable presented in a T-scope. The three letters of the CVC were masked by a following pattern, but the mask also included another letter placed where a fourth letter would have been if the target had been a four-letter word. If the fourth letter were considered along with the three of the CVC, it might have a variety of effects: It might not change the sound of the vowel (CAR to CARS), or it might (CAR to CARE), or it might make the word orthographically illegal (CAR to CARJ). Subjects' vowel identification became worse in the order just given. Both orthographic and pronunciation factors are at work.

Naish (1980) presented in a T-scope a triplet of stimuli: target, primary mask, and secondary mask. The secondary mask was used to ensure that subjects could not report the primary mask. The target was always a word, and the primary mask might be a word or a nonword. If the primary mask resembled the target either physically or phonetically, the target was easier to identify. Once again, both graphemic and phonemic codes are developed and used in word recognition.

Désrouesné and Beauvois (1979) studied brain-damaged patients known as **phonological dyslexics,** who have nearly normal language capabilities except for an inability to code unfamiliar words or pseudowords phonetically. They found at least two types of phonological dyslexia: One type cannot make sense of letter clusters such as 'sh' or 'ai' and will pronounce the word with each letter separate; the other type cannot convert graphemes to phonological codes (see Chapter 11).

Theories of phonetic recoding must include a separate stage in which letter groups are formed, as well as a stage at which letters and letter groups are converted to a phonetic form. Taft (1982) has suggested a stage at which one grapheme may be transformed into others having the same sound: '-ai-'

into '-a-e' or '-eigh', for example. In his lexical decision experiments, nonwords which could be graphemically transformed into real words were harder to discriminate than were nonwords whose graphemic transformations did not lead to words. *Cheece* can be transformed into *cheese* by substituting an 's' for a 'c', and *breece* into *breeze* by substituting a 'z' for a 'c'. In many contexts, 'c' has the sound of 's' but never the sound of 'z'. Even though *cheese* and *breeze* rhyme, still it took longer to decide that *cheece* did not sound like a real word than to make the same decision for *breece.* These results suggest that the 'c–s', but not the 'c–z', transformation was tried, even though both would be phonetically the same in the given context.

The converse of phonetic recoding, namely, orthographic recoding of a heard word, can happen and may even be necessary on occasion. For example, Martin Taylor heard on the radio a comment about a ballet choreographed by /masi:n/, which he first interpreted as being spelled *Macine*, in correspondence with the author Racine. Not knowing of such a choreographer, he visualized a few alternate spellings, and came up with *Massine*, who was a well-known choreographer. At that moment, the previously obscure comment became clear. The sound pattern was insufficient for recognition; the visual image of the printed word was required.

When subjects were asked to determine whether an auditorily presented word rhymed with one held in memory, their responses were faster if the words were orthographically regular than if they were irregular (Donnenwerth-Nolan, Tanenhaus, & Seidenberg, 1981). The process may be closely related to the grapheme to grapheme transformation postulated by Taft (1982). It becomes a two-way street: grapheme → phonetic pattern → grapheme.

For homophones, orthographic access to meaning is essential. If access were only through the sound, it would be impossible to understand the following limerick:

> There was a young fellow named Tait
> Who dined with his girl at 8:8
> But I'd hate to relate
> What that fellow named Tait
> And his tête-a-tête ate at 8:8.
> —Carolyn Well (quoted by Reed, 1925)

Japanese talkers sometimes explicitly use orthographic recoding to make conversational speech understandable, according to the Japanese linguist Suzuki (1977). The celebrated example *shikaishikaishikai* is hard to understand when spoken but is easy to understand when written, because each of the syllables has its own unique Kanji with its unique meaning (see Chapter 4). Homophones pose bigger problems in Chinese. For example, one sentence consists of the syllable *shi* repeated 10 times (Cheng, 1982).

Clearly, there is a feedback loop in the phonetic coding system: Orthography goes to phonology and phonology to orthography. In whatever way words are sensed, both orthographic and phonetic codings are used.

Visual–Phonetic Dual Coding

A **dual-coding** model claims that both visual and phonetic routes are used to access words' meanings. It enjoys the support of many theorists: Sometimes the support is implicit, as in Huey's (1908) observations on inner speech; at other times it is explicit, as in the studies reported in this section. LaBerge and Samuels (1974), who developed a comprehensive model of reading, allow a direct visual route to meaning along with a phonetic one. So do others who reviewed the literature on phonetic recoding (e.g., Bradshaw, 1975; McCusker, Hillinger, & Bias, 1981). Marshall and Newcombe (1973) support dual coding in normal readers after reviewing the literature on people who appear to have lost one or other route after brain damage: Some patients are forced to use a direct visual–meaning route and others an indirect phonetic-recoding route, depending on the locus of brain damage (see Chapter 11).

Henderson (1982) considers that few of experiments supporting dual coding are conclusive, and thus he argues that there is only one route to meaning, which he calls "lexical analogy." His arguments, though logical, seem sometimes forced. We ourselves support dual coding, and consider here evidence for it.

DIRECT VISUAL ROUTE TO MEANING

It would be most efficient to get to meaning directly from print, bypassing phonetic recoding as well as subvocalization. Huey (1908) observed that to a rapid reader meaning is suggested immediately by the visual forms of words. Woodworth (1938) asks eloquently, if rhetorically: "Just as a picture, gesture, a spoken word, suggests a meaning, why may not the printed word come to suggest its meaning directly instead of by the round about route of auditory-motor speech [p. 717]?"

A familiar word tends to be recognized by its shape and its letter features. Lexical access by the direct visual route is faster than using the indirect route of phonetic recoding (e.g., Coltheart *et al.* 1977; Dennis & Newstead, 1981; Frith, 1979; Rayner & Posnansky, 1978; see also Chapter 9). C. Conrad (1978) showed that speed readers do not use much phonetic recoding, as judged from the lack of color–name interference in a Stroop test. Two groups of people—skilled readers and phonemic dyslexics—tend to rely primarily or exclusively on a direct visual route to meaning.

Barron and Baron (1977) traced the development of children's access to meaning. They required children in Grades 1, 2, 4, 6, and 8 to decide whether picture–word pairs rhymed (picture of a horn with the word *corn*) or went together in meaning (the picture of a pair of pants with the word *shirt*). The subjects in all five grades made more errors on the rhyming task when they were concurrently vocalizing *double* than when they were not; they did not make more errors on the meaning tasks. Barron and Baron concluded that there is no developmental shift from phonetic to visual coding: Children can get meaning from printed words in the same way that adults can—that is, directly from print without the use of an intermediate phonetic code.

In contrast, Doctor and Coltheart (1980) found evidence of a developmental shift from phonetic recoding to direct visual coding in a situation where both routes could be used. Children aged 6–11 (Grades 2–7 in Britain) judged whether short sentences such as the following were meaningful:

1. *He ran threw the street.*
2. *He ran sew the street.*

Sentence 1, which is meaningful when phonetically recoded, produced more errors than did 2, but the difference in error rates between the two diminished as the function of age. As the children grew older they relied less on the phonetically coded version and more on the visually coded one.

These two apparently contradictory findings can be resolved. Barron and Baron's (1977) tasks involved decisions based either on the sound or on the meaning of a word. Concurrent vocalizing inhibited rhyme detection at all ages because rhyme cannot be detected without a phonetic code; it did not affect decisions about the meaning, which can be accessed through a direct visual code. Even the phonetic route might have been used to get the meaning of the word, since concurrent vocalization may not interfere with phonetic coding for the purpose of lexical decision (Besner *et al.*, 1981; above).

Doctor and Coltheart's (1980) study, on the other hand, put the phonetic and the visual code into conflict, as well as asking for judgments of sentence anomaly. As we shall see, phonetic effects are more pronounced at the sentence level than at word level, so that the phonetically correct but visually anomalous *He ran threw the street* may well have been coded phonetically for interpretation by children whose visual sense of words was not terribly well developed. We all know how difficult it is for young children to learn correct English spelling, especially of irregular words like *through.* Furthermore, a reader is normally expected to make sense of something when possible. It is not surprising, therefore, that younger children were more likely to accept the phonetically valid sentence as correct than the one that was both phonetically and visually anomalous.

Neither of the two studies shed much light on whether there is a developmental sequence from using a primarily phonetic to using a primarily visual route to word meaning. In the "Summary and Conclusions" to this chapter we present our own hypothesis on the matter.

INDIVIDUAL DIFFERENCES: CHINESE VERSUS PHOENICIANS

Baron and Strawson (1976) characterized readers as either "Chinese" or "Phoenicians" according to their style of dealing with words. The Chinese tend to use the visual form of words more than do the Phoenicians, who tend to use phonetic analysis. (Actually, Baron and Strawson used the pun *Phonecians,* to indicate both the Phoenician alphabet and the phonetic style.)

Subjects in one experiment were preselected as Chinese or Phoenicians on their ability to identify homophones of English words (Phoenicians should be better) and to select the correctly spelled member of a homophonic pair (Chinese should be better). Chinese and Phoenician subjects read 10-item lists of regular words (SWEET), exception words (SWORD), or nonwords (SWIRD). Overall, the average times for the lists were 4.3 sec for regular words, 5.9 sec for exception words, and 7.8 sec for nonwords. However, Chinese subjects were faster on exception words than on regular words, provided that the words were in a single case. When the words were in mixed case, even the Chinese subjects were quicker on regular words, though not so much quicker as were the Phoenicians.

The relative preference of a reader for the phonetic or visual route may be controllable to some degree. In identifying words, pseudowords, and orthographically illegal and unpronounceable nonwords, if subjects expected a mixture, then words and pseudowords were better identified than were nonwords, but if they expected words only or nonwords only, then an unexpected pseudoword acted like a nonword (Carr, Davidson, & Hawkins 1978). According to Carr *et al.*, the visual mode is automatic, but the orthographic mode, which leads to phonetic coding, is under "strategic control." This pattern is the opposite of what seems to happen in Serbo-Croatian, whose orthography is phonologically very regular, and phonetic coding is obligatory (Feldman, 1981). Apparently, either visual or phonetic coding can appear to be obligatory and the other optional, depending on the normal mode in which readers of a script tend to operate.

HORSE RACE OR HOSE RACE?

Within dual coding models, two positions have been advocated: The different pathways can be conceptualized either as mutually exclusive or as complementing one another. On the basis of results from lexical decision experiments that contrasted spelling tasks with pronunciation tasks, Meyer and Ruddy (1973) propose one kind of mutually exclusive dual-coding model: A word meaning can be reached via either a visual or a phonetic route, depending on which finishes first. Call this a horse race model. When the phonetic route wins, a spelling check is carried out, and access is confirmed only if this check succeeds.

Baron (1977) espouses the view that "two hoses jointly fill up the same bucket," thus speeding up the water flow to the bucket. That is, two pathways complement one another. Other researchers also suggest that visual and phonetic inputs to the lexicon normally cooperate in locating an entry, rather than competing in a horse race (Davelaar, Coltheart, Besner, & Jonasson, 1978). In the lexical decision experiments of Davelaar *et al.*, although both visual and phonemic encoding occurred simultaneously, naive subjects tended to rely on the outcome of the phonetic route. When this reliance produced a high error rate (i.e., when the nonwords sounded like English words—

BRANE), the subjects were able to abandon their phonetic strategy and rely on the visual strategy instead.

Similar strategic flexibility occurred in recognizing words presented in a T-scope (Hawkins, Reicher, Rogers, & Peterson, 1976). For one list with a small proportion of homophones, reliance on phonemic information would lead to accurate recognition on most of the words, whereas in the other list with many homophones, it would result in a high error rate. Two groups of subjects used different strategies for the two lists to minimize errors.

Consider the following sentence: *The buoy and the none tolled hymn they had scene and herd a pear of bear feet in the haul.* In it, the visual shapes of the words convey meanings that disagree with their contextual requirements; only through phonetic recoding can the contextual correctness of the homophones be judged. Visual coding and phonetic coding are both occurring, but conflicting with each other, instead of reinforcing as they usually do. The result is that reading real homophones is even slower than reading pseudo-homophones (nonwords that sound like the real words). The two hoses fill different buckets—a hose race!

PHONETIC RECODING IN NON-PHONETIC SCRIPTS

Is phonetic recoding unique to phonetic writing systems, in which one letter codes one phoneme (in an alphabetic system) or one syllable (in a syllabary), or does it occur also in logographic systems in which one grapheme represents one morpheme primarily and one syllable secondarily? This section describes some studies involving users of Chinese characters.

Japanese readers saw a series of Kanji and then named the one that followed a probe Kanji. A comparable experiment in English would be to show a list such as *dog, cow, cat, rabbit, pig,* and then ask "What followed *cat*?" *Cat* might be the probe. When a list of Kanji consisted of homophonic pairs, confusion was far greater than when they consisted of visually or semantically similar pairs (Erickson, Mattingly, & Turvey, 1977). Saito (1978) asked Japanese subjects to judge whether two single Kanji were physically the same or different. Subjects' reaction times increased when the two Kanji were homophones, showing the influence of sound on what should have been a visual task. Inoue (1980) found that same–different judgments for a pair of two-Kanji words was slower if the words were homophonic than if they were either synonymous or unrelated.

In a test of recognition memory of single characters, the largest number of errors made by Chinese subjects were phonetic, next visual, and then semantic (Chu-Chang & Loritz, 1977). In another series of studies, Chinese speakers had to recall a number of Chinese characters and also judge the acceptability of sentences whose constituent characters were manipulated in phonemic similarity. Phonemic similarity impaired performance on both tasks, and the more similar the stimuli, the greater was the impairment (Tzeng *et al.*, 1977; see also Chapter 3, "Phonetic Recoding of Characters").

The same effect of phonetic similarity occurs in English as well. An English example is *Crude rude Jude chewed stewed food,* in which order anomalies such as *Crude rude chewed Jude stewed food* or word anomalies such as *Crude rude Jude queued stewed food* are much harder to detect than are similar anomalies in sentences such as *Dark-skinned Ian ate boiled meat* (Baddeley & Hitch, 1974; Baddeley & Lewis, 1981). Poets use rhyme and alliteration for special effects, but phonemic repetition does not help in making text easy to understand. First grade stories with lines like *Nan can fan Dan / Can Dan fan Nan?* (Bloomfield & Barnhart, 1961) must make reading difficult, if inadvertently (see Chapter 15).

Users of Chinese characters, be they Chinese, Japanese, or Korean, are sensitive to the sounds of characters and retain characters phonetically in short-term memory. However, as with familiar English words, a Chinese character need not be phonetically coded for lexical access. Indeed, it is possible for a reader to know the meaning of a character without remembering its sound; in this case, she could not have used a phonetic code to access the meaning. When an unfamiliar character is encountered, a reader has no choice but to commit its visual form to memory while dashing to the nearest dictionary. Under the same circumstances, an English speaker would commit the word's sound to memory.

ACTIVE-ANALYTIC PLUS PASSIVE-GLOBAL DUAL PROCESS

A fast visual and a slow phonetic route normally support and stabilize each other, according to the Bilateral Cooperative (BLC) model of reading (see Chapter 11). If the same result is being obtained by both routes, the faster needs only a small amount of evidence from the slower to permit confirmation of its result. But if the early evidence from the slow route is incompatible, then the fast route must hold off making its decision until more evidence—and perhaps an alternate interpretation—arrives from the slow route. Additionally, the slow route is usually more secure, so that it can resolve ambiguities produced by the fast route.

Broadbent and Broadbent (1980) discuss a "perceptual-cyclic" model, in which a passive process provides a set of possible recognitions, using "aspects of the stimulus such as the total shape of a word rather than local details such as letters or, still less, line segments [p. 420]." This stage is followed by an active-analytic process that works on the outputs of the first stage, testing hypotheses about what might have been presented. The analytic process works from "specific local details of the stimulus input rather than generalized global features of the type that activate the first phase [p. 421]."

Becker and Killion (1977) hypothesize two processes: a visual recognition process and a top-down verification process. The visual process is susceptible to degradations such as reduced stimulus intensity. Semantic or experimental context can reduce the effects of degradation in this process. The verification process selects one of a small number of hypotheses, which might be provided by the visually related process. It is not affected by the degradation caused by reduced stimulus intensity but is affected by the frequency of the target word.

Like these models, the Bilateral Cooperative model uses a global process to produce a set of reasonable possibilities for recognition and an analytic-local process that uses these possibilities to guide analysis. Unlike these models, the two processes of the BLC model operate in parallel, based on the same input. The global stage does not "feed" the verification stage, although it may guide it. The results of each process may be used by the other, but they both work on the same data.

The two ways in which the BLC model can be regarded as a dual-coding model are actually one. The visual route to meaning is the passive-global process, and phonetic coding is the active-analytic process. The BLC model is a more thoroughgoing dual-coding model than are the ones we have cited: Passive-global processes and active-analytic processes are in play at all levels, from creating letters out of visual patterns to understanding metaphoric references in the poetry of William Blake.

Phonetic Recoding and Memory

Phonetic recoding is just one of several possible routes to meaning, and in skilled reading it is not even the most used route. Its more important role may be to store printed words until they can be integrated and comprehended as a clause. It is in the phonetic form that words are held in short-term memory during sentence comprehension, presumably because the memory functions were originally evolved to help with processing speech. We now establish that short-term memory is phonetic and that STM is used in sentence comprehension.

PHONETIC NATURE OF SHORT-TERM MEMORY

STM tends to handle linguistic material in a phonetic form regardless of whether it is presented visually or auditorily. The evidence is seen in recall errors that tend to be based on sounds rather than shapes of letters or words presented visually. In recalling the letters 'BHKTCVR', 'T' may, in error, be replaced by a rhyming letter such as 'P', but will not be replaced by 'F' which looks similar to 'T' but sounds different (R. Conrad, 1964). In another study, recall for sets of acoustically similar letters ('EGCPTVB') was worse than for dissimilar ones ('FGOAYQR') (Wickelgren, 1965).

Noise or heard words can adversely affect serial recall of a sequence of visually presented digits (Salame & Baddeley, 1982). The interference was worse, the more closely the auditory material resembled digits phonetically. The interference was mostly in the earlier part of a 9-digit serial list, and was negligible for the last three digits, even though the error rate for them was quite high. Subvocalizing caused even more errors than the worst unattended speech, and during subvocalization, unattended speech had no extra effect on recall.

Poor readers do not use phonetic recoding as much as do good readers, at least to hold words in STM. In one study good readers from Grade 2 made more errors than did poor readers in recalling rhyming letters ('B,C,D', etc.) but not non-rhyming ones ('H,K,Q', etc.). The higher error rates of the good readers indicate that they coded the letters phonetically more than did the poor readers (Liberman, Shankweiler, Liberman, Fowler, & Fischer, 1977). Other researchers used words and sentences and found similar effects (Barron, 1978; Byrne & Shea, 1979; Mann, Liberman, & Shankweiler, 1980).

Apparently, children learn only slowly to use auditory images as a means of holding linguistic material in STM. Phonetic coding follows after subvocalization in the developmental sequence and increases with age while subvocalization is decreasing. According to R. Conrad (1971), children at age 5 start to resort to phonetic recoding in remembering objects. Beyond age 5, he found a systematic progressive advantage up to age 11 (the oldest age studied), when the pictures of the objects had unlike sounding names (*fish, clock*) as compared to performance with rhyming names (*rat, cat*). Conrad's findings may show a developmental trend toward using words as labels for objects in memory in place of their pictorial representations; the words themselves may be remembered equally phonetically at any age. Indeed, Alegria and Pignot (1979) found the rhyme effect even in children as young as 4.

Brain-damaged patients using only the RH have trouble processing phrases containing more than three critical content words (e.g., *Happy little girl jumping*). Such patients can recognize a substantial number of isolated words using the visual route, so the limit is not a vocabulary limit. Zaidel (1978a) attributes this deficit to the fact that verbal short-term memory in the right hemisphere is severely limited. The right hemisphere does not do phonetic coding in most people.

People who have been deaf all their lives cannot develop true auditory images of words. Suter (1982) found that subjects who became deaf before learning language showed no differences between left and right hemisphere EEG levels when watching a story presented in **Ameslan** (American Sign Language), whereas hearing interpreters of sign language showed a stronger left hemisphere involvement. If phonetic coding is required for STM, then the deaf should be poorer than hearing subjects in a memory task. They are, but only when ordered recall is required (Hanson, 1982). Deaf people are as good in free (unordered) recall of a list of printed words as hearing people, but are unaffected by whether the words are phonetically similar. In ordered recall even the deaf show some detrimental effects of phonetic similarity and are much worse at the task than hearing subjects.

Apparently, it is not so much memory for the words themselves as memory for their order that requires phonetic coding. Thus, a patient who had lost reading ability, called a "phonemic dyslexic," was unable to recall more than two words presented serially but could remember as many as seven all presented together (Nolan & Caramazza, 1982). The main problems of phonemic dyslexics are associated with an inability to do phonetic coding (Chapter 11).

Word order plays a key role in understanding written or spoken syntax, and in short-term memory, order is maintained in phonetic form. In Ameslan syntax, however, word order plays a subordinate role to "inflections" (movements made simultaneously with the basic signs) (Hanson & Bellugi, 1982). Ameslan syntax is partially parallel rather than sequential. Understandably, congenitally deaf readers seem to recode words into Ameslan rather than phonetic forms, thus avoiding both the problem of phonetic coding and the need to retain word order while they reconstruct the syntax of what they read (Treiman & Hirsh-Pasek, 1983).

PHONETIC CODING IN SENTENCE PROCESSING

Researchers study phonetic coding and/or subvocalization in sentence processing, either by phonetically manipulating key words in a passage or by using concurrent vocalization.

Cunningham and Cunningham (1978) used a passage about six fish, whose names were pronounceable (*doffit, mintex*) for one group of subjects, and unpronounceable (*dfofti, mnitxe*) for the other group. To minimize the orthographic variable, the researchers trained the subjects to associate pictures of the fish with the names (without pronunciation) before the reading proper. The subjects in the Pronounceable Group silently read the passage significantly faster than did the subjects in the Unpronounceable Group. After reading, the subjects were asked to point to the fish that had particular traits described in the passage. The Pronounceable Group did better on this comprehension–recall test too.

In the next group of studies, sentence processing was probed using the technique called **concurrent vocalizing**—subjects say irrelevant words repeatedly while reading. Pintner (1913) was the pioneer of this technique. His subjects counted continuously 13, 14, 15, and so on, while reading a passage. Reading was impaired at first, but after practice, the subjects read better while counting than not. Concurrent vocalization has been resurrected by contemporary psychologists as one of the main tools for studying subvocalization and phonetic recoding.

In B. A. Levy's (1975) study, subjects indicated, immediately following the presentation of a set of sentences, whether a test sentence was identical or changed from one of the three presented sentences. Suppose the original sentence was: *The airline stewardess seduced an attractive pilot.* A lexical change involved substituting a synonym for one of the nouns (*stewardess* with *hostess*). A semantic change involved interchanging the subject and direct object: *The airline pilot seduced an attractive stewardess.*

Suppression had an adverse effect on both lexical and semantic tasks. Subjects in the study read sentences at fixed rates, and the memory requirement, especially for specific words, was explicit. Normally, individual words of a sentence are purged from working memory soon after a sentence has been comprehended and a gist extracted (see Chapter 12). In a later study (B. A.

Levy, 1978), suppressing vocalization adversely affected detection of word changes in sentences but not detection of paraphrases of a paragraph.

Baddeley's (1979) subjects counted from 1 to 6 repeatedly while deciding whether a visually presented sentence was true or false. Counting had no effect on the time for sentence verification. The sentences tested were simple:

1. *Robins have red breasts.*
2. *Generals have red breasts.*

He concludes that the articulatory loop of working memory is not necessary for comprehending simple sentences. Such short sentences probably do not require the use of phonetically coded short-term memory. According to Zaidel (1978a), they can be effectively handled by the isolated right hemisphere of the brain, which has little capacity for phonetic short-term memory.

Overt counting increased the probability of missing the anomaly in the following complex sentence but did not affect comprehension of normal sentences (Baddeley, Eldridge, & Lewis, 1981):

She doesn't mind going to the dentist to have fillings, but doesn't like the rent when he gives her the injection at the beginning.

The counting was assumed to suppress subvocalization. Listening, without attention, to a tape of monosyllabic words had no effect on performance, either by itself or along with suppression by counting. Tapping while reading also had no effect, suggesting that counting is detrimental because it is speech rather than simply because it is a concurrent task.

In a study by Slowiaczek and Clifton (1980), comprehension in reading, but not in listening, was impaired by requiring subjects to count or say *colacola* aloud, which blocked subvocalization. The effect of blocking subvocalization was specific to tests that required integration of concepts within or across sentences, as contrasted with tests that required only memory for individual word concepts. One of their test items was:

The older students had come to see his performance. The high school teacher cheered the sad children.

(Test) The older students cheered the sad children (Yes or No?)

According to the researchers, subvocalization results in a more durable memory representation, needed for integration of concepts. It also assists the construction of a prosodic representation, needed for sentence comprehension.

Another study considers counting as an activity that impinges on working memory that would otherwise be available for reading comprehension (Glanzer, Dorfman, & Kaplan, 1981). Subjects read a paragraph, exposing each sentence when they wanted to. When counting (21–59) was imposed between sentences, the reading latencies increased; when it was imposed within sentences (counting while reading), accuracy of comprehension decreased as well. According to the researchers, counting between sentences attacks the carry-over of information from the preceding text; counting within sentences attacks, in addition, carrying of information generated during processing of the current sentence.

CONCURRENT VOCALIZING: EVALUATION

Concurrent vocalizing interferes with comprehending complex sentences, according to the preceding experiments. Does interference occur (*a*) because vocalizing blocks subvocalization, or (*b*) because it interferes with phonetic coding as well? Being an articulatory activity, vocalizing should be expected to block another articulatory activity, namely, subvocalizing. But before concluding that subvocalizing is necessary for comprehending complex sentences, let us consider explanation (*b*). Vocalizing may not block phonetic coding but it may interfere with the use of phonetic coding, both being speech activities. Recall that silent reading, like reading aloud, does involve the two speech areas of the cortex: Broca's area and the supplementary motor area (see "Precursors of Subvocalization"). The main effect of concurrent vocalization seems to be on interpreting and recalling complex sentences. If phonetic coding is a means of holding words in working memory, and if working memory is necessary for comprehending complex sentences, then this result follows.

Unattended speech should not and does not interfere with reading. People are well able to eliminate all but one voice at a party (the so-called "cocktail-party effect"). One's own speech is harder to eliminate, since one has to pay attention to it in speaking.

In sum, concurrent vocalization inhibits integrative and phonetic functions rather than word understanding. For normal readers, phonetic coding seems to be essential for analysis of complex syntactic material and for integration over extended passages, but not for understanding simple sentences or individual words.

Summary and Conclusions

Audible or inaudible vocalizing may accompany silent reading, especially if the reader is unskilled or the material is difficult. Subvocalizing appears to provide an unskilled reader with an additional and well-practiced means of perceiving printed words. One of the main techniques for studying subvocalization is electromyography, which detects minute muscle potentials in the speech organs. This technique records diffuse muscle activities, and hence shows only the overall activity level, not which sounds or words are being subvocalized. Nevertheless, it may be effectively used in reducing excessive subvocalization, which may slow reading.

Phonetic recoding is quite a different phenomenon from subvocalization.

A reader may convert seen words into auditory images mainly as a means to hold the order of the words in short-term memory. The individual words, processed to varying degrees, have to be held in this memory until they can be integrated into a clause or a sentence. Complex sentence processing is affected by concurrent vocalizing, which seems to interfere with phonetic short-term memory of words.

To find a word's meaning, skilled readers seem to use a visual route primarily and a phonetic route for special words, such as unfamiliar words or pseudowords. The visual route is a fast passive-global process, whereas phonetic coding is a slow active-analytic process. Poor readers and some brain-damaged patients may rely almost entirely on one or the other route.

Phonetic coding interacts with orthographic coding: Auditorily presented words may be orthographically coded, just as visually presented words are phonetically coded. In a complex alphabetic orthography, such as English or French, phonetic coding includes two stages: In one, letter groups are formed, and in the second, the letter groups are converted to a phonetic form.

Sensitivity to the phonetic form of words and the use of phonetic coding for holding them in STM are not confined to users of sound-coding scripts; users of logographic Chinese characters do it too.

Now we trace a possible developmental sequence for the several routes to meaning. The foundation for the sequence is laid in the first auditory images the child uses to recognize spoken words. Later, the child learns to read by reading aloud, gathering meaning through the well-practiced auditory channel. Still later, overt vocalization may be omitted, although covert control of the vocal musculature still occurs in the form of subvocalization. At the subvocalization stage, the child's articulatory control patterns may complement the auditory images and the two may gradually replace the sounds heard during the vocalization of the reading-aloud stage.

Next is the development of phonetic recoding—the formation of auditory images with little or no subvocalization. Visual recognition of the words is being learned in parallel with these phonetic processes, and as the child continues to learn to read, both phonetic and visual coding processes are being developed. Both improve with familiarity and practice, but the visual path continues to improve until a later age. Even when visual coding is well practiced and is the dominant mode of word recognition, phonetically recoded words are the primary content of the short-term memory involved in clause and sentence analysis.

The visual path is a route to meaning, the phonetic path a route to remembering.

11

The Bilateral Cooperative Model of Reading

And that's the way we read: we race along, making quick guesses at the meanings of little bunches of words, and quick corrections of these first guesses afterwards.
—Flesch (1949, p. 183)

United we conquer, divided we fall.

Introduction to the Bilateral Cooperative Model

We now develop a model that attempts to provide a framework for all aspects of reading, from letter recognition to deep understanding of whole texts.

According to the **Bilateral Cooperative** (BLC) model, reading involves two parallel streams or "tracks" of interacting processes (M. M. Taylor, 1983). The **LEFT track** deals with functional relationships, sequentially ordered material, phonetic coding, syntax, and most functions we commonly think of as "linguistic." It is the analytic and logical track. The **RIGHT track** performs pattern matching functions, seeks out similarities between the input patterns and previously seen patterns, evokes associations, and relates the meanings of words and phrases with real-world conditions. Its functions tend to be global, parallel, and passive. LEFT and RIGHT tracks cooperate in extracting the meaning from marks on a page (and indeed from speech as well, though speech is not the topic of this book). The two tracks interact in the way suggested by the quote from Flesch that starts this chapter: The RIGHT track makes quick guesses, and the LEFT corrects the guesses as well as linking the results into phrases, clauses and larger units.

It is important to distinguish LEFT and RIGHT tracks from left and right hemisphere processes. The location of the two tracks in the brain is of less importance than their functional relationship. The terms are intended simply as mnemonics. In normal right-handed males, and in most females and left-handed males, the LEFT processes are mainly restricted to the left hemisphere (LH). The RIGHT processes, on the other hand, can be performed by either hemisphere. When the LH is heavily loaded in performing the LEFT processes,

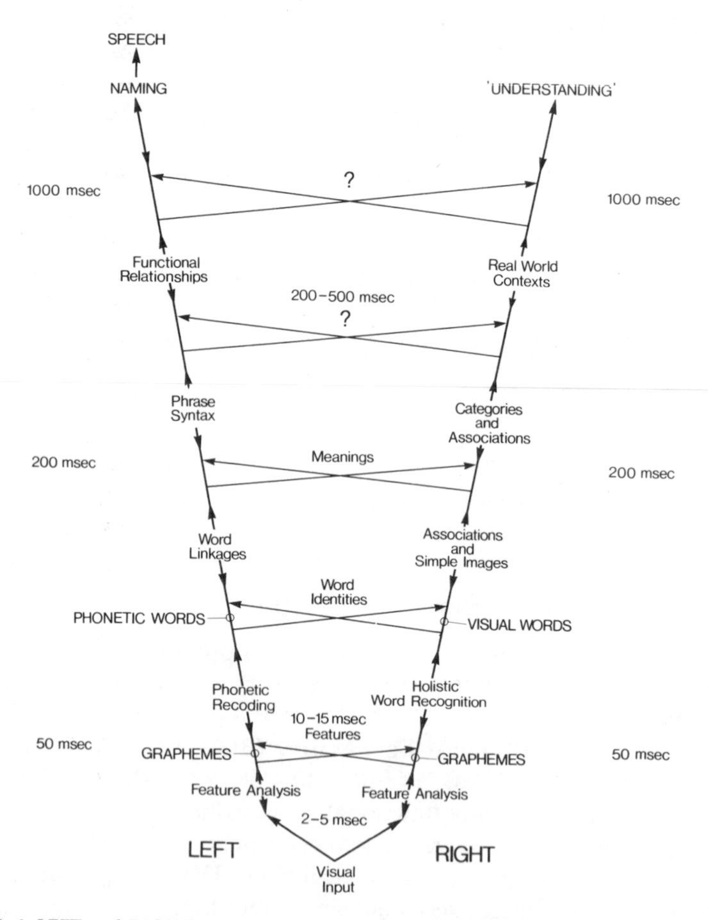

Figure 11-1 *LEFT and RIGHT tracks and their interactions in the Bilateral Cooperative model of reading. The two tracks are connected at a few discrete levels but otherwise are independent. The RIGHT track works by global pattern matching and association, ultimately linking the sense of items to the state of the real world; the LEFT works by analysis and rules, selecting appropriate pattern matches developed by the RIGHT and inhibiting inappropriate ones. The LEFT track is responsible for syntactic relations and phonetic coding of words.*

then the right hemisphere (RH) takes over the RIGHT processes. Only at the higher levels of understanding is there a clear preference of the RIGHT processes for the RH. The RH seems to be as essential for the understanding of jokes and metaphors as the left is for the production of speech.

A skeleton diagram for the BLC model is shown in Figure 11-1, which will be used to illustrate many of the ideas developed in the following sections. The important points about Figure 11-1 are:

- The processes on both LEFT and RIGHT tracks can operate independently of one another between interconnection points.
- The interconnections occur only at discrete points, between which the processes on the two tracks perform related tasks on similar data. Five crossover points have been postulated, but the actual number is unimportant.
- It takes longer to transfer data from one track to the other at the higher stages because of an increase in processing required to translate the representations of one track to those of the other. The crossovers require complicated processing in their own right, especially at the higher levels.

The processes in each track have a family resemblance: The low-level processes resemble the high-level processes within the same track much more closely than they resemble the same-level processes in the other track. Table 11-1 lists some of the major differences between LEFT and RIGHT processes, which will be elaborated throughout this chapter.

In each track, the lower levels deal with simple things such as letters or words, the higher levels with complex matters such as syntax or meaning. The LEFT track links words together, in the manner discussed in grammar books. The RIGHT combines the ideas behind the words, and connects them with the current real-world context; it fleshes out the skeleton built by the LEFT. Both tracks are heavily dependent on context, although it may not be evident from Fig 11-1. The data gathered from lower stages serves largely to confirm or deny expectations derived from patterns or rules active in the higher stages. Each stage is thus firmly linked to higher and lower stages in its own track, and to parallel stages in the other track.

Brain Function and Malfunction

Three kinds of people provide us with useful information about brain function: normal readers, people with localized brain damage, and people with surgically split brains (who have had the connections between the hemispheres cut). Each source of information has its problems. In normals, there is so much interconnection that one can seldom be sure just what processes are important at any moment; in patients with localized brain damage, each case is different, and the damage may affect more than the damaged area; in split-brain patients there is often some long-standing

Table 11-1 *Functions in the Bilateral Cooperative Model*

	LEFT track	RIGHT track
Cortical location	Left hemisphere	Both hemispheres, but mainly right in normal reading
Specialty	Labels, symbols, functional relationships, sequences	Patterns, colors, pictures, associations, collections
Processing style	Active, under attentional control Analysis into sub-units Seeks out differences Exact Unique result Serial, slow Handles material presented sequentially Time order Syntactic, rule based Pattern analysis Phonetically based Good short-term memory Speech output	Passive, automatic Global, wholistic Looks for similarities Approximate Many acceptable results Parallel, fast Handles material presented as a group Associations and spatial relations Meaning centered Approximate pattern matching Visually based Poor short-term memory Nonspeech output
Letter	Abstract letter identities Kanji phonetic and radical(?) Hangul and Kana	Isolated but not embedded letters Single or nonsense pairs of Kanji
Morpheme	Syntactic components Abstract elements	Content components Concrete elements
Word	Unfamiliar words Abstract words Embedded words Pseudowords	Familiar words Concrete, high-imagery words Words marked off by spaces
Sentence	Syntactic relations Make verbal gist	Meaning relations Visualization
Text	Functional and logical relations	Speed reading Humor and poetry

abnormality that could have led to changes from normal functioning. Hence, when the data from the three populations disagree, one must be cautious in making inferences about normal reading, but when they agree, the evidence is probably secure. (For a comprehensive review of hemispheric functions, see Moscovitch, 1979.)

Types of Acquired Dyslexia

Acquired dyslexia is loss of reading ability due to damage in the left hemisphere. Dyslexic patients can shed some light on the separation of functions in normal reading. If a patient retains one ability such as reading concrete words, while losing a closely related ability such as reading function words, we can be sure that the two abilities have at least one component process that differs. If another patient loses what the first retains, and vice versa, the pattern of ability loss is called double dissociation, and it demonstrates not only that there is something different between the abilities but also that the patients did not simply retain the "easier" ability.

If a particular ability is retained when another is lost, we can be sure that the two abilities use different processes. The reverse is not true, however. The fact that two abilities are usually lost together may mean: (*a*) they both use a process that is damaged; (*b*) they are mediated by processes performed in neighbouring brain areas that usually are damaged by the same accident; or (*c*) their underlying processes interact so that damage to one causes loss of the other ability. Each case of dyslexia is unique, but there exist certain syndromes representing abilities that tend to be lost together.

Acquired dyslexia can be classified into a few types, depending on the patterns of reading errors (Coltheart, Patterson, & Marshall, 1980; Marshall & Newcombe, 1973; Newcombe & Marshall, 1981; Patterson, 1981). The two main contrasting types are phonemic dyslexia and surface dyslexia.

PHONEMIC (DEEP) DYSLEXIA

Phonemic dyslexia is associated with well-defined damage to a large region of the left hemisphere, involving the speech areas. According to the BLC model, phonemic dyslexics cannot use a substantial portion of the LEFT track, and hence cannot convert letter strings into sound patterns. Inability to read pseudowords (e.g., DAKE) or to recognize homophones or rhymes is the most characteristic symptom of phonemic dyslexia. They can recognize familiar words, presumably by a visual route. Their reading errors are related to the correct words either semantically (e.g., *crocus* → "lilac"; *carpenter* → "nails"; *vice* → "wicked"), or visually (*ship* → "chip"; *hand* → "hound").

Phonemic dyslexics often have trouble with syntactic words and morphemes, which may be confused, ignored, or puzzled over. Thus, they may report *jumps, jumping, jumped* all as "jump . . . something." They may, however, use the meanings of function words to control their behavior, by choosing which of two birds in a picture is "above" or "below" the other, by putting things "in" or "on" other things, and so forth (Morton & Patterson, 1980a). Phonemic dyslexics usually have an easier time with nouns than with verbs, and may find adjectives almost as hard as function words. Many phonemic dyslexics can read high-imagery words better than low-imagery ones.

Characteristically, phonemic dyslexics either know a word and read it without hesitation or are unable to read it at all. Occasionally, a word can be primed by giving its category, as illustrated in this hypothetical dialogue:

> *Patient*: I don't know this word.
> *Experimenter*: It's a tool.
> *Patient*: Hammer.

Sometimes the reverse effect happens: A patient might know the category of an item without being able to say its name. For *hammer*, he might be able to say that it was a tool, but not which tool. This problem may tie in with the semantic errors these dyslexics sometimes make. It is as if they correctly decoded the word and made associations and categorizations, but were unable to develop the specific word label to a point where it could be used to check potential response words.

Phonemic dyslexics tend to have problems with short-term memory, particularly if the material is presented sequentially. The phonemic dyslexic studied by Nolan and Caramazza (1982) could remember only one or two items of a list presented sequentially but had no trouble remembering seven presented as a group. This patient's difficulties were by no means restricted to reading: He had just as much problem in repeating heard nonsense words or function words as in reading them.

Japanese phonemic dyslexics may not be able to read Kana although they can read Kanji. Sometimes they can read complex Kanji or multi-Kanji words of which they might not be able to read the constituent Kanji. They may be able to comprehend Kanji (select a correct picture) they cannot pronounce. One such patient said that he could not say the word although it was on the tip of his tongue. All the same, he could recognize the character instantly and understand its meaning (Sakamoto, cited by Sasanuma, 1980). Kanji are preferentially processed by RH, Kana by LH.

PHONOLOGICAL DYSLEXIA

Phonological dyslexics have LH lesions and are like phonemic dyslexics in that they cannot read pseudowords or unfamiliar words. In all other respects they seem to read more or less normally, having only minor problems with function words or syntax.

Phonological dyslexics can be subdivided into two classes: One class cannot combine letters into phonologically relevant clusters, whereas the other class cannot convert graphemes (letters and letter groups) into phonological codes (Beauvois & Dérouesné, 1979; Dérouesné & Beauvois, 1979). These two sub-processes are needed for phonetic coding in alphabetic languages like English or French, which have poor letter-to-sound correspondences. Phonological dyslexics lack all or part of one stage: the LEFT track phonetic coding stage.

SURFACE DYSLEXIA

Surface dyslexics have sustained a diffuse loss of brain tissue, usually in the LH, but outside the speech areas (Deloche, Andreewsky, & Desi, 1982; Marshall & Newcombe, 1973; Sasanuma, 1975; Warrington, 1975). The surface dyslexics retain LEFT track capabilities but lack direct visual access to word recognition, as well as much of the "understanding" system. In short, they are deficient in the RIGHT track.

Surface dyslexics can decode pseudowords but have trouble dealing with irregularly spelled common words, such as *yacht.* So long as the words can be worked out by rules, they can say them. On the other hand, they may have trouble understanding what they have read. They also tend to have problems with pictorial representation (Warrington, 1975).

A Japanese surface dyslexic has little trouble reading Kana but has lost most of the capability to read Kanji. In writing Kanji, the errors are often phonetic: The patient may write a Kanji for a syllable that sounds like the intended one. These patients also comprehend poorly what they read. When they try to read text written mainly in Kana, they have trouble identifying word boundaries, which require knowledge of the words (Sasanuma, 1975). In such text, the words are not visually marked in any way (see Chapter 4). Another correlate of surface dyslexia in Japan (in at least one patient) is an impairment of categorizing ability (Sasanuma, 1980), which is a RIGHT track function.

Right Hemisphere Involvement in Reading

J.W., A PATIENT WITH A PARTIALLY SPLIT BRAIN

For some brain pathologies such as intractable epilepsy, the recommended surgery may be to separate the two halves of the brain by cutting the connective tissue, the corpus callosum. This operation gives the patient what is known as a **split brain.** Usually the cut is complete, leaving no direct communication between the two cortical hemispheres. In one reported case, however, the patient, known as J.W., had a partial cut rather than a complete one. Later surgery completed the separation of the hemispheres, but the interesting data come from the period between the two operations (Sidtis, Volpe, Holtzman, Wilson, & Gazzaniga, 1981).

Speech is represented in the left hemisphere of almost all normal right-handed people and of most left-handed people as well. In keeping with this, J.W. was able to read words presented in the right side of his visual field (which projects to LH) easily and precisely. Words presented to the left side of his visual field (RH projection) caused some difficulty. He could obviously comprehend at least some of them, but to say the word he needed a complex strategy. As an example, when presented with the word *Knight*, he said: "I have a picture in mind but can't say it . . . Two fighters in a ring . . . Ancient and wearing uniforms and helmets . . . on horses . . . trying to knock each other off . . . Knights?"

This pictorial way of discovering the word typified J.W.'s procedure with RH presentations. He would visualize a scene incorporating the referent of the word in its center. For example, for *stove,* he might imagine a stove in the middle of a kitchen scene or a hardware store (both scenes apparently being simultaneously available to him), and then laboriously work out what the

Visual input → LH processing → naming → SPEECH
(meanings) ↑
→ RH processing → pictures → . . .

Figure 11-2. Processing channels available to J.W., who had a partially split brain.

word was. Clearly, the RH could identify the word and its meaning, but it could not pass the label to the LH, which controls speech output. The RH made a picture out of the word if it could, and the LH solved a puzzle to provide the spoken output. Although the word was not initially available for speech, when at last the correct word was found, its correctness could be checked by the RH against the original stimulus word.

A simplified description of the processing pathways available to J.W. for word naming might be as shown in Figure 11-2.

NORMAL READERS' CORTICAL ACTIVITIES

In recognizing letters and words in a T-scope, normal subjects tend to perform best with the left hemisphere, especially with unfamiliar words, isolated letters, and nonsense strings, or with Kana syllabics, Hangul syllable blocks, or multi-Kanji words. Familiar words, single Kanji, or nonsense Kanji pairs are either done equally well by both hemispheres or preferred by the right (see Chapters 1, 3, 4, and 5). The experiments are subtle and often open to different interpretations because of the many links between the hemispheres in normal readers. Both hemispheres can get information rapidly no matter which hemisphere first processed a stimuls (see "Interhemispheric Crossover of Information in Same-Different Judgments" later in this chapter).

Electrical signals recorded from the scalp (EEG) provide a gross measure of brain activity. In subjects reading continuous text, EEG signals were relatively stronger from the LH if the material was technical, and from the RH if it was a high-imagery story (Ornstein, Herron, Johnstone, & Swencionis, 1979). In subjects reading sentences that might end in a semantically anomalous word, signals were stronger in the LH for the first few words (which determine the syntactic structure) of the sentence, but stronger from the RH for the semantically anomalous last word (Kutas & Hillyard, 1982). The LH tends to deal with functional relationships, the RH with pictorial and semantic ones.

The activity of different regions of the brain may be measured by introducing radioactive atoms, which are carried along by the blood flow to the more active regions. A brain scan shows where these atoms have gone, moment by moment. In reading aloud, seven main areas are active in each hemisphere (Lassen *et al.*, 1978; see also Chapter 10). In silent reading, two of these areas, the motor control areas, are inactive. Each hemisphere shows approximately the same pattern of five active areas, as if corresponding regions in the two hemispheres had related activities.

In sum, the brain-scan work suggests that the two hemispheres work together; the split brain of J.W. shows that both can interpret printed words, though very differently; and the EEG work suggests that they tend to emphasize different kinds of material.

CAPABILITIES OF THE RIGHT HEMISPHERE

Few studies show obvious effects on simple reading processes following RH damage. This might be expected from the model, if both hemispheres are capable of the RIGHT processes. Nevertheless, the abilities of the two hemispheres differ more at higher levels of interpretation, such as judging the integrity or incongruity of stories (e.g., Moscovitch, 1979). In the study of Ornstein *et al.* (1979) mentioned above, readers of an emotional, high-imagery story showed greater RH involvement than did readers of technical material, presumably because RH handles associations, pictures, and meanings, whereas LH handles the functional relations among things.

J. W.'s word recognition, performed by the RH, is intensely pictorial and associative. Similarly, normal subjects presented with sentences or even short narratives for later recall will frequently visualize them if they describe concrete scenes. The words may be lost, but the imagery remains (e.g., Beaugrande, 1981; Begg & Paivio, 1969); on later recall, the sense can be restored from the visual image. This picturing of the text may well be RH processing, working on the outputs of the various levels of LH language processing where necessary, but based also on pattern interpretations developed internally.

Dennis and Whitaker (1976) reported on three children who had each lost one brain hemisphere before the age of 5 months. Two of them retained the RH and one the LH. The isolated RHs did learn syntactic functions, but not very well, and had problems with tasks such as replacing missing pronouns. The isolated LH could deal with semantic problems but had difficulty with visual association. These observations contrast with Hécaen's (1978) claim that there is complete transfer of capability between hemispheres if lesions occur at a young enough age. Perhaps both observations can be correct: The transfer of function from a small injured part of one hemisphere to the corresponding part of the other may be possible, but the transfer of total hemisphere function is just too much for the remaining hemisphere to handle.

Adult patients with damaged RH tend to show difficulties with integrating the sense of things. Such patients have problems with auditory as well as reading comprehension, although they can pronounce and read aloud quite well (Gainotti, Caltagirone, Micelli, & Masullo, 1981). They also have problems recognizing what parts of stories go together, determining whether items in a story are plausible in context, and understanding jokes (Brownell, Michel, Powelson, & Gardner, 1983; Wapner, Hamby, & Gardner, 1981). They tend not to see the intended meanings, but to accept literal readings of metaphoric statements without finding them funny (Winner & Gardner, 1977). In telling a story, they may fail to recognize it as fiction, and may inject themselves into the plot or argue with the story's premises (Gardner, 1982).

Zaidel (1978) carefully studied the linguistic capability of the RH in patients whose LH had been removed after language acquisition, or whose corpus callosum had been split. His major conclusions relevant to the BLC model follow:

- The RH recognizes patterns through template matching (in contrast to the LH, which recognizes by feature extraction and analysis.) The **template matching** procedure compares a pattern directly with a stored template, providing an output that is stronger, the more closely the pattern matches the template. It uses no analytic rules but uses the whole input pattern and the whole template globally. Thus, the RH sees 'C' as almost identical to 'G'; an analytic processor would concentrate on the cross-mark that differentiates the two letters.
- The RH can perceive an apparently disorganized or unrelated group of parts as a meaningful whole, but is poor at seeing a given configuration embedded in a larger, more complex pattern.
- The RH is capable of dealing with words written in mixed type faces (and hence must be able to translate letter features into letters, despite being unable to analyze words into their letters).
- The RH can provide "quick orientation to repeated linguistic patterns or gestalts" and can "tune in to the extra-linguistic context of utterances [p. 195]" (presumably for written material as well).
- The RH has a rich lexical structure, but its vocabulary tends to be connotative and associative rather than precise and denotative.
- The RH has very poor short-term memory and can relate no more than three or four content words.
- The RH comprehension is not impaired by syntactic complexity, but it has problems with longer strings of words.
- The RH has neither phonetic coding nor grapheme-to-phoneme conversion rules. (Some split-brain patients with long-standing neurological problems can perform phonetic tasks with the RH after callosal section; Sidtis, Volpe, Wilson, Rayport, & Gazzaniga, 1981).
- The RH cannot compose speech (although other researchers have claimed that it can produce stereotyped phrases such as *How are you*).

These generalizations about the RH correspond roughly to RIGHT track processes. They do not, however, prove that the RH is normally responsible for the RIGHT track functions. What Zaidel's (1978) work shows is that the RH is at least capable of performing the RIGHT processes. Sperry's (1982) patient who congenitally lacked a corpus callosum developed language in both hemispheres, but apparently at the expense of the usual nonverbal capabilities of the RH. In normal subjects, the LH can pass over some of its function to the RH when under pressure (Friedman, Polson, Dafoe, & Gaskill, 1982; Polson, Friedman, & Gaskill, 1981). Most likely, the RH normally performs the RIGHT processes when the LH is working on the LEFT processes. The RH may learn to do some LEFT processes habitually, if the need arises at a sufficiently early age. It may normally have the capacity for low-level LH processes, especially in people less lateralized than the typical right-handed male about whom we are making our stronger statements.

RIGHT HEMISPHERE AND ACQUIRED DYSLEXIA

If the RH performs all the functions listed by Zaidel (1978), one may ask some questions about the effects of RH damage on reading ability:

1. Why do RH lesions rarely, if ever, produce language difficulties parallel to those caused by LH lesions?
   • The RIGHT track functions can be performed by either hemisphere. The primary reason that they are done by the RH, if they are, is that the LH is usually busy performing the LEFT track processes. Hence, RH damage simply forces the LH to use its capability to do the work of both tracks. Deficits will be subtle, and will be demonstrated primarily in the complex, high-level RIGHT track functions, or under conditions of heavy task loading.
2. Why is surface dyslexia usually caused by diffuse lesions, often in the LH?
   • RIGHT track functions may well be less localized than LEFT, because they involve widespread parallelism and the interaction of many levels of association. Hence, diffuse loss of brain function is more likely to depress their level than to eliminate them, and focal damage is unlikely to affect them except in very specific areas of meaning. Surface dyslexia expresses RIGHT track problems, possibly also involving the LEFT track, and hence would be expected to occur only with diffuse lesions which generally depress brain function.
3. Even more significantly, why does the RH not show its language competence in the presence of a LH lesion for which it should be able to compensate?
   • Question 3 may have two answers: First, the RH probably does compensate to some extent for LH damage. The reading performance of phonemic dyslexics is characteristic of RH capabilities, and some authors regard phonemic dyslexia as RH reading (e.g., Saffran, Bogyo, Schwartz, & Marin, 1980). Benson (1981) describes a dyslexic patient who has recovered some reading ability a few years after LH damage. She read *living room* as "the place that my husband and I go after dinner to drink coffee and talk [p. 184]." This pictorial reading is reminiscent of the split-brained J.W. reading with his RH.

   Second, one function of the LEFT track is to control the RIGHT track activities by inhibiting inappropriate ones and assisting appropriate ones. When the LH is damaged, it may send noisy or false control signals to the RH, so that the RH function can be expressed only when the damaged LH tissue is cut out, or the brain hemispheres separated (e.g., Sperry, 1982).

Recognizing Words

We now consider the interactions of LEFT and RIGHT processes in recognizing letters and words, both in normal and abnormal readers. Later, we discuss the higher-level processes involved in understanding text.

From Feature Analysis to Word Recognition

FEATURES AND LETTERS—THE FIRST FIFTY MILLISECONDS

When a word is presented, information about it builds up over time. In the first 50 msec, both LEFT and RIGHT tracks turn the patterns of light and shade on the retina into visual features (see Chapter 9). This process seems to be similar, possibly identical, in the two hemispheres.

Moscovitch and his coworkers have used words and faces as stimuli that normally are preferentially processed by opposite hemispheres, words by the LH, faces by the RH. In the early stages of face processing, the two hemispheres behave similarly. Within 50 msec of the offset of a first face picture, both hemispheres can use the relatively unprocessed image of a second face equally well in a comparison with the first face. But by 100 msec, a RH advantage shows up (e.g., Moscovitch & Klein, 1980; Moscovitch, Scullion, & Christie, 1976). Wilkins and Stewart (1974) did a similar study using letters as stimuli. When two letters had the same name but were in different cases ("Is b the same as B?"), no hemisphere differences appeared if the two letters were separated by 50 msec, but a LH advantage showed up they were separated by 950 msec. When the two letters were the same case ("Is B the same as B?"), there was a RH advantage for the 50-msec separation but a LH advantage for the 950-msec separation. Unfortunately, Wilkins and Stewart did not use any intermediate intervals of separation.

In the first 50 msec, letters are not connected into sequences, although whole words may be recognized (Chapter 9). In Lefton and Spragins's (1974) study, the older the schoolchildren the faster they processed letter strings, and the more sensitive they were to order of approximation to English. No matter what the age, however, both first and fourth orders of approximation gave equally poor results when the stimuli were masked after 50 msec. The full effect of increasing order of approximation showed up only after 100 or 150 msec, and then it improved up to 200 msec.

Rayner and Posnansky (1978) labeled outline drawings with words or pseudowords that resembled the appropriate labels in various ways. A word's outer contour and perhaps its initial and final letters were all that were useful until some time between 40 and 80 msec (see "Shape, Letters, and Sound," in Chapter 9).

The first 50 msec of a reading fixation is used in acquiring the shapes of the words and the features necessary for decoding them. Both hemispheres participate in this initial activity. After the first 50 msec, however, the two hemispheres tend to do different things with the information gathered.

INTERHEMISPHERIC CROSSOVER OF INFORMATION IN SAME–DIFFERENT JUDGMENTS

Phonetic materials—alphabetics, Kana, Hangul—are better identified by the LH than by the RH. A single Kanji tends to be best recognized by the RH, but when two Kanji are presented together, they are recognized best by the LH if they combine to form a real word, but not otherwise (see Chapters 3, 4, and 5).

In a **same–different** experiment, the subject is asked to determine whether two or more stimuli are all the same in some aspect or other. For example, 'A' and 'a' are the same in name but not in shape. Generally, response patterns differ for the two kinds of judgments: "Different" judgments are slower, are done analytically, depend on the number of items, and are done better when the a stimulus is presented to the LH; "same" judgments are quicker, are done wholistically, do not depend on the number of items, and are done equally well by both hemispheres or better by the RH (Bradshaw, Gates, & Patterson, 1976; Keuss, 1977; Patterson & Bradshaw, 1975; Salmon & Rodwan, 1981; D. A. Taylor, 1976).

An ingenious study by Nishikawa and Niina (1981) illustrates the cross-over of information between the hemispheres at a low level in Figure 11-1. Japanese subjects performed a same–different judgment with different kinds of stimuli, alphabetics and Kana as well as Kanji, all of which might be presented right way up or upside down. Two different patterns of results were obtained, depending on the stimulus material. For alphabetics or Kana items, the response times increased with the number of items in the set, and LH presentation was quicker by 20–25 msec. For Kanji items or for upside-down alphabetics and Kana items, set size did not affect response times, and RH presentation was quicker by 20–25 msec. The pattern of results did not depend on which hemisphere received the initial visual data, but processing was delayed by 20–25 msec if the initial hemisphere was inappropriate to the stimuli, suggesting that the information was being transferred at an early stage to the other hemisphere if it was more appropriate.

The pattern of results is characteristic of the difference between LH and RH processing: LH is analytic, phonetic, and serial, taking a measurable time per item, whereas the RH shows no aptitude for analysis, working pictorially and in a parallel way on all items at once. Each can have access to the lower-level information, but it takes a finite time for the information to pass from one hemisphere to the other. The time increases further up in the processing chain.

COOPERATION BETWEEN THE HEMISPHERES IN LETTER RECOGNITION

Jones (1982) studied normal subjects' recognition of uppercase letters presented to either RH, LH, or both at once. He found two different types of subjects: One group recognized letters better when they were presented to RH, the other when they were presented to LH. The two groups differed in several ways:

1. RH-preferred subjects were better when the same letter was presented on both sides of the brain than when only one letter was presented to their preferred side, whereas LH-preferred were no better with bilateral presentation.
2. RH-preferred subjects appeared to integrate information from the two hemispheres before making any implicit recognition decision, whereas LH-preferred either ignored the RH information or were distracted by it.
3. The RH-preferred group confused 'O–Q' six times as readily as their next worst confusion, 'C–G', which was still more confusable than any pair confused by the LH-preferred group. The RH-preferred group found 'H' to be very distinctive, whereas the LH-preferred group confused it with several other letters, including 'U', 'N', 'K', 'M', 'D', and 'T'.
4. All differences between the two groups were stronger for males than for females, but even among female subjects there were still clear LH-preferred and RH-preferred groups.

As Jones interprets his results, the RH performs wholistic processing, the LH analytic, and some people prefer one or the other. 'O' and 'Q', and 'C' and 'G' are similar when compared by a template-matching procedure, but the extra marks on 'Q' and 'G' make them distinct from 'O' and 'C' when compared by a rule-based procedure.

In the BLC model, the LH is able to support both LEFT and RIGHT tracks, whereas the RH has only RIGHT track functions. When letters were presented to only one hemisphere, the LH-preferred subjects presumably used both tracks in the LH, whereas the RH-preferred did not. The RH-preferred subjects tended to use the RIGHT track in each hemisphere. When letters were presented to both hemispheres, the RH-preferred subjects now could add the LEFT track to their processing, whereas the LH-preferred subjects had been using both tracks anyway, and thus received no benefit from the bilateral presentation.

It is possible that Jones was lucky in his choice of exposure durations. He gave a 90 msec exposure, which is long enough for the LEFT track to begin work, but not long enough for it to perform optimally. Subjects who normally use the LEFT track heavily ("Phoenicians") might have time to do something useful with it, whereas others ("Chinese") would normally still be using their RIGHT track at that stage.

WORD RECOGNITION: RIGHT

Word recognition means different things in the two tracks: The RIGHT track extracts meaning, whereas the LEFT track codes graphemes into sounds. Any phonology developed by way of a RIGHT track recognition comes from the subsequent work of the LEFT track. The detectors of the RIGHT track are the feature detectors or "demons" described in Chapter 9, working at many different levels. A RIGHT detector is always examining its input for the particular pattern to which it is tuned. It will be likely to claim a detection if it has recently seen its pattern, or if a pattern with a related meaning has been encountered.

Morton (1969) described a similar mechanism for word detection which he incorporated in his concept of a logogen. A logogen was originally an internal representation of a word that acted both as a detector for spoken and written words, and as a source for the articulatory patterns needed in speaking the word. Morton (1979) has since separated the three main functions into different logogens: one for reading, one for listening, and one for speaking. The reading logogen is the one that behaves like our RIGHT-track word detectors.

When a **reading logogen,** or word detector, sees patterns that look like the word to which it is sensitive, its activity level rises. When the activity level rises above a fluctuating threshold value, the logogen signals that it has seen its word. The value of the threshold depends on whether the logogen's word or other associated words have occurred recently. Logogens for frequent words (*cat*) are more easily excited than are those for infrequent words (*cam*), but local context (a discussion of car motors) can lower the threshold for infrequent words such as *cam.*

A semantically related context can make a RIGHT detector or logogen more willing to claim a recognition, but it does not change the discriminative ability of the RIGHT detection system as a whole. Correct recognitions may be speeded and words detected more readily in blurred presentations, but this improvement comes at the cost of an increased likelihood of false recognitions (e.g., Becker, 1982; Broadbent & Broadbent, 1980).

RIGHT processes respond to contextual expectations, which are normally unconscious on the part of the reader. The expectations depend on syntax (LEFT track information) and on semantic associations (RIGHT track information). They can be of the form "function word is wanted here," which could turn off processing by content-word detectors, or they might be "we have been dealing with fruits—expect more," which would raise the sensitivity of detectors for fruit names. Word frequency behaves like a generalized contextual expectation: A high frequency word is never a surprise.

RIGHT recognition of words is based on gross visual features such as outer contour and perhaps the Bouma shapes of the first few letters (see Chapter 9). It does not involve phonology in any way but connects directly to word meaning. The pictorial processes reported by J.W., who had the partially split brain, are examples. Martin Taylor recently experienced a similar RIGHT track pictorial recognition while looking at an anagram in the children's section of a newspaper. The anagram, *Ugy Llefaure,* was labeled as the name of an athlete. It immediately evoked a picture of a well-known Montreal Canadien hockey player, along with a wealth of remembered information about his capabilities and personality. Despite all these cues, it took a good 10–15 sec of mental work before the name "Guy Lafleure" finally surfaced. The surname, at least, has almost the same outer contour as the anagram and could be recognized by the RIGHT track almost immediately, given the contextual clue *athlete.*

A recognition by the RIGHT track is never absolute and is seldom unique. Instead, many different detectors may be looking for somewhat similar patterns. The pattern for *stake* is like the pattern for *stoke*, and RIGHT detectors for both words (as well as many others) will have some output when *stoke* is presented. Two side effects come from the approximate and graded nature of the pattern-matching process: First, the process is fast and admits substantial variations in the acceptable forms; second, it recognizes only patterns with familiar identities. A RIGHT detector can handle distorted inputs that fit reasonable expectations, such as a pseudoword visually similar to the word for which it is tuned (*cosl* might be accepted as *coal* or *cost*), but it can never give a response indicating that an unfamiliar word has been seen (it could never report "cosl," no matter what was presented).

WORD RECOGNITION: LEFT

The processes of the LEFT track contrast strongly with those of the RIGHT. The LEFT track is able to deal with subparts of structures: It can analyze the letter clusters of pseudowords or extract the phonetics from Kanji. LEFT processes admit only one response to a stimulus pattern. If they cannot find a unique answer, they are likely to assert that there is no answer, or even that there is no stimulus requiring a response.

The main job of the LEFT track in word recognition is phonological coding. It alone can translate between visual and phonetic representations of words. LEFT processes may work by rule, by pattern matching, or by a combination of the two (see models of phonological coding in Chapter 10). Phonological coding is the first stage of syntactic analysis, which is completed by later stages of the LEFT track. Only the LEFT track can remember the order of things, which it does through its phonological coding. Deficient LEFT track function leads to a whole syndrome of effects, including poor short-term memory for sequential information (see "Acquired Dyslexia," above).

In some alphabetic languages, especially those with a phonologically irregular orthography, the phonological coding of the LEFT track is done in at least two separable stages: In the first stage, letter clusters with idiosyncratic pronunciations are isolated, and in the second stage the phonology is applied to these clusters (Dérouesné & Beauvois, 1979). In a highly regular orthography with few phonologically relevant letter clusters, such as Serbo-Croatian, there may be no orthographic clustering stage (Feldman, 1981; Feldman & Kostic, 1981). In reading such an orthography, more emphasis is placed on LEFT recognition processes than in a less regular orthography such as English.

The RH and the LH judge word length in a different manner. Schiepers (1976b) found that the lengths of real words were judged better than were the lengths of nonword strings. With left visual-field (LVF) presentation (RH processing), the word advantage held only for words of less than about six letters, whereas with RVF presentation (LH processing) it held for all lengths tested. The LH can process all kinds of words and letter strings, whereas the RH processes primarily familiar words. As familiar words tend to be short, long words have to be relegated for the LH to process. Long words that are familiar might still be recognized by the RH, but there are fewer of them than there are of long words that are unfamiliar. As always, the RH can perform only RIGHT processes, whereas the LH can do both.

Both phonemic dyslexics (who cannot code letter strings phonetically) and high-vocabulary normal readers show little variation in the time it takes to recognize a word (if it is recognized at all), whereas surface dyslexics (who cannot read irregular words) and low-vocabulary normal readers take longer for long words than for short ones. Phonemic dyslexics and skilled readers rely mainly on RIGHT recognition, which deals with long words as quickly as short ones, whereas surface dyslexics and poor readers must work out the words, using the LEFT processes, which take longer for long words.

WORD RECOGNITION: RIGHT AND LEFT TOGETHER

Neither RIGHT nor LEFT track by itself can recognize words well. The LEFT is slow, the RIGHT careless. Jointly, they work well and quickly. The RIGHT gives the LEFT some guesses to be checked, and checking the accuracy of a guess is easier than working out the solution of a puzzle from scratch. Thus, the LEFT can select which RIGHT guess is correct more quickly than it could analyze the word on its own. LEFT processes make decisions; RIGHT processes gather options.

Rausch (1981) asked subjects to tell whether words in the second half of a 60-word list were repeats of earlier words in the list. Subjects had temporal lobe lesions in either the LH or the RH. Neither kind of lesion affected the subjects' abilities to detect truly repeated words, but the lesion site strongly affected their tendencies to accept related words as having been presented earlier. LH-damaged patients tended to accept words from the same semantic category almost as readily as repeated words. They would often accept homophones and associates as repeats. They could use their RH to gather options, but were unable to reject the false ones. RH-damaged patients, on the other hand, were less likely than normals to accept related words as repeats, especially if the related words were homophones. They detected exact matches, but did not detect similarities as much as normals. Normals were more accepting of false repeats than the RH-damaged patients but less than the LH-damaged ones (see Figure 11-3).

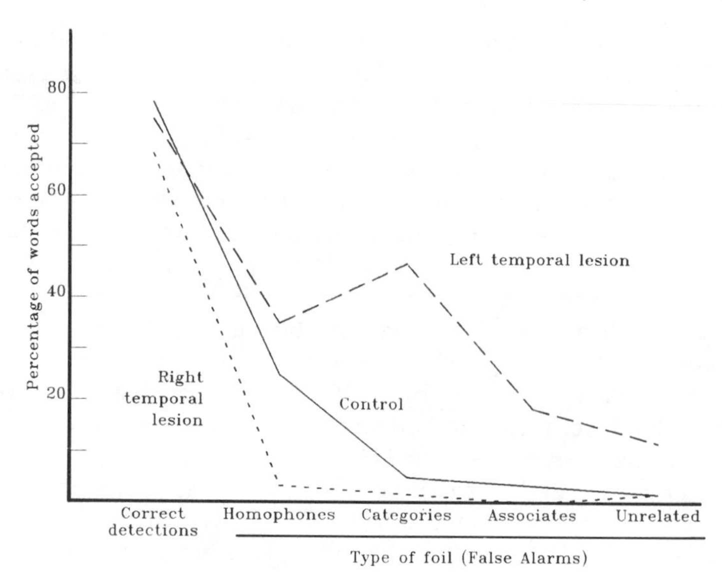

Figure 11-3. *RH acceptance versus LH rejection. Subjects judged whether words in a list had been presented earlier in the same list. Patients with Left temporal lesions, using their RH, accepted far more than normal numbers of foils (especially when the foil was from the same semantic category as an earlier word), whereas patients with Right temporal lesions, using their LH, accepted far fewer than the normal number of foils (Data from Rausch, 1981, reanalyzed).*

Frequently, one RIGHT candidate for word recognition will be much stronger than any other. Then, the LEFT need do no more than confirm its acceptability, and can do so rapidly. When there are no RIGHT candidates (the "text" consists of unfamiliar or nonsense words), the speed will just be that of the slow LEFT processing: Phonetic coding will be done, and the resulting sound patterns checked against a phonological lexicon. When the RIGHT processes do provide candidates that fail to fit the context, the LEFT not only must disconfirm them but also must discover the intended word. This event will normally happen only in the context of a joke, especially a pun, or in experimentally contrived sentences. The resulting delay is a form of Stroop interference and may well account for the faster reading of regular than irregular words and for the difficulty in reading sentences that are phonetically but not visually meaningful, as vividly illustrated in this notice (seen on a bulletin board in the Oxford University Psychology Department, May 1982): *Hear ewe ah sloe two reed, eye no; four wee waist thyme seaing reel homophones; yoo ar kwicker wyth non-wurd homofones, az thair shaips hav noe uther meening.*

Not all words can be recognized by the RIGHT process. Unfamiliar words and long words may excite detectors corresponding to their beginnings and perhaps their overall shapes. For these words, the direct RIGHT recognition process may fail or may provide an unwieldy number of options for the LEFT to work with. But while the RIGHT track is recognizing the words as best it can, the LEFT is busy extracting and identifying letters, which then are available for further processing by either track.

If words are written in mixed cases, fonts, or scripts, then the RIGHT track may base a second phase of wholistic recognition on the abstract letters produced by the LEFT process. The RIGHT recognition is wholistic and non-phonetic, whether it is based on abstract letters, visual features, or visual patterns. Generally, a RIGHT process at any level in the track may use information from any suitable lower level of either track to make a wholistic recognition. This assertion seems amenable to a future critical experiment of the following kind. Masks composed of letter fragments obscure letters better than they mask the words spelled by the letters, whereas other masking patterns can mask the words more than they mask the letters (e.g., Jacobson & Rhinelander, 1978; Johnston & McClelland, 1980). If the RIGHT word-recognition process does indeed use abstract letter identities as data, then masks composed of letter fragments should obscure mixed-case words much more heavily than they mask single-case words. Patterns that preferentially mask words should show equal masking strength whether the words are in mixed-case or single case form.

Acquired Dyslexia in the Bilateral Cooperative Model

PHONEMIC DYSLEXIA IN THE MODEL

"[In the phonemic dyslexic] all the defects of the various functions were reduced to a relative inefficiency to analyze parts out of a whole, on the one hand, and to a relative preference for synthesizing parts into a whole, on the other hand [Low, 1931; quoted by Marshall & Newcombe, 1980, p. 11]." With this statement, Low ended his careful analysis of a patient now classified as a phonemic dyslexic. The statement encapsulates the main characteristics of the damaged LEFT track functions and the preferred RIGHT track functions in the BLC model.

The phonemic dyslexics appear to lack most of the LEFT track functions up to "naming and speech," which remains functional most of the time. Some may retain syntactic capabilities in the higher stages of the LEFT track, but all lack the phonetic recoding and word function in the lower stages. Hence the information crossovers at the feature and word-label stages are probably ineffective, or pass erroneous information or noise.

The loss of LEFT functions includes the loss of ability to extract the individual letters from the word. For example, Faust's patient could identify the initial letter and use it to help recognize words, but only by covering up the rest of the word (cited by Marshall & Newcombe, 1980). The isolated RH of split-brain or hemi-decorticate patients has the same difficulty in extracting letters from words (Zaidel, 1978).

The loss of syntax in phonemic dyslexia is by no means complete, but syntax, when it is active, may work against the remaining functions rather than with them. When a phonemic dyslexic reads a sentence such as *He ran for the train*, the word *for* may be eliminated. If, now, a word such as *box* is substituted, as in *He ran box the train*, *box* cannot be read, even though it may be read in isolation (Andreewsky & Seron, 1975). The syntactic analysis of the sentence is apparently functioning well, but inhibiting the reading of some words that would otherwise be possible. On the other hand, phonemic dyslexics with this problem may correctly read a plural *-s* in a syntactic context demanding a plural form, without being able to read the same plural word on its own. For example, *houses* may be read as "house . . . something," whereas *many houses* is read correctly. Here, these dyslexics use syntactic context constructively.

The LEFT track informs the RIGHT that the word is a function word and therefore not suited to RIGHT track processing. The damaged LEFT track, however, fails to complete its processing and may in any case be sending erroneous control signals to the RIGHT. With a bound morpheme, even the erratic LEFT signals may aid the RIGHT to select the appropriate one of its several possibilities for interpreting the whole word, so long as the LEFT track retains some small syntactic ability. Not everything is lost.

Phonemic dyslexics suffer from a deficit in auditory short-term memory. Coltheart (1980) found this phenomenon difficult to encompass within theories of phonemic dyslexia, but we can predict it from the BLC model. Phonemic dyslexia revolves around difficulties with syntax and an inability to do phonetic recoding. Phonetic recoding is done so that auditory short-term memory can be used in developing syntactic relationships (see Chapter 10). The massive damage to the LEFT track that results in phonemic dyslexia must inevitably impair auditory short-term memory.

SPEED READING BY A PHONEMIC DYSLEXIC

The phonemic dyslexic P.C., who had been a speed reader before his lesion, maintained his speed reading even after his normal reading had been grossly impaired (Andreewsky, Deloche, & Kossanyi, 1980). When P.C. was not speed reading, he could read only slowly and with difficulty, like any other phonemic dyslexic. As he displayed all the usual symptoms of inability to handle function words, to derive phonology, and so forth, Andreewsky *et al.* actually entitled their chapter "Analogies between Speed Reading and Deep Dyslexia."

Speed reading uses the fast, associative processes of the RIGHT track, without much recourse to the slow analytic LEFT track processes that confirm RIGHT interpretations. Normal speed readers do not use much phonetic recoding, the primary LEFT track process, as shown in their insensitivity to Stroop interference (C. Conrad, 1978). Speed reading gets the gist of what is written about, without the exact sense. The stock-in-trade of speed reading are visual word recognition and semantic association—RIGHT track processes.

Speed readers skip function words and modifiers and in general do not use many LEFT track processes (see "Speed Readers and Skimmers" in Chapter 7).

SURFACE DYSLEXIA IN THE MODEL

Surface dyslexics have lost RIGHT track functions. They cannot make rapid word recognitions, cannot handle irregular words, and often cannot make sense out of what they can fluently read aloud. They take longer to read long words than short ones, because they are forced to use LEFT track analyses instead of RIGHT track pattern matching. Surface dyslexics seem to be less common than phonemic dyslexics, perhaps because the RIGHT functions depend on a host of parallel processes that may be less well localized and hence less susceptible to accidental damage than are the LEFT functions. At any rate, surface dyslexia seems not to happen with focal brain damage but is instead associated with diffuse lesions. The symptoms of surface dyslexia also seem to be more varied than those of phonemic dyslexia.

The "surface dyslexic" studied by Deloche *et al.* (1982) showed some provocative symptoms, in terms of the BLC model. In common with other surface dyslexics, and in contrast to phonemic dyslexics, he made more errors on long words than on short ones. He had more trouble with content words, especially nouns, than with function words. He could handle nonwords quite well, although perhaps using simplified orthographic rules. When words were followed after 140 msec by a pattern mask, his performance with content words improved and with nonwords declined dramatically. Without pattern masking, he recognized regular and irregular nouns equally well (unlike other surface dyslexics), but under pattern masking, he recognized regular words much better than irregular ones. Also, he falsely recognized as words nonwords that were homophonic to real words more often under pattern masking than without masking.

This patient may have had a RIGHT track problem, in common with other surface dyslexics, but the problem affected also the interaction between LEFT and RIGHT tracks. The RIGHT track recognition from outer contour and from letter identities worked reasonably well, but the confirmation from the LEFT track was erratic, sometimes inhibiting words that were correct. Masking after 140 msec could inhibit this LEFT track process, improving performance with the content words handled by the RIGHT track and making pseudowords hard to handle. Most likely, the performance of both tracks was reduced in comparison to normal. The patient may have been a mixed surface and phonemic dyslexic.

Because of the diffuse character of the brain lesion, many surface dyslexics might have problems with both tracks and be mixed dyslexics. As the illness causing surface dyslexia progresses, the semantic (RIGHT track) system is lost first, followed by a progressive deterioration in phonological processing that starts from the largest units (Shallice, Warrington & McCarthy, 1983).

Morpheme units are lost before syllables, then letter clusters, and finally the patient may become a letter-by-letter reader. This description is consistent with the idea that large units are processed as wholes.

Marcel (1980b) has noted some close analogies between the errors made by surface dyslexics and those made by beginning readers. Such a relationship is not surprising if the BLC model is correct. Beginning readers, at least those taught by the phonics method (see Chapter 15), are developing the LEFT track rules for word recognition, but have not yet had enough experience to use the RIGHT track effectively. They are, therefore, similar to surface dyslexics in having a LEFT track unsupported by the RIGHT.

Hyperlexia

Several pathways can lead to recognition of a word from the marks on the page. Skilled normal readers probably use all of them as the situation demands, but they differ in the emphasis they put on one or another method. "Chinese" and "Phoenician" subjects emphasize the RIGHT track and LEFT track, respectively. When, however, one or the other track is over-emphasized, some kind of reading abnormality results. This may occur because of accidental brain damage, as in phonemic or phonological dyslexia, or because of a failure in development, as in developmental dyslexia or hyperlexia.

Hyperlexia is a developmental syndrome which appears to be related to dyslexia. The hyperlexic child has general language and cognitive problems, but nevertheless learns very early to read. Usually this learning is spontaneous: The child reads avidly, even though he may be classified as autistic, not reacting much to people and things in the world around him. Most hyperlexic children have a family with some history of dyslexia (Healy, Aram, Horwitz, & Kessler, 1982). Oddly, hyperlexics may be much better than normal skilled readers at recognizing words composed of mutilated letters. In performing this task, they seem to use a particularly precise whole-word matching strategy with no analysis of the word parts, in contrast to the normal skilled readers, who tend to rely on analysis (Cobrink, 1982). Although hyperlexics are highly skilled in recognizing words, they are poor in integrating words into sentence contexts (Richman & Kitchell, 1981).

The hyperlexics appear to have overdeveloped the RIGHT track at the expense of the LEFT. Many hyperlexic children are autistic, and autistic children tend to lack LH specialization for language (Dawson, Warrenburg, & Fuller, 1982). Instead of providing the LEFT track with choices, the RIGHT has become a precise instrument for pattern matching in both hemispheres, using the resources which should have been used for analysis and hypothesis testing. Hyperlexics should therefore have problems similar to those of phonemic dyslexics, except that their problem began very early in life rather than in maturity.

Each type of disturbed reading has some limitation on processing resources. Resources already developed for one track may be lost in acquired dyslexia, or resources predisposed to one track may be taken over by the other in developmental dyslexia or hyperlexia. From this viewpoint, there is no discontinuity between the styles of normal reading and the different types of abnormal or pathological reading.

Words in Context: Mainly RIGHT Processes

Thus far, we have dealt with words as if word recognition were based primarily on the visual data. In experiments on word recognition, this basis may well be true most of the time. In normal, everyday reading, however, readers are hardly likely to pay the same attention to every word in a detective story as they would in an expository text on which they will be tested. A skilled reader probably "recognizes" only those words that are unexpected or hard to predict. So long as the RIGHT detectors produce adequate responses and their outputs continue to be meaningful, there is little need or opportunity for the LEFT track to verify most words. Words are no more recognized in text than letters are recognized in words.

This section deals with the relations between the RIGHT word detectors and the next level of RIGHT track processes, namely, associations. Associations are the key to meaning and to the coherence of a topic; they form the link to the higher level processes by which people understand language in all its metaphoric usages.

Focused Association

When we see an object, we see not just that object but also a host of associates that come with it. A cat may evoke feelings of friendliness or fright, the image of a dog, ideas of stealth and quickness, the memory of a friend, and so forth. When we see the word *cat* on the page, some of these same associations are evoked. Almost every content word comes surrounded by a cloud of associates, some of them common to most people, some idiosyncratic. The associations of a word, rather than its dictionary definition, carry most of its meaning. To understand the meaning of a word in context is to select the correct pattern of associates relating to that context.

Association is a RIGHT track function. When the RIGHT track detectors find a candidate for a word recognition, they excite all its associates, more or less strongly depending on the strength of the association and the context. The excited associates in their turn excite others, some of which are actually word detectors, others of which are higher-level concepts. Words that have many associates in common (e.g., *cat* and *dog*) will tend to "focus" excitement onto one another. If *cat* is seen, then the detector for *dog* will be excited, and it would not take too much visual data for the word *dog* to be accepted. If you read the phrase *They were fighting like a cat and hog,* did you at first see . . . *and dog?*

Word detectors can be sensitized by a context that includes their semantic neighbors (words having many associates in common with them). In such a state, the detectors are more willing to claim a detection, but without improving their powers of discrimination. RIGHT detectors provide reasonable approximations, and in a context, "reasonable" means "fitting the context." Words that do not fit the elephant may cause the reader to do a double take. What is a double take? It is the realization, at some level, that a word has not been properly predicted from context and that the incongruent elephant must be evaluated from the visual data. "Did the author really say ***that***?" The LEFT track is always following on, checking at least some of the words selected by the RIGHT, particularly if the RIGHT provided more than one reasonable candidate. When the LEFT track cancels a RIGHT candidate, the whole system must be reset, because the presumed context is wrong. A more careful rereading may be required, or possibly the word chosen by the LEFT recognition process can be incorporated by slightly reinterpreting the prior context.

SEMANTIC PRIMING: RIGHT CHECKED BY LEFT

The first function of association in reading is to provide a semantic context that allows RIGHT detectors to make fast claims to recognition, based on the first small, confirmatory data that come in from the visual feature detectors. When one reads a text, the topic usually stays the same and the content words all associate with it reasonably well. In experiments the place of a topic is usually taken by a single word.

The association effect is studied in the laboratory under the name **semantic priming,** sensitizing following "target" words by semantically related "priming" words that precede them. Shown in a T-scope is a target word, say NURSE, which the subject must say as fast as possible. If another word, called the **prime,** is presented before the target, it may make the response to the target faster or slower, compared with a control condition in which 'XXXXX' is presented. If the prime, say DOCTOR, is semantically related to the target, then the response to the target will be facilitated; if it is unrelated, say BREAD, the response will be inhibited. (Even the supposedly neutral control XXXXX may have some inhibitory effect; a more neutral control is provided by a real word such as BLANK repeated over many trials. Subjects quickly realize that BLANK provides no information, and seem to waste little time processing it; de Groot, Thomassen, & Hudson, 1982).

Semantic priming is a result of the focusing of associations activated by the prime. This mechanism would not, in itself, cause inhibition of targets unrelated to the prime, as RIGHT processes do not inhibit one another. Inhibition arises from the later work of the LEFT track. In fact, there seems to be no inhibition if the target closely follows the prime. Some delay between the prime and the target must occur before the inhibiting effect of unrelated primes can take effect (Stanovich & West, 1981).

Priming has two different effects, depending on the reason a target is difficult to recognize. In a study by Broadbent and Broadbent (1980), if the target was blurred by typing it through several sheets of overlying paper, then priming affected a passive-global process (i.e., the RIGHT track). The increase in correct recognitions was accompanied by an increase in "false alarms." A false alarm was a report of a semantically appropriate word when the target had been a similarly shaped but semantically incongruous word. If, on the other hand, the letters were clear but some were deleted, then priming affected an active-analytic process (i.e. the LEFT track). There were no false alarms; instead, there were many more correct reports for primed targets.

Priming a blurred stimulus word made subjects more willing to accept the stimulus as a word, whereas priming an incomplete stimulus word made subjects guess the correct word more easily. The two types of degradation also responded differently to the reliability of the primes. For deleted letters, unreliable primes were less effective than reliable ones, whereas for blurred words unreliable primes actually gave rise to more correct words than did reliable ones (presumably at the cost of more false alarms).

The LEFT track is not always required for checking the RIGHT recognitions. Blurred words are more likely to be recognized by the RIGHT processes with little LEFT assistance, because the LEFT track relies on letters, which are not easily seen when blurred. Because of the reduced LEFT-track checking, both correct and wrong (false alarm) responses are more likely with blurred stimuli than with equally difficult targets whose letters can be discriminated. When the primes are unreliable, the LEFT-track function is even more reduced, resulting in more correct as well as wrong responses. Words with missing letters are the wrong shape for the RIGHT detectors to recognize, so that LEFT rule-based processes must bear the lion's share of the work, regardless of the priming condition. When the primes are reliable, the LEFT track is able to produce more correct responses than when the primes are unreliable, since the primes are providing the possibilities ordinarily provided by the RIGHT track. The effect of unreliable primes can be understood as reduced effectiveness of LEFT processes, both for blurred words and for words with missing letters.

The semantic priming effect can come under top-down control. In Tweedy and Lapinski's (1981) study, the effect was strong when subjects expected a semantic relationship between the prime and the target. Eisenberg and Becker (1982) asked people to read or to skim an easy and a difficult passage. Some maintained their speed in both passages, whereas others slowed drastically when "skimming" the difficult passage. These two groups of subjects were then given a lexical decision task with semantic priming. The speed maintainers showed mainly facilitation with semantic priming and little interference from an unrelated prime, whereas those who slowed showed the reverse, namely, some facilitation and much interference.

The subjects who slowed would be ones who use the LEFT track to confirm difficult material, whereas the ones who maintained their speed could do so by inhibiting or ignoring the LEFT track to a greater degree. In the lexical decision experiment, the ones who could ignore the LEFT processes also showed little inhibition, whereas the ones who relied on the LEFT processes showed little facilitation. It would be interesting to see whether Eisenberg and Becker's (1982) speed maintainers are also "Chinese" and the subjects who slow down are "Phoenicians" in Baron and Strawson's (1976) terms. If such were the case, then it might be proper to talk about them as LEFT-dominant and RIGHT-dominant readers.

Most work on semantic priming has used one or two isolated words as primes, and one isolated word as a target. Stanovich and West (1983) did several experiments and reviewed the few studies that have used sentences as primes. In one such technique, the subject reads aloud the prime: *The whale was injured by the*... As the subject articulates the last word, the experimenter pushes a button to present the target, *harpoon*. In the neutral condition, the prime might be *They said it was the*..., and in the incongruous condition it might be *The skier lived in the*... The effects with sentence priming agreed with those normally obtained with isolated word priming, except that there seemed to be no effects of attentional control (Eisenberg & Becker, 1982; Tweedy & Lapinsky, 1981). Stanovich and West conjectured that sentence analysis required attentional control, which could then not be deployed in recognizing the target word.

CONSCIOUS AND UNCONSCIOUS PRIMING

Flash a prime briefly, following it with a pattern of random lines and curves. If the conditions are carefully chosen, the prime cannot be reported, but it nevertheless facilitates recognition of a related target (de Groot, in press; Fowler, Wolford, Slade, & Tassinary, 1981; Marcel, 1980a, in press). In a different procedure, an unattended word flashed together with a word to be categorized can affect how well subjects categorize, even when they are unaware of the existence of the unattended word (Underwood, 1981). The effect works for pictures as well: A picture used as a semantic prime can have an effect even when it is flashed at too short a duration for it to be named (McCauley, Parmelee, Sperber, & Carr, 1980). At first glance, these results smack of the discredited notion of "subliminal perception."

This "magical" priming effect actually resolves some conflicting results on ambiguous words used as primes. When the prime is an ambiguous word such as PALM, both senses of the word facilitate the recognition of related targets such as HAND and TREE (Holley-Wilcox & Blank, 1980). That this effect happens shows that neither sense is inhibited, even though subjects may be aware of only one sense of the ambiguous prime. If, however, one sense of the ambiguous prime has been sensitized by prior presentation of a related word (e.g., MONEY–BANK, versus RIVER–BANK), then only that sense serves to prime the target, and targets related to the other sense are inhibited. For example, MONEY–BANK facilitates CASH, whereas RIVER–BANK inhibits it (Schvaneveldt, Meyer, & Becker, 1976).

Marcel (1980a) used the double priming technique of Schvaneveldt *et al.* but masked the ambiguous word in some of his conditions. His results agreed with those of Schvaneveldt *et al.* if the ambiguous prime was not masked, but agreed with Holley-Wilcox and Blank if it was masked. With masking, both senses of the ambiguous prime facilitated recognition of the target, whereas without masking, the sense incongruent with the sensitizer was inhibited. Masking the prime can eliminate the inhibitory effect of an unrelated prime. An unrelated prime strongly inhibits recognition of the target if the prime is easily seen, but not if the prime is masked. A related prime facilitates recognition of the target, whether the prime is masked or not (de Groot, in press).

The magical priming occurs because the masked prime contains some information—enough to let the RIGHT process generate some plausible alternatives but not enough for the LEFT process to make a unique decision. Hence, no word is reported, but the semantic priming effects can occur. Also, the LEFT track inhibition from unrelated primes is avoided. If magical priming is due to RIGHT track facilitation operating without LEFT track inhibition, then different kinds of patterned masks should differentially affect it. Masks that obscure letters rather than words ought to increase the degree of magic, whereas patterns that preferentially mask words should eliminate it. Such masks have been discussed in Chapter 9.

CATEGORY EFFECT

Categories result from associative focusing. Most content words are labels for categories: *dog* means Saint Bernard, chihuahua, dachshund, collie, Labrador, and so on, and *Labrador* means Rover, Spot, Sheila, and so on. The category label refers to a concept that shares most of the associations of each of its members. Whereas each member has its own idiosyncratic association (Saint Bernards are huge and chihuahuas tiny), the category itself has few or none. As one goes to more and more abstract categories (dogs to animals to living things to entities), the pool of shared associations diminishes. However, when a category member is recognized, the associations that flow from it will focus on the category. In fact, they will focus on all categories of which the item is a member. Dogs, for example, are animals, but they are also (by reputation) cat fighters, friends of humans, furry, and so forth. To some of these categories they belong strongly but to some only weakly, in the sense that most of their associations are separate from those they share with the category.

Category names can be used for priming because of the association patterns they share with category members. Members with many idiosyncratic associations (weak category members) will be weakly excited, members with few (strong category members) more strongly excited, so that their thresholds for detection will become less stringent. This sensitization of categories shows up in a search task in which members of a category are sought in a background of non-members. Under some conditions, members of an expected category stand out immediately and automatically from a background of items of a different category. This "category effect" may be important in reading, for often the reader may know that a word represents an active verb, or a fruit, or a function word, before ever fixating on it.

A circle 'O' might be identified as either a letter or a numeral. Jonides and Gleitman (1972) used a circle as one of their targets among either numeric or letter distractors. If they called the circle *zero* and asked subjects to look for it among letters, it was found rapidly and with a speed independent of the number of letters. When the same circle was called *oh* subjects took longer, and their time depended on the number of letters. The same kind of reversal happened with the circle among the numeric distractors: Calling it *zero* made the task difficult. The category effect cannot be purely visual, although it shows up as if it were. Categories that work include numbers among letters, consonants among vowels, and even words distinguished by semantic category.

Often, experimenters on semantic priming use category names as the primes, because of their sensitizing effect. The category search task could be regarded as a variant of the lexical decision task: Instead of deciding whether a letter string is a word or not, the subjects must find a target belonging to a certain category. In this case, the prime sensitizes the RIGHT detectors for members of the category (if it is well enough specified), and as they work in parallel, the speed of detection is more or less independent of the number of distractors. If the category is not one that the RIGHT system can handle (being constructed by logical rules rather than based on frequently encountered relationships), then the LEFT track must cooperate, which implies sequential and slow operation.

SEMANTIC PRIMING IN SENTENCES

The effect of semantic priming in actual reading is hard to measure, because the experimental situation is likely to alter the reader's task from understanding the text to recognizing the words. The effect in listening to spoken sentences, however, can be measured. A subject is asked to push a button whenever a particular phoneme occurs. In the experimental sentences, the target phoneme is placed immediately after the word of interest. The delay in the button-push is assumed to indicate how long the subject took to process the word: If the word needs little processing, attention will quickly proceed to the next word, which has the target phoneme as its initial sound. Using this method, Foss (1982) found that words that were primed by the sentence topic, or by key words inserted earlier in the sentence, were processed faster than words in a similar but neutral context. Priming could be due to a key word some distance earlier in the text. If the same words were scrambled, to make a word list rather than a sensible text, then no priming was observed with even one word intervening between prime and target. Apparently, the coherence of the sentence context is required to maintain the associative framework. If word meanings are scattered, each one evokes a new set of associations that cancel or inhibit the old ones. Although this study was done with spoken material, there is no reason to believe the results would be very different in reading.

Semantic priming is a way of reinforcing the topic, ensuring that correct meanings are recognized in cases of ambiguity, and speeding understanding.

Syntax and Metaphor

Beyond the Word: Cooperation Between the Tracks

At levels above the stage of morpheme and word recognition, the LEFT and RIGHT processes become more distinct. They still retain their particular characters, with the LEFT being analytic and unique and the RIGHT global and approximate, but they try to do different things. At higher levels, the RIGHT track understands jokes and ambiguities, even though the LEFT may not be conscious of them. The RIGHT track continues its lower-level function of providing the LEFT track with a variety of choices to work on, and the LEFT track, in turn, continues its function of inhibiting false trails started by the multiple and approximate processes of the RIGHT. This tension between the literal and the poetic interpretations of text give the possibility of metaphor and the richness of skilled writing.

SEPARATION OF FUNCTIONAL AND SEMANTIC ASPECTS OF WORDS

The lower level processes in the two tracks have one result: the recognition of a word or a morpheme. From this point, what happens depends on what kind of morpheme was recognized. The stage of morpheme–word recognition has two outputs: (*a*) a phonological representation used for further analysis of how the word fits with other words, and (*b*) a semantic representation used to determine how the word fits into the real-world context. The syntactic function of the word or morpheme is transmitted to the LEFT track, its content to the RIGHT. Even the most functional of function words has some content, and the most concrete of content words has some function (Morton & Patterson, 1980b; Taylor & Taylor, in preparation).

The processing split into semantic and syntactic aspects of words further suggests that it is not so much words as morphemes that are useful. Morphemes, whether free (*walk*) or bound (*-ed*), are treated individually in English (see Chapter 8). In Kanji, morphemes are explicitly marked by being visually separated. In alphabetic writings morphemes are less well marked, and in alphabetic languages with regular letter–sound relations, they are hardly marked at all. In English the analysis into morphemes should be mainly a LEFT track process, although the RIGHT can extract some content morphemes. The RIGHT track might also recognize some frequent affixes, but then it immediately passes syntactic functions of the affixes to the LEFT for further use.

LEFT AND RIGHT TOGETHER IN COMPLEX SENTENCES

In syntactically complex sentences, the LEFT track may not have enough capacity to deal with all the functional relationships, so that the associative structures built by the RIGHT track may dominate the interpretation of the sentence. Consider the "verbal illusion" reported by Wason and Reich (1979): *No head injury is too trivial to ignore.* Almost everybody reads this sentence as an instruction to treat all head injuries. When it is carefully analyzed, it means the opposite, which is unreasonable in the real world. Its syntax contains many implicit reversals and is so complex that the LEFT process more or less abdicates to the reasonable presumption of the RIGHT process about head injuries being dangerous. To see that the sentence does actually mean the opposite of what it seems to mean, imagine what should be done about a less trivial head injury. Should it now be ignored? Another way to see the problem is to reverse a key word in the sentence: *No head injury is too trivial to treat.* Children have this kind of problem with syntax more than do adults.

The opposite effect can happen equally readily: If the words have associations that can be understood in more than one way when the words are scrambled, then the LEFT process is used to give them a unique interpretation. Is it *girl hits boy* or *boy hits girl*? Only the syntax knows for sure. If the verb had been *kisses,* would the syntax have mattered? The event would have been the same either way.

Metaphor

PROBLEMS WITH SYNTAX

The interaction of RIGHT and LEFT processes permits great flexibility in interpreting language. Early attempts at making computer-based systems for language understanding tended to rely on syntax, with unsatisfactory results. Many newer grammars embed some semantic information in their syntax, by refining categories like *noun* into finer and finer detail, such as "animate-inanimate," "male-female," "adult-child," and so forth. Each refinement further restricts verbs and adjectives appropriate to particular nouns.

Consider the following sentences:

1. *The dog bit the bone.*
2. *The bone bit the dog.*
3. *The jug bit the moon.*

In a grammar that embeds semantics into its syntactic restrictions, sentence 1 would be legal but 2 would not, because *bite* takes an animate agent, and bones are inanimate. To normal human readers, 2 is less wrong than 3, but in such a grammar, it would be "ungrammatical" for exactly the same reason as 2. The fact that the moon is inaccessible to any reasonable biter would be irrelevant. Only the inanimate nature of the jug would make 3 ungrammatical to such a grammar. When the semantics are embedded into the syntax, the interpreting process can become not only very complex and slow but also rigid and literal. Metaphor becomes hard to handle. The answer is not to find a yet more refined and extensive grammar, but to separate the grammar from the semantics. The LEFT track can handle the grammar, the RIGHT the semantics.

Even the best redefinition of word categories and properties would find it hard to deal with a sentence such as *The book leered up from the table.* This sentence conveys a great deal of implicit information to the reader. The grammar might know that *leer* means a particular kind of smile with some hidden intent behind it and that an animate, preferably human, subject is required. Such a sentence would be simply ungrammatical to a syntax that was controlled by semantic considerations. If the syntactic requirements are kept simple and the semantic understanding processes are dealt with separately, then it becomes possible to make sense of such sentences. *Book* is a noun, and therefore a reasonable subject for the verb *leer.* With a simple syntax, the sentence is quite grammatical. The BLC model suggests that humans do use a simple syntax, at least to make an initial pass at analyzing sentences. Sentences need not even be syntactically correct or complete; the BLC mechanisms can tolerate irregularities such as: *We thought, maybe, well anyway had an idea, but then, no.*

When the RIGHT and LEFT tracks work together, syntactic rules can remain simple. In the earlier example about the book leering up, the functions of the words are determined by their order, by the function words, and by the bound morphemes. All the content words have association patterns, which permit interpretation of the words in different modes, depending on which areas of the available association arena are emphasized by surrounding context. When the book leers up from the table, the verb *leer* forces an unusual association for *book,* which must take on some animate attribute, presumably reflected onto it by the person who sees the book on the table. The reader might reasonably interpret the sentence to mean that the book had been sought and not found, or in some other way had embarrassed the person seeing it *leer* up. Without the syntactic control, the relationships among the content words would remain mysterious, since neither *book* nor *table* is a suitable animate subject for *leer.* Without the associative proliferation, which can become quite far-reaching in the absence of LEFT track inhibition, the syntax would be quite hard to interpret.

Metaphor is the use of words in a nonliteral sense, taking a few of the features of the words to suggest something quite different from their literal sense. *He is a real lion of a man* does not mean that he walks on four legs, has yellow fur and roars, but that he is strong and courageous, and probably big.

Damage to the RH can cause difficulties in interpreting metaphor. In

Winner and Gardner's (1977) study, subjects were asked to select the correct picture from a set of four purporting to illustrate a metaphoric sentence. For example, the sentence *A heavy heart can really make a difference* was illustrated by (*a*) a crying person, (*b*) a person carrying a large red heart, (*c*) a picture of a 500 lb. weight, and (*d*) a picture of a large red heart. Normal people, and those with LH damage, tended to laugh at (*b*), but those with RH damage tended to select it as the correct illustration. The higher-level RIGHT processes seem to be more strongly lateralized to the RH than are the lower-level ones.

GENERALIZED AND FREE METAPHOR

Natural language is frequently carried on in metaphor. Words accrue meaning through consistent metaphoric usage, and meanings drift and multiply or die over time. A subpart of a meaning comes to dominate the original meaning. Who now remembers that *orient* once meant "to face to the east?" That meaning has split into two quite independent meanings: to face in a specific direction, and *The East.* The BLC model makes it quite easy to handle such shifts of meaning, by referring "meaning" to points at which many associations focus in the particular context.

The boundary between literal and metaphoric usage of a word is ill-defined. In the model, literal usage represents times when the strongest association for a word is appropriate, whereas metaphoric usage represents times when weaker associations prove to be correct. The metaphor consists of the discovery that the "true" meaning is not in the area of strongest association. One cannot create a metaphor by using a word that has no associations with what one means. It makes sense to say to somebody "You elephant" if they walk ponderously, but it is hard to think of a circumstance when it would make sense to say "You teacup." Elephants are noted for their heavy tread, but teacups have no obvious features with which to compare a person's characteristics.

Metaphors can be everyday phrases (idioms) that are so taken for granted that few people notice them to be metaphors. Consider:

- *Prices rose on the Stock Market today*
- *Poor Tony kicked the bucket*
- *He's a real live wire*
- *Psychological theories are built on shifting sands*

Sometimes these metaphors embed themselves into the language (another metaphor) so strongly that they live longer than the individual words in them. To be *hoist with one's own petard* is a well known phrase, but how many of those who use it know that a petard was a medieval hand-carried bomb? A *moot* was an assembly of the people, which evolved into democratic parliaments. A *moot point,* then, was a point needing general discussion. But now, outside law, where else is the word *moot* to be found? A *moot point* is one whose resolution is uncertain (in law, one whose resolution is unnecessary), and *moot* normally has meaning in no other context.

Such metaphors are fixed pattern of words, with meanings almost independent of the words in them, just as words have meanings independent of the letters in them. This kind of metaphor is recognized by RIGHT detectors acting at a level above words and separately from the associations derived from the constituent words. Like word detectors, phrase detectors may interact with the LEFT track to determine the correctness of various possible meanings, but usually one meaning clearly fits the context.

In addition to metaphors that have become fixed and rigid, there is a large group of metaphors that conform to well-defined patterns. Carbonell (1981) calls the patterns **generalized metaphors,** for example the "more-is-up" metaphor or the "conduit" metaphor. *Inflation is going through the roof* is not a pat phrase, but it is an instance of the generalized more-is-up metaphor. Because everyone understands that "more is up," this metaphor simply states that inflation is increasing dramatically and says it vividly. The conduit metaphor shows up in phrases such as *the generation gap, the language barrier.* Communication is seen as flowing from one person to another and something blocks the conduit. In the BLC model, generalized metaphors provide templates that are usually matched more approximately than those of the idiom group.

In normal reading, each phrase on the page consists of words that activate spreading RIGHT track association patterns. Usually the associations tend to focus on similar semantic areas; and those areas are consistent with prior context. When this happens, the phrase is said to be literal. When it does not happen, the pattern of associations may have additional foci. Possibly, secondary patterns of associations focus on areas that are consistent either with the context or with one another. When these unexpected foci provide the intended meaning for the phrase, it is said to be metaphoric. If the foci of secondary association are too weak, the phrase is nonsense.

The generalized metaphors help to fix the secondary association patterns, just as word detectors fix the recognition of misshapen or misspelled words. Although the main associative foci do not link sensibly, there are secondary ones that fit the generalized metaphor patterns. The meaning derived from the pattern is then a candidate for incorporation into sentence understanding.

The final class of metaphor is the **free metaphor** or creative metaphor, which is created freshly for its immediate purpose. Poets are very good at making free metaphors; the clouds of their words veil but glorify the sun of their intent. Free metaphors have no generalized metaphors on which they can hang. They must stand or fall by the combined strength of their associative patterns; like houses of cards, they can be strong if constructed properly, but they can collapse when the reader misunderstands the intended association. Free metaphors depend strongly on external context for support; generalized metaphors do not.

Free metaphors generally work best if the domain of the metaphor is consistent, unlike the (probably misquoted) British parliamentary complaint: "Mr. Speaker, I smell a rat; I see it forming in the air and darkening the sky. But mark my words, Mr. Speaker, I shall root it out; I shall nip it in the bud." All of the metaphors in this group, except possibly the second, are sufficiently conventional to be almost idioms. We know, more or less, what the talker meant. But if they had been free metaphors that no one ever used before, it is unlikely that anyone could have understood him.

This discussion of metaphor is a very small scratch on the surface of a very large topic (Ortony, 1979). Metaphor is at the heart of language, not merely an interesting sidelight (e.g., Rumelhart, 1979). Literal meanings are literal only because their strongest association patterns are consistent with the context. The strength of associations to words changes from time to time and from person to person. What may be a literal statement to one person may be a metaphor to another; a clever metaphor one year becomes next year's idiom, and soon turns to literary stone. These changes happen because the RIGHT track is flexible and approximate in its processing. They reflect the way language changes over time and across peoples. The BLC model encompasses these grand trends naturally.

Summary and Conclusions

The BLC model postulates two tracks of processes that complement one another at each of several stages in understanding text. The processes of one track are fast and global and attempt to find similarities between their inputs and familiar patterns. The processes of the other are slow and analytic and sort their inputs into elements in an attempt to find differences. The RIGHT (global) recognition is primarily template matching using a lax criterion to accept a match. The LEFT (analytic) recognition may use any of a variety of methods, including template matching and syntactic rules. The LEFT processes are done almost exclusively by the LH. The RIGHT processes can be performed by either brain hemisphere, but are done by the RH in normal readers because of competition for resources.

In the initial stages of reading, both tracks of the BLC model begin with visual processing of the patterns of marks on the page. The RIGHT track attempts a complete word recognition, whereas the LEFT looks for either words or part words. If the RIGHT track finds a word, it passes the meaningful elements to an associative, image-producing set of processes, while separating out the syntactic functions of the word for handling by the LEFT track. If the LEFT independently finds a word, it may do the same; if it does not, it can develop a phonological representation using subparts of the word. The result is a phonetically recoded version of the word, which can be linked into a processor evolved for handling spoken input.

At an intermediate stage of reading, the LEFT track has produced a representation evaluated through a phonological coding–decoding system, whereas the RIGHT has developed a series of associations based on the visual form of the word. It does not matter at this stage which track did the actual decoding work; both have the results. From this stage, both tracks have more work to do: The LEFT must analyze the syntactic function of the word while the RIGHT connects it with relevant meanings from other words it has seen. Both functions operate with feedback to earlier stages to sensitize inputs to appropriate following words and to desensitize detectors for inappropriate ones.

The RIGHT track is responsible for understanding metaphors, jokes and allusions. A metaphor exists because the strongest associations for a word, phrase, or story do not fit the context, but weaker associations do. A metaphor may be so common as to become an idiom, with its own RIGHT-track pattern detectors; it may be a novel member of a generalized metaphor, or it may be newly created within a context that permits it to be understood.

The time it takes to pass information between LEFT and RIGHT processes increases from around 20 msec at the lowest level to some hundreds of milliseconds at the higher levels. This difference could be due to hemispheric separation but is more likely to arise from the large amount of processing required to translate the representations of one track into those used by the other track.

The LH of the brain performs the LEFT track functions that we might call linguistic. It is no accident that the LH has been called the language hemisphere. According to the BLC model, however, reading can influence behavior and understanding through the RH as well. The RH specializes in the RIGHT track functions, which deal with images and impressions, global effects and associations. It can handle poetry, whose effect depends on the focusing of associations elsewhere than on the literal meanings of the words on the page.

In ending this chapter, we give you something for your RIGHT track to work on:[1]

A weeping willow is like a fairy castle
with a little fairy on each bough
A cloud is like marshmallows
Dark purple is like evening
A big nut is like a piece of gold
Clapping is like a bird flapping its wings
A cloud is like a big white feathery bird
A clock ticking is like silence
Colored pencils are like a miniature rainbow
The moon is like a wolf howling

—Mia Taylor (age 7)

[1]Reproduced with the poet's generous permission. Originally appeared in *Biline,* the bulletin of the Toronto French School (1970).

12

Reading and Writing Sentences

A sentence should read as if its author, had he held a plough instead of a pen, could have drawn a furrow deep and straight to the end.

—Henry David Thoreau[1]

Beautiful writing may not convey much information, and easy writing may not be beautiful. Dylan Thomas's poem, "In the Beginning," which adorns Chapter 9, is an example of beautiful writing that does not readily yield its content. Indeed, the elusiveness of its multifaceted content is precisely what intrigues the reader and continuously draws him back. In this and subsequent chapters we will deal mainly with writing for information, not for esthetic effect.

A sentence is an important unit of reading. Yet, so far, we have considered sentences only incidently, having been preoccupied with letters, words, and phrases. Now we tear ourselves from the fixation point of a T-scope and consider whole sentences. How are sentences written, read, analyzed, comprehended, and retained? In this chapter, we consider individual sentences, singly or in small groups; in the next, we consider sentences organized into paragraphs and passages.

Reading Clauses and Sentences

A good sentence uses a well-defined structure to express a single complete thought. In written English, it has a clear physical boundary, starting

[1]From "Sunday," *A Week on the Concord and Merrimack Rivers and Walden: Thoreau's Complete Works*. Boston: Houghton Mifflin, 1929, p. 110

with a capital letter and ending with a period. A clause is like a sentence in its syntactic structure, though not necessarily in its physical boundary. Sentences and clauses are treated in this chapter sometimes equivalently and sometimes differently.

Functional Roles of Individual Words

In a structured sentence each word plays a specific syntactic and semantic role. First we describe linguistic labels for those roles and then examine how readers use these roles in understanding sentences and clauses.

SYNTACTIC ROLES

A clause or sentence consists of two major constituents or parts, a subject and a predicate. The **subject** (S) is the part of a sentence about which something new (the predicate) is said; the **predicate** makes the assertion about the subject. A predicate must have at least one verb (V); in addition, it can have an object (O), a complement (C), and an adverbial (A). A subject or object may be a noun phrase or pronoun. A transitive verb requires an object, whereas an intransitive verb does not. A complement often is a noun phrase or adjective. Adverbial may be an adverb, an adverbial phrase, a prepositional phrase, and so on.

The position of an element within a sentence usually is a good clue to its syntactic role. The basic orders of elements in English declarative sentences are:

SV (subject, verb): *He sleeps.*
SVO_d (subject, verb, direct object): *He reads a book.*
SVO_dA (subject, verb, direct object, adverbial): *A car knocked it down.*
SVO_iO_dC (subject, verb, indirect object, direct object, complement): *I bought him those fresh.*

In other languages, other orders such as SOV in Japanese and Korean, are basic. Some languages are more definite than are others about requiring a specific order. Languages with less stringent order rules have other ways of signalling the syntactic roles of words, such as word inflections or the use of particles. The syntactic roles are the simplest descriptions of the functions of elements in a sentence. "Case roles" provide a little more information.

CASE ROLES

A sentence describes an event or state involving a few participants. Essentially, **case roles** sort out: Who did what to whom? And where, when, and how? Some of the formally designated case roles are Agentive, Instrumental, Dative, Factitive, Locative, and Objective (Fillmore, 1968); Agent, Counter-Agent, Object, Result, Instrument, Source, Goal, and Experiencer (Fillmore, 1971); or Agentive, Affected, Recipient, Locative, Instrumental,

Temporal, and Attribute (Quirk, Greenbaum, Leech, & Svartvik, 1979). A verb relates these cases in a sentence. Some important case roles are:

- Agent is a doer, an animate instigator of an event, a role typically assumed by the subject of a sentence.
- Affected (or Objective) is something animate or inanimate that does not cause an event but is directly involved in some other way. The direct object typically assumes this role.
- Recipient (or Dative or Experiencer) is usually an animate entity passively implicated by the happening or state. The role is assumed by an indirect object.
- The role of Attribute is taken by either the subject complement or the object complement: *He is a* ***student****; he fell* ***ill*** (subject complement, current and resulting attribute); *I prefer coffee* ***weak; overcooking*** *turned the coffee* ***bitter*** (object complement, current and resulting attribute).
- Instrument is an inanimate material cause of an event; its role can be taken by the subject or by "*with* + noun": ***The key*** *opened the door; He opened the door* ***with the key.***
- Locative or Temporal role can be taken by the subject or "preposition + noun": ***Chicago*** *is windy;* ***Today*** *is Sunday. I am* ***in the house on Sundays.***
- Goal or Source is the place to or from which something moves: *I wrote a letter* ***to the company from my school.***

A sentence can be simple (consisting of one independent clause), compound (two or more independent clauses), or complex (one independent clause and one or more dependent or subordinate clauses). Figure 12-1 shows a complex English sentence analyzed syntactically and by case role.

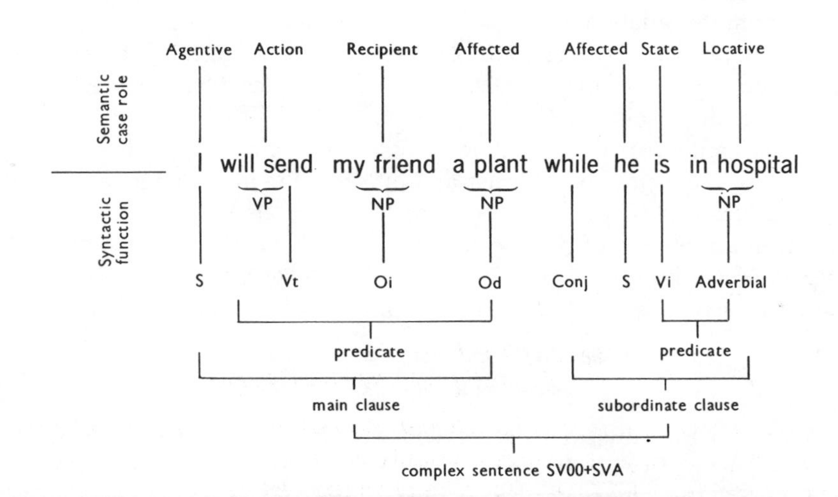

Figure 12-1. *A complex sentence analyzed for syntactic functions and case roles of words.*

SYNTACTIC OR CASE ROLES AND WORD ORDER

To understand a sentence, one of the tasks of a reader is to assign to each word its syntactic and case role. Suppose the sentence to be comprehended is: *A mother feeds her baby some milk.* The following may be steps in the reader's analysis:

1. *A mother* = NP (noun phrase): It is animate; it occurs early, so it probably is subject and agent.
2. *feeds* = action verb: so *mother* is subject and agent; *feeds* is a transitive verb, requiring a direct object and possibly an indirect object as well.
3. *her baby* = NP: It is an animate entity; word order does not indicate whether it is a direct or an indirect object, but semantically it is most likely to be the recipient rather than the affected.
4. *some milk* = NP: It is inanimate; it takes on the role of direct object/affected, confirming the syntactic and semantic role of *baby.*

It is not necessary for readers to know the linguistic labels or to articulate the rules in order to discover the relations among the words. But if they are made aware of the labels and rules, they seem to comprehend sentences better. Weaver (1977) trained Grade 3 children to attend to word order and case roles, and to the syntactic devices by which they are signaled. The children became better at solving sentence anagrams, and at comprehending and remembering sentences. When Christopherson (1978) taught case roles to college students, their delayed recall of prose was much better than that of controls, provided that case roles were taught before (rather than after) reading the prose. (One wonders whether the students' recall would have improved if aspects of the sentences other than case roles had been taught to them.)

Although Italian, like English, uses SVO order without case inflections, it permits far more variation in word order for pragmatic purposes. Accordingly, Italians rely primarily on semantic strategies whereas English listeners rely more on order to determine the roles of the words (Bates, McNew, MacWhinney, Devescovi, & Smith, 1982).

Young children make revealing errors. For example, English-speaking preschoolers use mainly word order and interpret the noun before a verb as the agent. Their strategy leads to correct interpretation of actives but to incorrect interpretation of passive sentences (*The car is bumped by the truck*) (Lempert & Kinsbourne, 1980). Even 7–8-year-olds (Grade 3 in England) misinterpret sentence 1 as 2, perhaps by using the same strategy (Reid, 1972):

1. *The girl standing beside the lady had a blue dress.*
2. *The girl was standing beside the lady, and the lady had a blue dress.*

When case roles are explicitly marked, as in Latin, Japanese, and Korean, word order can be flexible. In Japanese and Korean, over a dozen postposition particles explicitly indicate the case roles of words: *Mother-**ga** some milk-**o** her baby-**ni** feed.* This Japanese sentence (SO_dO_iV) can be written in the less preferred but still acceptable orders SO_iO_dV, O_dO_iSV, or O_iO_dSV, thanks to the postpositions that mark the case roles explicitly. The only rule in Japanese and Korean is that V must come at the end of a clause and S somewhere before V. In such languages, a reader must pay more attention to the postpositions than to word order. Japanese children begin to do so at age 4 and do so securely by age 5, at least for the two common cases (agent *-ga* and object *-o*). Before the emergence of the postpositional case strategy, children depend on word order, interpreting the first noun as the agent even when it is object-*o* (Hayashibe, 1975; Iwatate, 1980). Hebrew-speaking children also tend to rely more on word order at younger ages, even though Hebrew uses inflections rather than word order to provide syntactic information (Frankel, Amir, Frenkel, & Arbel, 1980; Frankel & Arbel, 1981).

Words in a sentence can be distinguished not only according to their syntactic and case roles but also according to other kinds of role, function and content.

FUNCTION WORDS

A sentence contains content words (roughly, nouns, verbs, adjectives, adverbs) and function words (the rest). Function words help to tie the content words together by clarifying their relationships—specifying their case roles, for example. They are few in number (between 100 and 200) and well fixed in a language; new ones seldom appear. In the following two sentences, function words are in uppercase letters: A short phrase contains A FEW content words AND A FEW function words. BY processing THE function words scantily OR not AT ALL, A reader CAN cut THE processing load BY half.

Here are several pieces of evidence that function words are indeed processed scantily. Count the occurrence of the letter 'f' in the following sentence:

> Finished files are the product of
> years of scientific research and
> the experience of practical knowledge.

How many did you find?[2]

In a letter-cancellation task, when 'e' was the target, its instances in the word *the* had the greatest probability of being missed (Corcoran, 1966). The target letter 't' in *the* was also left uncancelled in Healy's (1976) study. Other target letters such as 'a' tended to be missed in unstressed function words (Hatch, Polin, & Part, 1974; Smith & Groat, 1979). A target letter in a content word was easier to cancel when the passage was normal rather than scrambled, but the opposite was true for a target in a function word (Schindler, 1978). In proofreading, misprints were missed twice as often in function words as in content words of similar length (Haber & Schindler, 1981). When sentences were presented one word at a time rapidly (RSVP), function words,

[2] In good time, you should count six 'f's. In which words did you miss 'f' in your first count?

despite being short and familiar, were not reported as well as content words (Forster & Ryder, 1971; Potter *et al.*, 1980).

Taylor and Taylor's (in preparation) experiment provides direct evidence that function words are dispensable in passages. When asked to delete unimportant (but restorable) words from passages, subjects deleted many, but not all, of Fries's (1952) linguistically defined function words. According to Fries, words that can occupy the same position in sentences belong to the same class. For example, *a, the, no, my, every, John's, one,* etc. belong to the same class because each can replace the blank in a sentence such as: _____ *concert was good.*

In Taylor and Taylor's experiment, the words Fries groups together as one word class varied greatly in deletability. For example, *the* and *a* were highly deletable, whereas *no* was not deletable at all. The most deletable words were the articles (*the, a*), linking verbs (*is, was*), auxiliary verbs (*do, can*) and short frequent prepositions (*to, of*). Some linguistically defined function words (e.g., *not, several, between, despite,* etc.) were as undeletable as many content words. (Hence, *not* was considered as a content word and written in lowercase letters in the example earlier.) Besides position (or function) in a sentence, the factors that affect the deletability of a word seems to be its semantic content, frequency of occurrence, length, and membership in a closed or open class. The articles form a closed class with only two members, whereas the numbers (*one, two,* etc.) or proper nouns (*John, Mary,* etc.) form an open class.

In a second stage of Taylor and Taylor's experiment, texts were reduced by 20% by deleting the most deletable words. One group of subjects reading reduced texts comprehended them as well as intact texts, and a second group of subjects had little trouble restoring the deleted words. Other researchers have found similar results on the dispensability of some function words (Bassin & Martin, 1976; Tuinman, Blanton, & Gray, 1975).

What meanings do you get from the following two sentences? Sentence 1 retains five deletable function words, whereas 2 retains four undeletable content words:

1. *My* _____ *is* _____ *some* _____ *at a* _____ .
2. _____ *mother* _____ *buying* _____ *groceries* _____ *supermarket.* .

Although function words may be often deleted without destroying the meaning of a sentence, they can sometimes be crucial in sorting out the relations among the content words. Consider the difference a function word makes between these two sentences:

1. *The water poured* ***into*** *the bucket.*
2. *The water poured* ***from*** *the bucket.*

CONTENT WORDS

Instead of discussing the scanty processing of unimportant function words, let us discuss the converse process: A reader may pick up and attend mainly to key content words. Content words form 99.9% of a skilled reader's vocabulary, and new ones are being created every day in all living languages. Even languages sometimes thought to be dead are not immune to the invention of content words; witness the Latin word *helicopterum* invented by Pope John XXIII.

Eye movement studies show that content words are far more likely to be fixated than are function words. Speed readers, or non-speed readers forced to read like speed readers, tend to process mainly content words (see Chapters 7 and 11). One group of Aaronson and Scarborough's (1976) subjects had to answer yes or no to short questions after reading sentences that were displayed on a screen one word at a time, under the subjects' control. The subjects took longer to read major content words (subject and object) than they did function words.

In our Bilateral Cooperative model, readers construct the meaning of a sentence mainly from content words, using function words when necessary, that is, when the relations among the content words are not clear. This mode of reading is aided in Japanese and Korean text, in which key words and grammatical items are written in different types of script, with key words in visually prominent logographs, and grammatical items in simpler phonetic letters (see Chapters 4 and 5). It may well be the common mode of reading by skilled readers of any language. In English and many other languages, function words tend to be shorter than content words, and in German, nouns start with capital letters.

By concentrating mainly on content words, the RIGHT visual–associative process works with sentences of high imagery, such as: *A mother feeds her baby some milk sitting in an armchair. Mother* is one image; it combines with *milk* to form a higher-order or larger image; *mother–milk* combines with *baby* to form a yet more complex image, and so on. [(*mother* → *milk*) → *baby*] → *armchair*. The product of a reader's comprehension of this concrete sentence is a unitary imagery complex of a mother in an armchair feeding milk to the baby (not the syntactically correct image of "some milk sitting in an armchair being fed to a baby by its mother").

Clause Processing

In reading a clause, the ultimate goal of a reader is to comprehend its idea and retain the idea as a gist. The reader must recognize most of the words in a clause, assign to them syntactic and case roles, find their meanings in the context, organize them into larger processing units, and so on. He carries out these processes simultaneously, each interacting with the other, using a variety of steps. Differences in reading speed among college students can largely be attributed to differences in rates of processing such information within sentences rather than rates of integrating information across sentences in a passage (Graesser, Hoffman, & Clark, 1980).

CLAUSE AS A PROCESSING UNIT

A clause or sentence is a major processing unit; at its end, the reader can usually integrate the information sufficiently to extract a gist. Soon after gist extraction, most individual words as well as the syntactic structure of a clause are purged from working memory to make way for new clauses. Fodor, Bever, and Garrett (1974) adduce an impressive amount of evidence for a clausal unit from speech data; we have assembled some from reading.

If a clause (or a simple sentence) is a processing unit, the processing load should be high just at its end, where the sentence as a whole must be integrated or wrapped up. Appropriately, fixation tends to be longer on the last word than it is on other words in a sentence (Just & Carpenter, 1980). Whereas less than a third of pauses occur at clause boundaries in speech, almost all pauses occur at these locations in oral reading (Brown & Miron, 1971; Goldman-Eisler, 1968, 1972; Grosjean & Deschamps, 1975). Again in oral reading, the eye–voice span is shorter at the end of a sentence than it is at any other point, as the eyes hesitate there in order to give the voice time to express one thought clearly before a new thought is started (Buswell, 1920). In silent reading, too, readers pause at the ends of clauses and sentences, and such pauses are more related to content difficulty than to syntactic complexity (Mitchell & Green, 1978). (The end may take longer to be processed also because that is where important new information tends to be placed.)

If a clause is a unit, for two sentences of the same length, a complex sentence with two underlying clauses should be more difficult than a simple sentence with one clause. In rapid serial visual presentation (RSVP), there were fewer errors in reporting words for sentence 1 than for 2 (Forster, 1970):

1. *Alan has broken my mother's vase.*
2. *The truck Susan was driving crashed.*

If a clause is a processing unit, a word from the clause most recently processed should be retrieved faster and better than is a word from a preceding clause, independently of the number of intervening words. In Jarvella's (1971) study on speech, the likelihood of recalling a word was greatest if it was located in the same clause; intermediate if a word was located in a previous clause of the same sentence; and least likely if the word came from a clause of the previous sentence. Caplan (1972) found the same clause-boundary effect, whether subjects heard or saw a probe word after listening to test sentences. The effect was independent of intonation contours, serial position, and lexical material.

In Chang's (1980) study, subjects read two-clause sentences one word at a time at a self-paced rate. Following each sentence a probe word was presented, and the subjects decided if this word occurred in the sentence. Reaction times to probes from the final clause were shorter than to those from a preceding clause, when the same number of words intervened. For example, in the following two sentences, reaction times would be faster to *frogs* than to *afternoon*:

1. *As midsummer nears and the pond begins to shrink frogs crawl into the pond.*—**frogs**
2. *When the wind began to get stronger in the early afternoon the sun warmed us.*—**afternoon**

Frogs may have been more memorable, not only because it was in the second clause but also because it was the subject. The subject of a sentence tends to be the best remembered element of a sentence (Loosen, 1981).

Another team found a similar clause-boundary effect for some spoken sentences, such as sentence 1, but not for others, such as 2 (Marslen-Wilson, Tyler, & Seidenberg, 1978):

1. *Although Mary rarely cooks trout, when she does it is delicious.*—**trout**
2. *Even though they are quite small cats, they need a lot of space.*—**cats**

If you monitored your progress through 2, you probably felt that you came to a pause after the word *small,* and that *cats* came as a little surprise. Even though sentence 2 is perfectly grammatical and acceptable, a more natural way of expressing the same content seems to be 3:

3. *Even though these cats are quite small, they need a lot of space.*

One might be tempted to interpret sentence 2 as 4 instead:

4. *Even though they are quite small, cats need a lot of space.*

The findings of Marslen-Wilson *et al.* cannot be taken as evidence against the clause as a processing unit; rather, they may be considered as a warning that some clauses are better closed than others. The clause may be a clearly defined unit for grammarians, but it may not always be so well defined for readers.

PROCESSING WITHIN A CLAUSE

A reader processes a word as much as possible at the moment it appears and then puts the results in working memory until enough words are accumulated to form a larger unit such as a phrase or a clause. The immediate processing is revealed in a pattern of fixations, which tends to vary according to the physical and linguistic characteristics of each word encountered (see Chapter 7).

We emphasize that an individual word is processed as much as possible, but not necessarily fully, at the moment it appears—which is why not only preceding but also subsequent words in a sentence exert constraints on a word being processed (see Chapter 8). It is inefficient, in fact sometimes impossible, to obtain the full and accurate meaning of each word as it appears, because it may have either little meaning (*a, the, get*) or multiple meanings (*tears in his eyes/in his coat*); or because a critical constituent, such as the verb for the subject or the referent for a pronoun, may come later in a sentence. In processing a clause, the assignment of the first noun phrase (*the mother*) to the role of subject-agent is fully confirmed only when the action verb (*feeds*) appears. When a French verb was delayed until late in the clause, a simultaneous translator preferred to postpone translating incoming words until it appeared (Goldman-Eisler, 1980). In Korean and Japanese, a verb always comes at the end of a clause; furthermore, a marker added to the verb indicates whether a sentence is a question, negation, and so on.

In processing a clause or sentence, the smaller units are understood as much as possible, are disambiguated or confirmed using the subsequent units, and are accummulated to form larger units.

COMPREHENSION BY SYNTAX OR BY MEANING?

Ordinarily, a reader is not conscious of the syntactic analysis process; the meanings and associations of content words (*mother, feed, baby, milk*) often suffice to determine the sentence meaning, with a little help from word order and function words. But when the reader tries to comprehend a complicated sentence or a sentence in a foreign language, he becomes more conscious of the need for analysis. Try to understand the following sentences, both of which have the same syntactic structure:

1. *The boy whom the girl whom the man kissed saw left.*
2. *The cat that the dog that the man stroked bit miaowed.*

In sentence 1, since the girl might have kissed the man or the boy, and any of the three could have *saw* or *left,* the reader has to analyze the sentence carefully. But in sentence 2, the man would normally do the stroking, the dog the biting, and the cat the miaowing, so the sentence is relatively easy. In such oddly structured sentences, unambiguous associative-semantic linkages make matters a lot easier (see Schlesinger, 1968).

Both semantic and syntactic cues can help in understanding sentences, but even within syntax there are different cues such as word order, inflections, and so forth. In Hebrew sentences of the form *the bear pushes the horse,* either noun could semantically be the agent. Logically, object markers and gender–number agreement by themselves could have indicated the roles of the two nouns in many sentences. Yet, readers still took account of word order; they combined the three kinds of syntactic cues (word order, number, and gender) in a probabilistic way, rather than by a logical analysis (Frankel & Arbel, 1982). If probabilistic combination can occur even among purely syntactic cues, it is even more likely to occur when both semantic and syntactic cues can lead to sentence understanding. *The horse pushes the door* is much more likely than *The door pushes the horse,* regardless of syntactic markers.

According to the Bilateral Cooperative model of reading, the RIGHT associative process can provide plausible interpretations even though the materials may be difficult for the LEFT syntactic process (see Chapter 11). In normal sentence processing, and especially in speed reading, associative links often dominate understanding; syntax is useful primarily in corroborating and in disambiguating where necessary. Sentences are hard to understand only when the syntax is complex, and at the same time the associations are ambiguous.

French's (1981) findings support our model. He varied the syntactic complexity of his test sentences in four levels:

1. Simple: *The boy hit the ball.*
2. Compound: *The boy hit the ball and ran.*
3. Complex: *After hitting the sister, the brother cried.*
4. Scrambled: *the ate fat grass green cattle the.*

He varied semantics in three levels:

1. Well integrated: *The little baby drank the milk.*
2. Poorly integrated: *The aunt saw the door and left.*
3. Anomalous: *My tasty owner spilled the captain madly.*

French presented the sentences, word by word, in two speeds in rapid serial visual presentation (RSVP): slow, 14 words per sec; fast, 24 words per sec. (Even the slow speed is twice as fast as normal reading speed.) At the slow speed, both semantics and syntax had effects, but at the fast speed, only semantics mattered. That is, the well integrated sentences were read better than the poorly integrated ones, which in turn were read better than the anomalous ones.

Sentences are processed for and by their meanings first, and by their structures second.

GIST: A PRODUCT OF SENTENCE PROCESSING

After a clause or a sentence is comprehended, its structure as well as its individual words tend to be forgotten, but its meaning or gist is retained. In Sachs's (1967) study, recognition memory for the form of a sentence (arrangement of words or passive/active) declined much more rapidly than that for the meaning. In Lovett's (1979) study, Grades 1 and 2 children retained semantic, syntactic, and lexical information in that order, whether tested immediately, a little later, or much later.

Information on sentence structure or on individual words is not lost immediately after sentence comprehension; it appears to remain available for a little while (Garrod & Trabasso, 1973; Tzeng, 1975; Wright, 1972). For example, subjects verified and recognized more confidently old, previously studied sentences such as sentence 1 than they did new synonymous ones, such as 2 (Hayes-Roth & Hayes-Roth, 1977; J. R. Miller, 1981):

1. *The noise scared the babysitter.*
2. *The noise frightened the babysitter.*

These sentences are short and simple. The discrimination might be harder if the sentences were long and complex.

Some words of a sentence are better retained than others: Memory for family roles (e.g., *his wife*) exceed memory for names (*Rachel*); memory for proper names is higher than for pronouns; and memory for explicit clauses is better than memory for elliptical forms (Bates, Kintsch, Fletcher, & Giuliani,

1980). Memory for exact wording is lower in concrete than in abstract sentences, presumably because the former can be retained as a visual image (Begg & Paivio, 1969).

A gist may be a sequential verbal form or a wholistic visual image. In a verbal form, a gist may include only the basic elements of a sentence, agent–action–object, excluding goal or instrument (Goetz, Anderson, & Schallert, 1981):

1. *The customer wrote the company a complaint.*
2. *The housewife killed the cockroach with insecticide.*

The gists tended not to include *the company* in sentence 1, and *with insecticide* in 2. Furthermore, the subject–verb–object group was recalled completely or not at all. Loosen's (1981) Dutch subjects, after listening to a sentence, tended to recall only important words. (The importance of the words was rated by another group of subjects.) One of the three sentence types tested was:

Historical ***castles*** *with high, round towers* ***charm*** *interested* ***visitors.***

The three words in bold italics, especially the two nouns (the subject and the object), were recalled best, and the adjectives *high, round,* and *interested,* were recalled least. "Castles charm visitors" (SVO) makes a good gist.

Even in verbal form, a gist may not contain the exact words of the sentence; rather, it may contain words expressing synonymous concepts or "instantiated" words:

1. *The fish attacked the swimmer.*
2. *The housewife cooked chips.*

In recall of these sentences, instantiated specific terms—"shark" for *fish,* "fried" for *cooked*—were better cues than were the general terms that actually occurred (Anderson, Pichert, Goetz, Schallert, Stevens, & Trollip, 1976; Garnham, 1979). A gist may contain information not explicitly given but inferred by the reader (see "Implication and Inference").

A concrete sentence (*The farmer cut the wood*) is likely to be stored as a visual image, and an abstract sentence (*The lesson inspired devotion*) in a verbal form (Begg & Paivio, 1969; Garrod & Trabasso, 1973; Marschark & Paivio, 1977). A few short, related sentences (*The rock crushed the hut. The hut was at the river. The hut was tiny.*) may be integrated into one sentence (*The rock crushed the tiny hut at the river*) (Bransford & Franks, 1971). In referring to one scene, such a set of sentences may be stored as a single visual image.

The gist from each sentence or set of sentences is retained long enough to be used in comprehending subsequent sentences. This higher-level gist, in turn, may be forgotten after it has made its contribution to building a gist for a paragraph or a passage as a whole. What can you remember about any newspaper article you read this morning? Not a gist of each and every sentence, but a gist of the article itself, if that.

NETWORK GRAMMAR.

Here is yet another way a sentence might be syntactically and conceptually parsed using one version of **network grammar** (M. Taylor, 1974; I. Taylor, 1976). In this analysis, the central concept is the "open question" or "link." At each stage in understanding the sentence, what has been read leads the reader to expect that certain questions are going to be answered by what is yet to come. Consider the sentence *The book consists of three parts. The* signals that a static concept is to be expected. This expectation forms a "link," which is for the moment open and will probably be answered later. In this case, the link ties the coming concept with something already known and indicates to the reader "this will not be new." The word *book* fits the open link of *the* but leaves open links of its own: Something is going to be said about the book. The phrase *consists of* is a form of relation and requires a list of constituents of the book to satisfy it.

A sentence is parsed in this manner until few gaps in the pattern of knowledge remain. The period after *parts* indicates that the sentence is closed. The next sentence may start something like *It is,* in which case the *book* link is being filled; alternately, it may start something like *They are* or *The first,* in which case the *parts* link is being filled.

A network grammar indicates where in the body of knowledge the individual concepts (represented by content words) fit and where open links exist and just what concepts are needed to fill them. Links may be open both syntactically and associatively.

SENTENCE PROCESSING BY COMPUTER

It is instructive to compare the idea of open links of the network grammar with machine sentence processing. Several computer programs can interpret natural language to some degree (e.g., Winograd, 1972; Woods, 1970). Schank and Birnbaum's (1980) "expectation-based conceptual analysis system" is one such program. The sentence to be understood is:

Fred ate an apple.

Reading from left to right, the system first finds the word *Fred.* It understands this as a reference to some male human being named Fred and stores the reference in short-term memory. With the next word, *ate,* a case frame looks like:

(INGEST ACTOR (NIL) OBJECT (NIL)).

One of the expectations suggested by the meaning of *ate* is that the ACTOR of the INGEST concept, an animate being, may have already been mentioned. So the analyzer checks short-term memory, finds FRED there, and fills the ACTOR slot of the INGEST:

(INGEST ACTOR (FRED) OBJECT (NIL)).

There remains an unfulfillled expectation, which suggests that some mention will be made of what it is that Fred ate and that it should fill the OBJECT slot. The next word *an* creates an expectation for an indefinite reference. Finally, *apple* is read. The expectation created when *an* was read is satisfied, so APPLE is marked as an object not previously seen. The second expectation created when *ate* was read is also satisfied, so the OBJECT slot of the INGEST is filled. The system's current understanding of the input is represented as:

(INGEST ACTOR (FRED) OBJECT (APPLE REF (INDEF))).

There are no more words to read, so the process halts, having correctly assigned the relationships among the content words of the sentence.

Proposition and Processing

Sentences, though obvious linguistic and processing units, vary enormously in length and complexity. A sentence may contain only a single word (*Look!*) or a few hundred words (see "Suggestion 10" below). Actually, there is no limit to the length of a sentence. Clauses are shorter than sentences and vary less in length; propositions are even shorter and less variable than clauses.

PROPOSITIONAL ANALYSIS

A **proposition** consists of one or more concepts called **arguments** and one predicate that relates them. A proposition is similar to the case frames in the computer model of Schank and Birnbaum (1980). The arguments of a proposition fulfill different case roles, such as agent, object, and goal. Predicates are verbs, adjectives, adverbs, and conjunctions. A proposition may be written P (X, Y) or (P, X, Y). In either notation, the predicate P is written first and the arguments X and Y after P. Kintsch and his associates analyze the following text into a "text base" consisting of eight propositions in three levels (Kintsch, Kozminsky, Streby, McKoon, & Keenan, 1975):

The Greeks loved beautiful art. When the Romans conquered the Greeks, they copied them, and thus, learned to create beautiful art.

1. (LOVE, GREEK, ART)
2. (BEAUTIFUL, ART)
3. (CONQUER, ROMAN, GREEK)
4. (COPY, ROMAN, GREEK)
5. (WHEN, 3, 4)
6. (LEARN, ROMAN, 8)
7. (CONSEQUENCE, 3, 6)
8. (CREATE, ROMAN, 2)

The Greek text has three arguments: GREEK, ART, ROMAN. Proposition 2 is said to be subordinated to proposition 1, because it repeats the argument ART.

Propositions 3 and 4 are also subordinated to proposition 1 because of the repetition of GREEK. These three propositions are assigned to level 2 (indented one step). The remaining four propositions are assigned to level 3 (indented two steps), because they are all subordinated to one or more of the level 2 propositions.

Propositional analysis appears rigorously formal and precise, and yet there is no single agreed-upon algorithm (step-by-step mechanical procedure) for analyzing a sentence or text into a set of propositions or, conversely, for organizing a set of propositions into one or more sentences. As of 1980, a computer could not parse a text to derive a propositional representation (Miller & Kintsch, 1980).

In Kintsch *et al.*'s analysis, unless there is a title, the top level proposition is the one that comes first with a new concept. Thus, the relatively unimportant (LOVE, GREEK, ART) is treated as a top-level proposition. The proposition (BEAUTIFUL, ART) also is high in the hierarchy, even though adjectives are rated unimportant and tend to be dropped from a recalled gist (Loosen, 1981). P3 (subordinate clause) is in the same level as P4 (main clause) and in the higher level than P6 (another main clause).

PROPOSITION AS PROCESSING UNIT

Propositions seem to be valid processing units. Kintsch and Keenan's (1973) sentences had the same number of words but had between four and nine propositions. Reading time increased as more propositions were processed, and the longer the reading time, the fewer propositions were recalled. Superordinate propositions were recalled better than were subordinate ones. As Thorndyke (1975) points out, however, Kintsch and Keenan's test sentences with more propositions had to be syntactically more complex than did the sentences with fewer propositions. Graesser *et al.* (1980) studied the variables that affected the reading time of 12 narrative and expository passages. An increase in the number of propositions and of new argument nouns increased reading time, but not as much as did "low narrativity" (being less story-like and more exposition-like) of passages (see Chapter 13 for the two types of prose).

Ratcliff and McKoon (1978) presented sentences to subjects for study and then tested single words for recognition after giving a cue word. If the cue word and the target word were from the same proposition, the target was recognized faster than if they were from two different propositions making up a single sentence. This result is similar to that for clauses (Chang, 1980), which is not surprising, because a clause may include more than one proposition, but a proposition may not be split across clauses. Furthermore, most of Ratcliff and McKoon's "propositions" were indistinguishable from clauses. For example, they did not count the third proposition, conjunction, in the following sentence: *The host mixed a cocktail, but the guest wanted coffee.*

The proposition seems to be a psychologically valid unit. The question is whether it improves on the similar but more familiar and simple unit, the clause. Our own answer leans toward no (see also Chapter 13, "Models of Text Processing").

Transformed Sentences

TRANSFORMATION: LINGUISTIC DESCRIPTION

So far, we have described mainly simple-active-affirmative-declarative (SAAD) sentences. Let us take this most common basic structure and transform it into other structures, holding the semantic role of each element more or less constant. Table 12-1 lists the frequency of occurrence of each structure counted in a small but representative sample of written texts. Specifically, the sample (181 clauses) consists of 10 passages, each 150-words long, on a variety of subject matter covering a wide range of readability (Miller & Coleman, 1967; Taylor & Taylor, in preparation).

According to Chomsky (1957, 1965), a SAAD sentence is "generated" (a phrase structure is assigned) by a **phrase-structure grammar,**[3] which analyzes a sentence into progressively smaller units by a set of "rewrite rules" such as the following (→ means "can be rewritten as"):

1. Sentence → NP VP
2. NP → Art N
3. VP → V NP
4. Art (article) {*a, the*}
5. N → {*boy, book, apple,* . . . }
6. V → {*read, eat,* . . . }

Rules (5) and (6) use brace brackets to list a set of elements any one of which may be selected. These six rules generate many SAADs, such as *The boy read a book* and *The boy eats the apple.*

According to Chomsky's **transformational grammar** (1957, 1965), the sentences in Table 12-1 are related in that they derive from the same underlying string generated by a phrase-structure grammar. SAAD has not undergone optional transformations, whereas the others have: Each of P, N, and Q; each of PN, PQ, NQ; and PNQ, has been derived through increasingly complex transformational operations. For example, a passive is derived from the underlying string of its active sentence by three transformational operations: (*a*) move the subject into a *by* phrase to the right of the VP; (*b*) insert *be en* (*-ed*) as a past-tense marker; and (*c*) move the object into the subject position.

[3]For a linguistic introduction to Chomsky's grammar, see Lyons (1970) and Culicover (1982); for a psycholinguistic introduction, see Greene (1972) and I. Taylor (1976, Chapter 5). For the so-called extended standard grammar, see Chomsky (1975).

Table 12-1 *Frequency of Different Sentence Types*

Structure	Example	Occurrence (%)
SAAD	*He read the book.*	80.7
Passive (P)	*The book was read by him.*	13.8
Negative (N)	*He did not read the book.*	2.2
PN	*The book was not read by him.*	1.7
Imperative	*Read the book*	1.1
Wh-question	*Why dit he read the book?*	0.6
Question (Q)	*Did he read the book?*	0
PQ	*Was the book read by him?*	0
NQ	*Did he not read the book?*	0
PNQ	*Was not the book read by him?*	0

PROCESSING TRANSFORMED SENTENCES

Two decades ago, Chomsky's transformational grammar was often taken to be the model of how people comprehend and produce sentences. According to it, the more transformations a sentence had gone through, the harder should processing be. For a few years, studies supporting the model appeared thick and fast (e.g., Gough, 1965; Mehler, 1963; G. A. Miller, 1962; Miller & McKean, 1964; Savin & Perchonock, 1965). In Mehler's study, subjects tended to recall simpler structures better than they recalled complex ones, and most of their recall errors tended to be syntactic. Furthermore, the errors tended to produce a simpler form than the one given as a stimulus. In Miller and McKean's study, the more complex a structure, the longer it took to process.

Several points were overlooked in these experiments. To cite a few: First, as syntactic structures changed, so did the meanings, subtly or not so subtly. *Thou shalt not kill* and *Thou shalt kill* may be related in structure but will have opposite effects on readers. Second, the subjects' task—verbatim recall of unconnected sentences—is an unnatural form of sentence processing. Third, complex transformations occur seldom in our speech and text, and hence people are unfamiliar and unpracticed with them. In Table 12-1, SAAD is by far the most common structure. The overwhelming preponderance of SAAD (80–90%) and non-occurrence of complex transformations were observed also in speech by Goldman-Eisler and Cohen (1970). In speech there are fewer passives but more questions. A normal question requires an answer. In writing, can a question be other than rhetorical?

According to the linguist Givon (1979), SAAD occurs so frequently because it is the clause type most suitable for asserting new information, with the least **presupposition** (the information which a speaker assumes she and her listener share). Affirmatives assume that the reader lacks information and provide it. Negatives assume that the reader has information that is wrong and must be corrected or negated. (Ponder about then President Richard Nixon's celebrated remark on television, "I'm not a crook.") Wh-questions assume the reader's knowledge about the fact that somebody, for example, died; new information sought is "what /where/ when/ why/ how did he die?"

With these new perspectives on transformation, let us look at the structures listed in Table 12-1. Only the first three types—SAAD, P, N—occur sufficiently often to merit further consideration. SAAD has been discussed throughout the chapter; it will be further discussed indirectly in the following consideration of N and P.

NEGATIVE SENTENCE

In every language, negation is an indispensable part of communication. People need a way to reject or deny reality and to indicate unfulfilled expectation or nonexistence of expected events. In its primitive form (*No!*), it develops early in infant language. For example, one of the seven words a 16-month-old child used most frequently was *no* (Bloom, 1973). There are several ways to negate an affirmative statement such as *The ball is round.*

1. *The ball is not round.*
2. *No ball is round.*
3. *I deny that the ball is round.*
4. *The ball is nonround.*

Different expressions convey different nuances.

Superficially, the syntax for negation can be simple: A negative element is added to the verb of an affirmative sentence, as in the Korean (SOV) with the negative bound morpheme:

1. *John book read* ('John reads a book')
2. *John book* ***an****-read ('John does not read a book')*

People seem to understand first a sentence's positive sense and then take the second step of negating this positive sense. Negative sentences take longer to process than SAADs, presumably because of the extra step (Miller & McKean, 1964; Slobin, 1966).

A negative sentence is complex also because of its many possible meanings.

1. *John gave Mary a book.*
2. *John did not give Mary a book.*

What actually happened in 2? Did John give Mary a box? Did John give Jane a book? Did Tom give Mary a book? Did John sell Mary a book? Or none of these? Usually, context is required to clarify the situation, suggesting that a negative sentence is less self-contained than is a positive one (see "Context").

Certain negative sentences are completely misunderstood. Consider Wason and Reich's (1979) "verbal illusion":

1. *No missile is too small to be banned.*
2. *All missiles should be banned however small.*

If 1 equals 2, by parity of argument, then 3 equals 4:

3. *No head injury is too trivial to ignore.*
4. *All head injuries should be ignored however trivial.*

Almost everybody reads 3 as meaning "all head injuries should be treated" or "no head injury is too trivial to be noticed," which is presumably the intended meaning of the speaker. To see this, consider 5, which must be the opposite of 3:

5. *No head injury is too trivial to treat.*

In this sentence, we see another example in which the syntactic LEFT process is overwhelmed, and the sense must be made up by the RIGHT process, as explained by the BLC model.

Even simple negation is difficult for children. For instance, they find it easier to identify an object that is round and red than one that is round and not red (Neimark & Slotnick, 1970). In sentence–picture verification, negative sentences such as *The boy is not throwing the ball down the hill* resulted in guessing by the 3–6-year-old children studied (Gaer, 1969).

Some complex or subtle forms of negative are even more difficult for children to understand. Reid (1972) included some negatives in her study of sentence comprehension by 7–8-year-old (Grade 3) British children:

1. *Mary's dress was neither new nor pretty.*
2. *Mary's dress was not new and it was not pretty.*

Was Mary's dress new? (yes/no)
Was Mary's dress pretty? (yes/no)

More than 60% of the children answered yes to both questions in sentence 1, but not in 2. They did not interpret *neither–nor* as negatives, apparently ignoring *neither* and taking *nor* as *and.* It is not just negative structure but more properly negative content that is difficult. Thus, 3 was more difficult than 4:

3. *If only David had known, the dog was quite tame.*
4. *The dog was quite tame, but David did not know that.*

MULTIPLE NEGATIVES

In English two negatives are supposed to cancel each other and produce an affirmative: *He went out with other women, but not without telling his wife of his experiences and successes* = "He told his wife . . ." *Not un-* asserts a qualified positive. Thus, *He is not unhappy* is not the same as *he is happy:* He is expected to be unhappy, but actually he is not. Or, he is contented but not necessarily happy. Some double or triple negatives, however, are interpreted as emphasis, as in: *I ain't going to give nobody none of mine,* or *I ain't never marrying nobody.* According to the linguist Jespersen, such repeated negatives are usual in a great many languages whose negative element is small in phonetic bulk and is easily attracted to various words.

Sherman (1976) studied adults' comprehension of multiple negatives.

Subjects had to say yes or no for "reasonable" and "not reasonable" to sentences such as:

He was (6 ft.-5 inch, 4 ft.-10 in.) tall, and thus (everyone, no one) (believed, doubted) that he would (not) be (un)comfortable with very tall girls.

The subjects took longer and made more errors in responding to the sentences containing negatives, especially multiple negatives. Among the single negative sentences, those containing the word *doubted* were the most difficult, presumably because it makes a less extreme (or clear-cut?) statement than *no one, not,* or *un-*.

The following sentence from a psychology journal is almost incomprehensible because of its many negative twists: "If a distinction between pre and postlexical phonology can not be made, then the fact that non-words are not more affected by suppression than words can not be used as evidence that suppression fails to impair prelexical phonology [Besner *et al.*, 1981, p. 428]."

Wright and Wilcox (1979) varied the location and type of negative element in giving a set of instructions to subjects:

1. *Do not press unless the letter is P* (double negative ––).
2. *Do not press if the letter is P* (single negative –+).
3. *Press unless the letter is P* (single negative + –).
4. *Only press if the letter is P* (double positive ++).

The easiest instruction was ++; the instruction with the negative in the subordinate clause, + –, was easier than its reverse, – +; in fact, – +, for some reason, produced the most errors and longer responses than did the double negative – –.

To conclude, a negative sentence is generally harder to understand than its positive counterpart, because it is semantically and syntactically complex. Even so, we cannot indiscriminately follow the injunction of the composition teachers, Strunk and White (1972): "Put statements in positive form [p. 14]." They advice writers to replace *not important* by *trifling,* and *did not have much confidence in* by *distrusted.* Actually, the two kinds of expressions are not interchangeable: *He is not optimistic* denies the host of associations people have with optimism, but only temporarily; *He is pessimistic* brings to mind all the bad associations of pessimism and has a quite different meaning as well as affect.

The writer must try to produce sentences—affirmative or negative—that express the messages precisely, with all their shades of nuance intact.

PASSIVE SENTENCE

Passive sentences are far fewer than SAAD in normal text (13.8% to 80.7% in Table 12-1), but they are nevertheless the second commonest among the various structures. Technical writers tend to overuse passives, ignoring the writing teachers' prescription to use actives where possible. Why are actives preferable to passives?

1. *The boy hit the girl.*
2. *The girl was hit by the boy.*

Out of context, the active version 1 seems more direct and vivid in conveying more or less the same semantic content. It is also shorter and less complex than its passive version 2.

Passives are harder to understand, to learn, and to produce than their active versions (e.g., Coleman, 1965). They are also mastered late by children (Hayhurst, 1967; Lempert & Kinsbourne, 1980; Slobin, 1966). Certain passives take on active-like forms in long-term memory, after a delay of 2 min (J. R. Anderson, 1974). After listening to prose passages, subjects recalled sentences predominantly in the active, regardless of the original voice. After reading the passages, however, they recognized changes of voice better (Kerr, Butler, Maykuth, & Delis, 1982).

Japanese passives, even in auditory presentation, seem to be retained verbatim at a delay of 80 sec, perhaps because some of them have particular emotional implication for the speaker (Omura & Utsuo, 1981). In another Japanese study, subjects heard sentences and then reproduced them on cue. Their reaction times were slower for passives than for actives; their reaction times were shortest when a reproduced sentence matched the input sentence in voice, regardless whether it was a passive or an active (Itoh & Koyazu, 1981).

For English, there is little evidence that passives are routinely converted into actives before they are comprehended; on the contrary, a probe sentence is verified faster if it matches the voice of the original sentence (Garrod & Trabasso, 1973; Olson & Filby, 1972). The same is true in answering questions about sentences: Fewer errors occurred if the voice of question matched the voice of the sentence, regardless of the particular voice used (Wright, 1972). If you want a correct answer, ask a question in the passive voice about a passive sentence, and in the active voice about an active sentence.

Semantically, passive sentences can be either reversible or non-reversible:

1. *The boy was hit by the girl; The girl was hit by the boy*
2. *The doctor treated the patient*

In Harriot's (1969) study, subjects took longer to process passives than actives if the passives were reversible as in sentence 1, but took about equal time if they were non-reversible as in 2. Schoolchildren understand and produce non-reversible passives better than reversible ones (Turner & Rommetveit, 1967). Caramazza and Zurif's (1978) patients with LH damage and deficient STM can handle non-reversible passives better than reversible ones. The BLC model predicts such results: Semantically reversible sentences require the syntactic analysis of the LEFT track for their correct interpretation; non-reversible ones require only syntactic corroboration of what has already been understood by the RIGHT track.

Passives often do not have agents. In the following sentence, the actions done on the patient are the points of interest, and a passive sentence, especially in the form that omits agents, is appropriate: *The patient was wheeled into the operating room, anaesthetized, operated on, bandaged, and then wheeled out of the room.* Several possible agents—any number of orderlies, surgeons, nurses—being highly predictable or relatively unimportant for the message, are only implied in the passive version.

In English, roughly 90% of passives are agentless, or "truncated," and in languages like Ute, all passives are agentless (Givon, 1979). The passives and passive negatives from our own sample of the 10 passages (on which Table 12-1 is based) were 93% agentless. Slobin (1968) found that agentless passives are processed somewhat differently from full passives: They tend to be recalled verbatim and not as full passives or as actives. Truncated passives are produced at an earlier age and are easier than full passives for children to produce (Brown & Hanlon, 1970; Harris, 1976; Menyuk, 1969). When the agent is overtly expressed in a passive, it is the focus of new information.

Passives are especially useful when the agent is not known. Even if you do not know the identity of the thief, you can at least shout: *My money's been stolen!*

Knowledge and Sentence Processing

Anyone reading a sentence approaches the task armed with knowledge on a variety of matters. The writer, in turn, takes the reader's knowledge into consideration. How does the reader use his knowledge in processing sentences?

Given–New Information

Conveying new information is the main object of communication, but to facilitate this process, the writer fits the new information together with the given (old) information, which then provides links to something already known.

GIVEN–NEW INFORMATION: LINGUISTIC SIGNALS

Sentence structure partly indicates which information is new and which is previously given. In an active declarative sentence, the subject is usually the given information, and the predicate, the new information. The given information can be omitted so as to highlight the most important new information. The subject-agent is routinely omitted in active sentences of Chinese, Japanese, and Korean, not just in informal speech but also in formal writing. When two people are in a dialogue, they can be taken for granted more than any other elements. In English, too, given information is often omitted, if not in formal writing, then at least in informal speech. To the question *Who drank the juice?,* the answer can be simply *the maid.*

In speech, emphasis can be added to new information with stress: *The* ***maid*** *drank it.* In writing, one tool of emphasis is to depart from normal word order so as to bring to the beginning what normally comes at the end, and vice versa:

1. The question is whether to be or not to be.
2. The waters of old age are bitter, . . .
3. The Joneses are clever people.

In the hands of the two great writers, the first two mundane sentences are transformed into two memorable ones:

1. "To be or not to be, that is the question [Shakespear, *Hamlet*]."
2. "Bitter are the waters of old age, and tears fall inward on the heart [D. H. Lawrence]."
3. "They are clever people, those Joneses."

Although word order roughly signals which parts are old (come earlier in a sentence) and which new, the marking is indistinct, particularly for an active declarative sentence. For increasing focus, English syntax possesses the device **cleft transformation,** so called because it divides a single clause into two sections, each with its own verb. The following cleft transformations have the effect of emphasizing the words in boldface:

1. *It was* ***the juice*** *that the maid drank.*
2. *It was* ***the maid*** *who drank the juice.*
3. *What the maid did to the juice was* ***drink*** *it.*

The definite article *the* has no semantic content; it merely indicates that the referent is known to both the speaker and the listener, either because it has been already mentioned or because its existence is a piece of common knowledge. Neither does the indefinite article *a* have any semantic content; it signals that the referent is new:

1. *I found a letter and a bill in the mail box.*
2. *The letter, but not the bill, pleased me.*

For more subtle points, compare:

1. *Don't go; the train's coming.*
2. *Don't go; a train's coming.*

Sentence 1 implies "the train we are both expecting," whereas 2 implies a warning to avoid being hit (Halliday & Hasan, 1976).

PROCESSING GIVEN–NEW INFORMATION

On the differences between *the* and *a,* Loftus's (1975) subjects were more likely to report having seen a stop sign in a film clip if asked *Did you see the stop sign?* than if asked *Did you see a stop sign?* regardless of whether there had actually been a stop sign. De Villiers's (1974) subjects tended to process a set of sentences as being related if each of the sentences started with *the,* but not when it started with *a.* (Such a dramatic effect of *the* and *a* on reading or on speech is the exception rather than the rule; see "Function Words," above.)

The judgments of naive subjects tend to corroborate linguistic analysis of active and passive sentences. When asked to judge what active sentences were about, 62% of the raters said that they were about the agent. For passive sentences, 65% said that the sentences were about the affected or object. In both cases, the information at the beginning of the sentence was judged to be old, and by default, the information at the end was judged to be new (Hornby, 1972).

Understandably, readers and listeners pay more attention to new than to old information. In a sentence–picture verification task, listeners examined the part of a picture corresponding to the new portion of a sentence more carefully than that corresponding to old information (Hornby, 1974). In a retention task, information embedded in the new portion of a sentence was integrated into memory more reliably than was information from the old portion (Singer, 1976). In silent reading, readers fixate longer on new than old information (see Chapter 7).

In the simple task of describing a set of triplets of pictures, 3-year-old children could mark given–new information using such sentential devices as ellipsis, pronoun, emphatic stress, and the definite and indefinite articles. But there were some changes with age, and also differences between the languages studied—English, Hungarian, and Italian. For example, the use of ellipsis gradually decreased while the use of articles increased with increasing age (MacWhinney & Bates, 1978).

In Clark and Haviland's (1977) view, when people hear an assertion, they try (*a*) to distinguish the given from the new information; (*b*) to search memory for a direct antecedent for the given information; and (*c*) to integrate the new information into memory by attaching it to the antecedent. When they fail to find an antecedent, they have either to form an indirect antecedent by building an inferential bridge from something they know, or to restructure the given and new information in hopes of deriving a direct antecedent. Clark and Haviland seem to attach too much emphasis on processing the given information, when in fact it provides merely a background against which the new information is processed. People are preoccupied with processing new information; they pay attention to given information only when they would otherwise be unsure where the new information fitted.

CONTEXT

A word is read better in the context of a sentence than in isolation (see Chapter 8). Sentences—in particular, negatives or indirect requests—are understood better and faster in the context of other sentences than in isolation.

Negative sentences are normally harder than their affirmative counterparts, as discussed in "Negative Sentence," but when a negative is used for one of its natural functions—to contrast and distinguish the exception from the norm—it is quickly understood (Valle Arroyo, 1982; Wason, 1965). Given that everyone goes to work every day, saying *I went to work yesterday* does not convey any new information, but the negative *I didn't go to work yesterday* does.

A negative is understood fast also when it signals a change of meaning (Greene, 1970). Subjects took less time to decide that the first pair of sentences had a different meaning than to decide that the second pair had the same meaning (x and y are different numbers):

1. *x exceeds y. / x does not exceed y.*
2. *y exceeds x. / x does not exceed y.*

The sentence *Must you open the window* can function either as an indirect request meaning *Don't open the window* or literally as a query *Is it necessary that you open the window?* Out of context the interpretation of the sentence as a query was faster than that as a request, but in context of a story, the two interpretations were equally fast (Rumelhart, 1979).

Suppose you read a passage that starts with: *Approaching the enemy infantry, the men were worried about touching off landmines.*

1. *Regardless of the danger, the troops marched on.*

You would interpret sentence 1 literally, even without the first sentence. But if 1 is to be interpreted metaphorically, there has to be sufficient context, such as: *The children continued to annoy their babysitter. She threatened to spank them if they continued to stomp, run, and scream around the room.* The researchers had to provide five preceding sentences to induce metaphorical interpretation of sentence 1 (Ortony, Schallert, Reynolds, & Antos, 1978). Some metaphors, whether common or uncommon, can be clearly understood even without context. Examples might be: *No man is an island* or *The rushing cataract of her prose* (see Chapter 11).

An isolated sentence can be ambiguous, even incomprehensible:

1. *The stripes expanded.*

If sentence 1 is preceded by *The man blew up the striped balloon,* the meaning crystallizes (Franks, 1974).

Implication and Inference

TYPES OF IMPLICATION AND INFERENCE

A writer does not spell out every conceivable piece of information in her writing; instead, some information is left unsaid. A reader supplements or fills in the implied information with inferences. Implied information may turn out to be potent, as can be seen in an old joke supplied by one of I. Taylor's (1976) editors: "A ship's captain and his mate took turns writing up the daily ship's log. One day, angry, the captain wrote: 'Mate was drunk today.' Next day the mate saw this and took revenge by writing, 'Captain was sober today.'" The famed Word War II British commander, Viscount Montgomery, was once asked in an interview: "Who do you think were the three greatest commanders in history?" Replied Monty, without a moment's hesitation: "The other two were Alexander the Great and Napoleon."

There are at least two kinds of implication: logical and pragmatic (Brewer, 1977; Harris & Monaco, 1978). Logical implication is information that is necessarily implied by an utterance, as sentence 1 implies 2:

1. *Kathy is taller than Mary.*
2. *Mary is shorter than Kathy.*

Inference from pragmatic implication is not always correct but is probabilistic, as sentence 2 is from 1:

1. *The karate champion hit the cement block.*
2. *The karate champion broke the cement block.*

The champion could have broken his own hand instead of the block.

Singer (1980) found that recognition of necessary inferences was comparable to that of directly expressed ideas and was higher than for probable but unnecessary inferences. Hildyard and Olson (1978) found that children from Grades 4 and 6 could differentiate the two kinds of inference but that the older children were better at the task. What changed with age was not the ability to derive necessary inferences; rather, what changed was the ability to reject pragmatic inference as necessarily true.

EVIDENCE OF INFERENCE

That readers and listeners draw inferences can be demonstrated in various ways. One way is "false recognition" of correct inferences. Using a three-sentence "story," Paris and Carter (1973) showed that children from Grades 2 and 5 draw inferences. The children first heard:

1. *The bird is inside the cage.*
2. *The cage is under the table.*
3. *The bird is yellow.*

On a later test, some of the children falsely recognized a correct inference ("The bird is under the table") as having been originally heard; they did not falsely recognize an incorrect inference ("The bird is on top of the table"). Using similar procedures with good and poor readers, Waller (1976) found that both groups consistently recognized correct inferences that had not been presented.

Reading level does relate to skill in drawing inferences at an advanced level. Using a long story with 16 paragraphs, Johnson and Smith (1981) showed that Grade 3 children, but not Grade 5 children, made fewer inferences when premises for an inference were located in separate paragraphs than when they occurred in the same paragraph in the story.

An instrument such as *hammer* is often inferred when verb *pound* is used along with *nails*. Having heard sentence 1, adult subjects frequently reported in a later test that they had heard 2 (Johnson, Bransford, & Solomon, 1973):

1. *The boy pounded the nail to fix the birdhouse.*
2. *The boy was using the hammer to fix the birdhouse.*

One should expect a hammer to be part of the association complex aroused by 1, and hence to be acceptable when tested by 2.

Corbett and Dosher (1978) question cued recall (and false recognition?) as a reliable indication that people infer and encode instruments during reading. In their experiment, high probability instruments (*The lawyer cooked dinner on a stove*) were effective as recall cues even when alternate, low-probability instruments (*on a camp-fire*) were encoded during reading. Instruments were not inferred as a matter of routine. Highly probable items and events can be generated, out of our knowledge of the world, at the time of recall and recognition.

Certain inference is obligatory for comprehension and must be made at the time of reading: *The floor was dirty because Sally used the mop* can make sense only if added information, "the mop was dirty," is inferred. When this kind of sentence was embedded in short stories, subjects often falsely recognized the additional information as part of the story (Bransford & Johnson, 1973).

Another line of experiment on inference compares the time needed to process either an implicit or an explicit referent. Haviland and Clark (1974) asked their subjects to read one of two possible antecedent sentences 1 or 2 and then press a key as soon as they understood a closely related test sentences 3:

1. *We got some beer out of the trunk.*
2. *We checked the picnic supplies.*
3. *The beer was warm.*

The subjects took longer to comprehend the test sentence, if the antecedent sentence was 2 instead of 1, which explicitly mentions *beer.* Perhaps, "naive" subjects are not qualified to process this series of sentences. The writer or speaker normally would not use 2 and then 3, unless he habitually includes beer in picnic supplies and knows that the reader or listener knows this fact.

In one study, Grade 2 children with most prior knowledge on spiders answered more implicit questions after reading a passage on this topic than did children with least knowledge (Pearson, Hansen, & Gordon, 1979). You read sentences to add information to your knowledge base, but you do so under the constant influence of the same knowledge base.

Writing Sentences

Process of Sentence Production

What mental processes does a writer go through in producing sentences? Is producing sentences the exact inverse of comprehending them? There are few studies on how a writer produces sentences, forcing us to consider how a speaker produces sentences. It may turn out that a writer and a speaker goes through similar processes.

A speaker or writer produces a sentence when there is something to say. This "something" is conceived as a gist, which can take the form of a visual image, a topic word, or a few key words. Or, it may never even progress beyond a vague feeling, as shown in Figure 12-2.

CONTENT VERSUS STRUCTURE

Speakers appear to expend more time and effort in formulating contents than in formulating structures of sentences. When I. Taylor (1969) provided speakers with a set of topic words, the speakers' latencies to produce sentences were longer for infrequent and abstract topics than for frequent and concrete ones. Their latencies were not related to the types and complexities of sentence structures produced. In Deese's (1980a) study, when the content, but not the form, of speech was planned in advance, the sentences produced tended to be more fluent than in extemporaneous speaking. Goldman-Eisler (1968) manipulated content difficulties by giving subjects two different tasks: In one, subjects described, and in the other, they interpreted, a series of captionless cartoons. Interpretation presumably requires more cognitive activity than does description and should be accompanied by more hesitation pauses. She obtained the predicted results. In her other studies, structural complexity, in terms of the number of subordinate clauses, did not correlate with pauses (see also Butterworth, 1980). In yet other studies, Goldman-Eisler found that speakers hesitate before content words of high information (unpredictable).

Other studies examined speech errors or slips of the tongue to gain insight into sentence production (Dell & Reich, 1981; Fromkin, 1980; Garrett, 1976; Lashley, 1951; Shattuck-Hufnagel, 1979). Within a phrase, a noun tends to be exchanged with another noun: Thus, *(I've got to go home and) give my bath a hot*

Figure 12-2. *Process of producing a sentence (United Features Syndicate, Inc., 1972, reproduced with permission).*

back, is a more common error than *give my hot a bath back.* An anticipatory speech error, such as *they put their lips through their teeth,* shows that the idiomatic phrase was planned as a unit. This sort of anticipatory error occurs also in writing and within a clause (Hotopf, 1980): *Their success has also been reasonably successful* (the target was *prediction*).

In one of the few studies on writing processes, a team of researchers asked two groups of college students—freshmen and upperclassmen—to write an essay on a given topic for 30 min (Schumacher, Klare, Cronin, & Moses, 1982). Schumacher *et al.* examined pauses (10 sec or longer) occurring during writing, using videotapes combined with protocol analysis. The pauses were associated mostly with immediate planning, reviewing content, and word choice, and marginally with sentence structure, for both groups of subjects. Global planning also occurred, albeit less often as immediate planning.

Writers can plan many levels of content, sometimes simultaneously, sometimes sequentially—content word, phrase, clause, sentence, paragraph, passage, story, and book.

WORD AND PHRASE ORDER

Word order is specified by the syntax of a language. For example, an active-declarative sentence must be SV0 in English but SOV in Japanese and Korean. However, syntax does not have rules for ordering every element in a sentence. An English active-declarative sentence that contains a direct object and an indirect object can be SVO_dO_i or SVO_iO_d. According to linguists, the direct object is by far the more frequent kind of object, and it must be always present if there is an indirect object in the sentence. The direct object always follows the indirect object (Quirk *et al.*, 1979). According to psychologists, however, there seems to be a bias toward the direct–indirect object order (Bock & Brewer, 1974), despite that the preferred order requires an extra preposition (e.g., *John gave the book to Mary* is more likely than *John gave Mary the book*). The psychologically preferred order is acquired earlier than the linguistically preferred order in English (Osgood & Zehler, 1981), as well as in Chinese and Iranian (Salili & Hoosain, 1981). In this order, the action (giving) and the transfer object (book) are perceptually fused as "giving-of-a-book"; this unitary perceptual event is interrupted by inserting the recipient if it is phrased as "gave Mary a book."

In ordering phrases within a sentence, Bock (1982) argues that phrases containing more accessible information occur earlier in sentences. More accessible information tends to be: animate, familiar concrete, perceptually salient, already given, and repeated. For ordering clauses within a sentence, see our section "Suggestion 8."

Writing Effective Sentences

The preceding section described mostly speakers; the studies may describe writers equally well. But a writer must differ from a speaker at some point of sentence production: Having conceived a gist, a writer, unlike a speaker, can deliberate on the form of the sentences. Sometimes the writer agonizes over the choice of words, in search of *le mot juste*. At other times he tries out different structures: Passive or active? Two simple sentences or one complex sentence? If complex, the main clause before or after the subordinate clause? We have already dropped many hints for writers in the first part of the chapter (e.g., "Negative Sentences"). To supplement them, we now offer ten suggestions for choosing effective words and sentence structures, based largely on research findings. The experiments described here are on comprehension, which is what writers usually want to maximize.

SUGGESTION 1: USE SHORT COMMON WORDS

Vocabulary complexity is the major source of text difficulty, as pointed out by investigators who study readability (Bormuth, 1966; Dale & Chall, 1948; Fry, 1977; Klare, 1974–1975). These investigators recommend using short or frequent words. Frequent words tend to be short, familiar, and easily pronounced. For example, frequency has a correlation of .65 with familiarity and .54 with pronounceability (O'Neill, 1972). Zipf (1935) observed that the majority of the common words in many languages are monosyllables. Among the 100 most frequent words in Kucera and Francis's (1967) list, 94 are monosyllables. The list contains mostly function words, but it also contains 9 content words, which are all monosyllables: *new, time, now, year,* etc.

The relative frequencies of words strongly affect reading and speech: People learn, perceive, read, or guess frequent words faster and more accurately than they do infrequent ones (see Chapter 9). In one study, when 15% of the low frequency content words in a passage were replaced by high frequency ones of the same length (e.g., *judge* by *think, support* by *believe*), children understood the passage much better (Marks, Doctorow, & Wittrock, 1974). While reading a passage, most readers slow down when they encounter a word like *the lateral and medial cutaneous* ***antebrachials.*** A novel word tends to receive an extraordinarily long fixation, and so does a long word (Just & Carpenter, 1980; Rayner & McConkie, 1976). (In technical writing for a trained audience, however, long technical words may make the intended meanings precise.)

Unfamiliar acronyms can be worse than unfamiliar words, which often contain familiar prefixes and suffixes (**ante**brachial**s**). Read the following quote from a psychology journal:

> The first hypothesis suggests that CSP-HS-HP and CSP-LS-LP syllables should be easier to recall bimodally than ISP-HS-LP and ISP-LS-HP syllables. The second hypothesis implies that ISP-HS-LP should be easier to recall bimodally than ISP-LS-HP. Also, CSP-HS-HP should be easier to recall than CSP-LS-LP because both the spelling and pronunciation are higher in similarity to English in CSP-HS-HP than CSP-LS-LP [T. D. Nelson, 1969, p. 119].

True, the author did describe in the earlier part of his paper what the initials stood for. But would the reader memorize all these numerous initials, which will be useless beyond this particular paper? To make matters worse, the initials are made into a series of hard-to-differentiate sets.

Infrequent words and long sentences adversely affect reading time but not recall. Once the words have been decoded, their initial difficulty no longer matters, presumably because further processing occurs on a conceptual level that is unaffected by their original forms (Miller & Kintsch, 1980).

SUGGESTION 2: USE ACTIVE VERBS

The verb plays a central role in sentence comprehension. The linguist Jespersen (1949) considers it to be the center around which the subject and the object are grouped. In Japanese and Korean, a short declarative sentence may contain only a verb, as in *Will eat* ('[I] will eat [this meal]'). In Fillmore's (1968) case grammar and in proposition analysis the verb specifies a relation among its arguments. In predicting which sentences would be judged more alike, similarity of verbs was more important than that of the subjects and the objects (Healy & Miller, 1970). The main verb in active sentences are processed longer than other parts in some studies (Rayner, 1977; Wanat, 1976), but not in others (Aaronson & Scarborough, 1976; Just & Carpenter, 1980). A verb, however, was not recalled as well as a subject or an object (Loosen, 1981; Raeburn, 1979).

These studies did not distinguish two very different types of verb, the linking verbs and the rest, as in: *He* ***is*** *a psychology teacher* and *He* ***teaches*** *psychology.* The first type is a closed system, with 7 members (*be, been, is, was, are, were, am*); the other is an open system, with unspecifiably large membership (*drink, read, write,* etc.). A linking verb simply fulfills the function "verb" in a sentence and conveys little meaning. It is a "purely grammatical dummy," according to Lyons (1968). Next to the two articles, the linking verbs were the most deletable, and restorable, words in an experiment to see which words in a text are least important (Taylor & Taylor, in preparation). They are not required in some languages, such as Russian "This [is a] book." Overuse of such colorless linking verbs saps the vigor of a writer's sentences.

In another vein, concepts are easier to understand in the form of verbs than as derived nouns. Coleman (1964) selected sentences containing nominalized verbs, as in sentence 1, and then changed the nominalized verbs into their active forms, holding the number of words constant, as in 2:

1. *Analysis of aerial photographs requires a study and evaluation of the land forms, erosion, drainage, and other features of the terrain.*
2. *When we analyze aerial photographs, we must study and evaluate the land forms, erosion, drainage, and other features of the terrain.*

The active-verb versions such as 2 were understood, recalled, and learned more easily than were the nominalized versions. The use of active verbs simultaneously (*a*) shortens the clauses; (*b*) increases the number of verbs; (*c*) brings the subject and its verb close together; (*d*) renders the words short and familiar; and (*e*) makes meanings concrete.

SUGGESTION 3: RELATE SENTENCES BY REPEATING WORDS AND STRUCTURE

Successive sentences in a paragraph will relate in meaning when key words or concepts are repeated across them:

1. *Brian punched George.*
2. *George called the doctor.*
3. *The doctor arrived.*

When the object of one sentence was repeated as the subject of the next, reading time decreased and immediate recall increased, as compared with a parallel sentence in which a new noun was used as the subject (*Brian punched George. Arnold called the doctor.*) (Manelis & Yekovich, 1976).

Other items can be repeated with good effect. A structure is repeated in the following three consecutive sentences (that the sentences do not say much is beside the point): "Where children see little relevance in reading, then teachers must provide a model. Where children find little interest in reading, then teachers must change the situation. And where children have difficulty in reading, teachers must see that they are helped [F. Smith, 1978, p. 187]." A repeated structure gives coherence to the three sentences, speeds comprehension, as the structure developed for the first sentence can be reused for the second and the third, and renders the whole quote memorable.

Wisher (1976) found that sentences in one structure were processed faster and easier when they were presented in a block than when they were presented mixed with other structures. A tendency to read successive clauses in the same structure, maintaining the same subject, can be seen in a child's errors in oral reading (Goodman, 1982, p. 158):

1. (Text) *I'll light a fire in the fireplace and the porridge will be ready in a few minutes.*
2. (A child's reading) *I'll light a fire in the fireplace and I'll... and the porridge will be ready in a flash... a few minutes.*

SUGGESTION 4: RELATE SENTENCES BY USING ANAPHORA

Against the beneficial effects of repeating the same sounds, words, and structures, one must weigh the deadly monotony of seeing the same items again and again. "Like many habit-forming drugs, repetition can be both a stimulant and a soporific, depending on the dosage [W. W. Watt, 1964, p. 90]." Repeating words not only is monotonous but also has its hazard: The words' meanings may change subtly in different sentence contexts. Repeating a noun within a sentence (rather than substituting its pronoun) may signal a special meaning such as emphasis in sentence 1, or that the same noun has two referents as in sentence 2 (Lesgold, 1972):

1. *God is great and God is good.*
2. *The king is dead; long live the king.*

To establish commonality of reference across clauses and sentences, but to combat monotony while doing so, writers can use **anaphora,** which are linguistic devices for referring to previously mentioned constituents, called the referents (Halliday & Hasan, 1976). When the referent is a verb, a writer can delete it, leaving in such pro-verbs as *can* and *do,* as in the following quote attributed to ex-president Lyndon Johnson: "I can walk and chew gum. Gerry Ford can too, but not at the same time." When the referent is a noun, a pronoun usually substitutes for it. To comprehend a passage fully readers must identify referents for pro-verbs and pronouns. Not surprisingly, the ability to identify referents is correlated with the ability to comprehend a passage (Dutka, 1980; Frederiksen, 1981b). College-student readers with a large working memory span were better than those with a small span in identifying the referent of a pronoun, especially if there were many words separating them (Daneman & Carpenter, 1980).

In "ecologically valid" passages (taken straight out of children's textbooks and basal readers), how often do pronouns occur? In Grade 4 materials, whether narrative or expository, 30 pronouns occurred within a 250-word passage. The most of the referents were to previous sentences (Kameenui & Carnine, 1982). After reading these materials, Grade 4 children could answer pronoun-specific as well as general comprehension questions better when the pronouns were replaced by the referents than when they were left as was. But pronoun replacing worked only with expository passages; it did not improve comprehension of narrative passages, which presumably were easy enough to read using the original pronouns. High school students, too, take longer to read a sentence containing a pronoun than one containing a repeated noun phrase (Frederiksen, 1981b).

Some substitutions are harder to process than others. Lesgold's (1974) Grades 3 and 4 subjects found pro-verbs in sentences 1 and 2 more difficult than a personal pronoun in 3 or a noun substitute in 4:

1. *Joe is sick.* ***So is*** *Bill.*
2. *John likes Mary.* ***So does*** *Bill.*
3. *Joe left.* ***He*** *had....*
4. *Those dishes are expensive, but this* ***china****....*

Grade 3 children found it harder to identify the referent for a pronoun than to identify the repetition of the noun; they found it hardest to identify the referent for an omitted noun (Richek, 1976–1977).

The length of substitution matters: A pronoun referring to a noun or a noun phrase is more easily understood than one referring to a clause or a sentence (Barnitz, 1980; Dutka, 1980). The reference order also matters: referent before pronoun, *the book...it,* is easier than *it...the book* (Barnitz, 1980), and referent before category word, *a robin...the bird,* is easier than the reverse (Garrod & Sanford, 1977).

A pronoun can be located within the same sentence as its referent or in different sentences. Dutka (1980) found the distance between the referent and its substitute to be the second best predictor of difficulty after the length of the referent substituted. In Clark and Sengul's (1979) study, a four-sentence paragraph contained a pronoun in the fourth sentence whose referent was in the first, second, or third sentence. Less time was needed to comprehend sentences with the referent one sentence back (in the third sentence) than those with it two or three sentences back. The referent was easier to retrieve in the last clause, whether it was a subordinate or a main clause.

This shows how cautious the writer should be in using substitutes. The use we just made of *this* to refer to a complex, distant, and almost unidentifiable referent is one of the worst misuses of pronominals. Writers and speakers should use referents that are "on stage" (or in short-term memory) and not refer to items that have to be sought out from the wings. The referent of a pronoun may be hard to locate if the discourse scene or theme changes (Chafe, 1976; Rosenberg, 1976). It is safe to reintroduce a referent when a paragraph changes, or even when one sentence intervens between a substitute and its referent. Anaphora give economy, and perhaps elegance, to writing. They integrate ideas across clauses and sentences. On the other hand, they may adversely affect comprehension.

SUGGESTION 5: KEEP SUBJECT AND VERB CLOSE TOGETHER

Perceiving the subject–verb relation is the most critical part of sentence comprehension (Fry, Weber, & Depierro, 1978; Hamilton & Deese, 1971). See how a subject and its verb can become further and further separated as you move from sentence 1 to 2 and then to 3. In the **self-embedded** sentence 3, a clause is embedded into a second clause, which in turn nests into a third, like a set of Chinese boxes; 4 turns the nest inside out:

1. *The rat ran.*
2. *The rat (that the cat chased) ran.*
3. *The rat (that the cat (that the dog teased) chased) ran.*
4. *The dog teased the cat that chased the rat that ran.*

To process sentence 2, *the rat* has to be kept in working memory until *that the cat chased* has been processed, and the rat's own verb, *ran*, appears. In 3, both *the rat* and *the cat* have to be stored while *that the dog teased* is processed, and then *the cat* is retrieved to be processed along with *chased,* and so on. All this storing and interpreting is carried out in working memory that has only a limited capacity. Even though sentences 3 and 4 contain the same words, the memory load is heavier and comprehension more difficult in 3 than in 4, in which a reader is concerned only with what happens after the point where he is reading.

A modifying phrase can separate a predicate from its subject, and may confuse young readers. Reid (1972) gave a pair of sentences to children aged 7–8:

1. *The girl standing beside the lady had a blue dress.*
2. *The girl was standing beside the lady and the lady had a blue dress.*

The first version was interpreted by 59% of the children as though its extended version was sentence 2.

SUGGESTION 6: USE COMMAS TO SEGREGATE CONSTITUENTS

Gertrude Stein (1935), in her essay "Poetry and grammar," observed: "And what does a comma do, a comma does nothing but make easy a thing that if you like it enough is easy enough without the comma [p. 221]." Of course a comma does something: It segregates units within a sentence. Compare sentence 1 and 2:

1. *That that is is that that is not is not.*
2. *That that is, is; that that is not, is not.*

Commas and other punctuation marks were described by a grammarian in the early seventeenth century as follows: "The Use of these points, Pauses, or Stops, is not only to give a proper Time for Breathing: but to avoid Obscurity, and Confusion of the Sense in joining Words together in a sentence."

According to Baldwin and Coady (1978) (to whom we owe the above quote), a comma is critical in sentence 1, in which *John* might be read as the object of the verb *eat;* it is redundant in 2, in which the word order signals the syntactic roles of the words:

1. *Why can't we eat, John?*
2. *John, why can't we eat?*

Grade 5 children appeared to ignore a comma, even when it was syntactically critical. In contrast, adult subjects were profoundly affected by the presence or absence of commas in sentences such as 1, which they comprehended very poorly without commas, but with commas, almost as well as sentences such as 2.

Baldwin (1977) studied how children read the following types of sentences:

1. *If you can, skip along.*
2. *Skip along, if you can.*

Grade 3 children reading silently comprehended sentence 2 better than 1. In reading aloud, they made fewer intonation miscues at clause boundaries in 2.

A comma has another function: It introduces differences in nuance or adds emphasis:

1. *The master beat the student with a strap.*
2. *The master beat the student, with a strap.*

According to Fowler (1958), these sentences demonstrate the gulf between matter-of-factness and indignation.

SUGGESTION 7: LINK RELATED CLAUSES WITH CONJUNCTIONS

Conjunctions specify how what is to follow connects to what has gone before. The connection could be temporal (*and, after*), causal (*so, for*), contrasting (*but, although*), or of some other kind. *I flunked the exam. I feel rotten.* Most skilled adult readers link these two sentences with an implicit conjunction *so*, or its equivalent (Marshall & Glock, 1978–1979). Schoolchildren prefer to have causal relations explicitly stated. Furthermore, they tend to include an unstated conjunction in their verbatim recall of individual sentences (Pearson, 1974–1975).

Even when a set of clauses do not share a common subject, they can be linked with *and* if they describe the same scene. Consider this "freight-train" sentence from *Farewell to Arms* by Ernest Hemingway: "It was a hot day and the sky was very bright and blue and the road was white and dusty." The reader of the above sentence forms one complex experience, rather than three separate ones, as Kane and Peters (1966) point out. It is in such sentences that the associative process of the RIGHT track dominates, producing one imagery complex: "hot day, bright blue sky, white dusty road." Highly evocative, it almost passes as a Chinese poem.

SUGGESTION 8: ARRANGE CLAUSES IN A NATURAL OR IMPORTANCE ORDER.

How should a main clause and a subordinate clause be arranged in a complex sentence? The answer depends partly on the types of conjunction and partly on the skill of subjects. Preschoolers prefer an order of clauses that mirrors the order of events. Of four ways of arranging clauses containing *before* and *after,* 1 and 2 were easier for them to comprehend and act out than 3 and 4 (H. L. Johnson, 1975):

S1 = you drink juice; S2 = you eat cookies

1. S1 before S2—*You drink juice before you eat cookies.*
2. After S1, S2—*After you drink juice, you eat cookies.*
3. Before S2, S1—*Before you eat cookies, you drink juice.*
4. S2 after S1—*You eat cookies after you drink juice.*

In type 4 sentences, young children tend to misunderstand *after* as *then* (E. Clark, 1971).

With college students, however, no memory benefit derives from correspondence between order of mention and order of occurrence. Instead, in the following pair of sentences, subjects remembered 1 (main before subordinate clause) better than 2 (subordinate before main) (Clark & Clark, 1968):

1. *John talked to the doctor after he had his accident.*
2. *After he had his accident, John talked to the doctor.*

In another study with college students, the question "What happened first?" following a *before* or *after* sentence was answered more quickly than was "What happened second?" (Smith & McMahon, 1970).

In a study by Bever and Townsend (1979), *if* clauses tended to act most like independent clauses, as their content can be processed independently of the main clause; *though* clauses acted least like independent clauses, as the adversative relation required the two clauses to be processed together. However, in judging the reasonableness of heard sentences, young children found the *if*-first sentence 1 easier to deal with than the *if*-second sentence 2, perhaps because in 1, order of mention and temporal order are congruent (Emerson, 1980):

1. *If she became ill, she stayed home from school.*
2. *She stayed home from school if she became ill.*

SUGGESTION 9: WRITE SHORT BUT VARIED CLAUSES

Whenever you can shorten a sentence, do. One always can. The best sentence? The shortest.

—Gustave Flaubert

If a word can possibly be cut, cut it.

—George Orwell

This advice from the two illustrious writers is sound enough, considering that a long sentence tends to be structurally complex, taxing the reader's working memory. Studies on readability associate long sentences with difficult passages and short sentences with easy passages (Bormuth, 1966; Fry, 1977; Klare, 1974–1975). Flesch (1949) has a prescription for shortening sentences: "Go after complex sentences. Look for the joints where the conjunctions are—'if, because, as' and so on—and split your sentences up [p. 142]." This advise cannot always be followed. If two clauses are closely related to each other, they must be linked in one complex sentence, their relation marked with a conjunction (see Suggestion 7).

Coleman (1962) found that technical passages broken up into short sentences were more comprehensible than their long counterparts, but only slightly. He suggests that sentence is the wrong unit to shorten; what should be shortened are clauses, so as to bring the subject and its verb close together. Miller and Kintsch (1980) found that sentence length adversely affected reading time but not recall.

The average length of a written sentence is 19.2 words, according to Kucera and Francis (1967), who examined over 1 million words in a variety of types of writing. The average length in this book ranges from 18.4 words in this and the next chapter to 22.1 words in Chapter 11. Here is a piece of sound advice on sentence length (note also the repetition of sentence structure in the quote):

> If you find the majority of them [sentences] containing more than thirty words, the chances are that they need breaking up; if you find the majority of them under ten words, the chances are that some of them need to be combined. If you find most of them about the same length, the chances are that they need revision for the sake of variety [Manly, Rickert, & Freeman, 1937, p. 48].

A long sentence, even one with a simple structure, can be undesirable because it tends to contain unimportant verbiage that obscures the main point. A sentence in technical writing might read: *These experimental findings by numerous researchers, in particular by Jastrezembski, Schvanervoldt, and Donnanverth-Nolandt and their coworkers (1985; see also 1986b), lead us to conclude unequivocally that people do not read letter by letter.* The most important message, "people do not read . . .," is buried under a load of vacuous verbiage. Proper nouns are often harder to read than common nouns. Remedy: Put the main message first, cut the rest, and tack on the obligatory reference at the end in ( ) so that those who do not need it can easily skip it. (The names in the example are fictitious, despite their resemblance to names referenced elsewhere in the book.)

Here is a French–English bilingual sign found in a W.C. somewhere in Canada:

> Voulez-vous, s'il vous plaît, faire opérer l'eau sous pression dans cette closette d'eau après chaque besoin.[4]
>
> Please flush.

SUGGESTION 10: WATCH OUT FOR AMBIGUITY

Potential ambiguities abound in writing. They result from lack of commas, multiple meanings of words, careless uses of pronouns, or faulty arrangement of words and phrases. In conversation, ambiguity can be resolved by questioning the speaker, but in reading, there is no such recourse.

Flying planes can be dangerous is interpretable in two ways:

1. *Planes that are flying can be dangerous.* (planes = the subject)
2. *For you to fly planes can be dangerous.* (planes = the object)

Our favorite example of this sort of ambiguity comes from a girl who said: "I like swimming, dancing, and exciting boys."

Double entendres exploit alternate meanings of words for humor, usually risqué. Multiple meanings of a word may delight connoisseurs of double entendres, but they can be sources of processing difficulty. After reviewing the literature, Levelt (1978) concluded that ambiguity caused longer reactions in a variety of tasks, in particular judging compatibility between two sentences (Cairns, 1973).

MacKay (1966) presented subjects with a clause plus one following word, typed on an index card, and asked them to complete the sentence as quickly as possible:

1. *After making the right turn at the intersection, I . . .*
2. *After making the left turn at the intersection, I . . .*

[4]'Will you, if you please, operate the water under pressure in this water closet after each need.' (quoted by Gunning, 1968, p. 105)

Clauses with more than one meaning took longer to complete than those with just one. The subjects were more likely to stutter, repeat themselves, become ungrammatical, and even titter on ambiguous than on unambiguous clauses. Yet, these people were often not even aware of the ambiguity. The LEFT track had selected one version, but the RIGHT saw the joke.

According to Olson and MacKay (1974), words whose primary meanings are strongly favored are processed like unambiguous words. Words whose alternate senses are equally favored cause the most difficulty, increasing processing time and errors. For such words, both meanings are activated; perceiving one meaning requires the other to be suppressed, taking additional time.

Children process the more common meanings of words better than they do the secondary ones. For example, in the sentence *The bat flew out of the tree,* they might read *bat* as a baseball bat rather than a flying animal, even though it violates the context (Mason, Kniseley, & Kendall, 1979).

The relation between a pro-verb or pronoun and its referent can be ambiguous:

1. *John loves his wife. The milkman does too.*
2. *If the baby does not thrive on raw milk, boil it.*
3. *John told Robert's son that he must help him.*

Sentences 1 and 2 with their double meanings may evoke smiles, but 3 may confuse a reader, as it is capable of six different meanings (1 comes from Coleman, 1980; 2 and 3, from Jespersen, 1949). Frederiksen (1981b) found that the number of potential referents available within a paragraph increased reading time for high school students.

Journalists write newspaper headlines as concisely as possible, and readers give the headlines hurried glances. As there is no further context to resolve ambiguities, some headlines are ambiguous:

"QUIT OR LOSE ALL ALCOHOLICS BEING TOLD."

Is it "Quit or lose, all alcoholics being told" or "Quit or lose all, alcoholics being told"?

Faulty arrangements of constituents can cause ambiguity: "He advertised for a steady young man to look after a horse of the Baptist faith." *Only* is a tricky word to place in a sentence. Fowler (1958), that redoubtable arbiter of English usage, observes: "I read the other day of a man who 'only died a week ago,' as if he could have done anything else more striking or final [p. 405]."

Of course, writers should try to be aware of potential ambiguity and take steps to reduce it. Beyond a certain point, however, further reduction of ambiguity is achieved only at a cost, most often in excessive redundancy and diminished clarity. If one looks hard enough, just about any statement is ambiguous. Legal language aims above all at removing every possible ambiguity. It is sparing of pronouns, on the one hand, and makes an excessive use of qualifying words, on the other. The following quote is only a part of a long and complex "sentence" from a legal document (A recently proposed amendment to Canada's Income Tax Act). In trying to comprehend this sentence, and failing dismally, the reader can appreciate what we have been saying about taxing working memory.

> For the purposes of paragraph 1(e) an amount that is a reasonable standby charge for the automobile for the aggregate number of days in a taxation year during which it was made available by an employer, or by a person related to the employer, shall be deemed to be the amount equal to the product obtained when (a) where the employer or the person related to the employer owned the automobile at any time in the year, an amount in respect of its cost to the employer equal to the percentage thereof obtained when 2 per cent is multiplied by the quotient obtained when such of the aggregate number of days herein before referred to as were days during which the employer or the person related to the employer owned the automobile is divided by 30 (except that if the quotient so obtained is not a full number and exceeds one it shall be taken to the nearest full number or, if there is no nearest full number, then to the full number next below it)...[175 words so far; and the sentence continues for 49 more lines]...[Quoted in the Toronto *Globe and Mail*, 13 April 1983].

On rereading this monstrosity, we have changed our mind: The aim of this kind of sentence is not to remove ambiguity but to provide work for more lawyers trying to keep taxpayers out of jail.

Summary and Conclusion

A clause (or a simple sentence) is a syntactic, semantic, and processing unit. Syntactically, it may be analyzed into its elements, which are subject, verb, object, complement, and adverbial. The elements have specific orders (e.g., SVO). Semantically, a clause describes an event in which each element takes on a case role such as agent, affected, goal, instrument, and recipient.

To comprehend a clause, a reader analyzes it according to the syntactic and case roles of the elements, in addition to finding the words' meanings. The words thus processed (to varying degrees) are held in working memory until they form a clause. The clause is comprehended as a unit, and its content is retained as a gist, while its words and structure are soon, but not immediately, forgotten. A gist may be in the form of a visual image or in verbal form as SVO, stripped of modifiers, goals and instruments.

A proposition is a linguistic and processing unit that underlies a sentence. It consists of one or two arguments and one predicate that relates them (P, X, Y). The more propositions a sentence contains, the longer it takes to process. Propositional analysis is too rigorously formal and imprecisely defined for use by untrained people. As a descriptive unit, a proposition may not improve substantially on a clause.

The most common sentence structure is simple-active-affirmative-declarative, with a sprinkling of negatives, passives, and negative-passives.

Transformationally complex structures like passive-question, negative-question, or passive-negative-question seldom occur in text. A speaker's presuppositions dictate the type of sentence he produces.

A negative sentence is indispensable for communication, but for both syntactic and semantic reasons it is harder to comprehend than is its affirmative counterpart. In an appropriate context, it may be quickly understood. Double negatives are especially hard to comprehend.

Passive sentences may also be harder to understand than are their active versions, but they have their uses and misuses. Agentless passives and non-reversible passives are more common and are easier than full passives and reversible passives.

A text is bound to contain some implicit information. A reader infers necessary information from context and from general knowledge about the world. Inferred information, if it is plausible, is so potent that it may be falsely recognized as having been part of the original sentences.

Various linguistic devices are available for signaling emphasis, and for distinguishing which information is given and which new. They include ellipsis, pronoun, stress, word order, *the/a,* passive, and cleft-transformation.

To ease a reader's task, a writer must choose words and sentence structures with care. Use common and short words; use active verbs (rather than linking verbs or verbs made into nouns); and avoid unfamiliar acronyms. Bring together closely two constituents requiring joint processing, such as a subject and its verb or a referent and its pronoun, thus easing the load on a reader's working memory and avoiding misunderstanding. Long sentences tend to be structurally complex and/or wordy, but a steady diet of short sentences soon becomes monotonous.

Ambiguity can be caused by double meanings of words, mismatches between a referent and its substitute, faulty arrangements of constituents, and lack of necessary commas. Ambiguity can cost processing time and accuracy.

The BLC model of reading extends to the level of sentence: The LEFT syntactic processes work on the structure of the sentence to fit words together; the RIGHT semantic processes evoke associations and imagery of content words and the meaning of the sentence.

13

Prose: Narrative and Expository

"Once," said the Mock Turtle at last,... "I was a real Turtle."...Alice was very nearly getting up and saying, "Thank you, Sir, for your interesting story," but she could not help thinking there ***must*** *be more to come...*

—Lewis Carroll[1]

You read to be informed, entertained, or moved. What you read is a collection of sentences, a prose passage. Broadly, prose can be classified into narration, which tells a story, and exposition, which explains facts and ideas. The two types of prose differ not only in content and purpose but also in structure, which is the main topic of this chapter. First we discuss narrative, in particular, stories.

Narrative Prose

In many cultures reading is introduced to young children through stories, which tend to be far easier than expository texts. Stories are read faster and recalled better than expository passages (Graesser *et al.*, 1980). And, more comprehension questions are answered on them than on expository passages (Kameenui & Carnine, 1982). Good stories enchant children; they often contain moral lessons as well.

The questions asked in this section are: What are the elements of a story, and how are they arranged? Is there a story grammar? If so, is it universal or

[1]In chapter 9 "The Mock Turtle's Story," from *Alice's Adventures in Wonderland.*

culture specific? Does it guide people's comprehension and retention of stories? What makes a story interesting, comprehensible, and memorable?

Structure of a Story

What is a typical story like? Here is an old folktale "The Magic Mortar" (the Japanese version; 420-words long), which has many of the elements and structure found in folktales everywhere.[2]

The Magic Mortar

Once upon a time there were two brothers in a little village in Japan. The elder brother worked hard all the time, but the younger brother was lazy and good-for-nothing.

One day the elder brother went off to the mountains to work. While he was working, an old man appeared and gave him a stone mortar, the kind used for grinding grain into flour. "This is a magic mortar which will give you anything you wish for," said the old man.

Overjoyed, the elder brother rushed home with the mortar. "Please give me rice." So saying, he put the stick in the mortar. All at once out came rice, bags and bags of it. There was so much rice that he gave it to everyone in the village. "This is wonderful! Thank you very much." The happy villagers thanked him profusely.

The lazy brother alone was not happy. "I wish I had the mortar; I'd make better use of it," he grumbled to himself. And one day he stole the magic mortar and ran away. "No one will be able to catch me if I get to the ocean," he thought. He took a small rowboat and rowed out to sea, far out and right in the middle of the big waves.

Then he wondered what he wanted to ask the mortar for. "I have it! I would like a lot of nice, sweet little cakes." And he began to grind at the mortar with the stick, saying "Give me cakes!" Fine white cakes, lots of them, rolled out of the mortar. "My! How good they are!" He ate every one of them. He had eaten so many sweet cakes that he felt like having something salty to take the sweet taste out of his mouth.

So he ground at the mortar again and said: "Give me salt. I want salt." And now salt came pouring out of the mortar, all white and gleaming. And it kept coming and coming. "Enough," he cried, "I've had enough. Stop!" But the salt kept coming and coming, until the boat began to fill up and get heavy. And still the salt kept coming, and now the boat was so full it started to sink. And as the brother sank with the boat, he was still crying: "Enough! Enough!"

But the mortar kept on giving out salt and more salt, even down at the bottom of the ocean, and it is still doing it. And that is why the sea is salty.

ELEMENTS OF A STORY

A story contains four essential elements: character, plot, theme, and setting.

A story is about what **characters** do over time. Characters are so important that a story is sometimes named after the principal character, a hero or

[2]The story has been slightly revised from the version included in *Urashima Taro and Other Japanese Children's Stories*, edited by Florence Sakade, Tokyo: Charles E. Tuttle, 1959.

heroine, such as Peter Pan or Cinderella. Going beyond folktales, we find such memorable characters as Scrooge and Don Quixote, who have even given the language a noun *scrooge* and an adjective *quixotic.* A character usually has personality—stupid, greedy, noble, miserly, quixotic, or whatever—which plays a large, even a decisive, role in how the story develops.

The **plot** is a chart by which a story is navigated: A story sets sail from one harbor and ends at a destination far away. In between the two harbors, it encounters rough and smooth weather and water; the more of them it encounters, the better the story. A good story should be a "page-turner" that keeps a reader asking "What happens next?" Think of the plot for *Romeo and Juliet*. Romeo and Juliet fall in love at first sight. But the path of their romance is strewn with obstacles because of an ancient feud between the two families. The climax is tragic—Romeo kills himself, and then Juliet kills herself, all through misunderstanding. In an epilogue, the two feuding families reconcile, belatedly.

The **theme** or **moral** is rarely stated but is always implied; it must be extracted by the reader. A theme sums up the whole story: What does a story say, in a nutshell? Or, what is the moral of it? Our story "The Magic Mortar" is on the theme of "virtue is rewarded but greed costs you all," a universal theme found in folktales of many cultures.

A **setting** is the natural or artificial environment in which characters live and act. Sometimes the setting is almost ignored; sometimes it is crucial. In "The Magic Mortar," episode 1 is set in a Japanese village but could have been anywhere in the world. Episode 2, in contrast, depends on its sea setting. Can one think of *Robinson Crusoe* without its unique setting?

GRAMMAR FOR STORIES?

A **story grammar** specifies a set of story parts and their relations. It does so by formalizing the concept of "story structure" as a set of rules, in the same way as Chomsky's (1965) phrase-structure and transformational grammars formalize sentence structure (see Chapter 12). In principle, a story grammar should be able to generate all possible legitimate stories and no nonstories. A grammar should predict that an "ungrammatical story" would be difficult to comprehend and that in recall it would be modified into a grammatical form. In the past ten years it has been fashionable among linguists and psychologists to write story grammars. Let us consider a few of them.

The rules of Thorndyke's (1977) grammar are as follows:

1. Story → Setting + Theme + Plot + Resolution
   A story consists of four elements: Setting, Theme, Plot, and Resolution.
2. Setting → Characters + Location + Time
   Setting, in turn, consists of lower level elements, which are Characters, Location, and Time.
3. Theme → (Event)* + Goal
   Theme is the Goal of a main character, with a series of (optional) Events that initiated it.

4. Plot → Episode*
   A Plot is a series of episodes.
5. Episode → Subgoal + Attempt* + Outcome
   Episode consists of a Subgoal, repeated Attempts, and an Outcome.
6. Attempt → $\left\{ \begin{matrix} \text{Event} \\ \text{Episode} \end{matrix} \right\}$

   Attempt is a series of Events or Episodes.

→ = is rewritten as, or decomposed into
* = repeatable
( ) = optional
{ } = choose one or the other

Further rules state that Outcomes and Resolutions can be either Events (actions, happenings) or States (state of mind, condition of the world) but that Goals, Subgoals, and Characters, Locations, and Time descriptions must be States. By recursive rules, an episode itself can contain an episode, and an event can contain an event. By this grammar, the higher the level assigned to a story statement (i.e., the shorter its derivational path), the better that statement will be remembered. For example, the Theme (Rule 3) of a story would be better remembered than any Attempt (Rule 6).

In Mandler and Johnson's (1977) grammar, a story decomposes first into Setting and Event Structure. Event Structure in turn decomposes into a number of Episodes, each of which consists of Beginning, Development, and Ending. Development decomposes into Reaction and and Goal Path, and Goal Path into Attempt and Outcome. (See "The War of the Ghosts" in the following section). A story will have six "nodes" in the following order: Setting, Beginning, Reaction, Attempt, Outcome, and Ending. Connections between these nodes can be either temporal or causal. Transformational rules specify conditions under which a story node can be deleted or moved around.

Stein and Glenn's (1978) grammar starts with Setting + Episode. Episode has five categories: initiating event, internal response, attempt, consequence, and reaction. Episodes in a story are connected by AND, THEN, and BECAUSE (see "The Tiger's Whisker" in the following section)

These story grammarians all agree that a story consists of several parts, which can be labeled, and which are related temporally or causally. However, they disagree on the numbers, types, and order of nodes or categories. Black and Wilensky (1979) question the necessity and adequacy of these story grammars, as both formal grammars and as processing models. They find many acceptable stories that the grammars cannot generate, as well as one major class of nonstory (procedural expositions) that grammars do generate. They also contend that grammars would add nothing to semantic models such as "schema" that focus on the story content (see "Schema" later in this chapter). Recall that Chomsky's sentence grammars, on which story grammars are modeled, do not reflect the ways people produce or understand sentences (see Chapter 12).

Loose Story Structure

We will take a middle ground in the controversy about story grammars: We do not endorse a rigidly formal grammar patterned after sentence syntax, but at the same time we do not dismiss the idea of story structure altogether. Stories have a loose and flexible structure that can accommodate a variety of story contents.

WELL-FORMED AND ILL-FORMED STORIES

Let us analyze three stories to see what makes a good story. The first is an Amerindian folktale made famous among psychologists by Bartlett (1932). The grammar labels (in capitals) are those supplied by Mandler and Johnson (1977, pp. 136–137):

The War of the Ghosts

One night two young men from Egulac went down to the river to hunt seals, and while they were there it became foggy and calm (SETTING). Then they heard war-cries (BEGINNING), and they thought: "Maybe this is a war-party" (SIMPLE REACTION). They escaped to the shore, and hid behind a log (ATTEMPT). Now canoes came up, and they heard the noise of paddles, and saw one canoe coming up to them. There were five men in the canoe (ENDING), and they said:

"What do you think? We wish to take you along. We are going up the river to make war on the people" (BEGINNING).

One of the young men said: "I have no arrows" (ATTEMPT).

"Arrows are in the canoe," they said (OUTCOME).

"I will not go along. I might be killed. My relatives do not know where I have gone. But you," he said turning to the other, "may go with them" (ATTEMPT).

So one of the young men went, but the other returned home (OUTCOME).

And the warriors went on up the river to a town on the other side of Kalama (BEGINNING). The people came down to the water, and they began to fight (ATTEMPT), and many were killed (OUTCOME). But presently the young man heard one of the warriors say: "Quick, let us go home: that Indian has been hit" (BEGINNING). Now he thought: "Oh, they are ghosts." He did not feel sick (SIMPLE REACTION), but they said he had been shot (ACTION).

So the canoes went back to Egulac (ENDING), and the young man went ashore to his house, and made a fire (BEGINNING). And he told everybody and said: "Behold I accompanied the ghosts, and we went to fight. Many of our fellows were killed, and many of those who attacked us were killed. They said I was hit, and I did not feel sick."

He told it all (ACTION), and then he became quiet (ENDING). When the sun rose he fell down. Something black came out of his mouth. His face became contorted (BEGINNING). The people jumped up and cried (ACTION).

He was dead (ENDING).

According to Mandler and Johnson's grammar, this 330-word story often lacks one or more nodes in each episode: Simple Reaction and Goal in the early three episodes, and Outcome in the later three episodes. ("Action" is not one of the six nodes of their grammar.) It also lacks causal links between episodes.

According to our own (conventional) idea of story, "The War of the Ghosts" lacks some other essential elements. The main protagonist has no character, and his actions have no motivation. The events may occur chronologically but not causally. Neither a plot nor a theme/moral is easily recognizable. Nevertheless, "The War of the Ghosts" evokes an eerie mood, which is more than can be said about some "grammatical" stories written by story grammarians.

"The Tiger's Whisker" was written to conform to Stein and Glenn's grammar (Nezworski, Stein, & Trabasso, 1982):

	The Tiger's Whisker
Setting	Once there was a woman who lived in a forest.
Initiating event	One day she was walking up a hill and she came upon the entrance to a lonely tiger's cave.
Internal response	She really wanted a tiger's whisker and decided to try to get one.
Attempt	She put a bowl of food in front of the opening of the cave and she sang soft music.
Consequence	The lonely tiger came out and listened to the music. The lady then pulled out one of his whiskers and ran down the hill very quickly.
Reaction	She knew her trick had worked and felt very happy.

This 97-word story is perfectly grammatical, having all the six categories, and presenting them in the right order. Yet, it is not very engrossing, because it is weak in the four story elements. Why, for example, did the woman want the tiger's whisker?

"The Sunflower" is a Korean tale (translated into English by Insup Taylor):

The Sunflower

Once upon a time, there lived two sisters, an older and a younger. The two sisters worshipped the sun with all their hearts, and longed day and night to go to the sun and live with him.

One night the older sister thought: "The dear sun is mine alone; why must I share him with my sister?" So she killed the younger sister. And then, alone she tried to ascend to the sky to be with the sun. But the sun, outraged, let her fall to the ground and die.

A flower sprung up on the spot where she died. The flower is always looking toward the sun. People call it the sunflower.

In terms of a story grammar, this 114-word long tale lacks Setting (location) and the protagonist's Reaction. The category membership of the second sentence "The two sisters worshipped..." is not clear. In terms of our loose story structure, it is part of introducing the protagonists. This story, brief as it is, contains all the essential elements of a conventional story: The main protagonist has a definite character, and her actions have motivation and outcome. Events occur chronologically and causally following a recognizable plot. Because of the presence and arrangment of these elements, a theme or moral emerges. The story contains even an epilogue, which increases the charm of the story enormously.

STORY ELEMENTS REVISITED

A story has a beginning, a development, and an ending, which unfold according to a plot. The beginning, usually brief, contains an optional setting and introduces the protagonists. Sometimes it is elaborate, especially in a long complex story, "containing in it the seeds of future developments [Brooks & Warren, 1979, p. 195]." The ancient and deep feud between the houses of Capulet and Montague in *Romeo and Juliet* is such a beginning. If a story is short and well-structured, readers can generate, at the point where the beginning ends and the development starts, a set of hypotheses about subsequent events in a story (Olson, Mack, & Duffy, 1981).

A long middle develops the story through the characters' actions. A story is not worth telling if development lacks twists and turns, or complications and conflicts. Then comes the ending, which may contain any, or all, of the following events: outcome of actions, resolution of plot, climax, denouement, punch line, and epilogue. If a story has these elements and structure, a theme is likely to emerge.

In the story grammars, the introduction of characters is subsumed under Setting, which also includes Location and Time. Characters are indispensable, whereas Location and Time are dispensable. Characters are introduced not merely to point out their existence but to say something about their personalities that usually bears on the outcome of a story. In the story grammars, events and states are finely decomposed into Initiating Event, Attempt, Reaction, Outcome, and the like. These parts, whether they are called "nodes" or "categories," seem arbitrary, rigid, and unnecessary. Even the story grammarians disagree on the type, size, and number of these parts. Certain parts, especially Reaction, are often omitted in a story. In Whaley's (1981a) study, readers from Grade 6 and 11 did not always expect each of the story categories to be present, and they did not always expect Reaction and Outcome to appear in specific places.

In the English version of "The Magic Mortar," entitled "Why the Sea is Salt," episode 1 has a subplot that explains how the poor brother earned a magic mill. (In the English story, the two characters are the poor brother and the rich brother, and the instrument is the mill.) The poor brother had just begged a side of bacon and a loaf of bread from his rich brother. But when an old man appeared and begged for some food, the poor brother offered to share his meager ration. The grateful old man told the poor brother about a bunch of gnomes who owned a magic mill that produced anything except bacon, and instructed him how to bargain with the gnomes for the magic mill.

The subplot is unnecessarily elaborate for the theme of the story and hence is distracting. More is not always better. The English version also introduces another character, a sea captain, in the final episode. It is the captain who goes to the sea with the mill to meet the tragic fate. Why the innocent captain deserves such a rotten fate does not follow from the plot. In short, the reader's dissatisfaction does not stem from the omission of this or that story part; it stems from a serious defect in the plot. No moral (such as "greed loses all") can emerge from the English version.

PROCESSING STORY PARTS

Whaley (1981b) asked children from Grades 3, 6, and 11 to predict what should occur next in incomplete stories. Mandler and Johnson's (1977) grammar described to some extent the readers' expectation, especially in the two older groups, in that five of the six major nodes were produced in protocols. Outcome and Ending were the best predicted nodes, and Reaction the worst. Whether particular nodes were well predicted depended to some degree on the particular story. Mandler and Johnson's subjects recalled the six story nodes differently, depending on their ages. Children (Grades 1 and 4) recalled Setting, Beginning, Outcome, Attempt, Ending, and Reaction, in that order. Adults showed a similar pattern, except that they recalled Attempt better than Outcome and recalled a greater number of propositions.[3]

The category best recalled from "The Tiger's Whisker" by children (kindergarten and Grade 3) was Consequence, the second to last category (Nezworski *et al.*, 1982). However, when the protagonist's motivation for wanting the whisker (as a medicine for her sick husband) was added to a different category in five altered versions of the story, the added information was well recalled, independent of which category it appeared in. In recall, Reaction was most often changed into Consequence. In short, the best remembered information is the important information, regardless of its grammatical category and location in a story.

Mandler and Goodman (1982) wrote ten stories that conformed to Mandler and Johnson's (1977) story grammar, making sure each story node (now called "unit" or "constituent") has two sentences of similar length. Subjects' reading time varied for five of the six units tested (from slow to fast): Beginning, Outcome, Attempt, Ending, and Complex reaction. Furthermore, reading was fast within a unit and slow across units, demonstrating the unit property of the story constituents. That is, the second sentence in each unit was read faster than the first one. When the same units were removed from the context of a story, these effects disappeared. A more straightforward test of the unit property of story parts is to ask people to segment randomly selected ***natural*** (not written by story grammarians) stories into parts and to label the parts. Would they agree on story parsing as much as people do on sentence parsing, after receiving a comparable amount of instruction?

[3] "Proposition" is sometimes used synonymously with clause, simple sentence, or statement, rather than as (P, X, Y) (see Chapter 12).

STORY ENDING

Mandler and her associates found fast reading and poor recall of Reaction, and also of Ending. The result on Ending is surprising. Is Ending processed poorly because it is unimportant or because it is defined and categorized inappropriately? Reexamine "The War of the Ghosts": Of the four Endings Mandler and Johnson listed we would agree with them unhesitatingly only on the last Ending "He was dead." Many of Bartlett's (1932) subjects remembered this brief yet striking ending long after they read the story, even though the story is noted for its alien structure.

Using Mandler and Johnson's grammar but different stories, other researchers obtained good recall of Ending, especially Ending of the last episode; it was the second best recalled node after Beginning (Haberlandt, Berian, & Sandson, 1980). Whaley's (1981b) subjects predicted best the occurrence of Outcome and Ending. In reading a clause, sentence, or paragraph, the end is processed longer than other parts, presumably because that is where important information tends to appear, and where the unit as a whole is integrated (see Chapters 7 and 12).

In a multi-episode story, the ending of the last episode is the real ending, which subsumes all preceding endings under it. It is this superordinate, grand ending that story writers take extra care to make memorable, believing that it is the part most likely to linger in the reader's memory. Climax is "the point toward which the characters must move all along. He [the writer] must have planned it with utmost strategy, sneaking in forecasts of it almost from the beginning [Shyer, 1980, p. 314]." Early on in a story, where the story beginning ends, readers could forecast this kind of climax. They later read the climactic sentence more slowly than other sentences (Olson *et al.*, 1981). A climax of this kind occurs at the end of episode two of the Japanese version of "The Magic Mortar," but not of its English version. This is why the former is so much more satisfying than the latter.

Among story grammarians, Rumelhart (1977) would allow a later or last episode to dominate earlier episodes in importance. In one study, the ending of the second and final episode of a story provided more "closure" (it took longer to read) than the ending of the first episode (Haberlandt *et al.*, 1980).

If "ending" means an epilogue that comes after a climax, then it can be anticlimactic and forgettable, as is the epilogue to *Romeo and Juliet*. But the epilogue to "The Magic Mortar," being interesting and charming, might be highly memorable. We predicted that subjects recalling "The Magic Mortar" would (*a*) include the two main characters with their contrasting personalities; (*b*) organize the story in the two episodes; (*c*) describe the characters' contrasting actions centered around the magic mortar; and (*d*) include the climax, and probably the epilogue.

To test our predictions, Edmund Coleman (at that time our coauthor) asked college students in a class to read "The Magic Mortar." Immediately after reading it, and also 1 month later, he asked them to write down all they could remember. The subjects' immediate recall was too complete for our purpose, which was to distill the essential story elements. Thus, we scored only the recall that took place 1 month after reading the story. Our predictions were confirmed, except that we should have predicted "certain" rather than "probable" recall of the epilogue: All subjects included the epilogue in their recall.

ARRANGEMENT OF EPISODES AND ELEMENTS

Stories vary in the number of episodes and in the relations among the episodes. Main characters, setting, plot, and theme sometimes change, sometimes repeat, from one episode to another. In a multi-episode story, the relations among episodes can be embedded, cyclic, sequential, causal, contrasting, and so on. In "The Magic Mortar," episode 1 exists merely to set a stage for episode 2. The most famous example of an embedded story is *The Arabian Nights,* in which Sheherazade spun out one story within another and that inside another to fill 1001 nights. For example, the "Tale of King Sindibad and his Falcon" is told by the Wazin in the "Tale of the Wazin and the Sage Derban," which is a story told by the fisherman in the "Tale of the Fisherman and the Jinni," a story told by Sheherazade. (Sheherazade performed quite a memory feat in keeping these embedded stories straight.)

An example of a cyclic story is "Careful Hans," whose basic contents are as follows:

> Episode 1: Hans visits his grandma, who gives him a needle to take to his mother. Hans sticks it into a load of hay on a cart that was moving in front of him. Arriving at home, he cannot produce the needle. His mother tells him to carry a needle in his coat sleeve.
>
> Episode 2: Grandma gives Hans a knife, which he puts in his sleeve, as told, and loses it. His mother tells him to carry a knife in his pocket.
>
> Episode 3: Grandma gives Hans a puppy, which he pushes into his pocket, as told. The puppy is dead when he gets home. His mother tells him that he should tie a string around a dog's neck and lead it behind him.
>
> Episode 4: Grandma gives Hans a piece of meat, which he drags with a string around it. A pack of dogs eat the meat. The mother tells him to wrap a piece of meat in paper and carry on his head.
>
> Episode 5: Grandma gives Hans a pound of sweet butter, which he carries on his head as his mother instructed. He comes home drenched in melted butter. The end of the story: That's the last time Hans went visiting his Grandmother.

Children under age 3 have difficulty handling a story with multiple episodes (Gardner, 1982). A cycle of brief episodes should not be too difficult for them, since the structure understood for the first episode can be recycled for the remaining episodes. Cirilo (1980) found that the average reading time for an episode was shorter when it repeated the structure of the episode before it. Also, somewhat more lines were remembered from the second episode of parallel structures than from a second episode whose structure differed from the first.

Within an episode or a story, the elements are arranged to reflect the way events occur in the world: (setting), introduction of characters, characters' motivation for actions, actions, outcome of actions, (epilogue). People prefer a story sequence that mirrors the sequence of events in the world; they dislike flashbacks. Even in flashback, although the outcome of each episode or of an entire story may be presented first, events leading to it are usually presented chronologically. For example, in a detective story a murder scene may be presented first, and then the events leading to it are chronologically traced.

Baker (1978) found that readers' decisions about the order of two events were faster and more accurate for a chronological than for a flashback sequence. But in memory the readers did not reorder the flashback sequence to the natural order. Each of Baker's "stories" was short, containing five sentences and describing three events, only two of which could be changed around. The sentences in flashback had clear time signals: *Before that* and *Later.* When longer stories without time signals were used, Mandler's (1978) subjects reordered systematically disordered propositions, and Stein and Nezworski's (1978) subjects reordered randomly ordered statements into the "canonical" order, the order specified by their respective grammars. The question is, Do we need a grammar to specify people's preference for a natural order? Even for sentences, a grammar does not specify an order of clauses within a sentence (see Chapter 12, "Suggestion 8").

In one study, stories in which the order of sentences was randomized were harder to comprehend and remember than were their original versions. But when referential continuity in the randomized version was restored by replacing pronouns and other terms with fuller and more appropriate noun phrases, the ill effects of randomization was ameliorated. For example, the randomized story might start with *She had just won it and*. . . In the revised version, *she* is replaced by *Jenny,* and *it* by *a new balloon.* Story grammars have little role to play in accounting for the better recall of the revised randomized stories (Garnham, Oakhill, & Johnson-Laird, 1982).

To see whether causal relations are stronger than temporal ones, Black and Bern (1981) altered the relation between two sentences from causal to temporal by changing a single word:

The child was {*pulling* / *pointing*} *at a bottle. It fell to the floor and broke.*

Subjects tended to recall the causally related sentence pair as a unit, sometimes marking the relation with conjunctions (*and, so,* etc.). The causally related sentences were better recalled than the temporally related ones.

In the global structure of a story, a causal relation necessarily requires a temporal relation, but the reverse is not true. For example, in "The Magic Mortar," episode 2 must come after episode 1 for the story to make its point. Within episode 2, the bad brother eats a lot of sweet cakes, and then/therefore craves for salt. Juliet kills herself when/because she finds Romeo dead. A later event is often caused by an earlier event, whether so stated explicitly or not. "Time relations are often causal in disguise [Pearson & Johnson, p. 227]." Even when they are not, people often believe them to be.

Schema

The term *schema* (*schemata* is its plural) was made popular in psychology by Bartlett (1932). He defined it as "an (active) organisation of past reactions, or of past experiences, which must always be supposed to be operating in well-adapted organic responses [p. 201]."

MANY-FACETED SCHEMA

Bartlett himself disliked the term *schema*, complaining that it is at once too definite and too sketchy. Schema may be a useful concept but is so vague and elusive that it spawns a variety of definitions among contemporary psychologists. Actually, each psychologist may be looking at a different facet of the same concept, like the proverbial six blind men each feeling a different part of the same elephant. Here we sample several of the definitions.

A schema is a Plan: "A human being—and probably other animals as well—builds up an internal representation, a model of the universe, a schema, a simulacrum, a cognitive map, an Image [Miller, Galanter, & Pribram, 1960, p. 7]."

There are "textual schemata" for organizing textual materials (story, letter, technical report, etc.), and "content schemata," which are what the reader already knows about a topic (Anderson, Pichert, & Shirey, 1979).

Minsky's (1975) "frame" is a data-structure for representing a stereotyped situation, such as being in a certain kind of living room or going to a child's party. Attached to each frame are several kinds of information, such as about what one can expect to happen next, and about what to do if these expectations are not confirmed.

A schema is a "script," a giant temporal and causal chain of conceptualizations that have been known to occur in a particular order many times before (Schank & Abelson, 1977). It sets up expectations about events that are likely to follow in a given situation. Consider a restaurant script: One goes to a restaurant, sits at a table, orders a meal, eats it, pays the bill, leaves the place, and so on. When the first few events are given, the rest can be filled in from the restaurant script. A script resembles what we might call a well-worn routine.

Rumelhart (1980) likens schemata to plays, to theories, to procedures, and to parsers, all in one breath.

For Kintsch and Greene (1978), a story schema is a set of expectations about the conventions observed within a culture. For Mandler and Johnson (1977) and Stein and Nezworski (1978), a story schema is an idealized representation of the parts and their relations of a typical story and is synonymous with a universal story grammar. For Black and Wilensky (1979), there is no story-specific schema called story grammar; stories follow a general-purpose schema, such as a script.

So, a **schema** is an organized body of knowledge about an event. It is abstracted and acquired through many experiences with restaurants, reports, concepts, stories, and so on; and once acquired, it guides people—by setting up expectations—in interpreting and remembering new instances of restaurants, reports, concepts, stories, and so on.

SCHEMA AND RECONSTRUCTIVE VERSUS REPRODUCTIVE MEMORY

In his seminal study on remembering, Bartlett (1932) asked his college student subjects to read "The War of the Ghosts" and then to recall it at various intervals as opportunities offered: soon after, weeks later, months later, and in one case even 10 years later. In the subjects' recall protocols, anything that appeared incomprehensible or "queer" was either omitted or explained, reasons were invented and unfamiliar words and expressions changed to familiar ones. According to Bartlett, an unfamiliar story is reconstructed (as opposed to reproduced) in memory to conform to the subjects' schema. "The War of the Ghosts" is not only remembered poorly but also read with difficulty: When Olson *et al.* (1981) asked college students to talk aloud between sentences about their reactions, none of them seemed to formulate a coherent hypothesis about its global organization. The subjects were particularly confused about the sentence that mentions ghosts for the first time. The time to read this story was longer than that to read three Western stories.

Bartlett (1932) asked two groups of college students, one in England and the other in East India, to reproduce serially the Congo story (192 words) entitled "The Son who Tried to Outwit his Father." In serial reproduction, the story recalled by subject A is given as reading material to subject B, whose recall protocol becomes the stimulus for C, and so on. The basic plot of the story is: A son, to outwit his father, changed himself into one of the three kernels of a peanut—a fowl swallowed the peanut—a bush cat ate the fowl—a dog ate the cat—the dog was swallowed by a python, who was snared in a fish trap. The father, while fishing, pulled the fish trap, in which he found a python, in which he found a dog, in which he found a cat, in which he found a fowl, from which he took a peanut, in which was revealed his son. The son was so dumbfounded that he never again tried to outwit his father.

The story went through 20 reproductions for the English group and 10 reproductions for the Indian group, with the basic sequences of events intact. Only *fowl* was changed to "bird" or "hen" and *bush cat* to "cat" early in the series. Both groups, however, injected personality and motivation to the boy: "he was afraid of his father" or "he was up to mischief" for the English group, and "he was indolent and shirked work" for the Indian group.

College student subjects in the United States did not introduce serious distortions in five sequential retellings of a story with a schema belonging to their own culture, but they did in retelling a story with an alien Amerindian schema (Kintsch & Greene, 1978). One wonders how Amerindian subjects would recall their own stories vis-à-vis Western stories.

Accommodative reconstruction may or may not occur, depending on the nature of subsequent information. In the study by Spiro (1980), when subsequent information was inconsistent with the story as it had been understood up to that point, recall of the story contained distortions and importations (from the subjects' general knowledge) to reconcile the two inconsistent kinds of information. On the other hand, few recall errors occurred when cognitive states at recall were consistent with earlier states and when instructions for recall were conventional.

Subjects reconstruct or reproduce depending also on types of instruction, such as: (*a*) be accurate; (*b*) accept inference; (*c*) be compatible with the meaning of a passage. With delays of 24 hours or 7 days, distant statements are more likely to be accepted than immediately (Brockway, Chmielewski, & Cofer, 1974).

SCHEMA, INFERENCE, AND RECOGNITION

A schema influences the kind of inferences people draw, and it can be activated by a title. In a study by Sulin and Dooling (1974), one group of subjects read a brief biographical passage about a famous person, such as Adolf Hitler. They could draw on their prior knowledge of Hitler, a richly elaborated schema, to aid them in understanding and remembering the passage. The other group of subjects read the same passage, but as a story about a fictional character named G. Martin. The Hitler passage, more than the Martin passage, produced false recognitions of statements that asserted well-known facts about Hitler without actually occurring in the story. There were more false recognitions at longer (1 week) than at shorter (5 min) retention intervals (see also Hasher & Griffin, 1978).

When a title (e.g., "Washing Clothes") was not as schema rich as "Hitler," recognition of explicit information was not influenced by its presence. That is, a no-title group recognized explicit information as well as did a title group. This result obtained even though the no-title group considered the test passage to be incomprehensible and recalled it poorly (Alba, Alexander, Hasher, & Caniglia, 1981).

Some inferences are made during the time information is being stored. Harris and Monaco's (1978) subjects read a passage that contained a paragraph such as the following: *Jose arose early in the morning. After dressing, he ate breakfast and then went over to the neighborhood school. He was pleased that the sun was shining today.* In a subsequent recognition-of-information test, one group of subjects identified as "true" such statements as:

1. *Jose was a student.*
2. *Jose walked to school.*

Inference such as statement 1 was made even when the subjects had been told at the beginning of the passage that Jose was a teacher. (If Jose had been called "Mr. Brown," "Mr. Brown is a teacher" would have been a more likely inference.) The subjects made fewer inferences such as 1 and 2 when they were informed, before the passage was presented, that a later test would be multiple choice than when they were informed that it would be an essay test.

Reder (1979) measured reaction times of subjects judging plausibility of queried inferential statements after reading ten stories, either with or without titles. Prior exposure, high plausibility, and immediate probing produced faster reaction times than no exposure, moderate plausibility, and delayed probing. Reder concludes that many inferences are made while reading. Some of these inferences and of the input propositions are later retrieved in order to reconstruct the inferential propositions and to judge whether they are true.

Story Structure and Content: Conclusion

A story is about characters and their actions, which unfold according to a plot. A theme emerges from a story as a whole.

Several researchers have written formal story grammars, all of which predict readers' comprehension and recall of some stories by some subjects. But they are too formal and rigid to describe the wide variety of stories that exist, on the one hand, and they do not touch on the essential elements of a story that make it worth reading, on the other. We presented a loose and flexible description of story structure, illustrating it with several different types of stories.

A story is generally easy to process, even for very young children, partly because of its simple and predictable structure: beginning (introduction of characters, setting), development (complications in the plot), and ending (resolution of the plot, epilogue). The conventional story structure may have evolved so as to present new contents in a familiar container for easy prediction, comprehension, and retention.

Besides easy structure, children's stories must have contents that appeal to their readers' intellect and emotion. Because basic human emotions and aspirations are the same everywhere, some story themes (e.g., virtue is rewarded and vice punished) are universal, allowing easy transfer from one culture to another. Such universal themes may also be considered to be schemata. The child psychologist Bettelheim (1976) observes: "By dealing with universal human problems, particularly those which preoccupy the child's mind, these stories speak to his budding ego and encourage its development, while at the same time relieving preconscious and unconscious pressures [p. 6]."

Popular in many cultures are interesting epilogues such as "that's why there are cripples on earth" (Chinese) and "that's why cats and mice became enemies" (Korean). Rudyard Kipling's *Just So Stories* are all of this kind. Stories with this kind of title or epilogue even have their own label, "Pourquoi Tales." Magic, supernatural elements, and fantasy are important ingredients of folk-tales everywhere. Even some characters are universal, or at least stereotyped: Stepmothers are wicked, and brothers and sisters have contrasting personalities and fortunes. Animals often feature as characters; moreover, the same animal has similar traits in different cultures. Is there any culture in which a fox is portrayed other than being sly and crafty (and at the same time, stupid)?

Expository Prose

That writer does the most, who gives his reader the most knowledge, and takes from him the least time.

—C. C. Colton[4]

Exposition explains facts and ideas; its material tends to be organized according to the logical relations of the ideas. Some books in the upper grades of primary schools, and most materials in secondary schools and colleges are expository texts, covering such content areas as biology, economics, and psychology. Rhetoricians and writing teachers since ancient Greek times have been instructing writers how to organize their contents. Psychologists and educators show by experiments how the structural quality of a text affects its comprehension and retention.

Technical Writing

ORGANIZATION OF A TEXTBOOK

Let us start with a large unit, a book. We do not have to look far afield for an example of an expository textbook: You are reading one. A book certainly has a structure, which can be laid out in a table of contents. While writing this book, we kept for each chapter a detailed table of contents, which was automatically updated by a computer whenever it was changed in the text. The present chapter is divided into "Narrative Prose" and "Expository Prose." Table 13-1 is the table of contents for the latter. Uncluttered by the details of the contents, a table lets the authors (and the readers) see at a glance whether all the relevant topics are included, and whether they are in a logical relation to one another. The level of a section's heading indicates its relative importance in the chapter and in the book.

Our organizing principle is: Divide a book into many writing and reading sections, each of which is a self-contained unit with its own title and sometimes with its own introduction and conclusion or summary. A section often contains several paragraphs, and without an informative title, the reader (and the writer) may lose sight of the theme. Headings in every level should be informative enough to form a skeleton summary when arranged in a table of contents. They can also serve as cues for skimmers.

FORMAT OF A TECHNICAL PAPER

In a technical paper, the research finding is the most important information, and the other parts exist only to make it comprehensible and credible.

[4]An English epigrammatic writer (1780–1832). The quote appeared in *Lacon*: Preface.

Table 13-1 *Structure of the Second Part of Chapter 13*

- Expository Prose
  - Technical Writing
    - Organization of a Textbook
    - Format of a Technical Paper
  - Paragraph Structure
    - Paragraph Size and Boundary
    - Topic Sentence and its Development
    - Cohesion Between Sentences
    - Children's Sensitivity to Paragraph Structure
  - Test of Comprehension and Recall
    - Rating, Question, Paraphrase, and so on.
    - Cloze Test and the Use of Redundancy
    - Idea Units and Structural Importance
    - Modified Idea Units with a Topic Unit
  - Models of Text Processing
    - Content Structure and Top-Level Structure
    - Text Grammar
    - Text World
    - Macro-Structure
    - Gist: A Product of Prose Processing
  - Learning Techniques
    - Interpolated Questions and Reading Goals
    - Underlining and Note Taking
    - Advance Organizer
    - How Learning Techniques Work

Over the years, an effective, if rigid, format for technical writing has been developed. The parts and their sequence are:

1. Abstract (one paragraph)
2. Introduction (possibly not labeled)
3. Method; Results; Discussion (repeated for Experiment 1, 2, etc.)
4. General Discussion
5. Summary and Conclusions

An abstract is given at the very beginning, since comprehensibility, not suspense, is the most desirable quality of a technical paper. The abstract also enables readers to decide quickly whether they want to read the rest of the paper. Method can have several subsections, such as Subjects, Materials, Design, Instrumentation, and Procedures.

Such a rigid format helps the writer to organize her materials effectively. For example, when she is writing the Method, she should not wander into the Results, and vice versa. The reader can easily locate and digest desired information, since pieces of information in one area, such as Results, are already assembled in one known place.

Paragraph Structure

Expository as well as narrative prose can be segmented into paragraphs. However, paragraph structure differs somewhat between the two types of prose. In narrative prose, a paragraph changes with a change in an event, scene, or speaker, and its size varies enormously. In expository prose, a paragraph changes when one topic has been fully developed, and its size tends to be less variable, though still by no means uniform.

PARAGRAPH SIZE AND BOUNDARY

The beginning of a paragraph is easy to spot, as it starts with an indentation or is separated from other paragraphs by an extra space. Few readers may be aware of the importance of such visual breaks in a page. Open any book: If its pages have no visual breaks, the book is not inviting. In writing this book, we tried to have at least a few paragraph breaks in every page, thus providing visual as well as thought breaks at regular intervals.

A short paragraph is useful now and then to break a monotonous rhythm and to highlight a point.

The end of a paragraph signals to the readers that they should assimilate the material just presented and prepare for a new idea. And readers do indeed heed the signal: A fixation pause, which reflects processing time, tends to be long at the end of a paragraph (Just & Carpenter, 1980). Too frequent paragraph breaks mean that not enough material was presented for developing a topic or that the topic jumps around too much. Long paragraphs may be repetitive, loaded with details and irrelevant information, or the writer may not have noticed a change in a topic. A paragraph is sufficiently clear that people can mark paragraph boundaries if given coherent text from which the visible paragraph breaks have been removed (Koen, Becker, & Young, 1969).

TOPIC SENTENCE AND ITS DEVELOPMENT

A **paragraph** has not only a physical boundary but also an internal structure: It consists of a topic sentence and several sentences that support and develop it. The **topic sentence** often comes at the beginning of a paragraph (as in this one), but it may also come in the middle or at the end of a paragraph. Readers can often recognize a topic sentence even when the sentences in a paragraph are scrambled (Pfafflin, 1967). They tend to choose the first sentence as the topic, but only if it is sensible to do so (Kieras, 1978). For maximum clarity, put the topic sentence first.

The topic sentence is memorable, if it is explicit, prominently placed at the beginning, and well supported by all the sentences in the paragraph. The topic is the most useful information to keep alive in working memory because it is needed to comprehend the other information in the paragraph, and ultimately it is used in summing up the entire passage. The topic sentence can serve as a cue for retrieving the other information in the paragraph.

Some techniques for supporting the topic sentence are restatement, comparison, definition, illustration, analysis, cause and effect, qualification, and conclusion. Actually, it is not easy to characterize and label every supporting sentence, as shown in the following paragraph:

A paragraph is a device for organizing contents around a topic (topic sentence). Ideally, all the sentences in one paragraph are on one and only one topic (restatement). However, it is sometimes difficult to decide when one topic ends and another begins (qualification). For example, we wondered whether this paragraph should have been a continuation of the last one, but decided against the idea for the sake of having uniformly sized paragraphs (effect? justification?). After all, the topic has changed subtly: The last paragraph lists constituents of a paragraph, and this one illustrates them (cause? conclusion?).

COHESION BETWEEN SENTENCES

Let us see how paragraphs can be well or poorly structured. Kieras (1978) prepared "good" and "bad" paragraphs. In the good paragraph shown below, all propositions but the first (1) have links to earlier ones (e.g., 4 to 3; 6 to 5), whereas in the bad paragraph, four of the first five propositions bring only new concepts into the picture, with no links to what went before. The linked propositions, those incorporating already given concepts, are marked with a 'g', and the ones having only new concepts, with an 'n':

Good paragraph:	**Bad paragraph**
1 n: The ants ate the jelly.	4 n: The kitchen was spotless.
2 g: The ants were hungry.	7 n: The table was wooden.
3 g: The ants were in the kitchen.	2 n: The ants were hungry.
4 g: The kitchen was spotless.	3 g: The ants were in the kitchen.
5 g: The jelly was grape.	5 n: The jelly was grape.
6 g: The jelly was on the table.	6 g: The jelly was on the table.
7 g: The table was wooden.	1 g: The ants ate the jelly.

Kieras's subjects took longer to read the bad paragraph and recalled less of its content than they did of the good paragraph. Their difficulty occurred mainly on the initial sentences, which could not be immediately integrated.

Repeating the predicate of a preceding sentence as the subject of the current sentence promotes cohesion between sentences (see Chapter 12, "Suggestion 3"). This device is used in 3–4 and 6–7 of the good paragraph above. Because of it the following paragraph on a complex topic, "The Use of Mathematical Models in Business," is easy to read:

> The type of information processing, which attempts to predict future data based upon a set of interrelated events, is called a simulation model. A simulation model describes the problem with a set of conditonal relationships. These conditional relationships, . . . reflect the logic of the model.

Kissler and Lloyd's (1972) subjects who read the preceding paragraph answered short questions better than those who read the same paragraph in which the sentences were scrambled. Each question required the subjects to recall information from at least two sentences in a paragraph.

Vande Kopple (1982) prepared two kinds of paragraphs. In a topically linked paragraph, the given information is closely related to previous sentences through repeating words, using pronouns, or naming necessary, probable, or possible parts and characteristics. Sentences in the paragraph move from given to new information. Here is the first five sentences of a topically linked paragraph, with its topics italicized:

> Currently *the Marathon* is the best waxless ski for recreational cross-country skiing. *Its weight* is a mere two pounds. Yet *its two-inch width* allows the skier to break a trail through even the heaviest snow. *Its most unique characteristic* is the fishscale design for its bottom. *The Marathon* is almost as effective as most waxable skis.

By changing the cues of given and new information in the above sentences, Vande Kopple produced the following variant paragraph that should frustrate the given–new strategy. What seems to be given in each sentence is actually new, and vice versa:

> Currently *the best waxless ski for recreational cross-country skiing* is the Marathon. *A mere two pounds* is its weight. Yet *the skier* can break a trail through even the heaviest snow with its two-inch width. *The fishscale design for its bottom* is its most unique characteristics. *Most waxable skis* are only slightly more effective than the Marathon.

Most subjects, high school students, chose the topically linked paragraph as more readable. A few of the comments made by the subjects on the variant paragraph were: "it caused me to look back several times before I could follow it"; "I was held to the end of the sentence to find what the subject is." One subject labeled a variant paragraph "backward." The subjects comprehended and recalled the topically linked paragraphs better than its variant.

CHILDREN'S SENSITIVITY TO PARAGRAPH STRUCTURE

Good paragraph structure should help readers of all ages. But adults' sensitivity to structure may be more developed than that of children. In Danner's study (1974) most Grade 2 children could distinguish between organized and disorganized texts and could abstract the main idea to some extent. But it was not until Grade 6 that most children could use topic sentences as retrieval cues for later recall of paragraphs.

In Mosenthal's (1979) study, children's (aged 7–9) recall from paragraphs depended on their schemata structure or their modes of recalling a sequence of picture events. The children who expected the topic sentence to appear initially recalled best if it indeed was given initially. They also recalled more than did any other group. The children who expected the topic to appear at the end recalled best in that condition. The subjects without topic expectation recalled least and recalled about equally under the three conditions.

Tests of Comprehension and Recall

Researchers as well as teachers have many occasions to test readers' comprehension and retention of text. Requirements for a good test include:

- Validity—It tests what readers have comprehended or retained from the text itself.
- Objective—and reliable Procedures for constructing and scoring tests should be objective and simple so that different people using the tests, or the same people using them at different times, produce similar results.
- Ease of use—The test should be convenient for school teachers or researchers to construct and score consistently.

There are several different testing methods, each having advantages and disadvantages. Carroll (1972a) reviewed them, but before the concept of "idea units" (see the following section) had become popular.

RATING, QUESTION, PARAPHRASE, AND SO ON

In a rating test, readers are asked to rate a number of passages on how easy each of them was to read. Alternatively, they rate how well they feel they have comprehended a passage. Rating is simple but is subjective and gives only coarse measures.

Asking questions about a text, for all its venerable tradition, has some problems. A tester can ask easy questions about difficult passages, and vice versa. Sometimes the questions themselves are hard to understand. Essays, paraphrases, and summaries are easy to request but difficult to score objectively and rapidly. Their qualities are as strongly influenced by the testee's writing skill as by his comprehension of the text. As for paraphrasing, it is appropriate only for difficult text.

When the reading material is a set of instructions, such as a recipe, the best evidence of comprehension is the reader's ability to follow them. Following a set of instructions could be a pure measure of comprehension when the instructions are available during the test. Such a test, however, is rarely convenient to conduct in a classroom.

Multiple-choice tests overcome many of these disadvantages but have disadvantages of their own. Good multiple-choice questions are hard to prepare: The number and type of foils (plausible wrong choices), as much as the questions themselves, determine the ease of a test. Sometimes the questions themselves provide clues so that they can be answered without even reading the text (Tuinman, 1973–1974).

In Carver's (1970) version of a multiple-choice test, each alternative is a "chunk" of the original text—a clause, a phrase, or a word. One chunk, however, is changed in meaning by a substituted word or phrase. Apparently, people who have not read the original text are unable to score much above chance on this kind of multiple-choice test. But the test might encourage readers to pay undue attention to exact wordings rather than to the substance of the text.

CLOZE TEST AND THE USE OF REDUNDANCY

In a cloze test, occasional words, say every fifth word, are deleted from a passage, and the reader is asked to restore them. Good comprehension is shown by correct restoration of most words. Some authors suspect that cloze scores reflect only the reader's ability to make use of local redundancy within each sentence (Carroll, 1972b; Shanahan, Kamil, & Tobin, 1982; Weaver & Kingston, 1963; see also Chapter 8, "Restoring Words in Context"). Their suspicion may be put to rest, since cloze scores correlate highly with with judged difficulties of passages, .93 (Aquino, 1969).

Cloze scores correlate well also with other comprehension tests: .70–.85 with standard reading tests (Bormuth, 1969; Divesta *et al.*, 1979); .55–.64 with scores on multiple-choice tests (Entin & Klare, 1978). In a cross-language comparison of Grade 5 children, correlations between cloze scores and global comprehension were not so high but were still positive: .59, .57, and .65 for Japanese, Swedish, and English (U.S.), respectively (Grundin *et al.*, 1978). High verbal skill probably is responsible for both high cloze scores and global comprehension. Also, high cloze scores may be prerequisites to global comprehension, though not the reverse.

Cloze tests are objective and simple and show positive correlations with other measures of comprehension. Obviously, they can be useful as reading tests. Yet, a cloze test cannot be ***the*** test of comprehension because it does not reveal what content a reader can comprehend and remember. For example, can he draw necessary inferences, distinguish important ideas from unimportant ones, and abstract and retain the theme of the passage?

IDEA UNITS AND STRUCTURAL IMPORTANCE

Sentences are major linguistic and processing units, but they vary enormously in length and structure (see Chapter 12). Researchers look for units that are less variable. R. E. Johnson (1970) devised a technique of segmenting a passage by having groups of subjects mark the separations between units with slashes. An **idea unit** may contain one idea or may mark a place where a reader might pause. It resembles a clause and contains on average five words. Those units on which over half the subjects agree are considered valid. The passage is then retyped to show one unit per line. A second group of subjects rate the importance of each unit to the theme of the passage: They cross out, perhaps using a blue pencil, one-fourth of the least important units. The same procedure is repeated twice (once using a green pencil, and once a red pencil), until only one-fourth of the units, the most important, remain. In Johnson's original experiment, each of three different subject groups crossed out one-fourth of the passage.

Johnson found that the relative importance of units, or **structural importance,** was related to recall: Units with high importance ratings were better remembered than were other units, whether tested immediately or 63 days later. In other studies, both good and poor readers, whether listening or reading, were sensitive to the levels of structural importance, remembering important idea units better than unimportant ones. The good readers remembered more of the idea units, especially the important ones, than did the poor readers (Smiley, Oakley, Worthen, Campione, & Brown, 1977).

Rating units for importance requires skill. According to Eamon (1978–1979), good readers from college are better than poor readers at evaluating the relevance of material to the topic of the passage. In a study by Brown and Smiley (1977), there was considerable agreement among groups of college students and Grade 7 children, but not among Grades 3 and 5 children, on importance ratings. All the same, at all ages more of the important than of the unimportant units of stories were recalled.

With expository text, children are not so good at differentially processing important and unimportant information. In Baumann's (1981) study of Grades 3 and 6 children, in only one instance (Grade 3 children answering multiple-choice tests) did the children comprehend the main, gist ideas better than the two lower-level ideas. The children's recall did not parallel the three levels of ideas. In fact, Grade 6 children's cued recall was best for the lowest-level ideas and worst for the main ideas. In these "ecologically valid" experiments, the children read in their classrooms passages taken directly from the textbooks at their grade levels. The study shows either that the children's ability was low or that the textbooks were not well written.

The Soviet psychologist Bol'shunov (1977) segmented two passages—one on literature, and the other on popular science—into "semantic units" that resemble idea units. The relative importance of the units was ranked by a group of subjects. The percentage of subjects reporting each unit was calculated for two conditions: complete retelling and basic contents. The correlations between the recall data and the semantic significance were .65 and .77 (literature) and .34 and .51 (science) for the two conditions, respectively. However, a few unimportant units—emotive and/or vivid details—were well recalled. Conversely, a few important items were either omitted or reworded, perhaps because of their complex wordings.

Deese's team also found a correlation between the importance level of an idea unit and the probability that the essential information in that unit would be recalled (Deese, 1980b; Estes & Shebilske, 1980). However, the correlation was small. For example, it was .39 and .48 for college students reading Grade 10 text and college (biology) text, respectively. Deese's team used a rating technique different from that of the others: The subjects rated each idea unit as either important or unimportant in five degrees of strength, yielding 10 levels of importance.

The texts used by Deese's team, especially the Grade 10 biology text, were poorly written. When one member of the team, Wetmore (1980), improved the texts by using such devices as writing unimportant ideas briefly without vivid examples and enumerating important points, the correlation between importance level and recall increased from .39 to .54. The studies by Deese's team alert us that some textbooks, even widely used ones, are not well structured. Such texts also must be studied to see how they are read and how they can be improved.

Shebilske and Fisher (1981), other members of the team, studied how the importance level of units influenced eye movements. Two subjects (college graduates) read twice a long extract from the same Grade 10 biology text. On the first reading, the readers modulated their reading rate according to the familiarity of information, spending more time on new than on old information, but on the second reading, they modulated their rate according to the importance level of idea units, reading important units more slowly than unimportant ones. They made longer fixations and more regressions on important than on unimportant idea units in both readings.

People rate the importance of units differently, depending on the perspective from which they read a passage. In the study by Pichert and Anderson (1977), a passage contained some information important for a burglar (e.g., coin collection), and other information for a home buyer (leaky roof). One group of subjects rated the passage from the perspective of a burglar, and another group, from that of a home buyer. A control group was given no perspective. The three groups ranked the importance of idea units differently, and the importance ratings from a given perspective were the best predictors of the recall of subjects who read the passage from that perspective.

MODIFIED IDEA UNITS WITH A TOPIC UNIT

R. E. Johnson's (1970) notion of idea units and structural importance has been adopted by many investigators, sometimes in a modified form. The test is valid, reliable, and flexible. But it can be improved. In segmenting a passage into idea units, a few objective procedures can be used in place of Johnson's cumbersome procedure of having one or more groups of subjects segmenting a passage in three steps. The task can be done by one person, the tester herself, in one step. Moreover, no idea units have to be declared invalid on account of disagreements among subjects.

We suggest one basic procedure for segmenting a text: Count as one unit a simple sentence, a clause, a phrase, or a word, that is or could be bounded by a punctuation mark. After all, the punctuation marks—period, comma, colon, and so on—signal syntactic and semantic boundaries and instruct readers to pause (see Chapter 12, "Suggestion 6"). One auxiliary procedure is to count as a unit a long modifying phrase (three or more words), or an embedded clause, even if it is not punctuated. The complex sentence *A topic on which the majority agreed is chosen* ontains two clauses: *A topic is chosen* and *on which the majority agreed.* In our procedure the two are separated, and the second clause is typed below the first with an indentation (see the following discussion on "topic unit"). This procedure is the only concession, a slight one, to the underlying (as opposed to surface) syntactic relations within a sentence.

This section on topic unit is segmented into idea units following the preceding procedures and then typed one unit per line:

> A topic is the most important piece of information
> about a passage.
> Yet,
> Johnson's structural importance does not single it out.
> Since topic extraction cannot be codified
> as a set of procedures,
> a group of readers do the task.
> A topic is chosen,
>   on which the majority agreed,
> and is typed on a card by itself.
> Then,
> the readers rate each idea unit for importance,
> on a four-point scale.
> Importance is judged
> in relation to the topic,
> which,
> being on a card by itself,
> can be placed next to each unit
> for easy rating.

Our unit contains on average five words, as does Johnson's (1970) unit. Rating on a four-point scale not only is simple but also may show how readable a passage is: Conceivably, a difficult passage contains more units ranking high in importance than does an easy passage. Readers' levels of comprehension and retention are tested in two ways: Good readers extract a topic and rate units for importance faster and better than do poor readers. They also remember more units, especially topic and important units, than do poor readers.

Models of Text Processing

Some researchers are concerned not so much with measuring retention of information in a text as with developing a model of how it is done. They too start by segmenting a text into processing units, which are often labeled.

CONTENT STRUCTURE AND TOP-LEVEL STRUCTURE

Meyer (1975) analyzed text into "lexical propositions," which show the case roles of words within sentences, and "rhetorical propositions," which establish the relations among sentences and paragraphs. "Rhetorical predicates" specify the relationships within these propositions and order them into a hierarchical relationship called a content structure. The content structure is similar to the traditional outline but is far more detailed and complex than the outline, as it analyzes, labels, and orders every content word of a text. It can be used only by people trained in its procedures.

Meyer predicted that idea units high in the content structure would be comprehended and recalled better than those low in the structure. Her prediction was confirmed in an experiment in which college students listened to two well-written science passages (Meyer & McConkie, 1973; see also Waters, 1978). It was contradicted, however, in an experiment in which Grades 3 and 6 children read a set of passages randomly selected from pools of social studies texts for these grades (Baumann, 1981; see also B. M. Taylor, 1980; Tierney, Bridge, & Cera, 1979). Perhaps content structure is used best by skilled readers listening to or reading well-structured passages.

Meyer and her associates now identify five top-level organizational patterns or rhetorical relationships, called top-level structures. These patterns are: problem–solution, adversative (facts are contrasted in pros and cons), antecedent–consequence, description, and attribution (facts are organized as a list).

In one study, good comprehenders organized their recall protocols with a top-level structure the same as the author's. The effect of structure was more pronounced in delayed than in immediate recall (Meyer, Brandt, & Bluth, 1980). In another study, given a week of training on how to identify and use top-level structures, Grade 9 children recognized these structures better than did controls and recalled twice as much information as did the controls (Bartlett, 1978). In still another study, subjects' recall was increased by changing the top-level structure from attribution to adversative (Meyer, Freedle, & Walker, 1978). This finding, however, was not replicated in the study by Elliott (1980).

One wonders how well the same content can be organized according to different top-level structures. After all, different top-level structures are available because different contents require them. Adversative structure, effective as it may be for some materials, may not suit others. Attribution can be effective when printed in the form of a bullet list or a numbered list, of which there are many in this book. In a multi-paragraph passage, a writer is likely to use varied top-level structures within and between paragraphs.

TEXT GRAMMAR

Just and Carpenter (1980) divided each of 15 passages (paragraphs) on a scientific topic into "sectors" (similar to idea units or clauses), which they labeled and cast into a five-level hierarchical structure. The levels of the grammar were confirmed by subjects, who rated the sectors according to their relative importance:

1. topic
2. subtopic
3. definition, setting, consequence, cause
4. expansion
5. detail

According to the researchers, the integration time per content word for each type of sector reflects their importance level in the text grammar. The higher-level units take more time to integrate because their integration is essential to the reader's goal, and because it involves more relations to be computed and more retrievals to be made. In their eye-movement data, the sector that was processed the longest was the third level "definition/cause/consequence," and not the topic or the subtopic. The detail sectors took less time than all other types of sectors. Recall probabilities were lowest for details, then increased in the order of expansions, subtopics, definitions/causes/consequences, and topics.

The results are clear on unimportance of details but not so clear on importance of topics and subtopics.

TEXT WORLD

Consider the following passage from a story:

> A great black and yellow rocket stood in a desert. Empty, it weighed five tons. For fuel it carried eight tons of alcohol and liquid oxygen. Everything was ready. Scientists and generals withdrew to some distance and crouched behind earth mounds. Two red flares rose as a signal to fire the rocket.

In Beaugrande's (1981) text-world model, a person reading the preceding text would set up in his mind a configuration of concepts connected by relations, such as "agent-of," "location-of," "attribution-of," as shown in Figure 13-1. The ensuing processing would steadily expand this configuration by adding onto already created nodes where feasible, in this case, mostly to the *rocket* node, the topic concept. In this purely concept-based model, left-to-

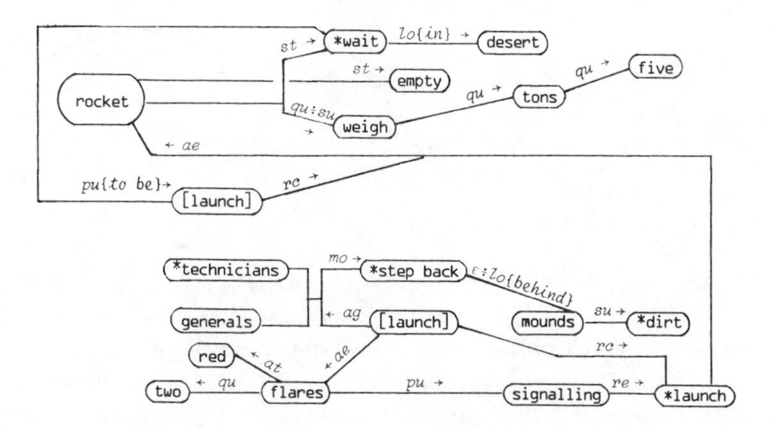

Figure 13-1. *Text world: Section of a reader's recall protocol. Key: ae,* affected entity; *ag,* agent of; *at,* attribute of; *lo,* location of; *mo,* motion of; *pu,* purpose of; *qu,* quantity of; *rc,* recurrence of; *re,* reason of; *st,* state of; *su,* substance of; *ε,* entry (from Beaugrande, 1981, p. 291, reprinted with permission of the author and the International Reading Association).

right chaining of words, indeed some of the surface words themselves, are either converted to concepts or discarded. Discarded along with them are the conventional linguistic units like sentences. On the other hand, inferences are included in the model.

According to Beaugrande, a main advantage of the model is that an ideal pattern of concepts and relations is obtained against which the patterns of readers' reports of the content can be matched. In recall protocols, readers are more concerned with maintaining coherence than with reproducing faithfully what has been read. Readers appear to lose whole regions of the network, rather than isolated nodes and links. A disadvantage of the model is that it does not capture the visual image that readers tend to form about the scene. (The "rocket" text describes a scene and is particularly amenable to visualizing.)

As we see it, the model's dismissal of surface features of text has an advantage as well as a disadvantage: The advantage is that the model can be used with any language; the disadvantage is that it has nothing to say about the considerable influence of surface features on text processing (see Chapter 12 and this chapter).

MACRO-STRUCTURE

Kintsch and van Dijk (1978) describe the process of building a macro-structure. Units in their model are micro-propositions, one or more arguments related by a predicate as (P, X, Y); and **macro-propositions,** which are gists of a set of propositions or paragraphs. They analyzed a five-sentence paragraph from "Bumperstickers and the Cops," which is a part of a 1300-word research article. Its first sentence is analyzed into a set of 7 propositions:

A series of violent, bloody encounters between police and Black Panther Party members punctuated the early summer days of 1969.

1. (SERIES, ENCOUNTER)
2. (VIOLENT, ENCOUNTER)
3. (BLOODY, ENCOUNTER)
4. (BETWEEN, ENCOUNTER, POLICE, BLACK PANTHER)
5. (TIME: IN, ENCOUNTER, SUMMER)
6. (EARLY, SUMMER)
7. (TIME: IN, SUMMER, 1969)

The reader builds a memory representation of the text in cycles that occur at both micro- and macro-structural levels, as shown in Figure 13-2. In Cycle 1, the short-term memory buffer is empty, and the propositions derived from the first sentence are the input. P4 (proposition 4) is selected as the superordinate proposition because it is the only proposition in the input set that is directly related to the title: It shares with the title the concept POLICE. Propositions P1, P2, P3, and P5 are directly subordinated to P4 because of the shared argument ENCOUNTER; P6 and P7 are subordinated to P5 because of the repetition of

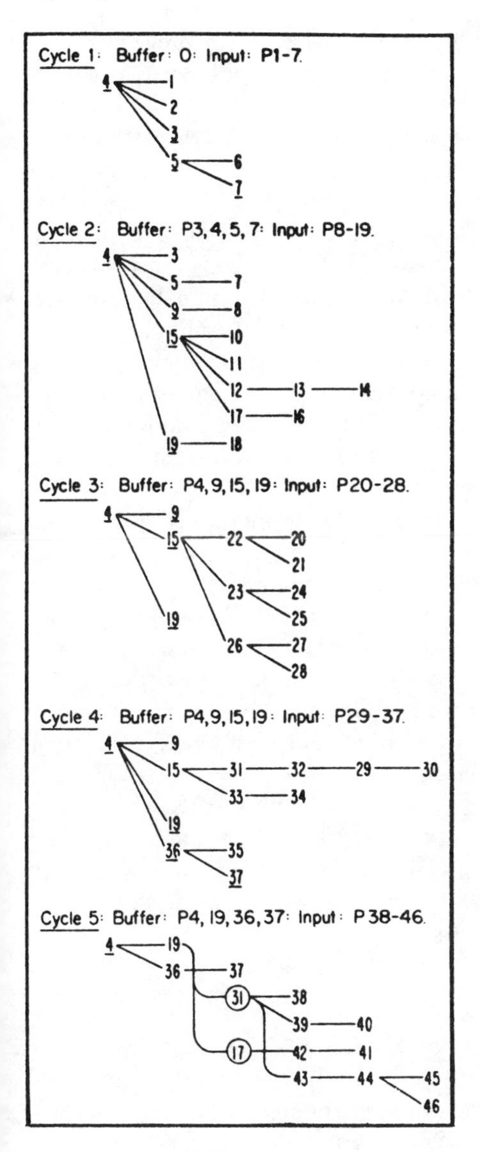

Figure 13-2. *The cyclical construction of the coherence graph for the propositions (P) (from Kintsch & van Dijk, 1978, p. 378, reproduced with permission of the American Psychological Association).*

SUMMER. In selecting the propositions to be maintained in the buffer from one cycle to the next, superordinate and recent ones are favored.

Problems arise in Cycle 5 for the fifth sentence (P38–46): *This is a report of a study that I undertook to assess the seriousness of charges.* In this sentence the input propositions do not share a common argument with any of the propositions in the buffer, requiring a long-term memory search. (The writer, having noticed a slight change in the topic, should have started a new paragraph with this sentence.) In other cases the lack of argument overlap may necessitate drawing inferences or reorganizing the propositions in the memory network. A text is considered difficult if it requires many inferences and reorganizations.

The model predicts which propositions will be recalled at various intervals or included in summaries. The topic proposition P4 will be the best remembered proposition because it recycles in the buffer. Other studies show that a thematic clause or sentence takes longer to read than does a less important one, suggesting that its good retention is due to long or deep processing (Cirilo & Foss, 1980). The two explanations are not mutually exclusive, and both may account for the memorability of a thematic sentence.

In chapter 12 we expressed our reservation about propositional analysis, which is unnecessarily complex and tedious. The same model may be built or tested using conventional linguistic units, such as phrase, clause, and sentence, and less conventional but similar idea units. Shebilske and Reid (1979) used the sentence as a unit, and Boccacio's *Decameron* as the text, in their study of macro-structure. Sentences that were directly related to a macro-proposition were read faster than were sentences that had to be integrated with others to construct a macro-proposition. When the same sentences were read out of context, reading rates did not differ between the two kinds of sentence.

In another study using a sentence as a unit, Cirilo (1981) presented a story sentence by sentence on a display scope under the subjects' control. Greater distances between a precursor sentence and a target, and lack of coreference between the two, lengthened reading times, but only when micro-processes were emphasized (verbatim recall of a segment of stories extracted from larger stories). Reading times were faster when the precursor was structurally important, but only when macro-processes were emphasized. In that condition, stories were read in their entirety as a filler task, with the main task being concept formation. Then, without prior warning, subjects were asked to recall the stories. Their protocols were scored for the presence or absence of the gist of the target sentence and the critical precursor.

GIST: A PRODUCT OF PROSE PROCESSING

One goal of reading an expository passage is to retain at least a gist of the passage. If a passage describes a scene, the gist can be a visual image. More often, it is in a verbal form, containing a few of the most important clauses. Occasionally, details, if they are vivid or important, may also be retained.

Readers construct a gist for a clause or sentence (Chapter 12); they use this gist to comprehend the second sentence; then they use the gist of the second sentence to comprehend the third sentence, and so on. At the end, they can construct a gist for a paragraph as a whole. Replace *sentence* by *paragraph,* and the preceding describes gist construction for a multi-paragraph passage. Gist construction should be helped by the presence of a clear topic, which is well supported by logically connected series of units, be they propositions, clauses, sentences, or paragraphs.

In reading a passage, the reader constructs a gist at an ever higher level of structure. The higher the level of a gist, the more likely it is to be retained.

Learning Techniques

Readers can use a variety of extra and overt activities to enhance their learning from expository text. They can underline, take notes, pose or answer questions, summarize, or paraphrase.

INTERPOLATED QUESTIONS AND READING GOALS

In reading a long passage continuously, one's attention tends to falter, and as a consequence, learning suffers. The patterns of eye movements of people reading continuously for 4 hours deteriorated, starting after only 30 min (Hoffman, 1946). When short series of questions were interpolated in a text, subjects could maintain their reading efficiency over a 6-hour session, even without feedback on the correctness of their answers (Carmichael & Dearborn, 1947).

It is critical how and where questions are inserted in a passage. In a typical study on inserted questions, subjects read a passage in which questions are placed either before or after the section to be tested. Then, after reading the entire passage, they are given another test, which can be either an "intentional test" (identical to the inserted questions) or an "incidental test" (not included among the inserted questions). The subjects taking either or both tests constitute a questioned group, and the subjects who do not see any interpolated questions constitute a control group.

The questioned group learns better than does the control group, if the questions are placed ***after*** the section of the passage wherein they are answered. In this condition, the questioned group is better than the control group certainly on the intentional items, and to a lesser degree on the incidental items as well. In the "before" condition, the questioned group is worse on the incidental items, presumably because their attention is focused on finding the answers to the questions, to the detriment of other information (Anderson & Biddle, 1975; Rothkopf & Bisbicos, 1967). The effectiveness of the questions as reading aids is not as great with middle grades (3–8) as with high school and college students (Memory, 1982). One should not be overzealous with questions: A question after each sentence breaks the flow of a narrative, impairing subjects' ability to remember sentences and to draw inferences (Moeser, 1978).

Reading goals influence reading patterns. In the study by Rothkopf and Billington (1979), high school students read a long passage on science after having memorized several specific learning goals. A sample goal: "What is the name of the scale used by oceanographers when recording the color of water?" The information relevant to each goal always was contained in a single sentence. Eye-movement data showed two inspection modes: relatively rapid inspection of incidental text and slow processing of the goal sentences. Goal-relevant sentences attracted over twice as many fixations, each fixation being slightly longer than those on incidental sentences.

In a different procedure, key sentences were recalled better when they were cued prominently (in capitals or boldface print) than when they were not cued. The cued sentences comprised only 10% of the text, and a recall test was given 1 hour after reading (Foster, 1979). This kind of physical cue to important information should help skimmers (see Chapter 7).

UNDERLINING AND NOTE TAKING

To learn well from text, the reader can underline and take notes. In these two activities, the student actively selects important information for later learning and gives extra processing to the noted and underlined items. Rickards and August (1975) examined the effects of active versus passive underlining on an 80-sentence passage in which one sentence per paragraph was underlined either by the reader (active) or by the researcher. The active group recalled both the underlined and the incidental material better than did the passive group in an immediate free-recall test.

Note taking is even more effective than underlining. In reading an 845-word passage, note-taking high school students recalled better than did the underliners, who, in turn, were better than controls (read only) on two types of tests, constructed response and multiple choice. Note taking required more time than did the other conditions (Kulhavy, Dyer, & Silver, 1975). In another study with college students, note taking improved substantive information (general ideas), whereas rereading improved factual information. The presence of the original text during study was essential to further learning (Dyer, Riley, & Yekovich, 1979).

ADVANCE ORGANIZER

Advance organizers are kinds of cognitive scaffolds into which new information can be incorporated. They are introductory materials at a higher level of abstractness, generality, and inclusiveness than is the passage itself (Ausubel, 1968, 1978). "Expository organizers" are used when a passage is completely unfamiliar. They provide a frame relevant both to previously known ideas and to details in the to-be-learned passage. "Comparative organizers" are used when material is relatively familiar. They may point out similarities and differences between the old and new materials.

Mayer (1982) reports that a concrete model of a computer was helpful before or after reading a passage about computers. In the model for a computer, input is a ticket window; memory, an erasable scoreboard; executive control, a shopping list; and output, a message pad. The group given an advance organizer excelled on creative use of the presented information in problem solving, whereas the group given a post-organizer excelled on test items involving retention of the information. The advance-organizer group recalled more of the conceptual information, whereas the post-organizer group recalled technical facts.

Perhaps a good summary can serve as a sort of organizer. Reder and Anderson (1980) found that new information is learned better if related information was learned previously in summary form than in full text. Organizers are useful when the materials to be learned are difficult or novel, or when the learner's ability is low (Faw & Waller, 1976).

HOW LEARNING TECHNIQUES WORK

The usefulness of different learning techniques depends on the kind of text and the purpose and skill of the learner. Good advance organizers may require considerable skill, time, and effort to prepare. Inserted questions and learning goals may require little skill but appreciable time and effort to prepare. They are useful if the intentional items are truly important and general and incidental items are less important. Questions seem to cause a backward review of the questioned and related materials, as well as a forward set to learn the same types of materials (McGaw & Grotelueschen, 1972; Rickards, 1979; Rothkopf & Bisbicos, 1967).

In note taking and underlining, it is the learner himself who differentiates important from unimportant information. If one is good at this skill, and if one's goal is to learn mainly the important items or ideas, the technique should save time and effort, compared with rereading. One also learns more incidental material than does the reader whose goals are chosen by the tester.

In writing this book, much of the task of reading the vast quantity of literature, in an assortment of languages, fell on Insup Taylor. To extract rapidly information that was at once important ***and*** relevant to this book, the following methods were used:

1. While reading through an article or a book, mark the parts that look noteworthy (mark faintly in the margin, to be erased later).
2. Reread only the marked parts, distinguishing once more the important and relevant from unimportant and irrelevant information (judged now in the context of the whole book or article).
3. Incorporate the selected information in the text, usually paraphrased.

The information distilled in this manner is often ingrained in memory, even though memorizing it was not the intention.

The more you study, and the more actively, selectively, and deeply you study, the more you learn.

Summary and Conclusions

Narrative prose tells a story, which is about characters and their actions as they unfold in a chronological–causal order and according to a plot. A theme (or moral) emerges from the story as a whole. A story may contain one or more episodes, whose arrangements can be contrasting, cyclic, embedded, and so on.

A story grammar specifies the number and type of story parts and their relations. The parts might be Setting, Goal, Attempt, Reaction, Outcome, and so on, but not Character, which is subsumed under Setting.

Some say there is a universal story grammar; some say there is a culture-specific grammar; and some question even the necessity of a grammar. We say there is a loose and flexible story structure that can accommodate a variety of stories.

Related to the idea of story grammar is a schema, an organized body of knowledge about an event. People acquire a schema through much experience with numerous instances of an event, and once acquired, the schema guides the way people understand and remember a similar event, be it a story or a restaurant routine. A conventional structure as well as common themes may be considered as story schemata.

Expository prose explains facts and ideas in a textbook or a technical paper. In a textbook, a table of contents helps the writer and the reader organize facts and ideas. In technical writing, an abstract is given at the beginning, and types of section are marked and sequenced for easy search and comprehension of desired information.

A passage should be broken into paragraphs in order to provide readers with regular visual and thought breaks. A good paragraph starts with a topic sentence, and its sentences are arranged in a logical sequence, in support of the topic sentence. Sentences within a paragraph cohere when key words are repeated, and anaphora and conjunctions are used. A good paragraph is easy to read, and its gist is easy to extract and remember.

Traditional tests of comprehension and retention have advantages and disadvantages. Multiple-choice tests and cloze tests can be rapidly and objectively scored, but they do not test some important aspects of comprehension, such as distinguishing important from unimportant information and extracting a gist or theme. Essays are better for tapping these aspects, but their scoring can be time consuming and subjective.

In a new method of testing comprehension and retention, a passage is segmented into clause-like idea units, either by a group of subjects or by the tester. Two to four levels of importance, plus a topic unit, can be differentiated. Readers are sensitive to the levels of importance, recalling more of the important than of the unimportant units, especially if a text is well structured. Certain details, if they are vivid, may be recalled well. This sensitivity develops with age and reading skill.

The right kind of questions placed at strategic spots in a long passage can aid students in learning the passage. Test items placed after to-be-learned sections are the best. Readers who underline and take notes are actively differentiating important from unimportant information and at the same time learning more of the former at the expense of the latter.

In comprehending a passage, a reader builds a gist at an ever higher level in his memory. At a low level, a phrase, proposition, clause, or sentence is comprehended as a unit, and its gist is kept in working memory until the next unit is comprehended. At a higher level, a paragraph is comprehended, and its gist is kept in working memory to be used in comprehending the next paragraph. This process repeats in cycles until an overall theme for the passage is formed and put in long-term memory. Thus, some time after reading a long passage, the reader may not remember individual phrases, propositions, clauses, sentences, and paragraphs, but will at least remember the gist of the passage as a whole.

III

Learning to Read

14

Early Readers and Reading Readiness

Very young children can acquire reading, provided it is made easy and gentle and pleasant.
—Quintilian, the Roman schoolmaster

Some infants are taught to read at home, and some preschoolers pick up reading on their own. How they do so not only is interesting in its own right but also sheds valuable light on how children learn to read at school. One important question early readers can answer is, When are children ready to read?

Preschoolers can Learn to Read

Early Readers

Young children were taught to read in ancient times and in many parts of the world. To give just one example, around 620 B.C. and in Europe until recent times, Jewish infants were taught to recognize Hebrew letters, and as soon as they were toilet-trained, sent to infant schools to be taught to read (Smethurst, 1975). In recent times in Europe and North America, many great writers and philosophers have learned to read early, at ages 1:6 to 5.[1] To enumerate several early readers: Jeremy Bentham, Jonathan Swift, Thomas Hobbes, Charles

[1] 1:6 = 1 year and 6 months.

Dickens, Ralph Waldo Emerson, Voltaire, Macaulay, John Stuart Mill, and J. P. Sartre (Engelmann & Engelmann, 1966; Smethurst, 1975).

By **early readers** we mean children who read before entering primary school at the age of 5 (in Great Britain, New Zealand), of 6 (in the United States, Canada, South Korea, Japan, and many other European countries), or of 7 (in China, Finland and other Scandinavian countries).

Durkin (1966) tested over 5000 children entering Grade 1 in one city in California. Among them she identified 49 children (29 girls and 20 boys) who could read already. For 6 years she tested the 49 children and interviewed their families. Later, she carried out in New York City a larger study with 156 early readers (80 girls and 76 boys), who constituted 4% of all school entrants. The early readers came from varied racial and socioeconomic backgrounds. Although preschoolers with an IQ as low as 82 could learn to read, most early readers tended to be above average in intelligence. The median IQs of early readers were 121 (range 91–161) and 133 (82–170) in the California study and the New York City study, respectively. Durkin's early readers tended to be far better readers in later school years than their equally bright classmates who did not learn to read early. Parents and teachers portrayed them as having good memory, concentration, curiosity, and persistence.

On the question of intelligence, all of Hollingworth's (1942) 12 subjects with IQs 180 or above picked up reading before going to school, at an average age of 3. One boy could say the alphabet at 12 months, and at 16 months he said it backward, just for the sake of change. Most of these bright early readers read voraciously once they learned how.

King and Friesen (1972) in Canada found about 1% of kindergartners in Calgary to be readers, even though reading is not taught in kindergartens. Like Durkin's early readers, 31 readers (20 girls and 11 boys) had higher IQs than did 31 prereading controls, but only slightly (111 versus 101). But unlike Durkin's early readers, the early readers in Calgary came from a higher socioeconomic class and smaller families than did the controls. M. Clark (1976) in Scotland found that early readers come from varied social backgrounds and have above average IQs (mean 122.5). In her study, more boys (20) than girls (12) were early readers. When these children entered Grade 1 at age 5, their reading ages ranged between 7:6 and 10.

Most preschoolers who learn to read do so largely on their own, with a little help from family members. Some learn to read from TV. Only a minority of the early readers' parents deliberately set out to teach their children reading, and in many of those cases the children may have prompted the parents by their own curiosity about letters and words. What some parents did was to provide models for their children by being voracious readers themselves, by reading to the children, or by having reading materials around the house. A Japanese survey shows that the earlier the parents (usually the mothers) began to read to the children, the more fluently the children read at age 5 (Sugiyama & Saito, 1973). In a Canadian study, almost all early readers had stories read to them daily (Patel & Patterson, 1982).

"Spontaneous" reading has been studied in Scotland (Clark, 1976); in the United States, where 1–4% of school entrants could read (Durkin, 1966); in Canada, where 1% of kindergartners could read (King & Friesen, 1972; Patel & Patterson, 1982); in Finland, where 15% of the school entrants (aged 7) already read at a Grade 2 level (Kyöstiö, 1980); and in Japan, where most school entrants (aged 6) know enough Hiragana letters to read simple sentences (Muraishi & Amano, 1972; see Chapter 4). The type of writing system may partly account for such large differences in the percentages of early readers in different countries. English and Finnish are alphabetic systems, but English codes its phonemes irregularly, whereas Finnish codes them regularly; Japanese Kana code syllables, which are more stable than phonemes as units, and code them consistently.

Parent–Teachers

When very young children are given reading instruction, the instructors are usually their parents. In Sumeria, around 3500 B.C., literacy was passed on from father to son (Smethurst, 1975). In modern times, parent–teachers successful enough to write up their stories have been keenly interested in their children's achievement; some, but not all, of them were highly educated as well. Nonprofessional though they may be, parents have some strong advantages over a professional teacher: They have to teach only one or two children, who want to learn to read and who are likely to be bright. And they are with the children for long periods, in appropriate and informal situations.

The noted psychologist Lewis Terman studied a 26-month-old girl, Martha, who could read any Grade 1 book. He was so impressed by Martha's feat that he persuaded her lawyer–father to write about her story in the *Journal of Applied Psychology*, and wrote the introduction to it himself (Terman, 1918). Winifred Sackville Stoner, an energetic and strong-minded advocate of early education, taught her 16-month-old daughter of the same name to read. Mrs. Stoner dedicated herself to giving Winifred an early all-around education and wrote about her experience in two books (Stoner, 1914, 1916). Winifred published her first volume of poetry at age 7 and later joined her mother in *Who's Who*.

Steinberg and Steinberg (1975), two psycholinguists, devised a four-phased program to teach their son Kimio to read. In the first phase, alphabet familiarization, they got 6-month-old Kimio interested in letters and words pasted on his crib. In the second phase, they taught him to identify designated letters by picking the right cards. In the third phase, they taught him to recognize words, phrases such as *Mama's key,* and sentences such as *What's that?* as whole patterns. By age 2, Kimio could identify 48 of these items, 15 of which he could pronounce. During his 27th month, it became apparent that Kimio knew the sound values of some letters. For example, seeing *clock* he said: "k-k-k-, What's this, Mommy?" By age 3:6, Kimio was able to read short sentences fluently, often reading new words at first sight. By age 5, he was reading at Grade 3 level and beyond, and by age 8 at Grade 3, his speed and accuracy equalled eleventh graders.[2]

The Swedish linguist Söderbergh (1971) wrote a book giving a detailed account of how her 2-year-old daughter learned to read. Though Astrid Söderbergh was taught by whole-word memorization, she soon showed signs of having induced letter–sound relations. In the third month of instruction, she noted that the Swedish word *precis* ('exactly') was like the previously learned *pappa*: She pointed to 'p' and observed that *pappa* had three of them. In the fifth month, she lay *ned* ('down') and *med* ('with') side by side and pointed out the differences and similarities. In the sixth month, she began trying to guess new words before her mother told her what they were. By the tenth month, at age 3:4, Astrid was trying to guess all the new words and was succeeding on about half of them.

The journalist–educator Ledson (1975) taught reading to his two young daughters, 3:9-year-old Eve and 2:8-year-old Jean. He used a contrasting teaching method, **phonics:** The first day he taught the girls the sounds of the first three letters, 'a, b, c'; in later lessons, he taught the girls to say the isolated sounds in "cuh.a.buh" or "buh.a.cuh" and to blend them into *cab* or *bac* (back). (Ledson's method was not simon-pure phonics, for he did teach a few irregularly spelled words, such as *I, you, a, the, am,* by the whole-word method.) By the seventh day, the girls learned the sounds of 'a, b, c, s, u, t', and were sounding out words such as *cab, scab, bat, us.* Their sounding out at this stage required much help, coaxing, and rewards such as raisins. On the seventeenth day, the little girls read their first sentence *I see you.*

By the second month, the girls could read about 180 words and many sentences. During the fourth month the girls' instruction was taken over by a 13-year-old baby-sitter, who instructed her charges about 9 hours a week. By the eighth month, the girls were checking children's books out of the library and reading as many as 30 of them in a single week. Although they had first been rewarded for every correct response, they quickly began to look upon reading as a reward in itself. For example, they would brush their teeth especially long and briskly to be allowed to read in bed before the lights were turned out.

Miño-Garcés (1981) taught his two sons, Nando and Javier, to read in English and Spanish, using Lado's whole-word method (at home) combined with Montessori's phonics method (at kindergarten). Actually, Nando, at age 3:10, was taught to read in English, his second language, but he transferred his English reading skill to Spanish reading without special training. (Transfer from English to Spanish reading should be easier than the other way around, for the two use the same Roman alphabet but Spanish is more regular in its letter–sound relations than is English.) When he entered school in the United States, Nando was placed at the Grade 2 level in reading. Lee (1977) taught his

[2]Postscript: Kimio Steinberg is now at the University of California, Berkeley. His father wrote to us recently: "I'm glad to report that even at 18 years of age he has not forgotten how to read. Again, further proof as to the efficacy of our reading program [Steinberg, 1982]!"

preschooler daughter to read in two unrelated languages and scripts, English and Korean.

Non-Parent Teachers

Instructors need not be highly educated, nor need they be parents: Anybody who can read and is interested in the pupil can do the task. Grandmothers, older siblings, baby-sitters, masters, and slaves (in ancient Greece and Rome), are known to have been effective teachers, even though they did not publish their success stories.

Williams (1982) taught a 2:6-year old subject to read using phonics. He taught the girl the seven letters ('u, a, i, p, s, t, n') and their sounds, taught her to blend them, and then taught her to build the words *up, us, at, it, an, in* from them. Williams prepared "books" simple enough to be read on the first day of instruction (see Chapter 15, "Cost–Benefit Analysis of Beginning Materials.") One of the first books used the single word *no,* which always appeared on a page by itself in 3-inch letters. The first page showed a picture of a baby standing on her head on a ball balanced on a chair that is balanced on a table. Her terrified mother far below shouted "_____," which the tiny pupil would read (or predict). The other pages showed the baby doing something equally silly and forbidden. Each time the book was reread, first one, then two, then three of the *no's* would be changed to *don't* or *stop,* thereby progressing to more reading and less predicting. The pupil could predict the word using story context, and she could build up the word by using the known sounds of the letters.

Young children can be taught not only at home individually but also in classrooms. In a Japanese nursery school, over 8 months, a class of six 2-year-olds and a class of fifteen 3-year-olds were taught about 100 words and a few phrases, 80% of them in Kanji (Steinberg & Steinberg, 1980). The children were not exceptional in any way, and came from middle-class families. They were taught by nursery school teachers who used the whole-word method. In France, R. Cohen (1977) reports good results of teaching a large number of preschoolers to read words and sentences. Daily group teaching for 10–20 min duration lasted for 8 months. Although the 4–5-year-olds scored higher in tests, even some 3–4-year-olds met the criterion of reading 75% of the test items correctly.

Levels of Reading to be Attained

Learning to read is too complicated a task to take in one bite. To make it seem less complicated, let us consider it in four levels, which are no more than convenient signposts planted along a continuum.[3]

[3]These levels are based partly on material supplied by Edmund Coleman (1980), who also provided information on Williams's (1982) thesis.

Level 1: Letter and Word Recognition

"When a child has learned to read two words, he has mastered one of the most staggering abstractions he will ever have to deal with in life: he can read words," observed Doman (1964, p. 119).

We divide Level 1 into a lower and a higher Level 1. The lower Level 1 skill, that of matching a visual pattern directly to an object, is not all that staggering. Even chimpanzees attain this level of reading. For example, Sarah learned about 130 words, colored shapes that stood for objects (Premack, 1971). A human infant should be able to attain this level of reading before the tenth month—certainly before he learns to talk. At 12 months, Kimio Steinberg could identify four words (*boy, car, baby,* and *girl*) by picking the correct flash cards when asked to do so, though he could not say any of them. One of Sarah's trainers taught four of the chimp's plastic words to her own daughter at 10 months, before the child was talking.

Congenitally deaf preschoolers have been taught to recognize many words and simple phrases in Sweden (Söderbergh, 1976) and in Japan (Steinberg *et al.*, 1982; Chapter 4). Children of deaf parents try to sign their first words as early as six months, several months before normal children make their first spoken words. Apparently, language is delayed not so much by its cognitive difficulty as by the fine muscular control needed to operate the articulators of speech. Reading at this level may actually be easier than talking.

At the higher Level 1, to read a word is to match the visual pattern with a sound pattern already known to refer to something in the world. The sound pattern is a first-order abstraction, and the visual pattern for this sound pattern is a second-order abstraction. Matching a visual pattern of a word to its sound pattern, and learning to match the same visual pattern to a concept, represent the two parallel sides of reading, according to the Bilateral Cooperative model of reading (see Chapter 11). Matching to the sound pattern is the LEFT-track function; matching to the concept, the RIGHT-track function. Humans must learn both kinds of matching before they can read effectively.

Level 2: Sentence Reading

Sarah the chimpanzee could read and compose sentences. For example, she once wrote the command *Give apple Gussie,* and the apple was promptly given to the other chimp. The mistake was never repeated—One trial learning! She also was able to read slightly more complex but still concrete sentences such as *Sarah take banana if-then Mary no give chocolate.* Sarah, who dearly loved chocolate, would not take the banana.

All the early readers just described attained this level as soon as they learned a small number of words. In principle, a child needs to learn only one or two words to read simple sentences such as *Look!* and *Dad ran.*

Level 3: Story Reading

At Level 3, a child reads stories with plots. If stories are written sufficiently simply and yet interestingly, even a 2:6-year-old could be enticed to read. In Williams's (1982) book, a child would be taught, first, to arrange three to six pictures in a sequence that follows a plot; next, to apply a one-word caption that describes each picture sequence ("No," "Yes," "Don't!"); then to predict, by saying aloud the one-word caption, what would come next in a sequence. This level can come before or after the sentence level, but it is probably not accessible to chimpanzees.

Level 4: Reading for Its Own Sake.

At Level 4, and perhaps at Level 3, we must say goodbye to chimps and concentrate on children. Chimpanzees seem to use reading and writing only as a means to manipulate their immediate environment, and not for the pleasure of finding out about events that happened "in days of yore and times and tides long gone."

A child reads for its own sake—that is, because she enjoys reading and wants to find out what will happen next in a story. Or, she wants to find out events that are happening in faraway places and that happened long ago. When a child has learned to read, she reads to learn. A child is not an accomplished reader unless she attains this level. Ledson's (1975) two little girls certainly reached this level by about ages 3 and 4: They would ***work*** to be allowed to read.

Perceptual, Cognitive, and Linguistic Readiness

Do children require specific perceptual, cognitive, and linguistic skills before they can start to learn to read? It is anticlimactic even to raise such a question after reading about early readers. However, some educators in the United States insist that children have to be at least 6 to 7 years old, and that the children require high levels of "readiness skills." Thus, they subject the children to "readiness tests" and "readiness training."

Readiness Tests

During the 1930s and 1940s, there was almost universal acceptance in the United States of the idea that children should have attained a mental age (MA) of 6:6 before being instructed in reading. This acceptance was largely based on Morphett and Washburne's (1931) study that showed that Grade 1 children below this MA had little success in reading, on the one hand, and children above this MA were as good as they were going to be, on the other. During the

1950s and 1960s, beginning instruction was restricted to children with MA 6:6, despite that the original study was not replicated.

Readiness tests are standardized instruments designed to assess a child's expected ability to profit from formal instruction in reading. There are several different tests, of which the best known is the Metropolitan Readiness Test. All readiness tests are supposed to tap the perceptual, cognitive, and linguistic skills assumed to be used for reading. Current readiness tests assess the following four areas of skills (Nurss, 1979):

1. Visual: nonverbal visual matching and memory, copying
2. Auditory: auditory matching and memory, sound–letter relation
3. Language comprehension: word matching, following directions
4. Quantitative: number concepts

More subjective assessments are also made by observing classroom behavior and the home environment.

Perceptual and Cognitive Skills

What kinds of tests predict children's reading? Stevenson and his team assessed the effectiveness of a battery of 11 cognitive and 11 psychometric tasks for predicting achievement in reading and arithmetic in Grades 1–3 (Stevenson, Parker, Wilkinson, Hegion, & Fish, 1976). The tests were administered to 255 children before they started kindergarten. The children's later achievements could be predicted more accurately by a small number of psychometric and cognitive measures than by teachers' ratings or by the Metropolitan Readiness Test.

In the study by Stevenson *et al.*, visual tasks such as matching, remembering, and copying picture stimuli correlated poorly with reading. The following four verbal tasks related well with reading:

1. Naming letters: The child names uppercase letters, matches letters, and says the first two letters of his name.
2. Visual–auditory paired associates: The child indicates which of the five possible responses spoken by the examiner is the correct match to a visual stimulus.
3. Reversals: The child selects a match for a two- or three-letter combination presented in correct and reversed orders (e.g., 'nu': 'un, un, nu, un').
4. Categories: The child produces class names for groups of three words.

The measures that correlated well with later arithmetic performance also tapped verbal skills, suggesting that the tests measure a more general intelligence factor. (At higher grades, arithmetic and verbal skills are likely to be less highly correlated.)

The correlations between the cognitive–psychometric measures and achievement in Grades 1, 2, and 3, respectively, were .62, .69, and .61 for reading, and .60, .69, and .59 for arithmetic. Preschool tests retained much of their power for predicting reading and arithmetic achievement over a period of 4 years. However, over comparable intervals of time, Grade 1 tests of reading achievement tended to predict later reading achievement even better.

In a study that compared racial groups, correlations between readiness tests given at kindergarten and reading achievements in Grade 2 were consistently high for middle- and lower-class white children but not for lower-class black and Mexican American children (Oakland, 1978).

Letter Naming

Knowledge of letter names in kindergarten or at the beginning of Grade 1 was one of the best predictors of reading achievement at the end of Grade 1. But the ability to name letters and to count dots was not related with continued success in reading and arithmetic in Grades 2 and 3 (Stevenson *et al.*, 1976).

Because in many studies letter naming has been found to be the best predictor of early reading achievement, it deserves a section by itself. Bond and Dykstra (1967) compiled the findings of studies involving several thousand children who were taught to read by six different methods. At the end of Grade 1, the best predictor of reading success was the Letter Recognition subtest of the Murphy Durrell Reading Readiness Analysis. The finding was repeated when the studies were extended to Grade 2 (Dykstra, 1968). According to Richek (1977–1978), the ability to recognize letters was one general skill that predicted success among kindergartners, regardless of the method of instruction used.

The high correlation between letter naming and reading does not mean, of course, that naming is directly responsible for good reading, although Stevenson *et al.* (1976) entertain the possibility that knowing the alphabet may give children information and confidence. More likely, common variables (e.g., interest in, and facility with, printed material) underlie both letter naming and reading. This observation may explain why teaching children letter names did not improve their reading (R. J. Johnson, 1970; Samuels, 1972), and why children can learn to read words without being able to name even a single letter (Steinberg & Steinberg, 1980).

Examine the letter names of the English alphabet: Some names indicate the sounds of the letters ("vee" for 'v'); some do so unreliably "see" for 'c', which, in different words, sounds /s, k/ or nothing at all); some have no relation with the letter's sound ("aitch" for 'h'). In Japanese, Kana names are the sounds of the Kana, and in Korean Hangul, the name of each consonant symbol contains the symbol's sound at both initial and final positions. For Kana and Hangul, then, letter names are useful and worth teaching. Even for English, though, letter names may arouse a child's interest in printed materials and help a teacher to communicate with her pupils. At any rate, the majority of children entering Grade 1 already know the letter names (Mason, 1980).

A Critical Look at Readiness Training

As recently as the 1970s, belief in the concept of readiness was firm in the United States: Austin and Morrison's (1974) national survey showed that 85% of schools routinely used readiness tests to prescribe readiness instruction. It was not unusual for one or more children in a Grade 1 class to spend the entire year "getting ready to read" by performing such challenging exercises as circling pictures of animals resembling a standard. Fortunately, some educators are now questioning the need for this kind of extended readiness instruction.

As Stevenson *et al.* (1976) point out, the most reasonable use of their own predictor tasks is as a screening device to identify children who merit further observation, rather than as a means of assigning children to special groups for readiness training. The concept of reading readiness should apply mainly to the question of whether a child is old enough to withstand the "rigor" of formal instruction at school (being able to sit still for 15 min, behave as a member of a group, and so on). For this kind of readiness, or physical and social maturity, the child may well have to be aged 3 or 4 chronologically, but not necessarily mentally.

The concept of readiness is peculiarly American. In Britain and New Zealand, children start kindergarten at age 4 (where some learn to read) and school at age 5. (Teaching materials tend to be simpler in these countries than in the United States, according to Downing & Leong, 1982). Yet, so far, no one has found schoolchildren in these countries to be inferior to American children in reading achievement. On the contrary, fewer school children are retarded readers in Britain than in the United States (see Chapter 16). In Japan, Korea, and China, the concept of readiness was unheard of until recently. Yet, almost all children learn to read, some even before going to school.

We object to readiness training not because it is useless but because it is far, far less useful than reading instruction itself. Moreover, reading itself may foster some readiness skills, rather than other way around, as we shall see. Based on their research, Singer and Balow (1981) point out: "If you want pupils to learn a particular skill [reading] or knowledge, it is more efficient to teach it directly than to expect it to transfer from other learnings [p. 309]."

Even without all the other evidence, the fact that there exist children who learn to read at the tender ages of 2 or 3 should shake one's belief in readiness tests. Not all these children were at the genius level (140–180 IQ), but the mental age of even the genius children would still be well below 6:6. Conversely, children of any mental age can be retarded in reading (see Chapter 16).

Reflect for a moment how children acquire speech: No one gives infants a speech readiness test before they are allowed to pick up speech; no one gives them extended lessons in distinguishing a "moo" from a "miaow"; no one instructs them what phonemes, morphemes, and words are. Infants just start talking. Why should not children be allowed to "just start reading" as well?

Linguistic Awareness: A Prerequisite to Reading?

Some educators and psychologists believe that **linguistic awareness,** rather than reading readiness, is a prerequisite to reading instruction. To Ryan (1980), linguistic awareness (which she also calls "metalinguistic knowledge") is "the ability to focus attention upon the form of language in and of itself, rather than merely as the vehicle by which meaning is conveyed [p. 39]." To Liberman and her associates, linguistic awareness is **segmenting ability,** the ability to segment words into syllables and phonemes.

> First, he [the beginning reader] must realize that spoken words consist of a series of separate phonemes. Second, he must understand how many phonemes the words in his lexicon contain and the order in which these phonemes occur. Without this awareness, he will find it hard to see what reading is all about [Liberman & Mann, 1981, p. 126].

Liberman and her associates base their argument on the findings that children who are good at segmenting are good also at reading (e.g., Liberman *et al.*, 1977). Fox and Routh (1976) also found that children who were proficient at segmenting a syllable into phonemes benefited from phonic blend training more than did children who were not. These studies do not rule out the possibility that a common skill underlies both tasks. After all, segmenting and blending are both LEFT-track functions involved in phonetic coding (see Chapter 11).

The conclusion that segmenting ability is a prerequisite to reading does not make intuitive sense. A child first perceives speech at the level of meaning. To a very young child, perhaps up to age 3, a sentence such as *Don't touch!* (marked by intonation) is one meaningful unit; to a slightly older child, aged around 5, a phrase such as *gonna (going to), napple (an apple), don't,* or even *red apple* is one indivisible unit (Ehri, 1975; Holden & MacGinitie, 1972; Hottenlocher, 1964; Karpova, 1977). We have heard of adults in the southern United States who think *Damnyankee* is one word. For children, function words are especially hard to separate from the content words with which they form a phrase. The phrase *of the* is the seventeenth most common "word" in English.

In speech, children never have to differentiate isolated phonemes, though of course they respond to phonemic differences by distinguishing *dig* from *big,* or *big* from *pig.* The phoneme in speech is a meaningless, small, abstract, unnatural, and unstable unit, to which the children need not respond directly; when they responds to it, they do so indirectly, via word meaning. Children may appreciate alliterations and rhymes, but only as parts of words.

Written language, on the other hand, is cut into visible segments. When the children are introduced to printed alphabetic material, they have a chance for the first time to become aware of phonemic segments, since each phoneme, more or less, has its corresponding letter. Their awareness of the word as a unit becomes more secure, for words in print are clearly separated by spaces. At school, as part of reading instruction children are often explicitly taught the concept of word—where a word begins and ends, and how many words a sentence contains.

Linguistic Awareness: A By-Product of Reading

We shall now try to show that segmenting ability, rather than being a prerequisite to learning to read, is a by-product of reading and writing. Segmenting words into syllables, which are large and stable phonetic units, is relatively easy. In the United States, 46% of 4-year-olds could do it. This ability did not improve much between ages 4 and 5 (46% to 48%), but did so substantially (to 90%) at age 6, the age when children receive intensive instruction in reading and writing (Liberman, Shankweiler, Fischer, & Carter, 1974).

In Ehri's (1975, 1976) studies, beginning readers were far more aware of words and syllables as linguistic units than were prereaders. In a learning task (associating orally given words with nonsense figures), kindergarten readers required fewer trials to criterion than did age-matched prereaders. Two groups of readers, one from kindergarten and the other from Grade 1, did not differ. Goldstein (1976) compared two groups of 4-year-olds: One group was given 13 weeks of reading instruction, and the other group was not. The children's skill in word analysis–synthesis predicted their reading achievement. But the analysis–synthesis skill itself improved after reading instruction, especially in the children who had been the poorest in this skill.

Let us now consider the influence of the script on syllable segmenting. Syllable segmenting is particularly easy in Japanese because its reading unit is the syllable, whose structure is simple (V, CV). A high percentage (60%) of Japanese preschoolers, 4- and 5-year-olds, can do the task even when they cannot read any Hiragana. But the percentage shoots up to 90% as soon as the preschoolers can read 1 to 5 Hiragana, and close to 100% when they read 60 or more Hiragana. The task of locating a designated syllable in a word, say /ko/ in *kotori,* is more difficult, and only 20% of the preschoolers can do the task before they are able to read their first Hiragana; the percentage jumps to 42% when the children can read 1 to 5 Hiragana, and to 95% when they can read all 71 basic Hiragana (Amano, 1970). On the other hand, even adult Japanese may find it difficult to segment syllables into phonemes. This inability is never a handicap to a Japanese reader; why should it be?

One of the scripts used in Liberia, Africa, is a syllabary called Vai, which is written without word division. Scribner and Cole (1981) compared Vai-script literates with English- or Arabic-script literates, as well as with illiterates, on various linguistic and cognitive tasks. The Vai-script literates were better at comprehending and remembering sentences broken into syllables than were the other groups. When the sentences were presented word by word, however, the Vai-script literates had no advantage over the other literates.

Segmenting words and syllables into phonemes is difficult, but it can develop when people learn to read in an alphabet, and by phonics. In Portugal, illiterate adults scored far poorer than controls (who became literate in adulthood) in phoneme deletion and addition tasks (*farm* → "arm," *ant* → "pant"). In fact, 50% of the illiterates failed every single test, whereas none of the literates did (Morais, Cary, Alegria, & Bertelson, 1979). In the study by Liberman *et al.* (1974), the percentages of children who could do phoneme segmenting at ages 4, 5, and 6 were 0, 17, and 70, respectively. Once again, the segmenting ability developed dramatically when children started reading and writing.

In Belgium, one group of Grade 1 children had been taught for 4 months by a whole-word method and the other by a phonics method. The phonics group did somewhat better on syllable segmenting, but spectacularly better on phoneme segmenting, than did the whole-word group (Alegria, Pignot, & Morais, 1982). The segmenting task required the children to reverse two segments in a French word. For example, children produced /dira/ from /radi/ (*radis* 'radish') or /os/ from /so/ (*sceau* 'bucket'). In Canada, preschool readers, despite their Grade 2 reading level, did poorly on phoneme segmenting and blending tasks. These children had learned to read largely on their own by the whole-word method (Patel & Patterson, 1982).

Segmenting ability is strongly influenced by learning to read, to an extent that depends on the method of learning and the script in which reading is learned. One has to conclude that reading leads to segmenting ability, and not vice versa. Baron and Treiman (1980) reached the same conclusion from their own research on word learning. Segmenting ability was more highly correlated with the use of rules (phonics method) than with use of whole-word recognition. However, segmenting ability did not predict learning from rule-emphasis instruction any better than it did learning from whole-word instruction. Baron and Treiman conclude: Segmenting ability plays a smaller role in learning to read than has been thought.

Holden and MacGinitie (1973) studied the relation between word awareness and cognitive development, which was measured by the Piagetian seriation test (children insert 9 additional sticks into an ordered array of 10 sticks of different lengths). Children who pass the test are considered to have reached "concrete operational thinking." Word awareness was more related to reading achievement than to cognitive development. In this experiment, too, readers were more aware of words as units than were prereaders.

Which comes first, linguistic awareness or reading? The issue is not trivial: If a teacher believes that awareness is a prerequisite to reading, she will spend excessive time in "awareness training" that could bring higher dividends if it were spent on more direct instruction in reading.

Language Development and Reading

Printed language is bound to spoken language, but in traditional school instruction, reading tends to be taught independently of, and subsequent to, speech development. We now give a brief summary of speech development that provides background, as well as some tips, to reading instruction.

Speech Development

An "infant" (from the Latin word for "not speaking") starts life without any speech and with a brain that is not fully developed. During the period when the brain is developing, between birth and the early teens, children acquire language(s) readily, not through formal instruction but by being immersed in a sea of speech. Beyond this "critical period," people learn languages less readily. Even with long formal instruction and continued use, adult immigrants can seldom master their adopted language to the point of sounding exactly like native speakers (Lenneberg, 1967; I. Taylor, 1978). "Attic" or "wild" children, if they are discovered in their teens, learn a language with difficulty rather than acquire it easily (Curtiss, 1977).

In phonological development, children first acquire phonemes with gross and clear feature contrasts and move on to phonemes with more subtle and finer contrasts. They can correctly articulate vowels and simple consonants (/m, b, p/) at age 2 and complex consonants (/z, v, θ, ð/) at ages 6–8. When the children enter school they have not yet established firm phonological rules or production rules for consonant clusters (Menyuk, 1972). They acquire complex phonological rules, such as the vowel-shift rule, through learning to read (Moskowitz, 1973; see Chapter 6). On the other hand, Read (1971) found that some preschoolers have an implicit knowledge of certain aspects of the sound system of English. Consider the preschooler's spelling error, "AODOV" (out of): 'D' is phonetically correct, because in some dialects there is no contrast between /t/ and /d/ when they occur between vowels.

In vocabulary development, a typical child starts with 3 words at age 1; thereafter, the size of her vocabulary doubles and redoubles until it expands to 5000 words at age 6–7 (M. E. Smith, 1926; Rinsland, 1945). The early vocabulary consists of expressive words (*hi, no, stop*), names of people (*Eve, Mommy, Daddy*), and of objects and actions that are important in the child's life (K. Nelson, 1974). These are basically action- and imagery-related words of the RIGHT track.

As children grow older, they acquire fine and complex distinctions among the senses of words. For example, the differentiated senses of *long, wide,* and *tall* evolve from an amorphous concept of bigness, positive senses (long, wide) emerging before negative ones (short, narrow) (Brewer & Stone, 1975). The verbs *sell* and *buy* involve a more complex set of distinctions (transfer of money) than do *give* and *take.* Accordingly, a 4-year-old uses only the simple verbs correctly, but an 8-year-old can use more complex verbs correctly (Gentner, 1975).

Before the age of 6 or 8, children organize words in their memory according to specific real world situations, especially personal experiences; later, like adults, they organize them according to linguistic relations, especially grammatical classes. In a word-association test, to the stimulus word *dark* a child may respond with *room*; an adult, with *light* (Anglin, 1977; Cramer, 1968; Entwisle, Forsyth, & Muus, 1964; Ervin, 1961; Petrey, 1977).

Such a shift in organization may reflect children's growing implicit knowledge of the grammatical roles of words in sentences.

In morphological development, English-speaking children learn bound morphemes in an order that is governed not so much by the articulatory difficulty or frequency of their phonemes as by conceptual difficulty. Thus, plural (-*s*) emerges before the possessive (-*s*), which in turn emerges before the third-person singular verb (-*s*) (R. Brown, 1973; de Villiers & de Villiers, 1973). The developmental trend is from concrete-imagic to syntactic forms. At one stage, around age 6, children may learn the morphological rules so well that they generalize the rules even to words where they are inapplicable (*go–goed*).

In syntactic development, at age 1 a child starts with single-word utterances such as *no, stop, gone.* The child chooses one word that singles out one salient feature of the perceptual–cognitive complex she wants to communicate (Bloom, 1973; Braine, 1974). A little later, she combines two words into primitive patterns, which might be: *Eve eat* (agent–action); *Eat lunch* (action–object); *Eve lunch* (agent–object). These are associative rather than syntactic structures. Two-term relations later evolve into a three-term syntactic sentence *Eve eat lunch* (agent–action–object, or subject–verb–object). At age 3, a child can produce a six-word interrogative sentence that is syntactically correct, or nearly so: *Why the kitty can't stand up?*

Up to age 3:6, a child may disregard word order and use instead "probable event" strategy in interpreting improbable sentences such as *The baby feeds the mother.* That is, she considers the mother as the agent (Bever, 1970; Strohner & Nelson, 1974). (This strategy remains even in adult language understanding, when the syntax is too complex.) Around age 4 or 5, a child starts to use word order to interpret sentences, considering a noun to be an agent if it occurs before a verb. This strategy leads to correct interpretation of actives such as *The car bumps the truck,* and even of inverted clefts such as *It's the truck that the car bumped,* but it leads to incorrect interpretation of passives such as *The truck is bumped by the car* (Lempert & Kinsbourne, 1980).

Up to the age of 5, a child has difficulty processing syntax without the support of a situational context, or without being dominated by semantic and pragmatic considerations. But around age 6, he comprehends syntactic structures in their own right, even if they do not match with real events (e.g., Caramazza & Zurif, 1978; Cromer, 1976; Patel, in press; Scholes, 1978).

Even older children (Grade 3) have difficulty with certain forms of anaphora, negatives, and other complex structures, as discussed in Chapter 12. Other investigators document evidence of syntactic development that goes well beyond age 6, up to 9 or 12 (C. Chomsky, 1969; Entwisle & Frasure, 1974; Palermo & Molfese, 1972; Scholes, 1978).

In many of these skills, speech understanding precedes production by some months. In one study, children aged between 2 and 4 were tested to see how well they could imitate, understand, and produce several syntactic contrasts (e.g., active versus negative, *boy draws* versus *boys draw*). On every item, the score went down from imitation to understanding, and then to production (Fraser, Bellugi, & Brown, 1963). A 10-month-old baby can point to parts of her body such as mouth and nose upon command, though she cannot produce the words herself. In fact, even at age 2, she may still be unable to pronounce *mouth,* using instead a pronunciation indistinguishable from *mouse.* But if an adult pronounces the two words, the child will have no difficulty in pointing to the correct object.

Children everywhere acquire language(s) seemingly effortlessly and rapidly, following a similar sequence. This is so because children everywhere go through a similar physical–perceptual–cognitive maturational sequence, on the one hand, and because they are exposed to similar kinds of speech (plenty of simple, clearly articulated utterances) used in similarly simple contexts (here and now), on the other. Children everywhere have compelling needs to communicate for their well-being, if not for their survival.

Speech and Reading

Children acquire speech readily by being immersed in a sea of talk. Any industrialized nation now has the means to immerse its children similarly in a sea of printed language. Television, through such popular programs as *Sesame Street* (which started in the 1960s) and *The Electric Company* (started in 1971), has been exposing a huge number of children to animated print.[4] Computer-controlled learning devices using animated letters and words are now on the market. Some of the successful teacher–parents used a similar technique even before TV and computers became popular: Stoner (1914, 1916) and Steinberg and Steinberg (1975) surrounded their babies with large, colored letters and words. Miño-Garcés (1981) argues that children should acquire reading like speech, not learn it like a foreign language. That is, they should pick up reading effortlessly, just because they are exposed to printed words and just because these words convey meanings.

In our view, bright children in a literate environment may acquire reading largely by themselves, with a lot of encouragement but with a minimum of instruction. But most children have to be instructed in reading, especially when phonics is involved. Even with adequate instruction, some intellectually normal children fail to learn to read (see Chapter 16).

Early speech is closely tied to the child's vital and immediate communicative needs: When in dire distress, a child can scream *Help!*; when warned with a shrill *Hot!*she heeds. Reading is seldom used in this urgent manner. Nevertheless, most children want to know what happens in a story or what labels on objects say, and this desire can be kindled and fostered.

In speech development, understanding precedes speaking. Accordingly, the Steinbergs did not require their 12-month-old baby to pronounce the

[4] *Sesame Street* teaches preschoolers numbers, letters, and about 20 English and Spanish words as sight vocabulary. *The Electric Company* gives supplementary instruction in basic reading skills to 7–10-year-old children with reading difficulties (Gibbon, Palmer, & Fowles, 1975).

letters and words that he could discriminate and identify by pointing. There are also children who have adequate receptive speech but lack articulatory speech (e.g., delayed speech, deaf, cerebral palsied). For these children, rudimentary reading with logographs (lower Level 1: word recognition) provides a valuable means of communication. A logograph can be directly associated to its meaning, bypassing its sound if necessary (see Chapters 3 and 4).

Children will be motivated to read if they obtain useful or interesting information from printed material, as can be seen in Japanese kindergartners: The more time preschoolers spend in kindergarten, the more Hiragana they can read, even though reading is not formally taught there (see Figure 4-1). What does happen in kindergarten is that writing is used to identify owners of objects, to give simple instructions, and so on. In the United States, Goodman and Goodman (1979) suggest that a classroom should be a literate environment full of things pupils will need and want to read. On the streets, there are signs like *Stop* and *One way,* and commercial logos like *Coca-Cola* and *K mart.* At home, children can pick favorite TV programs, read notes from parents, or find out how to make a sock puppet from instruction booklets.

Initially, the words learned in reading should be those children use in speech. Thus, in teaching 2-year-olds, Doman (1964) starts with *Mommy* and *Daddy.* Even with school-age children, the language-experience approach follows a similar philosophy: By asking the child what words he wants to learn, the teacher ensures that the words are in the child's speaking vocabulary. Since children's utterances start with single-word "sentences," Williams (1982) started his 2:6-year-old subject reading with words like *Stop* and *No.* Similarly, Lado's method starts with single words such as *Run* and *Jump,* which can be pronounced and then acted out (Lado & Andersson, 1976).

Sentence structures should be kept simple at first, since even 5- or 6-year-olds may misinterpret passives and negatives. Even among simple active structures, children use some structures more than others. Sentences and passages constructed in the syntactic patterns that occur frequently in children's speech tend to be better understood in reading than are those of infrequent patterns (Ruddell, 1965; Tatham, 1970). On the other hand, there is a danger that children's reading material may be simpler than their own speech, thus depriving them of an opportunity to increase their linguistic sophistication through reading (Sampson, 1982). After all, adults read a far wider variety of words than they ever hear in conversation. Why should children not have the same opportunity?

Dialect, Second Language, and Reading

One distinct dialect in the United States is **Black English** (BE), which originated with slaves in Africa (Dillard, 1972). According to Dillard, 80% of black people speak BE, which differs from standard English (SE) in phonology (*that→dat; test→tess; seed→see*); vocabulary (*savvy* = to understand; *heap* = very,

very much); and syntax (BE, unlike SE, distinguishes continuous versus momentary action):

1. *He be workin' when de boss come in* = the work went on before and after the boss's entry.
2. *He workin' when de boss come in* = he worked only when the boss was present.

Some educators believe that this kind of language difference will interfere with black children's learning to read in SE, noting that black children lag far behind white children in reading achievement. Among the disadvantaged in New York City, 83% of black children, compared with 45% of white children, were already 1–3 years behind in reading by Grade 3 (S. A. Cohen, 1969). Singer and Balow (1981) report on a 1965 study on black reading achievement in Riverside, California, where schools are integrated. At Grade 1, black reading achievement was only slightly lower than white achievement; at Grade 6, it was two grades below the norm, whereas white achievement was slightly ahead of the norm.

To minimize the assumed interference between BE and SE, some educators advocate using BE-based readers initially. Thus Stewart (1969) would introduce SE in three stages:

1. pure BE—*Darryl and Kevin, dey runnin.*
2. one SE feature—*Darryl and Kevin, dey are runnin.*
3. full SE—*Darryl and Kevin are running.*

Such practices have dubious value. Young SE speakers' utterances also differ from SE by being "telegraphic": "What doing?" or "Baby high chair." No sensible educator would imitate such utterances in reading materials for preschoolers. For one thing, preschoolers can understand full sentences, if they are simple; for another, they may develop the use of inflectional endings and function words through early reading of full sentences.

Other educators advocate reading standard materials in BE, or training in SE before learning to read, or using the language-experience approach. All strive to move the black children toward fluency in reading SE, but at different rates and through different routes. The compelling reason for teaching BE speakers to read SE from the beginning is that there is hardly any reading materials in BE, but there is a vast amount in SE.

Do research findings justify these educational alternatives? One study shows that black children are not sensitive to certain syntactic markers: They understood *When I passed by, I read the posters* as being in the past tense less than half the time (Labov, 1970). But another study shows that Grade 3 black children may fail to discriminate certain phonological features auditorily but comprehend as well as white children the same features in oral and silent reading (Melmed, 1971). Still another study shows that training in SE phonology did not affect the reading achievement of black children (Rystrom, 1970). In several studies, Black children from Grades 2 through 4 read BE and SE texts either equally well or read SE texts better than BE versions (e.g., Marwit & Newman, 1974; Nolan, 1972).

The evidence of BE interference in reading remains equivocal, and the educational alternatives considered earlier are premature, according to four critical reviews (Hall & Guthrie, 1980; Harber & Bryen, 1976; Shuy, 1979; Simons, 1979). In any case, today black children watch the same children's TV programs that white children watch, and hence they are likely to understand SE quite well. One black preschooler, aged 4, in a working-class home, picked up reading all by himself from TV commercials. He spoke BE but read books in SE without trouble (Torrey, 1969). Perhaps because of the equalizing effect of TV and for other reasons, three National Assessments of Reading between 1970 and 1980 show that the largest gain was made by 9-year-old black pupils (E. B. Fry, 1981). One thing is certain: Teachers of black children should be aware of differences between BE and SE and be sympathetic to BE speakers.

The United States is not the only country where languages used in reading and speaking can differ. In China, Switzerland, England, and many other countries, children who speak dialects must learn the standard language along with reading; in fact, reading is the main vehicle through which the standard language is learned. In China, a dialect and the standard language can differ much more than do BE and SE in the United States. In Canada, Walker's (1975) Grade 3 children who speak the Newfoundland dialect could read standard English texts faster with fewer errors than texts in their own dialect.

In some other countries, children learn a new language through reading, as did Korean children during the Japanese occupation. In bilingual countries some children learn to read in two languages. They read none the worse for their language "handicaps." In one long-term (over 7 years) project in Canada, English-speaking children in French immersion classes learned English just as well as did English controls, along with fully functional (though not native-like) French. Furthermore, reading skills transferred between the two languages (Bruck, Lambert, & Tucker, 1977). In these countries, a whole school class switches, usually abruptly, to a new dialect or language. Dialect or native speakers are not necessarily a disadvantaged minority group, as BE or Spanish speakers often are in the United States. In the right home environment, even speaking a minority language is not a handicap. Miño-Garcés's (1981) two early reading sons were native Spanish speakers in the United States who were fluent in their second language, English. He observes: "Early reading seems to be very helpful in second language acquisition [p. 3]."

Summary and Conclusions

Some children learn to read early, before they enter school at around age 6. Early readers tend to come from a home that values reading, even though it may not be high in SES. They tend to be bright and to remain good readers in later life. Most of them pick up reading on their own, with some help from family members. Some preschoolers are taught, usually by their parents, who may use look–say, phonics, or a combination of the two. Initially, reading materials should be easy and gentle and pleasant, and not too high a level of achievement should be expected.

In the United States, a belief persists that children must have attained a certain level of perceptual–cognitive–linguistic skills (equal to a mental age of 6:6) before they can begin to read. As a result, children are denied reading instruction until they can pass readiness tests. Some of these skills, especially verbal ones such as knowledge of letter names, do correlate with later reading achievement, perhaps because common variables underly letter naming and reading. However, positive correlations between the two skills do not justify extended readiness training, which is far less useful than reading itself.

The so-called linguistic awareness is more a by-product of reading than a prerequisite to it. The ability to segment words into phonemes should develop with reading, and does so, especially if the script is an alphabet, and phonics is emphasized. Syllable segmenting is less dependent on reading experience, but it too improves with reading. Learning to read with a syllabary helps a Japanese child to do the sophisticated task of locating a designated syllable in a word.

All normal children acquire speech when raised in a speech environment. They acquire the basics of their native tongue (the sound system, vocabulary, and syntax) by age 6, but acquire the more complex and subtle aspects of their language throughout childhood. Understanding tends to precede production. Beginning reading should parallel children's speech abilities. At the same time, reading can be used to accelerate speech development: Reading makes children aware of linguistic units, but far more importantly, it expands the vocabulary and simple syntax of speech, because both tend to be more varied and complex in printed materials than in speech.

Some children experience a "mismatch" between home language and school language. A mismatch can be between two dialects (e.g., BE and SE), or between two different languages (French and English). A mismatch per se need not be a handicap in learning to read; a mismatch together with low-SES might be.

If you want to teach a child how to read, teach her how to read words and sentences, instead of how to count dots and phonemes.

15

Reading Instruction at School

Once a child has learned to read, she can read to learn.

—Anon

Most children must be instructed in reading, usually at school. Let us now consider several factors that influence reading instruction at school, such as the teacher and method, the materials, and the child.

Teaching Methods

Methods of teaching reading have been contentious among educators and parents throughout the history of school education. A child, if she is bright, learns to read whether she is explicitly taught or not, and whatever the method of teaching. But not all children are bright, and teaching methods differ in relative efficiency. There are several methods, but the two most important ones, look–say and phonics, are the main topics of this chapter. Three other methods—the ABC method, the linguistic approach and the language-experience approach—will be briefly mentioned.

TEACHERS FOR EARLY GRADES

Before getting deeply involved with the highly controversial problem of teaching methods, let us give a quick look at a simpler topic, the teacher. In a cooperative study of reading achievements of Grade 1 children, teachers' experience and efficiency had only slight correlation with pupils' achievements (Bond & Dykstra, 1967). By contrast, Chall (1967), after reviewing 85 studies on teaching methods, concluded: "It was ***what the teacher did*** with the method, the materials, and the children rather than the method itself that seemed to make the difference [p. 270]." Other studies find the teacher to be an important factor in the success of reading instruction (Feitelson, 1973; Gray, 1956). Among children predicted to fail in reading, those taught by competent teachers had a lower rate of failure than those placed in classes of teachers judged to be poor (Jansky & de Hirsch, 1972). The statement, "There are no reading disabilities, just teacher disabilities," may contain a grain of truth.

A successful teacher plays the role of a strong leader. In their study of 100 Grade 1 and 50 Grade 3 classrooms, Stallings and Kaskowitz (1974) recorded what each child in a classroom was doing every 15 min throughout the day. The time spent attending to reading or mathematics yielded higher correlations with achievement than did any of the other activities. Nonacademic activities (e.g., arts and crafts, and reading stories to a group) were negatively correlated with achievement. The use of textbooks, workbooks, and other instructional materials yielded positive correlations with achievement, whereas the use of toys, puzzles, and even academic games always yielded negative correlations.

Effective teaching involves "direct instruction," which refers to academically focused, teacher-directed instruction using structured materials. Teaching goals are clear to pupils, time allocated for instruction is sufficient and continuous, coverage of content is extensive, performance of pupils is monitored, feedback to them is immediate, and questions are easy enough that they can produce many correct responses (Rosenshine, 1979). High-achieving classrooms tend to be convivial, cooperative, democratic, and warm.

Whole-Word Method versus Phonics

As beginners, children learn mostly to recognize words. In Chapter 14 we described preschoolers who were taught to recognize words by the whole-word method, by phonics, or by a combination of the two. In this chapter we describe school children who are taught by these as well as other methods.

WHOLE-WORD OR LOOK–SAY

Five thousand years ago, in the Sumerian schools, learning to read meant memorizing by rote long written lists of words grouped by subject: parts of the body, trees, and so on (Claiborne, 1974). This method, we now believe, emphasizes the RIGHT-track processes of word recognition and of association, which reinforce one another (see Chapter 11). It is probably not too bad a method for its purpose. In the United States, the "word method" appeared in the nineteenth century, as a revolt against teaching nonsense syllables (*ba, be, bi,* etc.). The method spread widely during the second half of the nineteenth century. Since then, it has waxed and waned in popularity.

By the whole-word or look–say method, a child learns to associate the visual pattern of a whole word with its meaning. Learning to read by look–say is easy, because it associates meaning directly to a word, and because it does not require any kind of analysis, especially phonetic analysis, of words. Direct association between words and meanings is the quickest and easiest way for getting the process of reading under way. Naturally enough, this is the method used by most early readers who learn to read largely on their own. It is also the method commonly used by some parents to teach their young children to read (e.g., Söderbergh, 1971; Steinberg & Steinberg, 1975).

By look–say, and by bypassing sounds, even a chimpanzee can learn to read and write (Premack, 1971); language-disabled Japanese preschoolers as young as 1:5 learned to recognize a few hundred Kanji and Kana words and phrases (Rees-Nishio, 1981; Steinberg *et al.*, 1982); reading-disabled American children learned 30 or so Chinese characters (Rozin *et al.*, 1971); mentally retarded adults (mean IQ 37) learned to read 16 logographs, which were simple line drawings (House *et al.*, 1980). Some cerebral palsied children learn logographic Blissymbols in a similar way. At least some of these groups (especially chimpanzees) seem to have a deficient LEFT track, making the RIGHT track whole-word method particularly suitable for them.

PHONICS: ANALYTIC AND SYNTHETIC

In England, John Hart in the sixteenth century advocated a phonics approach that used a consistent phonetic alphabet of his own design. Phonics was eclipsed during the nineteenth century while the pendulum swung to the whole-word method, but in the twentieth century it has made a comeback.

Using the phonics method, children learn letter–sound relations and sound blends so that they can sound out unfamiliar printed words. In "analytic phonics," or top-down, reading starts with sentences and moves down to words and word parts. Since words are learned as whole patterns, the label "analytic phonics" is misleading and confusing. In (synthetic) phonics, or bottom-up, individual sounds are associated with letters; the sounds are built into blends and syllables, which are then built into words. The sounds of individual letters are learned by rote memorization, but words are sounded out by letter–sound correspondence rules. Some preschoolers have been taught by synthetic phonics (Ledson, 1975; Williams, 1982; Chapter 14).

Writing Systems and Teaching Methods

In choosing a teaching method, one should examine the writing system to be taught: One teaching method is suitable for one writing system, another method for another system. First we briefly review teaching methods in Chinese, Japanese, and Korean. Then, we shall consider reading instruction in a few different alphabetic writing systems. All alphabets have a limited number of simple letters, between 20 and 50, but they differ in their degree of grapheme–phoneme correspondence. English is low in correspondence, whereas Finnish, German, and Hebrew are high.

CHINESE, JAPANESE, AND KOREAN

The whole visual pattern of a Chinese character is associated with its meaning (morpheme) and sound (syllable), whether the language is Chinese, Japanese, or Korean. Since a character does not code a sound directly, its sound is learned with the aid of added phonetic symbols. In writing, though perhaps not in reading, a character is analyzed into an ordered set of strokes (it is written stroke by stroke in a prescribed order.)

Children in all these Oriental countries seem to learn characters in three phases: In the first phase, they learn a handful of characters as wholes; in the second, they confuse characters that share a common subpart; and in the third, they make the correct associations between the assemblage of strokes and the character's sound and meaning, based on more secure knowledge of subparts. In mainland China, during the 5 or 6 years of primary and the 5 years of middle school, a child learns about 5000 characters.

In Japan, each Kana as a whole pattern is associated with its unique sound, a whole syllable, without having to analyze it into phonemes and without having to blend it with other Kana sounds. During the 6 years of primary school plus the 6 years of middle and high school, a child learns 106 Hiragana, 106 Katakana, and 2000 Kanji.

In Korean, each Hangul syllable-block as a whole pattern can be associated with its unique syllable; at the same time, the syllable-block itself can be analyzed into its constituent phonemes. A child learns about 2000 types of syllable-blocks, most of them by induction. During the 6 years of primary school, a child learns and uses only Hangul; later, during the 6 years of middle and high school, she learns 1800 Kanji.

In these three languages, at least three facts make initial learning easy: The unit of writing system is the stable syllable; sign–sound correspondence is regular when it exists; and meaning can often be associated to a single sign. But learning to read and write thousands of Chinese characters takes time and constant practice.

ENGLISH ORTHOGRAPHY

Children can discover letter–sound relations even when taught by look–say, and they have to learn common irregular words by look–say even when basically taught by phonics. A combination of look–say and phonics is the most suitable strategy for English, as half of its common words are regular and half are irregular (see Chapter 6).

In regular words, each letter represents the sound most commonly associated with it. Regular words such as *mat* and *log* can be easily learned by phonics, and once phonics is mastered, new words with a similar sound structure, such as *rat* and *fog,* can be sounded out with assurance. Each of these short words, though originally learned by phonics, may eventually come to be recognized as a whole visual pattern if it occurs frequently enough.

For irregular words such as *a, of, the, are, come* and *laugh,* letter–sound relations are not much help. The linguist Bloomfield advocated that teaching irregular words be postponed until many regular words have been taught (Bloomfield & Barnhart, 1961). Because many of the most common words are irregular, sentences built using only regular words will be stilted, containing infrequent words (e.g., *Can Sam tag Pam?*). Stories will be worse, as we shall see. Why not teach common irregular words by look–say? Because common words will be recognized as whole words later in life, it would probably be better to start them that way.

Learning to decode words in English is hard and takes time. In the United States, up to Grade 3 or 4, most school children are learning decoding techniques. The ability to apply letter–sound generalizations continues to develop at least through Grade 8 (Calfee, Venezky, & Chapman, 1969). The difficulties of word decoding also produce some reading casualties, as documented in Chapter 16.

INITIAL TEACHING ALPHABET

To help beginning readers, several educators have devised modifications of English printing (e.g., E. B. Fry, 1964; Laubach, 1962). Sir James Pitman developed the best-known modification, the initial teaching alphabet (i.t.a.), in the early 1960s (see Chapter 6 for its history). It has been tested widely in Britain, and to less extent in other English-speaking countries such as the United States, Canada, New Zealand, and Australia.

Using i.t.a., the child's learning centers on associating a sound with its letter. Not only phonics but also writing is stressed. Advocates of i.t.a., such as Downing (1967, 1973), claim that by the end of one year, the great majority of children easily transfer to traditional orthography (t.o.) at a level of reading comprehension far beyond that possible with a traditional basal series. Furthermore, they claim that there are only half as many poor readers in the i.t.a. groups as there are in the t.o. group. According to Gasper and Brown (1973), i.t.a. is beneficial to a child in two ways: in forming a positive attitude toward reading, and in developing vocabulary.

In England, Thackray (1971) reports that after 3 years of instruction, i.t.a. groups were superior to t.o. groups in oral reading but not in comprehension. In the United States, too, i.t.a. groups were superior to t.o. groups only in the initial stage of reading, and only in specific word-decoding skills, such as word reading and spelling in i.t.a. (Gillooly, 1973). These results are to be expected, since i.t.a. can affect only the phonological coding aspects of the LEFT track of the BLC model, not the semantic processes of the RIGHT track (see Chapter 11). Learning by i.t.a. may, after transfer to t.o., cause minor problems for the RIGHT track in its attempts to recognize words using their whole visual patterns.

GERMAN

Among the languages closely related to English, German has a relatively regular orthography. One letter or letter cluster tends to have one consistent sound, even though any particular sound may be represented by a few different letters or letter clusters (e.g., /f/ by 'f, ff, v'). Thanks to a high degree of letter–sound correspondence, German children make only one fifth as many mistakes on vowels when reading word lists as do their American counterparts.

School starts at age 6. The popular teaching method is "analytic" method (global, whole-word), which begins with a short story. Teaching proceeds in three overlapping stages:

1. Primitive global, sight reading of a limited number of words (about 80).
2. Analysis of the words by noting similar letters and sounds, until children learn all common letters and their sounds.
3. In synthesis, a word once broken into letters and syllables is built up again. By changing one letter in a known word, a set of new words (*h-and, s-and, l-and,* etc.) are learned.

During the first stage, the children might learn a poem like this:

Drei Rosen im Garten	'Three roses in the garden
drei Tannen im Wald	three firs in the wood
im Sommer ists lustig	in summer it is lovely
im Winter ists kalt.	in winter it is cold.'

All these processes are done in meaningful context, not as a drill of isolated letters and letter combinations. The cycle of story–sentence–phrase–word–syllable–letter sound (analytic part) and back (synthetic part) is repeated within every unit, which may last 1–3 weeks. Programmed exercises are parts of the units.

Within the first 1 or 2 years using this method, German children learn to read completely new texts with only a few known words, because they have learned both to analyze the sounds and to extract meanings. The method roughly corresponds to "Three-Phased Learning," discussed later in this chapter. Illiteracy in Germany is low, below 1%. (Based on Biglmaier, 1964, 1973.)

FINNISH

Finnish belongs to the Finno-Ugric language group, but it uses the Roman alphabet, as do most Indo-European languages. The Finnish script uses 13 consonant letters, 8 vowels, 16 diphthongs, and in some loan words, 6 foreign letters. All consonant and vowel letters have unique sounds, and the letter names of the vowels are identical with their sounds. Writing was cultivated properly in the sixteenth century, and spelling was standardized around the nineteenth century. Perhaps because of this late development of writing and the small proportion of foreign words, sounds correspond closely to their orthographic representations.

School in Finland starts at age 7, but before entering school, most children pick up some basic reading skills at home. About 15% of school entrants are able to read well enough to go straight into Grade 2. (In the United States, the corresponding number is 1–4%; see "Early Readers" in Chapter 14.) The order of formal teaching is: letter names, sounds of the letters, syllables, words, and sentences. The letters are learned approximately in the order of their frequency. The children learn long vowels, doubled consonants, and consonantal gradation in inflective forms (*lakki–lakin* [nominative–genitive]). The advantage of regular orthography is perhaps greater for spelling than for reading. Spelling errors, as revealed in dictation tests, are usually on foreign consonants, doubled consonants, and letters omitted at the end of words.

In sum, because of near-perfect letter–sound correspondence, word decoding is learned rapidly using phonics. At the end of Grade 1, children can read nearly any word, real or nonsense. (Based on Kyöstiö, 1980; Venezky, 1973).

HEBREW IN ISRAEL

Hebrew has a unique problem: For many children it is neither the language spoken at home nor the language in which the children's parents received their education.

Hebrew is a Semitic language, and its script is a non-Roman alphabet, though, like the Roman alphabet, it descended from the ancient Semitic syllabary. It has 31 symbols, consisting of 22 basic consonants and 9 vowels. At the end of a word, 5 consonants change form, and 3 change sound, depending on the presence or absence of a dot. A single dot can signal 7 different vowels. In reading, consonants usually precede the vowels written below them. The writing direction is from right to left.

Letter-to-sound correspondence is highly consistent, whereas the sound-to-letter correspondence is much less so. Many sounds are represented in more than one way, analogous to English 'f' and 'ph'. Spelling is therefore more of a problem than word decoding. Vowels are either omitted or, being small, are "tucked away" beneath consonants. The "invisible" vowels cause problems to beginning readers, who are largely unaware of the modifying effects of vowels. In a reading-aloud test at the end of Grade 1, vowel errors were more frequent than any other kind. (For adults, however, the presence or absence of the vowel signs does not seem to affect the latency for pronunciation, Navon & Shimron, 1981).

Of the 22 consonants, 20 are squarish, disconnected, and of uniform height. There are no capital, ascending or descending letters, and hence all words have much the same outer shape apart from their length. Both noun and verb forms of a word are derived from the same basic set of consonants, and clusters of numerous words are just slightly changed forms of one another. Minor differences between letters—quite often no more than the location of a single dot—are significant, requiring attention to minute details.

Obviously, learning words by their shapes is inefficient for the Hebrew system. After the 1950s, when a large influx of immigrants came into Israel from Arab countries, schools began to report failure rates of 50% at the end of Grade 1. An entire classroom would be either successful or unsuccessful in acquiring reading skills. The successful classrooms had teachers who used phonics rather than a wholistic approach (reading in phrase units). Some parents helped their children overcome the harmful effect of a teacher's wholistic approach by teaching phonics at home.

In Hebrew, we see a writing system that is beset with numerous difficulties for a beginning reader even though it has a highly consistent letter–sound correspondence. (Based on Feitelson, 1973, 1980).

Other Teaching Methods

ABC OR ALPHABETIC METHOD

One of the oldest teaching methods is the ABC or **alphabetic method** practiced in ancient Greece and Rome. By this method, a child spells a word by naming the letters and then pronounces the word. Thus, "see-ai-tee" is *cat*. The first sentence in Webster's old spelling book reads: *No man may put off the law of God.* It was taught as follows: "En-o no, emm-ai-en man, emm-ai-wy may, pee-you-tee put, o-double-eff off, tee-aitch-ee the, ell-ai-double you, law, o-eff of, gee-o-dee God [Fernald, 1943]."

As Anderson and Dearborn (1952) point out, the whole word is lost to sight in the maze of the individual letters. Children taught by this method may eventually become accurate word callers, but meaning suffers, learning is slowed, and the fun of reading is spoiled. The alphabet method actually keeps words from the child. What do parents do to keep information from their child? Why, they spell out words they do not want him to understand!

LINGUISTIC APPROACH

Several noted linguists have definite ideas about how reading should be taught. They oppose the whole-word method, and at the same time, oppose teaching isolated letter–sound relations. Instead, they advocate using the **linguistic approach,** which teaches the sounds of letters indirectly, via words of the same sounds and spelling patterns. For example, Lesson 1 of Bloomfield and Barnhart's (1961) *Let's Read* teaches *can, Dan, fan, man, Nan, pan* and *van,* all words that fall into the pattern C-*an*,, regardless of their frequency of occurrence. The "story" using these words reads as follows:

Nan can fan Dan.
Can Dan fan Nan?
Dan can fan Nan.
Nan, fan Dan.
Dan, fan Nan.

The linguist Fries (1963) would have the children discover the print-to-speech code by presenting them with contrasting, rather than the same, spelling patterns, illustrated by the following word groups:

dan	*dane*	*dean*
ban	*bane*	*bean*
hat	*hate*	*heat*
fat	*fate*	*feat*

The linguistic approach has serious weaknesses: It neglects irregularly spelled words, which happen to be very common and indispensable for writing interesting and idiomatic sentences and stories. It withholds such valuable clues to word recognition as word length. It goes against a psychological principle as well: Sentences with similar sounding words are hard to read and are easily confused in short-term memory, in both alphabetic (English) and logographic (Chinese) writing systems (see Chapter 10). Read the "Nan can fan Dan" story once more, and try to recall it. This kind of story turns out to be difficult, not to mention boring.

Teaching sounds by word families is impractical when used all by itself, but it can be valuable when used along with other methods. In fact, the induction method which forms the basis of the linguistic approach is incorporated into many beginning reading programs.

LANGUAGE-EXPERIENCE APPROACH

In the **language-experience approach,** the teacher asks a child what words and stories she wants to learn and then transcribes them (Ashton-Warner, 1963; Stauffer, 1970). The approach advocates a close relation among experiencing life, reading, speaking, writing, and listening. Since the words and stories are what the child supplied, she is highly interested in seeing them printed and studied. For the child, the words are very meaningful and hence richly associative for whole-word reading. Naturally she learns them readily.

A negative aspect is that the children tend to supply colorful but uncommon words (*frightened, icecapade, knife*) rather than bland but useful words (*man, see*). The infrequent and irregular words children supply are not the most suitable for teaching letter–sound relations. Unless the teacher carefully keeps track of the material supplied by the children, the vocabulary may become unsystematic and lopsided. However, the exotic words will be few relative to the total number of words in the stories, and they can be supplemented by adding words that fill important gaps. The extra interest generated by the personal words may more than compensate for the problems they cause. Perhaps future computers may be able to produce on demand personalized stories using words supplied by the children.

In Ontario, Canada, current teaching uses topical words interesting to the children along with a core vocabulary. The children are not expected to remember the topical words beyond their time of interest, but they keep practicing the core vocabulary.

Teaching Materials

The teaching materials are inextricably intertwined with teaching methods, as they are selected and sequenced according to the teaching method and philosophy of their authors.

Basal Series

USE OF BASAL SERIES

Graded **basal series** form the core of reading instruction at school. The use of basal series differs from country to country: Some countries, such as France, have no basal series; others, such as East Germany, have one official series; yet others, including West Germany and the United States, have several series (Malmquist, 1975). In Far East, South Korea and Taiwan each has one series, whereas Japan has several. In the United States, over 90% of primary teachers and 80% of intermediate-grade teachers use basal series (e.g., Aukerman, 1981; Austin & Morrison, 1963; Barton & Wilder, 1964; Spache & Spache, 1977).

The first basal series in the United States was prepared by Noah Webster in 1790; it sold millions of copies before it was replaced by later series. The McGuffey series (1840–1920) controlled the difficulty of successive books by controlling word length. The contents were moralistic and patriotic with little relation to children's life experience. Throughout the 1950s and early 1960s, basal series in the United States tended to be of similarly low quality. They tended to be stilted and unrelated to the language spoken by the children. Phonics was neglected. (Apparently, the McGuffey series is coming back in certain parts of the United States; its moral rather than its reading lessons appeal to parents.)

Basal series have improved vastly since then. Today, they may consist of readers, workbooks, story books, audio-cassettes, and filmstrips for children, as well as manuals for teachers. They use advanced knowledge in typography, format, illustration, and readability. They provide a well-rounded selection of reading experiences, including both poetry and prose, factual and fictional matters, and multiracial and multicultural contents. They no longer show blatant bias against girls. They are eclectic in freely adopting any method or material.

Used with flexibility and skill, the basal series provide convenient and useful tools for teachers, who can:

- Emphasize both oral and silent reading
- Respond to individual differences by letting advanced readers occupy themselves with supplementary material
- Use children's workbooks as testing and diagnosing instruments
- Ask varied interesting questions on the pictures in preprimers and primers

- Foster comprehension skills by letting children select captions for stories, recall sequences of events, anticipate events, draw inferences, or follow directions

PRIMERS AND GRADE 1 READERS

In the United States, basal series are graded as follows. Readiness books start with picture books that can be developed into a child-centered story, and include other books that are designed to train the children in the kinds of perceptual, cognitive, and linguistic skills tapped by the readiness tests described in Chapter 14. Preprimers introduce pupils to printed words along with pictures. Typically 20–25 different words are introduced and repeated in each of 3 to 4 preprimers in a given series. Primers are the first hardback books in the series. They introduce 100–150 new words, using the same story characters the children met in the earlier books.

Basal readers have often been criticized for their bland, contrived contents, with empty sentences and endless repetitions of the same few words. Their writing tends to be more redundant than that found in the free-reading choices of children (Jones & Carterette, 1963). Bettelheim and Zelan (1982) observe: "Such texts do indeed confirm children in not wanting to read, because nobody in his right mind would want to learn to read in order to be able to read such stupid stories [p. 266]." By contrast, Aukerman (1981), who examined 15 recent basal series, extols their virtues: "Most basals provide a beautiful, varied, and interesting collection of reading materials, unequalled anywhere else in the world [p. 12]!"

Both observations may be right, except that each applies to a different kind of material. Judge for yourself the following two selections, the left one from Allyn and Bacon's *Pathfinder* (1977; Level 6), and the right one, "The Seasons" by Robert Louis Stevenson, from *Holt Basic Reading* (1980; Level 2, in the teachers' edition). The poem teaches the initial /s/ and /f/.

Help Matt.
Help Nat and Nan.
Help the man.
I am Matt.
I am Nat.
And I am Nan.

Sing a song of seasons,
Something bright in all,
Flowers in the summer,
Fires in the fall.

In many countries outside the United States, reading instruction starts earnestly with Grade 1 readers, not pussyfooting around with readiness books and preprimers. Most of them introduce a large number of words early. For example, in South Korea 400 words are taught in just the first half of Grade 1. In the Soviet Union even the first-grade reader contains stories by Tolstoy, because by the end of Grade 1, the vocabulary includes 2000 words (Bettelheim & Zelan, 1982).

In the United States, the several basal series published between 1972 and

1974 averaged over 500 words, up to and including the Grade 1 reader; in 1965, they had averaged 324 words (Barnard & DeGracie, 1976). According to Bond and Dykstra (1967), programs that introduced words at a rapid pace produced children with superior word recognition at the end of Grade 1. The speaking vocabulary of first graders may be as many as 5000 words (Rinsland, 1945), which is ten times the vocabulary in their reading material. If only the children could sound these words out, they could recognize their meanings. How well do words in basal readers reflect children's vocabulary? The average level of agreement between a sight-word vocabulary list based on speech produced by children (Grades 1–3) and six basal programs was 89% for function words but only 49% for content words. On the other hand, agreement among four lists of children's speech vocabularies (produced by four SES groups in Toronto) was high: 94% for function words and 76% for content words (Reich & Reich, 1979). These lists could be used to construct a sight vocabulary for widespread usage.

Grade 1 basal series differ widely in the way they introduce new words (Willows, Borwick, & Hayvren, 1981). *The Merrill Linguistic Reading Program* (1975) introduces only 290 new words, with on average 44 repetitions per word, whereas Holt's *Language Patterns* (1976) introduces 1011 words, with 12 repetitions per word. Merrill and Ginn's *Starting Points in Language Arts* (1976) starts with easy material and progresses in difficulty over the year, whereas Holt and Scott Foresman's *Basics in Reading* (1978) both use difficult material throughout the first year.

CODE- OR MEANING-EMPHASIS

Fifteen years ago Chall (1967) could categorize basal programs into two approaches. **Code emphasis,** under which phonics and the linguistic method fall, starts by teaching the printed code for the spoken language. It emphasizes word decoding more than it does story comprehension. **Meaning emphasis,** under which the whole-word method and the language-experience method fall, starts with story reading; it teaches words as wholes in the context of stories. It emphasizes comprehension of text more than it does word decoding.

Beck (1981) compared four code-emphasis programs with four meaning-emphasis ones (top four rows in Table 15-1), and Popp (1979) compared in depth one meaning-emphasis program with one code-emphasis one (bottom row).

Table 15-1 *Basal Series Grouped by their Approaches*

Code emphasis	Meaning emphasis
Palo Alto (1973)	Ginn Reading 720 (1976)
Distar I and II (1974)	Houghton Mifflin Linguistic (1976)
Programmed Reading (1973)	Bank Street Readers (1973)
Merril Linguistic (1975)	New Open Highways (1974)
New Reading System (1974)	Reading Unlimited (1976)

The contents and sequences of the two approaches differ as follows.

1. Letter naming: Letter-name instruction occurs in Grade 1 in all the eight programs examined by Beck, except in Distar, in which it occurs in Grade 2. No programs go overboard in letter-name instruction.
2. Isolating a phoneme versus inducing it from words: Code-emphasis programs teach the sounds of individual letters by telling a child that the letter 'e' makes the sound /e/ (see "Phonic Blending" below). Sometimes only the teacher, but not the child, pronounces a sound in isolation. The linguistic program and some meaning-emphasis programs do not make a child pronounce the sound of an isolated letter; instead, they let the child induce letter–sound relations by presenting them with a set of words that share the sound patterns. Or, they might tell the child that 'e' in *get* is the short /e/ vowel sound.
3. Phonic blending: In Distar, the child says the sounds in an extended manner—/iiifff/ and then synthesizes these extended phonemes into the word *if*. In *New Reading System's* "successive blending," the children are taught explicitly to produce /s/, /æ/ → /sæ/; /sæ/, /t/ → /sæt/; ending with the final decoding of *sat*. Palo Alto provides each child with many opportunities to manipulate letters and to read the resulting word (*him, ham; ham, Sam*). Meaning programs do not emphasize blending.
4. Decodable words: Code-emphasis programs use a high percentage of decodable words that can be sounded out using the letter–sound relations already learned. The mean percentage of decodable words in the first third of Grade 1 is .85 (range .69–1.00) in the four code-emphasis programs; it is only .04 (range 0–.13) in the four meaning-emphasis programs. In meaning-emphasis programs, words are learned because they occur in the stories read in the classroom, not because they are highly decodable. The words learned tend to be high-frequency, low-decodable words: *funny, face, the, Mother, look, in, mirror, make, a* and *Father* (Willows *et al.*, 1981). Initially, words may be recognized with the aid of contextual and picture cues. Both types of programs teach some common irregular words as sight words.
5. Sentence and story reading: In code-emphasis programs, phonics is taught before story reading. Words learned by phonics are used in progressively larger units, such as phrases and then sentences. In *New Reading System,* all children at the end of Grade 1 are expected to be able to read Read-Alone stories that contain restricted vocabulary and controlled sentence structures. In meaning-emphasis programs story reading occurs before letter–sound relations. For example, in *Reading Unlimited* the teacher tells a story while children follow pictures in their books. At first, she asks questions whose answers can be guessed from the pictures, but later she asks questions whose answers must be

"read," using plenty of cues. Stories tend to be more interesting in meaning- than in code-emphasis programs.

6. Writing: The sensorimotor task of writing may serve to focus attention on the shape of the letter being taught. In general, more time is spent on writing in the code-emphasis programs than in the meaning-emphasis programs.
7. Pronunciation rules: In certain code-emphasis programs children may be taught pronunciation rules such as—when they see the letter 'e' followed by one or more consonant letters, they should respond with the short /e/.

Beck considers teaching pronunciation rules to be a "worthless" practice. What may be worthless is memorizing rules parrot-fashion; what may be useful is learning some high-utility rules with many examples. According to Clymer (1963), rules vary in usefulness. An example of a useful rule is that words with double 'ee' have the sound /i:/—85 words (*seem*) confirm to the rule, and 2 words (*been*) do not, making the utility of the rule 97% (even *been* conforms in many dialects of English). An example of a low utility rule: When 'y' is the final letter, it has the sound of /ai/—29 words (*fly*) confirm to the rule, 170 (*funny*) do not, making the utility of this rule 15%.

In considering the utility of a rule, overall frequency may be taken into account. For example, 14 out of 19 words with 'ich' are pronounced as in *which* (versus *cliches*), giving the rule 74% utility. In sheer frequency, however, the consistency is 3636 out of 3770 occurrences (giving a utility of 99%), because the word *which* accounts for 94% of the occurrence of 'ich' in running text (Caldwell, Roth, & Turner, 1978).

Teaching Methods: Continuing Debates

Though most reading researchers and theorists support an eclectic approach, some advocate using exclusively one or the other teaching method or program.

CODE- VERSUS MEANING-EMPHASIS: DEBATE

In Chall's (1967) survey, the code-emphasis approach tended to be more effective than the meaning-emphasis approach, at least through Grade 3. Both Popp (1979) and Chall (1979) found a stronger decoding emphasis in basal programs produced since 1967. A code-emphasis program seems effective particularly with at-risk children: A 4-year evaluation in five communities shows that Distar has raised the average achievement of low-SES children to the level of their middle-SES peers (Stebbins, St. Pierre, Proper, Anderson, & Cerva, 1977).

According to its supporters, code-emphasis teaches word recognition effectively, and does so without impairing comprehension, on the one hand;

meaning-emphasis does not teach word recognition effectively and does not necessarily produce better comprehension than does code-emphasis, on the other (e.g., Beck, 1981; Resnick, 1978; Williams, 1978). The meaning-emphasis programs seem to teach phonics too late, too little, or too unsystematically, whereas the code-emphasis program seems to sacrifice the quality of the early stories and sentences in their effort to include mostly decodable words. The two approaches may have to get closer to each other, perhaps until there is only one approach. In fact, many basal series in the United States use an eclectic approach that takes the best from various methods (Aukerman, 1981).

WHOLE-WORD VERSUS PHONICS: DEBATE

Some educators and researchers advocate using only the whole-word method, pointing out that mature readers get meanings directly from whole words, and children must emulate them (e.g., Goodman, 1973; Smith, 1978; Steinberg & Steinberg, 1980). They claim that memorizing a large number of words by their shapes is no more a burden than memorizing them by their sounds in speech. English letter–sound relations are either too irregular or too irrelevant to be learned, and to the extent that letter–sound relations are relevant, children can induce them spontaneously. While children are figuring out the sounds of a word, they may lose track of its meaning. As a result, early and extended drill in phonics may cause children to lose interest in reading.

Other educators and researchers emphasize the necessity of phonics (e.g., Chall, 1979; Coleman, 1970; Flesch, 1981, Gleitman & Rozin, 1973). Their argument runs roughly like this: Look–say has several limitations when it is used exclusively to teach full-scale reading to a normal child beyond the initial stages. A normal child must learn several thousand words to become an accomplished reader. Since look–say relies on rote memorization of word shapes, adding a new word becomes increasingly difficult as the number of words to be learned increases; a new word looks like too many old words: *come, came, cone, cane.*

Word recognition is haphazard. There is a story about a child who had learned to read *chicken* on a flash card, but could not later recognize it in a book. Asked how he recognized it on the flash card, he replied, "By the smudge over in the corner." Look–say is a RIGHT-track process, which looks for whole patterns, including irrelevant but consistent marks. The moral of this story is not that flash cards are useless, but that they should be used with care. Several different ones, preferably in different type fonts, should be used for each word, in order to promote correct generalization to other stimuli.

With look–say some children are likely to be left helpless for a time when confronted by new words. There is little opportunity for transfer from familiar to unfamiliar words, since words are not formally analyzed into useful parts. Look–say "wastes" the sound-coding property of alphabetic writing. After all, about one half of the common words of English can be sounded out using regular letter–sound relations. Even irregular words can be partially sounded out, as they are bound to contain one or two consonant letters with regular sounds.

Phonics is necessary for secure decoding of many new words. And it cannot be left entirely to children to induce by themselves, for not all children are bright and not all materials are optimal for induction.

PHONICS VERSUS WHOLE WORD: RESEARCH

Which is the better teaching method, phonics or whole-word? The question has been debated for at least 4 centuries and put to numerous experiments in the present century. Results from classroom experiments are mixed, as might be expected, considering the many variables that are involved—writing systems, teachers, children, materials, and so on.

For recognizing words, especially new words, phonics has been found to produce better results at the end of Grade 1 (e.g., Bond & Dykstra, 1967; Katz & Singer, 1976). Disadvantaged children seem to benefit most from phonics (Stebbins *et al.*, 1977). In summarizing 60 years of research on beginning reading, Dykstra (1974) observes that early systematic instruction in phonics provides a child with the skills necessary to become an independent reader at an early age. At school, Grade 1 children taught for some months exclusively by the whole-word method show some skill in word decoding, but far less than those who are taught by phonics (Alegria *et al.*, 1982; Noh, 1975). Left alone, or even with teaching, some children never learn to decode words (Chapter 16).

For 6 months Barr (1975) observed Grade 1 children, one half of whom were taught by phonics and the other half by the whole-word method. For the phonics group, oral reading errors tended to come from their speaking vocabulary, or to be nonsense words sharing sounds with the correct words, whereas substitution errors were influenced by graphic cues. For the whole-word group, errors tended to come from the set of words taught at the same time. Similar findings were reported by Noh (1975) with Korean children learning to read in Hangul (see Chapter 5).

Laboratory experiments have their own shortcomings. Bishop (1964) and Jeffrey and Samuels (1967) trained subjects either by phonics or by whole-word to read a list of words written with novel letters. In a transfer task, the subjects were then taught to read a new list of words composed of the same novel letters as were used in the training task. Phonics, but not whole-word, training resulted in positive transfer. But would one expect transfer using the whole-word method in such an experiment?

Baron (1977) and Brooks (1977) taught adult subjects to associate spoken responses with strings of printed symbols from an artificial alphabet. In the "orthographic" condition, the symbols could be related to the responses using grapheme–phoneme correspondence rules, whereas in the paired-associate condition, the symbols were related arbitrarily to the responses. After 400 practice trials with the artificial words, the words in the orthography condition were read faster than the words in the paired-associate condition. Even after extensive practice, response times were influenced by the possibility of using grapheme–phoneme correspondence rules. Similarly, Spring (1978) found that over a long series of trials, pronouncing latencies for the phonics condition were shorter than for the whole-word condition, even though the rates at which the latencies declined over trials were similar for the two groups.

In all of these studies, a small number of artificial letters was used. For the phonics condition, letter–sound correspondence was perfect, thus facilitating learning and transfer; for the whole-word condition, all words had the same length, thus eliminating one of the effective cues for word recognition. As well, the response measures involved only pronunciation—either accuracy or time—and not meaning. These are precisely the conditions for which whole-word recognition is least useful (see Chapters 9 and 11).

Muter and Johns (1983) studied how well English-speaking college students recognize the meanings of up to 200 individual words written in Chinese characters and Blissymbols (by look–say), and Devanagari words and Esperanto words (by phonics). The meanings of logographs were recognized faster and more accurately than were those of aplphabetic words. It is likely, however, that learning by phonics an alphabetic orthography with regular letter–sound relations would confer a long-term advantage for vocabularies of thousands of words, and that look–say would be more and more difficult as thousands of logographs are learned.

The relative advantage of look–say and phonics in laboratory experiments depends on the kind of material and task, and hence the findings have little practical value to teachers of real writing systems.

THREE-PHASED LEARNING

The BLC model suggests that the learning sequence should have three phases: Learn a handful of words by their whole visual shapes (RIGHT whole-word recognition based on visual features); learn to analyze words into their parts (LEFT analysis); learn once more to recognize the wholes, based on the securer knowledge of parts (RIGHT whole word based on letter identities). Chinese children learn characters in the three phases, Swedish- and English-speaking preschoolers pick up reading in the three phases, and German children are taught to read at school in the three phases. School children in the United States are often taught by an eclectic approach mixing whole-word with phonics.

Three-phased learning applies not only to words, but also to letters and to higher units of reading such as phrases, paragraphs, and whole texts. At the letter level, the child learns several letters by their gross shapes; then she notes the same and different features (configurational or fragmental) in the letters; and in the third phase she recognizes the whole letters again, now based on secure knowledge of the features.

At the word level, teach a child a handful of words by look–say, ensuring that the vocabulary contains enough words with letters in common that the child can begin the analysis procedure. When the child notices that there is something similar between *cat* and *hat*, the analysis procedure should be encouraged, while at the same time, more look–say words are introduced to teach other letter–sound relations. By this means, the children develop both analytic and wholistic routes to word recognition. As fluent readers, they will read a familiar word as a whole visual pattern, and an unfamiliar word by phonetic analysis.

At the passage level, the child already knows from speech something about elementary syntax and semantic associations among words, so that reading presents few problems of a new kind. But the syntax of writing can be more complex than that of speech, requiring a repeat of the same kind of three-phased learning. The three phases here are simple exposure to written syntax, its analysis into constituents, and the direct recognition of how words in common patterns fit together.

Three-phased learning will happen no matter what a teacher does, but the teacher can encourage all three of the phases. At all levels, the analytic second phase is probably the one that can benefit most from formal training; the first phase requires exposure and practice; and the third phase will follow the second automatically. If our observation is true, teachers should concentrate their efforts on phonetic word analysis, syntax, and story structure, but should allow the children to practice whole-word recognition, association, and story reading.

Effective learning requires not only the development of the analytic-phonetic LEFT track and the wholistic-associative RIGHT track but also their full integration.

Cost–Benefit Analysis of Beginning Materials

Suppose one wanted to teach an English-speaking child to read using synthetic phonics: What are the optimal materials? They have to be easy and at the same time useful. For the past 15 years, Coleman and his students have calibrated reading materials for beginners, based on cost–benefit analysis. Let us say that cost is the difficulty of learning the unit; benefit is the frequency of using it.

LETTER–SOUND RELATIONS: COST MEASURES

To calibrate the letters according to the cost of learning to pronounce them, Coleman (1970) had preschoolers learn the most common sound of each letter or digraph. He then rank ordered the letters according to one measure of cost, mean errors to mastery: 's, ie, oe, oy, z, sh, oo, ow, j, m, k, ae, ee, th, p, f, l, ch, h, ue, r, g, v, w, n, b, d, t, o, y, a, u, e, i, aw'. The last letter–sound relation in the list, 'aw', costs more than seven times as many errors as the first, 's'. The difficult items are the short Vs and stop Cs, the easiest ones, the sibilant Cs and long Vs.

For school children (Grades 1–3), both for letter-to-sound and for sound-to-letter relations, the easiest items were long vowel sounds whose letter names are identical with their common sounds ('o, i'); consonants with which only one sound is associated; and the short /a/ sound, which by itself can be a word. The most difficult letter-to-sound relations were the short vowels and the three consonants ('c, g, x') that have two or three sounds (Hardy, Smythe, & Stennett, 1972).

The sequences of letter–sound relations taught at school do not appear to follow the sequences of difficulty found by either study. For example, the sequence taught up to the beginning Grade 2 of *Reading Unlimited Program* (meaning-emphasis) is basically Cs before Vs, and single letters before digraphs. Here are some examples of the letter–sounds taught early: initial Cs ('b, t, f'); C clusters ('br, fl'); Cs with common and uncommon sounds ('c, g'); single Vs with a few different sounds ('a, e, o, i'); V digraphs ('ow, oo').

In *New Reading System* (code-emphasis), Cs, Vs, and "patterns" are intermixed. But a letter's uncommon sounds seem to be taught later than its common sound. The sequence is: the commonest sound of Cs ('c, t') and of Vs ('a', 'e'); initial and final patterns ('ed, ing'); doubled Cs ('ff, tt'), C digraphs coding one sound ('ch, kn'). 'G' in *giant* or 'ow' in *brown* appear later than the above items, in the middle of Grade 2. (For the full list, see Popp, 1979, Table 10.3.)

PHONIC BLENDS: COST MEASURES

Skill in blending phonemes contributes far more to reading than does skill in associating an isolated letter to its sound. Because phonic blending is mastered by concept-induction, it can be made easy or difficult, largely depending on the exemplars the child starts with. Coleman (1970) studied the relative difficulty of different blends. The experimenter said the two sounds in isolation, and a preschooler tried to say the complete word. Each child was given most of the two-phoneme blends found in English (578 of them). Figure 15-1 shows concept-induction curves for VC and CV blends. The blends in each set of 25 were ones the children had never encountered before, and yet, one-third of the way into the experiment, 95% of the VCs were blended correctly. By the end of the experiment 18–23 days later, CVs were blended equally well. The concept was induced by mastering many exemplars.

In general, sounds that were difficult to pronounce in isolation were difficult to reblend when used as initial consonants: C.Vs (p.ay) were more difficult than V.Cs (a.pe). Longer components (tele.vision) were easier than shorter ones (u.p). The practice blends (tea.cher; ba.by; can.dy) were blended correctly by almost all children from the first presentation. D. L. Brown (1971) found that kindergartners were better at blending syllables than phonemes. Surprisingly, it was easy for Coleman's subjects to blend consonant clusters,

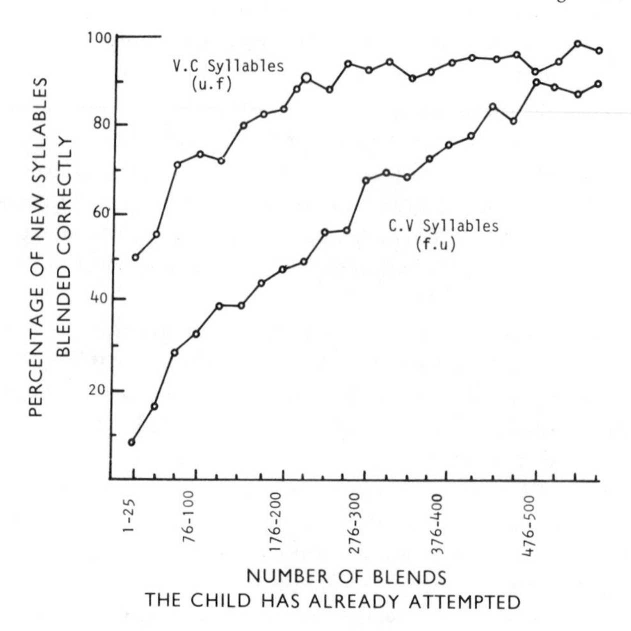

Figure 15-1. *The increasing percentage of new* V.C *and* C.V *syllables that the preschooler blended correctly as the experiment proceeded (from Coleman, 1970, reproduced with the author's permission).*

especially at the final positions (bran.d). Blends such as -VC.C (stam.p) and -V.CC (po.rch) were easy enough to be introduced at the beginning of instruction, even before the child fully comprehended the concept of phonics and word analysis. There were also difficult blends such as CC.V- (shr.ink) and C.CV- (s.kate).

By starting with the easy blends and progressing systematically to the difficult ones, Coleman's student Williams (1982) was able to help a 2:6-year-old girl master short blends of the kind with which even many school-age children have difficulty (see "Non-Parent Teacher" in Chapter 4).

SOUND-OUT WORDS: COST–BENEFIT MEASURES

If a child learns a word by blending its individual sounds, the cost of adding a word to his vocabulary can be roughly calculated from the cost of learning each letter–sound relation plus the cost of mastering the blend itself. Short words with two sounds cost less than longer words, but even within words of the same length, *up* is a lot easier than *to, do, be, he.*

To find cost measures for the most common words, Coleman (1970) had a large group of kindergartners learn to read 160 frequently used words, and then rank ordered the words according to their mean numbers of pronunciation errors during learning. Words such as *then, think, this* cost roughly five times as much in errors to criterion as words such as *kitten, cow, Bill, milk, up, go.* The most difficult words were function words that start with difficult sounds, such as the two sounds of 'th' in *through* and *this.*

Benefit measures are more complicated to compute. The word's frequency of usage is a convenient starting point, but an adequate measure must consider other factors such as: (*a*) the word's frequency of occurrence as a part of larger words (*at* is worth more than *if* because *at* is a part of more words); (*b*) the ease with which the word can be built into a larger word (*at* can be built into *sat* more easily than *go* into *got,* because the latter has a vowel change); and (*c*) the frequency of usage of the larger words.

WORDS AND SENTENCES: COST–BENEFIT MEASURES

For words, frequency of usage is the simplest measure of usefulness; it can also serve as a rough measure of cost, provided that function words and content words are considered separately. Frequent content words are slightly easier to learn than are infrequent ones, but frequent function words such as *the, a, is, of* are harder to learn than are infrequent ones such as *between, each,* probably because the former tend to be less meaningful than the latter. To obtain word frequency in preschoolers' sentences, Chitwood (1973) used a wireless microphone and collected all the sentences spoken by 43 preschoolers over a period of 8 hours. He then rank ordered all 1-, 2-, 3-, and 4-word sentences. Combining these measures with others, Coleman (1981) compiled a short list of words that can generate a large number of useful, easily learned sentences:

No.	I	can	get	up
Yes.	it	can't	go	down
See?	mommy	will	take	in
Stop.	daddy	won't	make	out
Look.	you			
Don't!				
What?				

The list has several one-word sentences (Column 1). Each of the words can be combined with many of the other words to generate two-word sentences (*I can; You can; Look out; Get up;* etc.) as well as three- and four-word sentences (*You can go; Get it down; I can get up;* etc.) In fact, the list, short as it is, can generate sentences too long for beginning materials (*No, Daddy won't make you get it down,* etc.)

For sentences, benefits can hardly be judged by frequency of use, because only the simplest sentences will ever be exactly repeated. Rather, the benefits might be assessed in terms of the range of situations in which sentences are useful. Some sentences would have greater benefit than others because they are better suited to the easily understood, action-packed plots of children's stories. However, since children do not learn sentences as such, it is probably not worthwhile to evaluate sentences for benefits.

Sentence length provides an obvious cost measure: One-word sentences are easier than two-word sentences, which in turn are easier than three-word sentences, and so on. Within sentences of the same length, obviously some are learned or understood more easily than others. It may be possible to develop some kind of structural cost measure: For example, actives are easier than passives or negatives, and simple sentences are easier than complex ones.

Development of Reading Skills

Beginning readers read fewer than 80 words per minute (WPM), but college students read over 250 WPM. Beginners' reading skills gradually approach those of adults, some skills developing earlier than others. In closing a three-volume series on early reading instruction, Resnick (1979) points out that there is a surprisingly small amount of data on development of reading skills, and longitudinal studies are especially lacking. Thus we are forced to rely on cross-sectional data in tracing the development of several reading skills, the two major ones being word decoding and comprehension.

Development of Word Decoding

MASTERING SUBSKILLS TO AUTOMACITY

LaBerge and Samuels (1974), the most articulate proponents of a subskills approach, view word decoding as a cluster of subskills, such as selecting and scanning features, unitizing the features into letter codes, associating letters with sounds, associating word sounds with meanings, and so on. They suggest that reading instruction should single out these subskills—from lower to higher levels—for training and testing and then sequence them appropriately. They use two criteria of mastery for each subskill, accuracy and automaticity. Mastery of one subskill at the automatic level frees a child to allocate his attention to the subskill at the next higher level. For example, the less attention a child needs to allocate for letter–sound processing, the more he has available for the sound blending task. Similarly, when decoding is fast and automatic, more resources are available for comprehension. Perfetti and Hogaboam (1975) found that the latency to vocalize single words was shorter for skilled than unskilled comprehenders, presumably because the skilled comprehenders had to spend less resources on decoding than did the unskilled.

Subskills may be mutually facilitative rather than independent. For normal Grade 3 readers (but not for disabled readers), the various decoding subskills were highly correlated (Guthrie, 1973b). Instead of training each subskill to the level at which it becomes automatic before tackling the next one, as suggested by LaBerge and Samuels, we believe in training a few related subskills together, emphasizing one or another as conditions demand. The grounds for our belief are: (*a*) There is no clear boundary where the need for one subskill ends and another starts; (*b*) The smaller and lower the subskill, the less meaningful and interesting it tends to be; (*c*) The more finely and definitely is word decoding divided into subskills, the more difficult it will be to integrate the subskills again; (*d*) When one skill is learned, a cluster of its subskills may be partially acquired. For example, selecting, scanning, and unitizing letter features seem to be acquired largely spontaneously in the learning of letters and words. Calfee and Drum (1978) point out that pre-reading kindergartners handle graphic symbols in much the same way as do adults, when allowance is made for the role of memory and encoding, and that programs for enhancing visual perception are seldom effective. Sensitivity to orthographic structure might be considered as one of the subskills involved in word recognition. But is it sensitivity that facilitates word recognition, or vise versa?

SPEED OF DECODING

Doehring (1976) conducted a cross-sectional study of speed of response in several skills. Subjects were 150 average children (75 boys and 75 girls) spanning the school grades from Kindergarten to Grade 11, and ages from 5 to 16. Doehring studied four skills: visual matching, auditory–visual matching, oral reading, and visual scanning. He tested each skill with seven to eleven types of material, including numbers, meaningful and meaningless CVC syllables, and color naming. For example, in a matching task, a child matches a common CVC word such as *did* to one of the three choices provided: *lid, did* and *dip*. The stimulus was given visually in visual–visual matching, and auditorily in auditory–visual matching. In preparing Figure 15-2 from Doehr-

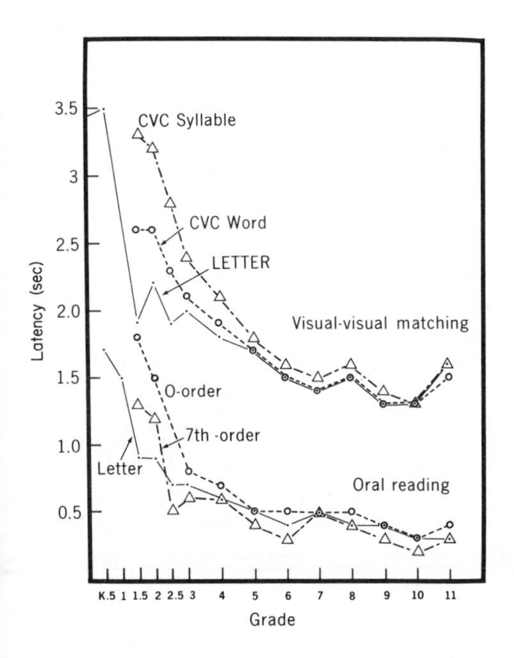

Figure 15-2. *Latency in visual–visual matching and oral reading (sec per syllable) decreases in higher school grades (based on Doehring, 1976).*

ing's data, we have chosen two skills, visual–visual matching and oral reading, and three representative types of test material for each skill.

In Figure 15-2 the following trends are discernible:

- The latency of response decreases gradually from Kindergarten to Grade 11, the steepest decrease occurring at Grade 1.5 for the letters in all three tasks. (In every skill and material tested, at Grade 11 there occurs a slight reversal in the decreasing trend. Doehring attributes it to statistical sampling error.)
- Meaningful, or sequentially constrained, materials have shorter latency than meaningless materials: Familiar CVC words are matched faster than CVC nonsense syllables, and words in seventh-order of approximation (*on a rock and wiped his head to*) are read faster than are words in zero-order (*the ago over end made for year*).
- Auditory–visual matching is slower, especially at earlier grades, than visual–visual matching, whatever the stimuli.
- Latencies for words become as short as those for single letters by Grade 5, and latencies for syllables as short as those for single letters by Grade 6.

Coding speed is related with comprehension. In Speer and Lamb's (1976) study, the number of letters named in 1 min (an index of fluency) doubled from the beginning to the end of Grade 1. Furthermore, the fluency scores correlated highly with Gates–MacGinitie scores (vocabulary and comprehension) given at the end of Grade 1. De Soto and De Soto (1983) found that even as late as Grade 4, the factor labeled "Verbal Coding Speed" (time to read words and pseudowords, or to name pictures) was positively correlated with reading comprehension.

Throughout the school years children become faster, perhaps eventually becoming automatic, in processing lexical, orthographic, semantic, and syntactic information. The development is especially rapid in the first few years, but it continues more slowly throughout the later grades.

DEVELOPMENT OF PERCEPTUAL AND DECODING SKILLS

Eye-movement patterns seem to have all but stabilized by Grade 5 according to Buswell (1922), but only by Grade 10 according to Ballentine (1951). The number and duration of fixations and regressions steadily decline from Grade 1 to college, the steepest decline occurring between Grades 1 and 2 (see Figure 7-1). The use of parafoveal vision is more developed in Grade 5 than in Grade 2 (Fisher & Montanary, 1977).

The size of the perceptual unit grows with age. Grade 5 children and adults used the initial clusters (BL-) as perceptual units, but Grade 2 poor readers relied on single letters as units (Santa, 1976–1977). The ability to use a word rather than its letters as a unit increases with age and reading skill. The number of letters of familiar words perceived in a T-scope increases rapidly from Grades 1 to 3, but slowly thereafter, both for good and for poor readers (Hoffmann, 1927; see Figure 8-1). The ability to process familiar words up to 6-

letters long as a whole is not well developed in Grade 2, but by Grade 4 or 6, it is almost as fully developed as it is in college (Samuels *et al.*, 1978). The ability to read by phrase keeps improving until Grade 4, according to Levin and Turner (1968), or until college, according to Resnick (1970).

Sensitivity to orthographic structure can be found in Grade 1 children, if tasks are simple (e.g., recognizing a letter in a 3-letter word versus in isolation, Lott & Smith, 1970). In a more difficult task, children had to point out which was "more like a word" in compairing a pronounceable letter string (DINK) with an unpronounceable string (XOGL). Grade 1 children could not do this task: Success rates were 50%, 69%, and 80% at Grades 1, 3, and 5, respectively (Rosinski & Wheeler, 1972). Ability to apply letter–sound generalizations continues to develop at least through Grade 8 (Calfee *et al.*, 1969). The use of spelling strategies also develops with age, especially between Grades 2 and 5 (Marsh *et al.*, 1980; see Figure 6-1). Strategies for spelling regular words develop earlier than those for spelling irregular words

Development of Comprehension Skills

Enough has been said about word decoding; what about the other major component of reading, namely, comprehension?

COMPREHENSION SUBSKILLS

To comprehend a sentence or a passage means to extract an idea conveyed in it. We have scrutinized the processes of comprehending clauses, sentences, stories, and expository passages in Chapters 12 and 13. We now recapitulate from these two chapters the salient points or **subskills of comprehension.** Similar comprehension subskills are involved in whatever languages or scripts children, or adults for that matter, may read.

In reading sentences, children must learn to:

- Recognize words
- Assign syntactic and case roles to words
- Construct a message based on content words, with the help of function words if necessary
- Identify the referents of anaphora
- Organize words into larger syntactic units, such as phrase and clause
- Extract the gist from a sentence

In reading stories children must learn to:

- Identify the motive of a hero or heroine
- Follow the sequence of events or the plot
- Anticipate an outcome or climax
- Extract a theme or moral

In reading expository prose, children must learn to:

- Identify the topic

- Distinguish important from unimportant idea units, processing the former more than the latter
- Follow a sequence of directions or logical ideas
- Draw inferences or conclusions
- Sort out cause–effect relations
- Extract the gist of a passage

A reader has other, higher-level tasks. She must separate facts from opinions; evaluate the relevance of materials to the author's thesis or to her reading goals; appreciate the beauty, aptness, or novelty of expressions; grasp the point of a joke, irony, or sarcasm; and above all, retain at least the main points of what has been read.

GROWTH OF COMPREHENSION SKILLS

Older children are better than younger children in processing text. In Doehring and Hoshko's (1977) study of children from Grades 1 through 11, the older the children, the faster they could restore missing words in sentences. In Danner's (1974) study, most Grade 2 children could distinguish between organized and disorganized texts, and could abstract the main idea to some extent. But it was not until Grade 6 that most children could use topic sentences as retrieval cues for later recall of paragraphs. On the other hand, when reading expository passages randomly chosen from their grade level textbooks, even Grade 6 children were not proficient in processing important and unimportant idea units differently (Baumann, 1981).

D. A. Resnick (1982) found a clear developmental trend in children's ability to paraphrase or judge figurative proverbs (e.g., *A mouse with one hole is quickly caught*). For example, in proverb–story matching, the number of items correct (out of 10) were 4.9, 6.2, 6.9, 7.8, and 9.6, for Grades 3, 4, 5, 6, and 7, respectively.

Brown and Day (1983) found a developmental trend in summarizing skills. Older high school and college students were able to use the advanced strategy of integrating information across paragraphs and rephrasing, in contrast to Grades 5 and 7 children who relied on the simpler strategy of deleting unimportant or redundant information and then copying what was left.

Teachers can help children to develop comprehension skills by explaining syntax and text structure, by using plenty of examples of good and bad sentences and paragraphs, and by asking questions that test these skills. Children can develop the skills by reading a lot of stories and passages, as well as writing examples for comment or correction by teachers. The Greek philosopher and teacher Epictetus (first century A.D.) advised: "If you wish to be a good reader, read."

TESTING READING SKILLS

Testing is an integral part of reading instruction at school. In Chapter 13 we compared several methods of testing comprehension ("Test of Comprehension and Recall"). A few of these methods, especially mutliple-choice and cloze tests, are used in the two types of reading tests used in schools. Our brief description of these two types of test is based on Pearson and Johnson (1978).

Suppose a teacher wants to find out whether a particular pupil reads below his grade level, and if so by how much. If the child managed 22 items correct on a particular 50-item test, he would be assigned a grade level score of 3.1, for he got as many items correct as the average for pupils at the beginning of the third grade. Because the child was tested on a **standardized test** (norm-referenced test), a table of norms allows the teacher to translate the child's raw score to a grade norm score. The norm represents a standard against which one can compare the reading achievement of a child, a classroom, a school, or a district.

Some of the widely used reading tests are: *Iowa Test of Basic Skills, The Metropolitan Achievement Tests,* and *Stanford Achievement Test*. These tests give separate scores at least for the two major components of reading, namely, vocabulary and comprehension.

A **criterion-referenced test** sets an absolute standard for achievement. For example, a criterion of 70 percent correct might be set for a reading test following a unit in a basal reader. If a child correctly answers 7 out of 10 test items, she moves on to the next unit; if she does not, she may have to repeat the old unit, or she might be given special remedial help. Criterion-referenced tests tend to provide anywhere from 5 to 10 to 30 subtest scores for comprehension (and even more for decoding skills). Thus, they are able to pinpoint the child's strong and weak subskills and hence are diagnostically more useful than are norm-referenced tests. Most basal readers have end-of-unit or end-of-book tests designed to help a teacher decide whether or not a child has mastered the skills of the unit or book.

In addition to these tests, there are the National Assessments of Reading, which reveal gains or losses made by different groups of readers over time. For example, between 1970 and 1980, 9-year-olds made significant gains from the first to the third assessments, whereas 13-year-olds and 17-year-olds remained stable. Among 9-year-olds, pupils who gained most were black, or from the Southeast, or from rural communities, or from disadvantaged urban communities (E. B. Fry, 1981).

If some schoolchildren in the United States read inadequately, let it never be said that insufficient testing is the cause.

Summary and Conclusions

Reading is usually taught at school by a teacher. An effective teacher "teaches"; that is, she engages her pupils in reading activities proper, not in "fun and games," and does so systematically, using structured materials.

Of several teaching methods, two contrasting ones are phonics and look–

say. Phonics teaches how to sound out letters and letter sequences, and is suitable for teaching regular words. Armed with phonics skills, children can decode new words on their own. The contrasting method, look–say, associates a whole word with its meaning and sound, and is the quickest and easiest way to introduce young children to reading. It is particularly suitable for teaching irregular words. In look–say, letter–sound relations are left to children to induce from known words. English has both regular and irregular words, requiring a combination of the two methods for teaching children (or adults) to read.

The linguistic approach teaches words of the same or contrasting sound and letter pattern as a group, and the language-experience approach lets the child choose the words he wants to learn. These two approaches may be incorporated with the basic phonics-plus-whole-word methods as an integrated set of techniques. The three-phased learning sequence is: whole-word, analysis into parts, and mature whole-word synthesis of the parts. The three-phased learning may help the child to integrate the two parallel processing tracks, the RIGHT pattern matching and the LEFT phonetic analysis, needed for skilled reading. Higher-level skills develop in three similar phases.

At school, graded basal series form the core of the teaching material in many countries. The modern basal series in the United States consist of manuals for teachers, readers and workbooks for children, and many other teaching aids. They are supposed to introduce a limited number of easy and yet useful words in interesting stories in each advancing grade. However, basal series differ widely the way they implement this principle.

The basal series can be categorized into two main approaches: A code-emphasis program first teaches the sounds of individual letters and letter sequences so that children can decode new words on their own. Beginning sentences and stories contain a high percentage of decodable words. A meaning-emphasis program starts with stories that allow children to use context and pictures to guess, and later to read, words. Stories contain many high-frequency, irregular words that are learned as wholes. Letter–sound relations are later induced from the known words.

Recently, the two types of programs have borrowed good features from each other. An effective basal series would emphasize letter–sound relations as well as meaning from the beginning, starting with easy and useful materials and progressing to more complex ones.

Reading skills develop gradually throughout primary (up to age 9), intermediate (13), and senior grades (17). Some simple skills develop rapidly between Grades 1 and 2, and slowly thereafter. Some complex skills keep developing throughout intermediate and senior grades. This kind of trend is observed whether one measures speed or accuracy of response.

Along with skills for word decoding, children must develop skills for comprehending sentences, stories, and expository passages. Such skills as distinguishing important from unimportant items, drawing inferences and conclusions, and extracting a gist can be trained with a three-phased cycle of plenty of reading (exposure to whole patterns), syntactic and structural analysis (with a teacher's help), and more "mature" reading.

Learning to read contains some rote learning and drill, but it also contains the fun of reading interesting stories, obtaining useful information, and mastering skills. The most important idea to get across to children is:

Reading is the magic key that unlocks the door to the wonderland of stories and information.

16

Developmental Dyslexia

For a long time he [Gustave Flaubert] could not understand the elementary connection that made of two letters one syllable, of several syllables a word.

—Carolin Commanville[1]

Identifying Developmental Dyslexics

Developmental dyslexia is a severe and persistent difficulty suffered by intellectually normal children in learning to read. A research group of the World Federation of Neurology defined **specific developmental dyslexia** as:

> A disorder manifested by difficulty in learning to read despite conventional instruction, adequate intelligence, and socio-cultural opportunity. It is dependent upon fundamental cognitive disabilities which are frequently of constitutional origin [Critchley, 1970, p. 11].

The definition raises some questions: What are "adequate intelligence and socio-cultural opportunity"? What are "fundamental cognitive disabilities"? What is meant by "constitutional origin"? When is a child considered to be having "difficulty in learning to read"? This chapter tries to answer these and other questions.

[1]Flaubert's niece, in *Souvenirs intimes*. J.P. Sartre also mentions Flaubert's difficulties in learning to read in his biography of Flaubert, entitled *L'idiot de la famille*.

Criteria for Selecting Dyslexic Subjects

READING TWO YEARS BELOW GRADE OR NONREADING

Conventionally, a child is labeled dyslexic when, despite adequate intelligence, he reads 2 or more years below his grade level. As a deficit of two years represents a more severe disability in younger than in older children, some researchers use a sliding scale. For example, Lyle and Goyen (1969) add a half year retardation for every grade. Thus, a child is dyslexic if he is 1 year retarded at Grade 2; 1.5 years retarded at Grade 3; 2 years retarded at Grade 4, and so on. Similarly, Vellutino's (1979) youngest subjects (Grade 2) are 1 or more years below grade level, but his older subjects are 2 or more years below grade level. Children meeting these criteria fall below a level between the fourth and tenth percentile on an oral reading test. In the experiments covered in this chapter, the reading discrepancy between dyslexics and controls ranges from 1 to 7 years, with "2 or more years" being most common. Reading "2-years below grade" is a convenient yardstick but perhaps is too loose.

Another definition focuses on the discrepancy between obtained reading level and that expected on the basis of age and IQ (Eisenberg, 1978; Rutter, 1978). Yet another convenient means of selecting dyslexic subjects is that they are taking remedial reading classes, their deficiency being severe enough to demand special training. Vernon (1957) used a more stringent definition of "backward reading," (which seems to be the label used in Great Britain for dyslexia.) Backward readers are **nonreaders,** who can probably guess a few simple words at sight, but have not grasped the mechanics of reading after a few years' instruction and cannot be said to read in any real sense.

DYSLEXIA, LEARNING DISABILITY, AND POOR READING

The literature on dyslexia is confusing. Some confusion is caused by the different criteria used to select dyslexic subjects, and some by the profusion of terms used to refer to dyslexia. Do the terms *dyslexia, nonreading, poor reading, backward reading, disabled reading, learning disability,* and so on, all refer to the same disorder? As a step toward reducing the confusion, at least *dyslexia* and *poor reading* should be distinguished.

According to Critchley (1970), dyslexia differs from poor reading by being associated with: (*a*) persistence to adulthood; (*b*) peculiar and specific nature of the errors in reading and spelling; (*c*) familial incidence of the defect; (*d*) greater incidence in males than in females; and (*e*) normal if not high intelligence. Over a 5-year span, Rutter and Yule (1975) in England compared what they call "general reading backwardness" (poor reading) with "specific reading retardation (dyslexia)." The dyslexics showed most of the characteristics Critchley enumerated. In addition, they enjoyed adequate socioeconomic status. The dyslexics made less progress in reading and spelling over the 5 years than did the poor readers with lower IQs. On the other hand, the dyslexics made better progress in arithmetic than did the poor readers.

According to the U.S. federal law that deals with the education of the handicapped, **specific learning disability** (LD) is an imperfect ability to listen, think, speak, read, write, spell, or to do mathematical calculation. The term includes such conditions as perceptual handicaps, brain injury, dyslexia, and developmental aphasia.

"Poor readers" refer to mildly retarded readers, specifically those scoring below the 27th percentile (one standard deviation below the mean) on a standard reading test. A simpler procedure is to designate the bottom one-third or one-quarter of a class as poor readers. Dyslexia and learning disability are the main topics of this chapter; poor reading has been already covered throughout the text. When we discuss the different studies, we will generally use whatever label was used by the original researchers, describing their criteria for selecting subjects when we can.

INTELLIGENCE

To avoid including subjects whose low reading achievement is caused by mental retardation, researchers usually ensure that their dyslexic subjects have "adequate intelligence," that is, an IQ above 80 or 90, as determined by one of the standard intelligence tests for children, such as the Wechsler Intelligence Scale for Children (WISC). Sometimes either Performance or Verbal IQ is used instead of Full IQ.

More boys than girls are dyslexic readers. At higher levels of IQ, the preponderance of males among retarded readers becomes more striking (Lovell, Shapton, & Warren, 1964): IQ less than 90, 1.2 boy to 1 girl; IQ between 90 and 99, 5 boys to 1 girl; IQ more than 100, 10 boys to 1 girl. These figures suggest strongly that there is more to dyslexia than just a lack of skill in reading. Among high IQ children, reading retardation may usually be due to dyslexia, but among low IQ children, other causes may contribute.

Many, if not all, dyslexic readers tend to score lower on Verbal than on Performance IQ, often by as much as 20 points (e.g., Kinsbourne & Warrington, 1963; Owen, Adams, Forrest, Stolz, & Fisher, 1971; Rabinovitch, 1968; Rourke, Dietrich, & Young, 1973). This result is not simply the cumulative effect of prolonged reading disability, because the difference between reader groups at Grade 1 is of the same magnitude as in Grade 6 (Lyle & Goyen, 1969). The dyslexics with lower Verbal than Performance IQ have characteristically different problems than do other dyslexics (see "Subtypes of Dyslexia," later in the chapter).

SOCIOECONOMIC STATUS (SES)

Low SES and large family size tend to be associated both with low verbal intelligence and with poor reading attainment, reflecting genetic as well as environmental influences (Rutter & Madge, 1976). In Barton and Wilder's (1964) nationwide survey of elementary schools, reading retardation rose steadily through the first six grades for low-social-class children. By Grade 4, about half of the children in low-SES classrooms were reading 1 year below grade level, whereas upper-class children tended to become advanced from the first grade and to maintain this advantage throughout the school years.

Some researchers ensure that their dyslexic subjects and controls are matched in SES. However, even when the two groups are selected from one social class, dyslexics tend to have less favorable family environments. In Germany, when Valtin (1980) matched dyslexics and controls according to their fathers' professions, the dyslexics' mothers tended to have lower education and a larger number of children than did the controls' mothers. The dyslexics also tended to be born later in the family order. In Baltimore, when 125 matched pairs of dyslexics and controls from the same disadvantaged class were compared, more dyslexics than normals (*a*) had mothers with low education; (*b*) came from a family with many children; (*c*) lived with unrelated males; and (*d*) lived without natural mothers (Kappelman, Rosenstein, & Canter, 1972).

Whether poor reading associated with low SES should be excluded from "pure" dyslexia is a matter of debate.

Incidence around the World

A worldwide survey of dyslexia is nearly impossible because of the lack of a uniform definition and the lack of interest in many countries. What follows is an extremely limited survey. Remember that at least two different definitions may have been used at different times and places: one, "2 years below grade level," which gives a rate of over 10%; the other, nonreading, which typically gives a low rate (6% or less).

UNITED STATES

Eisenberg (1966) surveyed 12,000 children in their fifth month of Grade 6 in a metropolitan (Baltimore) public school system. In this population, 27.5% of the children were 2 or more years behind the national norm for their grade, whereas 8.6% were 2 or more years ahead. Public schools tended to produce more retarded readers than did suburban schools, especially suburban private schools. In Minneapolis, an economically successful and homogeneous (few minority groups) city, only 3% of Grade 5 children read 2 years below grade (Stevenson *et al.*, 1982).

The United States is a heterogeneous society, and low reading achievement is endemic among disadvantaged groups, especially among blacks (Barton & Wilder, 1964; S. A. Cohen, 1969; Singer & Balow, 1981). One study reports that one-fifth of all Grade 3 children tested in three schools in a racially mixed, urban inner-city were "total nonreaders" (Gottesman, Croen, & Rotkin, 1982). Baron and Treiman (1980) report high rates of nonreaders among black working-class children in Philadelphia. The nonreaders could not read any of the test words, which were familiar exception words (*was, said, come,* etc.), regular words (*has, maid, dome,* etc.), and pseudowords (*mas, haid, gome,* etc.).

For all types of schoolchildren, the most frequently cited rate is 15%, representing 8 million children (B. B. Brown, 1978). Other rates often cited are 5% and 10%. The percentage of incidence seems to shrink when reading retardation associated with low SES is excluded. (Most "standard" reading tests have been standardized on middle-class children.) Reading disorder is the major single cause of the 700,000 yearly school dropouts in the educational system (Silberman, 1964). It is also a major reason for referrals to clinics and juvenile courts (B. B. Brown, 1978; Mendelson, Johnson, & Stewart, 1971).

OTHER COUNTRIES WITH ALPHABETS

Consider first other English-speaking countries. In Australia, Farrar and Leigh (1972) examined the results of Schonell's Word Recognition Test given to over 1000 children: 13% failed the test, reading at least 2 years behind their grade level. In England, the incidence differed markedly between urban and rural areas. In the Isle of Wight, an area of small towns, 3.5% were retarded readers at age 10, and 4.5% at age 14. By contrast, in inner London 7.6% were retarded readers at age 10 (Rutter & Yule, 1975). In one large-scale reading test in Leeds, England, 19% of 9–10-year-olds were reading 2 or more years below their age, but only 6.9% of the children were nonreaders (Vernon, 1957).

Among non-English-speaking nations, some reported incidence rates are 6% in Austria (Kowarik, 1976); 5% in the Netherlands (Dumont, 1976); and 2% in Czechoslovakia (Matejcek, 1976). The Bergen Project involving Norway, Denmark, and Sweden, finds 7% of early school graders to be dyslexic (Skagseth, 1982).

Tamil–English bilingual readers' errors are revealing. Aaron (1982) examined errors made by 8–10-year-old Tamil-speaking boys reading Tamil and English passages. Tamil is a highly inflected language in which suffixes mark such grammatical functions as tense, number, and case. On the other hand, the Tamil script has near perfect letter–sound relations (see Chapter 2, "Other Alphabets"). In Tamil, four error-prone boys seldom mispronounced words, but they often omitted or substituted suffixes. In English, however, they mispronounced or omitted entire words, even familiar words such as *went, play, car, put.* Aaron concludes that about 10% of the 40 Tamil-speaking boys he studied are disabled readers. One wonders whether the figure of 10% can apply to both English and Tamil. The four boys have difficulties with word decoding in English but not in Tamil. For comprehending text, suffix errors in Tamil should not be as disruptive as are decoding errors in English.

In many poor and underdeveloped countries in Africa and East Asia, the concept of reading retardation is a luxury too remote for immediate concern; a more pressing concern must be to reduce the staggeringly high rate of illiteracy.

FAR EASTERN COUNTRIES

No term corresponding to "developmental dyslexia" exists in Korea, Japan, or China. The absence of a term, of course, does not automatically mean the absence of dyslexia. But one would think that if a disorder were so widespread as to afflict 5–10% of schoolchildren, it would surely be noticed and labeled. In these countries primary education is compulsory, and almost all school-age children are at school. According to Makita's (1968) survey in Japan and Kuo's (1978) survey in Taiwan, the incidence is extremely low, about 1%.

An American educator, Duke (1977), in his article entitled "Why Noriko can Read! Some Hints for Johnny," notes the absence of remedial specialists and facilities in Japan, as do Sakamoto and Makita (1973). Every Japanese child in a Grade 3 class of 43 that Duke visited was a reader. By contrast, in the United States, a Grade 3 class of 30 typically contains 1 or 2 nonreaders and several poor readers.

Is the low incidence of nonreaders in Far Eastern countries attributable to their use of writing systems that are easy to learn? Some educators and researchers believe so (e.g., Liberman & Mann, 1981; Makita, 1968; Rozin & Gleitman, 1977). We agree with them, for several reasons (see also Chapters 3, 4, 5, and 14).

The writing and reading unit of the Chinese, Japanese, and Korean scripts is a syllable, which is large, concrete, and stable, compared with the unit of an alphabet, the phoneme. In the three scripts, individual signs have consistent and stable sound values that do not change when they combine with other sounds to form a word, as in the Japanese words *sa.ra, sa.ku.ra,* and *sa.yo.na.ra.* Contrast this with the problem of the English-speaking child learning *rations* after *tigers;* four of the letters in the two words are the same, but none has the same sound. The syllable signs confer another advantage: They reduce the problems of sequencing. *Sara* has two syllables and is written with two Kana; *tigers,* too, has two syllables but is written with six letters. Sequence errors tend to increase appreciably for strings of more than four items.

Learning a sign as a whole pattern is far easier than learning it by analysis, so long as there are not too many signs to learn. A Chinese character is learned as a whole pattern, not through phonic analysis and blending. So is a Kana sign and a Hangul syllable-block.

Japanese and Korean children learn syllable signs quickly (say, within 6 months), and once they know most of the letters, they are assured of being able to sound out any new words. Most children in Japan, and some in South Korea, accomplish this feat before entering school. People do not have to look up in a dictionary how a word is pronounced or spelled: Just sound a word as it is spelled and spell it as it sounds. In these two countries, there may be many kinds of contests, but there never is a spelling bee.

Closeness between the units of script and meaning probably helps in learning to read. Almost all single Chinese characters, many single Hangul blocks, and some single Kana are morphemes. In English, there are two single-letter words: *I* and *a.* When it comes to two-letter words, English still has only a handful, all of which are function words with little meaning (*in, to, of,* etc.); Japanese has many two-Kana words: *tora* ('tiger'), *hana* ('flower'), *Kana* .

The forms of letters may also be of some relevance. A few Chinese characters, Kana, and Hangul syllable-blocks do look similar enough to cause confusion, but not as much as do the notorious mirror-image letters 'b/d' and 'p/q' in English. Kana are seldom confused in reading, though they are, transiently, in writing (Makita, 1968; Muraishi & Amano, 1972).

The basic difficulty of many dyslexics is with the LEFT-track process of word decoding, including sequencing, as will be made clear in the rest of the chapter. If a script promotes easy word decoding, it follows that it will not produce many dyslexic children of this major type. There will be poor readers in these Far Eastern countries, as anywhere else, as long as poor readers are defined as those who fall in the bottom one-third of a class, or those who score below the 27th percentile on a reading test. There will be disabled readers also if they are defined as those who read 2 years below grade level. Not only in relative terms but also in absolute terms there will be poor readers, those who read inadequately for reasons other than difficult decoding (e.g., lack of interest, material, and time).

Stevenson *et al.* (1982) tested Grade 5 children in three countries—the United States, Japan, and Taiwan, and found that 3%, 2%, and 8%, respectively, were reading 2 years below grade. But by Grade 5, Japanese children are well past the stage of learning to read with Kana, and Chinese children no longer need the phonetic signs. If they read poorly, the difficulty is due to insufficient knowledge of a large number of complex Kanji, which are learned largely (but not exclusively) by rote memory and which require constant use to prevent them from being forgotten. A limited number of Kanji are easy to learn, but a large number of Kanji are hard to learn, as pointed out in Chapters 3 and 4.

In the three Far Eastern countries, respect for education and authority, which perhaps stems from the Confucian tradition, is both deep and pervasive. It can be found even in low-SES families, although today it seems to have lost its grip on some teenagers. Thus, as far as attitude toward learning is concerned, low-SES children are not disadvantaged. Respect for education and authority, in turn, lead to disciplined classroom behavior. Children are disciplined despite classes that tend to be very large, about two or three times as large as Western standards accept.

Even children from low SES and with "cognitive disabilities of constitutional origin" may learn to read, though perhaps only poorly, if their script is easy to decode.

Predicting Dyslexia

NEED FOR EARLY DETECTION

Delacato (1966) observed: "Children have reading problems long before they enter school [p. 29]." He went on to say that the school merely points out the problems. As in many other disorders or diseases, early diagnosis may lead to a good prognosis, because a child's behavior is malleable and because he has an opportunity to escape from the spiraling effects of reading failure. Strag (1972) reports that remedial success was 82%, 46%, and 10–15% for diagnoses made at Grades 1, 3, and 5–7, respectively. It is possible, however, that the easier cases tend to cure themselves with or without treatment, leaving only the harder cases to be discovered in the later grades, as Kinsbourne (1981) points out.

According to Spreen's (1982) own study as well as his review of other studies, most children who are referred to a clinic for reading or learning disability do not catch up. Children with IQ above 90 and without minimal brain damage tend to have better outcomes than do those with IQ lower than 80 or with brain damage. The younger the referral, the better the outcome is likely to be.

SCREENING TEST BATTERIES

Over a dozen screening test batteries have been constructed in the past few decades. They tap cognitive and linguistic skills that are assumed to be components of early reading, and are administered to kindergartners.

Jansky and de Hirsch's (1972) battery called Screening Index was standardized on 508 children in New York City and consists of the following five tests (given in order of their predictive power):

1. Letter naming (name six printed letters)
2. Picture naming (name 22 pictures)
3. Gates Word Matching (find words that are alike)
4. Bender Motor Gestalt (copy six designs)
5. Binet Sentence Memory (repeat a list of sentences)

Given at kindergarten, the battery predicted 79% of those who became failing readers in Grade 2 but misclassified 25% of those who became good readers. Among children predicted to fail, those taught by competent teachers (as judged by their principals) had a lower percentage of failures than those placed in classes of teachers judged to be poor.

An abbreviated battery used by another team includes the following tests, listed in order of predictive capability (Satz, Taylor, Friel, & Fletcher, 1978):

1. Finger localization
2. Alphabetic recitation
3. Recognition and discrimination
4. Peabody IQ
5. Visual–motor integration
6. Auditory discrimination
7. Dichotic listening
8. Socioeconomic status

The battery was standardized on all (458) white male children in a county in Florida. It was successful in predicting those who would become severely disabled readers and superior readers but was far less successful in predicting mildly disabled readers and average readers.

Verbal tests predict reading achievement better than do perceptual tests. When Sampson (1962) studied 50 children longitudinally from age 18 months to 8 years, reading correlated well with speech measures (.58–.68), but somewhat less with a nonverbal test of IQ (.45). Stevenson *et al.* (1976) also report that verbal tests predict reading achievement better than do visual ones. A simple and yet accurate predictor appears to be alphabetic recitation or letter naming, since it was the most successful test in Jansky and de Hirsch's battery and the second best in Satz *et al.*'s battery. (See also Chapter 14, "Letter Naming.")

Perceptual and Memory Deficiencies

"It [dyslexia] is dependent on fundamental cognitive disabilities . . . ," according to the definition of dyslexia given at the beginning of the chapter. We shall examine dyslexics' perceptual and memorial skills.

Perceptual Problems

EYE MOVEMENTS

Dyslexic readers often have poor eye-movement patterns, which can be described as a symptom of dyslexia in some cases and a cause in others. In one study, five 7-year-old dyslexics showed great individual differences in reading text and also in moving their eyes along series of large 'X's, which simulated reading without the factor of comprehension (Elterman, Abel, Daroff, Dell'Osso, & Bornstein, 1980). One dyslexic boy had considerable difficulty with all reading material, and often reread a line of text. By contrast, he showed an excellent eye movement pattern when scanning the series of 'X's. Two of the dyslexics showed abnormal patterns on both the 'X's and words. One girl's difficulty was so severe that she could not move her eyes sequentially across the 'X's even when each was pointed out individually. Another boy made return "staircase" movements (multiple, small, leftward saccades) during the 'X' scanning, something he never did during regular reading.

Pirozzolo's (1979) two subtypes of dyslexics differed in their eye-movement patterns. In reading easy text, the auditory-linguistic subtypes showed a pattern similar to that of normal readers, whereas visual-spatial dyslexics showed atypical patterns with many instances of faulty right-to-left scanning and inaccurate return sweeps. Pavlidis's (1981) unclassified dyslexic subjects (2 or more years retarded in reading; normal vision and IQ) showed erratic eye movements not only in reading but also in following sequentially illuminated light sources. Fisher (1979) notes sharply reduced peripheral-visual processing among the severely reading disabled.

Most people have one eye that is dominant for eye movement. The dominant eye moves to the target, and the other eye follows. Stein and Fowler (1982) tested the dominance pattern of dyslexics and controls from the same schools, matched by the age and by Performance IQ. All but one of the 80 controls had one eye that was consistently dominant, but 50 of the 80 dyslexics showed an inconsistent pattern of dominance. When the dyslexics were later categorized as "visual" or "other" dyslexics, 52 were of the visual type, including all 50 of those with inconsistent eye dominance.

Stein and Fowler hypothesized that eye dominance is related to lateralization of eye movement control. Inconsistent connections between the language centers of the LH and the eye-movement control centers might be a cause of reading difficulty. Both as a test of their hypothesis and as a treatment, they asked randomly selected children from all groups to wear glasses (that blocked out the left eye) for 6 months when doing close visual work, including reading. The glasses made no difference to the reading performance of the normals or of the "other" types of dyslexics, but they dramatically improved the reading performance of the "visual" dyslexics, even beyond the trial period. Many dyslexics said that the words stopped moving around or reversing themselves, and one said, "Why didn't you give these [glasses] to me before? [p. 60].

PERCEPTUAL VERSUS VERBAL TESTS

There is a large body of literature on perceptual deficits in dyslexia, with conflicting findings. Vellutino (1979) reviews them, arguing for the verbal-deficit rather than the perceptual-deficit theory of dyslexia. To test whether dyslexics' difficulties lie in visual–visual or visual–verbal association learning, Vellutino and his associates used the following three kinds of material and task (Vellutino, Steger, Harding, & Phillips, 1975):

1. Object or picture naming: Associate four nonsense syllables (*mog, pex, wib, yag*) to four novel colored cartoon animals.
2. Letter–sound association: Associate the same four syllables to four novel letter-like symbols.
3. Associate simple geometric forms to auditory responses (cough, "ssss").

The dyslexic group scored worse than did the control group only on tests 1 and 2, which contain a verbal component.

The following tests contained neither a verbal nor a STM component, and yet they distinguished impaired readers from normal readers. Tallal (1980) gave an auditory discrimination and temporal-order perception test to normal readers and reading-impaired children (in a remedial school). The stimuli were computer-generated tones composed of frequencies within the speech range. Some but not all of the reading impaired had difficulty discriminating the order of two nonverbal auditory stimuli when they were presented rapidly but not when they were presented slowly. There was a high correlation between the number of errors made on a phonics reading test (nonsense word reading) and the number of errors made in responding to the auditory-perceptual tests. A later study identified the dyslexics with auditory-perceptual deficit to be language impaired.

Another study compared controls with 8–14-year-old dyslexics (2 years behind) in visual processing (Di Lollo, Hanson, & McIntyre, 1983; see also Lovegrove & Brown, 1978). In backward-masking tasks, whether the stimulus was a letter or a pair of dot matrices, the dyslexics showed slower rates of processing than did the controls. In a temporal-integration task, the subjects had to detect a temporal gap separating two vertical lines displayed briefly on a computer scope twice in rapid succession. To detect the gap, the dyslexics required longer intervals between the two lines than did the controls.

Some dyslexics' auditory and visual systems cannot process rapidly presented sequential materials as well as can the perceptual systems of normal people.

Sequencing Error and Orientation Confusion

"Was, saw, was, saw. How were they so sure which it was?" This was the anguished question Simpson asked when she was suffering from dyslexia. Later she wrote a book about her own conquest of dyslexia, entitling it, appropriately, *Reversals* (Simpson, 1979). When children read *was* as "saw" or *there* as "three," they are making **sequencing errors,** or **reversals.** When they confuse mirror-image letters ('b' for 'd', and 'q' for 'p'), they are making **orientation confusions.**

SEQUENCING AND ORIENTATION ERRORS: RESEARCH

To study sequencing errors and orientation confusions, researchers construct word lists that provide many opportunities for making errors. In one study, dyslexic readers generally copied correctly *din–bin, cob–cod, sung–snug, lion–loin*, but even as late as Grade 6 they made a large number of orientation and sequencing errors in reading these words aloud (Vellutino, Steger, & Kandel, 1972).

In another study, reversals and orientation confusions accounted for only a small proportion of poor readers' errors—15 and 10%, respectively, whereas 75% of their errors were sound confusions (Liberman, Shankweiler, Orlando, Harris, & Berti, 1971). Reversals persisted at least into Grade 3. The error rates were unstable between tests, and sequencing and orientation errors by the same children were not correlated with one another. Many errors on symmetrical letters were often sound confusions rather than orientation confusions: Thus, 'b' was more confused with 'p' than with 'd'. Liberman *et al.* point out that not all of their poor readers (the bottom one-third) made reversals, which may loom larger in importance in certain children with severe and persisting reading difficulties.

A team of researchers in Finland described a 15-year-old girl whose instability of spatial vision is a cause of her dyslexia (Nyman, Laurinen, &

Hyvarinen, 1982). She has a strong and systematic tendency to misperceive the spatial order of symbols or objects lying on the same horizontal level and within a few degrees (.5) of visual angle. Thus, 'AV' may be seen as 'VA' if the stimulus is presented longer than 10 msec. Consequently, her reading is visually noisy, unstable, and difficult.

SEQUENCING AND ORIENTATION ERRORS: MISPERCEIVING OR MISREADING?

Liberman *et al.* (1971) and Vellutino *et al.* (1972) conclude that the orientation and sequencing errors so often observed in the reading and writing of dyslexic readers may be linguistic intrusion errors rather than visual-spatial distortions. That is, when dyslexics name 'b' as 'd', *was* as "saw," it is not because they misperceive them but because they misread them.

If the orientation confusion is solely a linguistic problem, why does 'm/w' but not 'm/n' confusion occur frequently? Why does 'A/V' reversal occur at all? If the two mirror-image letters, 'b/d', had dissimilar sounds, or even no sounds, would confusion between the two disappear? Not likely. Coleman's (1980) prereading subjects had merely to point to the right letter without pronouncing it. Yet, they confused 'b/d'. When 'b' was oriented slightly differently from 'd', confusions decreased. Similarly, Japanese children unused to Roman letters frequently confuse 'b/d'. As in American studies, confusions in this Japanese study decreased markedly at age 6, when children start to learn to read Japanese (Gibson, Gibson, Pick & Osser, 1962; Tanaka & Yasufuku, 1975).

Disabled readers who suffer left–right confusion are among the most severe cases and comprise about a quarter of the children who need remedial help in reading. Their confusion is not confined to reading but extends to discriminating body parts and object relations (Belmont & Birch, 1963; Benton, 1978; Corballis & Beale, 1976; Ginsberg & Hartwick, 1971). Orientation confusions and reversals are prevalent among dyslexics with visuo-spatial deficiencies who have normal language abilities.

There is something intrinsically difficult about discriminating right–left orientation. Remember that a shape is more salient and more useful in form perception than is orientation. In fact, it may sometimes be better to ignore orientation. A predator (say, lion) should be distinguished from a prey (deer) by their differences in shape, but a lion or a deer moving to the left should be recognized as the same animal when it moves to the right. Many animal species show difficulty in discriminating mirror-image shapes, according to Corballis and Beale (1976), who speculate that inter-hemispheric fiber systems, such as the corpus callosum, act to symmetrize memory traces and thus to preserve structural symmetry. Such a mirror representation is in fact present in the visual cortex (Cowey, 1979). Memory processes serve to generalize the record of events to their left–right mirror images, presumably for adaptive advantage.

Whatever is difficult for normal people, be it irregular letter–sound correspondence or discrimination of mirror-image shapes, tends to be magnified for dyslexics.

Short-Term Memory

Memory is heavily involved in reading, as we have discussed throughout this book, particularly in Chapters 1, 10, 12, and 13. Some researchers suggest that dyslexics generally have poor memories. However, more and more researchers are trying to pinpoint specific aspects of memory in which dyslexics are deficient. Apparently, the main deficiency is in short-term memory (STM) and not in long-term memory (LTM) (Jorm, 1979). Dyslexics' poor word knowledge and poor recall of linguistic items suggest that their linguistic LTM also may be deficient. Nevertheless, we shall concentrate on STM, and consider several issues.

PERCEPTUAL OR MEMORIAL DEFICIT?

Where in the various stages of information processing do dyslexic and normal readers differ? To answer the question, researchers presented briefly—in groups of eight—letters, geometric forms, and abstract forms, to two groups of subjects, normal readers and disabled readers (2 or more years below grade level) (Morrison, Giordani, & Nagy, 1977). Both groups of subjects were 12-years old and had average or above average intelligence. In a "partial report technique," the subjects reported the stimulus to which an indicator pointed by picking it out on a response card that contained all eight of the original stimuli. The presentation of the response card was delayed until after the stimulus was turned off.

During the "perceptual phase" (0–300 msec), the two groups of subjects did not differ (but see "Perceptual versus Verbal Tests," above.) During the encoding-memory phase (300–2000 msec), however, the disabled readers performed worse than did the good readers. They performed poorly on all three kinds of stimulus, not just the letters.

VERBAL CODING AND REHEARSAL

Reading-disabled children may do poorly on perceiving and remembering visual or auditory patterns because of their inadequate use of verbal codes. Blank and Bridger (1966) asked disabled readers and normal readers (Grades 1 and 4) to match patterns of flashing light presented in a time sequence with spatial representations of the same patterns. Disabled readers from both grades did worse than did controls. Both groups tried to code the patterns verbally, but the controls were much more efficient than the disabled readers. The controls were facile in coding two dimensions at once and in imposing their own organizational scheme on the patterns.

Bryden (1972) reached a similar conclusion: Namely, poor readers use inefficient verbal codes. He compared poor readers (1.5 years below grade level; below tenth percentile) with good readers for their performance on same–different judgments for various combinations of auditory sequential, visual sequential, and visual-spatial patterns. The poor readers were deficient on all the materials, presumably because of their deficient verbal coding. For example, a dot pattern like .. ... may be coded as "2–3" by a good reader, but either coded improperly as 5 dots or left uncoded by a poor reader.

Material to be remembered has to be rehearsed, usually in a verbal code. Is the poor memory of dyslexics a result of inadequate verbal rehearsal? Torgesen and Goldman's (1977) reading-disabled subjects scored worse than controls in a delayed serial recall task. The reading disabled rehearsed less than did the controls during the delay interval. When disabled readers were instructed in the use of verbal rehearsal, both rehearsal and recall differences between the two groups were eliminated. According to the researchers, disabled readers experience difficulties in the "management" of STM rather than being limited in its capacity. Other studies show that verbal rehearsal becomes fully efficient by age 13 in children with learning disabilities compared with age 11 in controls (Taver, Hallahan, Cohen, & Kauffman, 1977).

SEQUENTIAL VERSUS NON-SEQUENTIAL MATERIAL

Reading is a sequential process. In reproducing a heard series of digits or letters, memory for order was correlated with reading, whereas memory for items was not (Mason, Katz, & Wicklund, 1975; Stanley, Kaplan, & Poole, 1975). Poor readers made more errors than did good readers in retaining temporal sequences of figures and letters, but only when these materials were meaningful (Bakker, 1972). In another study, Grade 2 good readers (above 80th percentile) were better than poor readers (below 40th percentile) in their ability to order a five-item series that could be easily recoded as words (*horse, fish,* etc.), but not in their ability to order five unlabelable doodles (Katz, Shankweiler, & Liberman, 1981).

Corkin (1974), on the other hand, reports that "inferior" readers were poorer than average readers in reproducing a tapping sequence in the Knox cubes test after a 6-sec delay. It is possible that the average readers may have used, implicitly, verbal coding and rehearsal.

What happens if verbal rehearsal is prevented in a memory task? Noelker and Schumsky (1973) compared memory for form with memory for position in 9-year-old controls and reading retards (reading age at least 2 years below MA or 1 year below grade placement). The subjects' task was to reproduce a given series by placing a card or cards with black circles in the correct position within a series of other cards. Verbal rehearsal was prevented by requiring subjects to count aloud during the 10-sec interval between seeing and reproducing the series. Almost all subjects did well on the form task, but the two groups differed in the position task. Not only did the reading retards make many more errors but also they made them at all positions. The controls showed a bow serial-position effect, with no errors at the two ends.

Dyslexics score poorer than controls on the Digit Span subtest of WISC, but only slightly. Dyslexics' difficulty is magnified in serial lists longer than their memory span (Senf & Freundl, 1972). In a study by Cohen and Netley (1978), when a supraspan list of nine digits was auditorily given, LDs' recall was much poorer than controls' recall over all serial positions probed, including the first three and last three, which normally are recalled well.

Dyslexic children have poor STM for visual as well as auditory material, especially sequential material; they seem to have deficient STM management as well as capacity.

Decoding and Comprehension Deficits

Dyslexics have most difficulty with word decoding and spelling. But they also have difficulty with other aspects of reading and writing such as syntax, use of context, and ultimately text comprehension.

Word Decoding

A dyslexic might read *laugh* correctly, or as "funny" or "log," or not at all (Boder, 1971). Dyslexic readers are, in Vernon's (1957) words, "hopelessly uncertain and confused as to why certain successions of printed letters should correspond to certain phonetic sounds in words." The former dyslexic Simpson (1979) writes: "Those who learned to read without difficulty can best understand the labor reading is for a dyslexic by turning a page of text upside down and trying to decipher it [p. 42]." Dyslexia is sometimes referred to as "word blindness."

SLOW AND ERROR-PRONE WORD DECODING

Dyslexics have trouble decoding words, that is, converting printed words into sounds. Fisher's (1980) reading disabled readers (2 years behind and in a remedial school) and Shankweiler and Liberman's (1972) poor readers could do as well as controls at repeating orally presented words but not at recalling or reading aloud visually presented words. Snowling's (1980) dyslexic subjects did as well as controls in visual–visual matching of pseudowords (*sond–snod*) but did a lot worse than the controls in visual–auditory matching of the same stimuli. Calfee (1982) reports that his learning disabled group (identified at schools) not only decodes words worse than average readers and poor readers (the bottom quartile), but also shows little improvement in decoding through Grade 4, and is still performing poorly in Grade 6, the highest grade studied.

A coding test can distinguish good readers from poor readers and dyslexics from poor readers. Mackworth and Mackworth (1974) gave their version of a coding test to children in each of six grades (1–6), who formed three groups—five good and five poor readers from each grade, and eight dyslexics from an institute. All groups had IQs above 100. The subjects judged whether pairs of visually presented pictures, letters, or words, looked or sounded the same.

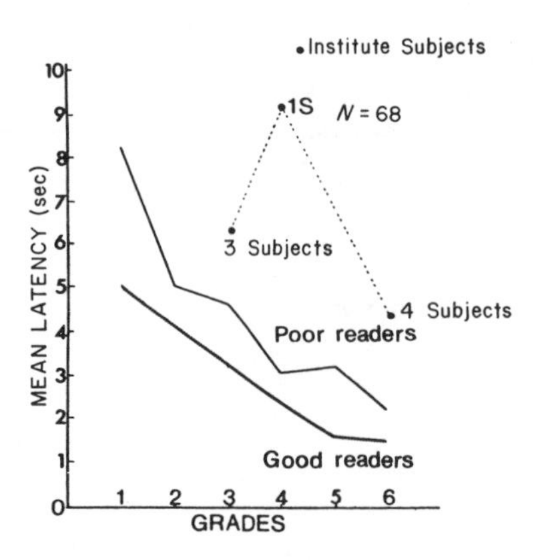

Figure 16-1. *Coding test: time to respond to letter and word pairs by good, poor, and dyslexic readers. N = 68 is the total number of good and poor readers (from Mackworth & Mackworth, 1974, p. 300, reproduced with permission of the authors and the National Reading Conference).*

Examples of word pairs were *road–read* and *pair–pear*. In each grade, the poor readers made more errors than the good readers, and the dyslexics made more errors than the poor readers. (The picture stimuli did not distinguish the groups.) The same pattern was obtained on speed of coding: In each grade the poor readers were slower than the good readers, and the dyslexics were slower still, as shown in Figure 16-1.

Bouma and Legein (1980) in the Netherlands compared dyslexics (1–4 years below the normal reading level) and controls (4–6 grade level) in their speed of letter recognition. The two groups did equally well in identifying and naming isolated letters, but the dyslexics were slower than the controls in identifying embedded letters ('xcx', 'xfx') and words, whether seen foveally or parafoveally. Long latencies and many errors tended to go together. The long latencies may give time for visual information to disappear from volatile visual stores before it can be put into a more stable speech code. Thus, Bouma and Legein trace the source of dyslexics' difficulty to phonetic coding of visually presented linguistic material. Their interpretation may well be true, but the effect may be part of a more general LEFT-track deficiency that shows up both in analysing internal letters and in performing phonetic coding.

BIZARRE VERSUS PHONETIC SPELLING

Some dyslexics' spelling errors are bizarre, and their handwriting uncertain, as can be seen in Figure 16-2.

By examining spelling errors, Thompson (1964) diagnosed the assassin of President John F. Kennedy, Lee Oswald, as a dyslexic and not a functional illiterate. In his Russian journal, Oswald spelled "giued" (*guide*), "Sovite" (*Soviet*), "wacth" (*watch*), "fonud" (*found*)," and so on. Oswald's words contained all the required letters but in the wrong order.

Most dyslexics are poor spellers, but not all poor spellers are dyslexics (Naidoo, 1972). Some good readers are poor spellers. In fact, a few good readers, and even good writers, are atrocious spellers. The great Danish writer of children's stories, Hans Christian Andersen, is said to have been a terrible speller. Nelson and Warrington (1974) could distinguish two types of children:

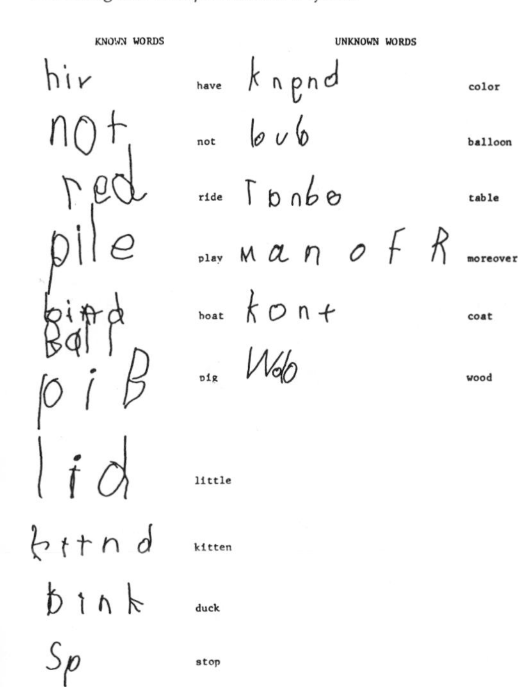

Figure 16-2. *Nonphonetic spelling of a dyslexic boy (mixed subtype), $8\frac{1}{2}$-years-old (Grade 3), IQ 120 (Verbal 110, Performance 128) (from Boder, 1971, p. 307, reproduced with permission of Grune & Stratton).*

those retarded only in spelling and those retarded in both spelling and reading. The latter tend to have lower Verbal than Performance IQs, and to produce nonphonetic spelling errors. Frith (1980) reports similar results. Her examples of phonetic errors are "coff, cof" and of nonphonetic ones "couge, coft" for *cough.*

DEFICIENT WORD KNOWLEDGE

One requirement for being a skilled reader is to have rapid access to the meanings of a large number of words. Many studies find substantial correlations between vocabulary and reading comprehension in normal readers (e.g., Davis, 1968; Graesser *et al.*, 1980; Singer & Crouse, 1981; Stevenson *et al.*, 1982; Thorndike, 1973). Poor readers are less fluent and know fewer words than good readers. Their definitions of words are less mature than those of the good readers: They tend to give descriptive definitions (a bike has wheels) rather than categorical definitions (a bike is a vehicle) (Fry, Johnson, & Muehl, 1970).

Even when they know words, dyslexic readers seem to be slow at retrieving them. Denckla and Rudel (1976) compared dyslexics and average readers aged 7–12 on "rapid automatic naming task." The subjects had to produce names of common objects, colors, letters, words, and numbers, which were presented visually. The dyslexic readers made more errors and took longer than did the average readers on this task. Without time pressure, the dyslexic readers had no difficulty naming most of these common objects. Wiig and Semel (1975) found the same kinds of differences between good and LD adolescent readers (2 years behind). For example, in naming verbal opposites, the LD adolescents were less quick and accurate than were controls.

Subtypes of Dyslexics

Dyslexics are not all the same but can be divided into subtypes. One of the earliest classifications into subtypes was made by Kinsbourne and Warrington (1963), who divided a small clinical population of backward readers into two groups based on a discrepancy of more than 20 points between Verbal and Performance IQs: In one group (7 cases) VIQ was higher than PIQ, whereas in the other group (6 cases) it was lower. Other evidence of language disorder, besides simple reading retardation, was found only in the group with lower VIQ.

Reading involves at least two basic components: visual and phonetic-linguistic. Dyslexics can be selectively deficient in either. In most studies, the phonetically deficient subtype occurs far more frequently than the visually deficient subtype (Cotterell, 1972; Ingram, Mason, & Blackburn, 1970; Mattis, French, & Rapin, 1975; Myklebust, 1965; Pirozzolo, 1979).

PHONETIC-LINGUISTIC DYSLEXIA

Boder (1971) studied 107 dyslexics (92 boys and 15 girls), aged 8–16, who had IQs 90 or higher and came to her clinic from a wide range of social classes. She classified the children according to their errors in reading and spelling words that were either within or outside their sight vocabulary. The dyslexics' spelling errors differed both qualitatively and quantitatively from those of normal readers.

A majority (63%) of Boder's cases were **phonetic-linguistic dyslexics,** who have difficulty in converting letters into sounds and hence read words globally. They can extract meanings from the visual forms of words, as long as the words are within their sight vocabulary. The most striking errors, observed primarily in reading but also in spelling, are substitutions of words closely related semantically but not phonetically, such as "funny" for *laugh* and "animal" for *cattle.* As is seen in Figure 16-2, a phonetic dyslexic's correctly written words stand out in a hodgepodge of misspellings, among which the original words can seldom be identified even by the writer.

Mattis (1978) also reports that 63% of his 400 dyslexic subjects (aged between 8 and 10) had language disorders. An additional 10% showed the syndrome of "articulatory and graphomotor dyscoordination." Pirozzolo's (1979) audio-linguistic group have language disorders, lower Verbal than Performance IQs, greater trouble with function than with content words, and faulty grapheme–phoneme matching in reading. Their eye movements are normal, at least in reading easy text.

Mitterer (1982) gave a battery of tests to Grade 3 good readers and poor readers (taking remedial programs). Poor readers divided into two distinct groups: One group depended primarily on whole-word recognition and did not decode words into sounds; the other group was the reverse. The tendency to use one route or the other was not related either to reading ability or to intelligence. The "whole-word poor readers" read regular words no better than irregular words; were adversely affected by case-alternation; did poorly on lexical decision; and were not affected adversely by concurrent vocalizing during lexical decision.

VISUAL-PERCEPTUAL DYSLEXIA

A small proportion of dyslexics—9% in Boder's sample and 5% in Mattis's sample—are **visual-perceptual dyslexics,** who find it difficult to perceive letters and words as visual wholes or Gestalts. They can read laboriously, using phonetic analysis, word lists up to or near their grade level, missing only words that cannot be decoded phonetically. *Laugh* may not be read at all, or may be read as "log" or "loge"; *talk* may come out as "talc."

A visual-perceptual dyslexic spells as he reads, phonetically, by ear. His misspellings are not so bizarre as are those of the phonetic type, and intended words can be readily identified. Examples might be "laf" for *laugh* and "tok" for *talk.* Simple irregularly spelled words in his limited sight vocabulary are usually written incorrectly, whereas a long and unfamiliar regular word not in his sight vocabulary may be written correctly.

Pirozzolo's visual-spatial dyslexics are weak in visual, spatial, and occulomotor skills such as directional and topographical orientation. They show atypical eye-movement patterns, and find it difficult to recognize words presented in parafoveal vision. Mitterer's "recoding poor readers" read regular words better than irregular ones; were not affected by case-alternation; did well on lexical decision; and were adversely affected by concurrent vocalizing.

MIXED AND OTHER TYPES OF DYSLEXIA

A child who has both phonetic and visual dyslexia shows the most severe reading impairment. Such a child shows letter orientation confusion more than do the children in the preceding two subtypes. Boder estimates 22% of her dyslexic subjects to be of this type, and 6% to be unclassifiable. Other researchers also have a mixed class or an unspecifiable subclass (e.g., Dalby & Gibson, 1981; Ingram *et al.*, 1970).

Using a statistical method (Q-technique of factor analysis), a team of Canadian researchers classified 88 reading-disabled children who had average IQs but were 2 or more years delayed in reading (Doehring, Trites, Patel, & Fiedorowicz, 1981). Three types emerged: (*a*) Type O (oral reading deficit) include 33 subjects who were poor on oral reading; (*b*) Type A (association deficit) include 22 who were poor on matching printed and spoken materials and showed LH dysfunction; and (*c*) Type S (sequential deficit) include 17 who were poorer in reading words and nonsense syllables than in reading letters and numbers. All three groups seem to be subsumed under the phonetic-linguistic type. Perhaps their sample size, 88, is not large enough to reveal visual subtypes.

Satz and Morris (1981) also used a statistical method (cluster analysis), both to search for the target group and to compare subtypes of the target group. Of 236 white boys (mean age 11) tested, 89 could be labeled as learning disabled because of their depressed reading performance (a 2-year deficit). The LDs fell into five subtypes: (*a*) 27 children with global language impairment; (*b*) 14 with naming difficulty; (*c*) 23 with perceptual–motor deficiency; (*d*) 10 with both (a) and (c); and (*e*) 12 with unexpected LD (average on cognitive and IQ tests). Subtypes (a) and (c), but not (b) and (e), showed a trend toward low SES, and included a high proportion of neurological "soft signs" (see "Minimal Brain Dysfunction" below).

As Doehring *et al.* (1981) point out, the types of reading disabilities identified may depend on the number and types of tests, the population sampled, and the method of classification. They predict that more rather than fewer types will be identified as classification methods improve.

ARE SUBTYPES REAL?

May not the reading–spelling patterns of phonetic or visual dyslexics actually reflect methods of teaching rather than different patterns of deficit? Boder's (1971) answer is "not likely." She points out that for the last 10 years, reading instruction in the Los Angeles city schools has been eclectic as a matter of policy, using both whole-word and phonics methods. Furthermore, each child has had many teachers, who presumably emphasize different patterns. Regardless of which method is introduced initially, a normal reader usually discovers the other pattern of reading for himself. Mitterer (1982) found two distinct subgroups among a population who had all been taught by the same methods.

Boder suggests that a genetic factor may exist in each of the three reading–spelling patterns. All but two of the sets of dyslexic siblings in her sample—a total of 39 siblings from 16 families—fell into the same reading–spelling pattern group. Fried (1979) reports that phonetic, but not visual, dyslexics showed inadequate cerebral dominance (see "Neurological and Constitutional Factors").

"Homogeneous" normal readers (undergraduates in one college) can be classified as visual or linguistic readers, depending on the strategy they use in verifying whether a given sentence describes a given picture. A smaller group of subjects uses a visual-spatial strategy whereas a larger group uses a linguistic strategy. About one-seventh of the subjects cannot be classified into either type (MacLeod, Hunt, & Mathews, 1978). Normal readers differ similarly in their strategies of word recognition: Some are "Chinese" (whole-word readers), others "Phoenicians" (recoding readers) (see Chapter 10, "Individual Differences").

Dyslexics, who are known for their heterogeneity, should be classifiable into at least two basic types, plus the inevitable non-classifiable type. (Acquired dyslexia is routinely classified into several subtypes. See Chapter 11 and later in this chapter.) Yet, not all students of developmental dyslexia use even the two basic subtypes. In most research, results are averaged for a whole dyslexic group, which sometimes includes non-dyslexic poor readers. This lack of selectivity glosses over probable differences between subtypes.

Deficient Comprehension and Integration

Severe difficulty in word decoding is bound to affect comprehension adversely. To begin with, when many of the words making up a text are decoded incorrectly, the text becomes a collection of nonsense words. The former dyslexic Simpson (1979) recalls: "I clutched at recognizable words, guessed at others, and invented what I thought would make a suitable connective," until her aunt thundered: "What is this gibberish [p. 14]?"

Rapid and accurate word decoding is not the only prerequisite to good comprehension; the connections among words and sentences must also be understood. Thus, training poor readers to read a list of words rapidly does not improve their comprehension of a passage made up using the words in the list (Fleisher *et al.*, 1979–1980). A reader must learn to read in large units, to use context, syntax, and text structure (see Chapters 8, 12, and 13).

READING UNIT

Large reading units lighten the processing load and help comprehension. Several studies show that poor readers tend to use small reading units. Cromer (1970) identified one form of reading difficulty among junior college students as failure to organize incoming reading material into large meaningful units. This group had adequate intelligence, language skills, and vocabulary, but had difficulty comprehending, presumably because they read word by word rather than in phrases and clauses.

Cromer presented a set of stories in four modes:

1. Regular sentence: *The cow jumped over the moon.*
2. Single words: (one word per line)
3. Phrase: *The cow jumped   over the moon.*
4. Fragmented grouping: *The cow   jumped over the   moon.*

The group with deficient organization answered fewer questions in multiple-choice tests than did the good readers. More interestingly, they comprehended better on the phrase mode than on the other three modes. By contrast, the group deficient in vocabulary were best on the single-word mode, not on the phrase mode. The two groups did not differ from normal readers in reading aloud the words presented singly, showing that adequate word identification was insufficient for comprehending text. Other studies extended Cromer's findings to an elementary school population (Gioffi, 1982; Isakson & Miller, 1976).

USE OF CONTEXT

Context provides a great deal of semantic and syntactic information about an individual word. Poor readers make use of context, but not as efficiently as do good readers, as discussed in Chapter 8. Guthrie (1973b) studied the use of context by three groups of children: 10-year-old disabled readers (in remedial classes) and two groups of normal readers, 10-years-old and 7-years-old. The Peabody (vocabulary) IQs of the three groups were 100.1, 105.6, and 108.3, respectively. Their task was to select one word out of three possibilities for sentence completion:

Both { *horses* / *flowers* / *talk* } *lifted their ears.*

All test sentences appeared within the context of larger passages, which the children read silently. The disabled readers were inferior to both groups of normal readers in comprehending the materials, despite possessing an adequate sight vocabulary.

SYNTAX, SENTENCE, AND TEXT

Vogel (1974) showed that the syntactic skills of young dyslexics are poorer than those of normal readers, even in oral tests. Wiig and Semel (1975) showed that syntactic deficits in dyslexic children persist into adolescence. In the use of syntax, normals achieved their highest level of usage by age 11; the learning disabled (LD), by 15. When required to form a sentence using words such as *coat, after,* and *belong*, LD adolescents produced many ungrammatical and incomplete sentences, such as "After the ball game," or "After the school." Asked if the sentences were complete, none of them was able to answer; nor could they complete their partial sentences. Their sentences, even when complete, tended to be declarative and simple, with few subordinating and conjoining clauses. LD adolescents' speech lacked specificity, containing many function words, interjections, filled pauses, and word repetitions. The written language of LDs showed many deviations from that of normals. A major difference, as determined by the Picture Story Language Test, was in Productivity (verbal output): They showed a deficit in total words, total sentences, and words per sentence.

In Fisher's (1980) study, disabled readers (2 years behind and in a remedial class) and normal readers of the same age were comparable in learning individual ideographs (stick figures and symbols). In reading a sentence constructed with the ideographs, the disabled performed worse than did the controls. And, in producing their own sentences using the ideographs, they made shorter and simpler sentences than did the controls.

In Calfee's (1982) study, LDs did not comprehend text as well as did average readers and bottom-quartile poor readers at the three Grades tested: 2, 4, and 6. Furthermore, comprehension was much worse in reading than in listening for the LDs, whereas it was slightly better in reading than in listening for the average readers and the poor readers. Idea units (roughly, clauses) making up a text differ in structural importance (see Chapter 13). In both reading and listening to stories, good readers recalled more idea units, especially important ones, than did poor readers (in a remedial program, 2 or more years below the grade level) (Smiley *et al.*, 1977).

Conclusion: Mostly Verbal but Some Perceptual Deficit

Two major theories on dyslexia are "perceptual deficit" and "verbal deficit." Orton (1937) believed that poorly established hemispheric dominance results in an unstable spatial organization of letters and words. Modern students of dyslexia, such as Vellutino (1979), Jorm (1979), and Fisher (1980) argue against the perceptual deficit theory and for the verbal deficit theory of dyslexia. Specifically, they assert that reading problems result from deficiencies in one or more aspects of linguistic functioning, or from a specific disorder in visual–verbal integration.

Visual–perceptual–motor problems are more prevalent in young children (ages 5–7), whereas language-related problems persist or become apparent in older children (11–14) (Fletcher & Satz, 1980). With increasing age the relation between perceptual skills and reading decreases (Hartlage, 1975; Miller & McKenna, 1981). For beginning readers, all letters are new and complex, requiring close visuo-spatial analysis.

The literature surveyed in this chapter leads us to endorse the verbal deficit theory. At the same time, we would not completely bury the perceptual deficit theory. Perceptual tests have some predictive power for reading, albeit less than that of verbal tests, and some dyslexics are deficient in processing rapid sequential materials, be they auditory or visual. Recall that 9% (Boder, 1971) or 5% (Mattis, 1978) of dyslexic children have visual-perceptual problems. Perceptual deficits may underly some verbal deficits, or some dyslexics may have a perceptual deficit which is important for some kinds of material. After all, reading has several components, and dyslexics are heterogeneous.

Of the dyslexic with a verbal deficit, there are at least two types, depending on whether the deficiency is mainly in the LEFT or the RIGHT track. A deficient LEFT track leads to poor phonetic coding, poor syntactic integration, poor sequencing, and poor STM. A deficient RIGHT track leads to poor visual word recognition, poor comprehension of associations and real-world relationships, and perhaps poor LTM. Studies which lump both kinds of dyslexic together, perhaps also with other retarded readers, are likely to find small inconsistent deficiencies of all kinds.

Neurological and Constitutional Factors

"It [dyslexia] is dependent upon fundamental cognitive disabilities which are frequently of constitutional origin." In the last section, we concentrated on the fundamental cognitive disabilities; here, we consider constitutional origin, specifically, cerebral functions and genetic factors.

Abnormal Neurological Functioning

Dyslexic children with gross and overt brain damage are often excluded from subject pools for research purpose. Nevertheless, some of the remainder appear to have subtle neural deficiencies. Five basic methods of studying cortical functions are (*a*) direct examination of the brain for any structural damage, sometimes postmortem; (*b*) behavioral deviations; (*c*) comparison with acquired dyslexia which is caused by known brain lesions; (*d*) psychological tests that tap hemispheric processing; and (*e*) recording evoked potentials from the cortex.

ANATOMICAL ABNORMALITY

The Orton Society has begun collecting postmortem brain specimens of dyslexic and normal individuals.[2] Initial findings are expected in the early 1980s (Sobotowicz & Evans, 1982). Meanwhile, there is anatomical evidence of slowed development in the left hemisphere of one male dyslexic who died in an accident (Galaburda & Kemper, 1979; Geschwind, 1979). In normal people's cortex, the planum temporale, part of Wernicke's area, is markedly larger in the left than in the right hemisphere. In the deceased dyslexic's cortex, the discrepancy between the two hemispheres in the size of the planum temporale was much reduced. Furthermore, there was a large island of cortical tissue in an abnormal location below the left planum. The case was left-handed and had also suffered a seizure.

In computerized brain tomograms (CAT scans), 10 of 24 adolescent and adult dyslexics had brains that were wider in the right parieto–occipital region than in the left. This group also had a lower Verbal IQ than subjects whose left parieto–occipital region was wider or equal to the right (Hier, LeMay, Rosenberger, & Perlo, 1978).

MINIMAL BRAIN DYSFUNCTION

The label **minimal brain dysfunction** (MBD) applies to a child who has no clear "hard" neurological signs but has **soft signs** that may be responsible for language retardation, motor clumsiness, perceptual deficits, right–left confusion, hyperactivity, poor directional sense, poor hand–eye coordination, poor body image, and so on. These behavioral deviations, if they persist strongly beyond age around 8, suggest abnormal functioning of the central nervous system, even though such a diagnosis is not revealed in the standard neurological examination. Some LD children show soft signs, some do not. Conversely, not all children with soft signs suffer from LD (see Gaddes, 1980; Nichols & Chen, 1981; Satz & Morris, 1981; Spreen, 1982).

DEVELOPMENTAL VERSUS ACQUIRED DYSLEXIA

Acquired dyslexia is loss of reading ability due to brain damage. By comparing symptoms between acquired and developmental dyslexia, it may

[2]The Orton Society is an association of people interested in dyslexia. Samuel Orton (1937) was the pioneer investigator of dyslexia in the United States.

be possible to learn about cortical deficiencies of the latter. Acquired dyslexia is often classified into several types, depending on the patterns of symptoms and lesions. In one taxonomy based largely on reading errors, there are phonemic dyslexia, surface dyslexia, and a few others, as discussed in Chapter 11.

The problems of phonemic dyslexia appear similar to those of phonetic-linguistic developmental dyslexia. In both groups, LEFT track and STM are deficient, impairing their abilities to decode letters into sounds, to recognize function words, and to decipher complex syntax. The most telling similarities between the two groups are seen in reading errors that differ from the correct words in sounds and appearances but resemble them in meaning: for phonemic dyslexics, *ill* → "sick" or *jail* → "prison"; for Boder's (1971) phonetic dyslexics, *laugh* → "funny," or *cattle* → "animal."

A team of British researchers tested the phonetic coding abilities of 15 dyslexic boys, using the lexical decision tasks designed for adult phonemic dyslexics (Baddeley, Ellis, Miles, & Lewis, 1982). Whereas Patterson and Marcel's (1977) two adult phonemic dyslexics could do a lexical decision task but showed no evidence of phonetic coding of nonwords, the dyslexic boys made lexical decisions slowly and inaccurately but were able to do some phonetic coding of nonwords. Baddeley *et al.* chose to conclude that their dyslexic boys differ qualitatively from Patterson and Marcel's phonemic dyslexics.

This conclusion appears to be unjustified. Patterson and Marcel's tests tap only part of all the varied and complex facets of phonemic dyslexia (see Chapter 11); their two patients have massive damage in the LH, whereas dyslexic children are assumed to have subtle deficiencies in the LH. Baddeley *et al.*'s 15 dyslexic boys were considered as one homogeneous group, when some may have been of the phonetic-linguistic type, some visual-perceptual.

Adult surface dyslexics recognize words based entirely on phonetic coding, which is defective. Surface dyslexics somewhat resemble Boder's visual dyslexics. Holmes (1978) tested two adults with surface dyslexia and four boys with developmental dyslexia on the same 800-word list. The boys' errors bore striking similarities to the adults's errors. Examples of errors made by both groups are *bike* → "[bik]"; *wage* → "wag"; *insect* → "insist"; *gorge*→"[goug]" (the response words shown in [ ] are nonwords). In both groups the stimuli and the errors are similar in sounds but dissimilar in meanings.

In a taxonomy based on the locations of lesions, acquired dyslexia, or **alexia,** is classified into three types (Benson, 1981; see Figure 1-1 for the areas of the cortex). Posterior alexia results from a lesion that disconnects visual information from the LH speech areas. For example, when the left occipital lobe as well as the corpus callosum are damaged, visual information from the intact right occipital lobe cannot be interpreted by the speech areas of the left hemisphere. The patient loses reading ability without comparable impairment in writing or oral language. Central alexia results from damage in the left parietal–temporal lobe, often involving the angular gyrus. The patient cannot read or write. Some patients, after a number of years, comprehend some written language, especially concrete words, making such characteristic errors as *infant* → "baby." The RH seems to have taken over the functions of reading. Anterior alexia, which accompanies Broca's aphasia, involves difficulty with syntax, especially with function words.

Three types of alexia may have counterparts in developmental dyslexia (Aaron, Baker, & Hickox, 1982). Aaron *et al.* assessed linguistic, perceptual, and cognitive skills of three groups of subjects: 17 college students with reading disability (who responded to an ad); 15 children (Grades 3 and 4) who read 2 grades below expectation; 5 normal readers (mean age 8:9). Both groups of dyslexics (but none of normal readers) could be classified into the three types of adult alexia based on the patterns of their test scores. About one-third of the older and one-quarter of the younger dyslexics did not match any of the the three types.

In sum, there is a good resemblance between some types of acquired dyslexia and some types of developmental dyslexia, even though the symptoms of the developmental dyslexics are seldom as clear-cut or as severe as those of the acquired dyslexics.

EEG AND EVOKED POTENTIALS

EEG shows the spontaneous electrical activity of the brain. One large-scale study found a high incidence of EEG abnormalities in children with learning disability and those at risk for various neurological disorders (Ahn, Prichep, John, Baird, Trepetin, & Kaye, 1980). In a review of the literature, the incidence of EEG abnormality is higher in dyslexics than in normal controls. The dyslexics' abnormal patterns are of several types, which may be related to different patterns of reading difficulty (Hughes, 1982).

A team of researchers measured **evoked potentials** to two types of stimuli, words and flashes, at a left parietal site of normal readers and dyslexics (Preston, Guthrie, Kirsch, Gertman, & Childs, 1977). The difference between the responses to words and to flashes reflects additional processing in the verbal task. This additional processing may be impaired in disabled readers, who showed small word–flash difference.

Other teams studied the differences in waveform of evoked potentials to words and to musical chords (Fried, 1979; Fried, Tanguay, Boder, Doubleday, & Greensite, 1981; Wood, Goff, & Day, 1971). The differences were greater over the left (LH) than over the right hemisphere (RH) in normal as well as in visual dyslexic subjects but not in phonetic dyslexics. (Visual dyslexics differed from normals in overall latencies but not in cerebral dominance.) The greater waveform differences over the LH, compared with the RH, may reflect the LH capacity to differentiate between verbal and nonverbal stimuli in normal adults and children. This capacity may be impaired in phonetic dyslexics.

PSYCHOLOGICAL TESTS OF LATERALITY

Psychological tests of brain laterality compare processing of information presented to one or the other ear, hand, or visual field of either eye. In each case, the left side is represented in the RH, and the right side in the LH.

In a **dichotic test,** an investigator presents acoustic stimuli to a subject's two ears simultaneously. For verbal (words, digits) material, a normal subject shows a **right-ear advantage**; that is, he processes better the verbal material presented to his right ear than to his left ear, implying LH processing. For nonverbal material, a normal listener shows a left-ear advantage (Kimura, 1961, 1964). Similarly, a normal subject shows a right visual-field advantage for visually presented verbal material, and left visual-field advantage for shape, as described in Chapters 1, 3, 4, and 11.

Findings with dyslexics are thoroughly confusing. For verbal material, some researchers report a right ear/visual-field advantage in normal readers as well as in dyslexics, but to a lower degree in dyslexics than in normal readers (e.g., Bryden, 1970; Keefe & Swinney, 1979; Leong, 1976; Marcel, Katz, & Smith, 1974; Mercure & Warren, 1978; Newell & Rugel, 1981; Witelson, 1977). Some researchers found no ear or eye asymmetry, or a slight left ear/visual-field advantage (RH processing) for dyslexics (Marcel & Rajan, 1975; McKeever & Van Deventer, 1975; Thomson, 1976; Witelson & Rabinovitch, 1972; Zurif & Carson, 1970). In contrast to the preceding studies, one study found that poor readers showed either a right visual-field advantage (LH processing) or a trend toward it, whereas good readers showed no right visual-field advantage (Yeni-Komshian, Isenberg, & Goldberg, 1975). Some researchers find that ear asymmetry does not distinguish dyslexics from normal readers in younger children (7–8), but it does in older children (11–12) (Bakker, 1969; Malatesha, 1977; Satz & Sparrow, 1970).

In Naylor's (1980) review of the literature, asymmetry (LH better than RH), in relation to controls, was greater in the reading disabled in 3 studies, equal in 21, and less in 15. We may conclude, if gingerly: Although the direction of laterality is similar for dyslexic and normal readers, the degree of LH specialization is less for the dyslexics, especially among the older ones.

A few studies considered dyslexics in subgroups. Pirozzolo and Rayner (1979) compared dyslexics and controls on their recognition of words and faces seen either in the left or right visual field (LVF, RVF). The dyslexics were 12-year-olds of the auditory-linguistic type, who were delayed in reading by 2 years and whose Verbal IQ (95) was lower than their Performance IQ (114). The Verbal and Performance IQs of the controls were equal (105). For faces, LVF recognition was superior for both groups, implying normal RH processing. For words, the dyslexic readers showed no RVF advantage (which suggests inadequate LH processing), whereas the controls did. Dalby and Gibson (1981) also found evidence of right lateralization of verbal material in 11 of 15 phonetic dyslexics but not in 15 visual or 15 non-specific dyslexics. Kerschner (1977) compared three groups of readers: gifted, good, and disabled. The RVF advantage for words (LH processing) was highest for the gifted, next for the good, and lowest for the disabled readers.

Abnormal LH processing by dyslexics was suggested some decades ago, notably by Orton (1937). Modern psychological tests often point to abnormal LH processing in dyslexics. In what way is it abnormal? Is the maturation of the LH delayed (Geschwind, 1965; Kinsbourne & Hiscock, 1978) or incomplete (Zurif & Carson, 1970)? Is LH's normal function interfered with because the LH is also used for RH spatial function (Witelson, 1977)? Is LH–RH integration deficient (Vernon, 1977)? Is transmission of linguistic information within LH slow (Pirozzolo & Rayner, 1979)? Are words processed by a RH-based perceptual coding (Kerschner, 1977)? Is there a time lag in transferring information from the RH to the LH (Davidson, 1982)? Is RH deficient (Yeni-Komshian *et al.*, 1975)?

Perhaps sex differences may shed some light on this controversy. More boys than girls, by four to one, are dyslexic. Why? Anatomically, males show larger asymmetry of the cortex in comparison with females (Wada, Clark, & Hamm, 1975). Functionally, men show greater LH specialization for verbal processing and greater RH specialization for spatial processing than do women (J. Levy, 1972). Inglis and Lawson's (1981) reanalysis of data from over a dozen different studies supports McGlone's (1978) earlier finding on male–female differences: Only the male patients showed a lateralized effect of brain damage, those with LH damage being impaired on the Verbal Scale and those with RH damage being impaired on the Performance Scale. The female patients did not show selective deficits on these scales after comparable brain damage in one hemisphere or the other.

Hier (1979) suggests that early and strong hemispheric specialization of boys could add to their risk of becoming dyslexic because they cannot easily compensate for any neural damage or deficiency. In disorders other than dyslexia too, boys are more susceptible than are girls. For example, more boys than girls, by five to one, stutter. Most color-blind people are male, as are most hemophiliacs. These are all sex-linked genetically controlled conditions.

Genetic Factors

DYSLEXICS' FAMILIES

Dyslexia seems to run in families. Owen *et al.* (1971) compared 76 controls matched with 76 "educationally handicapped" children (reading and/or spelling 1.5–2 years below grade level) and their family members. Here are some of their findings on the families of the handicapped:

- Their same-sex siblings were slightly below grade level in reading; the controls' siblings were 1 year above.
- Their siblings were retarded 1 year in spelling; the controls' siblings were retarded by 3 months.
- Their fathers obtained poorer scores on a reading test than the fathers of the controls.
- Their fathers and mothers had poorer grades in high school English than did the fathers and mothers of the controls.

Children whose Performance IQ exceeded their Verbal IQ on the WISC by 15 or more points represented the most "pure" dyslexic group, and their same-sex siblings showed many similar impairments. Other investigators tested the cognitive abilities of 58 reading-disabled children, matched controls, and their nuclear families (Foch, DeFries, McLearn, & Singer, 1977). The male relatives of the disabled children showed deficits in reading, spelling, auditory memory, perceptual speed, and verbal reasoning. Their mothers and sisters appeared to be less severely affected.

In one of the largest multi-pedigree studies, Hallgren (1950) in Stockholm studied 116 subjects (86 boys and 27 girls). The percentages of affected relatives were 47% brothers versus 35% sisters, and 47% fathers versus 38% mothers. Thus, 47% of male members and 37% of female members were affected. Dyslexia could be observed in families for three successive generations.

Gorden (1980) in Israel found that dyslexic children (2 years behind) were consistently better on tests of RH than of LH function. Most (90%) of the first-degree family members of the dyslexics also had the same profile, even though most of them claimed never to have had reading problems.

In a large-scale study of 7-year-old children in multiracial, low-SES communities in the United States, Nichols and Chen (1981) found that learning disabilities run in families. Because the estimated risks of LD to full and half-siblings of affected were nearly identical, and because risks to other relatives did not vary systematically by degree of relationship, this strong familial association appeared to be environmentally determined.

By contrast, studies of twins suggest genetic transmission. Monozygotic (MZ) twins, who come from a single egg, show a higher rate of concordance for dyslexia than dizygotic (DZ) twins, who come from two separate eggs. Through organizations for twins, Bakwin (1973) contacted 193 MZ male and female pairs and also 210 DZ male and female pairs. All were aged between 8 and 18, and came from middle income families. The overall incidence of reading disability among the twins was 14.5%, which is higher than the rate of 10% found in the general population. More MZ pairs (84%) than DZ pairs (29%) showed concordance for the disorder. In Zerbin-Rudin's (1967) summary of eight reports on twins, all 17 MZ twins were concordant for dyslexia, whereas only 12 of 34 DZ twins were so.

Summary and Conclusions

Dyslexic children read 2 or more years below their grade level, or could not read at all, despite having normal IQ. Many of them have a lower Verbal than Performance IQ.

Dyslexics seem deficient in cognitive skills, especially in their use of STM and in their processing of sequential material. Some show atypical eye movements, and some perceive poorly stimuli presented in a rapid sequence.

Early screening tests, especially the letter-naming test, can predict later reading difficulties. The earlier the diagnosis, the better the prognosis.

Dyslexic children experience difficulty learning letter–sound relations.

Some of them make orientation confusions and reverse letters. Their vocabulary is limited and their word retrieval is slow. Perhaps for all these reasons, their word decoding is slow and error prone. Over and above poor word decoding, they have deficient syntax, small reading units, inadequate use of context, and insensitivity to relative importance of idea units. Many of these skills develop through much reading, which dyslexics do not or cannot do.

Dyslexic children can be classified into at least two subtypes. The phonetic-inguistic type have difficulty in letter sequencing and in phonetic coding of words; they recognize words mainly by visual shape; and they resemble adults who suffer from phonemic dyslexia after a massive LH lesion. The visual type have trouble in perceiving words as visual wholes, and use phonetic coding to recognize words; they resemble adult surface dyslexics.

Dyslexic children may not have gross neural impairment but many (at least among the phonetic-linguistic type) seem to have a subtle deficiency in left-hemisphere processing. Dyslexia tends to run in families, especially among male members. There is evidence for both genetic and environmental transmission.

If dyslexia is defined as nonreading, and if noneading associated with low SES is excluded, the incidence of dyslexia is around 5% among school children in the developed countries that use alphabets. More boys than girls are dyslexic.

The apparent rarity of dyslexia in Japan, Korea, and Taiwan, suggests that learning to read is easy with a syllabary or Chinese characters. Even children with "cognitive disabilities of constitutional origin" may succeed in becoming no worse than poor readers if their scripts are easy for word decoding and sequencing.

So, after all,

> developmental dyslexia is a disorder manifested by difficulty in learning to read despite conventional instruction, adequate intelligence, and socio-cultural opportunity. It is dependent upon fundamental cognitive disabilities which are frequently of constitutional origin.

Epilogue

Reading has turned out to be far more complex than fluent readers have ever imagined. It is at once visual, phonetic, linguistic, cognitive, and neural.

Familiar words are recognized wholistically using a fast pattern-matching process, which can be done by both brain hemispheres but is usually done by the right. Unfamiliar words and pseudowords are coded from their letters using a slow, analytic–phonetic process in the left hemisphere.

In learning to read, both sets of processes must be developed and integrated, using whole-word and phonics methods. Learning proceeds in a series of three-phased cycles: recognizing a unit as a whole; analyzing it into subparts; and recognizing it as a whole again, based on securer recognition of its subparts. Poor or disabled reading results from failure to develop some part of the cycle.

Over the 5000 year history of writing, people have devised a variety of scripts, some now extinct, some still in use. They can be broadly classed as logographies, syllabaries, and alphabets, depending on the linguistic units coded by the individual symbols. Initially, logographs favor wholistic, whereas phonetic symbols favor analytic, recognition. But at some stage, logographs require some analysis, just as phonetic symbols involve wholistic recognition.

The goal of readers in any script is to comprehend the text and retain its gist. To realize this goal, they organize incoming material into larger units, distinguish important units from unimportant ones, and draw inferences. They carry out these comprehension processes in working memory, using mostly phonetic codes. Ultimately, the readers incorporate the gist in long-term memory or knowledge of the world.

Over 7 decades ago, Huey (1908) understood the supreme complexity of reading, when he said:

> And so to completely analyze what we do when we read would almost be the acme of a psychologist's achievements, for it would be to describe very many of the most intricate workings of the human mind, as well as to unravel the tangled story of the most remarkable specific performance that civilization has learned in all its history [p. 6].

Appendix: Some Acronyms Used in this Book

BE: Black English
BLC: Bilateral Cooperative (model of reading)
C: consonant
CVC: consonant–vowel–consonant (syllable)
DZ: dizygotic (fraternal twins)
EEG: electroencephalogram (a record of brain waves)
EMG: electromyogram (a record of minute muscle movements)
EVS: eye–voice span
IQ: intelligence quotient
i.t.a.: initial teaching alphabet
LD: learning disabilities
LH: left hemisphere (of the cortex)
LTM: long-term memory
LVF: left visual field (of each eye)
MA: mental age (as opposed to chronological age)
MZ: monozygotic (twins from a single egg)
NP: noun phrase, or negative–passive (sentence)
NQ: negative–question
PN: passive–negative
PNQ: passive–negative–question
P (X, Y) or (P, X, Y): (proposition) = Predicate (argument X, argument Y)
RH: right hemisphere
RVF: right visual field (of each eye)
RSVP: rapid serial visual presentation (of words)
SAAD: simple-active-affirmative-declarative sentence
SE: Standard English
SES: socioeconomic status
SVO: subject–verb–object (sentence)
STM: short-term memory
T-scope: tachistoscope
V: verb
V: vowel
VP: verb phrase
WISC: Wechsler Intelligence Scale for Children
WPM: words-per-minute
WSE: word superiority effect

References

Aaron, P. G. The neuropsychology of developmental dyslexia. In R. N. Malatesha, & P. G. Aaron (Eds.), *Reading disorders: Varieties and treatments*. New York: Academic Press, 1982.

Aaron, P. G., Baker, C., & Hickox, G. L. In search of the third dyslexia. *Neuropsychologia*, 1982, *20*, 203–208.

Aarons, L. Subvocalization: Aural and EMG feedback in reading. *Perceptual and Motor Skills*, 1971, *33*, 271–306.

Aaronson, D., & Scarborough, H. S. Performance theories for sentence coding: Some quantitative evidence. *Journal of Experimental Psychology: Human Perception and Performance*, 1976, *2*, 56–70.

Aaronson, D., & Scarborough, H. S. Performance theories for sentence coding: Quantitative models. *Journal of Verbal Learning and Verbal Behavior*, 1977, *16*, 277–303.

Aborn, M., Rubenstein, H., & Sterling, T. D. Sources of contextual constraint upon words in sentences. *Journal of Experimental Psychology*, 1959, *57*, 171–180.

Adams, M. J. Models of word recognition. *Cognitive Psychology*, 1979, *11*, 133–176.

Ahn, H., Prichep, L., John, E. R., Baird, H., Trepetin, M., & Kaye, H. Developmental equations reflect brain dysfunctions. *Science*, 1980, *210*, 1259–1262.

Ai, J. W. A report on psychological studies of the Chinese language in the past three decades. *Journal of Genetic Psychology*, 1950, *76*, 207–220.

Alba, J. W., Alexander, S. G., Hasher, L., & Caniglia, K. The role of context in the encoding of information. *Journal of Experimental Psychology: Human Learning and Memory*, 1981, *7*, 283–292.

Albrow, K. H. *The English writing system: Notes towards a description*. London: Longmans, 1972.

Alegria, J., & Pignot, E. Genetic aspects of verbal mediation in memory. *Child Development*, 1979, *50*, 235–238.

Alegria, J., Pignot, E., & Morais, J. Phonetic analysis of speech and memory codes in beginning readers. *Memory & Cognition*, 1982, *10*, 451–456.

Allen, J., Carlson, R., Granstrom, B., Hunnicutt, S., Klatt, D., & Pisoni, D. *Conversion of unrestricted English text to speech*. Cambridge, Mass: MIT, 1979.

Allington, R. L. Sensitivity to orthographic structure as a function of grade and reading ability. *Journal of Reading Behavior*, 1978, *10*, 437–439.

Alper, T. G. A diagnostic spelling scale for the college level: Its construction and use. *Journal of Educational Psychology*, 1942, *33*, 273–290.

Amano, K. Formation of the act of analyzing phonemic structure of words and its relation to learning Japanese syllabic characters (Kanamoji). *Japanese Journal of Educational Psychology*, 1970, *18*, 76–89, (in Japanese with English abstract).

Anderson, I. H. Studies in the eye movements of good and poor readers. *Psychological Monographs*, 1937, *48*, 1–35.

Anderson, I. H., & Dearborn, W. F. *The psychology of reading*. New York: Ronald, 1952.

Anderson, J. R. Verbatim and propositional representation of sentences in immediate and long-term memory. *Journal of Verbal Learning and Verbal Behavior*, 1974, *13*, 149–162.

Anderson, J. R., & Bower, G. H. Recognition and retrieval processes in free recall. *Psychological Review*, 1972, *29*, 97–123.
Anderson, R. C., & Biddle, W. B. On asking people questions about what they are reading. In G. H. Bower (Ed.), *Psychology of learning and motivation* (Vol. 9). New York: Academic Press, 1975.
Anderson, R. C., Pichert, J. W., Goetz, E. T., Schallert, D. L., Stevens, K. V., & Trollip, S. R. Instantiation of general terms. *Journal of Verbal Learning and Verbal Behavior*, 1976, *15*, 667–679.
Anderson, R. C., Pichert, J. W., & Shirey, L. L. *Effects of the reader's schema at different points in time*. Report 119, Center for the Study of Reading: Urbana, Ill, April, 1979.
Andreewsky, E., Deloche, G., & Kossanyi, P. Analogies between speed-reading and deep dyslexia: Towards a procedural understanding of reading. In M. Coltheart, K. E. Patterson, & J. C. Marshall (Eds.), *Deep dyslexia*. London: Routledge & Kegan Paul, 1980.
Andreewsky, E., & Seron, X. Implicit processing of grammatical rules in a case of agrammatism. *Cortex*, 1975, *11*, 379–390.
Anglin, J. M. *Word, object and conceptual development*. New York: W. W. Norton, 1977.
Aquino, M. R. The validity of the Miller–Coleman readability scale. *Reading Research Quarterly*, 1969, *4*, 342–357.
Aschcroft, S. C. Blind and partially seeing children. In L. M. Dunn (Ed.), *Exceptional children in the schools*. New York: Holt, Rinehart and Winston, 1967.
Ashton-Warner, S. *Teacher*. New York: Simon and Schuster, 1963.
Atkinson, R. C., & Shiffrin, R. M. The control of short-term memory. *Scientific American*, 1971, *225*, 82–90.
Aukerman, R. C. *The basal reader approach to reading*. New York: Wiley, 1981.
Austin, M. C., & Morrison, C. *The first R: The Harvard report on reading in elementary schools*. New York: Macmillan, 1963.
Austin, M. C., & Morrison, C. Early school screening practices. *Journal of Learning Disabilities*, 1974, *7*, 55–59.
Ausubel, D. P. *Educational psychology: A cognitive view*. New York: Holt, Rinehart and Winston, 1968.
Ausubel, D. P. In defense of advance organizers: A reply to the critics. *Review of Educational Research*, 1978, *48*, 251–257.
Baddeley, A. D. Working memory and reading. In P. A. Kolers, M. E. Wrolstad, & H. Bouma (Eds.), *Processing of visible language* (Vol. 1). New York: Plenum, 1979.
Baddeley, A. D., Eldridge, M., & Lewis, V. The role of subvocalization in reading. *Quarterly Journal of Psychology*, 1981, *33A*, 439–454.
Baddeley, A. D., Thomson, N., & Buchanan, M. Word length and the structure of short-term memory. *Journal of Verbal Learning and Verbal Behavior*, 1975, *14*, 575–589.
Baddeley, A. D., Ellis, N. C., Miles, T. R., & Lewis, V. J. Developmental and acquired dyslexia: A comparison. *Cognition*, 1982, *11*, 185–199.
Baddeley, A. D., & Hitch, G. J. Working memory. In G. A. Bower (Ed.), *The Psychology of learning and motivation* (Vol. 8). London: Academic Press, 1974.
Baddeley, A. D., & Lewis, V. L. Inner active processes in reading: The inner voice, the inner ear, and the inner eye. In A. M. Lesgold, & C. A. Perfetti (Eds.), *Interactive processes in reading*. Hillsdale, N.J.: Lawrence Erlbaum Associates, 1981.
Baker, L. Processing temporal relationships in simple stories: Effects of input sequence. *Journal of Verbal Learning and Verbal Behavior*, 1978, *17*, 559–572.
Bakker, D. J. Ear asymmetry with monaural stimulation: Task influence. *Cortex*, 1969, *5*, 36–42.
Bakker, D. J. *Temporal order in disturbed reading*. Rotterdam: Rotterdam University Press, 1972.
Bakwin, H. Reading disability in twins. *Developmental Medicine and Child Neurology*, 1973, *15*, 184–187.
Baldwin, R. S. Clause strategies as a factor in reading comprehension. In P. D. Pearson, & J. Hansen (Eds.), *Reading: Theory, research and practice*. (26th Yearbook of the National Reading Conference), Clemens, S.C.: National Reading Conference, 1977.

Baldwin, R. S., & Coady, J. M. Psycholinguistic approaches to a theory of punctuation. *Journal of Reading Behavior*, 1978, *10*, 363–375.

Ballentine, F. A. Age changes in measures of eye-movements in silent reading. In *Studies in psychology of reading*. Monograph in Education No. 4, Ann Arbor: University of Michigan Press, 1951.

Barnard, D. P., & DeGracie, J. Vocabulary analysis of new primary reading series. *Reading Teacher*, 1976, *30*, 177–180.

Barnitz, J. G. Syntactic effects on the reading comprehension of pronoun–referent structures by children in grades two, four and six. *Reading Research Quarterly*, 1980, *15*, 268–289.

Baron, J. Mechanisms for pronouncing printed words: Use and acquisition. In D. LaBerge, & S. J. Samuels (Eds.), *Basic processes in reading: Perception and comprehension*. Hillsdale, N.J.: Lawrence Erlbaum Associates, 1977.

Baron, J., & Strawson, C. Use of orthographic and word-specific mechanisms in reading words aloud. *Journal of Experimental Psychology: Human Perception and Performance*, 1976, *2*, 386–393.

Baron, J., & Treiman, R. Use of orthography in reading and learning to read. In J. F. Kavanaugh, & R. L. Venezky (Eds.), *Orthography, reading and dyslexia*. Baltimore: University Park Press, 1980.

Barr, R. The effect of instruction on pupil reading strategies. *Reading Research Quarterly*, 1975, *10*, 555–582.

Barron, R. W. Reading skill and phonological coding in lexical access. In M. M. Gruneberg, P. E. Morris, & R. N. Sykes (Eds.), *Practical aspects of memory*. London: Academic Press, 1978.

Barron, R. W. Visual and phonological strategies in reading and spelling. In U. Frith (Ed.), *Cognitive processes in spelling*. London: Academic Press, 1980.

Barron, R. W., & Baron, J. How children get meaning from printed words. *Child Development*, 1977, *48*, 587–594.

Bartlett, B. J. *Top-level structure as an organizational strategy for recall of classroom text*. (Doctoral dissertation), Tempe: Arizona State University, 1978.

Bartlett, F. C. *Remembering: An experimental and social study*. Cambridge: Cambridge University Press, 1932.

Barton, A. H., & Wilder, D. E. Research and practice in the teaching of reading: A progress report. In M. B. Miles (Ed.), *Innovation in education*. New York: Bureau of Applied Research, Columbia University, 1964.

Bassin, C. B., & Martin, C. J. Effect of three types of redundancy reduction on comprehension, reading rate, and reading time of English prose. *Journal of Educational Psychology*, 1976, *68*, 649–652.

Bates, E., Kintsch, W., Fletcher, C. R., & Giuliani, V. The role of pronominalization and ellipsis in texts: Some memory experiments. *Journal of Experimental Psychology: Human Learning and Memory*, 1980, *6*, 676–691.

Bates, E., McNew, S., MacWhinney, B., Devescovi, A., & Smith, S. Functional constraints on sentence processing: A cross-linguistic study. *Cognition*, 1982, *11*, 245–299.

Baumann, J. F. Effect of ideational prominence on children's reading comprehension of expository prose. *Journal of Reading Behavior*, 1981, *13*, 49–56.

Bayle, E. The nature and cause of regressive movements in reading. *Journal of Experimental Education*, 1942, *11*, 16–36.

Beaugrande R., Design criteria for process models of reading. *Reading Research Quarterly*, 1981, *16*, 261–315.

Beauvois, M. F., & Dérouesné, J. Phonological alexia: Three dissociations. *Journal Neurology, Neurosurgery and Psychiatry*, 1979, *42*, 1115–1124.

Bebko, J., Saida, S., & Ikeda, M. *Does the useful visual field size vary with the sentence difficulty?* Paper presented at the meeting of the Japan Applied Physics Society, Tokyo, March, 1978.

Beck, I. L. Reading problems and instructional practices. In G. E. MacKinnon, & T. G. Waller (Eds.), *Reading research: Advances in theory and practice* (Vol. 2). New York: Academic Press, 1981.

Becker, C. A. The development of semantic context effects: Two processes or two strategies. *Reading Research Quarterly*, 1982, *17*, 482–502.

Becker, C. A., & Killion, T. H. Interaction of visual and cognitive effects in word recognition. *Journal of Experimental. Psychol: Human Perception and Performance*, 1977, *3*, 389–401.

Beers, J., & Henderson, H. A study of developing orthographic concepts among first graders. *Research in the Teaching of English*, 1977, *11*, 133–148.

Begg, I., & Paivio, A. Concreteness and imagery in sentence meaning. *Journal of Verbal Learning and Verbal Behavior*, 1969, *8*, 821–827.

Beilin, H., & Horn, R. Transitionl probability effects in anagram problem solving. *Journal of Experimental Psychology*, 1962, *63*, 514–518.

Belmont, L., & Birch, H. G. Lateral dominance and right–left awareness in normal children. *Child Development*, 1963, *34*, 257–270.

Benson, D. F. Alexia. In J. T. Guthrie (Ed.), *Aspects of reading acquisition*. Baltimore: Johns Hopkins University Press, 1976.

Benson, D. F. Alexia and the neuroanatomical basis of reading. In F. J. Pirozzolo, & M. C. Wittrock (Eds.), *Neuropsychological and cognitive processes in reading*. New York: Academic Press, 1981.

Benton, A. L. Neurological aspects of developmental dyslexia and reading disorders. In A. L. Benton, & D. Pearl (Eds.), *Dyslexia: An appraisal of current knowledge*. New York: Oxford University Press, 1978.

Besner, D., Davies, J., & Daniels, S. Reading for meaning: The effects of concurrent articulation. *Quarterly Journal of Psychology*, 1981, *33A*, 415–437.

Bettelheim, B. *The uses of enchantment: The meaning and importance of fairy tales*. New York: Alfred A. Knopf, 1976.

Bettelheim, B., & Zelan, K. *On learning to read*. New York: Alfred A. Knopf, 1982.

Bever, T. G. The cognitive basis for linguistic structure. In J. R. Hayes (Ed.), *Cognitive development of language*. New York: Wiley, 1970.

Bever, T. G., & Townsend, D. J. Perceptual mechanisms and formal properties of main and subordinate clauses. In W. E. Cooper, & E. C.T. Walker (Eds.), *Sentence processing: Psycholinguistic studies presented to Merrill Garrett*. Hillsdale, N.J.: Lawrence Erlbaum Associates, 1979.

Biederman, I. Perceiving real-world scenes. *Science*, 1972, *177*, 77–80.

Biederman, I., & Tsao, Y.-C. On processing Chinese ideographs and English words: Some implications from Stroop-test results. *Cognitive Psychology*, 1979, *11*, 125–132.

Biemiller, A. The development of the use of graphic and contextual information as children learn to read. *Reading Research Quarterly*, 1970, *6*, 75–96.

Biemiller, A. Relationships between oral reading rates for letters, words, and simple text in the development of reading achievement. *Reading Research Quarterly*, 1977–1978, *13*, 222–253.

Biglmaier, F. *Lesestorungen, Diagnose und Behandlung*. München: Reinhalt, 1964 (1971).

Biglmaier, F. Germany. In J. Downing (Ed.), *Comparative reading*. New York: MacMillan, 1973.

Bishop, C. H. Transfer effects of word and letter training in reading. *Journal of Verbal Learning and Verbal Behavior*, 1964, *36*, 840–847.

Bjork, E. L., & Murray, J. T. On the nature of input channels in visual processing. *Psychological Review*, 1977, *84*, 472–484.

Black, J. B., & Bern, H. Causal coherence and memory for events in narratives. *Journal of Verbal Learning and Verbal Behavior*, 1981, *20*, 267–275.

Black, J. B., & Wilensky, R. An evaluation of story grammars. *Cognitive Science*, 1979, *3*, 213–230.

Blank, M., & Bridger, W. H. Deficiencies in verbal labeling in retarded readers. *American Journal of Orthopsychiatry*, 1966, *36*, 840–847.

Bliss, C. K. *Semantography*. (2nd Edition), Sydney, Australia: Semantography, 1965.

Bloom, L. *One word at a time: The use of single word utterances before syntax*. The Hague: Mouton, 1973.

Bloomfield, L. *Language*. New York: Holt, 1933.

Bloomfield, L., & Barnhart, C. L. *Let's read. A linguistic approach*. Detroit: Wayne State University Press, 1961.

Bock, J. K. Toward a cognitive psychology of syntax: Information processing contributions to sentence formulation. *Psychological Review*, 1982, *89*, 1–47.

Bock, J. K., & Brewer, W. F. Reconstructive recall in sentences with alternative surface structures. *Journal of Experimental Psychology*, 1974, *74*, 837–843.

Boder, E. Developmental dyslexia: Prevailing diagnostic concepts and a new diagnostic approach. In H. R. Myklebust (Ed.), *Progress in learning disabilities* (Vol. 2). New York: Grune & Stratton, 1971.

Bolinger, D. L. *Aspects of language*. New York: Harcourt Brace Jovanovich, 1968.

Bol'shunov, Ya V. Recall of semantically nonequivalent parts of a coherent text. *Soviet Psychology*, 1977, *16*, 70–80.

Bonavia, D. China's war of words. *Visible Language*, 1977, *11*, 75–78.

Bond, G. L., & Dykstra, R. The cooperative research program in first-grade reading instruction. *Reading Research Quarterly*, 1967, *2*, entire summer issue.

Bormuth, J. R. Readability: A new approach. *Reading Research Quarterly*, 1966, *1*, 79–132.

Bormuth, J. R. Factor validity of cloze tests as a measure of reading comprehension. *Reading Research Quarterly*, 1969, *4*, 358–368.

Bormuth, J. R. Value and volume of literacy. *Visible Language*, 1978, *12*, 118–161.

Bouma, H. Interaction effects in parafoveal letter recognition. *Nature*, 1970, *226*, 177–178.

Bouma, H. Visual recognition of isolated lower-case letters. *Vision Research*, 1971, *11*, 459–474.

Bouma, H. Visual search and reading: Eye movements and functional visual field: a tutorial review. In J. Requin (Ed.), *Attention and performance* (Vol. 7). Hillsdale, N.J.: Lawrence Erlbaum Associates, 1978.

Bouma, H. Personal communication, April 1982.

Bouma, H., & Legein, C. P. Dyslexia: A specific reading deficit? An analysis of response latencies for letters and words in dyslectics and in average readers. *Neuropsychologia*, 1980, *18*, 285–298.

Bouma, H., & van Rens, A. *Reading processes: On the recognition of single words in eccentric vision*. Eindhoven, Netherlands: IPO Annual Progress Report 5, 1970.

Bouwhuis, D. G. Word knowledge and letter recognition as determinants of word recognition. In P. A. Kolers, M. E. Wrolstad, & H. Bouma (Eds.), *Processing of visible language* (Vol. 1). New York: Plenum Press, 1979a.

Bouwhuis. D. G. *Visual Recognition of Words*, Doctoral dissertation, Eindhoven, Netherlands: Institute for Perception Research, 1979b.

Bouwhuis, D. G., & Bouma, H. Visual word recognition of three-letter words as derived from the recognition of the constituent letters. *Perception & Psychophysics*, 1979, *25*, 12–22.

Bradshaw, J. L. Peripherally presented and unreported words may bias the perceived meaning of a centrally fixated homograph. *Journal of Experimental Psychology*, 1974, *103*, 1200–1202.

Bradshaw, J. L. Three interrelated problems in reading: A review. *Memory & Cognition*, 1975, *3*, 123–134.

Bradshaw, J. L., Bradley, D., Gates, A., & Patterson, K. Serial, parallel or holistic identification of single words in the two visual fields? *Perception & Psychophysics*, 1977, *21*, 431–438.

Bradshaw, J. L., Gates, A., & Patterson, K. Hemispheric differences in processing visual patterns. *Quarterly Journal of Experimental Psychology*, 1976, *28*, 667–681.

Brady, M. *Toward a computational theory of early visual processing in reading*. Memorandum AI-M-593, MIT Artificial Intelligence Laboratory, September, 1980.

Braine, M. D. Length constraints, reduction rules, and holophrastic processes in children's word combinations. *Journal of Verbal Learning and Verbal Behavior*, 1974, *13*, 448–456.

Bransford, J. D., & Franks, J. J. The abstraction of linguistic ideas. *Cognitive Psychology*, 1971, *2*, 331–350.

Bransford, J. D., & Johnson, M. K. Considerations of some problems of comprehension. In W. G. Chase (Ed.), *Visual information processing*. New York: Academic Press, 1973.

Brewer, W. F. Memory for the pragmatic implications of sentences. *Memory & Cognition*, 1977, *5*, 673–678.
Brewer, W. F., & Stone, B. J. Acquisition of spatial antonym pairs. *Journal of Experimental Child Psychology*, 1975, *19*, 299–307.
Bridge, C. A., & Winograd, P. N. Readers' awareness of cohesive relationships during cloze comprehension. *Journal of Reading Behavior*, 1982, *14*, 299–312.
Broadbent, D. E., & Broadbent, M. H. P. Priming and the active/passive model of word recognition. In R. S. Nickerson (Ed.), *Attention and performance* (Vol. 8). Hillsdale, N.J.: Lawrence Erlbaum Associates, 1980.
Brockway, J., Chmielewski, D., & Cofer, C. N. Remembering prose: Productivity and accuracy constraints in recognition memory. *Journal of Verbal Learning and Verbal Behavior*, 1974, *13*, 194–208.
Brooks, C., & Warren, R. P. *Modern rhetoric*. New York: Harcourt Brace Jovanovich, 1979.
Brooks, L. Visual patterns in fluent word identification. In A. Reber, & D. Scarborough (Eds.), *Toward a psychology of reading*. Hillsdale, N.J.: Lawrence Erlbaum Associates, 1977.
Brown, A. L., & Day, J. D. Macrorules for summarizing texts: The development of expertise. *Journal of Verbal Learning and Verbal Behavior*, 1983, *22*, 1–14.
Brown, A. L., & Smiley, S. S. Rating the importance of structural units of prose passage: A problem of metacognitive development. *Child Development*, 1977, *48*, 1–8.
Brown, B. B. Foreword. In A. L. Benton, & D. Pearl (Eds.), *Dyslexia: An appraisal of current knowledge*. New York: Oxford University Press, 1978.
Brown, D. L. Some linguistic dimension in auditory blending. In *Reading: The right to participate*. (20th Yearbook of the National Reading Conference), Clemson, S.C.: National Reading Conference, 1971.
Brown, E., & Miron, M. S. Lexical and syntactic predictors of the distribution of pause time in reading. *Journal of Verbal Learning and Verbal Behavior*, 1971, *10*, 658–667.
Brown, H. D. Categories of spelling difficulty in speakers of English as a first and second language. *Journal of Verbal Learning and Verbal Behavior*, 1970, *9*, 232–236.
Brown, R. *A first language: The early stages*. Cambridge, Mass.: Harvard University Press, 1973.
Brown, R., & Hanlon, C. Derivational complexity and order of acquisition in child speech. In J. R. Hayes (Ed.), *Cognition and the development of language*. New York: Wiley, 1970.
Brownell, H. H., Michel, D., Powelson, J., & Gardner, H. Surprise but coherence: Sensitivity to verbal humor in right-hemisphere patients. *Brain and Language*, 1983, *18*, 20–27.
Bruck, M., Lambert, W. E., & Tucker, G. R. Cognitive consequences of bilingual schooling: The St. Lambert Project through grade six. *International Journal of Psycholinguistics*, 1977, *6*, 13–30.
Bryant, P. E., & Bradley, L. Why children sometimes write words which they do not read. In U. Frith (Ed.), *Cognitive processes in spelling*. London: Academic Press, 1980.
Bryden, M. P. Laterality effects in dichotic listening: Relations with handedness and reading ability in children. *Neuropsychologia*, 1970, *8*, 443–450.
Bryden, M. P. Auditory-visual and sequential-spatial matching in relation to reading ability. *Child Development*, 1972, *43*, 824–832.
Buswell, G. T. *An experimental study of the eye–voice span in reading*. Supplementary Education Monograph 17, Chicago: University of Chicago Press, 1920.
Buswell, G. T. *Fundamental reading habits: A study of their development*. Chicago: Chicago University Press, 1922.
Butler, B. E. Sequential and parallel operations in tachistoscopic recognition. *Canadian Journal of Psychology*, 1978, *28*, 241–256.
Butler, B. E., & Hains, S. Individual differences in word recognition latency. *Memory & Cognition*, 1979, *7*, 68–76.
Butler, B. E., & Morrison, I. *Do letter features migrate?: An analysis of errors with tachistoscopic recognition*. Unpublished report, Queen's University, Kingston, Ontario, 1982.
Butterworth, B. Evidence from pauses in speech. In B. Butterworth (Ed.), *Language production* (Vol. 1). London: Academic Press, 1980.

Buurman, R. den, Roersema, T., & Gerrissen, J. F. Eye movements and the perceptual span in reading. *Reading Research Quarterly*, 1981, *16*, 227–235.

Byrne, B., & Shea, P. Semantic and phonetic memory codes in beginning readers. *Memory & Cognition*, 1979, *7*, 333–338.

Cairns, H. S. Effects of bias on processing and reprocessing of lexically ambiguous sentences. *Journal of Experimental Psychology*, 1973, *97*, 337–343.

Caldwell, E. C., Roth, S. W., & Turner, R. R. A consideration of phonic generalizations. *Journal of Reading Behavior*, 1978, *10*, 91–96.

Calfee, R. C. Cognitive models of reading: Implications for assessment and treatment of reading disability. In R. N. Malatesha, & P. G. Aaron (Eds.), *Reading disorder: Varieties and treatments*. New York: Academic Press, 1982.

Calfee, R. C., & Drum, P. A. Learning to read: Theory, research and practice. *Curriculum Inquiry*, 1978, *8*, 183–249.

Calfee, R. C., Venezky, R. L., & Chapman, R. S. *Pronunciation of synthetic words with predictable and unpredictable letter-sound correspondences*. Technical Report 71, Wisconsin Research and Developmental Center for Cognitive Learning, 1969.

Campbell, R., & Besner, D. This and thap—constraints on the pronunciation of new, written words. *Quarterly Journal of Experimental Psychology*, 1981, *33A*, 375–396.

Caplan, D. Clause boundaries and recognition latencies. *Perception & Psychophysics*, 1972, *12*, 73–76.

Caramazza, A., & Zurif, E. B. Comprehension of complex sentences in children and aphasics: A test of the regression hypothesis. In A. Caramazza, & E. B. Zurif (Eds.), *Language acquisition and language breakdown*. Baltimore: Johns Hopkins University Press, 1978.

Carbonell, J. G. *Metaphor: An inescapable phenomenon in natural language comprehension*. CMU-CS-81-115, Carnegie Mellon University, Department of Computer Science, May, 1981.

Carmichael, L., & Dearborn, W. F. *Reading and visual fatigue*. Boston: Houghton Mifflin, 1947.

Carpenter, P. A., & Just, M. A. Reading comprehension as eyes see it. In M. A. Just, & P. A. Carpenter (Eds.), *Cognitive processes in comprehension*. Hillsdale, N.J.: Lawrence Erlbaum Associates, 1977.

Carr, T. H., Davidson, B. J., & Hawkins, H. L. Perceptual flexibility in word recognition: Strategies affect orthographic computation but not lexical access. *Journal of Experimental Psychology: Human Perception and Performance*, 1978, *4*, 674–690.

Carr, T. H., Lehmkuhle, S. W., Kottas, B., Astor-Stetson, E. C., & Arnold, D. Target position and practice in the identification of letters in varying contexts: A word superiority effect. *Perception & Psychophysics*, 1976, *19*, 412–416.

Carroll, J. B. Defining language comprehension: Some speculations. In J. B. Carroll, & R. D. Freedle (Eds.), *Language comprehension and the acquisition of knowledge*. Washington D. C.: VH Winston, 1972a.

Carroll, J. B. The case for ideographic writing. In J. F. Kavanagh, & I. G. Mattingly (Eds.), *Language by ear and by eye*. Cambridge, Mass: MIT Press, 1972b.

Carver, R. P. Analysis of "chunked" test items as measures of reading and listening comprehension. *Journal of Educational Measurement*, 1970, *7*, 141–150.

Carver, R. P. *Sense and nonsense in speed reading*. Silver Spring, Md.: Revrac, 1971.

Carver, R. P. Toward a theory of reading comprehension. *Reading Research Quarterly*, 1977–1978, *13*, 8–63.

Cattell, J. M. The time it takes to see and name objects. *Mind*, 1886, *11*, 63–65.

Chafe, W. Giveness, contrastiveness, definiteness, subjects, topics, and points of view. In C. Li (Ed.), *Subject and topic*. New York: Academic Press, 1976.

Chall, J. *Learning to read: The great debate*. New York: McGraw-Hill, 1967.

Chall, J. The great debate: Ten years later, with a modest proposal for reading stages. In L. B. Resnick, & P. A. Weaver (Eds.), *Theory and practice of early reading* (Vol. 1). Hillsdale, N.J.: Lawrence Erlbaum Associates, 1979.

Chamberlain, B. H. *A practical introduction to the study of Japanese writing*. London: Crosby Lockwood & Sons, 1905.

Chang, F. R. Active memory processes in visual sentence comprehension: Clause effects and pronominal reference. *Memory & Cognition*, 1980, *8*, 58–64.
Chastain, G. Phonological and orthographic factors in the word-superiority effect. *Memory & Cognition*, 1981, *9*, 389–397.
Chen, K. Acoustic image in visual detection for deaf and hearing college students. *Journal of General Psychology*, 1976, *94*, 243–246.
Cheng, C.-C. In defense of teaching simplified characters. *Journal of Chinese Linguistics*, 1977, *5*, 314–341.
Cheng, C.-M. Typewriters for Chinese characters. *Chinese Journal of Psychology*, 1978, *20*, 614–618, (in Chinese).
Cheng, C.-M. Computational analysis of present-day Mandarin. *Journal of Chinese Linguistics*, 1982, *10*, 281–358.
Chitwood, A. *Recording the spontaneous speech of preschool children*. Unpublished M.A. thesis, University of Texas at El Paso, 1973.
Chomsky, C. *Acquisition of syntax in children from 5 to 10*. Cambridge: MIT Press, 1969.
Chomsky, N. *Syntactic structure*. The Hague: Mouton, 1957.
Chomsky, N. *Aspects of the theory of syntax*. Cambridge, Mass: MIT Press, 1965.
Chomsky, N. Phonology and reading. In H. Levin, & J. P. Williams (Eds.), *Basic studies on reading*. New York: Basic Books, 1970.
Chomsky, N. *Reflections on language*. New York: Pantheon, 1975.
Chomsky, N., & Halle, M. *The sound pattern of English*. New York: Harper and Row, 1968.
Chong, J.-Y., Han, S.-J., & Kang, T.-J. *Manual for the Hangul Word Processor III.*, Toronto: Han Software, 1983.
Chou, H.-Hs. Chinese oracle bones. *Scientific American*, April 1979, *240*, 134–149.
Christie, J. F. The effects of grade level and reading ability on children's miscue patterns. *Journal of Educational Research*, 1981, *74*, 419–423.
Christopherson, S. Effects of knowledge of semantic roles on recall of written prose. *Journal of Reading Behavior*, 1978, *10*, 249–256.
Chu-Chang, M., & Loritz, D. J. Phonological encoding of Chinese ideograms in short-term memory. *Language Learning*, 1977, *27*, 344–352.
Cirilo, R. K. Some effects of story structure during comprehension. In M. L. Kamil, & A. J. Moe (Eds.), *Perspectives on reading research and instruction*. (29th Yearbook of the National Reading Conference), Clemson, S.C.: National Reading Conference, 1980.
Cirilo, R. K. Referential coherence and text structure in story comprehension. *Journal of Verbal Learning and Verbal Behavior*, 1981, *20*, 358–367.
Cirilo, R. K., & Foss, D. J. Text structure and reading time for sentences. *Journal of Verbal Learning and Verbal Behavior*, 1980, *19*, 96–109.
Claiborne, R. *The birth of writing*. New York: Time-Life Books, 1974.
Clark, E. V. On the acquisition of the meaning of *before* and *after*. *Journal of Verbal Learning and Verbal Behaviour*, 1971, *10*, 266–275.
Clark, H. H. The language-as-fixed-effect fallacy: A critique of language statistics in psychological research. *Journal of Verbal Learning and Verbal Behavior*, 1973, *12*, 335–359.
Clark, H. H., & Clark, E. V. Semantic distinctions and memory for complex sentences. *Quarterly Journal of Experimental Psychology*, 1968, *20*, 129–138.
Clark, H. H., & Haviland, S. E. Comprehension and the given–new contract. In R. O. Freedle (Ed.), *Discourse production and comprehension*. Norwood: Ablex, 1977.
Clark, H. H., & Sengul, C. J. In search of referents for nouns and pronouns. *Memory & Cognition*, 1979, *7*, 35–41.
Clark, M. *Young fluent readers*. London: Heinemann Educational Books, 1976.
Clay, M. M., & Imlach, R. H. Juncture, pitch and stress as reading behavior variables. *Journal of Verbal Learning and Verbal Behavior*, 1971, *10*, 133–139.
Clymer, T. The utility of phonic generalization. *Reading Teacher*, 1963, *16*, 252–258.
Cobrink, L. The performance of hyperlexic children on an "incomplete words" task. *Neuropsychologia*, 1982, *20*, 569–577.

Cohen, A. S. Oral reading errors of first grade children taught by a code emphasis approach. *Reading Research Quarterly*, 1974–1975, *10*, 616–650.
Cohèn, R. L., & Netley, C. Cognitive deficits, learning disabilities, and WISC verbal–performance consistency. *Developmental Psychology*, 1978, *14*, 624–634.
Cohen, R. *L'apprentissage précose de la lecture: A six ans est-il deja trop tard? ('Early reading: Is age six already too late?')*. Paris: Presses Universitaires de France, 1977.
Cohen, S. A. *Teach them all to read*. New York: Random House, 1969.
Coleman, E. B. Improving comprehensibility by shortening sentences.. *Journal of Applied Psychology*, 1962, *46*, 131–134.
Coleman, E. B. Approximations to English: Some comments on the method.. *American Journal of Psychology*, 1963, *76*, 239–247.
Coleman, E. B. The comprehensibility of several grammatical transformations. *Journal of Applied Psychology*, 1964, *48*, 186–190.
Coleman, E. B. Learning of prose written in four grammatical transformations. *Journal of Applied Psychology*, 1965, *49*, 332–341.
Coleman, E. B. Collecting a data base for a reading technology. *Journal of Educational Monograph*, 1970, *61 (4)*, 1–23.
Coleman, E. B. Personal communication, 1980.
Coleman, E. B. The educationl experiment station. In G. E. MacKinnon, & T. G. Waller (Eds.), *Reading research: Advances in theory and practice* (Vol. 2). New York: Academic Press, 1981.
Coltheart, M. Deep dyslexia: A review of the syndrome. In M. Coltheart, K. Patterson, & J. C. Marshall (Eds.), *Deep dyslexia*. London: Routledge & Kegan Paul, 1980a.
Coltheart, M. Reading, phonological recoding, and deep dyslexia. In M. Coltheart, K. Patterson, & J. C. Marshall (Eds.), *Deep dyslexia*. London: Routledge & Kegan Paul, 1980b.
Coltheart, M., Davelaar, E., Jonasson, J. T., & Besner, D. Access to the internal lexicon. In S. Dornic (Ed.), *Attention and performance* (Vol. 6). Hillsdale, N.J.: Lawrence Erlbaum Associates, 1977.
Coltheart, M., Patterson, K., & Marshall, J. C. (Eds.) *Deep dyslexia*. London: Routledge & Kegan Paul, 1980.
Conrad, C. Some factors involved in the recognition of words. In J. W. Cotton, & R. L. Klatzky (Eds.), *Semantic factors in cognition*. Hillsdale, N.J.: Lawrence Erlbaum Associates, 1978.
Conrad, R. Acoustic confusions in immediate memory. *British Journal of Psychology*, 1964, *55*, 75–84.
Conrad, R. The chronology of the development of covert speech in children. *Developmental Psychology*, 1971, *5*, 398–405.
Corballis, M. C., & Beale, I. L. *The psychology of left and right*. Hillsdale, N.J.: Lawrence Erlbaum Associates, 1976.
Corbett, A. T., & Dosher, B. A. Instrument inferences in sentence encoding. *Journal of Verbal Learning and Verbal Behavior*, 1978, *17*, 479–491.
Corcoran, D. W. J. An acoustic factor in letter cancellation. *Nature*, 1966, *210*, 658.
Corcoran, D. W. J., & Rouse, R. O. An aspect of perceptual organization involved in reading typed and handwritten words. *Quarterly Journal of Experimental Psychology*, 1970, *22*, 526–530.
Corkin, S. Serial-ordering deficits in inferior readers. *Neuropsychologia*, 1974, *12*, 347–354.
Cotterell, G. C. Teaching procedures. In J. F. Reid (Ed.), *Reading: Problems and practices*. England: Ward Lock Educational, 1972.
Cowey, A. Cortical maps and visual perception: The Grindley memorial lecture. *Quarterly Journal of Experimental Psychology*, 1979, *31*, 1–17.
Craik, F. I. M., & Levy, B. A. The concept of primary memory. In W. K. Estes (Ed.), *Handbook of learning and cognitive processes* (Vol. 4). Hillsdale, N.J.: Lawrence Erlbaum Associates, 1975.
Cramer, P. *Word association*. New York: Academic Press, 1968.
Critchley, M. *The dyslexic child*. London: William Heinemann Medical Books, 1970.
Cromer, R. Developmental strategies for language. In V. Hamilton, & M. D. Vernon (Eds.), *The development of cognitive processes*. New York: Academic Press, 1976.
Cromer, W. The difference model: A new explanation for some reading difficulties. *Journal of Educational Psychology*, 1970, *61*, 471–483.

Crowder, R. G. *The psychology of reading: An introduction*. New York: Oxford University Press, 1982.

Culicover, P. W. *Syntax*. New York: Academic Press, (Second edition) 1982.

Cunningham, J. P., Cooper, L. A., & Reaves, C. C. Visual similarity processes: Identity and similarity decisions. *Perception & Psychophysics*, 1982, *32*, 50–60.

Cunningham, P. M., & Cunningham, J. W. Investigating the "print to meaning" hypothesis. In P. D. Pearson, & J. Hansen (Eds.), *Reading: Disciplined inquiry in process and practice*. (27th Yearbook of the National Reading Conference). Clemson, S.C.: The National Reading Conference, 1978.

Curtiss, S. *Genie: A psycholinguistic study of a modern-day "wild child"*. New York: Academic Press, 1977.

Dalby, J. T., & Gibson, D. Functional cerebral lateralization in subtypes of disabled readers. *Brain and Language*, 1981, *14*, 34–48.

Dale, E., & Chall, J. S. A formula for predicting readability. *Ohio State U. Educational Research Bulletin*, 1948, *27*, 11–20.

Daneman, M., & Carpenter, P. A. Individual differences in working memory and reading. *Journal of Verbal Learning and Verbal Behavior*, 1980, *19*, 450–466.

Danner, F. W. *Children's understanding of intersentence organization in the recall of short descriptive passages*. Unpublished doctoral dissertation, University of Minnesota, 1974.

Davelaar, E, Coltheart, M., Besner, D., & Jonasson, J. T. Phonological recoding and lexical access. *Cognitive Psychology*, 1978, *6*, 391–402.

Davidson, R. J. The sight–speech gap. *Psychology Today*, 1982, *16*, 92.

Davis, F. B. Research in comprehension in reading. *Reading Research Quarterly*, 1968, *3*, 499–545.

Davis, F. B. Psychometric research on comprehension in reading. *Reading Research Quarterly*, 1972, *7*, 628–678.

Dawson, G., Warrenburg, S., & Fuller, P. Cerebral lateralization in individuals diagnosed as autistic in early childhood. *Brain and Language*, 1982, *15*, 353–368.

de Groot, A. M. B. The range of automatic spreading activation in word priming. *Journal of Verbal Learning and Verbal Behavior*, in press.

de Groot, A. M. B., Thomassen, A. J. W. M., & Hudson, P. T. W. Associative facilitation of word recognition as measured from a neutral prime. *Memory & Cognition*, 1982, *10*, 358–370.

De Soto, J. L., & De Soto, C. B. Relationship of reading achievement to verbal processing abilities. *Journal of Educational Psychology*, 1983, *75*, 116–127.

de Villiers, J. G., & de Villiers, P. A. A cross-sectional study of the acquisition of grammatical morphemes. *Journal of Psycholinguistic Research*, 1973, *2*, 267–278.

de Villiers, P. A. Imagery and theme in recall of connected discourse. *Journal of Experimental Psychology*, 1974, *103*, 263–268.

Deese, J. Text structure, strategies, and comprehension in learning from scientific textbooks. In J. Robinson (Ed.), *Research in science education: New questions, new directions*. Boulder, Colorado: Center for Educational Research and Evaluation, 1980a.

Deese, J. Pauses, prosody, and the demands of production in language. In W. Dechert, & M. Raupach (Eds.), *Temporal variables in speech: Studies in honor of Frieda Goldman-Eisler*. The Hague: Mouton, 1980b.

Deese, J. Personal communication, May 4, 1981.

DeFrancis, J. Language and script reform in China. In J. A. Fishman (Ed.), *Advances in the creation and revision of writing systems*. The Hague: Mouton, 1977.

Delacato, C. H. *Neurological organization and reading*. Springfield, Ill.: Charles C. Thomas, 1966.

Dell, G. S., & Reich, P. A. Stages in sentence production: An analysis of speech error data. *Journal of Verbal Learning and Verbal Behaviour*, 1981, *20*, 611–629.

Deloche, G., Andreewsky, E., & Desi, M. Surface Dyslexia: A case report and some theoretical implications to reading models. *Brain and Language*, 1982, *15*, 12–31.

Denckla, M. B., & Rudel, R. Naming of pictured objects by dyslexic and other learning disabled children. *Brain and Language*, 1976, *3*, 1–15.

Dennis, I., & Newstead, S. E. Is phonological recoding under strategic control? *Memory & Cognition*, 1981, *9*, 472–477.

Dennis, M., & Whitaker, H. A. Language acquisition following hemidecortication: Linguistic superiority of the left over the right. *Brain and Language*, 1976, *3*, 404–433.

Dérouesné, J., & Beauvois, M. F. Phonological processing in reading: Data from alexia. *Journal of Neurology, Neurosurgery and Psychiatry*, 1979, *42*, 1125–1132.

Dewey, G. *English spelling: Roadblock to reading*. New York: Teachers College, Columbia University, 1971.

Di Lollo, V. Temporal integration in visual memory. *Journal of Experimental Psychology: General*, 1980, *109*, 75–97.

Di Lollo, V., Hanson, D., & McIntyre, J. S. *Initial stages of visual information processing in dyslexia*. Unpublished manuscript, University of Alberta, 1983.

Dickinson, G. H. *Vocational speller*. Toronto: Sir Isaac Pitman and Sons, 1976? (year assumed)

Dillard, J. L. *Black English*. New York: Random House, 1972.

Diringer, D. *The alphabet (A key to history of mankind)*. New York: Funk and Wagnalls, 1968.

Divesta, F. J., Hayward, K. G., & Orlando, V. P. Developmental trends in monitoring text for comprehension. *Child Development*, 1979, *50*, 97–105.

Doctor, E. A., & Coltheart, M. Children's use of phonological encoding when reading for meaning. *Memory & Cognition*, 1980, *8*, 195–209.

Dodge, R., & Cline, T. S. The angle velocity of eye-movements. *Psychological Review*, 1901, *8*, 145–157.

Doehring, D. G. Acquisition of rapid reading responses. *Monographs of the Society for Research in Child Development*, 1976, *41* (2nd series No. 165).

Doehring, D. G., & Hoshko, I. M. A developmental study of the speed of comprehension of printed sentences. *Bulletin of the Psychonomic Society*, 1977, *9*, 311–313.

Doehring, D. G., Trites, R. L., Patel, P. G., & Fiedorowicz, C. A. M. *Reading disabilities*. New York: Academic Press, 1981.

Doman, G. *How to teach your baby to read: The gentle revolution*. New York: Random House, 1964.

Donnenwerth-Nolan, S., Tanenhaus, M. K., & Seidenberg, M. S. Multiple code activation in word recognition: Evidence from rhyme monitoring. *Journal of Experimental Psychology: Human Learning and Memory*, 1981, *7*, 170–180.

Downing, J. *Evaluating the initial teaching alphabet*. London: Cassell, 1967.

Downing, J. Linguistic environments, II. In J. Downing (Ed.), *Comparative reading*. New York: Macmillan, 1973.

Downing, J., & Leong, C.-K. *Psychology of reading*. New York: Macmillan, 1982.

Drewnowski, A., & Healy, A. F. Missing *-ing* in reading: Letter detection errors in word endings. *Journal of Verbal Learning and Verbal Behavior*, 1980, *19*, 247–262.

Drewnowski, A., & Healy, A. F. Phonetic factors in letter detection: A reevaluation. *Memory & Cognition*, 1982, *10*, 145–154.

Duke, B. C. Why Noriko can read! Some hints for Johnny. *The Educational Forum*, 1977, *41*, 230–236.

Dumont, J. J. Learning disabilities in the Netherlands. In L. Tarnopol, & M. Tarnopol (Eds.), *Reading disabilities—an international perspective*. Baltimore: University Park Press, 1976.

Dunn-Rankin, P. The visual characteristics of words. *Scientific American*, January 1978, *238*, 122–130.

Durkin, D. *Children who read early*. New York: Teachers College, Columbia University, 1966.

Dutka, J. T. Anaphoric relations, comprehension and readability. In P. A. Kolers, M. E. Wrolstad, & H. Bouma (Eds.), *Processing of visible language* (Vol. 2). New York: Plenum, 1980.

Dyer, F. N. Color naming interference in monolinguals and bilinguals. *Journal of Verbal Learning and Verbal Behavior*, 1971, *10*, 297–302.

Dyer, J. W., Riley, J., & Yekovich, F. R. An analysis of three study skills: Note-taking, summarizing, and reading. *Journal of Educational Research*, 1979, *73*, 3–7.

Dykstra, R. Summary of the second-grade phase of the cooperative research program in primary reading instruction. *Reading Research Quarterly*, 1968, *4*, 49–70.

Dykstra, R. Phonics and beginning reading instruction. In C. C. Walcutt, J. Lamport, & G. McCracken (Eds.), *Teaching reading: A phonic/linguistic approach to developmental reading*. New York: Macmillan, 1974.

Eamon, D. B. Selection and recall of topical information in prose by better and poor readers. *Reading Research Quarterly*, 1978–1979, *14*, 244–257.

Earhard, B. The line-in-object superiority effect in perception: It depends on where you fix your eyes and what is located at the point of fixation. *Perception & Psychophysics*, 1980, *28*, 9–18.

Earhard, B., & Armitage, R. From an object-superiority effect to an object-inferiority effect with movement of the fixation point. *Perception & Psychophysics*, 1980, *28*, 369–376.

Ebbinghaus, H. *Ueber das Gedaechtnis*. Leipzig: Duncker & Humblot, 1885.

Edfeldt, A. W. *Silent speech and silent reading*. Chicago: University of Chicago Press, 1960.

Ehri, L. C. Word consciousness in readers and prereaders. *Journal Educational Psychology*, 1975, *67*, 204–212.

Ehri, L. C. Word learning in beginning readers and prereaders: Effects of form class and defining contexts. *Journal of Educational Psychology*, 1976, *68*, 832–842.

Ehri, L. C. The role of orthography in printed word learning. In J. F. Kavanagh, & R. L. Venezky (Eds.), *Orthography, reading and dyslexia*. Baltimore: University Park Press, 1980.

Ehrlich, K., & Rayner, K. Pronoun assignment and semantic integration during reading: Eye movements and immediacy of processing. *Journal of Verbal Learning and Verbal Behavior*, 1983, *22*, 75–87.

Ehrlich, S. F., & Rayner, K. Contextual effects on word perception and eye movements during reading. *Journal of Verbal Learning and Verbal Behavior*, 1981, *20*, 641–655.

Eisenberg, L. Neuropsychiatric aspects of reading disability. *Pediatrics*, 1966, *37*, 17–33.

Eisenberg, L. Definitions of dyslexia: Their consequences for research and policy. In A. L. Benton, & D. Pearl (Eds.), *Dyslexia: An appraisal of current knowledge*. New York: Oxford University Press, 1978.

Eisenberg, P., & Becker, C. A. Semantic context effects in visual word recognition, sentence processing, and reading: Evidence for semantic strategies. *Journal of Experimental Psychology: Human Perception and Performance*, 1982, *8*, 739–756.

Ekstrand, B. R., & Dominowski, R. L. Solving words as anagrams. *Psychonomic Science*, 1965, *2*, 239–240.

Elliott, S. N. Children's knowledge and use of organizational patterns of prose in recalling what they read. *Journal of Reading Behavior*, 1980, *12*, 203–212.

Elman, J. L., Takahashi, K., & Tohsaku, Y. H. Lateral asymmetries for the identification of concrete and abstract Kanji. *Neuropsychologia*, 1981, *19*, 407–412.

Elterman, R. D., Abel, L. A., Daroff, R. B., Dell'Osso, L. F., & Bornstein, J. L. Eye movement patterns in dyslexic children. *Journal of Learning Disabilities*, 1980, *13*, 11–16.

Emerson, H. F. Children's judgments of correct and reversed sentences with 'if'. *Journal of Child Language*, 1980, *7*, 135–155.

Endo, M., Shimizu, A., & Nakamura, I. Laterality differences in recognition of Japanese and Hangul words by monolinguals and bilinguals. *Cortex*, 1981a, *17*, 1–9.

Endo, M., Shimizu, A., & Nakamura, I. The influence of Hangul learning upon laterality difference in Hangul word recognition by native Japanese subjects. *Brain and Language*, 1981b, *14*, 114–119.

Engelmann, S., & Engelmann, T. *Give your child a superior mind*. New York: Simon and Schuster, 1966.

Entin, E. B., & Klare, G. R. Some inter-relationships of readability, cloze, and multiple-choice scores on a reading comprehension test. *Journal of Reading Behavior*, 1978, *10*, 417–436.

Entwisle, D. R., Forsyth, D. F., & Muus, R. The syntagmatic–paradigmatic shift in children's word association. *Journal of Verbal Learning and Verbal Behavior*, 1964, *3*, 19–29.

Entwisle, D. R., & Frasure, N. E. A contradiction resolved: Children's processing of syntactic cues. *Developmental Psychology*, 1974, *10*, 852–857.

Erdmann, B., & Dodge, R. *Psychologische Untersuchungen uber das Lesen*. Halle: M. Niemeyer, 1898.

Erickson, D., Mattingly, I. G., & Turvey, M. T. Phonetic activity and reading: An experiment with Kanji. *Language and Speech*, 1977, *20*, 384–403.

Ericsson, K. A., Chase, W. G., & Faloon, S. Acquisition of a memory skill. *Science*, 1980, *208*, 1181–1182.

Eriksen, C. W., Pollack, M. D., & Montague, W. E. Implicit speech: Mechanisms in perceptual coding? *Journal of Experimental Psychology*, 1970, *84*, 502–507.

Ervin, S. M. Changes with age in verbal determinants of word association. *American Journal of Psychology*, 1961, *74*, 361–372.

Estes, T. M., & Shebilske, W. L. Comprehension: Of what the reader sees of what the author says. In M. L. Kamil, & A. J. Moe (Eds.), *Perspectives on reading research instruction*. (29th Yearbook of the National Reading Conference), Washington, D. C.: National Reading Conference, 1980.

Estes, W. K. The locus of inferential and perceptual processes in letter identification. *Journal of Experimental Psychology: General*, 1975, *104*, 122–145.

Estes, W. K. Similarity-related channel interactions in visual processing. *Journal of Experimental Psychology: Human Perception and Performance*, 1982, *8*, 353–382.

Fairbanks, G. The relation between eye-movements and voice in the oral reading of good and poor silent readers. *Psychological Monographs*, 1937, *48*, 78–107.

Farrar, J., & Leigh, J. Factors associated with reading failure. *Social Science and Medicine*, 1972, *6*, 241–251.

Faw, H. W., & Waller, T. G. Mathemagenic behaviors and efficiency in learning from prose materials: Review, critique, and recommendations. *Review of Educational Research*, 1976, *46*, 691–720.

Feitelson, D. I. Israel. In J. Downing (Ed.), *Comparative reading*. New York: Macmillan, 1973.

Feitelson, D. I. Relating instructional strategies to language idiosyncracies in Hebrew. In J. F. Kavanagh, & R. L. Venezky (Eds.), *Orthography, reading and dyslexia*. Baltimore: University of Park Press, 1980.

Feldman, J. M. Wh* N**ds V*w*ls? In F. B. Murray (Ed.), *The recognition of words*. Newark, Del.: International Reading Association, 1978.

Feldman, L. B. *Visual word recognition in Serbo-Croatian is necessarily phonological*. Status Report on Speech Research SR-66, Haskins Laboratories, April–June, 1981.

Feldman, L. B., & Kostic, A. *Word recognition with mixed alphabet forms*. Status Report on Speech Research SR-66, Haskins Laboratories, April–June, 1981.

Fernald, G. M. *Remedial techniques in basic school subjects*. New York: McGraw-Hill, 1943.

Fillmore, C. J. The case for case. In E. Bach, & R. T. Harms (Eds.), *Universals in linguistic theory*. New York: Holt, Rinehart and Winston, 1968.

Fillmore, C. J. Types of lexical information. In D. D. Steinberg, & L. A. Jakobovitz (Eds.), *Semantics: An interdisciplinary reader in philosophy, linguistics, and psychology*. London: Cambridge University Press, 1971.

Fisher, D. F. Reading and visual search. *Memory & Cognition*, 1975, *3*, 188–196.

Fisher, D. F. Dysfunctions in reading disability: There's more than meets the eye. In L. B. Resnick, & P. A. Weaver (Eds.), *Theory and practice of early reading* (Vol. 1). Hillsdale, N.J.: Lawrence Erlbaum Associates, 1979.

Fisher, D. F. Compensatory training for disabled readers: Research to practice. *Journal of Learning Disabilities*, 1980, *13*, 134–140.

Fisher, D. F., & Lefton, L. A. Peripheral information extraction: A developmental examination of reading process. *Journal of Child Psychology*, 1976, *21*, 77–93.

Fisher, D. F., & Montanary, S. P. Spatial and contextual factors in beginning reading: Evidence for PSG–CSG complements to developing automacity? *Memory & Cognition*, 1977, *5*, 247–251.

Fleisher, L. S., Jenkins, J. R., & Pany, D. Effects on poor readers' comprehension of training in rapid decoding. *Reading Research Quarterly*, 1979–1980, *15*, 30–48.

Fleming, J. T. Alternative interpretations of evidence for phonemic recoding in visual word recognition. *Journal of Reading Behavior*, 1976, *8*, 7–18.

Flesch, R. F. *The art of writing*. New York: Harper, 1949.

Flesch, R. F. *Why Johnny still can't read: A new look at the scandal of our schools*. New York: Harper and Row, 1981.

Fletcher, J. M., & Satz, P. Developmental changes in the neurological correlates of reading achievement: A six year longitudinal follow-up. *Journal of Clinical Neuropsychology*, 1980, *2*, 23–37.

Flom, M. C., & Weymouth, F. W. Visual resolution and contour interaction. *Journal of the Optical Society of America*, 1963, *53*, 1026–1032.

Foch, T. T., DeFries, J. C., McLearn, G. E., & Singer, S. M. Familial patterns of impairment in reading disability. *Journal of Educational Psychology*, 1977, *69*, 316–329.

Fodor, J. A., Bever, T. G., & Garrett, M. F. *The psychology of language*. New York: McGraw-Hill, 1974.

Ford, B., & Banks, W. P. Perceptual differences between reading handwritten and typed words. *Memory & Cognition*, 1977, *5*, 630–635.

Forster, K. I. Visual perception of rapidly presented word sequences of varying complexity. *Perception & Psychophysics*, 1970, *8*, 215–221.

Forster, K. I., & Ryder, L. A. Perceiving the structure and meaning of sentences. *Journal of Verbal Learning and Verbal Behavior*, 1971, *10*, 285–296.

Foss, D. J. A discourse on semantic priming. *Cognitive Psychology*, 1982, *14*, 590–607.

Fowler, C. A., Wolford, G, Slade, R., & Tassinary, L. Lexical access with and without awareness. *Journal of Experimental Psychology: General*, 1981, *110*, 341–362.

Fowler, H. W. *A dictionary of modern English usage*. London: Oxford University Press, 1958.

Fox, B., & Routh, D. K. Phonetic analysis and synthesis as word attack skills. *Journal of Educational Psychology*, 1976, *68*, 70–74.

Frankel, D. G., Amir, M., Frenkel, E., & Arbel, T. A developmental study of the role of word order in comprehending Hebrew. *Journal of Experimental Child Psychology*, 1980, *29*, 23–35.

Frankel, D. G., & Arbel, T. Developmental changes in assigning agent relations in Hebrew: The interaction between word order and structural cues. *Journal of Experimental Child Psychology*, 1981, *32*, 102–114.

Frankel, D. G., & Arbel, T. Probabilistic assignments of sentence relations on the basis of differentially weighted interpretive cues. *Journal of Psycholinguistic Research*, 1982, *11*, 447–464.

Franks, J. J. Toward understanding understanding. In W. B. Weimer, & D. S. Palermo (Eds.), *Cognition and symbolic processes*. Hillsdale, N.J.: Lawrence Erlbaum Associates, 1974.

Frase, L. T., & Schwartz, B. J. Typographical cues that facilitate comprehension. *Journal of Educational Psychology*, 1979, *71*, 197–206.

Fraser, C., Bellugi, U., & Brown, R. Control of grammar in imitation, comprehension, and production. *Journal of Verbal Learning and Verbal Behavior*, 1963, *2*, 121–135.

Frazier, L., & Rayner, K. Making and correcting errors during sentence comprehension: Eye movements in the analysis of structurally ambiguous sentences. *Cognitive Psychology*, 1982, *14*, 178–210.

Frederiksen, J. R. *Text comprehension and the effective visual field.*. Paper presented at the annual meeting of the Psychonomic Society, Washington, DC., 1977.

Frederiksen, J. R. *Word recognition in the presence of semantically constraining context*. Paper presented at the annual meeting of the Psychonomic Society, San Antonio, November, 1978.

Frederiksen, J. R. Sources of process interactions in reading. In A. M. Lesgold, & C. A. Perfetti (Eds.), *Interactive processes in reading*. Hillsdale, N.J.: Lawrence Erlbaum Associates, 1981a.

Frederiksen, J. R. Understanding anaphora: Rules used by readers in assigning pronoun referents. *Discourse Processes*, 1981b, *4*, 323–347.

French, P. Semantic and syntactic factors in the perception of rapidly presented sentences. *Journal of Psycholinguistic Research*, 1981, *10*, 581–591.

Fried, I. Cerebral dominance and subtypes of developmental dyslexia. *Bulletin of the Orton Society*, 1979, *29*, 101–112.

Fried, I., Tanguay, P. E., Boder, E., Doubleday, C., & Greensite, M. Developmental dyslexia: Electrophysiological evidence of subtypes. *Brain and Language*, 1981, *12*, 14–22.

Friedman, A., Polson, M. C., Dafoe, C. G., & Gaskill, S. J. Dividing attention within and between hemispheres: Testing a multiple resources approach to limited-capacity information processing. *Journal of Experimental Psychology: Human Perception and Performance*, 1982, *8*, 625–650.

Friedman, R. B. Identity without form: Abstract representations of letters. *Perception & Psychophysics*, 1980, *28*, 53–60.

Fries, C. C. *The structure of English*. New York: Harcourt Brace and World, 1952.

Fries, C. C. *Linguistics and reading*. New York: Holt, 1963.

Frith, U. Reading by eye and writing by ear. In P. A. Kolers, M. E. Wrolstad, & H. Bouma (Eds.), *Processing of visible language* (Vol. 1). New York: Plenum Press, 1979.

Frith, U. Unexpected spelling errors. In U. Frith (Ed.), *Cognitive processes in spelling*. London: Academic Press, 1980.

Fromkin, V. A. (Ed) *Errors in linguistic performance. Slips of the tongue, ear, pen and hand*. New York: Academic Press, 1980.

Fry, E. B. A diacritical marking system to aid beginning reading introduction. *Elementary English*, 1964, *41*, 526–529.

Fry, E. B. Fry's readability graph: Clarification, validity, and extension to level 17. *Journal of Reading Behavior*, 1977, *21*, 242–252.

Fry, E. B. *Do students read better now than 10 years ago?* Paper presented at the meeting of the National Reading Conference, Dallas, December, 1981.

Fry, E. B., Weber, J, & Depierro, J. A partial validation of the kernel distance theory of readability. In P. D. Pearson, & J. Hansen (Eds.), *Reading: Disciplined inquiry in process and practice*. (27th Yearbook of the National Reading Conference), Clemson, S.C.: National Reading Conference, 1978.

Fry, M. A., Johnson, C. S., & Muehl, S. Oral language production in relation to reading achievement among select second graders. In D. J. Bakker, & P. Satz (Eds.), *Specific reading disability: Advances in theory and method*. Rotterdam: Rotterdam University Press, 1970.

Fukuzawa, S. Developmental study on the factors of the difficulty in reading Kanji. *Science of Reading*, 1968, *11*, 16–21, (in Japanese with English summary).

Futch, O. A study of eye-movements in the reading of Latin. *Journal of General Psychology*, 1935, *13*, 434–463.

Gaddes, W. H. *Learning disabilities and brain function*. New York: Springer-Verlag, 1980.

Gaer, E. P. Children's understanding and production of sentences. *Journal of Verbal Learning and Verbal Behavior*, 1969, *8*, 289–294.

Gainotti, G., Caltagirone, C., Micelli, G., & Masullo, C. Selective semantic-lexical impairment of language comprehension in right-brain damaged patients. *Brain and Language*, 1981, *13*, 201–211.

Galaburda, A. M., & Kemper, T. L. Cytoarchitectonic abnormalities in developmental dyslexia: A case study. *Annals of Neurology*, 1979, *6*, 94–100.

Gardner, H. The making of a storyteller. *Psychology Today*, 1982, *16*, 49–63.

Garner, W. R. *Uncertainty and structure as psychological concepts*. New York: Wiley, 1962.

Garner, W. R., & Haun, F. Letter identification as a function of type of perceptual limitation and type of attribute. *Journal of Experimental. Psychology: Human Perception and Performance*, 1978, *4*, 199–209.

Garnham, A. Instantiation of verbs. *Quarterly Journal of Experimental Psychology*, 1979, *31*, 207–214.

Garnham, A., Oakhill, J., & Johnson-Laird, P. N. Referential continuity and the coherence of discourse. *Cognition*, 1982, *11*, 29–46.

Garrett, M. F. Syntactic processes in sentence production. In R. J. Wales, & E. Walker (Eds.), *New approaches to language mechanism*. Amsterdam: North-Holland, 1976.

Garrod, S., & Sanford, A. Interpreting anaphoric relations: The integration of semantic information while reading. *Journal of Verbal Learning and Verbal Behavior*, 1977, *16*, 77–90.

Garrod, S., & Trabasso, T. A dual-memory information processing interpretation of sentence comprehension. *Journal of Verbal Learning and Verbal Behavior*, 1973, *12*, 155–167.

Gasper, R., & Brown, D. *Perceptual processes in reading*. London: Hutchinson Educational, 1973.

Geiselman, R. E., Landee, B. M., & Christen, F. G. Perceptual discriminability as a basis for selecting graphic symbols. *Human Factors*, 1982, *24*, 329–337.

Gelb, I. J. *A study of writing*. Chicago: University of Chicago Press, 1963.

Gentner, D. Evidence for the psychological reality of semantic components: The verbs of possession. In D. A. Norman, D. E. Rumelhart, & LNR Research Group (Eds.), *Explorations in cognition*. San Francisco: Freeman, 1975.

Geoffrion, L. Positional uncertainty in lateral masking and the perceptual superiority of words. *Perception & Psychophysics*, 1976, *19*, 273–278.

Geschwind, N. Disconnexion syndromes in animals and man (Part 1). *Brain*, 1965, *88*, 237–274.

Geschwind, N. Specialization of the human brain. *Scientific American*, September 1979, *241*, 180–199.

Gibbon, S. Y., Palmer, E. L., & Fowles, B. R. Sesame Street, The Electric Company and Reading. In J. B. Carroll, & J. S. Chall (Eds.), *Toward a literate society*. New York: McGraw-Hill, 1975.

Gibson, E. J., Gibson, J. J., Pick, A. D., & Osser, H. A. A developmental study of the discrimination of letter-like forms. *Journal of Comparative and Physiological Psychology*, 1962, *55*, 897–906.

Gibson, E. J., & Guinet, L. Perception of inflections in brief visual presentations of words. *Journal of Verbal Learning and Verbal Behavior*, 1971, *10*, 182–189.

Gibson, E. J., & Levin, H. *The psychology of reading*. Cambridge: MIT Press, 1975.

Gillooly, W. B. The influence of writing system characteristics on learning to read. *Reading Research Quarterly*, 1973, *8*, 167–199.

Gilmore, G. C. Letter interactions in brief visual displays. *Quarterly Journal of Experimental Psychology*, 1980, *32*, 649–688.

Gilmore, G. C., Hersh, H., Caramazza, A., & Griffin, J. Multidimensional letter similarity derived from recognition errors. *Perception & Psychophysics*, 1979, *25*, 425–431.

Ginsberg, G. P., & Hartwick, A. Directional confusion as a sign of dyslexia. *Perceptual and Motor Skills*, 1971, *32*, 535–543.

Gioffi, G. Recognition of sentence structure in meaningful prose by good comprehenders and skilled decoders. *Journal of Reading Behavior*, 1982, *14*, 86–92.

Givon, T. *On understanding grammar*. New York: Academic Press, 1979.

Glahn, E. Chinese writing through four millennia. In A. Toynbee (Ed.), *Half the world*. New York: Holt, Rinehart and Winston, 1973.

Glanzer, M., Dorfman, D, & Kaplan, B. Short-term storage in the processing of text. *Journal of Verbal Learning and Verbal Behavior*, 1981, *20*, 656–670.

Glanzer, M., & Razel, M. The size of the unit in short-term storage. *Journal of Verbal Learning and Verbal Behavior*, 1974, *13*, 114–131.

Gleitman, L. R., & Rozin, P. Phoenician go home (a response to Goodman). *Reading Research Quarterly*, 1973, *8*, 494–501.

Glushko, R. J. The organization and activation of orthographic knowledge in reading aloud. *Journal of Experimental Psychology: Human Perception and Performance*, 1979, *5*, 674–691.

Goetz, E. T., Anderson, R. C., & Schallert, D. L. The representation of sentences in memory. *Journal of Verbal Learning and Verbal Behavior*, 1981, *20*, 369–385.

Goldman-Eisler, F. *Psycholinguistics: Experiments in spontaneous speech*. New York: Academic Press, 1968.

Goldman-Eisler, F. Pauses, clauses, sentences. *Language and Speech*, 1972, *15*, 103–113.

Goldman-Eisler, F., & Cohen, M. Is N, P, and NP difficulty a valid criterion of transformational operations? *Journal of Verbal Learning and Verbal Behavior*, 1970, *9*, 161–166.

Goldman-Eisler, F. Psychological mechanisms of speech production as studied through the analysis of simultaneous translation. In B. Butterworth (Ed.), *Language production* (Vol. 1). New York: Academic Press, 1980.

Goldstein, D. M. Cognitive-linguistic functioning and learning to read in preschoolers. *Journal of Educational Psychology*, 1976, *68*, 680–688.

Goodman, K. S. Cues and miscues in reading: A linguistic study. *Elementary English*, 1965, *42*, 640.

Goodman, K. S. The 13th easy way to make reading difficult: A reaction to Gleitman and Rozin. *Reading Research Quarterly*, 1973, *8*, 484–493.

Goodman, K. S. *Language and literacy* (Vol. 1). Boston: Routledge & Kegan Paul, 1982.

Goodman, K. S., & Goodman, Y. Learning to read is natural. In L. B. Resnick, & P. Weaver (Eds.), *Theory and practice of early reading* (Vol. 1). Hillsdale, N.J.: Lawrence Erlbaum Associates, 1979.

Gorden, H. W. Cognitive asymmetry in dyslexic families. *Neuropsychologia*, 1980, *18*, 645–655.

Gottesman, R. L., Croen, L., & Rotkin, L. Urban second grade children: A profile of good and poor readers. *Journal of Learning Disabilities*, 1982, *15*, 268–272.

Gough, P. B. Grammatical transformations and speed of understanding. *Journal of Verbal Learning and Verbal Behavior*, 1965, *4*, 107–111.

Gough, P. B., & Cosky, M. J. One second of reading again. In N.J. Castellan, D. B. Pisoni, & G. R. Potts (Eds.), *Cognitive theory*. Hillsdale, N.J.: Lawrence Erlbaum Associates, 1977.

Gould, J. D. Pattern recognition and eye movement parameters. *Perception & Psychophysics*, 1967, *2*, 399–407.

Graesser, A. C., Hoffman, N. L., & Clark, L. F. Structural components of reading time. *Journal of Verbal Learning and Verbal Behavior*, 1980, *19*, 135–151.

Grant, B. K. *A guide to Korean characters (Reading and writing Hangul and Hanja)*. Elizabeth, N.J. and Seoul, Korea: Hollym International, 1979.

Gray, W. S. *The teaching of reading and writing: An international survey*. Paris: UNESCO, 1956.

Greene, J. M. The semantic function of negatives and passives. *British Journal of Psychology*, 1970, *61*, 17–22.

Greene, J. *Psycholinguistics (Chomsky and psychology)*. Middlesex, England: Penguin, 1972.

Groat, A. The use of English stress assignment rules by children taught either with traditional orthography or with the initial teaching alphabet. *Journal of Experimental Child Psychology*, 1979, *27*, 395–409.

Grosjean, F., & Deschamps, A. Analyse contrastive des variables temporelles de l'anglais et du francais: Vitesse de parole et variables composantes, phenomenes d'hesitation. *Phonetica*, 1975, *31*, 144–184.

Grundin, H. U., Courtney, B. L., Langer, J., Pehrsson, R., Robinson, H. A., & Sakamoto, T. Cloze procedure and comprehension: An exploratory study across three languages. In D. Feitelson (Ed.), *Cross-cultural perspectives on reading and reading research*. Newark, Del.: International Reading Association, 1978.

Gunning, R. *The technique of clear writing*. New York: McGraw-Hill, 1968.

Guthrie, J. T. Models of reading and reading disability. *Journal of Educational Psychology*, 1973a, *65*, 9–18.

Guthrie, J. T. Reading comprehension and syntactic responses in good and poor readers. *Journal of Educational Psychology*, 1973b, *65*, 294–299.

Haber, L. R., Haber, R. N., & Furlin, K. R. Word length and word shape as sources of information in reading. *Reading Research Quarterly*, 1983, *18*, 165–189.

Haber, R. N., & Haber, L. R. The shape of a word can specify its meaning. *Reading Research Quarterly*, 1981, *16*, 334–345.

Haber, R. N., & Schindler, R. M. Error in proofreading: Evidence of syntactic control of letter processing? *Journal of Experimental Psychology: Human Perception and Performance*, 1981, *7*, 573–579.

Haberlandt, K., Berian, C., & Sandson, J. The episode schema in story processing. *Journal of Verbal Learning and Verbal Behavior*, 1980, *19*, 635–650.

Hagiwara, H. *Dissociations between reading syllabic and ideographic script in Japanese aphasic patients*. Paper presented at the annual meeting of BABBLE, Niagara Falls, March, 1983.

Hahn, G.-S. *Hangul (Korean alphabet and language)*. Seoul: Korean Overseas Information Service, 1981.

Hall, W. S., & Guthrie, L. F. On the dialect question and reading. In R. J. Spiro, B. C. Bruce, & W. F.

Brewer (Eds.), *Theoretical issues in reading comprehension*. Hillsdale, N.J.: Lawrence Erlbaum Associates, 1980.

Halle, M. Some thoughts on spelling. In K. S. Goodman, & J. T. Fleming (Eds.), *Psycholinguistics and the teaching of reading*. Newark, Del.: International Reading Association, 1969.

Hallgren, B. Specific dyslexia ("congenital word blindness"): A clinical and genetic study. *Acta Psychiatrica et Neurologica Scandinavica*, 1950, Supplement No.65.

Halliday, M. A., & Hasan, R. *Cohesion in English*. London: Longman, 1976.

Hamilton, H., & Deese, J. Comprehensibility and subject–verb relations in complex sentences. *Journal of Verbal Learning and Verbal Behavior*, 1971, *10*, 163–170.

Hampshire, B. *Working with Braille*. Paris: UN Educational, Scientific and Cultural Organization, 1981.

Hanna, P. R., Hanna, J. S., Hodges, R. E., & Rudorf, E. H. *Phoneme–grapheme correspondences as cues to spelling improvement*. Washington, D.C.: US Gov't Print Office, 1966.

Hanson, V. L. Short-term recall by deaf signers of American Sign Language: Implications of encoding strategy for order recall. *Journal of Experimental Psychology: Learning, Memory and Cognition*, 1982, *8*, 572–583.

Hanson, V. L., & Bellugi, U. On the role of sign order and morphological structure in memory for American Sign Language sentences. *Journal of Verbal Learning and Verbal Behavior*, 1982, *21*, 621–633.

Harber, J. R., & Bryen, D. N. Black English and the task of reading. *Review of Educational Research*, 1976, *46*, 387–405.

Hardy, M., Smythe, P. C., & Stennett, R. G. Developmental patterns in elemental reading skills: Phoneme–grapheme and grapheme–phoneme correspondences. *Journal of Educational Psychology*, 1972, *63*, 433–436.

Hardyck, C. D., Petrinovich, L. F., & Ellsworth, D. W. Feedback of speech muscle activity during silent reading: Rapid extinction. *Science*, 1966, *154*, 1467–1468.

Hardyck, C. D., & Petrinovich, L. F. Subvocal speech and comprehension level as a function of the difficulty level of reading material. *Journal of Verbal Learning and Verbal Behavior*, 1970, *9*, 647–652.

Harriot, P. The comprehension of active and passive sentences as a function of pragmatic expectations. *Journal of Verbal Learning and Verbal Behavior*, 1969, *8*, 116–169.

Harris, M. The influence of reversibility and truncation on the interpretation of the passive voice by young children. *British Journal of Psychology*, 1976, *67*, 419–427.

Harris, R. J., & Monaco, G. E. Psychology of pragmatic implication: Information processing between lines. *Journal of Experimental Psychology: General*, 1978, *107*, 1–23.

Hartlage, L. C. Differential age correlates of reading ability. *Perceptual and Motor Skills*, 1975, *41*, 968–970.

Hasher, L., & Griffin, M. Reconstructive and reproductive processes in memory. *Journal of Experimental Psychology: Learning and Memory*, 1978, *4*, 318–330.

Hatano, G., Kuhara, K., & Akiyama, M. Kanji help readers of Japanese infer the meaning of unfamiliar words. *Quarterly Newsletter of the Laboratory of Comparative Human Cognition*, 1981, *3*, 30—33.

Hatch, E., Polin, P., & Part, S. Acoustic scanning and syntactic processing. Three experiments—First and second language learners. *Journal of Reading Behavior*, 1974, *6*, 275–285.

Hatta, T. Asynchrony of lateral onset as a factor in difference in visual field. *Perceptual and Motor Skills*, 1976, *42*, 163–166.

Hatta, T. Lateral recognition of abstract and concrete Kanji in Japanese. *Perceptual and Motor Skills*, 1977a, *45*, 731–734.

Hatta, T. Recognition of Japanese Kanji in the left and right visual fields. *Neuropsychologia*, 1977b, *15*, 685–688.

Hatta, T. Recognition of Japanese Kanji and Hirakana in the left and right visual fields. *Japanese Journal of Psychology.*, 1978, *20*, 51–59, (in Japanese with English abstract).

Hatta, T. Hemispheric asymmetries for physical and semantic congruency matching of visually presented Kanji stimuli. *Japanese Journal of Psychology*, 1979, *50*, 273–278 (in Japanese with English abstract).

Hatta, T. Different stages of Kanji processing and their relations to functional hemispheric asymmetries. *Japanese Psychological Rsearch*, 1981a, *23*, 27–36.

Hatta, T. Task differences in the tachistoscopic Kanji recognition and their relations to hemisphere asymmetries. *Japanese Journal of Psychology*, 1981b, *52*, 139–144 (in Japanese with English abstract).

Hatta, T. Personal communication, May 9, 1981c.

Haviland, S. E., & Clark, H. H. What's new? Acquiring new information as a process in comprehension. *Journal of Verbal Learning and Verbal Behavior*, 1974, *13*, 512–521.

Hawkins, H. L., Reicher, G., Rogers, M., & Peterson, L. Flexible coding in word recognition. *Journal of Experimental Psychology: Human Perception and Performance*, 1976, *2*, 380–385.

Hayashi, R., & Hatta, T. Visual field differences in a deeper semantic processing task with Kanji stimuli. *Japanese Psychological Research*, 1982, *24*, 111–117.

Hayashibe, H. Word order and particles: A developmental study in Japanese. *Descriptive and Applied Linguistics*, 1975, *8*, 1–18.

Hayes-Roth, B., & Hayes-Roth, F. Prominence of lexical information in memory: Representation of meaning. *Journal of Verbal Learning and Verbal Behavior*, 1977, *16*, 119–136.

Hayhurst, H. Some errors of young children in producing passive sentences. *Journal Verbal Learning and Verbal Behavior*, 1967, *6*, 634–639.

Hayman, G. Task analysis of lexical decisions. Unpublished doctoral dissertation: McMaster University, Hamilton, Ontario, 1983.

Healy, A. F. Detection errors on the word THE: Evidence for reading units larger than letters. *Journal of Experimental Psychology: Human Perception and Performance*, 1976, *2*, 235–242.

Healy, A. F. The effects of visual similarity on proofreading for misspellings. *Memory & Cognition*, 1981, *9*, 453–460.

Healy, A. F., & Miller, G. A. The verb as the main determinant of semantic meaning. *Psychonomic Science*, 1970, *20*, 372.

Healy, J. M., Aram, D. M., Horwitz, S. J., & Kessler, J. W. A study of hyperlexia. *Brain and Language*, 1982, *17*, 1–23.

Hécaen, H. Right hemisphere contribution to language function. In P. A. Buser, & A. Rougeul-Buser (Eds.), *Cerebral correlates of conscious experience*. (INSERM Symposium No. 6), Amsterdam: Elsevier/North Holland Biomedical Press, 1978.

Hécaen, H., & Kremin, H. Neurolinguistic research on reading disorders resulting from left hemisphere lesions: Aphasic and "pure" alexias. In H. Whitaker, & H. A. Whitaker (Eds.), *Studies in neurolinguistics* (Vol. 2). New York: Academic Press, 1976.

Henderson, L. Wholistic models of feature analysis in word recognition: A critical examination. In P. A. Kolers, M. E. Wrolstad, & H. Bouma (Eds.), *Processing of visible language* (Vol. 2). New York: Plenum, 1980.

Henderson, L. *Orthography and word recognition in reading*. New York: Academic Press, 1982.

Henderson, L., & Chard, J. The reader's implicit knowledge of orthographic structure. In U. Frith (Ed.), *Cognitive processes in spelling*. London: Academic Press, 1980.

Hershensen, M. Stimulus structure, cognitive structure, and the perception of letter arrays. *Journal of Experimental Psychology*, 1969, *79*, 327–335.

Hier, D. B. Sex differences in hemispheric specialization: Hypothesis for the excess of dyslexic boys. *Bulletin of the Orton Society*, 1979, *29*, 74–83.

Hier, D. B., LeMay, M., Rosenberger, P. B., & Perlo, V. P. Developmental dyslexia: Evidence for a subgroup with a reversal of cerebral asymmetry. *Archives of Neurology*, 1978, *35*, 90–92.

Hildyard, A., & Olson, D. R. Memory and inference in the comprehension of oral and written discourse. *Discourse Processing*, 1978, *1*, 91–117.

Hink, R. F., Kaga, K., & Suzuki, J. An evoked potential correlate of reading ideographic and phonetic Japanese scripts. *Neuropsychologia*, 1980, *18*, 455–464.

Hirsch, E. D. Jr. *The philosophy of composition*. Chicago: University of Chicago Press, 1977.

Hochberg, J. Components of literacy: Speculations and exploratory research. In H. Levin, & J. P. Williams (Eds.), *Basic studies on reading*. New York: Basic Books, 1970.
Hodges, R. E. The language base of spelling. In V. Froese, & S. B. Straw (Eds.), *Research in the language arts*. Baltimore: University Park Press, 1981.
Hoffman, A. C. Eye movements during prolonged reading. *Journal of Experimental Psychology*, 1946, *36*, 95–118.
Hoffmann, J. Experimentell-psychologische Untersuchungen ueber Leseleistungen von Schulkindern. *Archiv fur die gesamte Psychologie*, 1927, *58*, 325–388.
Hogaboam, T. W., & McConkie, G. W. *The rocky road from eye fixations to comprehension.* Technical Report 207, Center for the Study of Reading, University of Illinois at Urbana-Champaign, May, 1981.
Holden, M. H., & MacGinitie, W. H. Children's conceptions of word boundaries in speech and print. *Journal of Educational Psychology*, 1972, *63*, 551–557.
Holden, M. H., & MacGinitie, W. H. *Metalinguistic ability and cognitive performance in children from five to seven*. New York: Teachers College, Columbia University, 1973.
Holender, D. Identification of letters in words and of single letters with pre- and postknowledge vs. postkowledge of the alternatives. *Perception & Psychophysics*, 1979, *25*, 313–318.
Holley-Wilcox, P., & Blank, M. A. Evidence for multiple access in the processing of isolated words. *Journal of Experimental Psychology: Human Perception and Performance*, 1980, *6*, 75–84.
Hollingworth, L. *Children above 180 IQ*. New York: World, 1942.
Holmes, J. M. "Regression" and reading breakdown. In A. Caramazza, & E. B. Zurif (Eds.), *Language acquisition and breakdown*. Baltimore, Md.: The Johns Hopkins University Press, 1978.
Holmes, V. M., & O'Regan, J. K. Eye fixation patterns during the reading of relative-clause sentences. *Journal of Verbal Learning and Verbal Behavior*, 1981, *20*, 417–430.
Horn, E. *Teaching spelling*. Washington, D.C.: AERA National Education Association, 1954.
Hornby, P. A. The psychological subject and predicate. *Cognitive Psychology*, 1972, *3*, 632–642.
Hornby, P. A. Surface structure and presupposition. *Journal of Verbal Learning and Verbal Behavior*, 1974, *13*, 530–538.
Hotopf, N. Slips of the pen. In U. Frith (Ed.), *Cognitive processes in spelling*. London: Academic Press, 1980.
Hottenlocher, J. Children's language: Word–phrase relationship. *Science*, 1964, *143*, 264–265.
House, B. J., Hanley, M. J., & Migid, D. F. Logographic reading by TMR adults. *American Journal of Mental Deficiency*, 1980, *85*, 161–170.
Huang, J.-T., & Liu, I.-M. Paired-associate learning proficiency as a function of frequency count, meaningfulness, and imagery value in Chinese two-character ideograms. *Chinese Psychological Journal*, 1978, *20*, 5–17, (in Chinese with English abstract).
Huey, E. B. *The psychology and pedagogy of reading*. Cambridge, Mass.: MIT Press, 1908 (1968).
Hughes, J. R. The electroencephalogram and reading disorders. In R. N. Malatesha, & P. G. Aaron (Eds.), *Reading disorders: Varieties and treatments*. New York: Academic Press, 1982.
Hull, C. L. Quantitative aspects of the evolution of concepts. *Psychological Monographs*, 1920, *28*, (Whole No. 123).
Ikeda, M., & Saida, S. Span of recognition in reading. *Vision Research*, 1978, *18*, 83–88.
Imai, K. Examination of instructional method of preschoolers' learning to read. *The Science of Reading*, 1979, *23*, 97–104, (in Japanese with English abstract).
Inglis, J., & Lawson, J. S. Sex differences in the effects of unilateral brain damage on intelligence. *Science*, 1981, *212*, 693–695.
Ingram, T. T. S., Mason, A. W., & Blackburn, I. A retrospective study of 82 children with reading disability. *Developmental Medicine and Child Neurology*, 1970, *12*, 271–281.
Inoue, M. Relations among the graphemic, phonemic, and semantic processing of Chinese characters (Kanji): A study by the graphemical matching task. *Japanese Journal of Psychology*, 1980, *51*, 136–144, (in Japanese, with English abstract).
Isakson, R., & Miller, J. Sensitivity to the syntactic and semantic cues in good and poor comprehenders. *Journal of Educational Psychology*, 1976, *9*, 12–20.

Ishii, I. *The mythology of Kanji*. Tokyo: Miyakawa Shoten, 1967, (in Japanese).

Ishikawa, S. *A follow-up study of letter reading ability of infants*. (The 1969 Annals of the Early Childhood Education Association of Japan), Tokyo: Froebel-kan, 1970, (in Japanese).

Itoh, Y., & Koyazu, T. Cued reproduction and paraphrase of a simple sentence. *Japanese Journal of Psychology*, 1981, *52*, 159–165, (in Japanese with English abstract).

Itsukushima, Y. Examination of mental mechanisms underlying order judgments in Japanese syllabary. *Japanese Journal of Psychology*, 1981, *51*, 310–317, (in Japanese with English abstract).

Iwatate, S. The word-order and case strategies in Japanese children. *Japanese Journal of Psychology*, 1980, *51*, 233–240, (in Japanese with English summary).

Jaarsveld, H. van *Practice effects in reading handwriting: Perceptual or conceptual*. Internal Report, A.T.W. Katholiek Universiteit Nijmegen (Netherlands), 1979.

Jaarsveld, H. van Personal communication, April, 1982.

Jackson, M. D., & McClelland, J. L. Sensory and cognitive determinants of reading speed. *Journal of Verbal Learning and Verbal Behavior*, 1975, *14*, 565–574.

Jackson, M. D., & McClelland, J. L. Processing determinants of reading speed. *Journal of Experimental Psychology: General*, 1979, *108*, 151–181.

Jacobson, J. Z. Interaction of similarity to words of visual masks and targets. *Journal of Experimental Psychology*, 1974, *102*, 431–434.

Jacobson, J. Z. Visual masking by homonyms. *Canadian Journal of Psychology*, 1976, *30*, 174–177.

Jacobson, J. Z., & Dodwell, P. C. Saccadic eye movements during reading. *Brain and Language*, 1979, *8*, 303–314.

Jacobson, J. Z., & Rhinelander, G. Geometric and semantic similarity in visual masking. *Journal of Experimental Psychology: Human Perception and Performance*, 1978, *4*, 224–231.

James, W. *The principles of psychology*. New York: Henry Holt, 1890.

Jansky, J., & de Hirsch, K. *Preventing reading failure*. New York: Harper and Row, 1972.

Jarvella, R. J. Syntactic processing of connected speech. *Journal of Verbal Learning and Verbal Behavior*, 1971, *10*, 409–416.

Javal, E. *Physiologie de la lecture et de l'ecriture*. Paris: Felix Alcan, 1906.

Jeffrey, W. E., & Samuels, S. J. The effect of method of reading training on initial reading and transfer. *Journal of Verbal Learning and Verbal Behavior*, 1967, *6*, 354–358.

Jensen, H. *Sign, symbol and script*. London: George Allen and Unwin, 1970.

Jensen, M. Relation between the qualifications of different groups of readers and different aspects of test. In P. A. Kolers, M. E. Wrolstad, & H. Bouma (Eds.), *Processing of visible language* (Vol. 1). New York: Plenum, 1979.

Jespersen, O. *A modern English grammar on historical principles, Part 1: Sound and spellings*, London: George Allen and Unwin, 1933.

Jespersen, O. *A modern English grammar on historical principles, Part 3: Syntax*, Copenhagen: Einar Munksgaard, 1949.

Johnson, H. L. The meaning of *before* and *after* for preschool children. *Journal of Experimental Child Psychology*, 1975, *19*, 88–99.

Johnson, H., & Smith, L. B. Children's inferential abilities in the context of reading to understand. *Child Development*, 1981, *52*.

Johnson, M. K., Bransford, J. D., & Solomon, S. K. Memory for tacit implications of sentences. *Journal of Experimental Psychology*, 1973, *98*, 203–205.

Johnson, R. E. Recall of prose as a function of the structural importance of the linguistic units. *Journal of Verbal Learning and Verbal Behavior*, 1970, *9*, 12–20.

Johnson, R. J. *The effect of training in letter names on success in beginning reading for children of differing abilities*. Paper presented at the meeting of the American Educational Research Convention, Anaheim, Cal., 1970.

Johnston, J. C. Effects of advance precuing of alternatives on the perception of letters alone and in words. *Journal of Experimental Psychology: Human Perception and Performance*, 1981, *7*, 560–572.

Johnston, J. C., & McClelland, J. L. Visual factors in word perception. *Perception & Psychophysics*, 1973, *14*, 365–370.

Johnston, J. C., & McClelland, J. L. Experimental tests of a hierarchical model of word identification. *Journal of Verbal Learning and Verbal Behavior*, 1980, *19*, 503–524.

Jones, B. The integrative action of the cerebral hemispheres. *Perception & Psychophysics*, 1982, *32*, 423-433.

Jones, D. *An English pronunciation dictionary*. London: Dent, 1917.

Jones, M. H., & Carterette, E. C. Redundancy in children's free-reading choice. *Journal of Verbal Learning and Verbal Behavior*, 1963, *2*, 489–493.

Jonides, J., & Gleitman, H. A conceptual vategory effect in visual search: O as letter or as digit. *Perception & Psychophysics*, 1972, *12*, 457–460.

Jorm, A. F. Children's reading processes revealed by pronunciation latencies and errors. *Journal of Educational Psychology*, 1977, *69*, 166–171.

Jorm, A. F. The cognitive and neurological basis of developmental dyslexia: A theoretical framework and review. *Cognition*, 1979, *7*, 19–33.

Juel, C. Comparison of word identification strategies with varying context, word type, and reader skill. *Reading Research Quarterly*, 1980, *15*, 358–376.

Juola, J. F., Ward, N. J., & McNamara, T. Visual search and reading of rapid serial presentations of letter strings, words, and text. *Journal of Experimental Psychology: General*, 1982, *111*, 208–227.

Just, M. A., & Carpenter, P. A. A theory of reading: From eye fixations to comprehension. *Psychological Review*, 1980, *87*, 329–354.

Just, M. A., Carpenter, P. A., & Woolley, J. D. Paradigms and processes in reading comprehension. *Journal of Experimental Psychology: General*, 1982, *111*, 228–238.

Kaiho, H., & Inukai, Y. An analysis of Gestalt characteristics of 881 Japanese/Chinese Kanji. *Japanese Journal of Psychology*, 1982, *53*, 312–315, (in Japanese with English abstract).

Kameenui, E. J., & Carnine, D. W. An investigation of fourth-graders' comprehension of pronoun constructions in ecologically valid texts. *Reading Research Quarterly*, 1982, *17*, 556–580.

Kane, T. S., & Peters, L. J. *A practical rhetoric of expository prose*. New York: Oxford University Press, 1966.

Kang, T.-J., Chong, J.-Y., & Taylor, I. Reading in all-Hangul or Hangul–Kanji mixed scripts. (In preparation).

Kappelman, M., Rosenstein, A., & Canter, R. Comparison of disadvantaged children with learning disabilities and their successful peer group. *American Journal of Diseases of Children*, 1972, *124*, 875–879.

Karlgren, B. *Sound and symbol in Chinese*. Hong Kong: Hong Kong University Press, 1962.

Karpova, S. N. *The realization of the verbal composition of speech by preschool children*. The Hague: Mouton, 1977.

Kates, B., MacNaughton, S., & Silverman, H. *Handbook of Blissymbolics*. Toronto: Blissymbol Communications Institute, 1978.

Katz, I., & Singer, H. *Effects of instructional methods on reading acquisition system: A reanalysis of first-grade study data*. Paper presented at the meeting of the International Reading Association, Anaheim, Cal., 1976.

Katz, L. Reading ability and single-letter orthographic redundancy. *Journal of Educational Psychology*, 1977, *69*, 653–659.

Katz, R. B., Shankweiler, D., & Liberman, I. Y. *Memory for item order and phonetic recoding in the beginning reader*. Status Report on Speech Research SR-66, Haskins Laboratories, 1981.

Kawai, Y. Physical complexity of the Chinese letters and learning to read it. *Japanese Journal of Educational Psychology*, 1966, *14*, 129–138, (in Japanese).

Keefe, B., & Swinney, D. On the relationship of hemispheric specialization and developmental dyslexia. *Cortex*, 1979, *15*, 471–481.

Keren, G., & Baggen, S. Recognition models of alphanumeric characters. *Perception & Psychophysics*, 1981, *29*, 234–246.

Kerr, N. H., Butler, S. F., Maykuth, P. L., & Delis, D. The effects of thematic context and presentation mode on memory for sentence voice. *Journal of Psycholinguistic Research*, 1982, *11*, 247–264.

Kerschner, J. R. Cerebral dominance in disabled readers, good readers, and gifted children: Search for a valid model. *Child Development*, 1977, *48*, 61–67.

Keuss, P. J. G. Processing of geometric dimensions in a binary classification task: Evidence for a dual process model. *Perception & Psychophysics*, 1977, *21*, 371–376.

Kibby, M. W. Intersentential processes in reading comprehension. *Journal of Reading Behavior*, 1980, *12*, 299–312.

Kieras, D. Good and bad structure in simple paragraphs: Effects on apparent theme, reading time, and recall. *Journal of Verbal Learning and Verbal Behavior*, 1978, *17*, 13–28.

Kimura, D. Cerebral dominance and the perception of verbal stimuli. *Canadian Journal of Psychology*, 1961, *15*, 166–171.

Kimura, D. Left–right differences in the perception of melodies. *Quarterly Journal of Experimental Psychology*, 1964, *14*, 355–358.

Kinda, H. *The Japanese language*. (Translated by U. Hirano), Tokyo and Rutland, Vermont: Charles E. Tuttle, 1978.

King, E. M., & Friesen, D. T. Children who read in kindergarten. *Alberta Journal of Educational Research*, 1972, *18*, 147–161.

Kinney, G. C., Marsetta, M., & Showman, D. J. *Studies in display symbol legibility, Part 12. The legibility of alphanumeric symbols for digitalized television*. ESD-TR-66-117, The Mitre Corporation, November, 1966.

Kinsbourne, M. Personal communication, February 2, 1981.

Kinsbourne, M., & Hiscock, M. Cerebral lateralization and cognitive development. In J. S. Chall, & A. F. Mirsky (Eds.), *Education and the brain*. Chicago: University of Chicago Press, 1978.

Kinsbourne, M., & Warrington, E. K. Developmental factors in reading and writing backwardness. *British Journal of Psychology*, 1963, *54*, 145–156.

Kintsch, W., & Greene, E. The role of culture-specific schemata in the comprehension and recall of stories. *Discourse Processes*, 1978, *1*, 1–13.

Kintsch, W., & Keenan, J. M. Reading rate and retention as a function of the number of propositions in the base structure of sentences. *Cognitive Psychology*, 1973, *5*, 257–274.

Kintsch, W., Kozminsky, E., Streby, W. J., McKoon, G., & Keenan, J. M. Comprehension and recall of text as a function of content variables. *Journal of Verbal Learning and Verbal Behavior*, 1975, *14*, 196–214.

Kintsch, W., & van Dijk, T. A. Toward a model of discourse comprehension and production. *Psychological Review*, 1978, *85*, 363–394.

Kissler, G. R., & Lloyd, K. E. Effect of sentence interrelation and scrambling on the recall of factual information. *Journal of Educational Psychology*, 1972, *64*, 187–190.

Klapp, S. T. Syllable-dependent pronunciation latencies in number naming: A replication. *Journal of Experimental Psychology*, 1974, *102*, 1138–1140.

Klare, G. R. Assessing readability. *Reading Research Quarterly*, 1974–1975, *10*, 62–102.

Kleiman, G. M. Speech recoding in reading. *Journal of Verbal Learning and Verbal Behavior*, 1975, *14*, 323–339.

Klein, G. A., & Klein, H. A. Word identification as a function of contextual information. *American Journal of Psychology*, 1973, *86*, 399–406.

Koen, F., Becker, A., & Young, R. The psychological reality of the paragraph. *Journal of Verbal Learning and Verbal Behavior*, 1969, *8*, 49–53.

Kolers, P. A. Three stages of reading. In H. Levin, & J. P. Williams (Eds.), *Basic studies on reading*. New York: Basic Books, 1970.

Kolers, P. A. Pattern-analyzing disability in poor readers. *Developmental Psychology*, 1975, *11*, 282–290.

Kolers, P. A., & Katzman, M. T. Naming sequentially presented letters and words. *Language and Speech*, 1966, *9*, 84–95.

Kolers, P. A., & Magee, L. E. Specificity of pattern-analyzing skills in reading. *Canadian Journal of Psychology*, 1978, *32*, 43–51.
Kolers, P. A., Palef, S. R., & Stelmach, L. B. Graphemic analysis underlying literacy. *Memory & Cognition*, 1980, *8*, 322–328.
Kolers, P. A., & Rudnicky, A. Personal Communication, October, 1982.
Kowarik, O. Reading–writing problems in Austria. In L. Tarnopol, & M. Tarnopol (Eds.), *Reading disabilities— an international perspective*. Baltimore: University Park Press, 1976.
Kratochvil, P. *The Chinese language today*. London: Hutchinson, 1968.
Krueger, L. E. Search time in a redundant visual display. *Journal of Experimental Psychology*, 1970, *83*, 391–399.
Kučera, H., & Francis, W. N. *Computational analysis of present-day American English*. Providence, R.I.: Brown University Press, 1967.
Kuennapas, T., & Janson, A.-J. Multidimensional similarity of letters. *Perceptual and Motor Skills*, 1969, *28*, 3–12.
Kulhavy, R. W., Dyer, J. W., & Silver, L. The effects of note taking and test expectancy on the learning of text material. *Journal of Educational Research*, 1975, *68*, 363–375.
Kuo, W. F. A preliminary study of reading disabilities in the Republic of China. *Collection of Papers by National Taiwan Normal University, Graduate School of Education*, 1978, *20*, 57–78.
Kuo, Z. Y. A behaviouristic experiment on inductive inference. *Journal of Experimental Psychology*, 1923, *6*, 247–293.
Kutas, M., & Hillyard, S. A. The lateral distribution of event-related potentials during sentence processing. *Neuropsychologia*, 1982, *20*, 579–590.
Kyöstiö, O. K. Is learning to read easy in a language in which the grapheme–phoneme correspondences are regular? In J. F. Kavanagh, & R. L. Venezky (Eds.), *Orthography, reading and dyslexia*. Baltimore: University Park Press, 1980.
LaBerge, D., & Samuels, S. J. Toward a theory of automatic information processing in reading. *Cognitive Psychology*, 1974, *6*, 293–323.
Labov, W. The logic of non-standard English. In F. Williams (Ed.), *Language and poverty*. Chicago: Markam, 1970.
Lado, R., & Andersson, T. *Early reading*. Washington, D.C.: Georgetown University Papers on Language and Linguistics 13, 1976.
Lashley, K. S. The problem of serial order in behavior. In A. Joffress (Ed.), *Cerebral mechanisms in behavior*. (The Hixon symposium), New York: Wiley, 1951.
Lassen, N. A., Ingvar, D. H., & Skinhøj, E. Brain function and blood flow. *Scientific American*, 1978, *239*, 62–71.
Laubach, F. C. *Learning English the new way*. Syracuse, N. Y.: New Readers Press, 1962.
Ledson, S. *Teach your child to read in 60 days*. New York: WW Norton, 1975.
Lee, J.-H. *Hun-min Jeoung Eum: An explanation and translation*. Seoul: Korean Library Science Research Institute, 1972, (in English and Korean).
Lee, O.-R. *Early bilingual reading as an aid to bicultural adjustment for a second-generation Korean child in the U.S.*. Unpublished doctoral dissertation, Washington, D.C.: Georgetown University, 1977.
Lefton, L. A., Spragins, A. B., & Byrnes, J. English orthography: Relation to reading experience. *Bulletin of the Psychonomic Society*, 1973, *2*, 281–282.
Lefton, L. A., & Spragins, A. B. Orthographic structure and reading experience affect the transfer from iconic to short-term memory. *Journal of Experimental Psychology*, 1974, *103*, 775–781.
Lempert, H., & Kinsbourne, M. Preschool children's sentence comprehension strategies with respect to word order. *Journal of Child Language*, 1980, *7*, 371–379.
Lenneberg, E. H. *Biological foundations of language*. New York: Wiley, 1967.
Leong, C. K. Hong Kong. In J. Downing (Ed.), *Comparative reading*. New York: Macmillan, 1973.
Leong, C. K. Lateralization in severely disabled readers in relation to functional cerebral development and syntheses of information. In R. M. Knights, & D. J. Bakker (Eds.), *The neuropsychology of learning disorders: Theoretical approaches*. Baltimore: University Park Press, 1976.

Lesevre, N. L'organization du regard chez des enfants d'age scolaire, lecteurs normaux et dyslexiques. *Revue de Neuropsychiatrie Infantile*, 1968, *16*, 323–349.

Lesgold, A. M. Pronominalization: A device for unifying sentences in memory. *Journal of Verbal Learning and Verbal Behavior*, 1972, *11*, 316–323.

Lesgold, A. M. Variability in children's comprehension of syntactic structures. *Journal of Educational Psychology*, 1974, *66*, 333–338.

Leslie, L., & Shannon, A. J. Recognition of orthographic structure during beginning reading. *Journal of Reading Behavior*, 1981, *13*, 313–324.

Levelt, W. J. M. A survey of studies in sentence perception: 1970–1976. In W. J. M. Levelt, & G. Flores d'Arcais (Eds.), *Studies in the perception of language*. New York: Wiley, 1978.

Levin, H., & Cohn, J. A. Studies of oral reading: XII. Effects of instructions on the eye–voice span. In H. Levin, E. J. Gibson, & J. J. Gibson (Eds.), *The analysis of reading skill*. Project No. 5-1213 (Vol. 5-1213), Ithaca, NY: Cornell University and U.S. Office of Education, 1968.

Levin, H., & Turner, A. Sentence structure and the eye–voice span. In H. Levin, E. J. Gibson, & J. J. Gibson (Eds.), *The analysis of reading skill*. (Project No. 5-1213), Ithaca, NY: Cornell University and U.S. Office of Education, 1968.

Levy, B. A. Vocalization and suppression effects in sentence memory. *Journal of Verbal Learning and Verbal Behavior*, 1975, *14*, 304–316.

Levy, B. A. Speech analysis during sentence processing: Reading and listening. *Visible Language*, 1978, *12*, 81–101.

Levy, J. Lateral specialization of the human brain: Behavioral manifestations and possible evolutionary basis. In J. A. Kiger (Ed.), *The biology of behavior*. Corvallis: Oregon State University Press, 1972.

Levy, J., & Trevarthen, C. Metacontrol of hemispheric function in human split-brain patients. *Journal of Experimental Psychology: Human Perception and Performance*, 1976, *2*, 299–312.

Liberman, I. Y., & Mann, V. A. *Should reading instruction and remediation vary with the sex of the child?* Status Report on Speech Research SR-65, Haskins Laboratories, 1981.

Liberman, I. Y., Shankweiler, D., Orlando, C., Harris, K. S., & Berti, F. B. Letter confusion and reversals of sequence in the beginning reader: Implications for Orton's theory of developmental dyslexia. *Cortex*, 1971, *7*, 127–142.

Liberman, I. Y., Shankweiler, D., Fischer, F. W., & Carter, B. Explicit syllable and phoneme segmentation in the young child. *Journal of Experimental Child Psychology*, 1974, *18*, 201–212.

Liberman, I. Y., Shankweiler, D., Liberman, A. M., Fowler, C., & Fischer, F. W. Phonetic segmentation and recoding in the beginning reader. In A. S. Reber, & D. L. Scarborough (Eds.), *Toward a psychology of reading*. Hillsdale, N. J.: Lawrence Erlbaum Associates, 1977.

Lindsay, P., & Norman, D. A. *Human information processing: An introduction to psychology*. New York: Academic Press, 1972.

Liu, I.-M. The function of word form and phonetic cues in the acquisition of word meaning. *National Science Council Monthly*, 1978, *6*, 1089–1098, (in Chinese with English abstract).

Liu, I.-M. Personal communication, May 17, 1979.

Liu, I.-M., & Chen, C.-L. Reading efficiencies for Chinese logography and phonographic simulation. *Journal of Chinese Psychology*, 1980, *22*, 23–28, (in Chinese with English abstract).

Liu, I.-M., Chuang, C.-J., & Wang, S.-C. *Frequency count of 40,000 Chinese words*. Taiwan: Luck Books Company, 1975, (in Chinese).

Liu, I.-M., Yeh, J.-S., Wang, L.-H., & Chang, Y.-K. Effects of arranging Chinese words as units on reading efficiency. *Journal of Chinese Psychology*, 1974, *16*, 25–32, (in Chinese with English abstract).

Llewellyn-Thomas, E. Eye movements in speed reading. In R. G. Stauffer (Ed.), *Speed reading: Practices and procedures*. Newark, Del.: University of Delaware Reading Center, 1962.

Llewellyn-Thomas, E. Movements of the eye. *Scientific American*, 1968, *219*, 88–95.

Locke, J. L. Phonemic effects in the silent reading of hearing and deaf children. *Cognition*, 1978, *6*, 173–187.

Loftus, E. F. Leading questions and the eyewitness report. *Cognitive Psychology*, 1975, *7*, 560–572.

Loosen, F. Memory for the gist of sentences. *Journal of Psycholinguistic Research*, 1981, *10*, 17–25.

Lott, D., & Smith, F. Knowledge of intraword redundancy by beginning reader. *Psychonomic Science*, 1970, *19*, 343–344.

Lovegrove, W., & Brown, C. Development of information processing in normal and disabled readers. *Perceptual and Motor Skills*, 1978, *46*, 1047–1054.

Lovell, K., Shapton, D., & Warren, N. S. A study of some cognitive and other disabilities in backward readers with average intelligence as assessed by a non-verbal test. *British Journal of Educational Psychology*, 1964, *34*, 58–64.

Lovett, M. W. The selective encoding of sentential information in normal reading development. *Child Development*, 1979, *50*, 897–900.

Low, A. A. A case of agrammatism in the English language. *Archives of Neurology and Psychiatry*, 1931, *25*, 556–597 (cited by Marshall & Newcombe, 1980).

Luce, R. D. *Individual choice behavior*. New York: Wiley, 1959.

Luce, R. D. Detection and recognition. In R. D. Luce, R. R. Bush, & S. E. Galanter (Eds.), *Handbook of mathematical psychology* (Vol. 1). New York: Wiley, 1963.

Lupker, S. J. On the nature of perceptual information during letter perception. *Perception & Psychophysics*, 1979, *25*, 303–312.

Lyle, J. G., & Goyen, J. Performance of retarded readers on the WISC and educational tests. *Journal of Abnormal Psychology*, 1969, *74*, 105–112.

Lyons, J. *Introduction to theoretical linguistics*. London: Cambridge University Press, 1968.

Lyons, J. *Chomsky*. London: William Collins, 1970.

McCauley, C., Parmelee, C. M., Sperber, R. D., & Carr, T. H. Early extraction of meaning from pictures and its relation to conscious identification. *Journal of Experimental Psychology: Human Perception and Performance*, 1980, *6*, 265–276.

McClelland, J. L. Preliminary letter identification in the perception of words and nonwords. *Journal of Experimental Psychology: Human Perception and Performance*, 1976, *2*, 80–91.

McClelland, J. L., & Miller, J. Structural factors in figure perception. *Perception & Psychophysics*, 1979, *26*, 221–229.

McClelland, J. L., & Rumelhart, D. E. An interactive activation model of context effects in letter perception: Part 1. An account of basic findings. *Psychological Review*, 1981, *88*, 375–407.

McConkie, G. W. Stimulus control in the study of reading. In P. D. Pearson, & J. Hansen (Eds.), *Reading: Disciplined inquiry in process and practice* (27th Yearbook of the National Reading Conference). Clemson, S.C.: National Reading Conference, 1978.

McConkie, G. W., & Rayner, K. The span of effective stimulus during a fixation in reading. *Perception & Psychophysics*, 1975, *17*, 578–586.

McConkie, G. W., & Rayner, K. An on-line computer technique for studying reading: Identifying the perceptual span. In H. Singer, & R. B. Ruddell (Eds.), *Theoretical models and processes of reading*. Newark, Del.: International Reading Association, 1976.

McConkie, G. W., & Zola, D. Is visual information integrated across successive fixations in reading? *Perception & Psychophysics*, 1979, *25*, 221–224.

McCusker, L. X., Gough, P. B., & Bias, R. G. Word recognition inside out and outside in. *Journal of Experimental Psychology: Human Perception and Performance*, 1981, *7*, 538–551.

McCusker, L. X., Hillinger, M. L., & Bias, R. G. Phonetic recoding and reading. *Psychological Bulletin*, 1981, *89*, 217–245.

McGaw, B., & Grotelueschen, A. Direction of the effect of questions in prose material. *Journal of Educational Psychology*, 1972, *63*, 580–588.

MacGinitie, W. H. Contextual constraint in English prose paragraph. *Journal of Psychology*, 1961, *51*, 121–130.

McGlone, J. Sex differences in functional brain asymmetry. *Cortex*, 1978, *14*, 122–128.

McGuigan, F. J. Feedback of speech muscle activity during silent reading: Two comments. *Science*, 1967, *157*, 579–580.

McGuigan, F. J. Covert oral behavior during the silent performance of language tasks. *Psychological Bulletin*, 1970, *74*, 309–326.

McGuigan, F. J., & Bailey, S. C. Longitudinal study of covert oral behavior during silent reading. *Perceptual and Motor Skills*, 1969, *28*, 170.

MacKay, D. G. To end ambiguous sentences. *Perception & Psychophysics*, 1966, *1*, 426–436.

MacKay, D. G. Phonetic factors in the perception and recall of spelling errors. *Neuropsychologia*, 1968, *6*, 321–325.

MacKay, D. G. Derivational rules and the internal lexicon. *Journal of Verbal Learning and Verbal Behavior*, 1978, *17*, 61–71.

McKeever, W. F., & van Deventer, A. D. Dyslexic adolescents: Evidence of impaired visual and auditory language processing associated with normal lateralization and visual responsivity. *Cortex*, 1975, *11*, 361–378.

Mackworth, J. F., & Mackworth, N. H. How children read: Matching by sight and sound. *Journal of Reading Behavior*, 1974, *6*, 295–303.

Mackworth, N. H. The line of sight approach to children's reading and comprehension. In S. F. Wanat, H. Singer, & M. Kling (Eds.), *Extracting meaning from written language*. Arlington, Virginia: Center for Applied Linguistics, 1977.

MacLeod, C. M., Hunt, E. B., & Mathews, N. Individual differences in the verification of sentence–picture relationships. *Journal of Verbal Learning and Verbal Behavior*, 1978, *17*, 493–507.

McLaughlin, G. H. Reading at impossible speeds. *Journal of Reading*, 1969, *12*, 449–454.

MacWhinney, B., & Bates, E. Sentential devices for conveying givenness and newness: A cross-cultural developmental study. *Journal of Verbal Learning and Verbal Behavior*, 1978, *17*, 539–558.

Makita, K. The rarity of reading disability in Japanese children. *American Journal of Orthopsychiatry*, 1968, *38*, 599–614.

Malatesha, R. N. Differences in hemispheric functions between dyslexics and normal readers (Doctoral dissertation, University of South Carolina, 1976). *Dissertation Abstracts International*, 1977, *38(1-A)*, 179–180.

Malmquist, E. An international overview of primary reading practices. *Journal of Reading*, 1975, *18*, 615–624.

Mandel, T. S. Eye movement research on the propositional structure of short texts. *Behavioral Research Methods and Instrumentation*, 1979, *11*, 180–187.

Mandler, J. M. A code in the node: The use of the story schema in retrieval. *Discourse Processes*, 1978, *1*, 14–35.

Mandler, J. M., & Goodman, M. S. On the psychological validity of story structure. *Journal of Verbal Learning and Verbal Behavior*, 1982, *21*, 507–523.

Mandler, J. M., & Johnson, N. S. Remembrance of things parsed: Story structure and recall. *Cognitive Psychology*, 1977, *9*, 111–151.

Manelis, L., & Yekovich, F. R. Repetitions of propositional arguments in sentences. *Journal of Verbal Learning and Verbal Behavior*, 1976, *15*, 301–312.

Manly, J. M., Rickert, E., & Freeman, M. *The writing of English*. New York: Henry Holt, 1937 (First edition 1919).

Mann, V. A., Liberman, I. Y., & Shankweiler, D. Children's memory for sentences and word strings in relation to reading ability. *Memory & Cognition*, 1980, *8*, 329–335.

Marcel, A. J. Conscious and preconscious recognition of polysemous words: Locating theselective effects of prior verbal context. In R. S. Nickerson (Ed.), *Attention and performance* (Vol. 8). Hillsdale, N.J.: Lawrence Erlbaum Associates, 1980a.

Marcel, A. J. Surface dyslexia and beginning reading: A revised hypothesis of pronunciation of print and its impairments. In M. Coltheart, K. Patterson, & J. C. Marshall (Eds.), *Deep dyslexia*. London: Routledge & Kegan Paul, 1980b.

Marcel, A. J. Conscious and unconscious perception: Visual masking, word recognition, and an approach to consciousness. *Cognitive Psychology*, In press.

Marcel, T., Katz, L., & Smith, M. Laterality and reading proficiency. *Neuropsychologia*, 1974, *12*, 131–139.

Marcel, T., & Rajan, P. Lateral specialization for recognition of words and faces in good and poor readers. *Neuropsychologia*, 1975, *13*, 489–497.

Marchbanks, G., & Levin, H. Cues by which children recognize words. *Journal of Educational Psychology*, 1965, *56*, 57–61.
Marks, C. B., Doctorow, M. J., & Wittrock, M. C. Word frequency and reading comprehension. *Journal of Educational Research*, 1974, *67*, 259–262.
Marr, D. Early processing of visual information. *Philosophical Transactions of the Royal Society of London*, 1976, *B 275*, 483–524.
Marr, D. *Vision*. San Fransisco: Freeman, 1982.
Marr, D., & Hildreth, E. Theory of edge detection. *Proceedings of the Royal Society of London*, 1980, *B 207*, 187–217.
Marschark, M., & Paivio, A. Integrative processing of concrete and abstract sentences. *Journal of Verbal Learning and Verbal Behavior*, 1977, *16*, 217–231.
Marsh, G., Friedman, M., Welch, V., & Desberg, P. The development of strategies in spelling. In U. Frith (Ed.), *Cognitive processes in spelling*. London: Academic Press, 1980.
Marshall, J. C., & Newcombe, F. Patterns of paralexia: A psycholinguistic approach. *Journal of Psycholinguistic Research*, 1973, *2*, 175–200.
Marshall, J. C., & Newcombe, F. The conceptual status of deep dyslexia: An historical perspective. In M. Coltheart, K. E. Patterson, & J. C. Marshall (Eds.), *Deep dyslexia*. London: Routledge & Kegan Paul, 1980.
Marshall, N., & Glock, M. D. Comprehension of connected discourse: A study into the relationships between the structure of text and information recalled. *Reading Research Quarterly*, 1978-1979, *14*, 10–55.
Marslen-Wilson, W. D., Tyler, L., & Seidenberg, M. Sentence processing and the clause-boundary. In W. J. M. Levelt, & G. Flores d'Arcais (Eds.), *Studies in the perception of language*. London: Wiley, 1978.
Martin, S. E. Nonalphabetic writing systems: Some observations. In J. F. Kavanagh, & I. G. Mattingly (Eds.), *Language by ear and by eye*. Cambridge, Mass.: MIT Press, 1972.
Marwit, W., & Newman, G. Black and white children's comprehension of standard and nonstandard English passages. *Journal of Educational Psychology*, 1974, *66*, 329–332.
Mason, J. M. When do children begin to read: An exploration of four year old children's letter and word reading competencies. *Reading Research Quarterly*, 1980, *15*, 203–227.
Mason, J. M., Kniseley, E., & Kendall, J. Effects of polysemous words on sentence comprehension. *Reading Research Quarterly*, 1979, *15*, 49–65.
Mason, M. Reading ability and letter search time: Effects of orthographic structure defined by single letter positional frequency. *Journal of Experimental Psychology: General*, 1975, *104*, 146–166.
Mason, M. The role of spatial redundancy in grapheme recognition: Perception or inference? *Journal of Experimental Psychology: Human Perception and Performance*, 1978, *4*, 662–673.
Mason, M. Reading ability and the encoding of item and location information. *Journal of Experimental Psychology: Human Perception and Performance*, 1980, *6*, 89–98.
Mason, M., Katz, L., & Wicklund, D. A. Immediate spatial order memory and item memory in sixth-grade children as a function of reader ability. *Journal of Educational Psychology*, 1975, *67*, 610–616.
Massaro, D. W. Stimulus control in the study of reading. In D. W. Massaro (Ed.), *Understanding language: An information-processing analysis of speech perception, reading, and psycholinguistics*. New York: Academic Press, 1975.
Massaro, D. W., Taylor, G. A., Venezky, R. L., Jastrzembski, J. E., & Lucas, P. A. *Letter and word perception: Orthographic structure and visual processing in reading*. Amsterdam, New York and Oxford: North-Holland, 1980.
Massaro, D. W., Venezky, R. L., & Taylor, G. A. Orthographic regularity, positional frequency, and visual processing of letter strings. *Journal of Experimental Psychology: General*, 1979, *108*, 107–124.
Masson, M. E. J. Cognitive processes in skimming stories. *Journal of Experimental Psychology: Learning, Memory and Cognition*, 1982, *8*, 400–417.

Matejcek, Z. Dyslexia in Czechoslovakian children. In L. Tarnopol, & M. Tarnopol (Eds.), *Reading disabilities—an international perspecrive*. Baltimore: University Park Press, 1976.

Matsuda, N., & Roffins, D. Prototype abstraction and distinctive feature learning: An application to learning Chinese characters. *Journal of Educational Psychology*, 1977, *69*, 15–23.

Mattis, S. Dyslexia syndromes: A working hypothesis that works. In A. L. Benton, & D. Pearl (Eds.), *Dyslexia: An appraisal of current knowledge*. New York: Oxford University Press, 1978.

Mattis, S., French, J. H., & Rapin, I. Dyslexia in children and young adults: Three independent neuropsychological syndromes. *Developmental Medicine and Child Neurology*, 1975, *17*, 150–163.

Mayer, R. E. Instructional variables in text processing. In A. Flammer, & W. Kintsch (Eds.), *Discourse processing: Advances in Psychology* (Vol. 8). Amsterdam: North-Holland, 1982.

Mayzner, M. S., & Tresselt, M. E. Anagram solution times: A function of letter order and word frequency. *Journal of Experimental Psychology*, 1958, *56*, 376–379.

Mayzner, M. S., & Tresselt, M. E. Tables of single letter and digram frequency counts for various word-length and letter-position combinations. *Psychonomic Monograph Supplements*, 1965, *1*, 13–32.

Mayzner, M. S., Tresselt, M. E., & Wolin, B. R. Tables of pentagram frequency counts for various word-length and letter-position combinations. *Psychonomic Monograph Supplements*, 1965a, *1*, 145–185.

Mayzner, M. S., Tresselt, M. E., & Wolin, B. R. Tables of tetragram frequency counts for various word-length and letter-position combinations. *Psychonomic Monograph Supplements*, 1965b, *1*, 79–142.

Mayzner, M. S., Tresselt, M. E., & Wolin, B. R. Tables of trigram frequency counts for various word-length and letter-position combinations. *Psychonomic Monograph Supplements*, 1965c, *1*, 33–78.

Mehler, J. Some effects of grammatical transformations on the recall of English sentences. *Journal of Verbal Learning and Verbal Behavior*, 1963, *2*, 250–262.

Melmed, P. A. *Black English phonology: The question of reading interference*. Monographs of the Language Behavior Research Laboratories 1, 1971.

Meltzer, E. S. Remarks on ancient Egyptian writing with emphasis on its mnemonic aspects. In P. A. Kolers, M. E. Wrolstad, & H. Bouma (Eds.), *Processing of visible language* (Vol. 2). New York: Plenum, 1980.

Memory, D. Written questions as reading aids in the middle grades: A review of research. In J. A. Niles, & L. A. Harris (Eds.), *New inquiries in reading research and instruction*. (31st Yearbook of the National Reading Conference), Rochester, N.Y.: National Reading Conference, 1982.

Mendelson, W., Johnson, N., & Stewart, M. A. Hyperactive children as teenagers: A follow-up study. *Journal of Nervous and Mental Disease*, 1971, *153*, 273–279.

Menyuk, P. *Sentences children use*. Cambridge, Mass.: M. I. T. Press, 1969.

Menyuk, P. *The development of speech*. Indiana: Bobbs Merrill, 1972.

Mercure, R., & Warren, S. Inadequate and adequate readers' performance on a dichotic listening task. *Perceptual and Motor Skills*, 1978, *46*, 709–710.

Merrill. *The Merrill Linguistic Reading Program*. Columbus, Ohio: Charles E. Merrill, 1975.

Mewhort, D. J. K. Sequential redundancy and letter spacing as determinants of T-scope recognition. *Canadian Journal of Psychology*, 1966, *20*, 435–444.

Mewhort, D. J. K. Accuracy and order of report in tachistoscopic identification. *Canadian Journal of Psychology*, 1974, *28*, 383–398.

Mewhort, D. J. K., & Beal, A. L. Mechanisms of word identification. *Journal of Experimental Psychology: Human Perception and Performance*, 1977, *3*, 629–640.

Mewhort, D. J. K., & Campbell, A. J. Processing spatial information and the selective masking effect. *Perception & Psychophysics*, 1978, *24*, 93–101.

Mewhort, D. J. K., Merikle, P. M., & Bryden, M. P. On the transfer from iconic to short-term memory. *Journal of Experimental Psychology*, 1969, *81*, 89–94.

Meyer, B. J. F. *The organization of prose and its effect upon memory*. Amsterdam: North Holland Publishing, 1975.

Meyer, B. J. F., Brandt, D. M., & Bluth, G. J. Use of top-level structure in text: Key for ninth graders' reading comprehension. *Reading Research Quarterly*, 1980, *16*, 72–103.

Meyer, B. J. F., Freedle, R. O., & Walker, C. H. *Effects of discourse on the recall of young and old adults*. Unpublished M.A. thesis, Arizona State University, 1978.

Meyer, B. J. F., & McConkie, G. W. What is recalled after hearing a passage? *Journal of Educational Psychology*, 1973, *65*, 109–117.

Meyer, D. E., & Ruddy, M. *Lexical memory retrieval based on graphemic representations of words*. Paper given at the meeting of the Psychonomic Society, St Louis, 1973.

Meyer, D. E., Schvaneveldt, R. W., & Ruddy, M. G. Functions of graphemic and phonemic codes in visual word-recognition. *Memory & Cognition*, 1974, *2*, 309–321.

Miller, G. A. The magical number seven, plus or minus two: Some limits on our capacity for processing information. *Psychological Review*, 1956, *63*, 81–97.

Miller, G. A. Some psychological studies of grammar. *American Psychologist*, 1962, *17*, 748–762.

Miller, G. A., Bruner, J. S., & Postman, L. Familiarity of letter sequences and tachistoscopic identification. *Journal General Psychology*, 1954, *50*, 129–139.

Miller, G. A., Galanter, E., & Pribram, K. *Plans and the structure of behavior*. New York: Henry Holt, 1960.

Miller, G. A., & McKean, K. O. A chronometric study of some relations between sentences. *Quarterly Journal of Experimental Psychology*, 1964, *16*, 297–308.

Miller, G. A., & Selfridge, J. A. Verbal context and the recall of meaningful material. *American Journal of Psychology*, 1950, *63*, 176–185.

Miller, G. R., & Coleman, E. B. A set of thirty-six prose passages calibrated for complexity. *Journal of Verbal Learning and Verbal Behavior*, 1967, *6*, 851–854.

Miller, G. R., & Coleman, J. E. A methodological critique of Fleming's alternative for phonemic encoding. *Journal of Reading Behavior*, 1978, *10*, 233–248.

Miller, J. R. Constructive processing of sentences: A simulation model of encoding and retrieval. *Journal of Verbal Learning and Verbal Behavior*, 1981, *20*, 24–45.

Miller, J. R., & Kintsch, W. Readability and recall of short prose passages: A theoretical analysis. *Journal of Experimental Psychology: Human Learning and Memory*, 1980, *6*, 335–354.

Miller, J. W., & McKenna, M. C. Disabled readers: Their intellectual and perceptual capacities at differing ages. *Perceptual and Motor Skills*, 1981, *52*, 467–472.

Miller, R. A. *The Japanese language*. Chicago: University of Chicago Press, 1967.

Milner, B. Psychological aspects of focal epilepsy and its neurological management. In *Advances in neurology* (Vol. 8). New York: Raven Press, 1975.

Miño-Garcés, F. *Early reading acquisition: Six psycholinguistic case studies*. Washington, DC: Georgetown University Press, 1981.

Minsky, M. A framework for representing knowledge. In P. H. Winston (Ed.), *The psychology of computer vision*. New York: McGraw-Hill, 1975.

Mitchell, D. C., & Green, D. W. The effects of context and content on immediate processing in reading. *Quarterly Journal of Experimental Psychology*, 1978, *30*, 609–636.

Mitterer, J. O. There are at least two kinds of poor readers: Whole-word poor readers and recoding poor readers. *Canadian Journal of Psychology*, 1982, *36*, 445–461.

Miura, T. The word superiority effect in a case of Hiragana letter strings. *Perception & Psychophysics*, 1978, *24*, 505–508.

Moeser, S. D. Effect of questions on prose utilization. *Journal of Experimental Psychology: Human Learning and Memory*, 1978, *4*, 290–303.

Monty, R. A., & Senders, J. W., (Eds.) *Eye movements and psychological processes*. Hillsdale, N.J.: Lawrence Erlbaum Associates, 1976.

Morais, J., Cary, L., Alegria, J., & Bertelson, P. Does awareness of speech as a sequence of phones arise spontaneously? *Cognition*, 1979, *7*, 323–331.

Morikawa, Y. Stroop phenomena in the Japanese language: The case of ideographic characters (Kanji) and syllabic characters (Kana). *Perceptual and Motor Skills*, 1981, *53*, 67–77.

Morphett, M. V., & Washburne, C. When should school children begin to read? *Elementary School Journal*, 1931, *31*, 496–503.

Morrison, F. J., Giordani, B., & Nagy, J. Reading disability: An information-processing analysis. *Science*, 1977, *196*, 77–79.

Morton, J. The effects of context upon speed of reading, eye movements and eye–voice span. *Quarterly Journal of Experimental Psychology*, 1964, *16*, 340–354.

Morton, J. Interaction of information in word recognition. *Psychological Review*, 1969, *76*, 165–178.

Morton, J. Facilitation in word recognition: Experiments causing change in the logogen model. In P. A. Kolers, M. E. Wrolstad, & H. Bouma (Eds.), *Processing of visible language* (Vol. 1). New York: Plenum Press, 1979.

Morton, J., & Patterson, K. E. Little words—no!. In M. Coltheart, K. E. Patterson, & J. C. Marshall (Eds.), *Deep dyslexia*. London: Routledge & Kegan Paul, 1980a.

Morton, J., & Patterson, K. E. A new attempt at an interpretation, or, an attempt at a new interpretation. In M. Coltheart, K. Patterson, & J. C. Marshall (Eds.), *Deep dyslexia*. London: Routledge & Kegan Paul, 1980b.

Moscovitch, M. Information processing and the cerebral hemispheres. In M. S. Gazzaniga (Ed.), *Handbook of behavioral neurobiology* (Vol. 2). New York: Plenum, 1979.

Moscovitch, M., & Klein, D. Material-specific perceptual interference for visual words and faces: Implications for models of capacity limitations, attention, and laterality. *Journal of Experimental Psychology: Human Perception and Performance*, 1980, *6*, 590–604.

Moscovitch, M., Scullion, D., & Christie, D. Early versus late stages of processing and their relation to functional hemispheric asymmetries in face recognition. *Journal of Experimental Psychology: Human Perception and Performance*, 1976, *2*, 401–416.

Mosenthal, P. Three types of schemata in children's recall of cohesive and noncohesive text. *Journal of Experimental Psychology*, 1979, *27*, 129–142.

Moskowitz, A. J. On the status of vowel shift in English. In T. E. Moore (Ed.), *Cognitive development and the acquisition of language*. New York: Academic Press, 1973.

Muraishi, S., & Amano, K. *Reading and writing abilities of preschoolers: A summary*. Tokyo: The National Language Research Institute, 1972 (in Japanese).

Murata, K. *Reading and writing of young children*. Tokyo: Baifukan, 1974 (in Japanese).

Murdock, B. Short-term memory. In G. H. Bower (Ed.), *The psychology of language and motivation* (Vol. 5). New York: Academic Press, 1972.

Murrell, G. A., & Morton, J. Word recognition and morphemic structure. *Journal of Experimental Psychology*, 1974, *102*, 963–968.

Muter, P., & Johns, E. E. The comparative ease of learning Blissymbolics, Chinese, Esperanto, and an unfamiliar alphabetic code. Unpublished manuscript, Department of Psychology, University of Toronto, 1983.

Myklebust, H. *Disorders of written language*. New York: Grune & Stratton, 1965.

Nachshon, I., Shefler, G. E., & Samocha, D. Directional scanning as a function of stimulus characteristics, reading habits, and directional set. *Journal of Cross-cultural Psychology*, 1977, *8*, 83–99.

Naidoo, S. *Specific dyslexia*. New York: Wiley, 1972.

Naish, P. The effects of graphemic and phonemic similarity between targets and masks in a backward visual masking paradigm. *Quarterly Journal of Experimental Psychology*, 1980, *32*, 57–68.

National Language Institute. *Reading and writing abilities of preschoolers*. Tokyo: National Language Institute, 1973 (in Japanese).

Navon, D., & Shimron, J Does word naming involve grapheme-to-phoneme translation?: Evidence from Hebrew. *Journal of Verbal Learning and Verbal Behavior*, 1981, *20*, 97–109.

Naylor, H. Reading disability and lateral assymetry: An information-processing analysis. *Psychological Bulletin*, 1980, *87*, 531–545.

Neimark, E. D., & Slotnick, M. S. Development of the understanding of logical connectives. *Journal of Educational Psychology*, 1970, *61*, 451–460.

Neisser, U. *Cognitive psychology*. New York: Appleton-Century-Crofts, 1967.

Nelson, H. E., & Warrington, E. K. Developmental spelling retardation and its relation to other cognitive abilities. *British Journal of Psychology*, 1974, *65*, 265–274.
Nelson, K. Concept, word, and sentence: Interrelations in acquisition and development. *Psychological Review*, 1974, *81*, 267–285.
Nelson, T. D. Spelling–pronunciation integration: Determinant of bimodal recall. *Journal of Verbal Learning and Verbal Behavior*, 1969, *8*, 118–122.
Newcombe, F., & Marshall, J. C. On psycholinguistic classifications of the acquired dyslexias. *Bulletin of the Orton Society*, 1981, *31*, 29–46.
Newell, D., & Rugel, R. P. Hemispheric specialization in normal and disabled readers. *Journal of Learning Disabilities*, 1981, *14*, 296–297.
Nezworski, T., Stein, N. L., & Trabasso, T. Story structure versus content in children's recall. *Journalof Verbal Learning and Verbal Behavior*, 1982, *21*, 196–206.
Nguy, T. V. H., Allard, F. A., & Bryden, M. P. Laterality effects for Chinese characters: Differences between pictorial and nonpictorial characters. *Canadian Journal of Psychology*, 1980, *34*, 270–273.
Nichols, P. L., & Chen, T. C. *Minimal brain dysfunction: A prospective study*. Hillsdale, N.J.: Lawrence Erlbaum Associates, 1981.
Niles, J. A., & Taylor, B. M. The development of orthographic sensitiiity during the school year by primary grade children. In D. Pearson, & J. Hansen (Eds.), *Reading: Disciplined inquiry in process and practice*. (27th Yearbook of the National Reading Conference), Clemens, S.C.: National Reading Conference, 1978.
Nisbett, R. E., Zukier, H., & Lemley, R. E. The dilution effect: Nondiagnostic information weakens the implications of diagnostic information. *Cognitive Psychology*, 1981, *13*, 248–277.
Nishikawa, Y., & Niina, S. Modes of information processing underlying hemispheric functional differences. *Japanese Journal of Psychology*, 1981, *51*, 335–342 (in Japanese with English abstract).
Nodine, C. F., & Simmons, F. G. Processing distinctive features in the differentiation of letterlike symbols. *Journal of Experimental Psychology*, 1974, *103*, 21–28.
Noelker, R. W., & Schumsky, D. A. Memory for sequence, form and position as related to the identification of reading retardates. *Journal of Educational Psychology*, 1973, *64*, 22–25.
Noh, M.-W. *The effects of instructional methods on the formation of reading strategies in beginning reading*. Unpublished M.A. thesis, Seoul University, Korea, 1975, (in Korean with English abstract).
Noh, M.-W., Hwang, I.-C., Park, Y.-S., & Kim, B.-W. A study on the development of adults' speed reading program. *Research Bulletin,* 1977 *10*, No. 97, Korean Institute for Research in the Behavioral Sciences, (in Korean with English summary).
Nolan, K. A., & Caramazza, A. Modality-independent impairments in word processing in a deep dyslexic patient. *Brain and Language*, 1982, *16*, 237–264.
Nolan, P. Reading nonstandard dialect materials: A study of grades two and four. *Child Development*, 1972, *43*, 1092–1097.
Nomura, Y. The information processing of Chinese characters (Kanji): Chinese reading, Japanese reading and the attachment of meaning. *Japanese Journal of Psychology*, 1978, *49*, 190–197, (in Japanese with English abstract).
Nomura, Y. The information processing of Kanji, Kana script: The effects of data-driven and conceptually-driven processing on reading. *Japanese Journal of Psychology*, 1981, *51*, 327–334, (in Japanese with English abstract).
Nooteboom, S. G., & Bouma, H. *On reading nonsense syllables, whole words and coherent text from a relatively long distance*. Eindhoven, Netherlands: IPO Annual Progress Report 3, 1968.
Novik, N. Parallel processing in a word-nonword classification task. *Journal of Experimental Psychology*, 1974, *102*, 1015–1020.
Nurss, J. R. Assessment of readiness. In T. G. Waller, & G. E. MacKinnon (Eds.), *Reading research: Advances in theory and practice* (Vol. 1). New York: Academic Press, 1979.
Nyman, G., Laurinen, P., & Hyvarinen, L. Topographic instability of spatial vision as a cause of dyslexic disorder: A case study. *Neuropsychologia*, 1982, *20*, 181–186.

Oakland, T. Predictive validity of readiness tests for middle and lower socioeconomic status Anglo, Black, and Mexican American children. *Journal of Educational Psychology*, 1978, *70*, 474–482.

Ohara, N. *Vicissitudes of Kanji*. Tokyo: Toho Shoten, 1980, (in Japanese).

Ohnishi, S. The recognition of letter sequences with different orders of approximation to the Japanese language: On the eye–voice span. *Japanese Journal of Research*, 1962, *4*, 43–47.

Oka, N., Mori, T., & Kakigi, S. Learning of reading Kanji and Kana Moji in young children. *Japanese Journal of Psychology*, 1979, *50*, 49–52, (in Japanese with English abstract).

Olson, D. R. The language of instruction: On the literate bias of schooling. In R. C. Anderson, & R. J. Spiro (Eds.), *Schooling and acquisition of knowledge*. Hillsdale, N.J.: Lawrence Erlbaum Associates, 1977.

Olson, D. R., & Filby, N. On the comprehension of active and passive sentences. *Cognitive Psychology*, 1972, *3*, 361–381.

Olson, G. M., Mack, R. L., & Duffy, S. K. Cognitive aspects of genre. *Poetics*, 1981, *10*, 283–315.

Olson, J. N., & MacKay, D. G. Completion and verification of ambiguous sentences. *Journal of Verbal Learning and Verbal Behavior*, 1974, *13*, 457–470.

Omura, A., & Utsuo, T. Recognition memory of Japanese active and passive sentences: An effect of pragmatics on sentence memory. *Japanese Psychological Research*, 1981, *23*, 18–26.

O'Neill, B. Defineability as an index of word meaning. *Journal of Psycholinguistic Research*, 1972, *1*, 287–298.

Ono, S. *Thoughts on the Japanese language*. Tokyo: Yomiuri Shinbunsha, 1967, (in Japanese).

Orbach, J. Differential recognition of Hebrew and English words in right and left visual fields as a function of cerebral dominance and reading habits. *Neuropsychologia*, 1967, *5*, 127–134.

O'Regan, K. Saccade size control in reading: Evidence for the linguistic control hypothesis. *Perception & Psychophysics*, 1979, *25*, 501–509.

O'Regan, K. "Convenient viewing position" hypothesis. In D. F. Fisher, R. A. Monty, & J. W. Senders (Eds.), *Eye movements: Cognition and visual perception*. Hillsdale, N.J.: Lawrence Erlbaum Associates, 1981.

Orgogozo, J. M., & Larsen, B. Activation of the supplementary motor area during voluntary movement in man suggests it works as a supramotor area. *Science*, 1979, *206*, 847–850.

Ornstein, R., Herron, J., Johnstone, J., & Swencionis, C. Differential right hemisphere involvement in two reading tasks. *Psychophysiology*, 1979, *16*, 398–404.

Orton, S. T. *Reading, writing and speech problems in children*. New York: Norton, 1937.

Ortony, A. (Ed.) *Metaphor and thought*. New York: Cambridge University Press, 1979.

Ortony, A., Schallert, D. L., Reynolds, R. E., & Antos, S. J. Interpreting metaphors and idioms: Some effects of context on comprehension. *Journal of Verbal Learning and Verbal Behavior*, 1978, *17*, 465–477.

Osgood, C. E., & Zehler, A. M. Acquisition of bi-transitive sentences: Prelinguistic determinants of language acquisition. *Journal of Child Language*, 1981, *8*, 367–383.

Owen, F. W., Adams, P. A., Forrest, T., Stolz, L. M., & Fisher, S. *Learning disorders in children: Sibling studies*. Monograph of the Society for Research in Child Development, 144, 1971.

Palermo, D. S., & Molfese, D. L. Language acquisition from age five onward. *Psychological Bulletin*, 1972, *78*, 409–428.

Palmer, J. C., MacLeod, C. M., Hunt, E., & Davidson, J. E. *Information processing correlates of reading: An individual differences analysis*. Psychology Department Technical Report, University of Washington, Seattle, Wash., 1980.

Paris, S. G., & Carter, A. Y. Semantic and constructive aspects of sentence memory in children. *Developmental Psychology*, 1973, *9*, 109–113.

Park, R. Performance on geometric figure copying tests as predictors of types of errors in decoding. *Reading Research Quarterly*, 1978–1979, *14*, 100–118.

Park, S., & Arbuckle, T. Y. Ideograms versus alphabets: Effects of script on memory in "biscriptual" Korean subjects. *Journal of Experimental Psychology: Human Learning and Memory*, 1977, *3*, 631–642.

Patel, P. G. Syntactic maturation: Some possible psycholinguistic correlates and conditions. In K.

Steckol, & R. N. St. Clair (Eds.), *Cognitive and developmental linguistics: Essays on normal and disordered children*. Baltimore: University Park Press, (in press).

Patel, P. G., & Patterson, P. Precocious reading acquisition: Psycholinguistic development, IQ, and home background. *First Language*, 1982, *3*, 139–153.

Patterson, K. E. Neuropsychological approaches to the study of reading. *British Journal of Psychology*, 1981, *72*, 151–174.

Patterson, K. & Bradshaw, J. L. Differential hemispheric mediation of nonverbal visual stimuli. *Journal of Experimental Psychology: Human Perception and Performance*, 1975, *1*, 246-252

Patterson, K. E., & Marcel, A. J. Aphasia, dyslexia and the phonological coding of written words. *Quarterly Journal of Experimental Psychology*, 1977, *29*, 307–318.

Patterson, K., & Kay, J. Letter-by-letter reading: Psychological descriptions of a neurological syndrome. *Quarterly Journal of Experimental Psychology*, 1982, *34A*, 411–441.

Pavlidis, G. Th. Do eye movements hold the key to dyslexia? *Neuropsychologia*, 1981, *19*, 57–64.

Pearson, P. D. The effects of grammatical complexity on children's comprehension, recall, and conception of certain semantic relations. *Reading Research Quarterly*, 1974–1975, *10*, 155–193.

Pearson, P. D., Hansen, J., & Gordon, C. *The effect of background knowledge on young children's comprehension of explicit and implicit information*. Technical Report 116, Champaign-Urbana: Center for the Study of Reading, University of Illinois, 1979.

Pearson, P. D., & Johnson, D. D. *Teaching reading comprehension*. New York: Holt, Rinehart and Winston, 1978.

Pearson, P. D., & Studt, A. Effects of word frequency and contextual richness on children's word identification abilities. *Journal of Educational Psychology*, 1975, *67*, 89–95.

Perfetti, C. A., Goldman, S., & Hogaboam, T. Reading skill and the identification of words in discourse context. *Memory & Cognition*, 1979, *7*, 273–282.

Perfetti, C. A., & Hogaboam, T. Relationships between single word decoding and reading comprehension skill. *Journal of Educational Psychology*, 1975, *67*, 461–469.

Petrey, S. Word associations and the development of lexical memory. *Cognition*, 1977, *5*, 57–71.

Pfafflin, S. M. Some psychological studies of sentence interconnections in written English prose. *Psychonomic Bulletin*, 1967, *1*, 17.

Pflaum, S., & Pascarella, E. T. Interactive effects of prior reading achievement and training disabled readers. *Reading Research Quarterly*, 1980, *16*, 138–158.

Pichert, J., & Anderson, R. C. Taking different perspectives on a story. *Journal of Educational Psychology*, 1977, *69*, 309–315.

Piette, E. Etudes d'ethnographic prehistorique. *L'Anthropologie*, 1896, *7*, 385–427.

Pillsbury, W. B. The reading of words: A study in apperception. *American Journal of Psychology*, 1897, *8*, 315–393.

Pintner, R. Inner speech silent reading. *Psychological Review*, 1913, *20*, 129–153.

Pirozzolo, F. J. *The neuropsychology of developmental reading disorder*. New York: Praeger Publishers, 1979.

Pirozzolo, F. J., & Rayner, K. Cerebral organization and reading disability. *Neurolopsychologia*, 1979, *17*, 485–491.

Pitman, J., & St. John, J. *Alphabets and reading*. London: Sir Isaac Pitman and Sons, 1969.

Pollatsek, A., Bolozky, S., Well, A. D., & Rayner, K. Asymmetries in the perceptual span for Israeli readers. *Brain and Language*, 1981, *14*, 174–180.

Polson, M. C., Friedman, A., & Gaskill, S. J. *Competition for left hemisphere resources: Right hemisphere superiority at abstract verbal information processing*. ICS Technical Report 105, Institute of Cognitive Science, University of Colorado, July, 1981.

Pomerantz, J. R., Sager, L. C., & Stoever, R. J. Perception of wholes and of their component parts: Some configural superiority effects. *Journal of Experimental Psychology: Human Perception and Performance*, 1977, *3*, 422–435.

Popp, H. M. Two approaches to initial reading instruction. In L. B. Resnick, & P. A. Weaver (Eds.), *Theory and practice of early reading* (Vol. 3). Hillsdale, N.J.: Lawrence Erlbaum Associates, 1979.

Potter, M. C., Kroll, J. F., & Harris, C. Comprehension and memory in rapid, sequential reading. In R. S. Nickerson (Ed.), *Attention and performance* (Vol. 8). Hillsdale, N.J.: Lawrence Erlbaum Associates, 1980.

Premack, D. Language in a chimpanzee? *Science*, 1971, *172*, 808–822.

Preston, M. S., Guthrie, J. T., Kirsch, I., Gertman, D., & Childs, B. VERs in normal and disabled adult readers. *Psychophysiology*, 1977, *14*, 8–14.

Preston, M. S., & Lambert, W. E. Interlingual interference in a bilingual version of the Stroop color–word task. *Journal of Verbal Learning and Verbal Behavior*, 1969, *8*, 295–301.

Purcell, D. G., & Stanovich, K. E. Some boundary conditions for a word superiority effect. *Quarterly Journal of Experimental Psychology*, 1982, *34A*, 117–134.

Purcell, D. G., Stanovich, K. E., & Spector, A. Visual angle and the word superiority effect. *Memory & Cognition*, 1978, *6*, 3–8.

Pynte, J. Implicit speech in the reading of numbers and meaningless syllables. In J. Requin (Ed.), *Attention and performance* (Vol. 7). Hillsdale, N.J.: Lawrence Erlbaum Associates, 1978.

Pynte, J., & Noizet, G. Optimal segmentation for sentences displayed on a video screen. In P. A. Kolers, M. E. Wrolsted, & H. Bouma (Eds.), *Visible language* (Vol. 2). New York: Plenum, 1980.

Quantz, J. O. *Problems in the psychology of reading*. New York: Macmillan, 1897.

Quirk, R., Greenbaum, S., Leech, G, & Svartvik, J. *A grammar of contemporary English*. London: Longman Group Ltd., 1979 (1972).

Rabinovitch, R. D. Reading problems in children: Definitions and classification. In K. Keeney (Ed.), *Dyslexia: Diagnosis and treatment of reading disorders*. St. Louis: C. V. Mosby, 1968.

Raeburn, V. P. The role of the verb in sentence memory. *Memory & Cognition*, 1979, *7*, 133–140.

Ratcliff, R., & McKoon, G. Priming in item recognition: Evidence for the propositional structure of sentences. *Journal of Verbal Learning and Verbal Behavior*, 1978, *17*, 403–417.

Rausch, R. Lateralization of temporal lobe dysfunction and verbal encoding. *Brain and Language*, 1981, *12*, 92–100.

Rayner, K. Parafoveal identification during a fixation in reading. *Acta Psychologica*, 1975, *39*, 271–282.

Rayner, K. Visual attention in reading: Eye movements reflect cognitive processes. *Memory & Cognition*, 1977, *5*, 443–448.

Rayner, K. Eye movements in reading and information processing. *Psychological Bulletin*, 1978, *85*, 618–660.

Rayner, K. Eye guidance in reading: Fixation locations within words. *Perception*, 1979a, *8*, 21–30.

Rayner, K. Semantic processing of words: Foveal and parafoveal differences in reading. In M. M. Gruneberg, P. E. Morris, & R. N. Syker (Eds.), *Practical aspects of memory*. New York: Academic Press, 1979b.

Rayner, K., & Habelberg, E. M. Word recognition cues for beginning and skilled readers. *Journal of Experimental Child Psychology*, 1975, *20*, 444–455.

Rayner, K., & Kaiser, J. S. Reading mutilated text. *Journal of Educational Psychology*, 1975, *67*, 301–306.

Rayner, K, & McConkie, G. W. What guides a reader's eye movements? *Vision Research*, 1976, *16*, 829–837.

Rayner, K., & Pollatsek, A. Eye movement control during reading: Evidence for direct control. *Quarterly Journal of Experimental Psychology*, 1981, *33A*, 351–373.

Rayner, K., & Posnansky, C. Stages of processing in word identification. *Journal of Experimental Psychology: General*, 1978, *107*, 64–80.

Read, C. Pre-school children's knowledge of English phonology. *Harvard Educational Psycyology*, 1971, *41*, 1–34.

Reder, L. M. The role of elaborations in memory for prose. *Cognitive Psychology*, 1979, *11*, 221–234.

Reder, L. M., & Anderson, J. R. A comparison of texts and their summaries: Memorial consequences. *Journal of Verbal Learning and Verbal Behavior*, 1980, *19*, 121–134.

Reed, L. *The complete limerick book*. London: Jarrold's, 1925.

Rees-Nishio, M. A. *Alternative modes of communication for the language disabled—evidence from brain function and neuropathology*. Unpublished M.A. thesis, University of Tokyo, 1979.

Rees-Nishio, M. A. Kanji reading by a pre-kindergarten language disabled child: A pilot study. *Brain and Language*, 1981, *13*, 259–289.

Reich, C. M., & Reich, P. A. The construction of an orally based sight-word vocabulary and its relationship to the vocabularies of beginning readers. *Journal of Educational Psychology*, 1979, *72*, 198–204.

Reicher, G. M. Perceptual recognition as a function of meaningfulness of stimulus materials. *Journal of Experimental Psychology*, 1969, *81*, 275–280.

Reid, J. F. Children's comprehension of syntactic features found in some extension readers. In J. F. Reid (Ed.), *Reading: Problems and practices*. London: Ward Lock Educational, 1972.

Resnick, D. A. A developmental study of proverb comprehension. *Journal of Psycholinguistic Research*, 1982, *11*, 521–538.

Resnick, L. B. Relations between perceptual and syntactic control in oral reading. *Journal of Educational Psychology*, 1970, *61*, 382–385.

Resnick, L. B. *Theory and practice in beginning reading instruction*. Pittsburgh: University of Pittsburgh Learning Research and Development Center, 1978.

Resnick, L. B. Toward a usable psychology of reading instruction. In L. B. Resnick, & P. Weaver (Eds.), *Theory and practice of early reading* (Vol. 3). Hillsdale, N.J.: Lawrence Erlbaum Associates, 1979.

Richek, M. A. Reading comprehension of anaphoric forms in varying linguistic contexts. *Reading Research Quarterly*, 1976–1977, *12*, 145–165.

Richek, M. A. Readiness skills that predict initial word learning using two different methods of instruction. *Reading Research Quarterly*, 1977–1978, *13*, 200–222.

Richman, L. C., & Kitchell, M. M. Hyperlexia as a variant of developmental language disorder. *Brain and Language*, 1981, *12*, 203–212.

Rickards, J. P. Adjunct postquestions in text: A critical review of methods and processes. *Review of Educational Research*, 1979, *49*, 181–196.

Rickards, J. P., & August, G. J. Generative underlining strategies in prose recall. *Journal of Educational Psychology*, 1975, *67*, 860–865.

Riley, J. A., & Lowe, J. D. Jr. A study of enhancing vs. reducing subvocalizing during reading. *Journal of Reading*, 1981, *25*, 7–13.

Rinsland, H. D. *A basic vocabulary of elementary school children*. New York: Macmillan, 1945.

Robinson, J. P. The changing reading habits of the American public. *Journal of Communication*, 1980, *30*, 141–152.

Rode, S. S. Development of phrase and clause boundary reading in children. *Reading Research Quarterly*, 1974–1975, *10*, 124–142.

Rosenberg, S. *Discourse structure*. Working Paper 130, MIT Artificial Intelligence Laboratory, Cambridge, Mass., 1976.

Rosenshine, B. V. Content, time, and direct instruction. In P. L. Peterson, & H. J. Walberg (Eds.), *Research in reading*. Berkeley, Calif.: McCutchan Publishing, 1979.

Rosewell, F., & Natchez, G. *Reading disability*. New York: Basic Books, 1971.

Rosinski, R. R., & Wheeler, K. E. Children's use of orthographic structure in word discrimination. *Psychonomic Science*, 1972, *26*, 97–98.

Rothkopf, E. Z., & Billington, M. Z. Goal-guided learning from text: Inferring a descriptive processing model from inspection times and eye movements. *Journal of Educational Psychology*, 1979, *71*, 310–327.

Rothkopf, E. Z., & Bisbicos, E. Selective facilitation effects of interspersed questions in learning from written materials. *Journal of Educational Psychology*, 1967, *58*, 56–61.

Rourke, B. P., Dietrich, D. M., & Young, G. C. Significance of WISC verbal–performance discrepances for younger children with learning disabilities. *Perceptual and Motor Skills*, 1973, *36*, 275–282.

Rozin, P., & Gleitman, L. R. The structure and acquisition of reading 2: The reading process and the acquisition of the alphabet principle. In A. S. Reber, & D. L. Scarborough (Eds.), *Toward a psychology of reading*. Hillsdale, N.J.: Lawrence Erlbaum Associates, 1977.

Rozin, P., Poritsky, S., & Sotsky, R. American children with reading problems can easily learn to read English represented by Chinese characters. *Science*, 1971, *171*, 1264–1267.

Rubenstein, H., Lewis, S. S., & Rubenstein, M. H. Evidence for phonemic recoding in visual word recognition. *Journal of Verbal Learning and Verbal Behavior*, 1971, *10*, 645–647.

Rubenstein, H., Richter, M. L., & Kay, E. J. Pronunceability and the visual recognition of nonsense words. *Journal of Verbal Learning and Verbal Behavior*, 1975, *14*, 651–657.

Rubin, D. C. The effectiveness of context before, after, and around a missing word. *Perception & Psychophysics*, 1976, *19*, 214–216.

Rubin, G. S., Becker, C. A., & Freeman, R. H. Morphological structure and its effect on visual word recognition. *Journal of Verbal Learning and Verbal Behavior*, 1979, *18*, 757–767.

Ruddell, R. B. The effect of oral and written patterns of language structure on reading comprehension. *The Reading Teacher*, 1965, *18*, 271–275.

Rumelhart, D. E. Notes on a schema for stories. In D. G. Bobrow, & A. Collins (Eds.), *Representation and understanding: Studies in cognitive science*. New York: Academic Press, 1975.

Rumelhart, D. E. Understanding and summarizing brief stories. In D. LaBerge, & J. Samuels (Eds.), *Basic processes in reading and comprehension*. Hillsdale, N.J.: Lawrence Erlbaum Associates, 1977.

Rumelhart, D. E. Some problems with the notion of literal meanings. In A. Ortony (Ed.), *Metaphor and thought*. New York: Cambridge University Press, 1979.

Rumelhart, D. E. The building blocks of cognition. In R. J. Spiro, B. C. Bruce, & W. F. Brewer (Eds.), *Theoretical issues in reading comprehension*. Hillsdale, N.J.: Lawrence Erlbaum Associates, 1980.

Rutter, M. Prevalence and types of dyslexia. In A. L. Benton, & D. Pearl (Eds.), *Dyslexia*. New York: Oxford University Press, 1978.

Rutter, M., & Madge, N. *Cycles of disadvantage: A review of research*. London: Heinemann Educational, 1976.

Rutter, M., & Yule, W. The concept of specific reading retardation. *Journal of Child Psychology and Psychiatry*, 1975, *16*, 181–197.

Ryan, E. B. Metalinguistic development and reading. In L. H. Waterhouse, K. M. Fischer, & E. B. Ryan (Eds.), *Language awareness and reading*. Newark, Del.: International Reading Association, 1980.

Ryder, R., & Graves, M. F. Secondary students' internalization of letter–sound correspondences. *Journal of Educational Research*, 1980, *73*, 172–178.

Rystrom, R. Dialect training and reading: A further look. *Reading Research Quarterly*, 1970, *5*, 581–589.

Sachs, J. Recognition memory for syntactic and semantic aspects of connected discourse. *Perception & Psychophysics*, 1967, *2*, 439–442.

Saffran, E. M., Bogyo, L. C., Schwartz, M. F., & Marin, O. S. M. Does deep dyslexia reflect right hemisphere reading? In M. Coltheart, K. Patterson, & J. C. Marshall (Eds.), *Deep dyslexia*. London: Routledge & Kegan Paul, 1980.

Saito, H. Human information processing of Kanji (Chinese characters). *Journal of the Literary Association of Kwansei Gakuin University*, 1978, *28*, 95–111, (in Japanese).

Sakamoto, T. Preschool reading in Japan. *Reading Teacher*, 1975, *29*, 240–244.

Sakamoto, T., & Makita, K. Japan. In J. Downing (Ed.), *Comparative reading*. New York: Macmillan, 1973.

Sakiey, E. The commonest syllables. In M. L. Kamil, & A. J. Moe (Eds.), *Reading research: Studies and applications*. (28th Yearbook of the National Reading Conference), Clemson, S.C.: National Reading Conference, 1979.

Salame, P., & Baddeley, A. Disruption of short-term memory by unattended speech: Implications for the structure of working memory. *Journal of Verbal Learning and Verbal Behavior*, 1982, *21*, 150–164.

Salapatek, P. Visual scanning of geometric figures by the human newborn. *Journal of Comparative & Physiological Psychology*, 1968, *66*, 247–258.

Salili, F., & Hoosain, R. Acquisition of bitransitive sentences in Persian and Chinese: Differences between comprehension and production tests. *Perceptual and Motor Skills*, 1981, *53*, 475–482.

Salmon, P., & Rodwan, A. Visual field sensitivity on a two-choice discrimination task. *Perceptual and Motor Skills*, 1981, *53*, 91–100.

Sampson, M. R. A comparison of the complexity of children's dictation and instructional reading materials. In J. A. Niles & L. A. Harris (Eds.) *New inquiries in reading research and instruction* (31st Yearbook of the National Reading Conference), Rochester, N.Y.: National Reading Conference, 1982

Sampson, O. C. Reading skill at eight years in relation to speech and other factors. *British Journal of Educational Psychology*, 1962, *32*, 12–17.

Samuels, S. J. The effect of letter-name knowledge on learning to read. *American Eudcational Research Journal*, 1972, *1*, 65–74.

Samuels, S. J., LaBerge, D., & Bremer, C. D. Units of word recognition: Evidence of developmental change. *Journal of Verbal Learning and Verbal Behavior*, 1978, *17*, 715–720.

Santa, C. M. Spelling patterns and the development of flexible word recognition strategies. *Reading Research Quarterly*, 1976–1977, *12*, 125–144.

Santa, C. M., & Santa, J. L. Vowel and consonant clusters in word recognition. *Perception & Psychophysics*, 1979, *25*, 235–237.

Santa, J. L., & Santa, C. M. Units of word recognition: Evidence for the use of multiple units. *Perception & Psychophysics*, 1977, *22*, 585–591.

Santee, J. L., & Egeth, H. E. Interference in letter identification: A test of feature-specific inhbibition. *Perception & Psychophysics*, 1980, *27*, 321–330.

Sasanuma, S. Kanji versus Kana processing in alexia with transient agraphia: A case report. *Cortex*, 1974, *10*, 89–97.

Sasanuma, S. Kana and Kanji processing in Japanese aphasics. *Brain and Language*, 1975, *2*, 369–383.

Sasanuma, S. Acquired dyslexia in Japanese: Clinical features and underlying mechanisms. In M. Coltheart, K. Patterson, & J. C. Marshall (Eds.), *Deep dyslexia*. London: Routledge & Kegan Paul, 1980.

Sasanuma, S., & Fujimura, O. Selective impairment of phonetic and non-phonetic transcription of words in Japanese aphasic patients: Kana versus Kanji in visual recognition and writing. *Cortex*, 1971, *7*, 1–18.

Sasanuma, S., & Fujimura, O. An analysis of writing errors in Japanese aphasic patients: Kanji versus Kana words. *Cortex*, 1972, *8*, 265–282.

Sasanuma, S., Itoh, M., Mori, K., & Kobayashi, Y. Tachistoscopic recognition of Kana and Kanji words. *Neuropsychologia*, 1977, *15*, 547–553.

Sasanuma, S., Itoh, M., Kobayashi, Y., & Mori, K. The nature of the task–stimulus interaction in the tachistoscopic recognition of Kana and Kanji words. *Brain and Language*, 1980, *9*, 298–306.

Sattath, S., & Tversky, A. Additive similarity trees. *Psychometrika*, 1977, *42*, 319–345.

Satz, P., & Morris, R. Learning disability subtypes: A review. In F. J. Pirozzolo, & M. C. Wittrock (Eds.), *Neuropsychological and cognitive processes in reading*. New York: Academic Press, 1981.

Satz, P., & Sparrow, S. Specific developmental dyslexia: A theoretical formulation. In D. J. Bakker, & P. Satz (Eds.), *Specific reading disability*. Lisse: Swets & Zeitlinger, 1970.

Satz, P., Taylor, H. G., Friel, J., & Fletcher, J. M. Some developmental and predictive precursors of reading disabilities: A six year follow-up. In A. L. Benton, & D. Pearl (Eds.), *Dyslexia: An appraisal of current knowledge*. New York: Oxford University Press, 1978.

Savin, H. B., & Perchonock, E. Grammatical structure and immediate recall of sentences. *Journal of Verbal Learning and Verbal Behavior*, 1965, *4*, 348–353.

Schank, R., & Abelson, R. P. *Scripts, plans, goals, and understanding*. Hillsdale, N.J.: Lawrence Erlbaum Associates, 1977.

Schank, R., & Birnbaum, L. *Memory, meaning, and syntax*. Technical Report 189, Yale University Department of Computer Science, 1980.

Schendel, J. D., & Shaw, P. A test of the generality of the word-context effect. *Perception & Psychophysics*, 1976, *19*, 383–393.

Schiepers, C. W. J. Global attributes in visual word recognition. Part 1: Length perception of letter strings. *Vision Research*, 1976a, *16*, 1343–1349.

Schiepers, C. W. J. Global attributes in visual word recognition. Part 2: The contribution of word length. *Vision Research*, 1976b, *16*, 1445–1454.

Schindler, R. M. The effect of prose context on visual search for letters. *Memory & Cognition*, 1978, *6*, 124–130.

Schlesinger, I. M. *Sentence structure and the reading process*. The Hague: Mouton, 1968.

Schmandt-Besserat, D. The earliest precursor of writing. *Scientific American*, 1978 June, *238*, 50–59.

Schmandt-Besserat, D. Decipherment of the earliest tablets. *Science*, 1981, *211*, 283–284.

Scholes, R. J. Syntactic and lexical components of sentence comprehension. In A. Caramazza, & E. B. Zurif (Eds.), *Language acquisition and language breakdown*. Baltimore: Johns Hopkins University Press, 1978.

Schuberth, R. E., & Eimas, P. D. Effects of context on the classification of words and nonwords. *Journal of Experimental Psychology: Human Perception and Performance*, 1977, *3*, 27–36.

Schumacher, G. M., Klare, G. R., Cronin, F. C., & Moses, J. D. *Cognitive processes during pauses in writing*. Paper presented at the meeting of the National Reading Conference, Clearwater, Fla., 1982.

Schvaneveldt, R. W., Meyer, D. E., & Becker, C. A. Lexical ambiguity, semantic context, and visual word recognition. *Journal of Experimental Psychology: Human Perception and Performance*, 1976, *2*, 243–256.

Schwantes, F. M. Effect of story context on children's ongoing word recognition. *Journal of Reading Behavior*, 1981, *13*, 305–311.

Scinto, L. F. Relations of eye fixations to old-new information of texts. In J. W. Senders, D. F. Fisher, & R. A. Monty (Eds.), *Eye movements and the higher psychological functions*. Hillsdale, N.J.: Lawrence Erlbaum Associates, 1978.

Scragg, D. G. *A history of English spelling*. Manchester, England: Manchester University Press, 1974.

Scribner, S., & Cole, M. *The psychology of literacy*. Cambridge, Mass.: Harvard University Press, 1981.

Sears, D. A. Engineers spell acoustically. *College Composition and Communication*, 1969, *20*, 349–351.

Sekuler, R., Tynan, P., & Levinson, E. Visual temporal order: A new visual illusion. *Science*, 1973, *180*, 210–212.

Selfridge, O. Pandemonium: A paradigm for learning. In *Symposium on the mechanisation of thought processes*. London: HM Stationery Office, 1959.

Senf, G. M., & Freundl, P. C. Sequential auditory and visual memory in learning disabled children. *Proceedings of the Annual Convention of the American Psychological Association*, 1972, *7*, 511.

Seybolt, P. J., & Chiang, G. K.-K. *Language reform in China (documents and commentary)*. White Plains, New York: M. E. Sharpe, 1978–1979.

Shallice, T., Warrington, E. K., & McCarthy, R. Reading without semantics. *Quarterly Journal of Experimental Psychology*, 1983, *35A*, 111-138.

Shanahan, T., Kamil, M. L., & Tobin, A. W. Cloze as a measure of intersentential comprehension. *Reading Research Quarterly*, 1982, *17*, 229–255.

Shankweiler, D., & Liberman, I. Y. Misreading: A search for causes. In J. K. Kavanagh, & I. G. Mattingly (Eds.), *Language by ear and by eye*. Cambridge, Mass.: MIT Press, 1972.

Shattuck-Hufnagel, S. Speech errors as evidence for a serial-ordering mechanism in sentence production. In W. E. Cooper, & E. C. T. Walker (Eds.), *Sentence processing: Psycholinguistic studies presented to Merrill Garrett*. Hillsdale, N.J.: Lawrence Erlbaum Associates, 1979.

Shaw, G. B. *Androcles and the Lion*. (Shaw Alphabet Edition), London: Penguin Books, 1962.

Shebilske, W. L., & Fisher, D. F. Eye movements reveal components of flexible reading strategies. In M. L. Kamil (Ed.), *Directions in reading: Research and instruction*. (30th Yearbook of the National Reading Conference), Washington, D. C.: National Reading Conference, 1981.

Shebilske, W. L., & Fisher, D. F. Eye movements and context effects during reading of extended discourse. In K. Rayner (Ed.), *Eye movements in reading: Perceptual and linguistic aspects*. New York: Academic Press, 1982.

Shebilske, W. L., & Reid, L. S. Reading eye movements, macro-structure and comprehension processes. In P. A. Kolers, M. E. Wrolstad, & H. Bouma (Eds.), *Processing of visible language* (Vol. 1). New York: Plenum, 1979.

Shen, E. An analysis of eye movements in the reading of Chinese. *Journal of Experimental Psychology*, 1927, *10*, 158–183.

Sherman, M. A. Adjectival negation and the comprehension of multiply negated sentences. *Journal of Verbal Learning and Verbal Behavior*, 1976, *15*, 143–157.

Shimamura, A. P., & Hunt, E. *Stroop interference tests with Kanji and Kana scripts*. Unpublished paper, University of Washington, Seatle, 1978.

Shimron, J., & Navon, D. The distribution of visual information in the vertical dimensions of Roman and Hebrew letters. *Visible Language*, 1980, *19*, 5–12.

Shulman, H. G., Hornak, R., & Sanders, E. The effects of graphemic, phonetic, and semantic relationships on access to lexical structures. *Memory & Cognition*, 1978, *6*, 115–123.

Shuy, R. W. The mismatch of child language and school language: Implications of beginning reading instruction. In L. B. Resnick, & P. A. Weaver (Eds.), *Theory and practice of early reading* (Vol. 1). Hillsdale, N.J.: Lawrence Erlbaum Associates, 1979.

Shyer, M. F. Story plots and themes. In A. S. Burack (Ed.), *The writer's handbook*. Boston: The Writer, Inc., 1980.

Sidtis, J. J., Volpe, B. T., Holtzman, J. D., Wilson, D. H., & Gazzaniga, M. S. Cognitive interaction after staged callosal section: Evidence for transfer of semantic activation. *Science*, 1981, *212*, 344–346.

Sidtis, J. J., Volpe, B. T., Wilson, D. H., Rayport, M., & Gazzaniga, M. S. Variability in RH language function after callosal section. *Journal of Neuroscience*, 1981, *1*, 323–331.

Silberman, C. *Cries in black and white*. New York: Random House, 1964.

Silverman, W. P. Can "Words" be processed as integrated units? *Perception & Psychophysics*, 1976, *20*, 143–152.

Simon, D. P., & Simon, H. A. Alternative uses of phonemic information in spelling. *Review of Educational Research*, 1973, *43*, 115–137.

Simon, H. A. How big is a chunk? *Science*, 1974, *183*, 482–488.

Simons, H. D. Black dialect, reading interference, and classroom interaction. In L. B. Resnick (Ed.), *Theory and practice of early reading* (Vol. 3). Hillsdale, N.J.: Lawrence Erlbaum Associates, 1979.

Simpson, E. *Reversals (A personal account of victory over dyslexia)*. Boston: Houghton Mifflin, 1979.

Singer, H., & Balow, I. H. Overcoming educational disadvantagedness. In J. T. Guthrie (Ed.), *Comprehension and teaching: Research review*. Newark, Del.: International Reading Association, 1981.

Singer, M. H. The primacy of visual information in the analysis of letter strings. *Perception & Psychophysics*, 1980, *27*, 153–162.

Singer, M. H., & Crouse, J. The relationship of context-use skills to reading: A case for an alternative experimental logic. *Child Development*, 1981, *52*, 1326–1329.

Singer, M. Thematic structure and the integration of linguistic information. *Journal of Verbal Learning and Verbal Behavior*, 1976, *15*, 549–558.

Singer, M. The role of case filling inferences in the coherence of brief passages. *Discourse Processes*, 1980, *3*, 185–201.

Skagseth, P. A. Dyslexia and visual problems. In Y. Zotterman (Ed.), *Dyslexia: Neuronal, cognitive and linguistic aspects*. Wenner-Gren Symposium Series (Vol. 35), New York: Pergamon, 1982.

Slobin, D. I. Grammatical transformations and sentence comprehension in childhood and adulthood. *Journal of Verbal Learning and Verbal Behavior*, 1966, *5*, 219–227.
Slobin, D. I. Recall of full and truncated passive sentences in connected discourse. *Journal of Verbal Learning and Verbal Behavior*, 1968, *7*, 876–881.
Sloboda, J. A. Visual imagery and individual difference in spelling. In U. Frith (Ed.), *Cognitive processes in spelling*. London: Academic Press, 1980.
Slowiaczek, M. L., & Clifton, C. Jr. Subvocalization and reading for meaning. *Journal of Verbal Learning and Verbal Behavior*, 1980, *19*, 573–582.
Smethurst, W. *Teaching young children to read at home*. New York: McGraw-Hill, 1975.
Smiley, S. S., Oakley, D. D., Worthen, D., Campione, J. C., & Brown, A. Recall of thematically relevant material by adolescent good and poor readers as a function of written versus oral presentation. *Journal of Educational Psychology*, 1977, *69*, 381–387.
Smith, F. *Understanding reading: A psycholinguistic analysis of reading and learning to read*. (2nd ed.), New York: Holt, Rinehart and Winston, 1978.
Smith, K. H., & McMahon, L. E. Understanding order information in sentences: Some recent work at Bell Laboratories. In G. B. Flores d'Acais, & W. J. M. Levelt (Eds.), *Advances in psycholinguistics*. Amsterdam: North-Holland, 1970.
Smith, M. E. An investigation of the development of the sentence and the extent of vocabulary in young children. *University of Iowa Studies in Child Welfare*, 1926, *3*, Whole Number 5.
Smith, P. T., & Baker, R. G. The influence of English spelling patterns on pronunciation. *Journal of Verbal Learning and Verbal Behavior*, 1976, *15*, 267–285.
Smith, P. T., & Groat, A. Spelling patterns, letter cancellation and the processing of text. In P. A. Kolers, M. E. Wrolstad, & H. Bouma (Eds.), *Processing of visible language* (Vol. 1). New York: Plenum Press, 1979.
Smith, P. T., & Sterling, C. M. Factors affecting the perceived morphemic structure of written words. *Journal of Verbal Learning and Verbal Behavior*, 1982, *21*, 704–721.
Snowling, M. J. The development of grapheme–phoneme correspondence in normal and dyslexic children. *Journal of Experimental Child Psychology*, 1980, *29*, 294–305.
Sobotowicz, W. S., & Evans, J. R. *Cortical dysfunctioning in children with specific reading disability*. Springfield, Ill: Charles C. Thomas, 1982.
Söderbergh, R. *A linguistic study of a Swedish preschool child's gradual acquisition of reading ability*. Stockholm: Almqvist and Wiksell, 1971.
Söderbergh, R. Learning to read between two and five: Some observations on normal hearing and deaf children. In C. Rameh (Ed.) *Semantics: Theory and application*. Washington, D. C.: Georgetown University Press, 1976.
Sokolov, A. N. *Inner speech and thought*. New York: Plenum, 1972.
Spache, G. D., & Spache, E. B. *Reading in the elementary school*. Boston: Allyn and Bacon, 1977.
Spector, A., & Purcell, D. G. The word superiority effect: A comparison between restricted and unrestricted alternative set. *Perception & Psychophysics*, 1977, *21*, 323–328.
Speer, O. B., & Lamb, G. S. First grade reading ability and fluency in naming verbal symbols. *Reading Teacher*, 1976, *29*, 572–576.
Sperling, G. The information available in brief visual presentations. *Psychological Monographs*, 1960, *74 (No. 498)*.
Sperry, R. W., Gazzaniga, M. S., & Bogen, J. E. Interhemispheric relationships: The neocortical commisures; syndromes of hemispheric disconnection. In P. J. Vinken, & G. W. Bruya (Eds.), *Handbook of clinical neurology* (Vol. 4). Amsterdam: North-Holland, 1969.
Sperry, R. Some effects of disconnecting the cerebral hemispheres. *Science*, 1982, *217*, 1223–1226.
Spiro, R. J. Accommodative reconstruction in prose recall. *Journal of Verbal Learning and Verbal Behavior*, 1980, *19*, 84–95.
Spoehr, K. T. Phonological encoding in visual word recognition. *Journal of Verbal Learning and Verval Behavior*, 1978, *17*, 127–141.
Spoehr, K. T., & Smith, E. E. The role of orthographic and phonotactic rules in perceiving letter patterns. *Journal of Experimental Psychology: Human Percption and Performance*, 1975, *104*, 21–34.

Spreen, O. Adult outcome of reading disorders. In R. N. Malatesha, & P. G. Aaron (Eds.), *Reading disorders: Varieties and treatments*. New York: Academic Press, 1982.

Spring, C. Automaticity of word recognition under phonics and whole-word instruction. *Journal of Educational Psychology*, 1978, *70*, 445–450.

Stallings, J. A., & Kaskowitz, D. H. *Follow through classroom observation evaluation 1972–73*. Menlo Park, Calif.: Stanford Research Institute, 1974.

Stallings, W. Approaches to Chinese character recognition. *Pattern Recognition*, 1976, *8*, 87–98.

Stanley, G., Kaplan, I., & Poole, C. Cognitive and nonverbal perceptual processing in dyslexics. *Journalof General Psychology*, 1975, *93*, 67–72.

Stanovich, K. E. Toward an interactive-compensatory model of individual differences in the development of reading fluency. *Reading Research Quarterly*, 1980, *16*, 32–71.

Stanovich, K. E., & West, R. F. The effect of sentence context on ongoing word recognition: Tests of a two-process theory. *Journal of Experimental Psychology: Human Perception and Performance*, 1981, *7*, 658–672.

Stanovich, K. E., & West, R. F. On priming by a sentence context. *Journal of Experimental Psychology: General*, 1983, *112*, 1–36.

Stauffer, R. G. *The language experience approach to the teaching of reading*. New York: Harper and Row, 1970.

Stebbins, L. B., St. Pierre, R. G., Proper, E. G., Anderson, R. B., & Cerva, T. R. *Education as experimentation: A planned variation model* (Vol. 4). Cambridge, Mass: Abt, 1977.

Stein, G. *Lectures in America*. New York: Modern Library, 1935.

Stein, N. L., & Glenn, C. An analysis of story comprehension in elementary school children. In R. Freedle (Ed.), *Discourse processing: Multidisciplinary perspectives*. Norwood, N.J.: Ablex, 1978.

Stein, N. L., & Nezworski, T. The effects of organization and instructional set on story memory. *Discourse Processing*, 1978, *1*, 177–194.

Stein, J. F., & Fowler, S. Towards the physiology of visual dyslexia. In Y. Zotterman (Ed.), *Dyslexia: Neuronal, cognitive and linguistic aspects*. Wenner-Gren Symposium Series (Vol. 35), New York: Pergamon, 1982.

Steinberg, D. D. Phonology, reading, and Chomsky and Halle's optimal orthography. *Journal of Psycholinguistic Research*, 1973, *2*, 239–258.

Steinberg, D. D. *Kanji are easier to learn to read than individual Kana*. Paper given at the meeting of the Japanese Psychological Association, Tokyo, September, 1977.

Steinberg, D. D. Personal communication, October 26, 1982.

Steinberg, D. D., Harada, M., Tashiro, M., & Yamada, A. One congenitally deaf 1-year-old learn to read. *Hearing Impaired*, 1982, *376*, 22–30 and 46, (in Japanese).

Steinberg, D. D., & Oka, N. Learning to read Kanji is easier than learning individual Kana. *Japanese Journal of Psychology*, 1978, *49*, 15–21, (in Japanese with English abstract).

Steinberg, D. D., & Steinberg, M. T. Reading before speaking. *Visible Language*, 1975, *9*, 197–224.

Steinberg, D. D., & Steinberg, M. T. *Early reading from infancy: A case study*. Working papers in linguistics, Department of Linguistics, University of Hawaii, 1980.

Steiner, R., Weiner, M., & Cromer, W. Comprehension training and identification of good and poor readers. *Journal of Educational Psychology*, 1971, *62*, 506–513.

Stern, J. A. Eye movements, reading, and cognition. In J. W. Senders, D. F. Fisher, & R. A. Monty (Eds.), *Eye movements and higher psychological functions* (Vol. 2). Hillsdale, N.J.: Lawrence Erlbaum Associates, 1978.

Stevenson, H. W., Parker, T., Wilkinson, A., Hegion, A., & Fish, E. Longitudinal study of individual differences in cognitive development and scholastic achievement. *Journal of Educational Psychology*, 1976, *68*, 377–400.

Stevenson, H. W., Stigler, J. W., Lucker, G. W., Lee, S.-Y., Hsu, Ch.-Ch., & Kitamara, S. Reading disabilities: The case of Chinese, Japanese and English. *Child Development*, 1982, *53*, 1164–1181.

Stewart, W. A. On the use of negro dialect in the teaching of reading. In J. C. Baratz, & R. W. Shuy

(Eds.), *Teaching black children to read*. Washington, D. C.: Center for Applied Linguistics, 1969.

Sticht, T. G., Beck, L., Hauke, R., Kleiman, G., & James, J. *Auding and reading: A developmental model*. Alexandria, Va.: Human Resources Research Organization, 1974.

Stoner, S. W. *Natural education*. Indianapolis: Bobbs-Merrill, 1914.

Stoner, S. W. *Manual of natural education*. Indianapolis: Bobbs-Merrill, 1916.

Stotsky, S. Toward reassessment of the principles underlying the choice of vocabulary and teaching of word analysis skills in reading instructional material. In M. L. Kamil (Ed.), *Directions in reading: Research and instruction* (30th Yearbook of the National Reading Conference). Washington D. C.: National Reading Conference, 1981.

Strag, G. A. Comparative behavioral ratings of parents with severe mentally retarded, special learning disability and normal children. *Journal of Learning Disabilities*, 1972, *5*, 52–56.

Strohner, H., & Nelson, K. E. The young child's development of sentence comprehension: Influence of event probability, nonverbal context, syntactic form, and strategies. *Child Development*, 1974, *45*, 567–576.

Stroop, J. L. Studies of interference in serial verbal reactions. *Journal of Experimental Psychology*, 1935, *18*, 643–662.

Strunk, W. Jr., & White, E. B. *The elements of style*. New York: Macmillan, 1972 (Second edition).

Sugishita, M., Iwata, M., Toyokura, Y., Yoshioka, M., & Yamada, R. Reading of ideograms and phonograms in Japanese patients after commisurotomy. *Neuropsychologia*, 1978, *16*, 417–426.

Sugiyama, Y., & Saito, T. Variables of parent reading in relation to social traits of kindergarten pupils. *Science of Reading*, 1973, *15*, 121–130, (in Japanese with English abstract).

Sulin, R. A., & Dooling, D. J. Intrusion of a thematic idea in retention of prose. *Journal of Experimental Psychology*, 1974, *103*, 255–262.

Sumby, W. H., & Pollack, I. Short-term processing of information. *HFORL Report Transactions*, 1954, 54–56.

Suter, S. Differences between deaf and hearing adults in task-related EEG asymmetries. *Psychophysiology*, 1982, *19*, 124–128.

Suzuki, T. On the twofold phonetic realization of basic concepts: In defence of Chinese characters in Japan. In F. C. C. Peng (Ed.), *Language in Japanese society*. Tokyo: University of Tokyo Press, 1975.

Suzuki, T. Writing is not language, or is it? *Journal of Pragmatics*, 1977, *1*, 407–420.

Taft, M. An alternative to grapheme–phoneme conversion rules? *Memory & Cognition*, 1982, *10*, 465–474.

Taft, M., & Forster, K. I. Lexical storage and retrieval of prefixed words. *Journal of Verbal Learning and Verbal Behaviour*, 1975, *14*, 638–647.

Takebe, Y. *Writing Japanese*. Tokyo: Tsunokawa Shoten, 1979, (in Japanese).

Tallal, P. Auditory temporal perception, phonics, and reading disabilities in children. *Brain and Language*, 1980, *9*, 182–198.

Tanaka, T. Development of letter recognition (3). *Japanese Journal of Psychology*, 1977, *48*, 49–53, (in Japanese with English abstract).

Tanaka, T., Iwasaki, J., & Miki, C. Development of the cognition of letters (1). *Japanese Journal of Psychology*, 1974, *45*, 37–45, (in Japanese with English abstract).

Tanaka, T., & Yasufuku, J. Development of the cognition of letters (2). *Osaka University of Education Report*, 1975, *24*, 85–99, (in Japanese with English abstract).

Tatham, S. M. Reading comprehension of materials written with select oral language patterns: A study at grade two and four. *Reading Research Quarterly*, 1970, *5*, 402–426.

Taver, S. G., Hallahan, D. P., Cohen, S. B., & Kauffman, J. M. Visual selective attention and verbal rehearsal in LD boys. *Journal of Learning Disabilities*, 1977, *10*, 26–35.

Taylor, B. M. Children's memory for expository text after reading. *Reading Research Quarterly*, 1980, *15*, 399–411.

Taylor, D. A. Holistic and analytic processes in the comparison of letters. *Perception & Psychophysics*, 1976, *20*, 187–190.

Taylor, I. Content and structure in sentence production. *Journal of Verbal Learning and Verbal Behavior*, 1969, *8*, 170–175.

Taylor, I. *Introduction to psycholinguistics*. New York: Holt, Rinehart and Winston, 1976.

Taylor, I. Acquiring vs. learning a second language. *Canadian Modern Language Review*, 1978, *34*, 455–472.

Taylor, I. The Korean writing system: An alphabet? a syllabary? a logography? In P. A. Kolers, M. E. Wrolstad, & H. Bouma (Eds.), *Processing of visible language* (Vol. 2). New York: Plenum, 1980.

Taylor, I. Writing systems and reading. In G. E. MacKinnon, & T. G. Waller (Eds.), *Reading research: Advances in theory and practice* (Vol. 2). New York: Academic Press, 1981.

Taylor, I., & Taylor, M. M. Which function words are deletable? (in preparation).

Taylor, M. M. The problem of stimulus structure in behavioral theory of perception. *South African Journal of Psychology*, 1973, *3*, 23–45.

Taylor, M. M. Speculations on biligualism and the cognitive network. *Working Papers on Bilingualism*, 1974, *2*, 68–124.

Taylor, M. M. The Bilateral Cooperative model of reading: A human paradigm for artificial intelligence. In A. Elithorn, & R. Banerji (Eds.), *Human and Artificial Intelligence*. New York: North Holland, 1983.

Taylor, S. E. An evaluation of forty-one trainees who had recently completed the "Reading Dynamics" program. In E. P. Bliesmer, & R. C. Staiger (Eds.), *Problems, programs, and projects in college adult reading* (11th Yearbook of the National Reading Conference). Milwaukee, Wis.: National Reading Conference, 1962.

Teng, E. L., & Sperry, R. W. Interhemispheric during simultaneous bilateral presentation of letters or digits in commissurotomized patients. *Neuropsychologia*, 1973, *11*, 131–140.

Tenney, Y. J. Visual factors in spelling. In U. Frith (Ed.), *Cognitive processes in spelling*. London: Academic Press, 1980.

Terman, L. M. Introduction to "An Experiment in infant education". *Journal of Applied Psychology*, 1918, *2*, 219–228.

Terry, P. R. The effect of orthographic transformations upon speed and accuracy of semantic categorizations. *Reading Research Quarterly*, 1976–1977, *12*, 166–175.

Terry, P. R., Samuels, S. J., & LaBerge, D. The effects of letter degradation and letter spacing on word recognition. *Journal of Verbal Learning and Verbal Behavior*, 1976, *15*, 577–585.

Thackray, D. V. *Reading for meaning with i.t.a. and t.o.*. London: Geoffrey Chapman, 1971.

Thompson, L. J. Did Lee Oswald have a specific language disability? *Orton Society Publication*, 1964, *14*.

Thomson, M. E. A. A comparison of laterality effects in dyslexics and controls using verbal dichotic listening tasks. *Neuropsychologia*, 1976, *14*, 243–246.

Thomson, M. E. An analysis of spelling errors in dyslexic children. *First Language*, 1981, *2*, 141–150.

Thorndike, R. L. *Reading comprehension education in fifteen countries: International studies in evaluation* (Vol. 3), New York: Halsted Press, 1973.

Thorndyke, P. W. *Cognitive structures in human story comprehension and memory*. Unpublished doctoral dissertation: Technical Report P-5513, Stanford University and the Rand Corporation, Santa Monica, 1975.

Thorndyke, P. W. Cognitive structures in comprehension and memory of narrative discourse. *Cognitive Psychology*, 1977, *9*, 77–110.

Tierney, R., Bridge, C., & Cera, M. The discourse processing operations of children. *Reading Research Quarterly*, 1979, *14*, 539–597.

Tinker, M. Recent studies of eye movements in reading. *Psychological Bulletin*, 1958, *55*, 215–231.

Torgesen, J. K., & Goldman, T. Rehearsal and short-term memory in reading disabled children. *Child Development*, 1977, *48*, 56–60.

Torrey, J. W. Learning to read without a teacher: A case study. *Elementary English*, 1969, *46*, 550–558.

Trager, G. L. Writing and writing systems. In T. A. Sebeok (Ed.), *Current trends in linguistics* (Vol. 12). The Hague: Mouton, 1974.

Trammell, R. L. The psychological reality of underlying forms and rules. *Journal of Psycholinguistic Research*, 1978, *7*, 79–94.

Treiman, R. A., Baron, J., & Luk, K. Speech recoding in silent reading: A comparison of Chinese and English. *Journal of Chinese Linguistics*, 1981, *9*, 116–124.

Treiman, R., & Hirsh-Pasek, K. Silent reading: Insights from second-generation deaf readers. *Cognitive Psychology*, 1983, *15*, 39–65.

Treisman, A. M. Focused attention in the perception and retrieval of multidimensional stimuli. *Perception & Psychophysics*, 1977, *22*, 1–11.

Treisman, A. M., & Gelade, G. A feature-integration theory of attention. *Cognitive Psychology*, 1980, *12*, 97–136.

Tsao, Y.-C., & Wu, M.-F. Stroop interference: Hemispheric difference in Chinese speakers. *Brain and Language*, 1981, *13*, 372–378.

Tsien, T.-H. *Written on bamboo and silk: The beginnings of Chinese books and inscriptions*. Chicago: Chicago University Press, 1962.

T'sou, B. K. A sociolinguistic analysis of the logographic writing system of Chinese. *Journal of Chinese Language*, 1981, *9*, 1–18.

Tuinman, J. J. Determining the passage dependency of comprehension questions in five major tests. *Reading Research Quarterly*, 1973–1974, *9*, 206–223.

Tuinman, J., Blanton, W. E., & Gray, G. A note on cloze as a measure of comprehension. *Journal of Psychology*, 1975, *90*, 159–162.

Tulving, E. Episodic and semantic memory. In E. Tulving, & W. Donaldson (Eds.), *Organization and memory*. New York: Academic Press, 1972.

Tulving, E., & Gold, C. Stimulus information and contextual information as determinants of tachistoscopic recognition of words. *Journal of Experimental Psychology*, 1963, *66*, 319–327.

Turner, E. A., & Rommetveit, R. The acquisition of sentence voice and reversibility. *Child Development*, 1967, *38*, 649–660.

Tversky, A. Features of similarity. *Psychological Review*, 1977, *84*, 327–352.

Tweedy, J. R., & Lapinski, R. H. Facilitating word recognition: Evidence for strategic and automatic factors. *Quarterly Journal of Experimental Psychology*, 1981, *33A*, 51–59.

Tzeng, O. J. L. Sentence memory: Recognition inferences. *Journal of Experimental Psychology: Human Learning and Memory*, 1975, *1*, 720–726.

Tzeng, O. J. L., & Hung, D. L. Reading in a nonalphabetic writing system. In J. F. Kavanagh, & R. L. Venezky (Eds.), *Orthography, reading and dyslexia*. Baltimore: University Park Press, 1980.

Tzeng, O. J. L., Hung, D. L., Cotton, B., & Wang, W. S.-Y. Visual lateralization effects in reading Chinese characters. *Nature*, 1979, *282*, 499–501.

Tzeng, O. J. L., Hung, D. L., & Wang, W. S.-Y. Speech recoding in reading Chinese characters. *Journal of Experimental Psychology: Human Learning and Memory*, 1977, *3*, 621–630.

Underwood, G. Lexical recognition of embedded unattended words: Some implications for reading processes. *Acta Psychologica*, 1981, *47*, 267–283.

Unger, J. Introduction: Primary school reading texts and teaching methods in the wake of the cultural revolution. *Chinese Education*, 1977, *10*, 4–29.

Vachek, J. *Written language*. The Hague: Mouton, 1973.

Valle Arroyo, F. Negatives in context. *Journal of Verbal Learning and Verbal Behavior*, 1982, *21*, 118–126.

Valtin, R. Dyslexia: Deficit in reading—or deficit in research? In J. K. Kavanagh, & R. L. Venezky (Eds.), *Orthography, reading and dyslexia*. Baltmore: University Park Press, 1980.

Van, Y.-Y., & Zian, C.-T. Beginning readers learn and remember characters. *Acta Psychologica Sinica*, 1962, *3*, 219–230.

Vanacek, E. Fixationsdauer und Fixationsfrequenz beim stillen Lesen von Sprach approximationen. *Zeitschrift fur Experimentelle und Angewandte Psychologie*, 1972, *19*, 671–689.

Vande Kopple, W. J. The given–new strategy of comprehension and some natural expository paragraphs. *Journal of Psycholinguistic Research*, 1982, *11*, 501–520.

Vanderheiden, G. C., & Harris-Vanderheiden, D. Communication techniques and aids for the nonvocal severely handicapped. In L. L. LLoyd (Ed.), *Communication assessment and intervention strategies*. Baltimore: University Park Press, 1976.

Vellutino, F. R. *Dyslexia: Theory and research*. Cambridge, Mass.: MIT Press, 1979.

Vellutino, F. R., Pruzek, R. M., Steger, J. A., & Meshoulam, L. I. Immediate visual recall in poor and normal readers as a function of orthographic-linguistic familiarity. *Cortex*, 1973, *9*, 368–384.

Vellutino, F. R., Steger, J. A., & Kandel, G. Reading disability: An investigation of the perceptual deficit hypothesis. *Cortex*, 1972, *8*, 106–118.

Vellutino, F. R., Steger, J. A., Harding, C. J., & Phillips, F. Verbal vs non-verbal paired-associates learning in poor and normal readers. *Neuropsychologia*, 1975, *13*, 75–82.

Venezky, R. L. English orthography: Its graphical structure and its relation to sound. *Reading Research Quarterly*, 1967, *2*, 75–106.

Venezky, R. L. *The structure of English orthography*. The Hague: Mouton, 1970.

Venezky, R. L. Letter–sound generalizations of first, second and third grade Finnish children. *Journal of Educational Psychology*, 1973, *64*, 288–292.

Venezky, R. L. *Theoretical and experimental base for teaching reading*. The Hague: Mouton, 1976.

Venezky, R. L. Letter–sound regularity and orthographic structure. In M. L. Kamil (Ed.), *Directions in reading: Research and instruction* (30th Yearbook of the National Reading Conference). Washington, D.C.: National Reading Conference, 1981.

Venezky, R. L., Chapman, R. S., & Calfee, R. C. *The development of letter–sound generalizations from second through sixth grade*. Technical Report 321, Winsconsin Research and Development Center for Cognitive Learning, 1972.

Vernon, M. D. *Backwardness in reading*. Cambridge: Cambridge University Press, 1957.

Vernon, M. D. Varieties of deficiency in the reading process. *Harvard Educational Review*, 1977, *47*, 396–410.

Vogel, S. A. Syntactic abilities in normal and dyslexic children. *Journal of Learning Disabilities*, 1974, *7*, 103–109.

Wada, J., Clark, R., & Hamm, A. Cerebral hemispheric asymmetry in humans: Cortical speech zones in adult and 100 infant brains. *Archives of Neurology*, 1975, *32*, 239–246.

Walker, L. Newfoundland dialect interference in oral reading. *Journal of Reading Behavior*, 1975, *7*, 61–78.

Walker, L. Comprehension of writing and spontaneous speech. *Visible Language*, 1977, *11*, 37–51.

Walker, W. Notes on native writing systems and the design of native literacy programs. *Anthropological Linguistics*, 1969, *11*, 148–166.

Waller, T. G. Children's recognition memory for written sentences: A comparison of good and poor readers. *Child Development*, 1976, *47*, 90–95.

Walley, R., & Weiden, T. Lateral inhibition and cognitive masking: A neuropsychological theory of attention. *Psychological Review*, 1973, *80*, 284–302.

Wanat, S. F. Relations between language and visual processing. In H. Singer, & R. Rudell (Eds.), *Theoretical models and processes of reading*. Newark, Del.: International Reading Association, 1976.

Wanat, S. F., & Levin, H. The eye–voice span: Reading efficiency and syntactic predictability. In H. Levin, E. J. Gibson, & J. J. Gibson (Eds.), *The analysis of reading skill*. (Project No. 5-1213), Ithaca, N. Y.: Cornell University and U.S. Office of Education, 1968.

Wang, F.-C. An experimental study of eye movements in the silent reading of Chinese. *Elementary School Journal*, 1935, *35*, 527–539.

Wang, W. S.-Y. The Chinese language. *Scientific American*, February 1973, *228*, 50–60.

Wang, W. S.-Y. Language structure and optimal orthography. In H. Singer, & O. Tzeng (Eds.), *Perception of print: Reading research in experimental psychology*. Hillsdale, N.J.: Lawrence Erlbaum Associates, 1981.

Wapner, W., Hamby, S., & Gardner, H. The role of the right hemisphere in the apprehension of complex linguistic materials. *Brain and Language*, 1981, *14*, 15–33.

Warrington, E. K. The selective impairment of semantic memory. *Quarterly Journal of Experimental Psychology*, 1975, *27*, 635–657.

Wason, P. C. The contexts of plausible denial. *Journal of Verbal Learning and Verbal Behavior*, 1965, *4*, 7–11.

Wason, P. C., & Reich, S. S. A verbal illusion. *Quarterly Journal of Experimental Psychology*, 1979, *31*, 591–597.

Watanabe, S. *Kanji and figural patterns*. Tokyo: NHK Books, 1976, (in Japanese).

Waters, H. S. Superordinate–subordinate structure in semantic memory: The roles of comprehension and retrieval processes. *Journal of Verbal Learning and Verbal Behavior*, 1978, *17*, 587–597.

Watt, T. S. Brush up your English. *Manchester Guardian*, 1954 June 21.

Watt, W. W. *An American rhetoric*. New York: Holt, Rinehart and Winston, 1964.

Weaver, P. A. *Improving reading comprehension: Effects of sentence organization instruction*. Unpublished M.A. thesis, Harvard University, 1977.

Weaver, W. W., & Kingston, A. J. A factor analysis of the cloze procedure and other measures of reading and language ability. *Journal of Communication*, 1963, *13*, 252–261.

Weber, R. M. First graders' use of grammatical context in reading. In H. Levin, & J. P. Williams (Eds.), *Basic studies on reading*. New York: Basic Books, 1970.

Weber, R. M. Learning to read: The linguistic dimension for adults. In T. P. Gorman (Ed.), *Language and literacy: Current issues and research*. Tehran, Iran: International Institute for Adult Literacy Method, 1977.

Wetmore, M. E. *Improving the comprehensibility of text*. Paper presented at the 30th annual meeting of the National Reading Conference, San Diego, 1980.

Whaley, C. P. Word–non-word classification time. *Journal of Verbal Learning and Verbal Behavior*, 1978, *17*, 143–154.

Whaley, J. F. Readers' reactions to temporal disruption on stories. In *Directions in reading: Research and instruction*. (30th Yearbook of the National Reading Conference). Washington, D.C.: National Reading Conference, 1981a.

Whaley, J. F. Readers' expectations for story structures. *Reading Research Quarterly*, 1981b, *17*, 90–114.

White, M. J. Feature-specific border effects in the discrimination of letter-like forms. *Perception & Psychophysics*, 1981, *29*, 156–162.

Whorf, B. L. The relationship of habitual thought and behavior to language. In L. Spier (Ed.), *Language, culture and personality*. Menosha, Wis.: The Sapir Memorial Publication Fund, 1941.

Wickelgren, W. W. Acoustic similarity and retroactive interference in short-term memory. *Journal of Verbal Learning and Verbal Behavior*, 1965, *4*, 53–61.

Wieger, L. *Chinese characters*. New York: Dover, 1965.

Wiig, E. H., & Semel, E. M. Productive language abilities in learning disabled adolescents. *Journal of Learning Disabilities*, 1975, *8*, 578–586.

Wijk, A. *Regularized English*. Stockholm: Almqvist-Wiksell, 1959.

Wijk, A. *Rules of pronunciation for the English language*. London: Oxford University Press, 1966.

Wildman, D. M., & Kling, M. Semantic, syntactic, and spatial anticipation in reading. *Reading Research Quarterly*, 1978–1979, *14*, 128–164.

Wilkes, A. L., & Kennedy, R. A. Relationship between pausing and retrieval latency in sentences of varying grammatical form. *Journal of Experimental Psychology*, 1969, *79*, 241–245.

Wilkins, A., & Stewart, A. The time course of lateral asymmetries in visual perception of letters. *Journal of Experimental Psychology*, 1974, *102*, 905–908.

Williams, A., & Weisstein, N. Line segments are perceived better in a coherent context than alone: An object–line effect in visual perception. *Memory & Cognition*, 1978, *6*, 85–90.

Williams, E. W. *Teaching a toddler to teach herself to read*. Unpublished M.A. thesis, University of Texas at El Paso, 1982.

Williams, J. *Has the psychology of reading helped the teaching of reading?* Paper presented at the meeting of the American Psychological Association, Toronto, 1978.

Williams, J. P., Blumberg, E. L., & Williams, D. V. Cues used in visual word recognition. *Journal of Educational Psychology*, 1970, *61*, 310–315.

Willows, D. M, Borwick, D., & Hayvren, M. The content of school readers. In G. E. MacKinnon, & T. G. Waller (Eds.), *Reading research: Advances in theory and practics* (Vol. 2). New York: Academic Press, 1981.
Willows, D. M., & MacKinnon, G. E. Selective reading: Attention to the "unattended" lines. *Canadian Journal of Psychology*, 1973, *27*, 292–304.
Willows, D. M., & Ryan, E. B. Differential utilization of syntactic and semantic information by skilled and less skilled readers in the intermediate grades. *Journal of Educational Psychology*, 1981, *73*, 607–615.
Winner, E., & Gardner, H. The comprehension of metaphor in brain-damaged patients. *Brain*, 1977, *100*, 717–729.
Winograd, T. *Understanding natural language*. New York: Academic Press, 1972.
Wisher, R. A. The effect of syntactic expectations during reading. *Journal of Educational Psychology*, 1976, *68*, 597–602.
Witelson, S. F. Developmental dyslexia: Two right hemispheres and none left. *Science*, 1977, *195*, 309–311.
Witelson, S. F., & Rabinovitch, M. S. Hemispheric speech lateralization in children with auditory-linguistic deficits. *Cortex*, 1972, *8*, 412–426.
Wolford, G. Perturbation model for letter identification. *Psychological Review*, 1975, *82*, 184–199.
Wolford, G., & Chambers, L. Lateral masking as a function of spacing. *Perception & Psychophysics*, 1983, *33*, 129–138.
Wolford, G., & Shum, K. H. Evidence for feature perturbations. *Perception & Psychophysics*, 1980, *27*, 409–420.
Wood, C. C., Goff, W. R., & Day, R. S. Auditory evoked potentials during speech perception. *Science*, 1971, *173*, 1248–1251.
Woods, W. Transition network grammars for natural language analysis. *Communications of the Association for Computing Machinary*, 1970, *13*, 591–606.
Woodworth, R. S. *Experimental psychology*. New York: Holt, 1938.
Wrenn, C. L. *The English language*. London: Methuen, 1949.
Wright, P. Some observations on how people answer questions about sentences. *Journal of Verbal Learning and Verbal Behavior*, 1972, *11*, 188–195.
Wright, P., & Wilcox, P. When two no's nearly make a yes: A study of conditional imperatives. In P. A. Kolers, M. E. Wrolstad, & H. Bouma (Eds.), *Processing of visible language* (Vol. 1). New York: Plenum, 1979.
Yeh, J.-S., & Liu, I.-M. Factors affecting recognition thresholds of Chinese characters. *Acta Psychologica Taiwanica*, 1972, *14*, 113–117, (in Chinese with English abstract).
Yeni-Komshian, G. H., Isenberg, S, & Goldberg, H. Cerebral dominance and reading disability: Left visual field deficit in poor readers. *Neuropsychologia*, 1975, *13*, 83–94.
Yik, W. F. The effect of visual and acoustic similarity on short-term memory for Chinese words. *Quarterly Journal of Experimental Psychology*, 1978, *30*, 487–494.
Yoshida, A., Matsuda, Y., & Shimura, M. *A study on instruction of Chinese characters*. Tokyo University Education Department Report 14, 1975, (in Japanese with English summary).
Yule, V. Is there evidence for Chomsky's interpretation of English spelling? *Spelling Progress Bulletin*, 1978, *18*, 10–12.
Zachrisson, R. E. *Anglic, a new agreed simplified English spelling*. Uppsala: Almqvist and Wiksell, 1931.
Zaidel, E. Lexical organization in the right hemisphere. In P. A. Buser, & A. Rougeul-Buser (Eds.), *Cerebral correlates of conscious experience*. (INSERM Symposium No. 6), Amsterdam: Elsevier/North Holland Biomedical Press, 1978a.
Zaidel, E. Concepts of cerebral dominance in the split brain. In P. A. Buser, & A. Rougeul-Buser (Eds.), *Cerebral correlates of conscious experience*. (INSERM Symposium No. 6), Amsterdam: Elsevier/North Holland Biomedical Press, 1978b.
Zangwill, O. L., & Blakemore, C. Dyslexia: Reversal of eye-movements during reading. *Neuropsychologia*, 1972, *10*, 371–373.

Zeitler, J. Tachistoskopische Versuche uber das Lesen. *Wundt's Philosophische Studien*, 1900, *16*, 380–464.

Zerbin-Rudin, E. Congential word blindness. *Bulletin of the Orton Society*, 1967, *17*, 47–54.

Zettersten, A. *A statistical study of the graphic system of present-day American English*. Lund, Sweden: Studentlitteratur, 1969.

Zhou, Y.-G. To what degree are the "phonetics" of present-day Chinese characters still phonetic? *Zhongguo Yuwen*, 1978, *146*, 172–177, (in Chinese).

Zimmerman, J., Broder, P. K., Shaughnessy, J. J., & Underwood, B. J. *A recognition test of vocabulary using signal detection measures and some correlates of word and nonword recognition*. Technical Report, Northwestern University, February, 1973.

Zipf, G. K. *The psycho-biology of language*. Boston: Houghton Mifflin, 1935.

Zurif, E. B., & Carson, G. Dyslexia in relation to cerebral dominant temporal analysis. *Neuropsychologia*, 1970, *8*, 351–361.

Zutell, J. Cognitive development, metalinguistic ability and invented spelling: Comparisons and correlations. In M. L. Kamil (Ed.), *Directions in reading: Research and instructions*. (30th Yearbook of the National Reading Conference). Washington, D.C.: National Reading Conference, 1981.

Name Index

C

D

G

M

Subject Index

153.6 T214p
Taylor, Insup.
The psychology of reading